Feminist Legal Theory
Volume I

The International Library of Essays in Law and Legal Theory
Series Editor: Tom D. Campbell

Schools

Natural Law, Vols I & II *John Finnis*
Justice *Thomas Morawetz*
Law and Economics, Vols I & II *Jules Coleman and Jeffrey Lange*
Critical Legal Studies *James Boyle*
Marxian Legal Theory *Csaba Varga*
Legal Reasoning, Vols I & II *Aulis Aarnio and D. Neil MacCormick*
Legal Positivism *Mario Jori*
American Legal Theory *Robert Samuel Summers*
Postmodernism and Law *Dennis Patterson*
Law and History *David Sugarman*
Law and Language *Fred Schauer*
Sociological Theories of Law *Kahei Rokumoto*
Rights *Carlos Nino*
Law and Psychology *Martin Lyon Levine*
Feminist Legal Theory, Vols I & II *Frances Olsen*
Law and Society *Roger Cotterrell*
Contemporary Criminological Theory *Francis T. Cullen and Velmer S. Burton Jr.*

Areas

Criminal Law *Thomas Morawetz*
Tort Law *Ernest J. Weinrib*
Contract Law, Vols I & II *Larry Alexander*
Anti-Discrimination Law *Christopher McCrudden*
Consumer Law *Iain Ramsay*
International Law *Martti Koskenniemi*
Property Law, Vols I & II *Elizabeth Mensch and Alan Freeman*
Constitutional Law *Mark V. Tushnet*
Procedure *D.J. Galligan*
Evidence and Proof *William Twining and Alex Stein*
Company Law *Sally Wheeler*
Privacy, Vols I & II *Raymond Wacks*
Lawyers' Ethics *David J. Luban*
Administrative Law *D.J. Galligan*
Child Law *Harry D. Krause*
Family Law, Vols I & II *Harry D. Krause*
Welfare Law *Peter Robson*
Medicine and the Law *Bernard M. Dickens*
Commercial Law *Ross Cranston*
Environmental Law *Michael C. Blumm*
Conflict of Laws *Richard Fentiman*
Law and Religion *Wojciech Sadurski*
Human Rights Law *Philip Alston*
European Community Law, Vols I & II *Francis Snyder*
Tax Law, Vols I & II *Patricia D. White*
Media Law *Eric Barendt*
Labour Law *David L. Gregory*
Alternative Dispute Resolution *Michael D.A. Freeman*

Legal Cultures

Comparative Legal Cultures *Csaba Varga*
Law and Anthropology *Peter Sack*
Hindu Law and Legal Theory *Ved Nanda*
Islamic Law and Legal Theory *Ian Edge*
Chinese Law and Legal Theory *Michael Palmer*
Russian Legal Theory *W. Butler*
Common Law *Michael Arnheim*
Japanese Law and Legal Theory *Koichiro Fujikura*
Law and Development *Anthony Carty*
Jewish Law and Legal Theory *Martin P. Golding*
Legal Education *Martin Lyon Levine*
Civil Law *Ralf Rogowski*
African Law and Legal Theory *Gordon Woodman and Akintunde Obilade*

Future Volume
Cumulative index

Feminist Legal Theory
Volume I

Edited by

Frances E. Olsen

University of California at Los Angeles
School of Law

NEW YORK UNIVERSITY PRESS
REFERENCE COLLECTION

First published in the U.S.A. in 1995 by
NEW YORK UNIVERSITY PRESS
Washington Square
New York NY 10003

Library of Congress Cataloging-in-Publication Data
Feminist legal theory / edited by Frances E. Olsen.
p. cm. – (The international library of essays in law and legal theory. Schools ; 15)
"New York University Press reference collection."
Includes bibliographical references.
ISBN 0-8147-6177-1 (set) – ISBN 0-8147-6179-8 (v. 1).
– ISBN 0-8147-6180-1 (v. 2)
1. Feminist jurisprudence. 2. Women–Legal status, laws, etc.
3. Feminist jurisprudence–United States. 4. Women–Legal status, laws, etc.–United States. I. Olsen, Frances E. II. Series.
K349.F46 1994
340'.1–dc20 94–3037
CIP

To

Margaret Pauline Olsen Rhine

12 April 1939–25 December 1976

and

Mary Joe Frug

13 November 1941–4 April 1991

Contents

Abortion: Privacy or Equality

Sexual Expression and Pornography

Scepticism or Embrace of Grand Theory

PART IV NEW DIRECTIONS

Acknowledgements

The editors and publishers wish to thank the following for permission to use copyright material.

Academic Press Limited for the essay: Frances E. Olsen (1990), 'Feminism and Critical Legal Theory: An American Perspective', *International Journal of the Sociology of Law*, **18**, pp. 199–215.

Blackwell Publishers for the essay: Nicola Lacey (1993), 'Theory into Practice? Pornography and the Public/Private Dichotomy', *Journal of Law and Society*, **20**, pp. 93–113.

Buffalo Law Review for the essay: Ellen C. DuBois, Mary C. Dunlap, Carol J. Gilligan, Catharine A. MacKinnon and Carrie J. Menkel-Meadow (1985), 'Feminist Discourse, Moral Values, and the Law – A Conversation', *Buffalo Law Review*, **34**, pp. 11–87.

Andrea Dworkin (1985), 'Against the Male Flood: Censorship, Pornography, and Equality', *Harvard Women's Law Journal*, **8**, pp. 1–29. Copyright 1985 by Andrea Dworkin. Reprinted by permission of Andrea Dworkin.

Feminist Studies Inc. for the essays: Christina Brooks Whitman (1991), 'Review Essay: Feminist Jurisprudence', *Feminist Studies*, **17**, pp. 493–507; Joan W. Scott (1988), 'Deconstructing Equality-Versus-Difference: Or, the Uses of Poststructuralist Theory for Feminism', *Feminist Studies*, **14**, pp. 33–50. By permission of the publisher, Feminist Studies Inc., c/o Women's Studies Program, University of Maryland.

Georgia Law Review Association Inc. for the essays: Jean Braucher (1991), 'Tribal Conflict Over Abortion', *Georgia Law Review*, **25**, pp. 595–624; Kathryn Abrams (1990), 'Ideology and Women's Choices', *Georgia Law Review*, **24**, pp. 761–801.

Harvard Law Review for the essays: Frances E. Olsen (1983), 'The Family and the Market: A Study of Ideology and Legal Reform', *Harvard Law Review*, **96**, pp. 1497–528; Mary Joe Frug (1992), 'A Postmodern Feminist Legal Manifesto (An Unfinished Draft)', *Harvard Law Review*, **105**, pp. 1045–75.

Melbourne University Law Review for the essay: Jenny Morgan (1988), 'Feminist Theory as Legal Theory', *Melbourne University Law Review*, **16**, pp. 743–59.

North Carolina Law Review for the essay: Ruth Bader Ginsburg (1985), 'Some Thoughts on Autonomy and Equality in Relation to *Roe v. Wade*', *North Carolina Law Review*, **63**, pp. 375–86. Copyright 1985 by the North Carolina Law Review Association. Reprinted with permission.

Series Preface

The International Library of Law and Legal Theory is designed to provide important research materials in an accessible form. Each volume contains essays of central theoretical importance in its subject area. The series as a whole makes available an extensive range of valuable material which will be of considerable interest to those involved in the research, teaching and study of law.

The series has been divided into three sections. The Schools section is intended to represent the main distinctive approaches and topics of special concern to groups of scholars. The Areas section takes in the main branches of law with an emphasis on essays which present analytical and theoretical insights of broad application. The section on Legal Cultures makes available the distinctive legal theories of different legal traditions and takes up topics of general comparative and developmental concern.

I have been delighted and impressed by the way in which the editors of the individual volumes have set about the difficult task of selecting, ordering and presenting essays from the immense quantity of academic legal writing published in journals throughout the world. Editors were asked to pick out those essays from law, philosophy and social science journals which they consider to be fundamental for the understanding of law, as seen from the perspective of a particular approach or sphere of legal interest. This is not an easy task and many difficult decisions have had to be made in order to ensure that a representative sample of the best journal essays available takes account of the scope of each topic or school.

I should like to express my thanks to all the volume editors for their willing participation and scholarly judgement. The interest and enthusiasm which the project has generated is well illustrated by the fact that an original projection of 12 volumes drawn up in 1989 has now become a list of some 60 volumes. I must also acknowledge the vision, persistence and constant cheerfulness of John Irwin and the marvellous work done by Mrs Margaret O'Reilly and Sonia Hubbard.

TOM D. CAMPBELL
Series Editor
The Faculty of Law
The Australian National University

Introduction

Feminist legal theory is barely over a decade old in the United States and even younger in most other countries. Yet the literature is extraordinarily rich and varied, with all indicators suggesting that it will become more so. Most major law schools in the US offer specialized courses on feminist legal theory, and its ideas have found their way into numerous other subjects. A growing number of legal theory or jurisprudence courses devote significant segments to feminist legal theory and, in one school or another, virtually every subject in law is taught with feminist materials integrated into the more conventional syllabus. At least one textbook in family law now uses feminist legal theory as a central organizing principle.[1] Over the next few years textbooks drawing equally strongly upon feminist theory will no doubt appear in other legal fields as well.

In 1983, *Harvard Law Review* and *Yale Law Journal*, the two most prestigious US legal periodicals, each published a major feminist lead article for the first time.[2] Since then, hundreds of feminist articles have been published in virtually every American law journal. While this proliferation of feminist law writing has been exciting and many of the articles have been worthwhile, the sheer volume makes it difficult to keep up with the literature; the tendency for feminist articles to be spread among a wide variety of journals, including obscure ones, has meant that, for anyone who does not have access to a large collection of English-language law journals, a large portion of the writing is for practical purposes unavailable. The essays in this volume have been drawn from 15 different journals. As with the rest of the volumes in this series, the chapters are unedited and double-paginated to facilitate citation to the original source.[3]

The first volume in this two-volume set introduces the field, presents important foundational essays, gives an overview of a few of the more interesting ongoing debates, and suggests some of the newer directions that seem among the most promising to me. The second volume is directed more to the teaching of law and to the relationship between feminist legal theory and other fields of law. Each volume is intended to be complete unto itself as well as complementary to the other. The first volume is suitable for an introductory feminist legal theory course, while the second may more usefully supplement a variety of courses. Both volumes could be read in an ambitious feminist legal theory course. Although the collection includes ideas with which I do not agree, I consider the essays to be the best English-language works of their length. To provide more variety, I favoured short contributions.

Part I, 'Defining the Field', introduces feminist legal theory from three perspectives. Clare Dalton first presents an accurate and readable history of the development of feminist legal theory in the US and links it usefully to post-modernism and other broader strands in critical thinking. In Chapter 2, Christina Whitman introduces feminist legal theory very effectively through a thoughtful, critical review of nine books and articles published between 1984 and 1990. Three of the articles she discusses appear in these volumes. Whitman's discussion may well warrant rereading after becoming familiar with the work she reviews. Lastly, Jenny Morgan introduces some of the major controversies that animated feminist legal theory in the 1980s and relates these controversies to the teaching of law, especially in Australia.

Part II, 'Foundations', begins with Catharine MacKinnon's *Signs* pieces, a two-part essay that appeared in this major interdisciplinary women's journal in 1982–83. This study put feminist legal theory on the intellectual and political map and introduced many of the themes that remain central to the field. Some people find the writing difficult, but it is well worth the effort; certainly the ideas are important enough to return to when they seem more familiar. My 'The Family and the Market' (Chapter 6) presents a feminist critique of the public-private distinction in law; I have included only Part I of the study here.

Part III – devoted to 'controversies' – begins with a discussion among five feminists – three lawyers, an historian and an educational psychologist. It illustrates the extensive use which feminist legal theorists have made of Carol Gilligan's finding that males and females typically engage in different forms of moral reasoning. Particularly important is the short debate between Carol Gilligan and Catharine MacKinnon concerning the origin and status of women's 'different voice' – the extent to which women's 'different voice' is primarily that of the oppressed or whether it is also a source for positive reconstruction. Their disagreement is sharp but thoughtful, respectful, and seemingly working towards a solution rather than scoring points, expressing anger or seeking attention (as in so many debates among male legal authors and even, unfortunately, among women).

The 'sameness and difference' debate, already introduced in Part I by Jenny Morgan, has consumed untold hours of discussion and reams of paper. Chapter 8 by Herma Hill Kay confronts the debate and proposes a pragmatic compromise of sorts, while in Chapter 9 Joan Scott demonstrates why she believes the debate is ill-conceived and how its terms are misleading. (I endorse a similar position on the sameness-difference debate in a legal history contribution reproduced as Chapter 18 in Volume II of this set.)

A woman's freedom to terminate a pregnancy, which in *Roe v. Wade*[4] received a degree of constitutional protection under the rubric of privacy, is thought by many feminists in the US to implicate questions of male control over and subordination of women more than questions of privacy as such. Ruth Bader Ginsburg's essay, based on a lecture she gave in 1984, is one of the best early presentations of this approach to abortion, although she has since updated and expanded her position.[5] Her initial statement (Chapter 10) holds an important place in the history of the development of feminist legal theory; it also presents a useful perspective on the sex discrimination litigation successes of the 1970s and early 1980s – successes in which Ginsburg, as litigator, played a major role. The relationship between women's subordination and coercive restrictions on abortion is developed further by Jean Braucher in Chapter 11, a critical review of a book in which Lawrence Tribe presents a liberal pro-choice, pro-compromise position on abortion. While Tribe's book recognizes that anti-abortion, anti-choice policies undermine a woman's opportunity to participate in the world as an equal to men, his book misses the more important point that these policies seem tolerable to others only because of the long history of the devaluation of women's work and women's humanity. In this sense, the subordinate position of women is a major cause, as well as one result, of coercive controls on women's reproductive decisions.

In Chapter 12, Andrea Dworkin presents one of the strongest statements of the major feminist anti-pornography position. She also introduces some of the reasons why pornography is considered by many American feminists to be such an important issue. Nicola Lacey's piece is one of the best feminist responses to the anti-pornography position. Lacey writes from an English perspective, but she is also thoroughly acquainted with the 'freedom of speech' focus of the American debate. More on the pornography issue can be found in Chapter 18 in this volume by Mary Joe Frug.

In the final chapter in Part III, Kathryn Abrams takes up a feminist debate that is just beginning to unfold in the US. The issue is the level of abstraction or degree of specificity at which feminist theory should proceed. I hope that a series of further articles on various aspects of this question may be forthcoming. Although the Abrams piece misrepresents my own position,[6] I consider it the best short introduction to these controversies available at this time.

The issue of the level of generalization has been raised by other feminists, both in the context of racism and as part of the post-modern critique of 'totalizing' theories. African-American feminists have criticized white women for referring to 'women' in the abstract when they really mean white women (much as feminists have criticized men for using 'people' when they really mean men). African-American women have in turn been criticized by Asian women and Latinas for referring to 'women of colour' when they really mean African-American women. Any generalization may homogenize and exclude, yet the most interesting and engaging theories and the most effective political actions often use abstraction and generalization. Specificity and fragmentation – the apparent alternative to generalization – may be theoretically limiting and politically immobilizing. In fact, the post-modern critique engages different issues from those occupying the racial critique. Rather than challenging such decisions as whether to address women as a single category or instead as subcategories (and how small to make the subcategories), the post-modern critique questions the use of categories altogether; it emphasizes the social construction and instability of any category, including that of 'woman' or 'woman of colour'.

Part IV, the final section, presents several essays that attempt to take feminist theory in new directions. Robin West argues that women's 'hedonic' experiences of pleasure and pain should be brought firmly into the public discourse and that laws should directly address the question of reducing women's pain and increasing their pleasure. Kimberle Crenshaw shows in Chapter 16 how the interaction between racism and sexism disadvantages women of colour and at the same time places them in a uniquely privileged position to improve society for everyone.

In Chapter 17 I construct a topology of feminist critiques of male dominance, relate this to an analogous one I develop of feminist critiques of law, and argue for a more comprehensive critique that would challenge the basic dualistic system of thought central to Western culture. The next chapter, by Mary Joe Frug, demonstrates the value of post-modern analysis to feminist legal theory. Through an examination of the ways that law sexualizes, terrorizes and maternalizes the female body, the essay shows, among other things, how law contributes to the production of femininity. Frug concludes with a complex critique of the efforts by some feminists to use civil rights ordinances to combat pornography.

Lama Abu-Odeh presents a sympathetic view in Chapter 19 of the choice which many Arab women have made to take up the veil. Situating herself as an Arab feminist 'who rejects the veil as a personal choice', Abu-Odeh describes the religious and social meaning of the veil to women of different classes, and the complex relationship between the 'honour' of Arab men and the bodies of their female relatives. The essay identifies multiple reasons to justify veiling – ranging from a woman's ambivalence regarding her body to the protection the veil offers against street sexual harassment – and various ways for feminists to relate to veiled women. I might add that veiling one's body does not cause as much physical harm as spike heel shoes, and that many Western women have adopted spike heel shoes under considerably less external pressure.

The final chapter in this volume again takes up the issue of the relationship between race and gender. Dorothy Roberts focuses on the image of the Black mother in American history and examines the ways that racism and patriarchy interact to create the social construct 'motherhood'. She stresses the importance of going beyond a recognition and acceptance of differences among women. Feminism is more than a critique of sexism; it is a movement of social emancipation to eradicate the domination that pervades our society. Women must combat racism as a central part of that struggle.

Notes

1 Weyrauch, Katz and Olsen (1994), *Cases and Materials on Family Law*, West Publishing Co.
2 See Frances Olsen (1983), 'The Family and the Market: A Study of Ideology and Legal Reform', *Harvard Law Review*, **96**, 1497; Ann E. Freedman (1983), 'Sex Equality, Sex Differences, and the Supreme Court', *Yale Law Journal*, **92**, 913.
3 There are two exceptions – essays whose original versions were too long for inclusion in these volumes. For Chapter 15 in Volume I and Chapter 16 in Volume II, I have used edited versions that appeared in Mary Joe Frug (1992), *Women and Law*, Foundation Press. In these two cases, the double pagination is to the Frug book, which provides the alternative citation.
4 410 U.S. 113 (1973). This is the case in which the US Supreme Court struck down as unconstitutional a law that barred women from obtaining an abortion.
5 See Ruth Bader Ginsburg (1992), 'Speaking in a Judicial Voice', *New York University Law Review*, **67**, 1185. This later article received considerable attention when President Clinton nominated Ruth Bader Ginsburg to the US Supreme Court. Some people interpreted her criticisms of the privacy rationale of *Roe v. Wade* to be a criticism of the decision itself, at a time when constitutional protection for women's access to abortion was under strenuous conservative attack. In addition to criticizing the rationale of the decision, she also further developed the suggestion in her earlier article (reproduced here) that abortion might have been more successfully secured at state level through legislative reform had the Supreme Court refrained from such a broad and sweeping decision as laid down in *Roe v. Wade*.
6 In (1989), 'Feminist Theory in Grand Style', *Columbia Law Review*, **89**, 1147, I was not justifying 'ideological determination' on 'strategic grounds' but trying to correct the common misunderstanding that MacKinnon's emphasis on coercive sexuality disparages the choices made and pleasures enjoyed by individual women. MacKinnon's focus is not a judgment upon individuals but a structural analysis that proceeds on a different level of generalization.

Part I
Defining the Field

[1]

COMMENTARY

Where We Stand:

Observations on the Situation of Feminist Legal Thought

Clare Dalton†

In September of 1987, a conference at Sag Harbor was the occasion for an organized discussion of "The Intellectual Wasteland" as a description of America today. The participants, mostly male, and white, were invited to join the sponsors in grumbling about the poverty of great thinking, and great thinkers, on the national scene. In October of 1987, senior sociologist Jessie Bernard, a woman, gave a lecture at Harvard University, on the subject of her new book, "The Feminist Enlightenment." She talked about now almost two decades of extraordinary intellectual contributions growing out of the women's movement—symbolized, for example, by the exponential increase in women's studies courses at universities around the country, from twenty in the academic year 1969-70, to 30,000 in the year 1986-87. These courses represent not only an amazingly speedy accumulation of enormous amounts of information about women and their lives, past and present, previously unavailable to thinkers, male or female, but the generation of new and challenging frames of inquiry, narratives and theories—collapsing disciplinary boundaries we previously took for granted and pushing beyond them.

The juxtaposition of these two events raises a set of interesting questions. Is there, in fact, a Feminist Enlightenment? If so, why do main-

† Assistant Professor of Law, Harvard Law School. B.A. (Hon.) Jurisprudence 1971, Somerville College, Oxford University; LL.M. 1973, Harvard Law School. In May of 1987 the faculty of the Harvard Law School failed, by a few votes short of the necessary two thirds majority, to grant Professor Dalton tenure. She and seventeen of her tenured colleagues asked that the decision be reviewed, on the grounds that both political and gender discrimination had influenced the outcome. In March of 1988, after a review which failed to investigate the charges of discrimination, Harvard University President Derek Bok affirmed the faculty decision. A gender discrimination suit filed by Professor Dalton remains pending against Harvard University.

stream intellectuals not embrace and celebrate it? Does the mainstream tend simply not to notice it? Does the Feminist Enlightenment actually reinforce or contribute to mainstream malaise? These are the questions I want to address, not at large, but locally; in the context of legal scholarship and legal education.

It has certainly been suggested, by both right- and left-leaning observers, that mainstream post-realist legal thought qualifies as an intellectual wasteland. In relation to which, then, feminist legal thought could be viewed as our corner of the Feminist Enlightenment. In a short compass here I want to describe what I mean by feminist legal thought and the characteristic kinds of projects being undertaken in that name. I hope to convey my sense that this body of thought is one of the most intellectually lively, challenging and provocative current bodies of legal scholarship and practice. And I hope to offer the beginnings of an explanation for the paradoxical co-existence of wasteland and Enlightenment.

To be a feminist today, I think it is fair to say, is to believe that we belong to a society, or even civilization, in which women are and have been subordinated by and to men, and that life would be better, certainly for women, possibly for everybody, if that were not the case. Feminism is then the range of committed inquiry and activity dedicated first, to describing women's subordination—exploring its nature and extent; dedicated second, to asking both *how*—through what mechanisms, and *why*—for what complex and interwoven reasons—women continue to occupy that position; and dedicated third to change.

To be engaged in feminist legal thought is to be a feminist who locates both her inquiry, and her activity, in relation to the legal system.[1] The legal system must here be understood broadly, as including the rules that constitute the formal body of law; the discourses in which those rules are situated, and through which they are articulated and elaborated; the institutions by means of which they are constantly subverted and modified in their implementation and administration; the specifically educational institutions through which legal culture is transmitted from generation to generation, and the various actors whose participation, as lawyers, clients, law enforcement officials, judges, jurors, arbitrators, mediators, social workers, legislators, bureaucrats, teachers or students, sustains the enterprise.[2]

---

[1] I should say at this point that while I do not think it impossible, in theory, to be male and a feminist, I use female pronouns out of the conviction that at least the overwhelming majority of feminists are women. Thus, while it is generally not a good idea for feminists to respond to our longstanding effacement behind male pronouns by practicing a parallel violence, in this particular context the "his or her" formulation would produce an unacceptable distortion of reality.

[2] Even this rather lengthy list is drastically truncated. It does not, for example, include all the witnesses, professional and lay, who assist in adjudicative settings, and all the experts who assist in legislative ones. Furthermore, if you view the legal system not as a self-contained entity, but as an arena of social practice inextricably intertwined with other arenas, it becomes

Feminist legal thought can be found today in many different settings: in print, in communities of women lawyers and legal academics committed to thinking together about the position of women in society and in law, in testimony against the nomination of certain Supreme Court hopefuls, in legislative reform efforts, and in law schools. I am going to put what I have to say in the framework provided by today's law schools, the context with which I (and probably some number of you) am most familiar.

In law schools today, feminist legal thought is most commonly offered as a specialized course. The earliest of these courses were usually called "Women and the Law," or "Sex Discrimination." Today, while those titles have not disappeared, others have appeared. "Feminist Jurisprudence" is a comparatively recent arrival on the scene, along with "Feminist Legal Theory" or the title I have used for this essay, "Feminist Legal Thought." There is no necessary link between course label and course content—all law school course titles are in some sense empty containers waiting to be filled, and each teacher is guided in her choice by a particular set of negative constraints and positive aspirations. Nonetheless, I want to suspend that understanding, for the time being, and structure what I have to say by asking what the differential implications of the different labels might be, if we took them seriously, and had no further information about course content to guide us.

It is important to recognize first, of course, that all the labels share one common problem. They all serve the conservative function of implying, or even insisting, that the concerns of women, and the contributions of feminists, can and should be contained in a single course, where they will neither affect nor infect the rest of the curriculum. Like segregation in the workplace, this separation out of "women's work" in legal theory probably contributes to its devaluation, which serves in turn as a further safeguard against the possibility that its influence might spread. On the other hand, the negative effects of segregation have to be measured against the advantages of obtaining a cloistered space within which to work—the intellectual equivalent of "A Room of One's Own."[3]

Let me begin where feminist legal thinking began,[4] in the courses which appeared in the curriculum in the early seventies under the titles

---

difficult to tell where law leaves off and something else—the market, for example, or medicine, or family, begins.

[3] VIRGINIA WOOLF, A ROOM OF ONE'S OWN (1929). I am departing from the usual practice of including only the author's last name and first initial so that readers may know the gender of the writer.

[4] In the account that follows, I have drawn, in particular, on: Marie Ashe, *Mind's Opportunity: Birthing a Poststructuralist Feminist Jurisprudence*, 38 SYRACUSE L. REV. 1129 (1988); Mary Joe Frug, The Role of Difference in the Study of Women in Law (July, 1987) (unpublished manuscript) (available from author, New England School of Law); Christine Littleton, *Equality and Feminist Legal Theory*, 48 U. PITT. L. REV. 1043 (1987); Ann Scales, *The Emergence of Feminist Jurisprudence: An Essay*, 95 YALE L.J. 1373 (1986).

"Women and the Law" or "Sex Discrimination."[5] "Women and the Law" sounds promisingly comprehensive and at the same time concrete. But it did not traditionally provide the comprehensiveness and concreteness it promised. First, in directing attention to particular doctrinal areas, the course obscured the way in which the problems of women were present in every area of the curriculum; the way in which their absence from many areas of traditional legal discourse was as significant as their presence in others. Second, the traditional areas of doctrinal coverage themselves imposed particular limitations. The alternative title, "Sex Discrimination," provides the key.

Born in and of the women's movement, and sharing its priorities, the courses were originally designed to track developing legal doctrine that addressed women's unequal treatment in law and in society. They focused on constitutional doctrine, and developing statutory standards, addressing discrimination against women in employment, in education, or as recipients of public benefits. This was a strategy that accepted, for the purpose of argument, the supposedly neutral norms and universal principles of the legal system, like equality, and challenged the arbitrariness with which they were being applied. It taught men how to refocus their vision, to some extent, and to see women's sameness where before they had seen difference. It was a strategy born of women's exclusion, and designed to secure access for women to the male arenas in which most of society's benefits were handed out.[6]

It was a strategy that brought women important gains,[7] the first crucial inroads on male monopoly. As time went by, however, its limitations became more visible. First, it turned out to have little power in

---

[5] The first casebooks in the field were published in 1973 and 1974. LEO KANOWITZ, SEX ROLES IN LAW AND SOCIETY: CASES AND MATERIALS (1973); KENNETH M. DAVISON, RUTH BADER GINSBURG & HERMA HILL KAY, TEXT, CASES AND MATERIALS ON SEX-BASED DISCRIMINATION (1974). Ruth Bader Ginsburg first taught a course in sex discrimination in 1970 at Rutgers Law School, Newark campus, then at Harvard in fall, 1971, and at Columbia from 1972 to 1979; Herma Hill Kay first taught a course on "Women and the Law" at Boalt Hall in the spring of 1972. Telephone interview with the chambers of Hon. Ruth Bader Ginsburg (March 21, 1988); interview with Prof. Herma Hill Kay, at Boalt Hall (March 14, 1988).

[6] An important early article developing equality theory in relation to women was Barbara Brown, Thomas Emerson, Gail Falk and Ann Freedman, *The Equal Rights Amendment: A Constitutional Basis for Equal Rights for Women*, 80 YALE L.J. 871 (1971). Among the most sophisticated current exponents of equality theory is Wendy Williams. *See, e.g.*, Williams, *The Equality Crisis: Some Reflections On Culture, Courts and Feminism*, 7 WOMEN'S RTS. L. REP. 175 (1982). This assimilationist model has also been characteristic of the positions taken by the NOW Legal Defense and Education Fund. *See, e.g.*, Brief Amici Curiae of the National Organization for Women; NOW Legal Defense and Education Fund; National Bar Association, Women Lawyers' Division, Washington Area Chapter; National Women's Law Center; Women's Law Project; and Women's Legal Defense Fund, In Support of Neither Party, California Fed. Sav. and Loan Ass'n v. Guerra, 107 S. Ct. 683 (1987) (No. 85-494) (LEXIS, Genfed Library, Briefs file).

[7] The gains can be seen most clearly in the area of employment discrimination. *See, e.g.*, Wengler v. Druggists Mutual Ins. Co., 446 U.S. 142 (1980); Frontiero v. Richardson, 411 U.S. 677 (1973); Phillips v. Martin Marietta Corp., 400 U.S. 542 (1971); Sail'er Inn, Inc. v. Kirby, 5 Cal. 3d 1, 488 P.2d 529, 95 Cal. Rptr. 329 (1971).

situations where women lacked the ability or the inclination to persuade men that they were "the same." "Women and the Law" courses had traditionally brought within their purview, and within their discrimination analysis, those areas of law encompassing precisely the areas of women's lives in which they seemed most inescapably and concretely unlike men—sexuality and reproduction. But despite heroic feminist efforts, *judicially* developing equality analysis proved unable to wrap itself around these intractably female issues, leaving the women's movement split on whether to continue to urge equality, or instead to concede difference.[8] Should women, for example, equate pregnancy with prostate trouble, or acknowledge the uniqueness of their childbearing capacity? This conflict and resulting uneasiness began to show up in the courses; the unifying framework provided by the original conception of equality, which in turn informed the original understanding of discrimination, began to lose its grip, and it became necessary to include in the course syllabi a variety of viewpoints, all claiming feminist status, on the best way out of the equal treatment/special treatment dilemma.

As this account suggests, the equality route had as one of its chief disadvantages its suppression of the concrete ways in which women's lives tend to be shaped differently from men's. The well-founded fear that where the law saw difference it would justify disadvantage, prevented women from insisting that the law take account of their reality. The price women paid was a theoretical legal equality which the actual, material constraints of their lives frequently left them unable to take advantage of. The equality model proposed, for strategic purposes, that what women wanted was access to a world already constituted; it stopped short of proposing that the workplace, or the university, or the professions, or the welfare system, or the family, should be re-envisioned or reconstructed by and with women's participation, to reflect women's reality.[9] These problems too threatened the original understanding of the "Women and the Law" project, and provided a catalyst for change.

---

[8] *See, e.g.*, Herma Hill Kay, *Equality and Difference: The Case of Pregnancy*, 1 BERK. WOMEN'S L.J. 1 (1985); Sylvia Law, *Rethinking Sex and the Constitution*, 132 U. PA. L. REV. 955 (1984); Ann Freedman, *Sex Equality, Sex Differences and the Supreme Court*, 92 YALE L.J. 913 (1983); Katharine Bartlett, *Pregnancy and the Constitution: The Uniqueness Trap*, 62 CALIF. L. REV. 1532 (1974).

[9] This approach justified men, too, in assuming that the admission of women into previously all-male institutions would leave the institutions unchanged. Dean Erwin Griswold, for example, said when women were finally admitted to the Harvard Law School as students in 1950:

> [I]t does not seem to me that this particular development is either very important or very significant. Most of us have seen women from time to time in our lives and have managed to survive the shock. We have even had a few around Langdell and Austin Halls for a good many years now, with no serious consequences. There seems to be no likelihood that we will have a very large proportion of women among our students. I think that we can take it and I doubt if it will change the character of the School or even its atmosphere to any detectable extent. As of today, I doubt if this change alone will require any of our faculty members to revise many of their lectures.

Dean Erwin Griswold, *Developments at the Law School*, HARVARD LAW SCHOOL YEAR BOOK 10 (1950).

"Feminist Jurisprudence" courses can be seen as one reaction to the proliferation of feminist legal theory produced by the unsettling developments of the late seventies and early eighties. They reflect the urgency of developing new approaches to the problems of women in law and in society, ones that will not founder on the rock of "equality," and they celebrate the range and power of the thinking and writing that has responded to this crisis. And yet, of all the possible titles for a course about women's situation with respect to law, "Feminist Jurisprudence" strikes me as in some respects the most problematic, the most expressive of dangers inherent in the project of feminist theory today.

"Feminist Jurisprudence" shares a very particular problem with Jessie Bernard's term "Feminist Enlightenment," which, in its effort to capture the energy and illumination emanating from the intellectual work driven by feminism, risks allying itself with a set of propositions ultimately foreign to feminism. The Enlightenment, after all, was about the Triumph of Reason, the exhilaration of Man's confidence that Truth and Justice were within his grasp. Jurisprudence—the philosophy of law—is, as it has been taught in our law schools, a prototypically Enlightenment project, having to do precisely with the eternals of truth and justice, dependent precisely on the power and priority of reason. Jurisprudence generates sentiments and aspirations like those expressed in the stone words engraved over the portals of Harvard Law School: "Not under Man, but under God and Law."

The problem was that when the men who ordered those words to be carved looked at God, they saw a man, and a man not unlike themselves. Women have long, if not always, held the suspicion, if not the knowledge, that what passed for point-of-view-less-ness was in fact His point of view. A point of view which did not always correspond to hers. Feminist epistemology starts from the premise that what has been presented as "the world" and "the truth" has obscured women's reality, and ignored women's perspective. It contains the explosive suggestion that what have passed as necessary, universal and ahistorical truths have never been more than partial and socio-historically situated versions of truth.[10] It is in this sense, then, that "Feminist Jurisprudence" seems like a contradiction in terms.

Today the Enlightenment project is in trouble all over the place—not only in feminist thought, but in theory more generally—because it rests on those few simple but basic assumptions that many no longer feel able to take for granted: the idea that a "self" can be singular or coher-

[10] The original "Women and the Law" project suppressed this core feminist insight, in order to claim the protection arguably offered to all, regardless of gender, under the supposedly neutral and objective system of legal entitlements. It was only as it became clear that this system, administered by men, would never in fact fulfill its expressed commitments, that this came to seem an unnecessary and potentially disabling strategy.

ent; the idea that knowledge can be objective (or the real-world-out-there correspond with the world-as-viewed-by-the-subject); the idea that certain minimal universal human needs or rights can be identified that are in no way contingent on the historical particulars of any given society, but for that very reason can be used to justify particular social and political structures. The multiplying challenges to the Enlightenment project in discipline after discipline go generally by the name of post-modernism. Feminism is, I believe, at its most powerful and best as a post-modern project.

Understood as a post-modern project, feminism has both positive and negative obligations. The positive obligations I will talk about later. The major negative obligations, I think, are two. First, a feminist narrative or theory should not imagine itself as *replacing* (but only as *displacing*) a male or masculinist one—how could feminists' situated claims to authority become absolute ones? Second, no single feminist narrative or theory should imagine that it can speak univocally for *all* women. We know that grand male theories have traditionally left out of their evidentiary bases and their intellectual formulations the experiences and perspectives not only of women (of all sorts) but also of minority or otherwise disadvantaged groups of men—why should we have different expectations of grand feminist theories?

Living with these limitations is not easy. Sometimes it seems that opposing the grandeur of "Jurisprudence" with anything else than another, perhaps differently gendered, "Jurisprudence" will be an exercise in futility—that proposing the demolition of a historic monument to make way for a variety of makeshift encampments is madness. Sometimes it seems as if humankind won't even have the luxury of a century or two to work this all out unless we feminists can substitute "our way" for "their way." But then again it seems that if feminists can only repeat the territorial battles of the past, if we cannot resist being drawn into the very expansionist warfare we have made it our job to criticize, our medium betrays our message.

This conviction makes me nervous about the kind of legal feminism that most aspires to "Jurisprudence," whether it is based on the core idea of "Woman" as "Mother," drawing usually on the theories of Chodorow,[11] Dinnerstein[12] and Gilligan,[13] or the core idea of "Woman"

---

11 NANCY CHODOROW, THE REPRODUCTION OF MOTHERING (1978). Chodorow suggests that in a society in which strong cultural norms exist about the proper attributes, roles and behaviors associated with femininity and masculinity, the disproportionate role played by women in the parenting of young children serves to "reproduce" mothering qualities in each succeeding generation of women, while reproducing the antitheses of those qualities in men, who struggle to separate out from mother by becoming everything she is not.

12 DOROTHY DINNERSTEIN, THE MERMAID AND THE MINOTAUR (1976). Dinnerstein, whose book predates Chodorow's, shares Chodorow's perception that the developmental task of separating out from mother, differently experienced by boy and girl children, helps to recreate the cultural differences we commonly see between men and women. More central to her account,

as "Sexual Subordinate," as represented in the work of Catharine MacKinnon.[14] Feminist theorists must struggle continually against the temptation of asserting new "necessary, universal and ahistorical truths"—about "Woman," or her adversary "Man"—against the temptation, that is, of reincorporating some new form of the Enlightenment project into feminist work. The danger here is that if we incorporate commonly held but unwarranted and essentialist assumptions about the nature of men, women, or their relationships one with another into feminist inquiry, our subjects will be robbed of other features that play important parts in the dynamic the inquiry seeks to understand. Race, class, sexual orientation, religion, ethnicity, gender *identity* (as opposed to gender attribution),[15] employment status, physical and mental health—all these interwoven elements play a more or less important part in how we constitute ourselves in relation to others.

On the other hand, there is an enormous amount that is illuminating in this feminist jurisprudence. It has taught many women new things about themselves as women, empowered them by showing them some of the structures of their disempowerment, offered them new critical tools to apply to the dismantling of those structures, and given them new words to try out in their struggles to communicate with one another, and with the world they would like to change. It is all useful theory. It becomes destructive only when it becomes insistent and inflexible, when it imagines all women molded by the experiences that are in fact somewhat particular to the kind of women who become law students and law professors, or forces even women law students and law professors to choose between the archetypes of "Mother" and "Sexual Subordinate," without reference to their many other differentiating experiences.

---

however, is the idea that the culturally constructed "mother" role makes successful separation-individuation extremely difficult for children of both genders, leaving men and women allied in a residual (unconscious) hatred and fear of mother, and women more generally. She traces the consequences of these attitudes towards women for adult relationships between men and women, and between men and the planet they inhabit and govern.

13 CAROL GILLIGAN, IN A DIFFERENT VOICE (1982). Gilligan suggests that there are two very different styles of thinking about moral questions, and the resolution of moral problems. One style, or ethic, stresses autonomy, rights, principles and exclusive solutions; the other stresses connection, contextual and consequentialist thinking, and inclusive solutions. The first ethic Gilligan found more prevalent in men, the second in women. Gilligan herself sees the results of her empirical work as confirming the psychoanalytic theory of Nancy Chodorow.

14 CATHARINE MACKINNON, FEMINISM UNMODIFIED (1987). This latest book builds on MacKinnon's earlier work in the areas of both sexual harassment and pornography, as well as her more theoretical contributions to the development of feminist legal theory.

15 In sociological literature, gender attribution is the process by which others come to assign gender to a person—to view them as male or female—whereas an individual's gender identity reflects the individual's own understanding of her- or himself as female or male. *See, e.g.*, SUZANNE J. KESSLER & WENDY MCKENNA, GENDER: AN ETHNOMETHODOLOGICAL APPROACH 1-20 (1978). While it may be relatively unusual for an individual to have a conscious and continuous sense of her- or himself as belonging to the other gender than the one attributed to her or him, psychoanalytic theory suggests that much more commonly, but unconsciously, individuals can take on an identification with the opposite gender as a more or less important aspect of their emotional constitution.

At this point I want to point out a complementary danger, which I think feminists have not yet faced as directly. In the work of some of those theorists who react against the kind of new essentialism I have been describing, the voice of gender risks being lost entirely, and this too seems to me something to be wary of.

Let me identify three quite different ways in which this can happen. One version involves the theorist who, as I have just done, critiques feminist analyses for their essentialism, but who moves on to underscore the differences among and between women, without ever returning to ask whether those differences entirely undercut the "essentialist" claim, or only complicate and modify it. This has happened, I think, in recent reactions to the work of Carol Gilligan, and the ethic of care she identifies as characteristically informing the moral reasoning of her women subjects.[16]

Another version of this dynamic finds support and expression in Lacan's arresting claim that "woman does not exist,"[17] or Luce Irigaray's account of "Ce sexe qui n'est pas un."[18] Taken to the extreme, this is a portrayal of "woman" as so constituted by her oppression that she has no authentic voice in which to speak, no position to urge—the space she inhabits teaches us only about her oppressor, never about herself. Within this framework, the feminist must aspire to root out of herself those attributes woman has been assigned within a patriarchal culture—among which, presumably, would be her ethic of care—and somehow refashion herself, as if she were her own to make.[19]

A third version of the dynamic seems to contain elements of both the prior two. In this version, as in the previous one, the "otherness" of gender, regardless of its particular content, is thought to give the feminist theorist a generic understanding of how dominant groups create "others," enabling her to speak on behalf of other "others" than herself. This feminism of method, to the extent that it orients inquiry towards the differences of handicap, race, religion, and so on, need never focus its gaze on the substance of women's lives. To that extent, it resembles the feminism that critiques feminist essentialism, without asking what is true

---

16 For a brief account of Gilligan's work in moral development, see *supra* note 13. For critiques, see, *e.g.*, Frug, *supra* note 4, at 34 (suggesting that "crude Gilliganism" "threatens to discredit women and their cause") and ELIZABETH SPELMAN, INESSENTIAL WOMAN: PROBLEMS OF EXCLUSION IN FEMINIST THOUGHT (forthcoming Beacon Press 1988).

17 20 JACQUES LACAN, LE SÉMINAIRE, ENCORE, *passim* (1975); JACQUES LACAN, TÉLÉVISION, *passim* (1974).

18 LUCE IRIGARAY, CE SEXE QUI N'EN EST PAS UN (1977), translated as THIS SEX WHICH IS NOT ONE (Catherine Porter, trans. 1985).

19 As MacKinnon puts it: "Feminism criticizes . . . male totality without an account of our capacity to do so or to imagine or realize a more whole truth. Feminism affirms women's point of view by revealing, criticizing, and explaining its impossibility." Catharine MacKinnon, *Feminism, Marxism, Method, and the State: Toward Feminist Jurisprudence*, 8 SIGNS 635, 637 (1983).

as well as what is false about those "essential" analyses.[20] Ironically enough, this care for others, to the exclusion of care for oneself, is exactly the behavior that the culture prescribes for women, and that the theorists attacked as essentialist describe as characteristic of women.

Why are feminists drawn away from specific questions about gender oppression and the mechanisms through which it operates? Out of the welter of possibilities let me identify three. One might be anger—an anger that leads us to reject (the existence or the value of) attributes, like caring, or sensitivity to others, that women develop, in significant part, because the important men in their lives insist on being taken care of. Another might be fear—that to acknowledge those attributes is to acknowledge the enemy within; is already to submit, or to be seen as submitting, to male demands that they be exercised, non-reciprocally, in the care and protection of men. In this view, denying the attributes is the only hope of resisting the appeal for their exercise. A third might be denial of a different kind, the kind that allows women, and especially feminists, to hide from ourselves the extent to which we do, in fact, submit to male demands for care and attention, for fear of what would happen if we did not.

Despite the legitimacy of both the anger and the fear that may shape these reactions, I wonder about the consequences, for women, of denying or withholding from themselves aspects of themselves they wish to deny or withhold from those whose claims they regard as illegitimate. There is, after all, a less self-mutilating option for each woman, which is to acknowledge, and even celebrate, those attributes in herself, while struggling to resist illegitimate demands for their exercise, and remaining aware of the extent to which she yields, of the extent to which resistance seems too costly.

For, as helpful as it is to be reminded that "woman," like other "others," is culturally constructed, the *women* whose lives are shaped by that construction, as it intersects with others, do indeed exist. They exist subordinated to men: poor, more than men; physically and sexually abused, more than men; paid less than men; promoted less than men; employed *and* managing a home, more than men; raising the children, more than men; underperforming relative to their male peers, in academic and professional settings; exploited, denigrated and stereotyped in popular cultural imagery, more than men; assigned the cultural function

---

20 The value of using feminist methodology in the service of other oppressed groups is well exemplified in the work of Martha Minow. *See, e.g.*, Minow, *The Supreme Court, 1986 Term—Foreword: Justice Engendered*, 101 HARV. L. REV. 10 (1987) (dealing with problems of "difference" in Supreme Court jurisprudence in the contexts of religion, ethnicity, race, and handicapping conditions, as well as gender), and Minow, *When Difference Has Its Home: Group Homes for the Mentally Retarded, Equal Protection and Legal Treatment of Difference*, 22 HARV. C.R.-C.L. L. REV. 111 (1987). My concern is only that feminists not be drawn away from specific attention to or advocacy on behalf of women by these other concerns.

of reflecting men "at twice their natural size."[21] They exist, sometimes colluding in their subordination, sometimes resisting it, using whatever their circumstances offer to piece a life together. And feminists, while continuing to acknowledge, celebrate and support the investigation of all the "differences" that divide and constitute both men and women, need not be embarrassed, and should not be afraid, to describe our work as being *about women,* and to imagine that our work is of a kind in which we have a special competence, and a special stake.

The feminist community within the nation's law schools needs to move on, fortified by the past, beyond the original conception of "Women and the Law," beyond "Feminist Jurisprudence," into the curriculum at large—questioning everything, inserting women everywhere. And as the central operations room, in which the agenda is developed, the first experimental studies are produced, the tools are forged and tempered, let us use the ample space provided by a reimagined and concretized conception of "Women and the Law," or by the comfortably modest and plural "Feminist Legal Thought."

When the women's movement began, post-modernism was still an alien in America. Now it is everywhere. Its minions live and work in a world of multiple realities, partial explanations, contingent truths, where scrupulous attention to the perspectived and fractured nature of your own understanding is your only hope of being able to enlarge it. At the same time, scrupulous attention to the perspectived and fractured nature of others' understandings serves the important function of dislodging theories and facts that claim to be neutral, detached, objective, without bias or taint, without perspective, and (as if that were not already enough) internally flawless, coherent and whole. Post-modernism focuses on the power that legitimates particular understandings and explanations of the world, on the link between power and knowledge, even while it also sees power as diffuse, and legitimation of power as local, plural and immanent. It generates new forms of scholarship (and here I'm going to borrow some language I can't improve upon):

> large narratives about changes in social organization and ideology, empirical and social-theoretical analyses of macro-structures and institutions, interactionist analyses of the micro-politics of everyday life, critical-hermeneutical and institutional analyses of cultural production, historically and culturally specific sociologies. . . . The list could go on.[22]

What a field day for feminists—finally able, within a still marginal

---

[21] The quotation is adapted from VIRGINIA WOOLF, A ROOM OF ONE'S OWN 35 (1929): "Women have served all these centuries as looking-glasses possessing the magic and delicious power of reflecting the figure of man at twice its natural size." It has recently been borrowed by Dale Spender and Sally Cline as the title for their new book, REFLECTING MEN AT TWICE THEIR NATURAL SIZE (1987), a funny and poignant account of the ways in which this male demand is structured and expressed, and of the sanctions attendant on the failure to fulfill it.

[22] Nancy Fraser & Linda Nicholson, *Social Criticism Without Philosophy: An Encounter Between Feminism and Postmodernism*, 10 COMMUNICATION, No. 3, at 345 (1988).

but increasingly influential intellectual framework, to articulate women's many realities, and critique the cultural frames and forms which in so many varieties and ways have cabined women's bodies and minds, and imposed such severe restrictions on the articulation of women's grievances. Now we can not only research what happens to women in the world shaped by law, law language and legal institutions,[23] but challenge even the structure of legal thought as contingent and in some culturally specific sense "male,"[24] implying the need for more radical changes than the ameliorative amendations we have offered in the past. Exposing the sites of legal education and practice as important creators and sustainers of the culture of gender, as well as the culture of law, we can assert the importance of studying the treatment of women, women's realities and women's concerns in legal education and the legal profession.[25] Our theory can be at the same time our practice; at work politically as we work professionally, we can give new meaning to the crucial insight of the women's movement that "the personal is political," "the private is also public."

I have left until last the question of how legal feminists may expect their work to be received, by the mainstream. In this as in other settings, it is already a disadvantage to be a woman. But to be a woman who teaches and writes as a woman, addressing women's concerns, is to be almost certainly beyond the pale. All post-modernism poses an insistent challenge to the work and identity of mainstream (malestream) academics, undercutting their claims to universality, threatening their aspiration to immortality. But academic father-slaying, by sons, while a terrifying prospect for both generations, is at the same time recognized as a generational dynamic, tamed by the cultural institutions in which it plays itself out, and in some sense as permissible as it is inevitable.[26] There is the further ameliorative factor that fathers have been sons in their time, and can identify, albeit only partially, with their aggressors. Whereas women, as mothers, but also as wives and daughters, have been assigned the function of admiring reflection, a task they doubly turn their backs on when they claim women as the subject of their study, and post-mod-

---

[23] *See, e.g.*, Marie Ashe, *Law-Language of Maternity: Discourse Holding Nature in Contempt*, 22 NEW. ENG. L. REV. 521 (1988); Martha Fineman, *Dominant Discourse, Professional Language and Legal Change in Child Custody Decision-Making*, 101 HARV. L. REV. 727 (1988).

[24] *See, e.g.*, Fran Olsen, *The Sex of Law*, __ INT'L J. SOC. L. __ (publication delayed at author's request); Robin West, *Jurisprudence and Gender*, 55 U. CHI. L. REV. 1 (1988).

[25] *See, e.g.*, Lucinda Finley, Gender Differences in Cognitive Approaches to Legal Problems and to the Law (July 30, 1987) (unpublished manuscript) (on file at the Berkeley Women's Law Journal); Carrie Menkel-Meadow, *The "Feminization" of the Legal Profession: The Comparative Sociology of Women Lawyers* in LAWYERS AND SOCIETY: A COMPARATIVE APPROACH (Richard Abel & Philip Lewis eds.) (forthcoming); Menkel-Meadow, *The Comparative Sociology of Women Lawyers*, 24 OSGOODE HALL L.J. __ (Fall 1986); Menkel-Meadow, *Portia in a Different Voice: Speculations on Women's Lawyering Process*, 1 BERK. WOMEN'S L.J. 39 (1985).

[26] For an extended treatment of this theme in an academic setting, see HAROLD BLOOM, THE ANXIETY OF INFLUENCE (1973).

ern feminist theory as their intellectual tradition. No cultural model exists which can contain the threat posed by this withdrawal, or curb the fears of those who cease to see their images admiringly reflected in women's work.

In this respect not much has changed since Virginia Woolf wrote in 1929:

> Whatever may be their use in civilized societies, mirrors are essential to all violent and heroic action. That is why Napoleon and Mussolini both insist so emphatically upon the inferiority of women, for if they were not inferior they would cease to enlarge. That serves to explain in part the necessity that women so often are to men. And it serves to explain how restless they are under her criticism; how impossible it is for her to say to them this book is bad, this picture is feeble, or whatever it may be, without giving far more pain and rousing far more anger than a man would do who gave the same criticism. For if she begins to tell the truth, the figure in the looking-glass shrinks; his fitness for life is diminished. How is he to go on giving judgement, civilising natives, making laws, writing books, dressing up and speechifying at banquets, unless he can see himself at breakfast and at dinner at least twice the size he really is?[27]

Except now the looking-glasses not only hang on the walls of dining rooms, but also stand in the halls of law schools, and their glass is less and less likely to magnify as it reflects. The distress and disorientation produced by this state of affairs can be diminished, it seems, only by the negotiation between mirror and mirrored of new relationships, and new imageries to instantiate and celebrate them.

---

[27] Virginia Woolf, A Room of One's Own 36 (1929).

[2]

REVIEW ESSAY

FEMINIST JURISPRUDENCE

CHRISTINA BROOKS WHITMAN

Real Rape. By Susan Estrich. Cambridge: Harvard University Press, 1987.

"Statutory Rape: A Feminist Critique of Rights Analysis." By Frances Olsen. *Texas Law Review* 63 (October 1984): 387-432.

"Jurisprudence and Gender." By Robin West. *University of Chicago Law Review* 55 (Winter 1988): 1-72.

"The Difference in Women's Hedonic Lives: A Phenomenological Critique of Feminist Legal Theory." By Robin West. *Wisconsin Women's Law Journal* 3 (1987): 81-145.

Making All the Difference: Inclusion, Exclusion, and American Law. By Martha Minow. Ithaca, N.Y., and London: Cornell University Press, 1990.

Justice and Gender. By Deborah L. Rhode. Cambridge: Harvard University Press, 1989.

"Telling Stories about Women and Work: Judicial Interpretations of Sex Segregation in the Workplace in Title VII Cases Raising the Lack of Interest Argument." By Vicki Schultz. *Harvard Law Review* 103 (June 1990): 1750-1843.

"Sapphire Bound!" By Regina Austin. *Wisconsin Law Review* 1989 (May 1989): 539-578.

"On Being the Object of Property." By Patricia Williams. *Signs* 14 (Autumn 1988): 5-24.

Feminist Studies 17, no. 3 (Fall 1991).

In the 1970s feminist legal theory furthered feminist legal practice. Feminist lawyers saw themselves as advocates of "women's rights," interested in winning legal victories in particular cases. Because their attention was focused on reform through legislation or litigation, the theory they developed was deliberately, if uncritically, grounded in what would be persuasive to those who held power in government institutions. They built directly upon the precedent made in race cases, precedent which assumed that the appropriate goal for social change was equality and defined equality as the similar treatment of similarly situated individuals. The key to the early legal victories[1] of the second wave was the assertion that women and men are similarly situated for all legally relevant purposes.

In the last decade, however, feminist jurisprudence has become less interested in arguing to judges. Instead, its attention has turned to the critique of law itself as a construct of patriarchy. As a practical matter this shift was provoked by the apparent deficiencies of the ostensibly neutral, formal equality strategy in cases involving problems, like pregnancy, that judges thought reflected bedrock biological differences between women and men.[2] Legal scholars, influenced by feminist critical theory in other disciplines, began to ask whether the standard methods of legal analysis necessarily distort what is at stake for women. In a move that parallels the feminist criticism of science, these scholars challenge the assumption that law establishes a neutral procedural framework that provides a fair hearing for all points of view.

One significant body of work within this critical movement argues that sex is not an issue that can be made to disappear through gender-neutral methods of analysis. This scholarship builds on the insights of Catharine MacKinnon, the only feminist legal theorist to come up with a unifying theory independent from legal precedent and the only one whose work has had a wide readership beyond the profession.[3] MacKinnon challenges the assumption that answers are to be found by comparing women to men. She argues that discrimination against women is based on dominance, rather than distinction, and that the key to understanding male dominance lies in the social construction of sexuality from a male perspective. The social meaning of sex as pleasurable for both sexes when men dominate and women submit justifies gender hierarchy. Women are seen as naturally subordinate in this most basic of biological activities and, by extension, naturally subordinate as political beings. Sex between women and men, which MacKinnon sees as coerced in fact but socially described as consensual, becomes for her the central subject of jurisprudential inquiry because it explains why sex inequality can be seen by law as the consequence of free individual choice.[4]

Examples of the way in which MacKinnon's work has influenced legal scholarship can be found in the legal reform work of Susan Estrich, the deconstructive work of Frances Olsen, and the more ambivalent, personally exploratory work of Robin West. Estrich fits within the tradition of the 1970s in that she argues for specific changes in legal rules, but when she writes about rape her central theme is the way in which criminal law has constructed sexual coercion as consent. Estrich also departs from earlier strategies for legal reform in her explicit rejection of objectivity and abstraction. She begins her discussions with a description of her own rape, and she goes beyond legal doctrinal analysis to the wider context of the reporting, investigation, prosecution, and disposition of rape cases. Unlike MacKinnon, Estrich is willing to adopt the language of consent. She would have the law find lack of consent when a woman has expressly refused to engage in intercourse ("No means no") or when her consent was coerced by threats or misrepresentation. This would leave unpunished those rapes in which consent or silence was coerced by more subtle means, but it would go beyond what is currently possible in the prosecution of rape by nonstrangers. Because Estrich is primarily interested in legal change, she has written her basic argument in two forms to two audiences, neither of which is the larger feminist community. Her work on rape initially appeared as a lengthy law review article addressed to lawyers[5] and was subsequently repackaged as a book, *Real Rape,* addressed to a lay audience. Although the article adopts the standard law-review format in that it consists of an extended discussion of cases and legislation, Estrich uses these materials to create a powerful narrative of the exclusion of the woman victim's perspective. Her theme throughout is that consent and coercion are defined from a male point of view. Criminal law has required, for example, that force be resisted in the way that men would respond to male aggression. And the due process concern that a defendant not be unfairly punished is exaggerated inappropriately by the male fear that women will cry rape. Although the book is addressed to a lay audience, it is in some ways less exciting than the article. The argument is more tightly written, focused on the problem of date rape, and Estrich carefully avoids the explicit feminism and anger that permeates the article. *Real Rape* is designed to persuade legislators to make changes that will facilitate the prosecution of date rape without requiring that they accept Estrich's more fundamental challenges to the way in which male perspectives are embedded in the criminal justice system.

Frances Olsen writes within the tradition of critical legal studies, which has challenged the consistency and coherence of the rights-based analysis that was used to achieve the early victories of the "women's rights" movement. Olsen's most powerful article may be "Statutory Rape: A Feminist Critique of Rights Analysis," which analyzes *Michael M. v. Superior Court of Sonoma County.*[6] In that case the Supreme Court upheld a sex-based statutory rape statute against an equal protection challenge. Olsen demonstrates how any approach to the case threatens women: upholding statutory rape law provides security for some women while intruding on the autonomy of others who are not allowed to consent to sex; striking the laws down furthers autonomy at the expense of security when consent is coerced. The trouble, Olsen suggests, is that, under present circumstances, the interests of some women would be best served by stressing autonomy, but other women would be best served by stressing security. Indeed, a particular woman might well be oppressed by both sexual freedom and societal control of her sexuality. She might be subject to coerced sex that does not fit the legal definition of rape and yet be prohibited from other activities on the grounds of her sexual vulnerability.[7] To treat women as autonomous bearers of legal rights ignores MacKinnon's insight into the way consent is coerced. *Michael M.* provides a case study that demonstrates how legal argument forces advocates to reach premature foreclosure. The answer, according to Olsen, is not to give up on law but to give up on the effort to achieve credibility with judges by articulating principles that purport to decide all cases for all time. Feminist lawyers should make explicitly political choices and challenge those particular rules that have most pernicious effects at any given time.

Olsen's work demonstrates that feminist insights, the introduction of the perspectives of women, can be done in a way that is compatible with and continuous with the best sort of legal analytic reasoning. Lawyers have always dealt with precedent through close textual reading that searches for unsupported assumptions and suppressed inconsistencies. Olsen turns these techniques to self-consciously political purposes in her critique of the arguments made by the Supreme Court, by lawyers, by feminists, and by feminist lawyers. She demonstrates not only that each argument leaves some important interests out but also that a particular position may actually interfere with the ability of the advocate to see what has happened to the real woman in the real case. She points out, for example, that another feminist scholar, who advocates gender-neutral laws, characterizes the rape in *Michael M.* as a "victimless crime" even though the adolescent defendant in that case sought the consent of the victim by slugging her in the face.

Olsen's work builds explicitly on MacKinnon's. Robin West's scholarship is more deeply ambivalent about MacKinnon's contribution, but its very preoccupations demonstrate the way in which issues of sexuality and dominance have become central to feminist jurisprudence. West, like Olsen, has been very prolific. I will discuss only two of her articles here. In "Jurisprudence and Gender," West argues that both liberal rights-based theory and critical legal theory are premised upon a definition of "human being" that is inapplicable to women. Both theories regard humans as fundamentally separate from each other, but women, West claims, are not in fact physically individuated from other people. Women, unlike men, "are in some sense 'connected' to life and to other human beings during at least four recurrent and critical material experiences": pregnancy, heterosexual penetration, menstruation, and breastfeeding. Although West acknowledges that not all women have all these experiences, she argues that most women are forced into them by male power disguised as biological imperative. In this respect she builds on MacKinnon, and, perhaps more than MacKinnon,[8] West appears to assume that these fundamental experiences are the same for all women despite race, class, and even sexual preference. West differs from MacKinnon in that she has a positive as well as a negative view of sexuality: the "potentiality for physical connection with others that uniquely characterizes women's lives has within it the seeds of *both* intimacy and invasion" (p. 53). MacKinnon accurately describes women's experience, West says, but so do her opponents who describe sex as pleasurable and affirming; each describes one side of the fundamental contradiction inherent in the material condition of women.

West's approach is reassuring to those who feel uncomfortable with MacKinnon's emphasis on sex as inevitably coerced. It provides a less political way to understand the strategic tensions described by Olsen. And it is particularly powerful in describing why a woman's perspective on such issues as rape and abortion may not be captured by legal concepts of autonomy and independence: "The fear of sexual and fetal invasion and intrusion is the fear of being occupied *from within,* not annihilated from without . . . of having one's own physical and material life taken over by the pressing physical urgency of another, not ended by conflicting interests of another. . . " (p. 41). West claims to provide a means of reconciling "cultural feminists" like Carol Gilligan and "radical feminists" like Catharine MacKinnon. But much of the apparent force of her approach is attributable to the reductive way in which she describes the positions of others, and the reconciliation she claims to achieve may be simply schizophrenic. That possibility becomes apparent in a second, more personal, and very thought-provoking article ponderously titled "The Difference in Women's Hedonic Lives: A Phenomenological Critique of Feminist Legal Theory."

"The Difference in Women's Hedonic Lives" is divided into two parts. In the first part, West uses examples from her own life to demonstrate that women's suffering is invisible to men because men lack similar experiences and because women are taught either to deny pain or to regard it as inevitable or pleasurable. The examples West uses are promiscuity, physically abusive relationships, and street harassment. Much of this material is powerfully supportive of MacKinnon's point that sex is socially constructed in ways that are destructive to women. But the second part of West's essay takes MacKinnon to task for silencing women who experience pleasure in sexual submission. West takes *The Story of O* as illustrative of the way in which giving men power can further women's pleasure. MacKinnon's approach, West argues, leads to a feminism that ignores the "experiential reality" that some women feel pleasure in pain and thus diminishes the "hedonic" content of women's lives. West's article is so consistently interesting and so obviously an effort to speak honestly and directly on matters that are seldom discussed in legal literature that it cannot be easily dismissed. Yet it doesn't form a coherent whole. The author of part 2 seems not to have learned from the author of part 1, and vice versa. If women are taught to lie to men and to themselves about the existence of pain, as West argues in part 1, how are we to use their experience of pleasure in pain as a basis for feminist theory?

West's attempt to reconcile MacKinnon with the insights of cultural feminism reflects the importance of Carol Gilligan, who has been the other major influence on feminist work challenging the accepted discourse of law. In fact, Gilligan has had an impact on feminist jurisprudence that may be more powerful and more enduring than her impact on any other discipline. Legal feminists came late to the question of difference. The constraints of litigation led them to continue to focus on what women and men have in common at a time when feminists elsewhere were beginning to be preoccupied with difference. Gilligan's *In a Different Voice: Psychological Theory and Women's Development*[9] was published just at the time when legal scholars were looking for an alternative to the gender-neutral jurisprudence of the 1970s. It seemed to provide an explanation for the alienation that many women feel while in law school and legal practice, while suggesting that an alternative jurisprudence could be built around themes of caring, relationships, and responsibility.

Yet Gilligan's "ethic of care" has not proven to be very useful for deciding particular cases or generating legal theory. West's effort to bridge MacKinnon's emphasis on invasion and Gilligan's emphasis on intimacy is provocative but unsuccessful. Another ambitious but ultimately unsatisfying attempt to build from Gilligan is Suzanna Sherry's "Civic Virtue and the Feminine Voice in Constitutional Adjudication."[10] Sherry identifies Gilligan's "different voice" with the tradition of civic republicanism currently enjoying a vogue among constitutional scholars and then argues that the opinions of Justice Sandra Day O'Connor, at least when compared to the opinions of other conservative Justices, exhibit relational thinking in that O'Connor is particularly sensitive to the claims of community. The result is a rather dazzling but very strained exhibition of how unlike can be made to seem (a little bit) alike. In order to make the comparisons work to even a limited extent, Sherry is forced to describe not only civic republicanism, but also O'Connor and Gilligan, in the most abstract and ummodulated terms.

A more successful, because less ambitious, effort to apply Gilligan's insights can be found in the work of Carrie Menkel-Meadow. Menkel-Meadow, who writes about alternative dispute resolution and the legal profession, focuses not on the substance of law but on the role of women in legal practice. In an article written in 1985 she speculated, on the basis of Gilligan's work, that a significant increase in the numbers of women lawyers might lead to changes in the practice and values of the law.[11] Menkel-Meadow thought women might become "innovators and critics of the profession," creating, for example, a "more cooperative, less war-like" alternative to the "advocacy-adversarial model" of law and a non-hierarchical, participatory structure of law firm organization. More recently, Menkel-Meadow admits that her own research and that of others "seems to indicate that women in law are being assimilated into the traditional culture of the profession rather than bringing . . . innovations" (p. 313).[12] A major strength of Menkel-Meadow's work is her care not to claim too much. She is not insensitive to the dangers of perpetuating stereotypes and takes pains to stress that she is talking about socially created differences between women and men, but she is committed as "an act of faith" to the proposition that women will make a difference. Her work is aspirational, self-described as an agenda for future research and an effort to encourage the development of more caring methods of lawyering. Because it has so little upon which to build, it is also frustratingly vague.

Menkel-Meadow does not, except in the most general sense, try to use Gilligan's work to decide substantive questions. Martha Minow's recent book, *Making All the Difference: Inclusion, Exclusion, and American Law* does exactly that. It is an ambitious effort at synthesis. Minow combines Gilligan's insights with American pragmatism, and other work in philosophy, social science, and literary criticism, to suggest that a wide range of legal questions involving difference ought to be resolved by "attention to relationships—relationships between people, between concepts, and between the observer and the observed." Minow does not limit herself to issues of gender difference but explores the ways in which cases involving race, ethnicity, religious minorities, children, the mentally and physically disabled, and even the separation of governmental powers can be productively resolved by attention to relationships. Her theme is that problems of difference have seemed intractable because difference has been thought to inhere in the "different" individual rather than to be a product of social construction. This mistake has led courts to ask how "special" needs can be accommodated into essentially unchanging environments rather than to observe how environments create difference by unnecessary failure to be inclusive. Minow argues that we can restructure relationships to include difference. The standard feminist example of this point would be the adoption of workplace structures and practices which assume workers have obligations to dependent family members. Minow generates others: developing hospital procedures that treat every patient as potentially HIV-positive; teaching sign language to the hearing students in a deaf child's class; finding another family to care for a Down's syndrome child whose parents are unable or unwilling to provide emotional support.

Minow does an effective job of explaining how pragmatist and feminist thinking can be used to challenge the "individual rights" analysis that has dominated law. Refreshingly undogmatic, she does not reject rights theory in favor of relational strategies but redefines rights as "communally recognized rituals for securing attention in a continuing struggle over boundaries between people" (p. 383). Despite the strength of her critique, however, Minow does not ultimately succeed in formulating an alternative decisional strategy. She herself sees the problem. It is one shared by many who have tried to articulate a theory of value based on caring: "This all sounds lovely, you may say, but awfully abstract, What actually happens?" (p. 381). Minow's response is to generate a series of actual case studies. They are all individually interesting but difficult to understand as part of a common strategy. Minow's "relational" solutions to particular problems—like, ironically, so many of the solutions generated by economic approaches to law—seem possible only because she makes factual assumptions that facilitate resolution. She assumes, for example, that there are enough resources to treat all hospital patients with extraordinary care. The deaf child appears to be in a class that is taught by a teacher who knows or can easily learn sign language and one in which no other disabled or disruptive students compete for accommodation; this ideal environment will apparently be recreated year after year. In the Down's syndrome example, which is based on actual litigation, the court has before it a family eager to be emotional parents to the child. Every case seems to turn on fortuities. Perhaps all Minow means to say is that the legal system ought to be open to taking advantage of those opportunities to restructure relationships that happen to exist. That is an important point but not one that promises a dramatic transformation in how law deals with difference.

The great temptation of legal thinking is the hope that the interests of women, like those of other groups, can be captured in a single narrative, or formula, or three- or four-part test to be applied to all cases. This would give litigators confidence that they are truly representing their clients' interests, and judges would be able to tell themselves that they are acting with appropriate neutrality. Cases, after all, must be decided, so lawyers must reach conclusions and come up with answers. Provisional, contingent solutions seem too political, too likely to be the result of unconscious or conscious bias. Yet feminist scholars, who have undergone their own temptation with unitary, foundational theory, have not been able to describe a theory that benefits some women without hurting others. There are real differences among women, and some of these have been exacerbated by the women's movement and its legal victories, which achieved access to power for some while removing traditional protections for others.[13] As Deborah L. Rhode puts it, "we need theory without Theory."

In her recent book, *Justice and Gender,* Rhode, like Minow, emphasizes the broader context in which legal rules are created. But unlike Minow, she addresses only questions involving gender and she reaches for no overarching method of analysis. Instead, Rhode discusses the full range of particular legal problems involving women, placing each one in its historical, social, and economic context before discussing the relevant judicial opinions and current legal arguments. Rhode herself makes very few suggestions for legal change, at least as ultimate solutions. There are aspects of this approach which are extremely frustrating. Rhode is so thorough in explicating the full range of arguments that she seems excessively balanced. Again and again she responds to hard questions with a simple call for more research. But Rhode has created the first true legal treatise on gender, and unlike most legal treatises, hers does not limit itself to doctrine. The book is crammed with information from secondary sources and exhaustive in describing the range of possible legal positions. It is not a comfortable book to read from cover to cover, largely because of its lack of a distinctive point of view, but it is a splendid resource.

Some of the most exciting scholarship now being produced

creates partial narratives. Much of it is innovative in its use of nonlegal methods of analysis, and some departs dramatically from traditional approaches to legal inquiry. In one recent article, for example, Vicki Schultz uses statistical methods to analyze the role in Title VII cases of employers' arguments that women are overrepresented in low-paying, low-status jobs because they are not interested in more highly rewarded work. Instead of considering each judicial opinion as an independent, self-contained text, Schultz looks at a data set of fifty-four cases and makes a quantitative analysis of the relationship between argument, evidence, and outcome. She finds that courts are more willing to credit the lack of interest argument when employers show that they have made special efforts to attract women and less likely to credit it when plaintiffs produce individual victims who can offer anecdotal evidence of discrimination. Schultz concludes that courts assume that patterns of sex segregation are attributable either to women's choices or to employer coercion. Judges believe that discrimination exists only where employers refuse to hire those women who enter the work world with the desire to take on nontraditional jobs. They overlook the possibility that women's choices are evolving, formed in part in reaction to structural features of employment that affect women's experience in the workplace. Relying on sociological research which supports this latter interpretation, Schultz proposes a new story which implicates employment practices in women's choices even when employers do not engage in deliberate exclusion or coercion. Because she does not focus on doctrinal argument but on underlying judicial assumptions about the nonlegal world, Schultz does not discuss whether Title VII provides an adequate vehicle for remedies against individual employers when segregation is caused by structural and cultural features of workplace organization. But she makes a powerful case that, if it does not provide such remedies, the statute is not responsive to the most serious and enduring problems of employment discrimination against women.

Schultz's work suggests that no single legal approach is adequate because workplace exclusion operates in different ways for different women. Narratives by Black feminist scholars pose a more fundamental challenge, not only to the perspective of white feminist jurisprudence,[14] but also to its lack of passion. In "Sapphire Bound!" Regina Austin, a writer who has been particularly interested in tactics of resistance,[15] calls for a jurisprudence that would "preach the justness of the direct, participatory, grass-roots opposition Black women undertake" (p. 544). She takes as her text *Chambers v. Omaha Girls Club,*[16] in which a court held that Title VII was not violated when a girls' club, administered primarily by whites for Black teenage girls, fired its arts and crafts instructor, an unmarried Black woman, because she became pregnant. The dismissal was found to be justified because Chambers was a "negative role model" for her students. Austin points out the irony of an employment practice that replicates the very condition the organization claims to address: club administrators hoped to discourage teenage pregnancy because of the economic hardship and social prejudice it entails, but Chambers's pregnancy was not "problematic" in this sense until she was fired. Like Schultz, Austin relies on sociological and cultural studies of the way in which structure affects individual choice. She describes adolescent pregnancy as a response to the material conditions in which many Black teenagers live, and Chambers's adult decision to become a mother as "an alternative social form that one might choose deliberately, rationally, and proudly" (p. 576). Role models, Austin argues, ought to be Sapphires, affirming the perspective of less powerful Black women rather than projecting "an assimilated person that is . . . unthreatening to white people" (p. 574).

Other Black scholars have refused to conform to traditional legal standards of politeness and coherence. Some of the most powerful work is by Patricia Williams, who is more explicitly autobiographical than Austin. Williams's recent essays are written in a fragmented, postmodern style that captures the contradictions of her life as a descendant of slaves and of slaveowners who has graduated from Harvard Law School and now teaches commercial transactions. In "On Being the Object of Property," Williams challenges conventional legal discourse by wrenching legal concepts away from their established meanings and using them evocatively and metaphorically. An illusory contract, for example, becomes not a contract in which consideration fails because it is nonexistent or unavailable but a metaphor for the way in which contract law is used to justify the brutal parting of a mother from her children – Mary Beth Whitehead, a "surrogate" mother, from her baby daughter; Williams's twelve-year-old great-great-grandmother, a slave raped by her owner, from her daughter, Williams's great-grandmother, Mary. Williams's essay is disturbing because it is open-ended and evolving. It doesn't end with a solution. It doesn't even formulate a problem in a form that a court could answer. Perhaps it therefore isn't "law." But it certainly should speak to lawyers.

Law has a tendency to marginalize, and even exclude, theories that are tentative, ambiguous, provisional. Yet some of the most exciting feminist jurisprudence, as well as some of the most banal, has been explicitly open-ended. Formal rules and structured analyses are the ways in which law protects itself against favoritism and arbitrary decision making. But feminist scholarship has found that the dangers of legal power lie not only in bias and interest but also in the false confidence that bias and interest have been eliminated. Feminist jurisprudence has developed a group of theories that can be used to critique results in particular cases and be a powerful challenge to the rhetorical claims of the law. It has complicated and challenged legal discussion. Its interdisciplinary reach is impressive, although little of it is, perhaps as a consequence, strikingly original.

Yet there is a sense in which much of current feminist jurisprudence seems unmoored, directionless. Perhaps more than anywhere else, the strains of the debate over essentialism have disrupted feminist strategies in the law. The formal equality model that accomplished so much through litigation in the 1970s cannot be reconciled with what feminists have come to know about the dangers of assuming similarity within gender as well as across gender lines. However, no alternative model has emerged that avoids these dangers and successfully appeals to the constitutive principles of our Constitution and laws. Courts are just beginning to accept the full implications of the view that groups, as well as individuals, can be holders of legal rights. The next, and more difficult, stage will be to retain the force of that understanding while making a legal space for more nuanced claims about the way that disadvantage varies within groups.

NOTES

1. In cases such as those challenging the legality under Title VII of policies that prohibit all fertile women from certain high-paying jobs on the ground that working conditions

are harmful to fetuses, International Union, UAW v. Johnson Controls, 111 S. Ct. 1196 (1991), some of these victories have come under attack. Important work is being done by scholars such as Mary Becker, who has demonstrated the powerful similarities between these policies and early-twentieth-century protective legislation held unconstitutional in the 1970s. See Becker, "From *Muller v. Oregon* to Fetal Vulnerability Policies," *University of Chicago Law Review* 53 (Fall 1986): 1219-73.

2. See Joan Williams, "Deconstructing Gender," *Michigan Law Review* 87 (February 1989): 797-845; Lise Vogel, "Debating Difference: Feminism, Pregnancy, and the Workplace," *Feminist Studies* 16 (Spring 1990): 9-32.

3. Catharine MacKinnon's work over the last decade has been influenced by her collaboration with Andrea Dworkin, who is not a lawyer. A representative sample of MacKinnon's speeches can be found in *Feminism Unmodified* (Cambridge: Harvard University Press, 1987); her most recent work in political theory is *Toward a Feminist Theory of the State* (Cambridge: Harvard University Press, 1989).

For reviews in the legal literature, both positive and negative, see Angela Harris, "Categorical Discourse and Dominance Theory," *Berkeley Women's Law Journal* 5 (January 1990): 181-96; Frances Olsen, "Feminist Theory in Grand Style," *Columbia Law Review* 89 (June 1989): 1147-78; Christina B. Whitman, "Law and Sex," *Michigan Law Review* 86 (May 1988): 1388-1403; and Katherine T. Bartlett, "MacKinnon's Feminism: Power on Whose Terms?" *California Law Review* 75 (July 1987): 1559-70.

4. Perhaps because MacKinnon's framework has so dominated the discussion of sexuality in feminist jurisprudence (as both inspiration and focus of attack), there has been very little development of a lesbian perspective. See Patricia A. Cain, "Feminist Jurisprudence: Grounding the Theories," *Berkeley Women's Law Journal* 4 (January 1989): 191-214.

5. Susan R. Estrich, "Rape," *Yale Law Journal* 95 (May 1986): 1087-1184. Estrich has continued to write as an advocate for legal reform to a specific professional audience. A recent article on abortion doctrine, coauthored with Kathleen Sullivan, is explicitly directed to Justice Sandra Day O'Connor, whom the authors describe as "in the position single-handedly to decide the future of abortion rights." Susan R. Estrich and Kathleen M. Sullivan, "Abortion Politics: Writing for an Audience of One," *University of Pennsylvania Law Review* 138 (November 1989): 119-55.

6. See Michael M. v. Superior Court of Sonoma County, 450 U.S. 464 (1981).

7. For example, in Dothard v. Rawlinson, 433 U.S. 321 (1977), the Supreme Court held that the exclusion of women from employment as prison guards in all-male maximum security prisons that housed sex offenders did not violate Title VII of the Civil Rights Act because the "unique" vulnerability of women to rape created an increased security risk that justified their exclusion.

8. Angela Harris, "Race and Essentialism in Feminist Legal Theory," *Stanford Law Review* 42 (January 1990): 581-616, criticizes both West and MacKinnon as privileging white experience and ignoring Black women. Harris argues that MacKinnon's emphasis on the sexual domination of women by men ignores the way in which social constructions of sexuality (for example, the response to rape) have been used to oppress Black men as well as women. Harris's attack on West goes directly to the core of West's theory. By making gendered experiences primary in the formation of women's sense of self, West overlooks the lives of Black women, for whom "the web of race and gender" cannot be disentangled.

9. Carol Gilligan, *In a Different Voice: Psychological Theory and Women's Development* (Cambridge: Harvard University Press, 1982).

10. Suzanna Sherry, "Civic Virtue and the Feminine Voice in Constitutional Adjudication," *Virginia Law Review* 72 (April 1986): 543-616.

11. Carrie Menkel-Meadow, "Portia in a Different Voice: Speculation on a Women's

Lawyering Process," *Berkeley Women's Law Journal* 1 (Fall 1985): 39-63.

12. Ibid., "Exploring a Research Agenda of the Feminization of the Legal Profession: Theories of Gender and Social Change," *Law and Social Inquiry* 14 (Spring 1989): 289-319.

13. See, for example, the impact on women of gender neutrality in divorce law described in Lenore J. Weitzman, *The Divorce Revolution* (New York: Free Press, 1985); and Kristen Luker's description of the abortion controversy as a dispute among women ignited by the Supreme Court's decision in Roe v. Wade, 410 U.S. 113 (1973). Kristen Luker, *Abortion: The Politics of Motherhood* (Berkeley: University of California Press, 1984).

14. For example, Patricia J. Williams, in "Alchemical Notes: Reconstructing Ideals from Deconstructed Rights," *Harvard Civil Rights-Civil Liberties Law Review* 22 (Spring 1987): 401-33, and Kimberle Crenshaw, in "Race, Reform, and Retrenchment: Transformation and Legitimation in Antidiscrimination Law," *Harvard Law Review* 101 (April 1988): 1331-87, have argued that some white feminists, and male critical legal scholars, have been too quick to jettison rights-based theory. Legal discourse of rights has, they argue, been a powerful tool for minorities, who do not consider its work complete.

15. In addition to the article under review here, also see Regina Austin, "Employer Abuse, Worker Resistance, and the Tort of Intentional Infliction of Emotional Distress," *Stanford Law Review* 41 (July 1988): 1-59; and Regina Austin, "Resistance Tactics for Tokens," *Harvard BlackLetter Journal* 3 (Spring 1986): 52-53.

16. 629 F. Supp. 925 (D. Neb. 1986), *affirmed*, 834 F.2d 697 (8th Cir. 1987), *rehearing denied*, 840 F.2d 583 (1988).

[3]

FEMINIST THEORY AS LEGAL THEORY

BY JENNY MORGAN*

[*The application of feminist theories to the structure of law has become a subject of increasing controversy. The author discusses the current American debate between the proponents of equal treatment by the law, and those who believe that women have different and special needs. The article examines attempts at deconstruction of the public/private distinction within law. Both threads of analysis are taken up in an examination of the potential impact of feminism on Australian legal education.*]

INTRODUCTION

This article sets out to indicate the centrality of the feminist legal project to law, legal scholarship and legal education in America. While the focus is American, the implications I draw from the material are, I believe, central to Australian legal education. Though the scope of American legal feminism is very broad, this article focuses on only two of the major theoretical debates in American feminist legal scholarship, and on some more practical applications of that theory.

The two theoretical areas addressed are firstly, the sameness/difference debate — are women the same as or different from men, or is this the wrong question; and secondly, the exploration by feminist legal scholars of the distinction, or lack thereof, between the so-called public and private dimensions of life. The reason I focus on these two areas is, in part, due to their prominent place in (American) feminist legal writing: there is a whole field of feminist legal scholarship with which many Australians may be unfamiliar and this article aims to introduce some of this work. Secondly, the two areas examined here are also part of the Australian legal tradition. Should we be unabashedly aiming for 'equal treatment' for women and men or should we be trying to envisage a new system? We are all familiar with the distinction between public and private law and are also familiar with the liberal distinction between the public (regulated by law) and the private (unregulated)[1] but we need to think how these distinctions may be oppressive to women and the role of the law in creating them.

I briefly describe the work of psychologist Carol Gilligan, perhaps the most influential non-legal writer on the American feminist legal project. Her work has influenced both these debates, though particularly the former. It suggests profound questions about women's 'difference' and has been used by legal scholars to suggest ways in which the law and legal education can respond to this

* B.A. (Hons) (Sydney); LL.B (U.N.S.W.); LL.M (Yale). Currently Lecturer in Law, University of Melbourne.

A number of people read and commented on this paper in its numerous drafts: thanks to all of them especially Hilary Charlesworth, Judith Gardam, Beth Gaze, Andrew Goldsmith, Reg Graycar, Peter Hanks, and Chris Ronalds.

[1] This particular formulation of the distinction between public and private as one distinguishing between that which is regulated by law and that which is unregulated comes from O'Donovan, K., *Sexual Divisions in Law* (1985).

perceived difference. Her work has also influenced another important area of feminist legal work, touched on briefly in this paper, the feminist critique of liberal rights formulations. I also describe the work of feminists in more 'black letter' legal areas such as contracts and remedies. The article concludes by addressing the implications for Australian legal education that may be drawn from this material and other feminist legal endeavours.

SAMENESS / DIFFERENCE DEBATE

Though perhaps not the most crucial debate in feminist legal scholarship, the sameness/difference controversy has probably absorbed the most energy.[2] Of course the reason for the centrality of the debate in America is in part because of the equality provisions in the American constitution.[3] Nevertheless, the debate is still worth describing to an Australian audience for gender equality, if not constitutionally central, is politically central.

The basic issue is whether women are the same as or different from men. Or in a more narrow or practical sense, should we be encouraging the legal system to accord women equal treatment (the underlying premise being that women are the same as men) or special treatment (where the underlying premise is that women are different from men)? The sameness/difference debate is played out at both a theoretical and practical level (which is hardly surprising, for feminist legal scholars would refuse to see that theory and practice have to be, or indeed can be, separated).

The debate has mostly occurred in the context of maternity leave provisions. Only four states in the U.S. have special maternity leave laws.[4] These have been challenged as being in violation of Federal anti-discrimination laws (Title VII and the Pregnancy Discrimination Act) on the grounds that they treat pregnant women better than non-pregnant workers who are unable to work for other reasons.[5] Such challenges have been supported by 'equal treatment' feminists who argue that 'pregnancy can or should be visualized as one human experience which in many contexts, most notably the workplace, creates needs and problems similar to those arising from causes other than pregnancy, and which can be handled adequately on the same basis as other physical conditions of employees'.[6]

[2] *E.g.* Wolgast, E., *Equality and the Rights of Women* (1980); Scales, A., 'Towards a New Feminist Jurisprudence' (1980) 56 *Indiana Law Journal* 375; Freedman, A., 'Sex Equality, Sex Difference and the Supreme Court' (1983) 92 *Yale Law Journal* 913; Krieger, L.J., and Cooney, P.N., 'The Miller-Wohl Controversy: Equal Treatment, Positive Action and the Meaning of Women's Equality' (1983) 13 *Golden Gate University Law Review* 513; Law, S., 'Rethinking Sex and the Constitution' (1984) 132 *University of Pennsylvania Law Review* 955; Williams, W.W., 'Equality's Riddle: Pregnancy and the Equal Treatment/Special Treatment Debate' (1984) 13 *New York University Review of Law and Social Change* 325; Finley, L.M., 'Transcending Equality Theory: A Way Out of the Maternity and the Workplace Debate' (1986) 86 *Columbia Law Review* 1118; Scales, A., 'The Emergence of Feminist Jurisprudence: An Essay' (1986) 95 *Yale Law Journal* 1373.

[3] The 14th Amendment to the American Constitution provides 'No State shall . . . deny to any person within its jurisdiction the equal protection of the laws'.

[4] Finley, *op. cit.* n. 2, 1128 n. 49.

[5] The most recent challenge was *California Federal Savings and Loan Association v. Guerra* 55 *US Law Week* 4077 (1987). For a brief explanation of Title VII and the Pregnancy Discrimination Act, see *infra* n. 19.

[6] Williams, *op. cit.* n. 2, 326.

Some of the feminist support for the equal treatment line has essentially pragmatic or tactical origins. Equal treatment advocates could suggest that it is difficult for women to argue that they want to be treated like men in some contexts, for example, in access to jobs seen as traditionally male, yet in other contexts to argue for special treatment, treatment that is better than that of men.[7] The equal treatment protagonists also argue that to single out pregnancy for special treatment perpetuates the view that pregnancy is solely women's responsibility,[8] and that it leaves the door open for arguments that have historically redounded to the detriment of women: that women have a 'special sphere' of activity at which they are particularly good and within which they should be confined.[9] They suggest that singling out pregnancy denies the humanity common to all people[10] and divides workers.[11] It may also, according to equal treatment advocates, mean that new structural barriers to women's employment are created: special pregnancy leave makes women more expensive to employ than men.[12]

Special treatment supporters, on the other hand, argue that pregnancy *is* unique and requires particular laws which are different from those for general sickness and disability leave.[13] Some of the attraction of this view lies in the very inadequate nature of sick leave provisions in America generally: if pregnant women are forced to rely on general disability provisions, the amount of leave allowed will be inadequate for their needs and thus they will, effectively, be back in the old position of losing their jobs because of pregnancy.[14] Special treatment advocates do not deny that other workers have disability leave needs too, but they are willing to work in a piecemeal fashion, starting with pregnant women, towards improving the position for all workers.[15] Special treatment proponents are also concerned that the equal treatment model accepts men as the norm: pregnancy leave is no longer special if you think of women workers as 'normal'.[16]

To an Australian, it may seem somewhat surprising that such a debate could occupy so much energy. After all, if we accept the equal treatment line, should Australian feminists organize to get rid of maternity leave provisions? Perhaps if

7 Williams, W., 'The Equality Crisis: Some Reflections on Culture, Courts and Feminism' (1982) 7 *Women's Rights Law Reporter* 175, 196 argues that a doctrinal approach which allows special treatment of pregnancy that is for the benefit of women also allows special treatment that works to women's detriment. She states 'If we can't have it both ways, we need to think carefully about which way we want it'.

8 Finley, *op. cit.* n. 2, 1146 and Williams, *op. cit.* n. 2, 351-5, 377.

9 See Williams, *op. cit.* n. 2, 358.

10 Williams, *op. cit.* n. 2, 326.

11 Williams, *op. cit.* n. 2, 371; Williams, *op. cit.* n. 7, 196.

12 Williams, *op. cit.* n. 2, 367; Williams, *op. cit.* n. 7, 196.

13 See, in particular, Scales (1981), *op. cit.* n. 2.

14 Finley, *op. cit.* 1147-8. Krieger and Cooney present a version of this argument by asserting that the equal treatment/special treatment debate about maternity leave laws should not be argued only at an abstract level, but account should also be taken of the material conditions of women's lives. See Krieger and Cooney, *op. cit.* n. 2, 569. Williams, an equal treatment advocate, maintains that the equal treatment approach can accommodate this argument: if a practice has the effect of creating a disparate impact on women, it should be found discriminatory under Title VII. Williams, *op. cit.* n. 2, 365-6, 378.

15 Krieger and Cooney, *op. cit.* n. 2, 570-2.

16 See Finley, *op. cit.* n. 2, 1147-8; Scales (1981), *op. cit.* n. 2, 427-35. And see Williams' refutation of this argument *op. cit.* n. 2, 366-8.

we go back a little further to the reason for the inclusion of pregnancy under American sex discrimination legislation, the concentration of energy seems less absurd. The Pregnancy Discrimination Act was enacted in response to the Supreme Court decisions in *Geduldig v. Aiello*[17] and *General Electric Company v. Gilbert*.[18] *Geduldig* was a challenge to the exclusion of pregnancy from a disability insurance program, the argument being that this amounted to discrimination on the grounds of sex, *i.e.* a failure to accord equal protection of the laws. The Supreme Court concluded that this was not sex discrimination, rather merely a distinction between pregnant and non-pregnant persons or, as Scales has described it 'that no discrimination exists if pregnant women and pregnant men are treated the same'.[19] The debate is reminiscent of a split within liberalism between equality of outcome or result and equality of treatment.[20] But it is also illustrative of a more profound debate within American (legal) feminism: that is, the whole issue of women's 'difference'.

That debate has been fuelled, perhaps particularly within legal circles, by the work of developmental psychologist Carol Gilligan.[21] Gilligan looked at much of Kohlberg's work[22] on moral development and noted that all his empirical work had been done on male children. Based on her own and other's work on female moral development, she suggested that Kohlberg had inadequately represented human development by only studying male development.

The attraction of Gilligan's work for legal thinkers comes particularly from her conceptions of rights and relationships as revealed in her account of Jake and Amy's responses to the Heinz dilemma.

The Heinz dilemma was developed by Kohlberg to measure moral develop-

17 417 U.S. 484 (1974).

18 429 U.S. 125 (1976). This was a challenge under Title VII, rather than the Constitution, to the exclusion of pregnancy in an employment disability plan.

19 Scales (1986), *op. cit.* n. 2, 1399. By way of clarification, Title VII of the Civil Rights Act 1964 (42 U.S.C. 2000(e) and following) is the Federal law concerned with discrimination in employment. 42 U.S.C. 2000e-2(a)(1) provides that it is an unlawful employment practice for an employer 'to discriminate against any individual with respect to his compensation, terms, conditions, or privileges of employment, because of such individual's race, colour, religion, sex, or national origin'. In 1978, the Civil Rights Act was amended via the Pregnancy Discrimination Act which added the following definition to the (brief) definition section: 42 U.S.C. 2000e (k) 'The terms "because of sex" or "on the basis of sex" include, but are not limited to, because of or on the basis of pregnancy, childbirth, or related medical conditions; and women affected by pregnancy, childbirth, or related medical conditions shall be treated the same for all employment-related purposes, including receipt of benefits under fringe benefit programs, as other persons not so affected but similar in their ability or inability to work . . .'. Whilst this amendment may have got over the initial problem in *Gilbert, i.e.* it established that discrimination on the ground of pregnancy was discrimination on the ground of sex, it does not resolve, however, the issue of 'special treatment' for pregnant women.

20 Finley, *op. cit.* n. 2, 1144; Olsen, F., 'Statutory Rape: A Critique of Rights Analysis' (1984) 63 *Texas Law Review* 387, 397.

21 Gilligan, C., *In a Different Voice: Psychological Theory and Women's Development* (1982); Gilligan, C., 'In a Different Voice: Women's Conceptions of the Self and of Morality' (1977) 47 *Harvard Educational Review* 481; Gilligan, C., 'Remapping the Moral Domain: New Images of Self in Relationship' in Watt, I. (ed.), *Reconstructing Individualism* (1986); Gilligan, C., 'Remapping Development: The Power of Divergent Data' in Cirillo, L. and Wapner, S. (eds) *Value Presuppositions in Theories of Human Development* (1986). *Cf.* Lyons, N., 'Two Perspectives: On Self, Relationships, and Morality' (1983) 53 *Harvard Educational Review* 125. For applications of Gilligan's work outside the scope of this article see, for example, Karst, K.L., 'Woman's Constitution' [1984] *Duke Law Journal* 447 and Sherry, S., 'Civic Virtue and the Feminine Voice in Constitutional Adjudication' (1986) 72 *Virginia Law Review* 543.

22 See Kohlberg, L., *The Philosophy of Moral Development* (1981), cited in Gilligan, C., *In a Different Voice* (1982), *op. cit.* n. 21, 18.

ment. Heinz has to decide whether to steal a drug which is needed to save his wife's life, and which he can't afford to buy. The druggist refuses to lower the price. Jake, the 11 year old boy, when asked if Heinz should steal, recognizes that the dilemma is constructed as a conflict between the values of life and property, decides that life is more important, and concludes that Heinz should steal the drug. He says that if Heinz got caught, the judge should give Heinz a very light sentence. As Gilligan states, Jake '[c]onsidering the moral dilemma to be "sort of like a math problem with humans", . . . sets it up as an equation and proceeds to work out the solution.'[23]

Amy, the 11 year old girl, for on the other hand, is, in Gilligan's words, 'evasive and unsure'.[24] Asked whether Heinz should steal the drug, Amy says 'Well, I don't think so. I think there might be other ways besides stealing it, like if he could borrow the money or make a loan or something but he really shouldn't steal the drug — but his wife shouldn't die either.'[25] Amy goes on to consider not the conflicting values of life and property, but what effect the theft would have on Heinz's relationship with his wife: 'If he stole the drug, he might save his wife then, but if he did, he might have to go to jail, and then his wife might get sicker again, and he couldn't get more of the drug and it might not be good. So, they should really just talk it out and find some other way to make the money.'[26] Gilligan states: '[Amy] see[s] in the dilemma not a math problem with humans but a narrative of relationships that extends over time . . .'.[27]

On the traditional moral development scale, Jake scores at a higher level than Amy. Gilligan suggests both responses are equally sophisticated, just different. She argues Amy's 'understanding of morality . . . aris[ing] from the recognition of relationship, [and] her belief in communication as the mode of conflict resolution . . . seems far from naive or cognitively immature.'[28] Jake reasons abstractly, taking the problem out of its context, uses a 'logic of fairness' and creates a hierarchy of winners and losers.[29] Amy sees the problem as 'a network of connection, a web of relationships that is sustained by a process of communication. With this shift, the moral problem changes from one of unfair domination, the imposition of property over life, to one of unnecessary exclusion, the failure of the druggist to respond to the wife.'[30] In other words, Jake reasons through a hierarchy or ladder of rights, and Amy through a web of connection.

How have Gilligan's insights affected feminist legal scholarship?[31] To some extent it has probably boosted the special treatment/difference side of the debate. After all, Gilligan's work suggests that women reason differently: as we come to recognise and validate more differences, it is but a short step to argue that the

23 Gilligan, C., *In a Different Voice* (1982) *op. cit.* n. 21, 26.
24 *Ibid.* 28.
25 *Ibid.*
26 *Ibid.*
27 *Ibid.*
28 *Ibid.* 30.
29 *Ibid.* 32.
30 *Ibid.*
31 This is perhaps stating the connection too strongly: Gilligan's work is just the most prominent example of a tendency in American feminism to explore, validate and celebrate women's difference which has influenced legal scholarship; furthermore, some of the feminist legal work is merely consistent with, rather than being dependent on, Gilligan's work.

legal system has a role in that recognition and validation.[32] It has assisted broad theoretical analyses of the legal system which criticize the abstract, detached ideal of legal reasoning, and argue for a contextualized, connected legal system. The latter is for some a more accurate description of how the legal system actually works, and for others, an ideal towards which feminist legal workers should be moving.

On a more practical level, it has given a theoretical underlay to some feminists' support of mediation as an alternative method of dispute resolution.[33] Mediation is seen as a form of dispute resolution that places the dispute in its social context, and aims to come up with a resolution of disputes that avoids a zero sum game. At this point, it is probably important to remind ourselves that to suggest that there is only one American legal feminism is to be totally misleading. For instance, to continue the mediation example, there are many feminists (in America, and Australia and England for that matter) who would oppose the use of mediation in many domestic disputes, suggesting that the inequality of bargaining power which exists between men and women makes mediation, with its emphasis on compromise, together with the privacy of mediation proceedings, a dangerous practice for women.[34] Given the historical and continuing subordination of women, it is argued that the procedural protection of a court system, the attempt at equalizing power relationships through legal representation and formality, and indeed, the legal system's emphasis on rights, may be essential in order to achieve justice for women.[35] Fineman has recently drawn attention to the use of mediation in custody disputes. She has argued that the emphasis on mediation has caused, or at least contributed to, the reification of joint custody as an ideal, an outcome which she suggests ignores the interests of divorced mothers. That is, not only must we be concerned about the individual dispute and individual inequalities of bargaining power, but also the broader

[32] One example of such a move or tendency is provided in Ann Scales' work. In her 1986 article she comments on her earlier (1981) work: 'my stance had the . . . basic flaw — an obsession with what differences between men and women the law could, in the abstract, take into account. Pregnancy and breastfeeding, I thought, had to be accounted for if the law were to take a sufficiently broad view of equality: Equality requires that a woman not be forced to choose between children and career, just as a man need not make that choice. I endorse my former view thus far. I then believed also that *only* pregnancy and breastfeeding could be taken into account, because those were the only two "objectively" determinable differences between the sexes. The law, I believed, needed to steer completely clear of the "subjective" phenomenon of stereotyping. I now see that limitation as unnecessarily reticent and guaranteed to achieve nothing, as many such liberal assumptions are.' Scales (1986), *op. cit.* n. 2, 1381 n. 46.

[33] Menkel-Meadow, C., 'Toward Another View of Legal Negotiation: The Structure of Problem Solving' (1984) 31 *U.C.L.A. Law Review* 754, 763 n. 28; Menkel-Meadow, C., 'Portia in a Different Voice: Speculations on a Women's Lawyering Process' [1987] *Berkeley Women's Law Journal* 39, 51-3.

[34] Bottomley, A., 'Resolving family disputes: a critical view' in Freeman, M.D.A. (ed.) *State, Law and the Family* 293-303; Bottomley, A., 'What is happening to family law? A feminist critique of conciliation' in Brophy, J. and Smart, C. (eds) *Women-in-Law: Explorations in Law, Family and Sexuality* (1985), 162-87; Schwarzkoff, J. and Morgan, J., *Community Justice Centres: A Report on the N.S.W. Pilot Project, 1979-1981* (1982), 174; Stallone, D.R., 'Decriminalization of Violence in the Home: Mediation in Wife Battering Cases' (1984) 2 *Law and Inequality* 493; Lerman, L.G., 'Mediation of Wife Abuse Cases: The Adverse Impact of Informal Dispute Resolution on Women' (1984) 7 *Harvard Women's Law Journal* 57; Germane, C., Johnson, M., and Lemon, N., 'Mandatory Custody Mediation and Joint Custody Orders In California: The Danger for Victims of Domestic Violence' (1985) 1 *Berkeley Women's Law Journal* 175.

[35] See, in particular, Bottomley in Brophy and Smart, *op. cit.* n. 34, 184-5.

effect of mediation on women as a group, through a change in the substantive law from sole to joint custody.[36]

Some legal feminists have rejected, or are at least highly sceptical of, Gilligan's work.[37] Catharine MacKinnon, a leading feminist legal scholar in America, has joined other feminists in criticizing Gilligan's failure to articulate a causal mechanism for women's 'different voice'; that is, the expression of a web of connection rather than a hierarchy of rights.[38] MacKinnon criticizes both sides of the equal treatment/special treatment debate, arguing that they both accept men as their norm, and that the question for feminists is not whether a practice treats women the same as or differently from men, but whether the practice subordinates women.[39] And she hesitates to embrace Gilligan's thesis, for she sees women's 'different voice' as arising out of women's oppression. To celebrate this voice, she asserts, is to play into stereotyped visions of femininity which will continue to oppress women.[40] MacKinnon states

> I do not think that the way women reason morally is morality in a different voice. I think it is morality in a higher register, in the feminine voice. Women value care because men have valued us according to the care we give them, and we could probably use some . . . When you are powerless, you don't just speak differently. A lot, you don't speak. Your speech is not just differently articulated, it is silenced . . . All I am saying is that the damage of sexism is real, and reifying it into differences is an insult to our possibilities.[41]

My own view of this is that both Gilligan and MacKinnon are correct. Gilligan's work is very moving, and resonates very clearly with the dissatisfaction of many women lawyers and law students with legal education and the legal system more generally. At the same time, MacKinnon is, I believe, sensible in hesitating to embrace a framework that can, as it stands, support biological determinism, and the view that women are inherently different and therefore less capable. She is probably correct that women's different voice (if there is one) does arise from oppression, but the values that Gilligan has identified as belonging to women, those of care and connection, rather than an abstract notion of rights, have a lot to offer law and legal education. I will return to this theme at the end of this article.

THE PUBLIC / PRIVATE DISTINCTION AND THE CRITIQUE OF RIGHTS

Feminist legal scholars have taken the feminist slogan 'The Personal is Political' seriously and explored how the dichotomy between the public and the private has been constructed and supported by the legal system, to the detriment

36 Fineman, M., 'Dominant Discourse: The Professional Appropriation of Child Custody Decision-Making', Institute for Legal Studies, Working Paper Series 2, University of Wisconsin-Madison Law School, also published as 'Dominant Discourse, Professional Language and Legal Change in Child Custody Decisionmaking' (1988) 101 *Harvard Law Review 727*.

37 See also Kerber, Greeno and Maccoby, Luria, Stack and Gilligan, 'On *In a Different Voice:* An Interdisciplinary Forum' (1986) 11 *Signs: Journal of Women in Culture and Society* 304.

38 'Feminist Discourse, Moral Values and the Law — A Conversation' (1985) 34 *Buffalo Law Review* 11, 74, hereinafter cited as 'Conversation'.

39 *Ibid.* 20-4; MacKinnon, C.A., *Sexual Harassment of Working Women: A Case of Sex Discrimination* (1979) 4-5, 101-41; MacKinnon, C.A., 'Difference and Dominance: On Sex Discrimination' in *Feminism Unmodified: Discourses on Life and Law* (1987) 32-45.

40 'Conversation' *op. cit.* n. 38, 74-5.

41 'Difference and Dominance' *op. cit.* n. 36, 39. *Cf.* Scales (1986), *op. cit.* n. 2, 1381 where she states that 'Gilligan's work . . . could also become the Uncle Tom's Cabin of our century.'

of women. At the most obvious level, this has involved critical analyses of, and action around, the law's failure to intervene in 'the private' and thus its failure to protect women from violence in the home, from marital rape and 'date rape', from incestuous assault as children — all areas of political legal activity by Australian legal feminists in recent years. At the same time, feminist legal scholars have challenged the view that the law does not intervene in the private (and in particular the family), drawing attention to the existing mass of regulation surrounding the family in tax law, criminal law, tort law, *etc.* which both impinges on the family and plays its part in constructing the very notion of family.[42] Some scholars have argued that state intervention in the family cannot be avoided and, indeed, that the whole concept of state intervention is totally incoherent.[43]

Related to this more profound critique of the public/private distinction are attempts to transcend the distinction. Olsen, for example, has argued for a transcendence of the public/private dichotomy, rather than merely an extension of the public legal world into the 'private' familial world or vice versa.[44] Her focus is on the dichotomy between the (private) family and the (public) market, particularly the employment market. She examines efforts to improve the status of women which focus on each of these worlds. She charts attempts to impose family ideology on the market and market ideology on the family, together with attempts to make each live up to its own ideals.

Attempts to make the family more like an ideal family recognise the exploitation of women which has occurred in the private sphere and thus try to make men more benevolent towards women. Here Olsen points to the delegalization movement in family law, a process also evident in Australia, with the increase in court counselling, and mediation. As suggested above, these strategies can hurt women by, for example 'forc[ing] the weaker party to accept a resolution that gives her far less than she would be entitled to in a formal adjudication.'[45]

[42] *E.g.* O'Donovan, K., *Sexual Divisions in Law* (1985); Daly, K.E., 'Structure and Practice of Familial-Based Justice in a Criminal Court' (1987) 21 *Law and Society Review* 267; Graycar, R. and Shiff, D. (eds), *Life Without Marriage* (1987); Law, S., 'Women, Work, Welfare and the Preservation of Patriarchy' (1983) 131 *University of Pennsylvania Law Review* 1249; Graycar, R., 'Hoovering as a Hobby: The Common Law's Approach to Work in the Home' (1985) 28 *Refractory Girl* 22; Graycar, R., 'Compensation for Loss of Capacity to Work in the Home' (1985) 10 *Sydney Law Review* 528; Land, H., 'The Family Wage' [1980] *Feminist Review* 55; Lahey, K., 'The Tax Unit in Income Tax Theory' in Pask, E.D., Mahoney, K.E., and Brown, C.A. (eds), *Women, the Law and the Economy* (1985); Edwards, M., *The Income Unit in Australian Tax and Social Security Systems* (1984); Grbich, J., 'The Position of Women in Family Dealing: the Australian Case' (1987) 15 *International Journal of the Sociology of Law* 309.

[43] Fran Olsen argues 'that the terms "intervention" and "nonintervention" [in the family] are largely meaningless. The terms do not accurately describe any set of policies, and as general principles, "intervention" and "nonintervention" are indeterminate.' Olsen, F.E., 'The Myth of State Intervention in the Family' (1985) 18 *University of Michigan Journal of Law Reform* 835. *Cf.* Minow, M., 'Beyond State Intervention in the Family: For Baby Jane Doe' (1985) 18 *University of Michigan Journal of Law Reform* 933, 934 who, in the context of decisions about treatment of severely handicapped newborns, 'reject[s] the framework of "state intervention" . . . showing that arguments cast in those terms overlook the variety of possible forms and directions of state intervention, and obscure the inevitable role of the state in any possible allocation of power to decide the infant's medical treatment.'

[44] Olsen, F.E., 'The Family and the Market: A Study of Ideology and Legal Reform' (1983) 96 *Harvard Law Review* 1497.

[45] *Ibid.* 1542.

Attempts to make the family more like the market focus on equality, a market value, and include Married Women's Property Acts, which imposed juridical equality, an ideal of the market. In fact, this legislation did little to improve women's lives, Olsen argues, because it did not 'force the husband to share his power over the family's wealth' but rather gave rights to separate property. Because women's domestic labour was unpaid and men earned most of the money, the practical effect on women's lives was minimal.[46] She concludes

> Although the reforms promote equality, they also undermine the altruistic bases of the family and thus leave women open to the kind of individualized, particularized domination characteristic of market relations. The reforms have tended to give women equal rights, but they have not democratized the family.[47]

Attempts have also been made to end women's oppression through making the market more like an ideal market, that is, taking its ideal of equality seriously. Initiatives here include anti-discrimination measures, again familiar to an Australian audience, which Olsen suggests are inadequate:

> Anti-discrimination law does not end the actual subordination of women in the market but instead mainly benefits a small percentage of women who adopt 'male' roles . . . It obscures for women the actual causes of their oppression and treats discrimination against women as an irrational and capricious departure from the normal objective operation of the market, instead of recognizing such discrimination as a pervasive aspect of our dichotomized system.[48]

Finally, she documents efforts to make the market more like the family or, as Olsen puts it, 'making the market more responsive to the needs of women'.[49] Strategies here are aimed at removing the individualism of the market and Olsen points to protective labour legislation for women which again failed to improve the status of women and indeed, in America, held up the development of decent health and safety protections for all workers and 'effectively degraded . . . [women] by treating the asserted differences as evidence of women's inferiority.'[50]

Olsen argues that both sets of attempts fail because they all accept a dichotomy between the public and the private which fragments people's lives in a way which neither fully reflects lived experience nor transforms that experience to make it whole. Such a transformation is necessary at both a conceptual and practical level. If we can move away from the dichotomous thinking, clearly characteristic of much legal thinking, and characteristic of both the public/private dichotomy and the family/market dichotomy, we may be able to start thinking about strategies that would empower women, recognize the specificity of their lives, ultimately transform both the domestic and public lives of all people, and even make such concepts redundant. She concludes 'Most of the time neither our family lives nor our market lives seem fully satisfactory, yet our dissatisfaction with each leads us to romanticize the other in a vicious cycle . . . Polarizing the family and the market does not increase the possibilities available to individuals and to the human personality.'[51]

[46] *Ibid.* 1532.
[47] *Ibid.*
[48] *Ibid.* 1552.
[49] *Ibid.* 1529.
[50] *Ibid.* 1556-7. See also Olsen, F.E., 'From False Paternalism to False Equality: Judicial Assaults on Feminist Community, Illinois 1869-1895' (1986) 84 *Michigan Law Review* 1518.
[51] *Ibid.* 1566-7.

The feminist critique of the public/private divide is by no means complete. Neither Olsen nor O'Donovan, an English feminist legal scholar who has engaged in a similar critique of 'Sexual Divisions in Law',[52] presents 'the answer' for transcending the public/private distinction. However, their critique provides ways of analysing the law's impact on women's subordination, ways which transcend doctrinal legal boundaries and reinforce the need for feminists to engage with law to transform the terms of the debate.

CRITIQUE OF RIGHTS

Both the sameness/difference debate and attempts at deconstruction of the public/private distinction, have influenced another feminist legal project, the critique of rights formulations. The feminist critique of rights also connects with the more discursive dissatisfaction of critical legal studies scholars with rights discourse. One of the best examples of feminist legal scholarship in this area is Fran Olsen's discussion of statutory rape laws.[53]

The analysis came out of a Supreme Court challenge to statutory rape laws by a 17 year old boy.[54] The particular statutory rape law challenged was not gender neutral, that is, it was an offence for a man to have sexual intercourse with a woman under 18 years of age, and he argued such a law denied him equal protection because he was being prosecuted and his 16 year old female 'partner' was not. His challenge was rejected by a majority of the Supreme Court, who held that because young women were exposed to the risk of pregnancy, there was no need for them to be additionally exposed to the risk of prosecution.

Olsen refers to feminist objections which describe (gendered) statutory rape laws as 'an unwarranted governmental intrusion into [young women's] . . . lives and an oppressive restriction upon their freedom of action', that is, they interfere with a young woman's 'right to privacy and her right to be as free sexually as her male counterpart'.[55] Furthermore, they treat young women as passive victims and men as aggressors thereby perpetuating a double standard.

Olsen notes that one suggested solution to these feminist objections is to make the laws gender neutral. The problem with this approach is that such a change in the law is not necessarily going to change legal practice. She argues 'it leaves untouched the repressive aspects of statutory rape laws. In our present society, these repressive aspects hurt females more than males'.[56]

Secondly, it could be argued that it is best to remove the state altogether from regulating this activity. However, this would leave women open to exploitation by individual men: 'Nice as it is to be freed from state oppression, domination by private individuals can be equally oppressive. Despite their negative aspects, statutory rape laws can provide some protection for females.'[57] She points out that rights analysis cannot help us decide which reform is best for women — the

52 O'Donovan, *op. cit.* n. 42. See also Finley, *op. cit.* n. 2.
53 Olsen, *op. cit.* n. 20.
54 *Michael M. v. Superior Court* 450 U.S. 464 (1981).
55 Olsen, *op. cit.* n. 20, 404-5.
56 *Ibid.* 411.
57 *Ibid.* 407.

right to privacy will isolate women and expose them to individual exploitation, and the right to equality does not recognize that women are more likely to be sexually exploited than men, or challenge that practice. Instead, we must face the political and moral questions involved away from the context of rights discourse.

Olsen goes on to consider, albeit somewhat speculatively, a strategy that would empower young women, while still providing some protection. She argues that, rather than completely ceasing to have statutory rape as an offence, the young woman should be able to decide whether to bring a prosecution; that is, the young woman's 'characterization of a sexual encounter as voluntary intercourse or as rape would be determinative'.[58] She recognizes that this strategy would expose young women to pressure from their parents, and may play into the stereotype that women make up claims of rape, but it recognizes that young women may be particularly vulnerable, and does something to reduce that vulnerability.

A similar critique of rights discourse has also occurred in the area of abortion, both in England and America. Feminists have pointed out that the rhetoric of 'the right to choose', or in American constitutional rhetoric, 'the right to privacy', presents an image of isolated women, disengages us from debates about how the right to choose should be exercised, and allows the state to justify a failure to support funded abortions for all women.[59] The American critique of the way abortion 'rights' have been constructed links the feminist discomfort with rights discourse to the critique of the public/private distinction: as MacKinnon says '[T]o fail to recognize the meaning of the private in the ideology and reality of women's subordination by seeking protection behind a right *to* that privacy is to cut women off from collective verification and state support in the same act'.[60]

I have tried to indicate two of the central theoretical debates in American legal feminism, and hinted at a number of others. I have not discussed some perhaps more practical American feminist struggles. These include the (fairly successful) struggle to get sexual harassment recognized as a form of sex discrimination[61] and the current attempts to address the issue of pornography.[62] The latter is probably the most controversial issue amongst American feminist legal workers

58 *Ibid.* 408-9.

59 See the discussion of *Roe v. Wade* 410 U.S. 113 (1973) and *Harris v. McRae* 448 U.S. 297 (1980) in MacKinnon, C., 'The Male Ideology of Privacy: A Feminist Perspective on the Right to Abortion' (1983) 17 *Radical America* 23 and MacKinnon, C., 'Privacy and Equality: Beyond *Roe v. Wade*' in *Feminism Unmodified* (1987); Kingdom, E., 'Legal Recognition of a Woman's Right to Choose' in Brophy, J. and Smart, C. (eds), *Women-in-Law: Explorations in Law, Family and Sexuality* (1985); Brown, 'Reproductive Freedom and the Right to Privacy: A Paradox for Feminists' in Diamond, I. (ed.), *Families, Politics and Public Policy: a Feminist Dialogue on Women and the State* (1983).

At the same time, some American legal feminists, particularly black feminists, have argued rights discourse is useful for women. *E.g.* Williams, P.J., 'Alchemical Notes: Reconstructing Ideals from Deconstructed Rights' (1987) 22 *Harvard Civil Rights-Civil Liberties Law Review* 401; Schneider, E.M., 'The Dialectic of Rights and Politics: Perspectives from the Women's Movement' (1986) 61 *New York University Law Review* 589 and Minow, M., 'Interpreting Rights: An Essay for Robert Cover' (1987) 96 *Yale Law Journal* 1860.

60 MacKinnon (1983), *op. cit.* n. 59, 33.

61 MacKinnon (1979) *op. cit.* n. 39; MacKinnon 'Sexual Harassment: Its First Decade in Court' in *Feminism Unmodified*, *op. cit.* n. 39.

62 *E.g.* MacKinnon, C., 'Not a Moral Issue' (1984) 2 *Yale Law and Policy Review* 321 and Chapters 11-16 in *Feminism Unmodified*, *op. cit.* n. 39.

at the moment. Catharine MacKinnon has drafted legislation, originally passed in two local government areas, which gives women a right to sue for damages for harm directly caused by pornography, and in limited circumstances to get an injunction to prevent further distribution of particularly violent pornography.[63] Such moves have been strongly criticized by other feminists who have concerns about free speech, and those who feel that the approach is inadequate because it fails to address the more pervasive and oppressive images of women in advertising in the general media.[64] The issue of pornography is presently central to American feminism, in a way that is perhaps not quite so true of British, or, for that matter, Australian legal feminism. This is, in part, because American feminists are more likely to be working in a radical feminist framework, a framework which sees sexuality as central to the oppression of women, in the way that Marxists use class as the central analytical category.[65] British feminism is more likely to be a socialist feminism and therefore is more concerned with the dual oppression of gender and class.[66]

BEYOND SEXUALITY AND THE FAMILY

The focus on empowerment of women is common to much feminist legal writing. The controversy over equal and special treatment can be seen as, in part, a debate about tactical questions as to which strategy is likely to be the most empowering to women. Gilligan's work has reinforced an interest in allowing women's voices and experiences to be heard in legal education and the legal profession more generally. And the critique of the public/private dichotomy is providing a way, at the very least, of understanding women's disempowerment by the legal system's insistence on non-regulation of the private. It could be suggested that the two areas I have concentrated on are essentially concerned with 'women's issues' — sexuality and the family — areas which have traditionally been seen as of concern to women legal workers. This is certainly not the limit of the feminist contribution to the legal project. Feminist legal scholarship also has important perspectives to throw onto traditional 'black letter' law.

Two pieces of North American legal scholarship are of particular interest here.[67] In one, Christine Boyle, a Canadian, reviews two books on remedies.[68]

63 Minneapolis Code of Ordinances, Title 7. Ch. 139 and 141, vetoed by the Mayor and Indianapolis Antipornography Ordinance No. 24 and No. 35 (1984); see Spahn, E., 'On Sex and Violence' (1984) 20 *New England Law Review* 629, 630. The Indianapolis ordinance was held unconstitutional in *American Booksellers v. Hudnut* 771 F.2d 323 (7th Cir. 1985), affirmed 106 S. Ct 1664 (1986).

64 *E.g.* Spahn, *op. cit.* n. 63; the Feminist Anti-Censorship Taskforce Amici Curiae Brief in *American Booksellers v. Hudnut* 106 S. Ct 1664 (1986). The arguments are summarized for an Australian audience in Gaze, B., 'Pornography and freedom of speech: An American feminist approach' (1986) 11 *Legal Service Bulletin* 123.

65 See MacKinnon, C., 'Feminism, Marxism, Method and the State: An Agenda for Theory' (1982) 7 *Signs: Journal of Women in Culture and Society* 515, 515-6: 'Sexuality is to feminism what work is to marxism: that which is most one's own, yet most taken away . . . Sexuality is that social process which creates, organizes, expresses, and directs desire, creating the social beings we know as women and men, as their relations create society. As work is to marxism, sexuality to feminism is socially constructed yet constructing, universal as activity yet historically specific, jointly comprised of matter and mind.' *Cf.* MacKinnon, 'Desire and Power' in *Feminism Unmodified op. cit.* n. 39.

66 *E.g.* Barrett, M., *Women's Oppression Today: Problems in Marxist Feminist Analysis* (1980); Segal, L., *Is the Future Female?: troubled thoughts on contemporary feminism* (1987).

67 See also Lahey, K., and Salter, S., 'Corporate Law in Legal Theory and Legal Scholarship: From Classicism to Feminism' (1985) 23 *Osgoode Hall Law Journal* 543.

68 Boyle, C., 'Book Review' (1985) 63 *Canadian Bar Review* 427 (reviewing Sharpe, R.J., *Injunctions and Specific Performance* and Waddams, S.M., *The Law of Damages*).

She draws attention to the use of 'he' as the universal pronoun in one, and the one paragraph on family law injunctions, as compared to the 68 paragraphs on injunctions to protect property. She is careful not to suggest that 'family law is a "women's subject"', but does argue 'that people who are concerned about the position of women in our society, would, on this issue-oriented level, look for material on injunctions for the protection of abused wives'.[69] She again draws on Gilligan's work to point to the abstract character of much of the writing and the worship of 'rationality' in one of the texts. She is concerned that Waddams overvalues rationality, a term he does not define. Does it mean unemotional, or making decisions without reference to morality, or something else? The first two are both modes of decision making that a feminist analysis would find deeply troubling. She states, in one of the great quotable quotes of feminist legal scholarship: '"Men and the Law" is tolerable as an area of intellectual activity, but not if it is masquerading as "People and the Law"'.[70]

The other article is by Mary Jo Frug, 'A Feminist Analysis of a Contracts Casebook'.[71] In some senses it is similar to Christine Boyle's piece, but it is more closely argued, detailed and devastating. Frug demonstrates how different readers interact with a casebook, and, in particular, how these various readers' notions of gender affect their absorption of legal principles, their understanding of women (and men), and for women law student readers, how their self-perception as future lawyers is affected.

She engages in a detailed analysis of women's appearances in the casebook. As authors of cases (judges) women are totally absent either because of their historical absence from the legal profession or because none of the judges are ever identified by their sex. Other legal authors such as commentators are always identified as males. As parties in the cases, women appear as housewives, sisters, fashion designers and hairdressers. As a law student audience, women are never addressed: all the commentators quoted refer to men as possible future lawyers. Frug deals with the expected criticism 'but that's how the world is', suggesting it is an 'ironic diversion'.[72] She argues that casebook editors rarely consider the issue of whether they are accurately representing 'the real world' when they select cases. She even concedes that the casebook editors may be able to justify their choice of cases in this or some other way. However, the fact remains that the selection reinforces rather than expands readers' views about gender, and while historically women may have been excluded from the legal profession, the book conveys a disconcerting view of current 'legal culture'. She also discusses the analytical and abstract character of the book and given that we associate these characteristics with males, she contends that this contributes to the maleness of the casebook. She argues that the authors' neutral stance, their failure to discuss the justice of case outcomes, and their failure to discuss developments in legal theory 'discourages readers from developing ethical, social and

69 *Ibid.* 431.
70 *Ibid.* 430-1.
71 Frug, M.J., 'Re-Reading Contracts: A Feminist Analysis of a Contracts Casebook' (1985) 34 *American University Law Review* 1065.
72 *Ibid.* 1079-80.

moral opinions on legal issues. Insofar as these questions and opinions seem feminine, because they involve attachment, compassion, and emotion, repressing these questions encourages readers to repress the feminine characteristics within themselves'.[73]

It can be seen that both the Boyle and the Frug pieces engage in a critique of the abstraction, rationality and neutrality of the law, and argue for a more contextualized, subjective and connected approach. That is, for another way of making women visible. This critique is probably the most threatening to traditional legal analysis, but also the most radical challenge to the devaluing of the female in law. Catharine MacKinnon has argued 'male dominance is perhaps the most pervasive and tenacious system of power in history . . . it is metaphysically nearly perfect. Its point of view is the standard for point-of-viewlessness, its particularity the meaning of universality. . . . Feminism claims the voice of women's silence . . . the centrality of our marginality and exclusion, the public nature of privacy, the presence of our absence.'[74] The work of Boyle and Frug is a concrete attempt to expose how the supposed universality or 'point of viewlessness' of legal discourse excludes women.

WHAT IS THE RELEVANCE OF THIS SCHOLARSHIP TO AUSTRALIAN LEGAL EDUCATION?

I believe that part of the feminist project in law schools is to make women visible. It disturbs me that in 1986 a woman student can come to me in tears saying she had spent 8 weeks in a course on human rights and women had not been mentioned. Were we not human? To my shame, I suggested that perhaps gender neutral language wasn't *that* important. As she said to me, 'if they can't even include women in the language they use, what hope have we got for changing *anything*?' We must examine the cases and, in particular, the hypotheticals used in lectures and tutorials and question what image of women is presented. It is a small but vital point — the reasonable man should be dead and buried by now.[75]

It can be argued that women are not invisible in Australian law courses — after all women's issues are discussed in the teaching of family law and sexual assault. Of course they are, and though many questions remain about the adequacy of our approach to these questions, the reach of feminism into the law is, and must be, much greater. A number of universities, though not very many in Australia, have established 'Women and the Law' courses. These are inclined to cover 'women's issues' — domestic violence, sexual assault and anti-discrimination. As Reg

73 *Ibid.* 1112.

74 MacKinnon, C., 'Feminism, Marxism, Method and the State: Towards Feminist Jurisprudence' (1983) 8 *Signs: Journal of Women in Culture and Society* 635, 638-9.

75 It is worth remembering here though that a mere change in language will not necessarily lead to a change in conception, and may more effectively hide a masculist discourse. As Lucinda Finley argues, 'the use of neutral language may mask underlying biases in the purportedly objective standard that were more apparent when the gender male was referred to specifically'. Finley, L., 'Laying Down the Master's Tools: A Feminist Revision of Torts', unpublished manuscript, p. 21, forthcoming 1988. *Cf.* Boyle, C., 'Criminal Law and Procedure: Who Needs Tenure?' (1985) 23 *Osgoode Hall Law Journal* 427, 433: 'Simply changing one's language does not necessarily reflect a change in perspective.'

Graycar has argued, the first two must be part of a compulsory criminal law course, whether or not they are also covered in more specialized courses.[76] Mary Jane Mossman, a Canadian feminist legal scholar, has pointed to the problems with the 'women and law' strategy.[77] She suggests that few students will take such a course as an option, and they are likely to be those students who are already alert to the masculist nature of most legal culture; enrolment in such courses may be stigmatizing, 'reinforcing the idea of women as Other' and, finally, they may 'dissipate efforts to create gender equality in the law school as a whole'.[78]

A somewhat more sustained challenge to gender inequality is made through Law and Gender courses such as the one taught at La Trobe University and the one recently established at the University of New South Wales. Such courses generally take a more global view of the role of law in creating gender inequality. Thus, they tend to take a more theoretical perspective, and rather than merely teaching a grab bag of women's issues, do not accept the false subject distinctions we create in our legal education. Thus one could create a section of such a course around the material I discussed above about the public/private divide, bringing in material on state regulation of the family, the labour market, sexuality and contracts, to name but a few. Or, to quote one of Reg Graycar's examples, '[i]deological concepts such as the "good mother" permeate cases about custody in family law, as we would expect them to, but they also arise in, for example, crime, in tort, in succession and others.'[79] Still, such courses do not meet all of Mary Jane Mossman's hesitations about women and the law courses: women are still seen as marginal, not in the course itself, but in the position of the course as an elective in law schools which in many other ways exclude and marginalize women.

Yet another approach has been implemented at the University of Oslo, where there is a separate department of women's law, and all compulsory courses must have a feminist component.[80] Mary Jane Mossman argues this may continue to marginalize women's concerns, for the 'feminist bit' will just be 'tacked on' at the end.[81] Still, I believe all these are small steps on the path that Mossman suggests we must take, to 'transform the normative tradition in law'.[82] The Norwegian approach at least addresses the issue of feminist perspective in the traditional 'black letter' courses. Gender affects all aspects of our lives and all aspects of the law: although it may be more difficult to raise these issues in a corporate or a tax course, feminist legal scholars, as I have demonstrated above, are producing analyses of these very areas of the law.

76 Graycar, R., '"to transform the normative tradition of law . . ." a comment on the feminist project in the law school' (1986) 58 *Australian Quarterly* 366, 369.

77 Mossman, M.J., '"Otherness" and the Law School: A Comment on Teaching Gender Equality' (1985) 1 *Canadian Journal of Women and the Law* 213.

78 *Ibid.* 214.

79 Graycar, *op. cit.* n. 76, 370.

80 Dahl, T.S., 'Taking Women as a Starting Point: Building Women's Law' (1986) 14 *International Journal of the Sociology of Law* 239.

81 Mossman, M.J., 'Feminism and Legal Method: The Difference it Makes' (1986) 3 *Australian Journal of Law and Society* 30, 46.

82 Mossman, *op. cit.* n. 77, 218.

Feminist academics have also addressed a different kind of invisibility of women, that is, women's lack of participation in the classroom. Spender and others[83] have documented the disproportionate participation of men in school and university classrooms, and students at both Yale Law School and Osgoode Hall in Canada have documented a similar phenomenon.[84] My own observations and conversations with colleagues in Australia have indicated that we have a similar problem. I believe some of this lack of participation has to do with the maleness of law and law teaching I have described above: notably the absence of women as actors in the law as presented in casebooks and hypotheticals. Some of it may also have to do with the abstraction and neutrality of the way legal principles are presented and taught. Perhaps 'the Amys' haven't quite all turned into 'Jakes'. Some of it, I have argued elsewhere, is related to the style of teaching.[85] Where lectures are held in large classes and student participation is expected, I believe we may be presenting or encouraging a style of discourse that is more congenial for male students. There is much evidence that men tend to dominate a discourse that is adversarial, that men tend to interrupt, whether literally, or by keeping their hands raised while others are talking (whereas women lower their hands) and that women are thereby excluded. Women, on the other hand, are more likely to participate in, and indeed dominate, co-operatively developed discourse. This is more likely to occur in seminars and tutorials. It is clearly not financially possible to move to seminar teaching for all law courses in all law schools, but we must be vigilant about who is talking in our classrooms, and develop more co-operative styles of teaching where we can. It is interesting to note here that the recent review of Australian legal education by C.T.E.C.[86], the Pearce Report, while it extolled the virtues of small group teaching, it did so without reference to any concern with women's participation in classrooms. It suggested that the University of New South Wales, which currently only teaches in seminars, could consider using more lectures; to make these suggestions without consideration of issues of co-operation versus competition and the particular impact on women law students of large classes, is to neglect a large body of literature and to perpetuate the invisibility of women in our law schools.

Once again, it will be clear that my comments on styles of teaching and women's silence are consistent with some of Gilligan's work described above, and I now return to some of the hesitations about her work previously mentioned. It could be argued that I am suggesting that women are both incapable of operating in the law school environment, and, given that we have an adversarial legal system, in the legal profession. Needless to say, nothing could be further from the truth. We might believe, as Mary Jo Frug seems to, that the characteris-

83 *E.g.* Sears, P.S., and Feldman, D.H., 'Teacher Interactions with Boys and with Girls' in Stacey, J., Bereaud, S., and Daniels, J., *And Jill Came Tumbling After: Sexism in American Education* (1974); Spender, D., *Invisible Women: The Schooling Scandal* (1982); Spender, D. and Sarah, E., *Learning to Lose: Sexism and Education* (1980); Project on the Status and Education of Women *The Classroom Climate: A Chilly One for Women*, (1982).

84 Submissions to Faculty from Women Students at Yale Law School: Women's Silence in the Classroom (undated); Attridge, I., *et al.* 'Gender in a Law School Classroom: Perceptions and Practices' Osgoode Hall Law School, May 1987.

85 Morgan, J.J., 'The Socratic Method: Silencing Cooperation' (Unpublished manuscript).

86 Pearce, D., Campbell, E., and Harding, D., Commonwealth Tertiary Education Commission. *Australian Law Schools: A discipline assessment*.

tics I am talking about are merely associated with the masculine (aggressive, adversarial, abstract), and the feminine (submissive, connected, contextual), with the characteristics associated with the feminine being devalued. Or we might believe that these characteristics in fact belong to (most) men and (most) women respectively. In any case, I would argue that the 'feminine' qualities are essential both for teaching law and practising law. And whether women have these qualities because of gender oppression, or because they just grew like Topsy, it is time to reevaluate legal teaching and legal practice so that they encompass these *human* qualities. After all, there is an awful lot more involved in practising law than the archetypal joust in court.[87] As Carrie Menkel-Meadow has suggested, 'Amy's approach is . . . plausible and legitimate . . . as a style of lawyering'.[88]

The critique of law and legal education undertaken by feminists does of course have similarities to critiques by others — for example, Marxists,[89] critical legal theorists[90] and humanists.[91] Feminist legal scholars may also belong to any of these intellectual traditions, and/or they may consider themselves liberal, socialist or radical feminists,[92] but they all share a focus that is absent from these other scholarly traditions. This is a focus on understanding the oppression of women through law/s and attempts to use law/s to end the subordination of women.

It is obvious that this article hardly accomplishes a 'transformation of the normative tradition in law', but it aims to describe the efforts made to do just that, or at the very least to address the issue of gender subordination and the empowerment of women. Why isn't the project like 'Law and Underwater Basket Weaving'?[93] The reference is clearly to the, perhaps apocryphal, Californian college course of the 70's. In the legal education context, Regina Graycar used it to refer to 'Women and the Law' courses, structured around a grab bag of 'women's issues'. This article has tried to demonstrate that the fundamental critique of other disciplines undertaken by feminists in recent years is also occurring in law.[94] To treat it as just another 'Law and . . .' initiative, is to misconceive the challenge raised by feminist legal scholarship.

87 For the sporting analogy see Menkel-Meadow, C., 'Portia in a Different Voice: Speculations on Women's Lawyering Process' (1985) 1 *Berkeley Women's Law Journal* 39, 51.

88 *Ibid.* 46.

89 *E.g.* Beirne, P. and Quinney, R. (eds), *Marxism and Law* (1982); O'Malley, P., *Law, Capitalism and Democracy: A Sociology of Australian Legal Order* (1983); *cf.* Klare, K.E., 'The Law-School Curriculum in the 1980s: What's Left?' (1982) 32 *Journal of Legal Education* 336.

90 *E.g.* Kennedy, D., *Legal Education and the Reproduction of Hierarchy: A Polemic Against the System* (1983) and Kennedy, D., 'Legal Education as Training for Hierarchy' in Kairys, D. (ed.), *The Politics of Law: A Progressive Critique* (1982).

91 Project for the Study of Humanistic Education in Law, *Humanistic Education in Law: Reassessing Law Schooling*; Himmelstein, J., 'Reassessing Law Schooling: An Inquiry Into the Application of Humanistic Educational Psychology to the Teaching of Law' (1978) 53 *New York University Law Review* 514.

92 For detailed exegeses of these schools of thought see Eisenstein, H., *Contemporary Feminist Thought* (1984) and Jaggar, A.M., *Feminist Politics and Human Nature* (1983).

93 Graycar, R., *op. cit.* n. 76, 370 where she said, in reference to courses on 'Law and Gender', '[they] are an improvement on "women and . . ." (here substitute law or underwater basket weaving)'.

94 *E.g.* Langland, E. and Gove, W. (eds), *A Feminist Perspective in the Academy: The Difference it Makes* (1981); Spender, D. (ed.), *Men's Studies Modified: The Impact of Feminism on the Academic Disciplines* (1981); Keller, E.F., *Reflections on Gender and Science* (1985); Harding, S., *The Science Question in Feminism* (1986); Harding, S. and Hintikka, M.B. (eds), *Discovering Reality: Feminist Perspectives on Epistemology, Metaphysics, Methodology, and Philosophy of Science* (1983).

Part II
Foundations

[4]

Feminism, Marxism, Method, and the State: An Agenda for Theory

Catharine A. MacKinnon

Sexuality is to feminism what work is to marxism: that which is most one's own, yet most taken away. Marxist theory argues that society is fundamentally constructed of the relations people form as they do and make things needed to survive humanly. Work is the social process of shaping and transforming the material and social worlds, creating people as social beings as they create value. It is that activity by which people become who they are. Class is its structure, production its consequence, capital its congealed form, and control its issue.

Dedicated to the spirit of Shelly Rosaldo in us all.

The second part of this article, which will appear in a forthcoming issue of *Signs* as "Feminism, Marxism, Method, and the State: Toward Feminist Jurisprudence," applies the critique developed here to theories of the state and to legal materials. Both articles are parts of a longer work in progress. The argument of this essay on the relation between marxism and feminism has not changed since it was first written in 1973, but the argument on feminism itself has. In the intervening years, the manuscript has been widely circulated, in biannual mutations, for criticism. Reflecting on that process, which I hope publication will continue (this *is* "an agenda for theory"), I find the following people, each in their way, contributed most to its present incarnation: Sonia E. Alvarez, Douglas Bennett, Paul Brest, Ruth Colker, Robert A. Dahl, Karen E. Davis, Andrea Dworkin, Alicia Fernandez, Jane Flax, Bert Garskoff, Elbert Gates, Karen Haney, Kent Harvey, Linda Hoaglund, Nan Keohane,

---

EDITORS' NOTE: *Central to feminist theory and feminist method, as Catharine A. MacKinnon shows, is consciousness raising. Through this process, feminists confront the reality of women's condition by examining their experience and by taking this analysis as the starting point for individual and social change. By its nature, this method of inquiry challenges traditional notions of authority and objectivity and opens a dialectical questioning of existing power structures, of our own experience, and of theory itself.*

[*Signs: Journal of Women in Culture and Society* 1982, vol. 7, no. 3]

Implicit in feminist theory is a parallel argument: the molding, direction, and expression of sexuality organizes society into two sexes—women and men—which division underlies the totality of social relations. Sexuality is that social process which creates, organizes, expresses, and directs desire,[1] creating the social beings we know as women and men, as their relations create society. As work is to marxism, sexuality to feminism is socially constructed yet constructing, universal as activity yet historically specific, jointly comprised of matter and mind. As the organized expropriation of the work of some for the benefit of others defines a class—workers—the organized expropriation of the sexuality of some for the use of others defines the sex, woman. Heterosexuality is its structure, gender and family its congealed forms, sex roles its qualities generalized to social persona, reproduction a consequence, and control its issue.

Marxism and feminism are theories of power and its distribution: inequality. They provide accounts of how social arrangements of patterned disparity can be internally rational yet unjust. But their specificity is not incidental. In marxism to be deprived of one's work, in feminism of one's sexuality, defines each one's conception of lack of power per se. They do not mean to exist side by side to insure that two separate spheres

---

Duncan Kennedy, Bob Lamm, Martha Roper, Michelle Z. Rosaldo, Anne E. Simon, Sharon Silverstein, Valerie A. Tebbetts, Rona Wilensky, Gaye Williams, Jack Winkler, and Laura X. The superb work of Martha Freeman and Lu Ann Carter was essential to its production.

I have rendered "marxism" in lower case and "Black" in upper case and have been asked by the publisher to explain these choices. It is conventional to capitalize terms that derive from a proper name. Since I wish to place marxism and feminism in equipoise, the disparate typography would weigh against my analytic structure. Capitalizing both would germanize the text. I also hope feminism, a politics authored by those it works in the name of, is never named after an individual. Black is conventionally (I am told) regarded as a color rather than a racial or national designation, hence is not usually capitalized. I do not regard Black as merely a color of skin pigmentation, but as a heritage, an experience, a cultural and personal identity, the meaning of which becomes specifically stigmatic and/or glorious and/or ordinary under specific social conditions. It is as much socially created as, and at least in the American context no less specifically meaningful or definitive than, any linguistic, tribal, or religious ethnicity, all of which are conventionally recognized by capitalization.

1. "Desire" is selected as a term parallel to "value" in marxist theory to refer to that substance felt to be primordial or aboriginal but posited by the theory as social and contingent. The sense in which I mean it is consonant with its development in contemporary French feminist theories, e.g., in Hélène Cixous, "The Laugh of Medusa: Viewpoint," trans. Keith Cohen and Paula Cohen, *Signs: Journal of Women in Culture and Society* 1, no. 4 (Summer 1976): 875–93; and in works by Gauthier, Irigaray, LeClerc, Duras, and Kristeva in *New French Feminisms: An Anthology*, ed. Elaine Marks and Isabelle de Courtivron (Amherst: University of Massachusetts Press, 1980). My use of the term is to be distinguished from that of Gilles Deleuze and Felix Guattari, *Anti-Oedipus: Capitalism and Schizophrenia* (New York: Viking Press, 1977); and Guy Hocquenghem, *Homosexual Desire* (London: Allison & Busby, 1978), for example.

of social life are not overlooked, the interests of two groups are not obscured, or the contributions of two sets of variables are not ignored. They exist to argue, respectively, that the relations in which many work and few gain, in which some fuck and others get fucked,[2] are the prime moment of politics.

What if the claims of each theory are taken equally seriously, each on its own terms? Can two social processes be basic at once? Can two groups be subordinated in conflicting ways, or do they merely crosscut? Can two theories, each of which purports to account for the same thing—power as such—be reconciled? Or, is there a connection between the fact that the few have ruled the many and the fact that those few have been men?

Confronted on equal terms, these theories pose fundamental questions for each other. Is male dominance a creation of capitalism or is capitalism one expression of male dominance? What does it mean for class analysis if one can assert that a social group is defined and exploited through means largely independent of the organization of production, if in forms appropriate to it? What does it mean for a sex-based analysis if one can assert that capitalism would not be materially altered if it were sex integrated or even controlled by women? If the structure and interests served by the socialist state and the capitalist state differ in class terms, are they equally predicated upon sex inequality? To the extent their form and behavior resemble one another, could this be their commonality? Is there a relationship between the power of some classes over others and that of all men over all women?

Rather than confront these questions, marxists and feminists have usually either dismissed or, in what amounts to the same thing, subsumed each other. Marxists have criticized feminism as bourgeois in theory and in practice, meaning that it works in the interest of the ruling class. They argue that to analyze society in terms of sex ignores class divisions among women, dividing the proletariat. Feminist demands, it is claimed, could be fully satisfied within capitalism, so their pursuit undercuts and deflects the effort for basic change. Efforts to eliminate barriers to women's personhood—arguments for access to life chances without regard to sex—are seen as liberal and individualistic. Whatever women have in common is considered based in nature, not society; cross-cultural analyses of commonalities in women's social conditions are seen as ahistorical and lacking in cultural specificity. The women's movement's focus

2. I know no nondegraded English verb for the activity of sexual expression that would allow a construction parallel to, for example, "I am working," a phrase that could apply to nearly any activity. This fact of language may reflect and contribute to the process of obscuring sexuality's pervasiveness in social life. Nor is there *any* active verb meaning "to act sexually" that specifically envisions a woman's action. If language constructs as well as expresses the social world, these words support heterosexual values.

upon attitudes and feelings as powerful components of social reality is criticized as idealist; its composition, purportedly of middle-class educated women, is advanced as an explanation for its opportunism.

Feminists charge that marxism is male defined in theory and in practice, meaning that it moves within the world view and in the interest of men. Feminists argue that analyzing society exclusively in class terms ignores the distinctive social experiences of the sexes, obscuring women's unity. Marxist demands, it is claimed, could be (and in part have been) satisfied without altering women's inequality to men. Feminists have often found that working-class movements and the left undervalue women's work and concerns, neglect the role of feelings and attitudes in a focus on institutional and material change, denigrate women in procedure, practice, and everyday life, and in general fail to distinguish themselves from any other ideology or group dominated by male interests. Marxists and feminists thus accuse each other of seeking (what in each one's terms is) reform—changes that appease and assuage without addressing the grounds of discontent—where (again in each one's terms) a fundamental overthrow is required. The mutual perception, at its most extreme, is not only that the other's analysis is incorrect, but that its success would be a defeat.

Neither set of allegations is groundless. In the feminist view, sex, in analysis and in reality, does divide classes, a fact marxists have been more inclined to deny or ignore than to explain or change. Marxists, similarly, have seen parts of the women's movement function as a special interest group to advance the class-privileged: educated and professional women. To consider this group coextensive with "the women's movement" precludes questioning a definition of coalesced interest and resistance[3] which gives disproportionate visibility to the movement's least broadly based segment. But advocates of women's interests have not always been class conscious; some have exploited class-based arguments for advantage, even when the interests of working-class *women* were thereby obscured.

For example, in 1866, in an act often thought to inaugurate the first wave of feminism, John Stuart Mill petitioned the English parliament for women's suffrage with the following partial justification: "Under whatever conditions, and within whatever limits, men are admitted to suffrage, there is not a shadow of justification for not admitting women under the same. The majority of women of any class are not likely to differ in political opinion from the majority of men in the same class."[4] Perhaps Mill means that, to the extent class determines opinion, sex is

3. Accepting this definition has tended to exclude from "the women's movement" and make invisible the diverse ways that many women—notably Blacks and working-class women—have *moved* against their determinants.

4. John Stuart Mill, "The Subjection of Women," in *Essays on Sex Equality*, ed. Alice S. Rossi (Chicago: University of Chicago Press, 1970), pp. 184–85.

irrelevant. In this sense, the argument is (to some persuasively) narrow. It can also justify limiting the extension of the franchise to women who "belong to" men of the same class that already exercises it, to the further detriment of the excluded underclass, "their" women included.[5]

This kind of reasoning is confined neither to the issue of the vote nor to the nineteenth century. Mill's logic is embedded in a theoretical structure that underlies much contemporary feminist theory and justifies much of the marxist critique. That women should be allowed to engage in politics expressed Mill's concern that the state not restrict individuals' self-government, their freedom to develop talents for their own growth, and their ability to contribute to society for the good of humanity. As an empirical rationalist, he resisted attributing to biology what could be explained as social conditioning. As a utilitarian, he found most sex-based inequalities inaccurate or dubious, inefficient, and therefore unjust. The liberty of women as individuals to achieve the limits of self-development without arbitrary interference extended to women his meritocratic goal of the self-made man, condemning (what has since come to be termed) sexism as an interference with personal initiative and laissez-faire.

The hospitality of such an analysis to marxist concerns is problematic. One might extend Mill's argument to cover class as one more arbitrary, socially conditioned factor that produces inefficient development of talent and unjust distribution of resources among individuals. But although this might be in a sense materialist, it would not be a class analysis. Mill does not even allow for income leveling. Unequal distribution of wealth is exactly what laissez-faire and unregulated personal initiative produces. The individual concept of rights that this theory requires on a juridical level (especially but not only in the economic sphere), a concept which produces the tension between liberty for each and equality among all, pervades liberal feminism, substantiating the criticism that feminism is for the privileged few.

The marxist criticism that feminism focuses upon feelings and attitudes is also based on something real: the centrality of consciousness raising. Consciousness raising is the major technique of analysis, structure of organization, method of practice, and theory of social change of the women's movement.[6] In consciousness raising, often in groups, the

5. Mill personally supported universal suffrage. As it happened, working-class men got the vote before women of any class.

6. Feminists have observed the importance of consciousness raising without seeing it as method in the way developed here. See Pamela Allen, *Free Space: A Perspective on the Small Group in Women's Liberation* (New York: Times Change Press, 1970); Anuradha Bose, "Consciousness Raising," in *Mother Was Not a Person*, ed. Margaret Anderson (Montreal: Content Publishing, 1972); Nancy McWilliams, "Contemporary Feminism, Consciousness-Raising, and Changing Views of the Political," in *Women in Politics*, ed. Jane Jaquette (New York: John Wiley & Sons, 1974); Joan Cassell, *A Group Called Women: Sisterhood & Symbolism in the Feminist Movement* (New York: David McKay, 1977); and Nancy

impact of male dominance is concretely uncovered and analyzed through the collective speaking of women's experience, from the perspective of that experience. Because marxists tend to conceive of powerlessness, first and last, as concrete and externally imposed, they believe that it must be concretely and externally undone to be changed. Women's powerlessness has been found through consciousness raising to be both internalized and externally imposed, so that, for example, femininity is identity to women as well as desirability to men. The feminist concept of consciousness and its place in social order and change emerge from this practical analytic. What marxism conceives as change in consciousness is not a form of social change in itself. For feminism, it can be, but because women's oppression is not just in the head, feminist *consciousness* is not just in the head either. But the pain, isolation, and thingification of women who have been pampered and pacified into nonpersonhood—women "grown ugly and dangerous from being nobody for so long"[7]—is difficult for the materially deprived to see as a form of oppression, particularly for women whom no man has ever put on a pedestal.

Marxism, similarly, has not just been misunderstood. Marxist theory *has* traditionally attempted to comprehend all meaningful social variance in class terms. In this respect, sex parallels race and nation as an undigested but persistently salient challenge to the exclusivity—or even primacy—of class as social explanation. Marxists typically extend class to cover women, a division and submersion that, to feminism, is inadequate to women's divergent and common experience. In 1912 Rosa Luxemburg, for example, addressed a group of women on the issue of suffrage: "Most of these bourgeois women who act like lionesses in the struggle against 'male prerogatives' would trot like docile lambs in the camp of conservative and clerical reaction if they had the suffrage. Indeed, they would certainly be a good deal more reactionary than the male part of their class. Aside from the few who have taken jobs or professions, the bourgeoisie do not take part in social production. They are nothing but co-consumers of the surplus product their men extort

Hartsock, "Fundamental Feminism: Process and Perspective," *Quest: A Feminist Quarterly* 2, no. 2 (Fall 1975): 67–80.

7. Toni Cade (now Bambara) thus describes a desperate Black woman who has too many children and too little means to care for them or herself in "The Pill: Genocide or Liberation?" in *The Black Woman: An Anthology*, ed. Toni Cade (New York: Mentor, New American Library, 1970), p. 168. By using her phrase in altered context, I do not want to distort her meaning but to extend it. Throughout this essay, I have tried to see if women's condition is shared, even when contexts or magnitudes differ. (Thus, it is very different to be "nobody" as a Black woman than as a white lady, but neither is "somebody" by male standards.) This is the approach to race and ethnicity attempted throughout. I aspire to include all women in the term "women" in some way, without violating the particularity of any woman's experience. Whenever this fails, the statement is simply wrong and will have to be qualified or the aspiration (or the theory) abandoned.

from the proletariat. They are parasites of the parasites of the social body."[8] Her sympathies lay with "proletarian women" who derive their right to vote from being "productive for society like the men."[9] With a blind spot analogous to Mill's within her own perspective, Luxemburg defends women's suffrage on class grounds, although in both cases the vote would have benefited women without regard to class.

Women as women, across class distinctions and apart from nature, were simply unthinkable to Luxemburg, as to most marxists. Feminist theory asks marxism: What is class for women? Luxemburg, again like Mill in her own context, subliminally recognizes that women derive their class position, with concomitant privileges and restrictions, from their associations with men. For a feminist, this may explain why they do not unite against male dominance, but it does not explain that dominance, which cuts across class lines even as it takes forms peculiar to classes. What distinguishes the bourgeois woman from her domestic servant is that the latter is paid (if barely), while the former is kept (if contingently). But is this a difference in social productivity or only in its indices, indices which themselves may be products of women's undervalued status?[10] Luxemburg sees that the bourgeois woman of her time

8. Rosa Luxemburg, "Women's Suffrage and Class Struggle," in *Selected Political Writings*, ed. Dick Howard (New York: Monthly Review Press, 1971), pp. 219–20. It may or may not be true that women as a group vote more conservatively than men, on a conventional left-right spectrum. The apparently accurate suspicion that they do may have accounted for left ambivalence on women's suffrage as much as any principled view of the role of reform in a politics of radical change.

9. Ibid., p. 220.

10. This question is most productively explored in the controversy over wages for housework. See Margaret Benston, "The Political Economy of Women's Liberation," *Monthly Review*, vol. 21, no. 4 (September 1969), reprinted in *From Feminism to Liberation*, ed. Edith Hoshino Altbach (Cambridge, Mass.: Schenckman Publishing Co., 1971), pp. 199–210; Peggy Morton, "Women's Work Is Never Done," in *Women Unite* (Toronto: Canadian Women's Educational Press, 1972); Hodee Edwards, "Housework and Exploitation: A Marxist Analysis," *No More Fun and Games: A Journal of Female Liberation*, issue 4 (July 1971), pp. 92–100; and Mariarosa Dalla Costa and Selma James, *The Power of Women and the Subversion of the Community* (Bristol: Falling Wall Press, 1973). This last work situates housework in a broader theoretical context of wagelessness and potential political power while avoiding support of wages for housework as a program; its authors have since come to support wages for housework, deducing it from the perspective presented here. See also Sylvia Federici, *Wages against Housework* (Bristol: Falling Wall Press, 1973); Wally Seccombe, "The Housewife and Her Labor under Capitalism," *New Left Review* 83 (January–February 1974): 3–24; Carol Lopate, "Women and Pay for Housework," *Liberation* 18, no. 9 (May–June 1974): 11–19; Nicole Cox and Sylvia Federici, *Counter-Planning from the Kitchen—Wages for Housework: A Perspective on Capital and the Left* (Bristol: Falling Wall Press, 1975); Wendy Edmond and Suzi Fleming, eds., *All Work and No Pay: Women, Housework and the Wages Due* (Bristol: Falling Wall Press, 1975); Jeanette Silveira, *The Housewife and Marxist Class Analysis* (Seattle, Wash.: By the author, 1975) (pamphlet available from the author, P.O. Box 30541, Seattle, Wash. 98103); Jean Gardiner, "Women's Domestic Labor," *New Left Review* 89 (January–February 1975): 47–55; Beth Ingber and Cleveland Modern Times Group, "The Social Factory," *Falling Wall Review*, no. 5 (1976), pp. 1–7;

is a "parasite of a parasite" but fails to consider her commonality with the proletarian woman who is the slave of a slave. In the case of bourgeois women, to limit the analysis of women's relationship to capitalism to their relations through men is to see only its vicarious aspect. To fail to do this in the case of proletarian women is to miss its vicarious aspect.

Feminist observations of women's situation in socialist countries, although not conclusive on the contribution of marxist theory to understanding women's situation, have supported the theoretical critique.[11] In the feminist view, these countries have solved many social problems, women's subordination not included. The criticism is not that socialism has not automatically liberated women in the process of transforming production (assuming that this transformation is occurring). Nor is it to diminish the significance of such changes for women: "There is a difference between a society in which sexism is expressed in the form of female infanticide and a society in which sexism takes the form of unequal representation on the Central Committee. And the difference is worth dying for."[12] The criticism is rather that these countries do not make a priority of working for women that distinguishes them from nonsocialist societies. Capitalist countries value women in terms of their "merit" by male standards; in socialist countries women are invisible except in their capacity as "workers," a term that seldom includes women's distinctive work: housework, sexual service, childbearing. The con-

---

Joan Landes, "Wages for Housework: Subsidizing Capitalism?" *Quest: A Feminist Quarterly* 2, no. 2 (Fall 1975): 17–30; Batya Weinbaum and Amy Bridges, "The Other Side of the Paycheck: Monopoly Capital and the Structure of Conscription," *Monthly Review* 28, no. 3 (July–August 1976): 88–103.

11. These observations are complex and varied. Typically they begin with the recognition of the important changes socialism has made for women, qualified by reservations about its potential to make the remaining necessary ones. Delia Davin, "Women in the Countryside of China," in *Women in Chinese Society*, ed. Margery Wolf and Roxane Witke (Stanford, Calif.: Stanford University Press, 1974); Katie Curtin, *Women in China* (New York: Pathfinder Press, 1975); Judith Stacey, "When Patriarchy Kowtows: The Significance of the Chinese Family Revolution for Feminist Theory," *Feminist Studies* 2, no. 2/3 (1975): 64–112; Julia Kristeva, *About Chinese Women* (New York: Urizen Books, 1977); Hilda Scott, *Does Socialism Liberate Women? Experiences from Eastern Europe* (Cambridge, Mass.: Beacon Press, 1974); Margaret Randall, *Cuban Women Now* (Toronto: Women's Press, 1974) (an edited collation of Cuban women's own observations); and *Cuban Women Now: Afterword* (Toronto: Women's Press, 1974); Carollee Bengelsdorf and Alice Hageman, "Emerging from Underdevelopment: Women and Work in Cuba," in *Capitalist Patriarchy and the Case for Socialist Feminism*, ed. Zillah Eisenstein (New York: Monthly Review Press, 1979).

12. Barbara Ehrenreich, "What Is Socialist Feminism?" *Win* (June 3, 1976), reprinted in *Working Papers on Socialism and Feminism* (Chicago: New American Movement, n.d.). Counterpoint is provided by feminists who have more difficulty separating the two. Susan Brownmiller notes: "It seems to me that a country that wiped out the tsetse fly can by fiat put an equal number of women on the Central Committee" ("Notes of an Ex-China Fan," *Village Voice*, quoted in Batya Weinbaum, *The Curious Courtship of Women's Liberation and Socialism* [Boston: South End Press, 1978], p. 7).

cern of revolutionary leadership for ending women's confinement to traditional roles too often seems limited to making their labor available to the regime, leading feminists to wonder whose interests are served by this version of liberation. Women become as free as men to work outside the home while men remain free from work within it. This also occurs under capitalism. When woman's labor or militancy suits the needs of emergency, she is suddenly man's equal, only to regress when the urgency recedes.[13] Feminists do not argue that it means the same to women to be on the bottom in a feudal regime, a capitalist regime, and a socialist regime; the commonality argued is that, despite real changes, bottom is bottom.

Where such attitudes and practices come to be criticized, as in Cuba or China, changes appear gradual and precarious, even where the effort looks major. If seizures of state and productive power overturn work relations, they do not overturn sex relations at the same time or in the same way, as a class analysis of sex would (and in some cases did) predict.[14] Neither technology nor socialism, both of which purport to alter women's role at the point of production, have ever yet equalized women's status relative to men. In the feminist view, nothing has. At minimum, a separate effort appears required—an effort that can be shaped by revolutionary regime and work relations—but a separate effort nonetheless. In light of these experiences, women's struggles, whether under capitalist or socialist regimes, appear to feminists to have more in common with each other than with leftist struggles anywhere.

Attempts to create a synthesis between marxism and feminism,

13. Stacey (n. 11 above); Janet Salaff and Judith Merkle, "Women and Revolution: The Lessons of the Soviet Union and China," *Socialist Revolution* 1, no. 4 (1970): 39–72; Linda Gordon, *The Fourth Mountain* (Cambridge, Mass.: Working Papers, 1973); Richard Stites, *The Women's Liberation Movement in Russia: Feminism, Nihilism, and Bolshevism* (Princeton, N.J.: Princeton University Press, 1978), pp. 392–421.

14. See Fidel Castro, *Women and the Cuban Revolution* (New York: Pathfinder Press, 1970); but compare Fidel's "Speech at Closing Session of the 2d Congress of the Federation of Cuban Women," November 29, 1974, *Cuba Review* 4 (December 1974): 17–23. Stephanie Urdang, *A Revolution within a Revolution: Women in Guinea-Bissau* (Boston: New England Free Press, n.d.). This is the general position taken by official documents of the Chinese revolution, as collected by Elisabeth Croll, ed., *The Women's Movement in China: A Selection of Readings, 1949–1973*, Modern China Series, no. 6 (London: Anglo-Chinese Educational Institute, 1974). Mao Tse-Tung recognized a distinctive domination of women by men (see discussion by Stuart Schram, *The Political Thought of Mao Tse-Tung* [New York: Praeger Publishers, 1969], p. 257), but interpretations of his thought throughout the revolution saw issues of sex as bourgeois deviation (see Croll, ed., pp. 19, 22, 32). The Leninist view which the latter documents seem to reflect is expressed in Clara Zetkin's account, "Lenin on the Woman Question," excerpted as appendix in *The Woman Question* (New York: International Publishers, 1951), p. 89. Engels earlier traced the oppression of women to the rise of class society, the patriarchal family, and the state, arguing that woman's status would be changed with the elimination of private property as a form of ownership and her integration into public production (Friedrich Engels, *Origin of the Family, Private Property and the State* [New York: International Publishers, 1942]).

termed socialist-feminism, have not recognized the depth of the antagonism or the separate integrity of each theory. These juxtapositions emerge as unconfronted as they started: either feminist or marxist, usually the latter. Socialist-feminist practice often divides along the same lines, consisting largely in organizational cross-memberships and mutual support on specific issues.[15] Women with feminist sympathies urge attention to women's issues by left or labor groups; marxist women pursue issues of class within feminist groups; explicitly socialist-feminist groups come together and divide, often at the hyphen.[16]

Most attempts at synthesis attempt to integrate or explain the appeal of feminism by incorporating issues feminism identifies as central—the family, housework, sexuality, reproduction, socialization, personal life—within an essentially unchanged marxian analysis.[17] According to

15. Sheila Rowbotham, *Hidden from History: Rediscovering Women in History from the Seventeenth Century to the Present* (New York: Random House, 1973); Mary Jo Buhle, "Women and the Socialist Party, 1901–1914," in Altbach, ed. (n. 10 above); Robert Shaffer, "Women and the Communist Party, USA, 1930–1940," *Socialist Review* 45 (May–June 1979): 73–118. Contemporary attempts to create socialist-feminist groups and strategies are exemplified in position papers: Chicago Women's Liberation Union, "Socialist Feminism: A Strategy for the Women's Movement," mimeograph (Chicago, 1972) (available from Women's Liberation Union, Hyde Park Chapter, 819 W. George, Chicago, Ill. 60657); Berkeley-Oakland Women's Union, "Principles of Unity," *Socialist Revolution* 4, no. 1 (January–March 1974): 69–82; Lavender and Red Union, *The Political Perspective of the Lavender and Red Union* (Los Angeles: Fanshen Printing Collective, 1975). Rosalind Petchesky, "Dissolving the Hyphen: A Report on Marxist-Feminist Groups 1–5," in Eisenstein, ed. (n. 11 above), and Red Apple Collective, "Socialist-Feminist Women's Unions: Past and Present," *Quest: A Feminist Quarterly* 4, no. 1 (1977): 88–96, reflect on the process.

16. Many attempts at unity began as an effort to justify women's struggles in marxist terms, as if only that could make them legitimate. This anxiety lurks under many synthetic attempts, although feminism has largely redirected its efforts from justifying itself within any other perspective to developing its own.

17. While true from a feminist standpoint, this sweeping characterization does minimize the wide varieties of marxist theories that have produced significantly different analyses of women's situation. Juliet Mitchell, *Woman's Estate* (New York: Random House, 1971); Sheila Rowbotham, *Women, Resistance and Revolution: A History of Women and Revolution in the Modern World* (New York: Random House, 1972); Zillah Eisenstein, "Some Notes on the Relations of Capitalist Patriarchy," in Eisenstein, ed. (n. 11 above); Eli Zaretsky, "Socialist Politics and the Family," *Socialist Revolution* 19 (January–March 1974): 83–99; Eli Zaretsky, "Capitalism, the Family and Personal Life," *Socialist Revolution* 3, nos. 1 and 2 (January–April 1973): 69–126, and no. 3 (May–June 1973): 19–70; Virginia Held, "Marx, Sex and the Transformation of Society," in *Women and Philosophy: Toward a Theory of Liberation*, ed. Carol C. Gould and Marx W. Wartofsky (New York: G. P. Putnam's Sons, 1976), pp. 168–84; Mihailo Marković, "Women's Liberation and Human Emancipation," ibid., pp. 145–67; Hal Draper, "Marx and Engels on Women's Liberation," in *Female Liberation*, ed. Roberta Salper (New York: Alfred A. Knopf, Inc., 1972), pp. 83–107. No matter how perceptive about the contributions of feminism or sympathetic to women's interests, these attempts cast feminism, ultimately, as a movement *within* marxism: "I want to suggest that the women's movement can provide the basis for building a new and authentic American socialism" (Nancy Hartsock, "Feminist Theory and the Development of Revolutionary

the persuasion of the marxist, women become a caste, a stratum, a cultural group, a division in civil society, a secondary contradiction, or a nonantagonistic contradiction; women's liberation becomes a precondition, a measure of society's general emancipation, part of the superstructure, or an important aspect of the class struggle. Most commonly, women are reduced to some other category, such as "women workers," which is then treated as coextensive with all women.[18] Or, in what has become near reflex, women become "the family," as if this single form of women's confinement (then divided on class lines, then on racial lines) can be *presumed* the crucible of women's determination.[19] Or,

Strategy," in Eisenstein, ed. [n. 11 above], p. 57). Attempts at synthesis that push these limits include Gayle Rubin, "The Traffic in Women: Notes on the 'Political Economy' of Sex," in *Toward an Anthropology of Women*, ed. Rayna R. Reiter (New York: Monthly Review Press, 1975), pp. 157–210; Sheila Rowbotham, *Women's Liberation and the New Politics*, Spokesman Pamphlet, no. 17 (Bristol: Falling Wall Press, 1971); Annette Kuhn and AnnMarie Wolpe, "Feminism and Materialism," in *Feminism and Materialism: Women and Modes of Production*, ed. Annette Kuhn and AnnMarie Wolpe (London: Routledge & Kegan Paul, 1978); Ann Foreman, *Femininity as Alienation: Women and the Family in Marxism and Psychoanalysis* (London: Pluto Press, 1977); Meredith Tax and Jonathan Schwartz, "The Wageless Slave and the Proletarian," mimeograph (1972) (available from the author); Heidi I. Hartmann, "Capitalism, Patriarchy, and Job Segregation by Sex," *Signs: Journal of Women in Culture and Society* 1, no. 3, pt. 2 (Spring 1976): 137–69, and "The Unhappy Marriage of Marxism and Feminism: Towards a More Progressive Union," *Capital and Class* 8 (Summer 1979): 1–33; advocates of "wages for housework" mentioned in n. 10 above; and work by Linda Gordon, *Woman's Body, Woman's Right: A Social History of Birth Control in America* (New York: Grossman Publishers, 1976), pp. 403–18. Also see Linda Gordon, "The Struggle for Reproductive Freedom: Three Stages of Feminism," in Eisenstein, ed. (n. 11 above). Charlotte Bunch and Nancy Myron, *Class and Feminism* (Baltimore: Diana Press, 1974) exemplifies, without explicitly articulating, feminist method applied to class.

18. This tendency, again with important variations, is manifest in writings otherwise as diverse as Charnie Guettel, *Marxism and Feminism* (Toronto: Canadian Women's Education Press, 1974); Mary Alice Waters, "Are Feminism and Socialism Related?" in *Feminism and Socialism*, ed. Linda Jenness (New York: Pathfinder Press, 1972), pp. 18–26; Weather Underground, *Prairie Fire* (Underground, U.S.A.: Red Dragon Collective, 1975); Marjorie King, "Cuba's Attack on Women's Second Shift, 1974–1976," *Latin American Perspectives* 4, nos. 1 and 2 (Winter–Spring 1977): 106–19; Al Syzmanski, "The Socialization of Women's Oppression: A Marxist Theory of the Changing Position of Women in Advanced Capitalist Society," *Insurgent Sociologist* 6, no. 11 (Winter 1976): 31–58; "The Political Economy of Women," *Review of Radical Political Economics* 4, no. 3 (July 1972). See also Selma James, *Women, the Unions and Work, or What Is Not to Be Done* (Bristol: Falling Wall Press, 1976). This is true for "wages for housework" theory in the sense that it sees women as exploited because they do work—housework.

19. Engels (n. 14 above); Leon Trotsky, *Women and the Family*, trans. Max Eastman et al. (New York: Pathfinder Press, 1970); Evelyn Reed, *Woman's Evolution: From Matriarchal Clan to Patriarchal Family* (New York: Pathfinder Press, 1975); Lise Vogel, "The Earthly Family," *Radical America* 7, nos. 4–5 (July–October 1973): 9–50; Kollontai Collective, "The Politics of the Family: A Marxist View" (paper prepared for Socialist Feminist Conference at Yellow Springs, Ohio, July 4–6, 1975); Linda Limpus, *Liberation of Women: Sexual Repres-*

the marxist meaning of reproduction, the iteration of productive relations, is punned into an analysis of biological reproduction, as if women's bodily differences from men must account for their subordination to men; and as if this social analogue to the biological makes women's definition material, therefore based on a division of *labor* after all, therefore real, therefore (potentially) unequal.[20] Sexuality, if noticed at all, is, like "every day life,"[21] analyzed in gender-neutral terms, as if its social meaning can be presumed the same, or coequal, or complementary, for women and men.[22] Although a unified theory of social inequality is presaged in these strategies of subordination, staged progression, and assimilation of women's concerns to left concerns, at most an uneven

sion and the Family (Boston: New England Free Press, n.d.); Marlene Dixon, "On the Super-Exploitation of Women," *Synthesis* 1, no. 4 (Spring 1977): 1–11; David P. Levine and Lynn S. Levine, "Problems in the Marxist Theory of the Family," photocopied (Department of Economics, Yale University, July 1978). A common approach to treating women's situation as coterminous with the family is to make women's circumstances the incident or focus for a reconciliation of Marx with Freud. This approach, in turn, often becomes more Freudian than marxist, without yet becoming feminist in the sense developed here. Juliet Mitchell, *Psychoanalysis and Feminism: Freud, Reich, Laing and Women* (New York: Pantheon Books, 1974); Eli Zaretsky, "Male Supremacy and the Unconscious," *Socialist Revolution* 21, no. 22 (January 1975): 7–56; Nancy Chodorow, *The Reproduction of Mothering: Psychoanalysis and the Sociology of Gender* (Berkeley: University of California Press, 1978). See also Herbert Marcuse, "Socialist Feminism: The Hard Core of the Dream," *Edcentric: A Journal of Educational Change*, no. 31–32 (November 1974), pp. 7–44.

20. Sometimes "reproduction" refers to biological reproduction, sometimes to the "reproduction" of daily life, as housework, sometimes both. Political Economy of Women Group, "Women, the State and Reproduction since the 1930s," *On the Political Economy of Women*, CSE Pamphlet no. 2, Stage 1 (London: Conference of Socialist Economists, 1977). Family theories (n. 19 above) often analyze biological reproduction as a part of the family, while theories of women as workers often see it as work (n. 18 above). For an analysis of reproduction as an aspect of *sexuality*, in the context of an attempted synthesis, see Gordon, "The Struggle for Reproductive Freedom: Three Stages of Feminism" (n. 17 above).

21. Henri Lefebvre, *Everyday Life in the Modern World* (London: Penguin Books, 1971); Bruce Brown, *Marx, Freud and the Critique of Everyday Life: Toward a Permanent Cultural Revolution* (New York: Monthly Review Press, 1973).

22. Herbert Marcuse, *Eros and Civilization: A Philosophical Inquiry into Freud* (New York: Random House, 1955); Wilhelm Reich, *Sex-Pol: Essays, 1929–1934* (New York: Random House, 1972); Reimut Reiche, *Sexuality and Class Struggle* (London: New Left Books, 1970); Bertell Ollman, *Social and Sexual Revolution: Essays on Marx and Reich* (Boston: South End Press, 1979); Red Collective, *The Politics of Sexuality in Capitalism* (London: Red Collective, 1973). This is also true of Michel Foucault, *The History of Sexuality*, vol. 1, *An Introduction* (New York: Random House, 1980). Although Foucault understands that sexuality must be discussed at the same time as method, power, class, and the law, he does not systematically comprehend the specificity of gender—women's and men's relation to these factors—as a primary category for comprehending them. As one result, he cannot distinguish between the silence about sexuality that Victorianism has made into a noisy discourse and the silence that has *been* women's sexuality under conditions of subordination by and to men. Lacan notwithstanding, none of these theorists grasps sexuality (*including desire itself*) as social, nor the content of its determination as a sexist social order that eroticizes potency (as male) and victimization (as female).

combination is accomplished. However sympathetically, "the woman question" is always reduced to some other question, instead of being seen as *the* question, calling for analysis on its own terms.

Socialist-feminism stands before the task of synthesis as if nothing essential to either theory fundamentally opposes their wedding—indeed as if the union had already occurred and need only be celebrated. The failure to contain both theories on equal terms derives from the failure to confront each on its own ground: at the level of method. Method shapes each theory's vision of social reality. It identifies its central problem, group, and process, and creates as a consequence its distinctive conception of politics as such. Work and sexuality as concepts, then, derive their meaning and primacy from the *way* each theory approaches, grasps, interprets, and inhabits its world. Clearly, there is a relationship between how and what a theory sees: is there a marxist method without class? a feminist method without sex? Method in this sense organizes the apprehension of truth; it determines what counts as evidence and defines what is taken as verification. Instead of engaging the debate over which came (or comes) first, sex or class, the task for theory is to explore the conflicts and connections between the methods that found it meaningful to analyze social conditions in terms of those categories in the first place.[23]

23. Marxist method is not monolithic. Beginning with Marx, it has divided between an epistemology that embraces its own historicity and one that claims to portray a reality outside itself. In the first tendency, all thought, including social analysis, is ideological in the sense of being shaped by social being, the conditions of which are external to no theory. The project of theory is to create what Lukács described as "a theory of theory and a consciousness of consciousness" (Georg Lukács, "Class Consciousness," in *History and Class Consciousness: Studies in Marxist Dialectics* [Cambridge, Mass.: MIT Press, 1968], p. 47). Theory is a social activity engaged in the life situation of consciousness. See Jane Flax, "Epistemology and Politics: An Inquiry into Their Relation" (Ph.D. diss., Yale University, 1974). In the second tendency, theory is acontextual to the extent that it is correct. Real processes and thought processes are distinct; being has primacy over knowledge. The real can only be unified with knowledge of the real, as in dialectical materialism, because they have previously been separated. Nicos Poulantzas, *Political Power and Social Classes* (London: Verso, 1978), p. 14. Theory as a form of thought is methodologically set apart both from the illusions endemic to social reality—ideology—and from reality itself, a world defined as thinglike, independent of both ideology and theory. Ideology here means thought that is socially determined without being conscious of its determinations. Situated thought is as likely to produce "false consciousness" as access to truth. Theory, by definition, is, on the contrary, nonideological. Since ideology is interested, theory must be disinterested in order to penetrate myths that justify and legitimate the status quo. As Louis Althusser warned, "We know that a 'pure' science only exists on condition that it continually frees itself from ideology which occupies it, haunts it, or lies in wait for it" (*For Marx* [London: Verso, 1979], p. 170). When this attempt is successful, society is seen "from the point of view of class exploitation" (Louis Althusser, *Lenin and Philosophy* [New York: Monthly Review Press, 1971], p. 8). A theory that embraced its own historicity might see the scientific imperative itself as historically contingent. (On the objective standpoint, see text, pp. 537–42.) The problem with using scientific method to understand women's situation is that it is precisely unclear and crucial what is thought and what is thing, so that

Feminism has not been perceived as having a method, or even a central argument, with which to contend. It has been perceived not as a systematic analysis but as a loose collection of factors, complaints, and issues which, taken together, describe rather than explain the misfortunes of the female sex. The challenge is to demonstrate that feminism systematically converges upon a central explanation of sex inequality through an approach distinctive to its subject yet applicable to the whole of social life, including class.

Under the rubric of feminism, woman's situation has been explained as a consequence of biology[24] or of reproduction and mothering, social organizations of biology;[25] as caused by the marriage law[26] or, as

the separation itself becomes problematic. The second tendency grounds the marxist claim to be scientific; the first, its claim to capture as thought the flux of history. The first is more hospitable to feminism; the second has become the dominant tradition.

24. Simone de Beauvoir, *The Second Sex* (New York: Alfred A. Knopf, Inc., 1970). Her existential theory merges, in order to criticize, social meaning with biological determination in "anatomical destiny": "Here we have the key to the whole mystery. On the biological level a species is maintained only by creating itself anew; but this creation results only in repeating the same Life in more individuals. But man assures the repetition of Life while transcending Life through Existence; by this transcendence he creates values that deprive pure repetition of all value. . . . Her misfortune is to have been biologically destined for the repetition of Life when even in her own view Life does not carry within itself its reasons for being, reasons that are more important than life itself" (p. 59). She does not ask, for example, whether the social value placed upon "repetition of life," the fact that it is seen as iterative rather than generative, or the fact that women are more identified with it than are men, are themselves social artifacts of women's subordination, rather than existential derivations of biological fiat. Shulamith Firestone substitutes the contradiction of sex for class in a dialectical analysis, but nevertheless takes sex itself as presocial: "Unlike economic class, sex class sprang directly from a biological reality; men and women were created different, and not equally privileged. . . . The biological family is an inherently unequal power distribution" (*The Dialectic of Sex: The Case For Feminist Revolution* [New York: William Morrow & Co., 1972], p. 3). Her solutions are consistent: "The freeing of women from the tyranny of their reproductive biology by every means available, and the diffusion of childbearing and the childrearing role to the society as a whole, men as well as women" (p. 206). Susan Brownmiller (in *Against Our Will: Men, Women and Rape* [New York: Simon & Schuster, 1976]) expresses a biological theory of rape within a social critique of the centrality of rape to women's subordination: "Men's structural capacity to rape and woman's corresponding structural vulnerability are as basic to the physiology of both our sexes as the primal act of sex itself. Had it not been for this accident of biology, an accommodation requiring the locking together of two separate parts, penis and vagina, there would be neither copulation nor rape as we know it. . . . By anatomical fiat—the inescapable construction of their genital organs—the human male was a natural predator and the human female served as his natural prey" (pp. 4, 6). She does not seem to think it necessary to explain why women do not engulf men, an equal biological possibility. Criticizing the law for confusing intercourse with rape, she finds them biologically indistinguishable, leaving one wondering whether she, too, must alter or acquiesce in the biological.

25. Adrienne Rich, *Of Woman Born: Motherhood as Experience and Institution* (New York: W. W. Norton & Co., 1976); Chodorow (n. 19 above); Dorothy Dinnerstein, *The Mermaid and the Minotaur: Sexual Arrangements and Human Malaise* (New York: Harper & Row, 1977); Suzanne Arms, *Immaculate Deception: A New Look at Women and Childbirth in America* (Boston: Houghton Mifflin Co., 1975).

26. I take Mill's "The Subjection of Women" (n. 4 above) to be the original articulation

extensions, by the patriarchal family, becoming society as a "patriarchy";[27] or as caused by artificial gender roles and their attendant attitudes.[28] Informed by these attempts, but conceiving nature, law, the family, and roles as consequences, not foundations, I think that feminism fundamentally identifies sexuality as the primary social sphere of male power. The centrality of sexuality emerges not from Freudian conceptions[29] but from feminist practice on diverse issues, including abortion, birth control, sterilization abuse, domestic battery, rape, incest, lesbianism, sexual harassment, prostitution, female sexual slavery, and pornography. In all these areas, feminist efforts confront and change women's lives concretely and experientially. Taken together, they are producing a feminist political theory centering upon sexuality: its social determination, daily construction, birth to death expression, and ultimately male control.

Feminist inquiry into these specific issues began with a broad unmasking of the attitudes that legitimize and hide women's status, the ideational envelope that contains woman's body: notions that women desire and provoke rape, that girls' experiences of incest are fantasies, that career women plot and advance by sexual parlays, that prostitutes are lustful, that wife beating expresses the intensity of love. Beneath each of these ideas was revealed bare coercion and broad connections to woman's social definition as a sex. Research on sex roles, pursuing Simone de Beauvoir's insight that "one is not born, one rather becomes a woman,"[30] disclosed an elaborate process: how and what one learns to become one. Gender, cross-culturally, was found to be a learned quality, an acquired characteristic, an assigned status, with qualities that vary independent of biology and an ideology that attributes them to nature.[31]

---

of the theory, generalized in much contemporary feminism, that women are oppressed by "patriarchy," meaning a system originating in the household wherein the father dominates, the structure then reproduced throughout the society in gender relations.

27. In her "notes toward a theory of patriarchy" Kate Millett comprehends "sex as a status category with political implications," in which politics refers to "power-structured relationships, arrangements whereby one group of persons is controlled by another. . . . Patriarchy's chief institution is the family" (*Sexual Politics* [New York: Ballantine Books, 1969], pp. 32, 31, 45).

28. Sandra L. Bem and Daryl J. Bem, "Case Study of Nonconscious Ideology: Training the Woman to Know Her Place," in *Beliefs, Attitudes and Human Affairs*, ed. D. J. Bem (Belmont, Calif.: Brooks/Cole, 1970); Eleanor Emmons Maccoby and Carol Nagy Jacklin, *The Psychology of Sex Differences* (Stanford, Calif.: Stanford University Press, 1974); and Shirley Weitz, *Sex Roles: Biological, Psychological and Social Foundations* (New York: Oxford University Press, 1977).

29. Nor does it grow directly from Lacanian roots, although French feminists have contributed much to the developing theory from within that tradition.

30. De Beauvoir (n. 24 above), p. 249.

31. J. H. Block, "Conceptions of Sex Role: Some Cross-cultural and Longitudinal Perspectives," *American Psychologist* 28, no. 3 (June 1973): 512–26; Nancy Chodorow, "Being and Doing: A Cross-cultural Examination of the Socialization of Males and Females," in *Women in Sexist Society*, ed. V. Gornick and B. K. Moran (New York: Basic

The discovery that the female archetype is the feminine stereotype exposed "woman" as a social construction. Contemporary industrial society's version of her is docile, soft, passive, nurturant, vulnerable, weak, narcissistic, childlike, incompetent, masochistic, and domestic, made for child care, home care, and husband care. Conditioning to these values permeates the upbringing of girls and the images for emulation thrust upon women. Women who resist or fail, including those who never did fit—for example, black and lower-class women who cannot survive if they are soft and weak and incompetent,[32] assertively self-respecting women, women with ambitions of male dimensions—are considered less female, lesser women. Women who comply or succeed are elevated as models, tokenized by success on male terms or portrayed as consenting to their natural place and dismissed as having participated if they complain.

If the literature on sex roles and the investigations of particular issues are read in light of each other, each element of the female *gender* stereotype is revealed as, in fact, *sexual*. Vulnerability means the appearance/reality of easy sexual access; passivity means receptivity and disabled resistance, enforced by trained physical weakness; softness means pregnability by something hard. Incompetence seeks help as vulnerability seeks shelter, inviting the embrace that becomes the invasion, trading exclusive access for protection . . . from the same access. Domesticity nurtures the consequent progeny, proof of potency, and ideally waits at home dressed in saran wrap.[33] Woman's infantilization evokes pedophilia; fixation on dismembered body parts (the breast man, the leg man) evokes fetishism; idolization of vapidity, necrophilia. Narcissism insures that woman identifies with that image of herself that man holds up: "Hold still, we are going to do your portrait, so that you can begin looking like it right away."[34] Masochism means that pleasure in violation becomes her sensuality. Lesbians so violate the sexuality implicit in female gender stereotypes as not to be considered women at all.

Socially, femaleness means femininity, which means attractiveness

Books, 1971); R. R. Sears, "Development of Gender Role," in *Sex and Behavior*, ed. F. A. Beach (New York: John Wiley & Sons, 1965).

32. National Black Feminist Organization, "Statement of Purpose," *Ms.* (May 1974): "The black woman has had to be strong, yet we are persecuted for having survived" (p. 99). Johnnie Tillmon, "Welfare Is a Women's Issue," *Liberation News Service* (February 26, 1972), in *America's Working Women: A Documentary History, 1600 to the Present*, ed. Rosalyn Baxandall, Linda Gordon, and Susan Reverby (New York: Vintage Books, 1976): "On TV a woman learns that human worth means beauty and that beauty means being thin, white, young and rich. . . . In other words, an A.F.D.C. mother learns that being a 'real woman' means being all the things she isn't and having all the things she can't have" (pp. 357–58).

33. Marabel Morgan, *The Total Woman* (Old Tappan, N.J.: Fleming H. Revell Co., 1973). "Total Woman" makes blasphemous sexuality into a home art, redomesticating what prostitutes have marketed as forbidden.

34. Cixous (n. 1 above), p. 892.

to men, which means sexual attractiveness, which means sexual availability on male terms.[35] What defines woman as such is what turns men on. Good girls are "attractive," bad girls "provocative." Gender socialization is the process through which women come to identify themselves as sexual beings, as beings that exist for men. It is that process through which women internalize (make their own) a male image of their sexuality *as* their identity as women.[36] It is not just an illusion. Feminist inquiry into women's own experience of sexuality revises prior comprehensions of sexual issues and transforms the concept of sexuality itself—its determinants and its role in society and politics. According to this revision, one "becomes a woman"—acquires and identifies with the status of the female—not so much through physical maturation or inculcation into appropriate role behavior as through the experience of sexuality: a complex unity of physicality, emotionality, identity, and status affirmation. Sex as gender and sex as sexuality are thus defined in terms of each other, but it is sexuality that determines gender, not the other way around. This, the central but never stated insight of Kate Millett's *Sexual Politics*,[37] resolves the duality in the term "sex" itself: what women learn in order to "have sex," in order to "become women"—woman as gender—comes through the experience of, and is a condition for, "having sex"—woman as sexual object for man, the use of women's sexuality by men. Indeed, to the extent sexuality is social, women's sexuality *is* its use, just as our femaleness *is* its alterity.

Many issues that appear sexual from this standpoint have not been seen as such, nor have they been seen as defining a politics. Incest, for example, is commonly seen as a question of distinguishing the real evil, a crime against the family, from girlish seductiveness or fantasy. Contraception and abortion have been framed as matters of reproduction and fought out as proper or improper social constraints on nature. Or they are seen as private, minimizing state intervention into intimate relations. Sexual harassment was a nonissue, then became a problem of distinguishing personal relationships or affectionate flirtation from abuse of position. Lesbianism, when visible, has been either a perversion or not, to be tolerated or not. Pornography has been considered a question of freedom to speak and depict the erotic, as against the obscene or violent. Prostitution has been understood either as mutual lust and degradation or an equal exchange of sexual need for economic need. The issue in rape has been whether the intercourse was provoked/mutually

35. Indications are that this is true not only in Western industrial society; further cross-cultural research is definitely needed.

36. Love justifies this on the emotional level. Firestone (n. 24 above), chap. 6.

37. Millett's analysis is pervasively animated by the sense that women's status is sexually determined. It shapes her choice of authors, scenes, and themes and underlies her most pointed criticisms of women's depiction. Her explicit discussion, however, vacillates between clear glimpses of that argument and statements nearly to the contrary.

desired, or whether it was forced: was it sex or violence? Across and beneath these issues, sexuality itself has been divided into parallel provinces: traditionally, religion or biology; in modern transformation, morality or psychology. Almost never politics.

In a feminist perspective, the formulation of each issue, in the terms just described, expresses ideologically the same interest that the problem it formulates expresses concretely: the interest from the male point of view. Women experience the sexual events these issues codify[38] as a cohesive whole within which each resonates. The defining theme of that whole is the male pursuit of control over women's sexuality—men not as individuals nor as biological beings, but as a gender group characterized by maleness as socially constructed, of which this pursuit is definitive. For example, women who need abortions see contraception as a struggle not only for control over the biological products of sexual expression but over the social rhythms and mores of sexual intercourse. These norms often appear hostile to women's self-protection even when the technology is at hand. As an instance of such norms, women notice that sexual harassment looks a great deal like ordinary heterosexual initiation under conditions of gender inequality. Few women are in a position to refuse unwanted sexual initiatives. That consent rather than nonmutuality is the line between rape and intercourse further exposes the inequality in normal social expectations. So does the substantial amount of male force allowed in the focus on the woman's resistance, which tends to be disabled by socialization to passivity. If sex is ordinarily accepted as something men do *to* women, the better question would be whether consent is a meaningful concept. Penetration (often by a penis) is also substantially more central to both the legal definition of rape and the male definition of sexual intercourse than it is to women's sexual violation or sexual pleasure. Rape in marriage expresses the male sense of entitlement to access to women they annex; incest extends it. Although most women are raped by men they know, the closer the relation, the less women are allowed to claim it was rape. Pornography becomes difficult to distinguish from art and ads once it is clear that what is degrading to women is compelling to the consumer. Prostitutes sell the unilaterality that pornography advertises. That most of these issues codify behavior that is neither countersystemic nor exceptional is supported by women's experience as victims: these behaviors are either not illegal or are effectively permitted on a large scale. As women's experience blurs the lines between deviance and normalcy, it obliterates the distinction between abuses *of* women and the social definition of what a woman *is*.[39]

38. Each of these issues is discussed at length in the second part of this article ("Toward Feminist Jurisprudence"), forthcoming.

39. On abortion and contraception, see Kristin Luker, *Taking Chances: Abortion and the Decision Not to Contracept* (Berkeley: University of California Press, 1975). On rape, see Diana E. H. Russell, *Rape: The Victim's Perspective* (New York: Stein & Day, 1977); Andrea

These investigations reveal rape, incest, sexual harassment, pornography, and prostitution as not primarily abuses of physical force, violence, authority, or economics. They are abuses of sex. They need not and do not rely for their coerciveness upon forms of enforcement other than the sexual; that those forms of enforcement, at least in this context, are themselves sexualized is closer to the truth. They are not the erotization *of* something else; eroticism *itself* exists in their form. Nor are they perversions of art and morality. They *are* art and morality from the male point of view. They are sexual because they express the relations, values, feelings, norms, and behaviors of the culture's sexuality, in which considering things like rape, pornography, incest, or lesbianism deviant, perverse, or blasphemous is part of their excitement potential.

Sexuality, then, is a form of power Gender, as socially constructed, embodies it, not the reverse. Women and men are divided by gender, made into the sexes as we know them, by the social requirements of heterosexuality, which institutionalizes male sexual dominance and female sexual submission.[40] If this is true, sexuality is the linchpin of gender inequality.

A woman is a being who identifies and is identified as one whose sexuality exists for someone else, who is socially male. Women's sexuality is the capacity to arouse desire in that someone. If what is sexual about a woman is what the male point of view requires for excitement, have male requirements so usurped its terms as to have become them? Considering women's sexuality in this way forces confrontation with whether there is any such thing. Is women's sexuality its absence? If being *for* another is the whole of women's sexual construction, it can be no more escaped by separatism, men's temporary concrete absence, than eliminated or qualified by permissiveness, which, in this context, looks like women emulating male roles. As Susan Sontag said: "The question is: *what* sexuality are women to be liberated to enjoy? Merely to remove the onus placed upon the sexual expressiveness of women is a hollow victory if the sexuality they become freer to enjoy remains the old one that converts women into objects. . . . This already 'freer' sexuality mostly reflects a

---

Medea and Kathleen Thompson, *Against Rape* (New York: Farrar, Straus & Giroux, 1974); Lorenne N. G. Clark and Debra Lewis, *Rape: The Price of Coercive Sexuality* (Toronto: Women's Press, 1977); Susan Griffin, *Rape: The Power of Consciousness* (San Francisco: Harper & Row, 1979); Kalamu ya Salaam, "Rape: A Radical Analysis from the African-American Perspective," in his *Our Women Keep Our Skies from Falling* (New Orleans: Nkombo, 1980), pp. 25–40. On incest, see Judith Herman and Lisa Hirschman, "Father-Daughter Incest," *Signs: Journal of Women in Culture and Society* 2, no. 1 (Summer 1977): 735–56. On sexual harassment, see my *Sexual Harassment of Working Women* (New Haven, Conn.: Yale University Press, 1979). On pornography, see Andrea Dworkin, *Pornography: Men Possessing Women* (New York: G. P. Putnam's Sons, 1981).

40. Ellen Morgan, *The Erotization of Male Dominance/Female Submission* (Pittsburgh: Know, Inc., 1975); Adrienne Rich, "Compulsory Heterosexuality and Lesbian Existence," *Signs: Journal of Women in Culture and Society* 5, no. 4 (Summer 1980): 631–60.

spurious idea of freedom: the right of each person, briefly, to exploit and dehumanize someone else. Without a change in the very norms of sexuality, the liberation of women is a meaningless goal. Sex as such is not liberating for women. Neither is more sex."[41] Does removing or revising gender constraints upon sexual expression change or even challenge its norms?[42] This question ultimately is one of social determination in the broadest sense: its mechanism, permeability, specificity, and totality. If women are socially defined such that female sexuality cannot be lived or spoken or felt or even somatically sensed apart from its enforced definition, so that it *is* its own lack, then there is no such thing as a woman as such, there are only walking embodiments of men's projected needs. For feminism, asking whether there is, socially, a female sexuality is the same as asking whether women exist.

Methodologically, the feminist concept of the personal as political is an attempt to answer this question. Relinquishing all instinctual, natural, transcendental, and divine authority, this concept grounds women's sexuality on purely relational terrain, anchoring women's power and accounting for women's discontent in the same world they stand against. The personal as political is not a simile, not a metaphor, and not an analogy. It does not mean that what occurs in personal life is similar to, or comparable with, what occurs in the public arena. It is not an application of categories from social life to the private world, as when Engels (followed by Bebel) says that in the family the husband is the bourgeois and the wife represents the proletariat.[43] Nor is it an equation of two spheres which remain analytically distinct, as when Reich interprets state behavior in sexual terms,[44] or a one-way infusion of one sphere into the other, as when Lasswell interprets political behavior as the displacement

41. Susan Sontag, "The Third World of Women," *Partisan Review* 40, no. 2 (1973): 180–206, esp. 188.

42. The same question could be asked of lesbian sadomasochism: when women engage in ritualized sexual dominance and submission, does it express the male structure or subvert it? The answer depends upon whether one has a social or biological definition of gender and of sexuality and then upon the content of these definitions. Lesbian sex, simply as sex between women, does not by definition transcend the erotization of dominance and submission and their social equation with maculinity and femininity. Butch/femme as *sexual* (not just gender) role playing, together with parallels in lesbian sadomasochism's "top" and "bottom," suggest to me that sexual conformity extends far beyond gender object mores. For a contrary view see Pat Califia, *Sapphistry: The Book of Lesbian Sexuality* (Tallahassee, Fla.: Naiad Press, 1980); Gayle Rubin, "Sexual Politics, the New Right and the Sexual Fringe," in *What Color Is Your Handkerchief: A Lesbian S/M Sexuality Reader* (Berkeley, Calif.: Samois, 1979), pp. 28–35.

43. Engels (n. 14 above); August Bebel, *Women under Socialism*, trans. Daniel DeLeon (New York: New York Labor News Press, 1904).

44. Reich (n. 22 above). He examines fascism, for example, as a question of how the masses can be made to desire their own repression. This might be seen as a precursor to the feminist question of how female desire *itself* can become the lust for self-annihilation.

of personal problems into public objects.[45] It means that women's distinctive experience as women occurs within that sphere that has been socially lived as the personal—private, emotional, interiorized, particular, individuated, intimate—so that what it is to *know* the *politics* of woman's situation is to know women's personal lives.

The substantive principle governing the authentic politics of women's personal lives is pervasive powerlessness to men, expressed and reconstituted daily *as* sexuality. To say that the personal is political means that gender as a division of power is discoverable and verifiable through women's intimate experience of sexual objectification, which is definitive of and synonymous with women's lives as gender female. Thus, to feminism, the personal is epistemologically the political, and its epistemology is its politics.[46] Feminism, on this level, is the theory of women's point of view. It is the theory of Judy Grahn's "common woman"[47] speaking Adrienne Rich's "common language."[48] Consciousness raising is its quintessential expression. Feminism does not appropriate an existing method—such as scientific method—and apply it to a different sphere of society to reveal its preexisting political aspect. Consciousness raising not only comes to know different things as politics; it necessarily comes to know them in a different way. Women's experience of politics, of life as sex object, gives rise to its own method of appropriating that reality: feminist method.[49] As its own kind of social analysis,

45. Harold Lasswell, *Psychoanalysis and Politics* (Chicago: University of Chicago Press, 1930).

46. The aphorism "Feminism is the theory; lesbianism is the practice" has been attributed to TiGrace Atkinson by Anne Koedt, "Lesbianism and Feminism," in *Radical Feminism*, ed. Anne Koedt, Ellen Levine, and Anita Rapone (New York: New York Times Book Co., 1973), p. 246. See also Radicalesbians, "The Woman Identified Woman," ibid., pp. 24–45; TiGrace Atkinson, "Lesbianism & Feminism," *Amazon Odyssey: The First Collection of Writings by the Political Pioneer of the Women's Movement* (New York: Links Books, 1974), pp. 83–88; Jill Johnston, *Lesbian Nation: The Feminist Solution* (New York: Simon & Schuster, 1973), pp. 167, 185, 278. This aphorism accepts a simplistic view of the relationship between theory and practice. Feminism reconceptualizes the connection between being and thinking such that it may be more accurate to say that feminism is the epistemology of which lesbianism is an ontology. But see n. 56 below on this latter distinction as well.

47. Judy Grahn, *The Work of a Common Woman* (New York: St. Martin's Press, 1978). "The Common Woman" poems are on pp. 61–73.

48. Adrienne Rich, "Origins and History of Consciousness," in *The Dream of a Common Language: Poems, 1974–1977* (New York: W. W. Norton & Co., 1978), p. 7. This means that a women's movement exists wherever women identify collectively to resist/reclaim their determinants as such. This feminist redefinition of consciousness requires a corresponding redefinition of the process of mobilizing it: feminist *organizing*. The transformation from subordinate group to movement parallels Marx's distinction between a class "in itself" and a class "for itself." See Karl Marx, *The Poverty of Philosophy* (New York: International Publishers, 1963), p. 195.

49. In addition to the references in n. 1, see Sandra Lee Bartky, "Toward a

within yet outside the male paradigm just as women's lives are, it has a distinctive theory of the *relation* between method and truth, the individual and her social surroundings, the presence and place of the natural and spiritual in culture and society, and social being and causality itself.

Having been objectified as sexual beings while stigmatized as ruled by subjective passions, women reject the distinction between knowing subject and known object—the division between subjective and objective postures—as the means to comprehend social life. Disaffected from objectivity, having been its prey, but excluded from its world through relegation to subjective inwardness, women's interest lies in overthrowing the distinction itself. Proceeding connotatively and analytically at the same time, consciousness raising is at once common sense expression and critical articulation of concepts. Taking situated feelings and common detail (common here meaning both ordinary and shared) as the matter of political analysis, it explores the terrain that is most damaged, most contaminated, yet therefore most women's own, most intimately known, most open to reclamation. The process can be described as a collective "sympathetic internal experience of the gradual construction of [the] system according to its inner necessity,"[50] as a strategy for deconstructing it.

Through consciousness raising, women grasp the collective reality of women's condition from within the perspective of that experience, not from outside it. The claim that a sexual politics exists and is socially fundamental is grounded in the claim of feminism *to* women's perspective, not from it. Its claim to women's perspective *is* its claim to truth. In its account of itself, women's point of view contains a duality analogous

Phenomenology of Feminist Consciousness," in *Feminism and Philosophy*, ed. Mary Vetterling-Braggin et al. (Totowa, N.J.: Littlefield, Adams & Co., 1977). Susan Griffin reflects/creates the process: "We do not rush to speech. We allow ourselves to be moved. We do not attempt objectivity. . . . We said we had experienced this ourselves. I felt so much for her then, she said, with her head cradled in my lap, she said, I knew what to do. We said we were moved to see her go through what we had gone through. We said this gave us some knowledge" (*Woman and Nature: The Roaring Inside Her* [New York: Harper & Row, 1978], p. 197). Assertions such as "our politics begin with our feelings" have emerged from the practice of consciousness raising. Somewhere between mirror-reflexive determination and transcendence of determinants, "feelings" are seen as both access to truth—at times a bit phenomenologically transparent—and an artifact of politics. There is both suspicion of feelings and affirmation of their health. They become simultaneously an inner expression of outer lies and a less contaminated resource for verification. See San Francisco Redstockings, "Our Politics Begin with Our Feelings," in *Masculine/Feminine: Readings in Sexual Mythology and the Liberation of Women*, ed. Betty Roszak and Theodore Roszak (New York: Harper & Row, 1969).

50. Fredric Jameson, *Marxism and Form* (Princeton, N.J.: Princeton University Press, 1971), p. xi. Jameson is describing dialectical method: "I have felt that the dialectical method can be acquired only by a concrete working through of detail, by a sympathetic internal experience of the gradual construction of a system according to its inner necessity."

to that of the marxist proletariat: determined by the reality the theory explodes, it thereby claims special access to that reality.[51] Feminism does not see its view as subjective, partial, or undetermined but as a critique of the purported generality, disinterestedness, and universality of prior accounts. These have not been half right but have invoked the wrong whole. Feminism not only challenges masculine partiality but questions the universality imperative itself. Aperspectivity is revealed as a strategy of male hegemony.[52]

"Representation of the world," de Beauvoir writes, "like the world itself, is the work of men; they describe it from their own point of view, which they confuse with the absolute truth."[53] The parallel between representation and construction should be sustained: men *create* the world from their own point of view, which then *becomes* the truth to be described. This is a closed system, not anyone's confusion. *Power to create the world from one's point of view is power in its male form.*[54] The male epistemological stance, which corresponds to the world it creates, is ob-

51. This distinguishes both feminism and at least a strain in marxism from Freud: "My self-analysis is still interrupted and I have realized the reason. I can only analyze my self with the help of knowledge obtained objectively (like an outsider). Genuine self-analysis is impossible, otherwise there would be no [neurotic] illness" (Sigmund Freud, Letter to Wilhelm Fleiss, #71, October 15, 1887, quoted in Mitchell, *Psychoanalysis and Feminism: Freud, Reich, Laing and Women* [n. 19 above], pp. 61–62, see also p. 271). Given that introspection is not analytically dispositive to Freud, the collective self-knowledge of feminism might be collective neurosis. Although it is interpersonal, it is still an insider to its world.

52. Feminist scholars are beginning to criticize objectivity from different disciplinary standpoints, although not as frontally as here, nor in its connection with objectification. Julia Sherman and Evelyn Torton Beck, eds., *The Prism of Sex: Essays in the Sociology of Knowledge* (Madison: University of Wisconsin Press, 1979); Margrit Eichler, *The Double Standard; A Feminist Critique of Feminist Social Science* (New York: St. Martin's Press, 1980); Evelyn Fox Keller, "Gender and Science," *Psychoanalysis and Contemporary Thought* 1, no. 3 (1978): 409–33. Adrienne Rich, "Toward a Woman-centered University," in *Woman and the Power to Change*, ed. Florence Howe (New York: McGraw-Hill Book Co., 1975).

53. De Beauvoir (n. 24 above). De Beauvoir had not pursued the analysis to the point I suggest here by 1979, either. See her "Introduction," in Marks and de Courtivron, eds. (n. 1 above), pp. 41–56.

54. This does not mean all men *have* male power equally. American Black men, for instance, have substantially less of it. But to the extent that they cannot create the world from their point of view, they find themselves unmanned, castrated, literally or figuratively. This supports rather than qualifies the sex specificity of the argument without resolving the relationship between racism and sexism, or the relation of either to class. Although historically receiving more attention, race and nation are otherwise analogous to sex in the place they occupy for, and the challenge they pose to, marxist theory. If the real basis of history and activity is class and class conflict, what, other than "false consciousness," is one to make of the historical force of sexism, racism, and nationalism? Similarly, positing a supra-class unit with true meaning, such as "Black people," is analytically parallel to positing a supra-class (and supra-racial) unit "women." Treating race, nation, and sex as lesser included problems has been the major response of marxist theory to such challenges. Any relationship *between* sex and race tends to be left entirely out of account, since they are considered parallel "strata." Attempts to confront the latter issue include Adrienne Rich,

jectivity: the ostensibly noninvolved stance, the view from a distance and from no particular perspective, apparently transparent to its reality. It does not comprehend its own perspectivity, does not recognize what it sees as subject like itself, or that the way it apprehends its world is a form of its subjugation and presupposes it. The objectively knowable is object. Woman through male eyes is sex object, that by which man knows himself at once as man and as subject.[55] What is objectively known corresponds to the world and can be verified by pointing to it (as science does) because the world itself is controlled from the same point of view.[56]

"Disloyal to Civilization: Feminism, Racism and Gynephobia," in *On Lies, Secrets and Silence: Selected Essays, 1966–1978* (New York: W. W. Norton & Co., 1979); Selma James, *Sex, Race and Class* (Bristol: Falling Wall Press, 1967); R. Coles and J. H. Coles, *Women of Crisis* (New York: Dell Publishing Co., Delacorte Press, 1978); Socialist Women's Caucus of Louisville, "The Racist Use of Rape and the Rape Charge" (Louisville, Ky., ca. 1977); Angela Davis, "The Role of Black Women in the Community of Slaves," *Black Scholar* 3, no. 4 (December 1971): 2–16; The Combahee River Collective, "A Black Feminist Statement," in Eisenstein, ed. (n. 11 above); Karen Getman, "Relations of Gender and Sexuality during the Period of Institutional Slavery in the Southern Colonies" (working paper, Yale University, 1980); E. V. Spelman, "Feminism, Sexism and Racism" (University of Massachusetts, 1981); Cherríe Moraga and Gloria Anzaldúa, eds., *This Bridge Called My Back: Writings of Radical Women of Color* (Watertown, Mass.: Persephone Press, 1981).

55. This suggests a way in which marxism and feminism may be reciprocally illuminating, without, for the moment, confronting the deep divisions between them. Marxism comprehends the *object* world's *social* existence: how objects are constituted, embedded in social life, infused with meaning, created in systematic and structural relation. Feminism comprehends the *social* world's *object* existence: how women are created in the image of, and as, things. The object world's social existence varies with the structure of production. Suppose that wherever the sexes are unequal, women are objects, but what it means to be an object varies with the productive relations that create objects as social. Thus, under primitive exchange systems, women are exchange objects. Under capitalism, women appear as commodities. That is, women's sexuality as object for men is valued as objects are under capitalism, namely as commodities. Under true communism, women would be collective sex objects. If women have universally been sex objects, it is also true that matter as the acted-upon in social life has a history. If women have always been things, it is also true that things have not always had the same meaning. Of course, this does not explain sex inequality. It merely observes, once that inequality exists, the way its dynamics may interact with the social organization of production. Sexual objectification may also have a separate history, with its own periods, forms, structures, technology, and, potentially, revolutions.

56. In a sense, this realization collapses the epistemology/ontology distinction altogether. What is purely an ontological category, a category of "being" free of social perception? Surely not the self/other distinction. Ultimately, the feminist approach turns social inquiry into political hermeneutics: inquiry into situated meaning, one in which the inquiry itself participates. A feminist political hermeneutics would be a theory of the answer to the question, What does it mean? that would comprehend that the first question to address is, To whom? within a context that comprehends gender as a social division of power. Useful general treatments of hermeneutical issues (which nevertheless proceed as if feminism, or a specific problematic of women, did not exist) include Josef Bleicher, *Contemporary Hermeneutics: Hermeneutics as Method, Philosophy and Critique* (London: Routledge & Kegan Paul, 1980); Hans-Georg Gadamer, *Philosophical Hermeneutics*, trans. David E. Linge (Berkeley: University of California Press, 1976); Rosalind Coward and John Ellis,

Combining, like any form of power, legitimation with force, male power extends beneath the representation of reality to its construction: it makes women (as it were) and so verifies (makes true) who women "are" in its view, simultaneously confirming its way of being and its vision of truth. The eroticism that corresponds to this is "the use of things to experience self."[57] As a coerced pornography model put it, "You do it, you do it, and you do it; then you become it."[58] The fetish speaks feminism.

Objectification makes sexuality a material reality of women's lives, not just a psychological, attitudinal, or ideological one.[59] It obliterates

---

Language and Materialism: Developments in Semiology and the Theory of the Subject (London: Routledge & Kegan Paul, 1977). Mary Daly approaches the ontological issue when she says that ontological theory without an understanding of sex roles can not be "really ontological" (*Beyond God the Father: Toward a Philosophy of Women's Liberation* [Boston: Beacon Press, 1973], p. 124). But both in this work, and more pervasively in *Gyn/Ecology: The Metaethics of Radical Feminism* (Boston: Beacon Press, 1978), the extent of the *creation* of women's *reality* by male epistemology, therefore the extent and nature of women's damage, is slighted in favor of a critique of its lies and distortions. Consider her investigation of suttee, a practice in which Indian widows are supposed to throw themselves upon their dead husband's funeral pyres in grief (and to keep pure), in which Daly focuses upon demystifying its alleged voluntary aspects. Women are revealed drugged, pushed, browbeaten, or otherwise coerced by the dismal and frightening prospect of widowhood in Indian society (Daly, *Gyn/Ecology*, pp. 113–33). Neglected—both as to the women involved and as to the implications for the entire diagnosis of sexism as illusion—are suttee's deepest victims: women who want to die when their husband dies, who volunteer for self-immolation because they believe their life is over when his is. See also Duncan Kennedy, "The Structure of Blackstone's Commentaries," *Buffalo Law Review* 28, no. 2 (1979): 211–12.

57. Dworkin (n. 39 above), p. 124. Explicitness is the aesthetic, the allowed sensibility, of objectified eroticism. Under this norm, written and pictured evocations of sexuality are compulsively literal. What it is to arouse sexuality through art is to recount events "objectively," i.e., verbally and visually to re-present who did what to whom. On the "dynamic of total explicitness" as stylization, explored in the context of the "foremost insight of the modern novel: the interweaving, the symbolic and structural interchange between economic and sexual relations," see George Steiner, "Eros and Idiom: 1975," in *On Difficulty and Other Essays* (New York: Oxford University Press, 1978), p. 100: "Chasteness of discourse [in George Eliot's work] acts not as a limitation but as a liberating privacy within which the character can achieve the paradox of autonomous life" (p. 107). This connects the lack of such liberating privacy for women—in life, law, or letters—with women's lack of autonomy and authentic erotic vocabulary.

58. Linda Lovelace, *Ordeal* (Secaucus, N.J.: Citadel Press, 1980). The same may be true for class. See Richard Sennett and Jonathan Cobb, *The Hidden Injuries of Class* (New York: Alfred A. Knopf, Inc., 1972). Marxism teaches that exploitation/degradation somehow necessarily produces resistance/revolution. Women's experience with sexual exploitation/degradation teaches that it also produces grateful complicity in exchange for survival and self-loathing to the point of the extinction of self, respect for which makes resistance conceivable. The problem here is not to explain why women acquiesce in their condition but why they ever do anything but.

59. The critique of sexual objectification first became visibly explicit in the American women's movement with the disruption of the Miss America Pageant in September 1968. Robin Morgan, "Women Disrupt the Miss America Pageant," *Rat* (September 1978), reprinted in *Going Too Far: The Personal Chronicle of a Feminist* (New York: Random House, 1977), pp. 62–67. The most compelling account of sexual objectification I know is con-

the mind/matter distinction that such a division is premised upon. Like the value of a commodity, women's sexual desirability is fetishized: it is made to appear a quality of the object itself, spontaneous and inherent, independent of the social relation which creates it, uncontrolled by the force that requires it. It helps if the object cooperates: hence, the vaginal

---

tained in the following description of women's depiction in art and the media: "According to usage and conventions which are at last being questioned but have by no means been overcome, the social presence of a woman is different in kind from that of a man. . . . A man's presence suggests what he is capable of doing to you or for you. By contrast, a woman's presence expresses her own attitude to herself, and *defines what can and cannot be done to her*. . . . To be born a woman has been to be born, within an allotted and confined space, into the keeping of men. The social presence of women has developed as a result of their ingenuity in living under such tutelage within such a limited space. But this has been at the cost of a woman's self being split into two. A woman must continually watch herself. She is almost continually accompanied by her own image of herself. . . . she comes to consider the surveyor and the surveyed within her as the two constituent yet always distinct elements of her identity as a woman. She has to survey everything she is and everything she does because how she appears to others, and ultimately how she appears to men, *is of crucial importance for what is normally thought of as the success of her life*. Her own sense of being in herself is supplanted by a sense of being appreciated as herself by another. One might simplify this by saying: men act; women appear. *Men look at women. Women watch themselves being looked at.* This determines not only most relations between men and women but also the relation of women to themselves. The surveyor of woman in herself is male: the surveyed, female. Thus she turns herself into an object—and most particularly an object of vision: a sight" (John Berger, *Ways of Seeing* [New York: Viking Press, 1972], pp. 46, 47 [my emphasis]). All that is missing here is an explicit recognition that this process embodies what the sexuality of women is about and that it expresses an inequality in social power. In a feminist context, aesthetics, including beauty and imagery, becomes the most political of subjects. See Purple September Staff, "The Normative Status of Heterosexuality," in *Lesbianism and the Women's Movement*, ed. Charlotte Bunch and Nancy Myron (Baltimore: Diana Press, 1975), pp. 79–83, esp. pp. 80–81.

Marxist attempts to deal with sexual objectification have not connected the issue with the politics of aesthetics or with subordination: "She becomes a sexual object only in a relationship, when she allows man to treat her in a certain depersonalizing, degrading way; and vice versa, a woman does not become a sexual subject simply by neglecting her appearance. There is no reason why a women's liberation activist should not try to look pretty and attractive. One of the universal human aspirations of all times was to raise reality to the level of art. . . . Beauty is a value in itself" (Marković [n. 17 above], pp. 165–66). Other attempts come closer, still without achieving the critique, e.g., Power of Women Collective, "What Is a Sex Object?" *Socialist Woman: A Journal of the International Marxist Group* 1, no. 1 (March/April 1974): 7; Dana Densmore, "On the Temptation to Be a Beautiful Object," in *Toward a Sociology of Women*, ed. C. Safilios-Rothschild (Lexington, Mass.: Xerox Publication, 1972); Rita Arditti, "Women as Objects: Science and Sexual Politics," *Science for the People*, vol. 6, no. 5 (September 1974); Charley Shively, "Cosmetics as an Act of Revolution," *Fag Rag* (Boston), reprinted in *Pink Triangles: Radical Perspectives on Gay Liberation*, ed. Pam Mitchell (Boston: Alyson Publication, 1980). Resentment of white beauty standards is prominent in Black feminism. Beauty standards incapable of achievement by any woman seem to fulfill a dual function. They keep women buying products (to the profit of capitalism) and competing for men (to be affirmed by the standard that matters). That is, they make women feel ugly and inadequate so we need men and money to defend against rejection/self-revulsion. Black women are further from being able concretely to achieve the standard that no woman can ever achieve, or it would lose its point.

orgasm;[60] hence, faked orgasms altogether.[61] Women's sexualness, like male prowess, is no less real for being mythic. It is embodied. Commodities do have value, but only because value is a social property arising from the totality of the same social relations which, unconscious of their determination, fetishize it. Women's bodies possess no less real desirability—or, probably, desire. Sartre exemplifies the problem on the epistemological level: "But if I desire a house, or a glass of water, or a woman's body, how could this body, this glass, this piece of property reside in my desire and how can my desire be anything but the consciousness of these objects as desirable?"[62] Indeed. Objectivity is the methodological stance of which objectification is the social process. Sexual objectification is the primary process of the subjection of women. It unites act with word, construction with expression, perception with enforcement, myth with reality. Man fucks woman; subject verb object.

The distinction between objectification and alienation is called into question by this analysis. Objectification in marxist materialism is thought to be the foundation of human freedom, the work process whereby a subject becomes embodied in products and relationships.[63] Alienation is the socially contingent distortion of that process, a reification of products and relations which prevents them from being, and being seen as, dependent on human agency.[64] But from the point of view of the object, objectification *is* alienation. For women, there is no

60. Anne Koedt, "The Myth of the Vaginal Orgasm," in Koedt et al., eds. (n. 46 above), pp. 198–207; TiGrace Atkinson, "Vaginal Orgasm as a Mass Hysterical Survival Response," in *Amazon Odyssey* (n. 46 above), pp. 5–8.

61. Shere Hite, *The Hite Report: A Nationwide Study of Female Sexuality* (New York: Dell Publishing Co., 1976), "Do you ever fake orgasms?" pp. 257–66.

62. Jean-Paul Sartre, *Existential Psychoanalysis*, trans. Hazel E. Barnes (Chicago: Henry Regnery Co., 1973), p. 20. A similar treatment of "desire" occurs in Deleuze and Guattari's description of man as "desiring-machine," of man in relation to the object world: "Not man as the king of creation, but rather as the being who is in intimate contact with the profound life of all forms or all types of beings, who is responsible for even the stars and animal life, and who ceaselessly plugs an organ-machine into an energy-machine, a tree into his body, a breast into his mouth, the sun into his asshole; the eternal custodian of the machines of the universe" (Deleuze and Guattari [n. 1 above], p. 4). Realizing that women, socially, inhabit the object realm transforms this discourse into a quite accurate description of the feminist analysis of women's desirability to man—the breast in his mouth, the energy machine into which he ceaselessly plugs an organ machine. Extending their inquiry into the extent to which this kind of objectification of woman is specific to capitalism (either as a process or in its particular form) does little to redeem the sex blindness (blind to the sex of its standpoint) of this supposedly general theory. Women are not desiring-machines.

63. Peter Berger and Stanley Pullberg, "Reification and the Sociological Critique of Consciousness," *New Left Review*, vol. 35 (January–February 1966); Herbert Marcuse, "The Foundation of Historical Materialism," in *Studies in Critical Philosophy*, trans. Joris De Bres (Boston: Beacon Press, 1972); Karl Klare, "Law-Making as Praxis," *Telos* 12, no. 2 (Summer 1979): 123–35, esp. 131.

64. Istvan Meszaros, *Marx's Theory of Alienation* (London: Merlin Press, 1972); Bertell Ollman, *Alienation: Marx's Conception of Man in Capitalist Society* (London: Cambridge University Press, 1971); Marcuse, *Eros and Civilization* (n. 22 above), pp. 93–94, 101–2.

distinction between objectification and alienation because women have not authored objectifications, we have been them. Women have been the nature, the matter, the acted upon, to be subdued by the acting subject seeking to embody himself in the social world. Reification is not just an illusion to the reified; it is also their reality. The alienated who can only grasp self as other is no different from the object who can only grasp self as thing. To be man's other *is* to be his thing. Similarly, the problem of how the object can know herself as such is the same as how the alienated can know its own alienation. This, in turn, poses the problem of feminism's account of women's consciousness. How can women, as created, "thingified in the head,"[65] complicit in the body, see our condition as such?

In order to account for women's consciousness (much less propagate it) feminism must grasp that male power produces the world before it distorts it. Women's acceptance of their condition does not contradict its fundamental unacceptability if women have little choice but to *become* persons who freely choose women's roles. For this reason, the reality of women's oppression is, finally, neither demonstrable nor refutable empirically. Until this is confronted on the level of method, criticism of what exists can be undercut by pointing to the reality to be criticized. Women's bondage, degradation, damage, complicity, and inferiority—together with the possibility of resistance, movement, or exceptions—will operate as barriers to consciousness rather than as means of access to what women need to become conscious of in order to change.

Male power is real; it is just not what it claims to be, namely, the only reality. Male power is a myth that makes itself true. What it is to raise consciousness is to confront male power in this duality: as total on one side and a delusion on the other. In consciousness raising, women learn they have *learned* that men are everything, women their negation, but that the sexes are equal. The content of the message is revealed true and false at the same time; in fact, each part reflects the other transvalued. If "men are all, women their negation" is taken as social criticism rather than simple description, it becomes clear for the first time that women *are* men's equals, everywhere in chains. Their chains become visible, their inferiority—their inequality—a product of subjection and a mode of its enforcement. Reciprocally, the moment it is seen that this—life as we know it—is not equality, that the sexes are not socially equal, womanhood can no longer be defined in terms of lack of maleness, as negativity. For the first time, the question of what a woman *is* seeks its ground in and of a world understood as neither of its making nor in its image, and finds, within a critical embrace of woman's fractured and alien image, that world women have made and a vision of its wholeness.

65. Rowbotham, *Women's Liberation and the New Politics* (n. 17 above), p. 17.

Feminism has unmasked maleness as a form of power that is both omnipotent and nonexistent, an unreal thing with very real consequences. Zora Neale Hurston captured its two-sidedness: "The town has a basketfull of feelings good and bad about Joe's positions and possessions, but none had the temerity to challenge him. They bowed down to him rather, because he was all of these things, and then again he was all of these things because the town bowed down."[66] If "positions and possessions" and rulership create each other, in relation, the question becomes one of form and inevitability. This challenges feminism to apply its theory of women's standpoint to the regime.[67]

Feminism is the first theory to emerge from those whose interest it affirms. Its method recapitulates as theory the reality it seeks to capture. As marxist method is dialectical materialism, feminist method is consciousness raising: the collective critical reconstitution of the meaning of women's social experience, as women live through it. Marxism and feminism on this level posit a different relation between thought and thing, both in terms of the relationship of the analysis itself to the social life it captures and in terms of the participation of thought in the social life it analyzes. To the extent that materialism is scientific it posits and refers to a reality outside thought which it considers to have an objective—that is, truly nonsocially perspectival—content. Consciousness raising, by contrast, inquires into an intrinsically social situation, into that mixture of thought and materiality which is women's sexuality in the most generic sense. It approaches its world through a process that shares its determination: women's consciousness, not as individual or subjective ideas, but as collective social being. This method stands inside its own determinations in order to uncover them, just as it criticizes them in order to value them on its own terms—in order to *have* its own terms at all. Feminism turns theory itself—the pursuit of a true analysis of social life—into the pursuit of consciousness and turns an analysis of inequality into a critical embrace of its own determinants. The process is transformative as well as perceptive, since thought and thing are inextricable and reciprocally constituting of women's oppression, just as the state as coercion and the state as legitimizing ideology are indistinguishable, and for the same reasons. The pursuit of consciousness becomes a form of political practice. Consciousness raising has revealed gender relations to be a collective fact, no more simply personal than class relations. This implies that class relations may also be personal, no less so for being at the same time collective. The failure of marxism to realize this may connect the

66. Zora Neale Hurston, *Their Eyes Were Watching God* (Urbana: University of Illinois Press, 1978), pp. 79–80.

67. In the second part of this article, "Feminism, Marxism, Method, and the State: Toward Feminist Jurisprudence" (forthcoming in *Signs*), I argue that the state is male in that objectivity is its norm.

failure of workers in advanced capitalist nations to organize in the socialist sense with the failure of left revolutions to liberate women in the feminist sense.

Feminism stands in relation to marxism as marxism does to classical political economy: its final conclusion and ultimate critique. Compared with marxism, the place of thought and things in method and reality are reversed in a seizure of power that penetrates subject with object and theory with practice. In a dual motion, feminism turns marxism inside out and on its head.

To answer an old question—how is value created and distributed?—Marx needed to create an entirely new account of the social world. To answer an equally old question, or to question an equally old reality—what explains the inequality of women to men? or, how does desire become domination? or, what is male power?—feminism revolutionizes politics.

Stanford Law School
Stanford University

[5]

VIEWPOINT

Feminism, Marxism, Method, and the State: Toward Feminist Jurisprudence

Catharine A. MacKinnon

I

Feminism has no theory of the state. It has a theory of power: sexuality is gendered as gender is sexualized. Male and female are created through the erotization of dominance and submission. The man/woman difference and the dominance/submission dynamic define each other. This is the social meaning of sex and the distinctively feminist account of gender inequality.[1] Sexual objectification, the central process within this

For A. D. and D. K. H. In addition to all those whose help is acknowledged in the first part of this article, "Feminism, Marxism, Method, and the State: An Agenda for Theory," *Signs: Journal of Women in Culture and Society* 7, no. 3 (Spring 1982): 515–44 (hereafter cited as part I), my students and colleagues at Yale, Harvard, and Stanford contributed profoundly to the larger project of which both articles are parts. Among them, Sonia E. Alvarez, Jeanne M. Barkey, Paul Brest, Ruth Colker, Karen E. Davis, Sharon Dyer, Tom Emerson, Daniel Gunther, Patricia Kliendienst Joplin, Mark Kelman, Duncan Kennedy, John Kaplan, Lyn Lemaire, Mira Marshall, Rebecca Mark, Martha Minow, Helen M. A. Neally, Lisa Rofel, Sharon Silverstein, Dean Spencer, Laurence Tribe, and Mary Whisner stand out vividly in retrospect. None of it would have happened without Lu Ann Carter and David Rayson. And thank you, Meg Baldwin, Annie McCombs, and Janet Spector.

Marxism appears in lower case, Black in upper case, for reasons explained in part I.

1. Much has been made of the distinction between sex and gender. Sex is thought the more biological, gender the more social. The relation of each to sexuality varies. Since I believe sexuality is fundamental to gender and fundamentally social, and that biology is its social meaning in the system of sex inequality, which is a social and political system that does not rest independently on biological differences in any respect, the sex/gender distinction looks like a nature/culture distinction. I use sex and gender relatively interchangeably.

[*Signs: Journal of Women in Culture and Society* 1983, vol. 8, no. 4]

dynamic, is at once epistemological and political.[2] The feminist theory of knowledge is inextricable from the feminist critique of power because the male point of view forces itself upon the world as its way of apprehending it.

The perspective from the male standpoint[3] enforces woman's definition, encircles her body, circumlocutes her speech, and describes her life. The male perspective is systemic and hegemonic. The content of the signification "woman" is the content of women's lives. Each sex has its role, but their stakes and power are not equal. If the sexes are unequal, and perspective participates in situation, there is no ungendered reality or ungendered perspective. And they are connected. In this context, objectivity—the nonsituated, universal standpoint, whether claimed or aspired to—is a denial of the existence or potency of sex inequality that tacitly participates in constructing reality from the dominant point of view. Objectivity, as the epistemological stance of which objectification is the social process, creates the reality it apprehends by defining as knowledge the reality it creates through its way of apprehending it. Sexual metaphors for knowing are no coincidence.[4] The solipsism of this ap-

2. This analysis is developed in part 1. I assume here your acquaintance with the arguments there.

3. Male is a social and political concept, not a biological attribute. As I use it, it has *nothing whatever* to do with inherency, preexistence, nature, inevitability, or body as such. It is more epistemological than ontological, undercutting the distinction itself, given male power to conform being with perspective. (See part 1, pp. 538–39, n. 56.) The perspective from the male standpoint is not always each man's opinion, although most men adhere to it, nonconsciously and without considering it a point of view, as much because it makes sense of their experience (the male experience) as because it is in their interest. It is rational for them. A few men reject it; they pay. Because it is the dominant point of view and defines rationality, women are pushed to see reality in its terms, although this denies their vantage point as women in that it contradicts (at least some of) their lived experience. Women who adopt the male standpoint are passing, epistemologically speaking. This is not uncommon and is rewarded. The intractability of maleness as a form of dominance suggests that social constructs, although they flow from human agency, can be less plastic than nature has proven to be. If experience trying to do so is any guide, it may be easier to change biology than society.

4. In the Bible, to know a woman is to have sex with her. You acquire carnal knowledge. Many scholarly metaphors elaborate the theme of violating boundaries to appropriate from inside to carry off in usable form: "a penetrating observation," "an incisive analysis," "piercing the veil." Mary Ellman writes, "The male mind . . . is assumed to function primarily like a penis. Its fundamental character is seen to be aggression, and this quality is held essential to the highest or best working of the intellect" (*Thinking about Women* [New York: Harcourt, Brace, Jovanovich, 1968], p. 23). Feminists are beginning to understand that to know has meant to fuck. See Evelyn Fox Keller, "Gender and Science," *Psychoanalysis and Contemporary Thought* 1, no. 3 (1978): 409–33, esp. 413; and Helen Roberts, ed., *Doing Feminist Research* (London: Routledge & Kegan Paul, 1981). The term "to fuck" uniquely captures my meaning because it refers to sexual activity without distinguishing rape from intercourse. At least since Plato's cave, visual metaphors for knowing have been central to Western theories of knowledge, the visual sense prioritized as a mode of verification. The relationship between visual appropriation and objectification is now only begin-

proach does not undercut its sincerity, but it is interest that precedes method.

Feminism criticizes this male totality without an account of our capacity to do so or to imagine or realize a more whole truth. Feminism affirms women's point of view by revealing, criticizing, and explaining its impossibility. This is not a dialectical paradox. It is a methodological expression of women's situation, in which the struggle for consciousness is a struggle for world: for a sexuality, a history, a culture, a community, a form of power, an experience of the sacred. If women had consciousness or world, sex inequality would be harmless, or all women would be feminist. Yet we have something of both, or there would be no such thing as feminism. Why can women know that this—life as we have known it—is not all, not enough, not ours, not just? Now, why don't all women?[5]

---

ning to be explored. "The knowledge gained through still photographs will always be . . . a semblance of knowledge, a semblance of wisdom, as the act of taking pictures is a semblance of wisdom, a semblance of rape. The very muteness of what is, hypothetically, comprehensible in photographs is what constitutes their attraction and provocativeness" (Susan Sontag, *On Photography* [New York: Farrar, Straus & Giroux, 1980], p. 24). See part 1, pp. 539–40, n. 59.

5. Feminism aspires to represent the experience of all women as women see it, yet criticizes antifeminism and misogyny, including when it appears in female form. This tension is compressed in the epistemic term of art "the standpoint of all women." We are barely beginning to unpack it. Not all women agree with the feminist account of women's situation, nor do all feminists agree with any single rendition of feminism. Authority of interpretation—the claim to speak as a woman—thus becomes methodologically complex and politically crucial for the same reasons. Consider the accounts of their own experience given by right-wing women and lesbian sadomasochists. How can patriarchy be diminishing to women when women embrace and defend their place in it? How can dominance and submission be violating to women when women eroticize it? Now what is the point of view of the experience of all women? Most responses in the name of feminism, stated in terms of method, either (1) simply regard some women's views as "false consciousness," or (2) embrace any version of women's experience that a biological female claims as her own. The first approach treats some women's views as unconscious conditioned reflections of their oppression, complicitous in it. Just as science devalues experience in the process of uncovering its roots, this approach criticizes the substance of a view because it can be accounted for by its determinants. But if both feminism and antifeminism are responses to the condition of women, how is feminism exempt from devalidation by the same account? That feminism is critical, and antifeminism is not, is not enough, because the question is the basis on which we know something is one or the other when women, all of whom share the condition of women, disagree. The false consciousness approach begs this question by taking women's self-reflections as evidence of their stake in their own oppression, when the women whose self-reflections are at issue question whether their condition is oppressed at all. The second response proceeds as if women are free. Or, at least, as if we have considerable latitude to make, or to choose, the meanings if not the determinants of our situation. Or, that the least feminism can do, since it claims to see the world through women's eyes, is to validate the interpretations women choose. Both responses arise because of the unwillingness, central to feminism, to dismiss some women as simply deluded while granting other women the ability to see the truth. These two resolutions echo the object/subject split:

The practice of a politics of all women in the face of its theoretical impossibility is creating a new process of theorizing and a new form of theory. Although feminism emerges from women's particular experience, it is not subjective or partial, for no interior ground and few if any aspects of life are free of male power. Nor is feminism objective, abstract, or universal.[6] It claims no external ground or unsexed sphere of generalization or abstraction beyond male power, nor transcendence of the specificity of each of its manifestations. How is it possible to have an engaged truth that does not simply reiterate its determinations? *Dis*-engaged truth only reiterates *its* determinations. Choice of method is choice of determinants—a choice which, for women as such, has been unavailable because of the subordination of women. Feminism does not begin with the premise that it is unpremised. It does not aspire to persuade an unpremised audience because there is no such audience. Its project is to uncover and claim as valid the experience of women, the major content of which is the devalidation of women's experience.

This defines our task not only because male dominance is perhaps the most pervasive and tenacious system of power in history, but because it is metaphysically nearly perfect.[7] Its point of view is the standard for

objectivity (my consciousness is true, yours false, never mind why) or subjectivity (I know I am right because it feels right to me, never mind why). Thus is determinism answered with transcendence, traditional marxism with traditional liberalism, dogmatism with tolerance. The first approach claims authority on the basis of its lack of involvement, asserting its view independent of whether the described concurs—sometimes because it does not. It also has no account, other than its alleged lack of involvement, of its own ability to provide such an account. How can some women see the truth and other women not? The second approach claims authority on the basis of its involvement. It has no account for different interpretations of the same experience or any way of choosing among conflicting ones, including those between women and men. It tends to assume that women, as we are, have power and are free in exactly the ways feminism, substantively, has found we are not. Thus, the first approach is one-sidedly outside when there is no outside, the second one-sidedly inside when someone (probably a woman) is inside everything, including every facet of sexism, racism, and so on. So our problem is this: the false consciousness approach cannot explain experience as it is experienced by those who experience it. The alternative can only reiterate the terms of that experience. This is only one way in which the object/subject split is fatal to the feminist enterprise.

6. To stress: the feminist criticism is not that the objective stance fails to be truly objective because it has social content, all the better to exorcise that content in the pursuit of the more truly point-of-viewless viewpoint. The criticism is that objectivity is largely accurate to its/the/a world, which world is criticized; and that it becomes more accurate as the power it represents and extends becomes more total. Analogous criticisms have arisen in the natural sciences, without being seen as threatening to the "science of society" project, or calling into question that project's tacit equation between natural and social objects of knowledge. What if we extend Heisenberg's uncertainty principle to social theory? (Werner Heisenberg, *The Physical Principles of the Quantum Theory* [Chicago: University of Chicago Press, 1930], pp. 4, 20, 62–65). What of the axiomatic method after Gödel's proof? (See Ernest Nagel and James R. Newman, *Gödel's Proof* [New York: New York University Press, 1958].)

7. Andrea Dworkin helped me express this.

point-of-viewlessness, its particularity the meaning of universality. Its force is exercised as consent, its authority as participation, its supremacy as the paradigm of order, its control as the definition of legitimacy. Feminism claims the voice of women's silence, the sexuality of our eroticized desexualization, the fullness of "lack," the centrality of our marginality and exclusion, the public nature of privacy, the presence of our absence. This approach is more complex than transgression, more transformative than transvaluation, deeper than mirror-imaged resistance, more affirmative than the negation of our negativity. It is neither materialist nor idealist; it is feminist. Neither the transcendence of liberalism nor the determination of materialism works for us. Idealism is too unreal; women's inequality is enforced, so it cannot simply be thought out of existence, certainly not by us. Materialism is too real; women's inequality has never not existed, so women's equality never has. That is, the equality of women to men will not be scientifically provable until it is no longer necessary to do so. Women's situation offers no outside to stand on or gaze at, no inside to escape to, too much urgency to wait, no place else to go, and nothing to use but the twisted tools that have been shoved down our throats. If feminism is revolutionary, this is why.

Feminism has been widely thought to contain tendencies of liberal feminism, radical feminism, and socialist feminism. But just as socialist feminism has often amounted to marxism applied to women, liberal feminism has often amounted to liberalism applied to women. Radical feminism is feminism. Radical feminism—after this, feminism unmodified—is methodologically post-marxist [8] It moves to resolve the

8. I mean to imply that contemporary feminism that is not methodologically post-marxist is not radical, hence not feminist on this level. For example, to the extent Mary Daly's *Gyn/Ecology: The Metaethics of Radical Feminism* (Boston: Beacon Press, 1978) is idealist in method—meaning that the subordination of women is an idea such that to think it differently is to change it—it is formally liberal no matter how extreme or insightful. To the extent Shulamith Firestone's analysis (*The Dialectic of Sex: The Case for Feminist Revolution* [New York: William Morrow & Co., 1972]) rests on a naturalist definition of gender, holding that women are oppressed by our bodies rather than their social meaning, her radicalism, hence her feminism, is qualified. Susan Griffin's *Pornography and Silence: Culture's Revolt against Nature* (San Francisco: Harper & Row Publishers, 1982) is classically liberal in all formal respects including, for instance, the treatment of pornography and eros as a distinction that is fundamentally psychological rather than interested, more deeply a matter of good and bad (morality) than of power and powerlessness (politics). Andrea Dworkin's work, esp. *Pornography: Men Possessing Women* (New York: Perigee Books, 1981), and Adrienne Rich's poetry and essays, exemplify feminism as a methodological departure. This feminism seeks to define and pursue women's interest as the fate of all women bound together. It seeks to extract the truth of women's commonalities out of the lie that all women are the same. If whatever a given society defines as sexual defines gender, and if gender means the subordination of women to men, "woman" means—is not qualified or undercut by—the uniqueness of each woman and the specificity of race, class, time, and place. In this sense, lesbian feminism, the feminism of women of color, and socialist feminism are converging in a feminist politics of sexuality, race, and class, with a left to right spectrum of its own. This politics is struggling for a practice of unity that does

marxist-feminist problematic on the level of method. Because its method emerges from the concrete conditions of all women as a sex, it dissolves the individualist, naturalist, idealist, moralist structure of liberalism, the politics of which science is the epistemology. Where liberal feminism sees sexism primarily as an illusion or myth to be dispelled, an inaccuracy to be corrected, true feminism sees the male point of view as fundamental to the male power to create the world in its own image, the image of its desires, not just as its delusory end product. Feminism distinctively as such comprehends that what counts as truth is produced in the interest of those with power to shape reality, and that this process is as pervasive as it is necessary as it is changeable. Unlike the scientific strain in marxism or the Kantian imperative in liberalism, which in this context share most salient features, feminism neither claims universality nor, failing that, reduces to relativity. It does not seek a generality that subsumes its particulars or an abstract theory or a science of sexism. It rejects the approach of control over nature (including us) analogized to control over society (also including us) which has grounded the "science of society" project as the paradigm for political knowledge since (at least) Descartes. Both liberalism and marxism have been subversive on women's behalf. Neither is enough. To grasp the inadequacies for women of liberalism on one side and marxism on the other is to begin to comprehend the role of the liberal state and liberal legalism[9] within a post-marxist feminism of social transformation.

As feminism has a theory of power but lacks a theory of the state, so marxism has a theory of value which (through the organization of work in production) becomes class analysis, but a problematic theory of the state. Marx did not address the state much more explicitly than he did women. Women were substratum, the state epiphenomenon.[10] Engels,

not depend upon sameness without dissolving into empty tolerance, including tolerance of all it exists to change whenever that appears embodied in one of us. A new community begins here. As critique, women's communality describes a fact of male supremacy, of sex "in itself": no woman escapes the meaning of being a woman within a gendered social system, and sex inequality is not only pervasive but may be universal (in the sense of never having not been in some form) although "intelligible only in . . . locally specific forms" (M. Z. Rosaldo, "The Use and Abuse of Anthropology: Reflections on Feminism and Cross-cultural Understanding," *Signs: Journal of Women in Culture and Society* 5, no. 3 [Spring 1980]: 389–417, 417). For women to become a sex "for ourselves" moves community to the level of vision.

9. See Karl Klare, "Law-Making as Praxis," *Telos* 12, no. 2 (Summer 1979): 123–35; Judith Shklar, *Legalism* (Cambridge, Mass.: Harvard University Press, 1964). To examine law as state is not to decide that all relevant state behavior occurs in legal texts. I do think that legal decisions expose power on the level of legitimizing rationale, and that law, as words in power, is central in the social erection of the liberal state.

10. Karl Marx, *Capital, Selected Works*, 3 vols. (Moscow: Progress Publishers, 1969), 2:120, 139–40; *The German Ideology* (New York: International Publishers, 1972), pp. 48–52; *Introduction to Critique of Hegel's Philosophy of Right*, ed. Joseph O'Malley, trans. Annette Jolin (Cambridge: Cambridge University Press, 1970), p. 139; Marx to P. V. Annenkov, 1846, in *The Poverty of Philosophy* (New York: International Publishers, 1963), pp. 179–93, 181.

who frontally analyzed both, and together, presumed the subordination of women in every attempt to reveal its roots, just as he presupposed something like the state, or state-like social conditions, in every attempt to expose its origins.[11] Marx tended to use the term "political" narrowly to refer to the state or its laws, criticizing as exclusively political interpretations of the state's organization or behavior which took them as sui generis. Accordingly, until recently, most marxism has tended to consider political that which occurs between classes, that is, to interpret as "the political" instances of the marxist concept of inequality. In this broad sense, the marxist theory of social inequality has been its theory of politics. This has not so much collapsed the state into society (although it goes far in that direction) as conceived the state as determined by the totality of social relations of which the state is one determined and determining part—without specifying which, or how much, is which.

In this context, recent marxist work has tried to grasp the specificity of the institutional state: how it wields class power, or transforms class society, or responds to approach by a left aspiring to rulership or other changes. While liberal theory has seen the state as emanating power, and traditional marxism has seen the state as expressing power constituted elsewhere, recent marxism, much of it structuralist, has tried to analyze state power as specific to the state as a form, yet integral to a determinate social whole understood in class terms. This state is found "relatively autonomous." This means that the state, expressed through its functionaries, has a definite class character, is definitely capitalist or socialist, but also has its own interests which are to some degree independent of those of the ruling class and even of the class structure.[12] The state as such, in this view, has a specific power and interest, termed "the political," such that class power, class interest expressed by and in the state, and state behavior, although inconceivable in isolation from one another, are nevertheless not linearly or causally linked or strictly coextensive. Such work locates "the specificity of the political" in a

11. I am criticizing Engels's assumptions about sexuality and women's place, and his empiricist method, and suggesting that the two are linked. Friedrich Engels, *Origin of the Family, Private Property and the State* (New York: International Publishers, 1942).

12. Representative works include Fred Block, "The Ruling Class Does Not Rule: Notes on the Marxist Theory of the State," *Socialist Revolution* 33 (May–June 1977): 6–28; Ralph Miliband, *The State in Capitalist Society* (New York: Basic Books, 1969); Nicos Poulantzas, *Classes in Contemporary Capitalism* (London: New Left Books, 1975), and *Political Power and Social Classes* (London: New Left Books, 1975); Goran Therborn, *What Does the Ruling Class Do When It Rules?* (London: New Left Books, 1978); Norberto Bobbio, "Is There a Marxist Theory of the State?" *Telos* 35 (Spring 1978): 5–16. Theda Skocpol, *States and Social Revolution: A Comparative Analysis of France, Russia and China* (Cambridge: Cambridge University Press, 1979), pp. 24–33, ably reviews much of this literature. Applications to law include Isaac Balbus, "Commodity Form and Legal Form: An Essay on the 'Relative Autonomy' of the Law," *Law and Society Review* 11, no. 3 (Winter 1977): 571–88; Mark Tushnet, "A Marxist Analysis of American Law," *Marxist Perspectives* 1, no. 1 (Spring 1978): 96–116; and Klare (n. 9 above).

mediate "region"[13] between the state as its own ground of power (which alone, as in the liberal conception, would set the state above or apart from class) and the state as possessing no special supremacy or priority in terms of power, as in the more orthodox marxist view.

The idea that the state is relatively autonomous, a kind of first among equals of social institutions, has the genius of appearing to take a stand on the issue of reciprocal constitution of state and society while straddling it. Is the state essentially autonomous of class but partly determined by it, or is it essentially determined by class but not exclusively so? Is it relatively constrained within a context of freedom or relatively free within a context of constraint?[14] As to who or what fundamentally moves and shapes the realities and instrumentalities of domination, and where to go to do something about it, what qualifies what is as ambiguous as it is crucial. Whatever it has not accomplished, however, this literature has at least relieved the compulsion to find all law—directly or convolutedly, nakedly or clothed in unconscious or devious rationalia—to be simply bourgeois, without undercutting the notion that it is determinately driven by interest.

A methodologically post-marxist feminism must confront, on our own terms, the issue of the relation between the state and society, within a theory of social determination adequate to the specificity of sex. Lacking even a tacit theory of the state of its own, feminist practice has instead oscillated between a liberal theory of the state on the one hand and a left theory of the state on the other. Both treat law as the mind of society: disembodied reason in liberal theory, reflection of material interest in left theory. In liberal moments the state is accepted on its own terms as a neutral arbiter among conflicting interests. The law is actually or potentially principled, meaning predisposed to no substantive outcome, thus available as a tool that is not fatally twisted. Women implicitly become an interest group within pluralism, with specific problems of mobilization and representation, exit and voice, sustaining incremental gains and losses. In left moments, the state becomes a tool of dominance and repression, the law legitimizing ideology, use of the legal system a form of utopian idealism or gradualist reform, each apparent gain deceptive or cooptive, and each loss inevitable.

Applied to women, liberalism has supported state intervention on behalf of women as abstract persons with abstract rights, without scrutinizing the content of these notions in gendered terms. Marxism

13. Poulantzas's formulation follows Althusser. Louis Althusser and Etienne Balibar, *Reading Capital*, trans. Ben Brewster (London: New Left Books, 1968). For Poulantzas, the "specific autonomy which is characteristic of the function of the state . . . is the basis of the specificity of the political" (*Political Power and Social Classes* [n. 12 above], pp. 14, 46). Whatever that means. On structural causality between class and state, see p. 14.

14. See Ernesto Laclau's similar criticism of Miliband in *Politics and Ideology in Marxist Theory* (London: New Left Books, 1977), p. 65.

applied to women is always on the edge of counseling abdication of the state as an arena altogether—and with it those women whom the state does not ignore or who are, as yet, in no position to ignore it. Feminism has so far accepted these constraints upon its alternatives: either the state, as primary tool of women's betterment and status transformation, without analysis (hence strategy) for it as male; or civil society, which for women has more closely resembled a state of nature. The state, with it the law, has been either omnipotent or impotent: everything or nothing.

The feminist posture toward the state has therefore been schizoid on issues central to women's survival: rape, battery, pornography, prostitution, sexual harassment, sex discrimination, abortion, the Equal Rights Amendment, to name a few. Attempts to reform and enforce rape laws, for example, have tended to build on the model of the deviant perpetrator and the violent act, as if the fact that rape is a crime means that the society is against it, so law enforcement would reduce or delegitimize it. Initiatives are accordingly directed toward making the police more sensitive, prosecutors more responsive, judges more receptive, and the law, in words, less sexist. This may be progressive in the liberal or the left senses, but how is it empowering in the feminist sense? Even if it were effective in jailing men who do little different from what nondeviant men do regularly, how would such an approach alter women's rapability? Unconfronted are *why* women are raped and the role of the state in that. Similarly, applying laws against battery to husbands, although it can mean life itself, has largely failed to address, as part of the strategy for state intervention, the conditions that produce men who systematically express themselves violently toward women, women whose resistance is disabled, and the role of the state in this dynamic. Criminal enforcement in these areas, while suggesting that rape and battery are deviant, punishes men for expressing the images of masculinity that mean their identity, for which they are otherwise trained, elevated, venerated, and paid. These men must be stopped. But how does that change them or reduce the chances that there will be more like them? Liberal strategies entrust women to the state. Left theory abandons us to the rapists and batterers. The question for feminism is not only whether there is a meaningful difference between the two, but whether either is adequate to the feminist critique of rape and battery as systemic and to the role of the state and the law within that system.

Feminism has descriptions of the state's treatment of the gender difference, but no analysis of the state as gender hierarchy. We need to know. What, in gender terms, are the state's norms of accountability sources of power, real constituency? Is the state to some degree autonomous of the interests of men or an integral expression of them? Does the state embody and serve male interests in its form, dynamics, relation to society, and specific policies? Is the state constructed upon the subordination of women? If so, how does male power become state power?

Can such a state be made to serve the interests of those upon whose powerlessness its power is erected? Would a different relation between state and society, such as may pertain under socialism, make a difference? If not, is masculinity inherent in the state form as such, or is some other form of state, or some other way of governing, distinguishable or imaginable? In the absence of answers to such questions, feminism has been caught between giving more power to the state in each attempt to claim it for women and leaving unchecked power in the society to men. Undisturbed, meanwhile, like the assumption that women generally consent to sex, is the assumption that we consent to this government. The question for feminism, for the first time on its own terms, is: what is this state, from women's point of view?

As a beginning, I propose that the state is male in the feminist sense.[15] The law sees and treats women the way men see and treat women. The liberal state coercively and authoritatively constitutes the social order in the interest of men as a gender, through its legitimizing norms, relation to society, and substantive policies. It achieves this through embodying and ensuring male control over women's sexuality at every level, occasionally cushioning, qualifying, or de jure prohibiting its excesses when necessary to its normalization. Substantively, the way the male point of view frames an experience is the way it is framed by state policy. To the extent possession is the point of sex, rape is sex with a woman who is not yours, unless the act is so as to make her yours. If part of the kick of pornography involves eroticizing the putatively prohibited, obscenity law will putatively prohibit pornography enough to maintain its desirability without ever making it unavailable or truly illegitimate. The same with prostitution. As male is the implicit reference for human, maleness will be the measure of equality in sex discrimination law. To the extent that the point of abortion is to control the reproductive sequelae of intercourse, so as to facilitate male sexual access to women, access to abortion will be controlled by "a man or The Man."[16] Gender, elaborated and sustained by behavioral patterns of application and administration, is maintained as a division of power.

Formally, the state is male in that objectivity is its norm Objectivity is liberal legalism's conception of itself. It legitimizes itself by reflecting its view of existing society, a society it made and makes by so seeing it,

15. See Susan Rae Peterson, "Coercion and Rape: The State as a Male Protection Racket," in *Feminism and Philosophy*, ed. Mary Vetterling-Braggin, Frederick A. Elliston, and Jane English (Totowa, N.J.: Littlefield, Adams & Co., 1977), pp. 360–71; Janet Rifkin, "Toward a Theory of Law Patriarchy," *Harvard Women's Law Journal* 3 (Spring 1980): 83–92.

16. Johnnie Tillmon, "Welfare Is a Women's Issue," *Liberation News Service* (February 26, 1972), in *America's Working Women: A Documentary History, 1600 to the Present*, ed. Rosalyn Baxandall, Linda Gordon, and Susan Reverby (New York: Vintage Books, 1976), pp. 357–58.

and calling that view, and that relation, practical rationality. If rationality is measured by point-of-viewlessness, what counts as reason will be that which corresponds to the way things are. Practical will mean that which can be done without changing anything. In this framework, the task of legal interpretation becomes "to perfect the state as mirror of the society."[17] Objectivist epistemology is the law of law. It ensures that the law will most reinforce existing distributions of power when it most closely adheres to its own highest ideal of fairness. Like the science it emulates, this epistemological stance can not see the social specificity of reflection as method or its choice to embrace that which it reflects. Such law not only reflects a society in which men rule women; it rules in a male way: "The phallus means everything that sets itself up as a mirror."[18] The rule form, which unites scientific knowledge with state control in its conception of what law is, institutionalizes the objective stance as jurisprudence. A closer look at the substantive law of rape[19] in light of such an argument suggests that the relation between objectification (understood as the primary process of the subordination of women) and the power of the state is the relation between the personal and the political at the level of government. This is not because the state is presumptively the sphere of politics. It is because the state, in part through law, institutionalizes male power. If male power is systemic, it *is* the regime.

17. Laurence Tribe, "Constitution as Point of View" (Harvard Law School, Cambridge, Mass., 1982, mimeographed), p. 13.

18. Madeleine Gagnon, "Body I," in *New French Feminisms,* ed. Elaine Marks and Isabelle de Courtivron (Amherst, Mass.: University of Massachusetts Press, 1980), p. 180. Turns on the mirroring trope, which I see as metaphoric analyses of the epistemological/political dimension of objectification, are ubiquitous in feminist writing: "Into the room of the dressing where the walls are covered with mirrors. Where mirrors are like eyes of men, and the women reflect the judgments of mirrors" (Susan Griffin, *Woman and Nature: The Roaring Inside Her* [New York: Harper & Row Publishers, 1979], p. 155). See also Mary Daly, *Beyond God the Father: Toward a Philosophy of Women's Liberation* (Boston: Beacon Press, 1975), pp. 195, 197; Sheila Rowbotham, *Women's Consciousness, Man's World* (Harmondsworth: Pelican Books, 1973), pp. 26–29. "She did suffer, the witch/ trying to peer round the looking/ glass, she forgot/ someone was in the way" (Michelene, "Reflexion," quoted in Rowbotham, p. 2). Virginia Woolf wrote the figure around ("So I reflected . . ."), noticing "the necessity that women so often are to men" of serving as a looking glass in which a man can "see himself at breakfast and at dinner at least twice the size he really is." Notice the doubled sexual/gender meaning: "Whatever may be their use in civilized societies, mirrors are essential to all violent and heroic action. That is why Napoleon and Mussolini both insist so emphatically upon the inferiority of women, for if they were not inferior, they would cease to enlarge" (*A Room of One's Own* [New York: Harcourt, Brace & World, 1969], p. 36).

19. Space limitations made it necessary to eliminate sections on pornography, sex discrimination, and abortion. For the same reason, most supporting references, including those to case law, have been cut. The final section accordingly states the systemic implications of the analysis more tentatively than I think them, but as strongly as I felt I could, on the basis of the single substantive examination that appears here.

II

Feminists have reconceived rape as central to women's condition in two ways. Some see rape as an act of violence, not sexuality, the threat of which intimidates all women.[20] Others see rape, including its violence, as an expression of male sexuality, the social imperatives of which define all women.[21] The first, formally in the liberal tradition, comprehends rape as a displacement of power based on physical force onto sexuality, a preexisting natural sphere to which domination is alien. Thus, Susan Brownmiller examines rape in riots, wars, pogroms, and revolutions; rape by police, parents, prison guards; and rape motivated by racism—seldom rape in normal circumstances, in everyday life, in ordinary relationships, by men as men.[22] Women are raped by guns, age, white supremacy, the state—only derivatively by the penis. The more feminist view to me, one which derives from victims' experiences, sees sexuality as a social sphere of male power of which forced sex is paradigmatic. Rape is not less sexual for being violent; to the extent that coercion has become integral to male sexuality, rape may be sexual to the degree that, and because, it is violent.

The point of defining rape as "violence not sex" or "violence against women" has been to separate sexuality from gender in order to affirm sex (heterosexuality) while rejecting violence (rape). The problem remains what it has always been: telling the difference. The convergence of sexuality with violence, long used at law to deny the reality of women's violation, is recognized by rape survivors, with a difference: where the legal system has seen the intercourse in rape, victims see the rape in intercourse. The uncoerced context for sexual expression becomes as elusive as the physical acts come to feel indistinguishable.[23] Instead of

20. Susan Brownmiller, *Against Our Will: Men, Women and Rape* (New York: Simon & Schuster, 1976), p. 15.

21. Diana E. H. Russell, *The Politics of Rape: The Victim's Perspective* (New York: Stein & Day, 1977); Andrea Medea and Kathleen Thompson, *Against Rape* (New York: Farrar, Straus & Giroux, 1974); Lorenne M. G. Clark and Debra Lewis, *Rape: The Price of Coercive Sexuality* (Toronto: The Women's Press, 1977); Susan Griffin, "Rape: The All-American Crime," *Ramparts* (September 1971), pp. 26–35; Ti-Grace Atkinson connects rape with "the institution of sexual intercourse" (*Amazon Odyssey: The First Collection of Writings by the Political Pioneer of the Women's Movement* [New York: Links Books, 1974], pp. 13–23). Kalamu ya Salaam, "Rape: A Radical Analysis from the African American Perspective," in *Our Women Keep Our Skies from Falling* (New Orleans: Nkombo, 1980), pp. 25–40.

22. Racism, clearly, is everyday life. Racism in the United States, by singling out Black men for allegations of rape of white women, has helped obscure the fact that it is men who rape women, disproportionately women of color.

23. "Like other victims, I had problems with sex, after the rape. There was no way that Arthur could touch me that it didn't remind me of having been raped by this guy I never saw" (Carolyn Craven, "No More Victims: Carolyn Craven Talks about Rape, and about What Women and Men Can Do to Stop It," ed. Alison Wells [Berkeley, Calif., 1978, mimeographed]), p. 2.

asking, what is the violation of rape, what if we ask, what is the nonviolation of intercourse? To tell what is wrong with rape, explain what is right about sex. If this, in turn, is difficult, the difficulty is as instructive as the difficulty men have in telling the difference when women see one. Perhaps the wrong of rape has proven so difficult to articulate[24] because the unquestionable starting point has been that rape is definable as distinct from intercourse, when for women it is difficult to distinguish them under conditions of male dominance.[25]

Like heterosexuality, the crime of rape centers on penetration.[26] The law to protect women's sexuality from forcible violation/expropriation defines the protected in male genital terms. Women do resent forced penetration. But penile invasion of the vagina may be less pivotal to women's sexuality, pleasure or violation, than it is to male sexuality. This definitive element of rape centers upon a male-defined loss, not coincidentally also upon the way men define loss of exclusive access. In this light, rape, as legally defined, appears more a crime against female monogamy than against female sexuality. Property concepts fail fully to comprehend this,[27] however, not because women's sexuality is not, finally, a thing, but because it is never ours. The moment we "have" it—"have sex" in the dual sexuality/gender sense—it is lost as ours. This may explain the male incomprehension that, once a woman has had sex, she loses anything when raped. To them we *have nothing* to lose. Dignitary harms, because nonmaterial, are remote to the legal mind. But women's loss through rape is not only less tangible, it is less

24. Pamela Foa, "What's Wrong with Rape?" in Vetterling-Braggin, Elliston, and English, eds. (n. 15 above), pp. 347–59; Michael Davis, "What's So Bad about Rape?" (paper presented at Annual Meeting of the Academy of Criminal Justice Sciences, Louisville, Ky., March 1982).

25. "Since we would not want to say that there is anything morally wrong with sexual intercourse per se, we conclude that the wrongness of rape rests with the matter of the woman's consent" (Carolyn M. Shafer and Marilyn Frye, "Rape and Respect," in Vetterling-Braggin, Elliston, and English, eds. [n. 15 above], p. 334). "Sexual contact is not inherently harmful, insulting or provoking. Indeed, ordinarily it is something of which we are quite fond. The difference between ordinary sexual intercourse and rape is that ordinary sexual intercourse is more or less consented to while rape is not" (Davis [n. 24 above], p. 12).

26. Sec. 213.0 of the *Model Penal Code* (Official Draft and Revised Comments 1980), like most states, defines rape as sexual intercourse with a female who is not the wife of the perpetrator "with some penetration however slight." Impotency is sometimes a defense. Michigan's gender-neutral sexual assault statute includes penetration by objects (sec. 520a[h]; 520[b]). See *Model Penal Code*, annotation to sec. 213.1(d) (Official Draft and Revised Comments 1980).

27. Although it is true that men possess women and that women's bodies are, socially, men's things, I have not analyzed rape as men treating women like property. In the manner of many socialist-feminist adaptations of marxian categories to women's situation, that analysis short-circuits analysis of rape as male sexuality and presumes rather than develops links between sex and class. We need to rethink sexual dimensions of property as well as property dimensions of sexuality.

existent. It is difficult to avoid the conclusion that penetration itself is known to be a violation and that women's sexuality, our gender definition, is itself stigmatic. If this is so, the pressing question for explanation is not why some of us accept rape but why any of us resent it.

The law of rape divides the world of women into spheres of consent according to how much say we are legally presumed to have over sexual access to us by various categories of men. Little girls may not consent; wives must. If rape laws existed to enforce women's control over our own sexuality, as the consent defense implies, marital rape would not be a widespread exception,[28] nor would statutory rape proscribe all sexual intercourse with underage girls regardless of their wishes. The rest of us fall into parallel provinces: good girls, like children, are unconsenting, virginal, rapable; bad girls, like wives, are consenting, whores, unrapable. The age line under which girls are presumed disabled from withholding consent to sex rationalizes a condition of sexual coercion women never outgrow. As with protective labor laws for women only, dividing and protecting the most vulnerable becomes a device for not protecting everyone. Risking loss of even so little cannot be afforded. Yet the protection is denigrating and limiting (girls may not choose to be sexual) as well as perverse (girls are eroticized as untouchable; now reconsider the data on incest).

If the accused knows us, consent is inferred. The exemption for rape in marriage is consistent with the assumption underlying most adjudications of forcible rape: to the extent the parties relate, it was not really rape, it was personal.[29] As the marital exemptions erode, preclusions for cohabitants and voluntary social companions may expand. In this light, the partial erosion of the marital rape exemption looks less like a change in the equation between women's experience of sexual violation and men's experience of intimacy, and more like a legal adjustment to the social fact that acceptable heterosexual sex is increasingly not limited to the legal family. So although the rape law may not now always assume that the woman consented simply because the parties are legally one, indices of closeness, of relationship ranging from nodding acquaintance to living together, still contraindicate rape. Perhaps this reflects men's experience that women they know meaningfully consent to sex with them. That cannot be rape; rape must be by someone else,

28. For an excellent summary of the current state of the marital exemption, see Joanne Schulman, "State-by-State Information on Marital Rape Exemption Laws," in *Rape in Marriage*, Diana E. H. Russell (New York: Macmillan Publishing Co., 1982), pp. 375–81.

29. On "social interaction as an element of consent," in a voluntary social companion context, see *Model Penal Code*, sec. 213.1. "The prior *social* interaction is an indicator of consent in addition to actor's and victim's *behavioral* interaction during the commission of the offense" (Wallace Loh, "Q: What Has Reform of Rape Legislation Wrought? A: Truth in Criminal Labeling," *Journal of Social Issues* 37, no. 4 [1981]: 28–52, 47). Perhaps consent should be an affirmative defense, pleaded and proven by the defendant.

someone unknown. But *women* experience rape most often by men we know.[30] Men believe that it is less awful to be raped by someone one is close to: "The emotional trauma suffered by a person victimized by an individual with whom sexual intimacy is shared as a normal part of an ongoing marital relationship is not nearly as severe as that suffered by a person who is victimized by one with whom that intimacy is not shared."[31] But women feel as much, if not more, traumatized by being raped by someone we have known or trusted, someone we have shared at least an illusion of mutuality with, than by some stranger. In whose interest is it to believe that it is not so bad to be raped by someone who has fucked you before as by someone who has not? Disallowing charges of rape in marriage may also "remove a substantial obstacle to the resumption of normal marital relations."[32] Depending upon your view of normal. Note that the obstacle to normalcy here is not the rape but the law against it. Apparently someone besides feminists finds sexual victimization and sexual intimacy not all that contradictory. Sometimes I think women and men live in different cultures.

Having defined rape in male sexual terms, the law's problem, which becomes the victim's problem, is distinguishing rape from sex in specific cases. The law does this by adjudicating the level of acceptable force starting just above the level set by what is seen as normal male sexual behavior, rather than at the victim's, or women's, point of violation. Rape cases finding insufficient force reveal that acceptable sex, in the legal perspective, can entail a lot of force. This is not only because of the way specific facts are perceived and interpreted, but because of the way the injury itself is defined as illegal. Rape is a sex crime that is not a crime when it looks like sex. To seek to define rape as violent, not sexual, is understandable in this context, and often seems strategic. But assault that is consented to is still assault; rape consented to is intercourse. The substantive reference point implicit in existing legal standards is the sexually normative level of force. Until this norm is confronted as such, no distinction between violence and sexuality will prohibit more in-

30. Pauline Bart found that women were more likely to be raped—that is, less able to stop a rape in progress—when they knew their assailant, particularly when they had a prior or current sexual relationship ("A Study of Women Who Both Were Raped and Avoided Rape," *Journal of Social Issues* 37, no. 4 [1981]: 123–37, 132). See also Linda Belden, "Why Women Do Not Report Sexual Assault" (City of Portland Public Service Employment Program, Portland Women's Crisis Line, Portland, Ore., March 1979, mimeographed); Diana E. H. Russell and Nancy Howell, "The Prevalence of Rape in the United States Revisited," in this issue; and Menachem Amir, *Patterns in Forcible Rape* (Chicago: University of Chicago Press, 1971), pp. 229–52.

31. Answer Brief for Plaintiff-Appellee at 10, People v. Brown, 632 P.2d 1025 (Colo. 1981).

32. Brown, 632 P.2d at 1027 (citing Comment, "Rape and Battery between Husband and Wife," *Stanford Law Review* 6 [1954]: 719–28, 719, 725).

stances of women's experienced violation than does the existing definition. The question is what is *seen as* force, hence as violence, in the sexual arena. Most rapes, as women live them, will not be seen to violate women until sex and violence are confronted as mutually definitive. It is not only men convicted of rape who believe that the only thing they did different from what men do all the time is get caught.

The line between rape and intercourse commonly centers on some measure of the woman's "will." But from what should the law know woman's will? Like much existing law, Brownmiller tends to treat will as a question of consent and consent as a factual issue of the presence of force.[33] Proof problems aside, force and desire are not mutually exclusive. So long as dominance is eroticized, they never will be. Women are socialized to passive receptivity; may have or perceive no alternative to acquiescence; may prefer it to the escalated risk of injury and the humiliation of a lost fight; submit to survive. Some eroticize dominance and submission; it beats feeling forced. Sexual intercourse may be deeply unwanted—the woman would never have initiated it—yet no force may be present. Too, force may be used, yet the woman may want the sex—to avoid more force or because she, too, eroticizes dominance. Women and men know this. Calling rape violence, not sex, thus evades, at the moment it most seems to confront, the issue of who controls women's sexuality and the dominance/submission dynamic that has defined it. When sex is violent, women may have lost control over what is done to us, but absence of force does not ensure the presence of that control. Nor, under conditions of male dominance, does the presence of force make an interaction nonsexual. If sex is normally something men do to women, the issue is less whether there was force and more whether consent is a meaningful concept.[34]

To explain women's gender status as a function of rape, Brownmiller argues that the threat of rape benefits all men.[35] She does not specify in what way. Perhaps it benefits them sexually, hence as a gender: male initiatives toward women carry the fear of rape as support for persuading compliance, the resulting appearance of which has been called consent. Here the victims' perspective grasps what liberalism applied to women denies: that forced sex as sexuality is not exceptional in relations between the sexes but constitutes the social meaning of gender: "Rape is a man's act, whether it is male or a female man and whether it is a man relatively permanently or relatively temporarily; and being raped is a woman's experience, whether it is a female or a male woman and whether it is a woman relatively permanently or relatively

33. Brownmiller (n. 20 above), pp. 8, 196, 400–407, 427–36.

34. See Carol Pateman, "Women and Consent," *Political Theory* 8, no. 2 (May 1980): 149–68.

35. Brownmiller (n. 20 above), p. 5.

temporarily."[36] To be rapable, a position which is social, not biological, defines what a woman *is*.

Most women get the message that the law against rape is virtually unenforceable as applied to them. Our own experience is more often delegitimized by this than the law is. Women radically distinguish between rape and experiences of sexual violation, concluding that we have not "really" been raped if we have ever seen or dated or slept with or been married to the man, if we were fashionably dressed or are not provably virgin, if we are prostitutes, if we put up with it or tried to get it over with, if we were force-fucked over a period of years. If we probably couldn't prove it in court, it wasn't rape. The distance between most sexual violations of women and the legally perfect rape measures the imposition of someone else's definition upon women's experiences Rape, from women's point of view, is not prohibited; it is regulated. Even women who know we have been raped do not believe that the legal system will see it the way we do. We are often not wrong. Rather than deterring or avenging rape, the state, in many victims' experiences, perpetuates it. Women who charge rape say they were raped twice, the second time in court. If the state is male, this is more than a figure of speech.

The law distinguishes rape from intercourse by the woman's lack of consent coupled with a man's (usually) knowing disregard of it. A feminist distinction between rape and intercourse, to hazard a beginning

36. Shafer and Frye (n. 25 above), p. 334. Battery of wives has been legally separated from marital rape not because assault by a man's fist is so different from assault by a penis. Both seem clearly violent. I am suggesting that both are also sexual. Assaults are often precipitated by women's noncompliance with gender requirements. See R. Emerson Dobash and Russell Dobash, *Violence against Wives: A Case against the Patriarchy* (New York: Free Press, 1979), pp. 14–20. Nearly all incidents occur in the home, most in the kitchen or bedroom. Most murdered women are killed by their husbands, most in the bedroom. The battery cycle accords with the rhythm of heterosexual sex (see Leonore Walker; *The Battered Woman* [New York: Harper & Row Publishers, 1979], pp. 19–20). The rhythm of lesbian S/M appears similar (Samois, eds., *Coming to Power* [Palo Alto, Calif.: Up Press, 1981]). Perhaps most interchange between genders, but especially violent ones, make sense in sexual terms. However, the larger issue for the relation between sexuality and gender, hence sexuality and violence generally, including both war and violence against women, is: What *is* heterosexuality? If it is the erotization of dominance and submission, altering the participants' gender is comparatively incidental. If it is males over females, gender matters independently. Since I see heterosexuality as the fusion of the two, but with gender a social outcome (such that the acted upon is feminized, is the "girl" regardless of sex, the actor correspondingly masculinized), battery appears sexual on a deeper level. In baldest terms, sexuality is violent, so violence is sexual, violence against women doubly so. If this is so, wives are beaten, as well as raped, *as women*—as the acted upon, as gender, meaning sexual, objects. It further follows that all acts *by anyone* which treat a woman according to her object label "woman" are *sexual* acts. The extent to which sexual acts are acts of objectification remains a question of our account of our freedom to make our own meanings. It is clear, at least, that it is centering sexuality upon genitality that distinguishes battery from rape at exactly the juncture that both the law, and seeing rape as violence not sex, does.

approach, lies instead in the *meaning* of the act from women's point of view. What is wrong with rape is that it is an act of the subordination of women to men. Seen this way, the issue is not so much what rape "is" as the way its social conception is shaped to interpret particular encounters. Under conditions of sex inequality, with perspective bound up with situation, whether a contested interaction is rape comes down to whose meaning wins. If sexuality is relational, specifically if it is a power relation of gender, consent is a communication under conditions of inequality. It transpires somewhere between what the woman actually wanted and what the man comprehended she wanted. Instead of capturing this dynamic, the law gives us linear statics face to face. Nonconsent in law becomes a question of the man's force or the woman's resistance or both.[37] Rape, like many crimes and torts, requires that the accused possess a criminal mind (mens rea) for his acts to be criminal. The man's mental state refers to what he actually understood at the time or to what a reasonable man should have understood under the circumstances. The problem is this: the injury of rape lies in the meaning of the act to its victims, but the standard for its criminality lies in the meaning of the same act to the assailants. Rape is only an injury from women's point of view. It is only a crime from the male point of view, explicitly including that of the accused.

Thus is the crime of rape defined and adjudicated from the male standpoint, that is, presuming that (what feminists see as) forced sex is sex. Under male supremacy, of course, it is. What this means doctrinally is that the man's perceptions of the woman's desires often determine whether she is deemed violated. This might be like other crimes of subjective intent if rape were like other crimes. But with rape, because sexuality defines gender, the only difference between assault and (what is socially considered) noninjury is the meaning of the encounter to the woman. Interpreted this way, the legal problem has been to determine whose view of that meaning constitutes what really happened, as if what happened objectively exists to be objectively determined, thus as if this task of determination is separable from the gender of the participants and the gendered nature of their exchange. Thus, even though the rape law oscillates between subjective tests and more objective standards invoking social reasonableness, it uniformly presumes a single underlying reality, not a reality split by divergent meanings, such as those inequality produces. Many women are raped by men who know the meaning of their acts to women and proceed anyway.[38] But women are also violated

37. Even when nonconsent is not a legal element of the offense (as in Michigan), juries tend to infer rape from evidence of force or resistance.

38. This is apparently true of undetected as well as convicted rapists. Samuel David Smithyman's sample, composed largely of the former, contained self-selected respondents to his ad, which read: "Are you a rapist? Researchers Interviewing Anonymously by Phone to Protect Your Identity. Call. . . ." Presumably those who chose to call defined their acts as rapes, at least at the time of responding ("The Undetected Rapist" [Ph.D. diss., Claremont Graduate School, 1978], pp. 54–60, 63–76, 80–90, 97–107).

every day by men who have no idea of the meaning of their acts to women. To them, it is sex. Therefore, to the law, it is sex. That is the single reality of what happened. When a rape prosecution is lost on a consent defense, the woman has not only failed to prove lack of consent, she is not considered to have been injured at all. Hermeneutically unpacked, read: because he did not perceive she did not want him, she was not violated. She had sex. Sex itself cannot be an injury. Women consent to sex every day. Sex makes a woman a woman. Sex is what women are *for*.

To a feminist analysis, men set sexual mores ideologically and behaviorally, define rape as they imagine the sexual violation of women through distinguishing it from their image of what they normally do, and sit in judgment in most accusations of sex crimes. So rape comes to mean a strange (read Black) man knowing a woman does not want sex and going ahead anyway. But men are systematically conditioned not even to notice what women want. They may have not a glimmer of women's indifference or revulsion. Rapists typically believe the woman loved it.[39] Women, as a survival strategy, must ignore or devalue or mute our desires (particularly lack of them) to convey the impression that the man will get what he wants regardless of what we want. In this context, consider measuring the genuineness of consent from the individual assailant's (or even the socially reasonable, i.e., objective, man's) point of view.

Men's pervasive belief that women fabricate rape charges after consenting to sex makes sense in this light. To them, the accusations *are* false because, to them, the facts describe sex. To interpret such events as rapes distorts their experience. Since they seldom consider that their experience of the real is anything other than reality, they can only explain the woman's version as maliciously invented. Similarly, the male anxiety that rape is easy to charge and difficult to disprove (also widely believed in the face of overwhelming evidence to the contrary) arises because rape accusations express one thing men cannot seem to control: the meaning to women of sexual encounters.

Thus do legal doctrines, incoherent or puzzling as syllogistic logic, become coherent as ideology. For example, when an accused wrongly but sincerely believes that a woman he sexually forced consented, he may have a defense of mistaken belief or fail to satisfy the mental requirement of knowingly proceeding against her will.[40] One commentator notes, discussing the conceptually similar issue of revocation of prior consent (i.e., on the issue of the conditions under which women are

39. "Probably the single most used cry of rapist to victim is 'You bitch . . . slut . . . you know you want it. You *all* want it' and afterward, 'there now, you really enjoyed it, didn't you?' " (Nancy Gager and Cathleen Schurr, *Sexual Assault: Confronting Rape in America* [New York: Grosset & Dunlap, 1976], p. 244).

40. See Director of Public Prosecutions v. Morgan, 2 All E.R.H.L. 347 (1975); Pappajohn v. The Queen, 11 D.L.R. 3d 1 (1980); People v. Mayberry, 15 Cal. 3d 143, 542 P.2d 1337 (1975).

allowed to control access to their sexuality from one time to the next): "Even where a woman revokes prior consent, such is the male ego that, seized of an exaggerated assessment of his sexual prowess, a man might genuinely believe her still to be consenting; resistance may be misinterpreted as enthusiastic cooperation; protestations of pain or disinclination, a spur to more sophisticated or more ardent love-making; a clear statement to stop, taken as referring to a particular intimacy rather than the entire performance."[41] This equally vividly captures common male readings of women's indications of disinclination under all kinds of circumstances.[42] Now reconsider to what extent the man's perceptions should determine whether a rape occurred. From whose standpoint, and in whose interest, is a law that allows one person's conditioned unconsciousness to contraindicate another's experienced violation? This aspect of the rape law reflects the sex inequality of the society not only in conceiving a cognizable injury from the viewpoint of the reasonable rapist, but in affirmatively rewarding men with acquittals for not comprehending women's point of view on sexual encounters.

Whether the law calls this coerced consent or mistake of fact, the more the sexual violation of women is routine, the more beliefs equating sexuality with violation become reasonable, and the more honestly women can be defined in terms of our fuckability. It would be comparatively simple if the legal problem were limited to avoiding retroactive falsification of the accused's state of mind. Surely there are incentives to lie. But the deeper problem is the rape law's assumption that a single, objective state of affairs existed, one which merely needs to be determined by evidence, when many (maybe even most) rapes involve honest men and violated women. When the reality is split—a woman is raped but not by a rapist?—the law tends to conclude that a rape *did not happen.* To attempt to solve this by adopting the standard of reasonable belief without asking, on a substantive social basis, to whom the belief is reasonable and why—meaning, what conditions make it reasonable—is one-sided: male-sided. What is it reasonable for a man to believe concerning a woman's desire for sex when heterosexuality is compulsory? Whose subjectivity becomes the objectivity of "what happened" is a matter of social meaning, that is, it has been a matter of sexual politics. One-sidedly erasing women's violation or dissolving the presumptions into the subjectivity of either side are alternatives dictated by the terms

41. Richard H. S. Tur, "Rape: Reasonableness and Time," *Oxford Journal of Legal Studies* 3 (Winter 1981): 432–41, 441. Tur, in the context of the Morgan and Pappajohn cases, says the "law ought not to be astute to equate wickedness and wishful, albeit mistaken, thinking" (p. 437). In feminist analysis, a rape is not an isolated or individual or moral transgression but a terrorist act within a systematic context of group subjection, like lynching.

42. See Silke Vogelmann-Sine et al., "Sex Differences in Feelings Attributed to a Woman in Situations Involving Coercion and Sexual Advances," *Journal of Personality* 47, no. 3 (September 1979): 420–31, esp. 429–30.

of the object/subject split, respectively. These are alternatives that will only retrace that split until its terms are confronted as gendered to the ground.

Desirability to men is commonly supposed to be a woman's form of power. This echoes the view that consent is women's form of control over intercourse, different but equal to the custom of male initiative. Look at it: man initiates, woman chooses. Even the ideal is not mutual. Apart from the disparate consequences of refusal, or openness of original options, this model does not envision a situation the woman controls being placed in, or choices she frames, yet the consequences are attributed to her as if the sexes began at arm's length, on equal terrain, as in the contract fiction. Ambiguous cases of consent are often archetypically referred to as "half won arguments in parked cars."[43] Why not half lost? Why isn't half enough? Why is it an argument? Why do men still want "it," feel entitled to "it," when women don't want them? That sexual expression is even framed as a matter of woman's consent, without exposing these presuppositions, is integral to gender inequality. Woman's so-called power presupposes her more fundamental powerlessness.[44]

III

The state's formal norms recapitulate the male point of view on the level of design. In Anglo-American jurisprudence, morals (value judgments) are deemed separable and separated from politics (power contests), and both from adjudication (interpretation). Neutrality, including judicial decision making that is dispassionate, impersonal, disinterested, and precedential, is considered desirable and descriptive. Courts, forums without predisposition among parties and with no interest of their own, reflect society back to itself resolved. Government of laws not men limits partiality with written constraints and tempers force with reasonable rule following. This law aspires to science: to the immanent generalization subsuming the emergent particularity, to prediction and control of social regularities and regulations, preferably codified. The formulaic "tests" of "doctrine" aspire to mechanism, classification to taxonomy. Courts intervene only in properly "factualized" disputes,[45] cognizing social conflicts as if collecting empirical data. But the de-

43. Note, "Forcible and Statutory Rape: An Exploration of the Operation and Objectives of the Consent Standard," *Yale Law Journal* 62 (1952): 55–56.

44. A similar analysis of sexual harassment suggests that women have such "power" only so long as we behave according to male definitions of female desirability, that is, only so long as we accede the definition of our sexuality (hence, ourselves, as gender female) to male terms. We have this power only so long as we remain powerless.

45. Peter Gabel, "Reification in Legal Reasoning" (New College Law School, San Francisco, 1980, mimeographed), p. 3.

marcations between morals and politics, the personality of the judge and the judicial role, bare coercion and the rule of law,[46] tend to merge in women's experience. Relatively seamlessly they promote the dominance of men as a social group through privileging the form of power—the perspective on social life—feminist consciousness reveals as socially male. The separation of form from substance, process from policy, role from theory and practice, echoes and reechoes at each level of the regime its basic norm: objectivity.

Consider a central example. The separation of public from private is as crucial to the liberal state's claim to objectivity as its inseparability is to women's claim to subordination. Legally, it has both formal and substantive dimensions. The state considers formal, not substantive, the allocation of public matters to itself to be treated objectively, of private matters to civil society to be treated subjectively. Substantively, the private is defined as a right to "an inviolable personality,"[47] which is guaranteed by ensuring "autonomy or control over the intimacies of personal identity."[48] It is hermetic. It means that which is inaccessible to, unaccountable to, and unconstructed by anything beyond itself. Intimacy occurs in private; this is supposed to guarantee original symmetry of power. Injuries arise in violating the private sphere, not within and by and because of it. Private means consent can be presumed unless disproven. To contain a systematic inequality contradicts the notion itself. But feminist consciousness has exploded the private. For women, the measure of the intimacy has been the measure of the oppression. To see the personal as political means to see the private as public. On this level, women have no privacy to lose or to guarantee. We are not inviolable. Our sexuality, meaning gender identity, is not only violable, it *is* (hence we are) our violation. Privacy is everything women as women have never been allowed to be or to have; at the same time the private is everything women have been equated with and defined in terms of *men's* ability to

46. Rawls's "original position," for instance, is a version of my objective standpoint (John Rawls, *A Theory of Justice* [Cambridge, Mass.: Harvard University Press, 1971]). Not only apologists for the liberal state, but also some of its most trenchant critics, see a real distinction between the rule of law and absolute arbitrary force. E. P. Thompson, *Whigs and Hunters: The Origin of the Black Act* (New York: Pantheon Books, 1975), pp. 258–69. Douglas Hay argues that making and enforcing certain acts as illegal reinforces a structure of subordination ("Property, Authority, and the Criminal Law," in *Albion's Fatal Tree: Crime and Society in Eighteenth Century England*, D. Hay et al., eds. [New York: Pantheon Books, 1975], pp. 17–31). Michael D. A. Freeman ("Violence against Women: Does the Legal System Provide Solutions or Itself Constitute the Problem?" [Madison, Wis., 1980, mimeographed], p. 12, n. 161) applies this argument to domestic battery of women. Here I extend it to women's situation as a whole, without suggesting that the analysis can *end* there.

47. S. D. Warren and L. D. Brandeis, "The Right to Privacy," *Harvard Law Review* 4 (1890): 193–205.

48. Tom Gerety, "Redefining Privacy," *Harvard Civil Right–Civil Liberties Law Review* 12, no. 2 (Spring 1977): 236.

have. To confront the fact that we have no privacy is to confront our private degradation as the public order. To fail to recognize this place of the private in women's subordination by seeking protection behind a right to that privacy is thus to be cut off from collective verification and state support in the same act.[49] The very place (home, body), relations (sexual), activities (intercourse and reproduction), and feelings (intimacy, selfhood) that feminism finds central to women's subjection form the core of privacy doctrine. But when women are segregated in private, one at a time, a law of privacy will tend to protect the right of men "to be let alone,"[50] to oppress us one at a time. A law of the private, in a state that mirrors such a society, will translate the traditional values of the private sphere into individual women's right to privacy, subordinating women's collective needs to the imperatives of male supremacy.[51] It will keep some men out of the bedrooms of other men.

Liberalism converges with the left at this edge of the feminist critique of male power. Herbert Marcuse speaks of "philosophies which are 'political' in the widest sense—affecting society as a whole, demonstrably transcending the sphere of privacy."[52] This does and does not describe the feminist political: "Women both have and have not had a common world."[53] Isolation in the home and intimate degradation, women share. The private sphere, which confines and separates us, is therefore a political sphere, a common ground of our inequality. In feminist translation, the private is a sphere of battery, marital rape, and women's exploited labor; of the central social institutions whereby women are deprived of (as men are granted) identity, autonomy, control, and self-determination; and of the primary activity through which male supremacy is expressed and enforced. Rather than transcending the private as a predicate to politics, feminism politicizes it. For women, the private necessarily transcends the private. If the most private also most "affects society as a whole," the separation between public and private collapses as anything other than potent ideology. The failure of marxism adequately to address intimacy on the one hand, government on the

49. Harris v. McRae, 448 U.S. 297 (1980), which holds that withholding public funds for abortions does not violate the federal constitutional right to privacy, illustrates. See Zillah Eisenstein, *The Radical Future of Liberal Feminism* (New York: Longman, Inc., 1981), p. 240.

50. Robeson v. Rochester Folding Box Co., 171 NY 538 (1902); Cooley, *Torts*, sec. 135, 4th ed. (Chicago: Callaghan & Co., 1932).

51. This argument learned a lot from Tom Grey's article, "Eros, Civilization and the Burger Court," *Law and Contemporary Problems* 43, no. 3 (Summer 1980): 83–99.

52. Herbert Marcuse, "Repressive Tolerance," in *A Critique of Pure Tolerance*, ed. Robert Paul Wolff, Barrington Moore, Jr., and Herbert Marcuse (Boston: Beacon Press, 1965), pp. 81–117, esp. p. 91.

53. Adrienne Rich, "Conditions for Work: The Common World of Women," in *Working It Out: Twenty-three Women Writers, Artists, Scientists, and Scholars Talk about Their Lives and Work*, ed. Sara Ruddick and Pamela Daniels (New York: Pantheon Books, 1977), pp. xiv–xxiv, esp. p. xiv.

other, is the same failure as the indistinguishability between marxism and liberalism on questions of sexual politics.

Interpreting further areas of law, a feminist theory of the state will reveal that the idealism of liberalism and the materialism of the left have come to much the same for women. Liberal jurisprudence that the law should reflect society and left jurisprudence that all law does or can do is reflect existing social relations will emerge as two guises of objectivist epistemology. If objectivity is the epistemological stance of which women's sexual objectification is the social process, its imposition the paradigm of power in the male form, then the state will appear most relentless in imposing the male point of view when it comes closest to achieving its highest formal criterion of distanced aperspectivity. When it is most ruthlessly neutral, it will be most male; when it is most sex blind, it will be most blind to the sex of the standard being applied. When it most closely conforms to precedent, to "facts," to legislative intent, it will most closely enforce socially male norms and most thoroughly preclude questioning their content as having a point of view at all. Abstract rights will authoritize the male experience of the world. The liberal view that law is society's text, its rational mind, expresses this in a normative mode; the traditional left view that the state, and with it the law, is superstructural or epiphenomenal expresses it in an empirical mode. Both rationalize male power by presuming that it does not exist, that equality between the sexes (room for marginal corrections conceded) is society's basic norm and fundamental description. Only feminism grasps the extent to which the opposite is true: that antifeminism is as normative as it is empirical. Once masculinity appears as a specific position, not just as the way things are, its judgments will be revealed in process and procedure, as well as adjudication and legislation. Perhaps the objectivity of the liberal state has made it appear "autonomous of class." Including, but beyond, the bourgeois in liberal legalism, lies what is male about it. However autonomous of class the liberal state may appear, it is not autonomous of sex. Justice will require change, not reflection—a new jurisprudence, a new relation between life and law.

University of Minnesota Law School

[6]

VOLUME 96 MAY 1983 NUMBER 7

HARVARD LAW REVIEW

THE FAMILY AND THE MARKET: A STUDY OF IDEOLOGY AND LEGAL REFORM

*Frances E. Olsen**

Reform strategies aimed at improving the lives of women in American society have ranged from efforts to ensure equal treatment for women in the marketplace to the establishment of family courts to promote fair treatment and harmony within the household. In this Article, Professor Olsen argues that most reform efforts have been conceived and carried out from within the confines of a particular world view, a world view that perceives social life to be divided between separate though interdependent spheres of market and family. She concludes that this structure of consciousness — the dichotomy between market and family — not only has limited the effectiveness of reforms actually undertaken, but also has sharply curtailed the range of possible strategies conceived by reformers. Professor Olsen draws upon Feuerbach's model of historical progress, as well as upon our understanding of relations between the state and civil society and between male and female, to speculate upon the possibilities for radically improving the lives of all individuals, men and women, by transcending the market/family dichotomy.

A new round of debate has developed regarding the family and family values. Some argue that the family is a reactionary institution and a primary locus for the oppression of women; others extol the sharing within family life and seek to reclaim family values as supportive of democratic and progressive goals. Although this debate is yet unresolved, it is already boring. Admittedly, it can stir strong emotions, but on some level we all know it will not lead to any solution. Rather than join the debate, this Article examines the terrain upon which the debate has been conducted.

---

* Goddard College, B.A., 1968; University of Colorado, J.D., 1971; Harvard University, candidate, S.J.D.

This Article is based in part on research supported by the Peter B. Livingston Fund of Harvard Medical School. I wish to express my appreciation to the Fund, to the editors of the *Harvard Law Review*, and to the dozens of friends and colleagues who offered helpful comments on earlier drafts. Mary Joe Frug, Chris Littleton, Martha Minow, and James B. White were particularly generous and supportive. Duncan Kennedy enriched my understanding of how helpful one person can be to another. I am grateful for his valuable insights, his numerous critical readings, and his unswerving encouragement. He has provided an example I hope to follow.

A central concern underlying the debate is the subordination of women to men. Both sides share the goal of equality and independence for women. Repeated efforts at reform have resulted in a significant measure of success, yet the subordination of women continues. Many different factors may help to explain why the reform strategies adopted have had ambiguous and even contradictory effects. One factor that often receives insufficient attention is the ideological foundations of social reforms. In particular, reforms are limited by their premises, by the unexamined assumptions upon which they are based.

One such assumption embodies the radical separation of the market and the family, the idea that the market structures our productive lives and the family structures our affective lives. In the nineteenth century, the family was seen to constitute a separate sphere of activity — a sphere particularly suited to women. "Woman's sphere" may no longer be considered to be just home and family, but we do continue to view the family as something sharply distinct from the market. The vision of the market and the family as a dichotomy[1] — the perception that social life comprises two separate though interdependent spheres — can be described as a structure of consciousness.[2] By structure of consciousness, I mean a shared vision of the social universe that underlies a society's culture and also shapes the society's view of what social relationships are "natural" and, therefore, what social reforms are possible.

In my discussion of the market/family dichotomy, I shall refer frequently to two other dichotomies — the ones between state and civil society and between male and female. The state/civil society dichotomy is crucially related to the complexities of the market/family dichotomy; and the dichotomy between male and female is particularly important both to the

---

[1] A "dichotomy" exists when a significant aspect of experience is divided sharply between two categories that are mutually exclusive but together account for the entire aspect. A pair of subclasses form a dichotomy when they are separated by a "vacuum boundary," *see* Katz, *Studies in Boundary Theory: Three Essays in Adjudication and Politics*, 28 BUFFALO L. REV. 383, 383–85 (1979), and together they constitute an important class. The class of human beings, for example, has been divided between male and female. Virtually everybody is placed in one gender category or the other, and almost nobody is placed in both. This can be contrasted with the division between child and adult, which is far less dichotomized because adolescents are thought of as children for some purposes and adults for other purposes.

[2] I do not intend to be making any claims about what might be called material reality. I am describing ideas and consciousness, not things or institutions. When I assert that there is a dichotomy between market and family, for example, I am obviously not claiming that the market and the family are separate in any physical sense.

ways in which the market/family dichotomy now affects human existence and to our hopes for constructing new ways of thinking about and leading our lives.

These three dichotomies are each distinct: none is logically dependent upon another and none necessarily entails another. Nevertheless, deep ties exist among them, and each reflects a way of thinking that entails a radical division of the world. All three dichotomies seem eternal; yet by transcending all three, by reconceiving the relationship between the two elements in each of the three pairs and restructuring our thoughts and lives to create, reflect, and reinforce those reconceptions, we have the greatest possibility for bringing about changes that would significantly improve our individual and collective lives.

I. The Ideology of the Family and the Market

The separate and unequal spheres constituted for men and women had two opposite effects on women: the woman's sphere both constrained women and provided them with valuable opportunities. In the early nineteenth century, as men's work was largely removed to the factory[3] while women's work remained primarily in the home, there came to be a sharp dichotomy between "the home" and "the [workaday] world."[4] This dichotomy took on many of the moral overtones developed in the theological dichotomy between heaven and earth.[5] Often the home was referred to as "sacred," and home life was celebrated as the reward for which men should be willing to suffer in the earthly world of work.[6] The family and home were seen as safe repositories for the virtues and emotions that people believed were being banished from the world of commerce and industry. The home was said to provide a haven from the anxieties of modern life — "a shelter for those moral and spiritual values which the commercial spirit and the critical spirit were threatening to destroy."[7]

At the same time that the home was being glorified, it was being devalued. The woman's sphere was for men "the object

---

[3] *See* V. Clark, History of Manufactures in the United States: 1607–1860 (1916); 1 J. Commons, History of Labour in the United States (1918); 2 *id.*

[4] *See* N. Cott, The Bonds of Womanhood 64–70 (1977).

[5] *See id.* at 65–70.

[6] *See id.* at 64.

[7] W. Houghton, The Victorian Frame of Mind, 1830–1870, at 343 (1957) (emphasis omitted).

of yearning, and yet of scorn."[8] Ann Douglas has pointed out that, while men sentimentalized the family and exalted domesticity, they continued to behave in the marketplace as if they believed that "profane," worldly goals represented the greatest good. "It is to their credit that they indirectly acknowledged that the pursuit of these 'masculine' goals meant damaging, perhaps losing, another good, one they increasingly included under the 'feminine' ideal. Yet the fact remains that their regret was calculated not to interfere with their actions."[9]

Further, while the world of the marketplace was decried for being selfish, debasing, and exploitative, it was also admired and esteemed. Self-reliance, progress, modernization — each had positive connotations that were associated with the world of commerce and industry. Rationality, discipline, and a focus on objective reality were considered desirable aspects of the "male" sphere of the market.[10] Moreover, although the values of domesticity were used to criticize the destructiveness of marketplace values and the pursuit of wealth, they nevertheless served to "undercut opposition to exploitative pecuniary standards in the work world, by upholding a 'separate sphere' of comfort and compensation, instilling a morality that would encourage self-control, and fostering the idea that preservation of home and family sentiment was an ultimate goal."[11]

Given this simultaneous glorification and denigration of both the home and the marketplace, it should be no surprise that the sharp split between the two spheres had complex effects upon women. The market/family dichotomy tended to exclude women from the world of the marketplace while promising them a central role in the supposedly equally important domestic sphere. The dichotomy encouraged women to be generous and nurturant but discouraged them from being strong and self-reliant; it insulated women from the world's corruption but denied them the world's stimulation. While the dichotomy tended to mask the inferior, degraded position of women, it also provided a degree of autonomy and a base from which women could and did elevate their status.[12]

Nancy Cott has perceptively noted that rather early in the nineteenth century "domestic occupations began to mean for

---

[8] N. COTT, *supra* note 4, at 62.

[9] A. DOUGLAS, THE FEMINIZATION OF AMERICAN CULTURE 12 (1977).

[10] *See generally* R. TRYON, HOUSEHOLD MANUFACTURES IN THE UNITED STATES, 1640–1860 (1917) (recounting rise of disciplined modes of production); M. WEBER, GENERAL ECONOMIC HISTORY (F. Knight trans. 1927) (same).

[11] N. COTT, *supra* note 4, at 69.

[12] For an excellent summary of the literature on the "woman's sphere," see *id.* at 197–206.

women what worldly occupations meant for men."[13] The very process of "distinguish[ing] 'home' and 'woman' from 'the world' and 'man' tended to make the two spheres analogous and comparable."[14] This Article will examine the "analogous and comparable" aspects of the family and the market and the importance that ideas about both have to the status of women and to feminist theory.

A. The Free Market and the Private Family: The Principle of Nonintervention

Although the woman's sphere has been described as "private" and contrasted with the "public sphere of the marketplace and government,"[15] such a characterization can be misleading. There are two different dichotomies involved in this contrast: on one hand, a dichotomy between the market, considered public, and the family, considered private; on the other hand, a dichotomy between the state, considered public, and civil society, considered private.[16] Both the market and the family are thought of as part of "private" civil society in opposition to the "public" state.[17] Calling both the marketplace and the state "public" can thus confuse our thinking about the two dichotomies.

It is important to recognize the distinction between the state/civil society dichotomy and the market/family dichotomy, because the former dichotomy plays itself out in an analogous manner on both sides of the latter.[18] In discourse on the market, the state/civil society dichotomy appears as the issue

[13] *Id.* at 73.

[14] *Id.* at 72.

[15] Taub & Schneider, *Perspectives on Women's Subordination and the Role of Law*, in THE POLITICS OF LAW 118 (D. Kairys ed. 1982); *see* Powers, *Sex Segregation and the Ambivalent Directions of Sex Discrimination Law*, 1979 WIS. L. REV. 55, 71.

[16] I am using "civil society" in Marx's sense rather than Hegel's. *Compare* K. MARX, *On the Jewish Question*, in WRITINGS OF THE YOUNG MARX ON PHILOSOPHY AND SOCIETY 216 (L. Easton & K. Guddat eds. 1967) [hereinafter cited as WRITINGS] (civil society contrasted with political state), *with* Knox, *Translator's Foreword* to G. HEGEL, PHILOSOPHY OF RIGHT at x–xi (T. Knox trans. 1952) (1st ed. 1821) (civil society as an abstract universal that can mature into a state through the educative influence of civil life).

[17] It may be true that the ease with which we use the language of public and private in both of these dichotomies reflects an actual connection between the dichotomies, but it is certainly a mistake to conflate the two or to assume too simple a relationship between them.

[18] Of course it is also true that a single dichotomy can reproduce both its elements on either side of itself.

of state regulation of the economy; in discourse on the family, it appears as the issue of state interference in the family. The classic laissez-faire arguments against state regulation of the free market find a striking parallel in the arguments against state interference with the private family. The two sets of arguments, and the ideals that underlie them, share a great deal more than just hostility to government. Both are constructed of similar elements and subject to similar attacks; our understanding of each is enriched by our understanding of the other.

1. The Free Market. — It is possible briefly to summarize the basic themes of laissez-faire theory without denying the richness or complexity of the theory.[19] Laissez-faire theory depends upon the notion of a free and autonomous market. Although the free market does not have to be considered an object or a thing, "the market" must at least be considered a coherent and sensible way of talking and thinking about economic relations among people. Further, laissez-faire theory posits that the market is "natural" in that it reflects actual supply and demand, and "autonomous" in that it was not created by the state and can function independently of the state.[20] Laissez-faire theory both assumes and asserts that it makes sense to advocate state neutrality with respect to the market. Economic and social inequalities that persist after the institution of the liberal state (that is, the institution of "political equality") are deemed to be natural and beyond the proper scope of state activity. Thus, although laissez-faire theorists believe that people should be considered equal in their relations with the state, these theorists characterize the domination and subordination that accompany economic and social inequality in civil society as private matters that do not implicate the political state. A departure from laissez-faire policies is asserted to constitute an effort by the state to alter an inequality

---

[19] Laissez-faire ideology has been discussed and criticized in detail elsewhere. *See, e.g.*, M. HORWITZ, THE TRANSFORMATION OF AMERICAN LAW, 1780–1860, at xv–xvii, 101–08, 253–66 (1977) (discussing role of judiciary in laissez-faire policies); Kennedy, *Distributive and Paternalist Motives in Contract and Tort Law, With Special Reference to Compulsory Terms and Unequal Bargaining Power*, 41 MD. L. REV. 563, 576–83 (1982) (description and critique of freedom-of-contract ideology) [hereinafter cited as Kennedy, *Motives*]; Kennedy, *Form and Substance in Private Law Adjudication*, 89 HARV. L. REV. 1685, 1746–48 (1976) (description and criticism of laissez-faire ideology) [hereinafter cited as Kennedy, *Form and Substance*]. For a classic statement of laissez-faire ideology, see A. SMITH, AN INQUIRY INTO THE NATURE AND COURSES OF THE WEALTH OF NATIONS (London 1776). A more recent restatement of these principles may be found in M. FRIEDMAN, CAPITALISM AND FREEDOM (1962).

[20] *See* A. SMITH, *supra* note 19, at 459–65.

that otherwise exists quite independently of the state.[21] Enforcement of contract, tort, and property law is compatible with laissez-faire doctrine only as long as the courts merely facilitate free market transactions without jeopardizing or compromising state neutrality.

Some critics of laissez faire accept the claim that laissez-faire policies would actually represent state neutrality with respect to an autonomous free market, but nevertheless reject these policies[22] and urge that the state should regulate the economy to lessen some of the damaging effects of free market inequality. Thus, proponents of laissez-faire policy have had to assert not only that nonintervention is possible, but also that it is preferable to any form of state intervention.

Two classic arguments have been advanced to support nonintervention. The first is based on the theory that, although the natural market functions effectively, it is fragile. Just as introducing rabbits into Australia disrupted the continent's natural ecology, so, too, the attempt to mitigate human suffering by tinkering with one aspect of the market may cause quite unexpected and severe suffering with regard to other aspects of the market.[23]

The second classic argument emphasizes the extreme strength and durability of the market. The claim here is that the free market is characterized by strong natural forces that will overcome and nullify any but the most radical efforts to impose state control on the economy, and that nothing less than socialism or total state abolition of the free market will have any lasting effect. Such theorists consider a court's refusal to enforce "harsh" or "oppressive" contract terms or a legislature's attempt to abolish cognovit notes to be reforms doomed to failure. The very same "unequal bargaining position" that is appealed to in support of such reforms can be used to demonstrate their futility. One contract term may be forbidden, but it will be replaced by another or by an adjustment in price; thus, assuming that the basic conditions of

---

21 *See, e.g.*, Ives v. South Buffalo Ry., 201 N.Y. 271, 294, 94 N.E. 431, 439–40 (1911) (holding workmen's compensation legislation unconstitutional on ground that right of property has foundation in fundamental law that cannot be changed by legislatures), *overruled*, Montgomery v. Daniels, 38 N.Y.2d 41, 340 N.E.2d 444, 378 N.Y.S.2d 1 (1975).

22 *See, e.g.*, Laski, *The Basis of Vicarious Liability*, 26 YALE L.J. 105, 134 (1916). *See generally* J. FREY, THE LABOR INJUNCTION: AN EXPOSITION OF GOVERNMENT BY JUDICIAL CONSCIENCE AND ITS MENACE (1922) (arguing that injunctions against labor unions are used to violate personal and property rights). For a critique of this position, see Kennedy, *Motives*, *supra* note 19, at 620–24.

23 This claim has been taken up again by some writers in law and economics. *See, e.g.*, R. POSNER, ECONOMIC ANALYSIS OF LAW (2d ed. 1977).

supply and demand remain unchanged, bargaining power will stay about the same, and parties will continue to form contracts that reflect this bargaining power.[24]

2. *The Private Family.* — The idea that the state should not intrude upon the family has, for most people today, a great deal more appeal than does classical laissez-faire economics. Partly for this reason, the parallels between the free market and the private family may not be obvious. In fact, given the dichotomous relationship between the family and the market, the breakdown of classical laissez-faire ideology and the "invasion" of the marketplace by the state might seem to be an additional reason for keeping the state out of the family. Just as the family was once seen as the repository for values being destroyed in the marketplace,[25] the family may also be seen as the sanctuary of privacy into which one can retreat to avoid state regulation. If the state/civil society dichotomy is perceived to be breaking down with respect to the market, many would therefore redouble their efforts to preserve the state/civil society dichotomy with respect to the family.

The basic assumptions that underlie arguments in favor of the private family are similar to those underlying the arguments in favor of the free market. The first assumption is that "the family" is a coherent way of talking about certain relations among people. Another assumption is that the family is capable of existing in some sense apart from state activity, as a natural formation rather than only as a creation of the state.[26]

The issue of state neutrality with respect to the family is more complicated than that of neutrality with respect to the market. Neutrality toward the market means treating the participants in economic life as juridical equals. The state is said to take a neutral stance toward the family, however, when it ratifies the preexisting social roles within the family.[27]

---

[24] For a description and very effective radical critique of the "unequal bargaining position" argument, see Kennedy, *Motives*, *supra* note 19, at 614–24.

[25] *See supra* p. 1499.

[26] Again, one need not believe that the family is an actual entity, just as it was not necessary to consider the market a thing, although both are often talked about and conceptualized as if they were concrete. It is necessary only to consider the family as a coherent concept and as something capable of attaining a degree of autonomy. Another way of putting this is that it must make sense to say that a particular family exists even if it is not recognized by the state.

This does not mean that the legal family cannot be seen as something defined solely by the law; indeed, some would define a legal family in just that way. But people also believe in the notion of a natural family, and the areas in which the legally defined family fails to overlap with the natural family create a certain tension. *See* Stanley v. Illinois, 405 U.S. 645, 651–52 (1972); Glona v. American Guar. & Liab. Ins. Co., 391 U.S. 73, 75–76 (1968).

[27] *See infra* pp. 1505–06.

In contrast to the market, in which universal selfish behavior is supposed to result in the betterment of society,[28] the family has generally been expected to be based on less individualistic principles. The good of all is to be achieved not by each family member's pursuit of individual goals, but rather by sharing and sacrifice among family members. At one time the social good was thought to require the husband to control his wife; and children were, and to an extent still are, expected to obey their parents for the sake of a better society. Parents have often been expected to sacrifice their immediate individual interests for the sake of their children.[29] The morality of altruism has been supposed to animate the family to the same extent that the morality of individualism has been supposed to pervade the marketplace.

The state has traditionally been expected to facilitate sacrifice and sharing within the family by ratifying the social roles assigned to family members; thus, it would be considered intervention for the state to treat the members of a family as juridical equals. At one time, for example, the father's social role entitled him to control the children. If the mother were to leave him and take the children with her, the courts would ordinarily be expected to force her to return them to him; for courts to refuse to do so would be considered state interference with the family.[30]

Today, courts are still ordinarily expected to ratify the social role of parents as disciplinarians. For example, if a court were to allow a child to recover tort damages from her parents for confining her to her room as punishment, most people would consider this a serious state intrusion into the

---

[28] *See infra* pp. 1520–21.

[29] *See* J. Locke, *An Essay Concerning the True Origin, Extent and End of Civil Government*, in SOCIAL CONTRACT 33 (E. Barker ed. 1960) (parents' duty to care for children); *id.* at 35–36 (children's subjection to parents until children are capable of fending for themselves); *id.* at 37 (suggesting that parents' dominion over children has as its objective making the children "most useful to themselves and *others*" (emphasis added)); *id.* at 47–48 (necessity of making husband the final arbiter of all clashes of will in the marital relationship).

[30] *See* People *ex rel.* Olmstead v. Olmstead, 27 Barb. 9, 31 (N.Y. Sup. Ct. 1857) (granting father habeas corpus remedy against mother and mother-in-law to obtain custody of child on ground that "[t]he paramount legal right of the father to the custody and education of his child can be interfered with by a court of equity only where he has been at fault in bringing about the separation"); People *ex rel.* Nickerson v. ———, 19 Wend. 16, 19 (N.Y. Sup. Ct. 1837) (granting father habeas corpus against wife to obtain custody of their child, and stating that "[t]he interference of the court with the relation of father and child . . . is a delicate and strong measure [that] should never be exerted except for the most sound and solid reasons"); F. Olsen, A History of Child Custody Law as Ideology (Feb. 4, 1982) (unpublished manuscript on file in Harvard Law School Library).

family, even though the parents' act would have been false imprisonment had it been committed by a third party.[31]

The notion of noninterference in the family depends upon some shared conception of proper family roles, and "neutrality" can be understood only with reference to such roles. For example, one of the bases upon which statutes limiting access to contraceptives have been struck down is that such statutes intrude upon the marital relation.[32] Governmental programs providing minors with access to contraceptives, however, are also condemned as state interference in the family.[33] Thus, "interference" is not a simple description of state action or inaction, but rather a way of condemning particular state policies, usually those aimed at changing the status quo. The status quo itself is treated as something natural and not as the responsibility of the state. Actual inequality and domination in the family — as in the free market — are represented as private matters that the state did not bring about, although it could undertake to change them.

The theory of the private family, like free market theory,[34] includes the assertion that particularized adjustments of seemingly unfair or inhumane results will not actually serve anybody's long-run interests. One attack made upon ad hoc adjustments by the state is based on the delicate quality of family relations.[35] Adherents of this position argue that what might seem to be a minor change in the law could have disastrous

---

[31] A modern court might allow tort recovery for serious physical harm caused by a parent's effort to discipline the child; nevertheless, different standards would be applied because the defendant was the parent. *See* MODEL PENAL CODE § 3.08(1)(a) (Proposed Official Draft 1962) (sanctioning use of force by parent against child "for the purpose of safeguarding or promoting the welfare of the minor"); RESTATEMENT (SECOND) OF TORTS § 147 & comment d (1975) (parents' privilege of discipline is broader than that of others); *see also* Holodook v. Spencer, 36 N.Y.2d 35, 324 N.E.2d 338, 364 N.Y.S.2d 859 (1974) (rejecting children's argument that, because their parents had failed properly to supervise them, the parents should be liable for resultant injury).

For the traditional view of parental liability for child beating, see State v. Jones, 95 N.C. 588 (1886) (refusing to hold parents criminally liable for disciplinary beatings).

[32] Griswold v. Connecticut, 381 U.S. 479, 485–86 (1965).

[33] The Reagan Administration's recent effort to require birth control clinics to notify the parents of women under 18 who were prescribed contraceptives was, in part, based on the idea that lack of notification was detrimental to the family. *See* N.Y. Times, Feb. 20, 1983, at E5, col. 4. (quoting Richard S. Schweiker, Secretary of Health and Human Services) ("Without this notification parents would not have a chance to participate.") Thus far, two federal district courts have held this "squeal rule" to be unlawful on statutory grounds. *See* New York v. Schweiker, Civ. No. 83-0726 (S.D.N.Y. Mar. 21, 1983); Planned Parenthood Fed'n of Am. v. Schweiker, Civ. No. 83-0037 (D.D.C. Mar. 2, 1983).

[34] *See supra* pp. 1503–04.

[35] This attack is analogous to the "fragile market" theory. *See supra* p. 1503.

unforeseen consequences. Thus, a member of England's House of Lords argued in 1838 that a bill allowing mothers to visit children living with their legally separated fathers could "ruin[] half the families in the kingdom."[36] It was said to be "dangerous . . . to tamper" with the "delicate" principles of family law.[37]

In a quite different argument analogous to the "durable market" theory,[38] it is claimed that state intervention to protect the weaker family member from abuse by the stronger is ineffective because powerful, underlying, "real" relations between family members will inevitably reassert themselves. Social intervention short of dismembering the family is likely to prove meaningless.

For example, it has been argued that battered wives cannot be helped by the state unless the state undertakes to protect them twenty-four hours a day.[39] The wife who does not leave her battering husband is in a position analogous to that of the weaker party entering a contract characterized by unequal bargaining power. Just as the fact that the weaker party chose to enter into the contract suggests that he thought he would profit from it, so the fact that the wife remains in her marriage suggests that, in her own estimation, she gains more from the relationship than she loses. For the police to watch or evaluate the husband's every abuse of the wife would be analogous to the state-drafted contracts that laissez-faire theorists believe must eventually result from any sustained effort to police abuse by the party in a superior commercial bargaining position. As long as the weaker party wants to enter into the contract and as long as the wife wants to stay in the marriage, the state's effort to eliminate particular terms, it is asserted, is bound to be futile.

According to these arguments, therefore, what might seem to be a minor reform either will have no effect or will have such drastic effects that the state might as well abolish families altogether and undertake to raise children itself.

---

[36] 44 PARL. DEB. (3d ser.) 772, 789 (1838) (statement of Lord Wynford).

[37] *Id.* at 788 (statement of Lord Brougham).

[38] *See supra* pp. 1503–04.

[39] Indeed, police are trained to avoid involvement in domestic situations, because such involvement would amount to intrusion on "private" relationships that police supposedly are unable to alter. *See* Bruno v. Codd, 90 Misc. 2d 1047, 396 N.Y.S.2d 974 (Sup. Ct. 1977), *rev'd*, 64 A.D.2d 582, 407 N.Y.S.2d 165 (1978), *aff'd*, 47 N.Y.2d 582, 393 N.E.2d 976, 419 N.Y.S.2d 901 (1979); Parnas, *The Police Response to the Domestic Disturbance*, 1967 WIS. L. REV. 914, 916–30; Truninger, *Marital Violence: The Legal Solutions*, 23 HASTINGS L.J. 259, 264, 272 (1971).

B. Standard Critiques of the Free Market and the Private Family

1. The Market. — The attack upon the accuracy and coherence of the laissez-faire image of the free market had two major components. First, the notion that the market is private and capable of existing separately from the state was challenged. Commentators argued that "systems advocated by professed upholders of *laissez-faire*" were "in reality permeated with coercive restrictions of individual freedom."[40] Furthermore, these coercive restrictions did not conform to "any formula of 'equal opportunity' or of 'preserving the equal rights of others.'"[41] State interference, it was claimed, was unavoidable and would inevitably "affect the distribution of income and the direction of economic activities."[42] Because government neutrality was an impossibility,[43] a laissez-faire economy was a false ideal.

The second component of this attack was a demonstration that the government was not in fact neutral, but instead benefited certain entrepreneurs at the expense of working people. In making this argument, some commentators assumed that it would be theoretically possible to fashion workable laissez-faire policies, but pointed out that in practice these were "never . . . carried out consistently."[44] The extreme version of this argument would suggest that laissez faire is a smokescreen used by representatives of large industries to limit popular control of business. The same industries, it could be argued, would not really want an across-the-board laissez-faire policy, because they actually depend upon probusiness regulation.[45]

An argument that draws on both components of the attack on laissez faire treats so-called "private law" as a state grant of partial sovereignty to one of the economic actors. Thus, contract law does not simply put into effect the agreement of the parties; rather, the mechanisms for enforcing contract put "the sovereign power of the state at the disposal of one party to be exercised over the other party."[46] Similarly, private

---

[40] Hale, *Coercion and Distribution in a Supposedly Non-Coercive State*, 38 POL. SCI. Q. 470, 470 (1923).

[41] *Id.*

[42] *Id.*

[43] *See id.*

[44] Cohen, *The Basis of Contract*, 46 HARV. L. REV. 553, 561 (1933).

[45] *See id.* at 562 ("A government so limited in its powers that it could do no harm would be useless, since it could do no good.").

[46] *Id.* at 586.

property is seen to confer on its owner the "sovereign power [of] compelling service and obedience"[47] from those who need access to the property.[48] This vision of property and contract law undermines the notion that the state can be a noncoercive, neutral arbiter in the market.

2. *The Family.* — Arguments similar to those developed in the attack on laissez faire have been used[49] to undermine the basis for state refusal to "intervene" in the private family.[50] One such argument attempts to demonstrate that the state cannot be neutral because it cannot help imposing coercive restrictions upon the freedom of family members. For example, although noninterventionists argue that the state should not interfere to prevent wife abuse,[51] courts will have to deal somehow with cases in which battered wives kill their husbands.[52] The simple principle of nonintervention in the family gives no clear direction for deciding such cases; it will not dictate whether criminal charges should be brought against these women or whether wife battering should mitigate or provide a defense to homicide. Yet the determination of such questions will inevitably affect the distribution of power within violent marriages and thus the social relations of families.[53]

---

[47] Cohen, *Property and Sovereignty*, 13 CORNELL L.Q. 8, 12 (1927).

[48] The Supreme Court decisions that treated freedom to contract as a property right were said to have "pass[ed] a certain domain of sovereignty from the state to the private employer." *Id.* at 11.

[49] *See, e.g.*, Easton, *Feminism and the Contemporary Family*, in 8 SOCIALIST REV., May–June 1978, at 11, *reprinted in* A HERITAGE OF HER OWN 555 (N. Cott & E. Pleck eds. 1979) [hereinafter cited as HERITAGE]; Taub and Schneider, *supra* note 15.

[50] In our earlier discussion of the battered wife, for example, *see supra* p. 1507, the noninterventionist argument would treat wife abuse as a private misfortune for which the state would not be responsible. Although the state might undertake to use its repressive apparatus to reduce the occurrence of interspousal violence by altering the legal consequences attendant upon it, to do so would, according to the noninterventionists, run such great risks of undermining the positive values of the private family that it should not be undertaken.

[51] *See supra* p. 1507 & notes 36 and 50.

[52] *See* Schneider, *Equal Rights to Trial for Women: Sex Bias in the Law of Self-Defense*, 15 HARV. C.R.-C.L. L. REV. 623 (1980); *cf.* Note, *Defense Strategies for Battered Women Who Assault Their Mates:* State v. Curry, 4 HARV. WOMEN'S L.J. 161 (1981) (discussing wife's assault on battering husband).

[53] It might be objected at this point that the state could indeed remain neutral with respect to the family by treating wife beating just as it would any other assault and by applying the same laws of self-defense and impaired capacity to the wife's self-help that it would apply generally. Regardless whether the legal treatment of cases involving married couples is identical to that of other cases, the particulars of that treatment will nevertheless affect the balance of power within a family. Given that husbands tend to be physically stronger than their wives and less socially conditioned against the use of violence, they will usually win a battle fought without

The second component of the attack on the private nature of the family is the claim that, even if the state could be neutral vis-à-vis the family, it in fact is not. The theory of the private family, it is argued, is not consistently carried out. Instead, the assertion that family affairs should be private has been made by men to prevent women and children from using state power to improve the conditions of their lives.[54] By insisting that the family should not be subject to state regulation, men have been able to retain their excessive power. Furthermore, men in fact use the coercive power of the state to reinforce and consolidate their authority over wives and children.

The argument that nonintervention serves to empower husbands to dominate their wives and children has been particularly useful in the attack upon the claimed neutrality of the state with respect to the family. During the first half of the

---

weapons. The husband's advantage is reduced when the wife has a gun or even a knife. Although statistically more husbands than wives kill their spouses, *see* Schneider, *supra* note 52, at 626, battered wives in general would probably benefit from a greatly expanded law of self-defense. In most families a relatively strong assault law and relatively weak homicide law would tend to shift power from the husband to the wife. Similarly, whether and how property is divided when a couple break up their household, and what value is placed on household services in quasi-contractual recovery, will affect the balance of power within most families. *See* Bruch, *Property Rights of De Facto Spouses Including Thoughts on the Value of Homemakers' Services*, 10 FAM. L.Q. 101 (1976). In other words, the effect of state regulation upon the family is not dependent upon the state's singling out married people for any special treatment. The state provides the legal ground rules for human association, and these affect the social power of individuals and thus human interaction.

Furthermore, although some have called for the state to disestablish marriage or free itself from any juridical recognition of marriage, not even the strongest advocates of children's rights have suggested the total delegalization of parenthood. And without such total delegalization, the state will continue to affect the underlying relations of power and affection that influence family life, as it does, for example, through state custody law, which inevitably affects the power relations between parents.

[54] Traditionally, courts regarded wife beating as the husband's prerogative. *See* Bruno v. Codd, 90 Misc. 2d 1047, 1048, 396 N.Y.S.2d 974, 975 (Sup. Ct. 1977), *rev'd*, 64 A.D.2d 582, 407 N.Y.S.2d 165 (1978), *aff'd*, 47 N.Y.2d 582, 393 N.E.2d 976, 419 N.Y.S.2d 901 (1979); 1 W. BLACKSTONE, COMMENTARIES *432–33; T. DAVIDSON, CONJUGAL CRIME 100–13 (1978); Eisenberg & Micklow, *The Assaulted Wife: "Catch 22" Revisited*, 3 WOMEN'S RTS. L. REP. 138, 138–39 (1977); Williams, *The Equality Crisis: Some Reflections on Culture, Courts, and Feminism*, 7 WOMEN'S RTS. L. REP. 175, 177 & n.9 (1982). Even though wife beating is no longer explicitly condoned by law, various state officials may actively encourage such conduct through a policy of failing to enforce prohibitions of wife beating, a policy that empowers wife beaters to act with the acquiescence of the state. Often, police fail to respond to calls about wife beating or decline to arrest husbands; prosecutors take a lax stance; and judges refuse to convict or else give very light sentences upon conviction. *See* sources cited *supra* note 36.

nineteenth century, state neutrality meant the ratification and reinforcement of social roles within the family that were openly hierarchical. Husbands were expected to control their wives, and wives were expected to obey their husbands.[55] Nineteenth century feminists attacked the state for granting husbands sovereignty within the family, and asserted that the state itself was creating inequality when it endorsed separate social roles and realms of activities for the different members of the family.[56] According to Lucretia Mott, the subjugation of wives by husbands was not apostolic but was "done by law and public opinion."[57] Lucy Stone and Henry Blackwell protested that the marriage laws "confer[red] upon the husband an injurious and unnatural superiority, investing him with legal powers which no honorable man would exercize, and which no man should possess."[58]

The feminist recognition that state empowerment of the husband enabled him to coerce the family finds a parallel in John Dawson's work on undue influence law,[59] which elaborates upon the basic contradiction that existed between different concepts of "freedom" in the late nineteenth century. Dawson explains:

> On the one hand, doctrines of undue influence were attempting to "free" the individual by regulating the pressures that restricted individual choice; on the other hand, theories of economic individualism aimed at an entirely different kind of freedom, a freedom of the "market" from external regulation. It was not yet fully recognized that the freedom of the "market" was essentially a freedom of individuals and groups to coerce one another, with the power to coerce reinforced by agencies of the state itself.[60]

---

[55] Children were also expected to obey their parents, and until recently, failure to observe this duty could result in incarceration for juvenile delinquency. *See* Katz & Teitelbaum, *PINS Jurisdiction, the Vagueness Doctrine, and the Rule of Law*, 53 IND. L.J. 1 (1977-1978).

[56] The Seneca Falls Declaration of 1848 charged that man had "usurped the prerogative of Jehovah himself" and had falsely claimed the right to assign to woman a particular sphere of action, whereas that right in fact "belong[ed] to her conscience and to her God." Declaration of Sentiments and Resolutions, Seneca Falls (July 19, 1848), *reprinted in* FEMINISM: THE ESSENTIAL HISTORICAL WRITINGS 76, 80 (M. Schneir ed. 1972) [hereinafter cited as FEMINISM].

[57] L. Mott, Not Christianity, but Priestcraft (1854), *reprinted in* FEMINISM, *supra* note 56, at 101 (speech to the Woman's Rights Convention in Philadelphia).

[58] L. Stone & H. Blackwell, Marriage of Lucy Stone Under Protest (1855), *reprinted in* FEMINISM, *supra* note 56, at 104 (statement by Lucy Stone and Henry Blackwell, read and signed at their marriage).

[59] Dawson, *Economic Duress — An Essay in Perspective*, 45 MICH. L. REV. 253 (1947).

[60] *Id.* at 266.

The parallel with nineteenth century family law is striking. Family law doctrine aimed at "freeing" the individual members of a family from external regulation. Feminists argued, however, that this freedom was essentially a freedom of husbands to coerce wives, "with the power to coerce reinforced by agencies of the state itself."[61]

One response to feminist attacks on the claimed neutrality of the state was the gradual enactment of laws that seemed more neutral. During the late nineteenth century and the twentieth century, much of the law providing for juridical superiority of the male was replaced by statutes and court decisions providing for juridical equality.[62] The effect of this legal change upon the actual subordination of women has been debated,[63] but what is of interest here is the extent to which the assertion of state neutrality between juridically equal husbands and wives is open to the same attacks as is the asserted state neutrality between juridically equal entrepreneurs and workers. The move toward legal equality does represent a change in the mode of explaining or denying the inferior status of women. It can be seen as a shift from a direct to an indirect mode of legitimating the subordination of women.[64] Just as the notion of different, essentially incomparable spheres had replaced the claim that God created women inferior to men,

---

[61] *Id.*

[62] *See, e.g.*, 1 J. SCHOULER, A TREATISE ON THE LAW OF MARRIAGE, DIVORCE, SEPARATION AND DOMESTIC RELATIONS § 4 (6th ed. 1921). Schouler observes:

> There was in this country and England, during the latter part of the nineteenth century, a remarkable movement for giving the wife equal rights in all respects with the husband, which has been so far successful that it can almost be said now that the modern wife has a legal right which, fortunately for all of us, she does not exercise, to leave home in the morning and go to work, collect and keep her own wages and leave her husband to do the housework and take care of the babies.

Id. at 5.

[63] *See, e.g.*, Powers, *supra* note 15, at 88–102.

[64] Women's inferior position is legitimated directly by claims that God or nature made women actually inferior. *See, e.g.*, 1 *Corinthians* 11:3–11:16; 1 *Timothy* 2:8–2:15. It is legitimated indirectly by claims that women are equal in ability and that their inferior position is due to their own behavior. For a discussion of the conditioning that leads women to accept their inferior position, see Bem & Bem, *Homogenizing the American Woman: The Power of an Unconscious Ideology*, in FEMINIST FRAMEWORKS 6–23 (A. Jagger & P. Struhl eds. 1978); *cf.* Freeman, *Legitimizing Racial Discrimination Through Antidiscrimination Law: A Critical Review of Supreme Court Doctrine*, 62 MINN. L. REV. 1049 (1978) (arguing that racism and antidiscrimination law work to legitimate the inferior position of racial minorities). Another kind of indirect legitimation of women's inferiority treats the particular failure of an individual woman to achieve success as a personal shortcoming rather than a societal one, and thus directs her energy toward inward-looking solutions rather than social change.

so the notion of separate spheres was supplanted by the claim that men and women were actually equal.

C. Stage Theory Parallel — The "Lag Theory"

Our present ways of thinking and talking about the market and the family are deeply affected by the history of our ideas about these concepts. One idea that has had a powerful impact is the notion that the family is moving away from feudalism more slowly than the market is; the market has seemed to be the more progressive institution, leading the way toward modernization, while the family has followed a slower but parallel development. According to this "lag theory," changes in the family reproduce but lag behind those in the market.[65] In our efforts to understand the lag theory and its effects on our current thinking,[66] it will be useful to examine popular beliefs about the historical stages of the market and of the family. It is not my goal to present a detailed account of the actual history of either institution. Rather, I will sketch out our conventional, somewhat simplistic, but nonetheless powerful beliefs about the historical development of the market and the family.

1. Stages of the Market. — During the feudal period, individuals were not expected to be equal.[67] Hierarchy was part of the natural order of things, and paying homage to superiors was as fitting as paying homage to God. Even if an individual might properly change his particular position in the existing hierarchy, to try to alter the hierarchy itself would be disgrace-

---

[65] There are many different explanations for why the family should lag behind the market; these vary from rather simplistic concepts of the family as part of the "superstructure" determined by the economic "base" of the market to less materialistic claims that the family captures and preserves past ideals to ease the path of change. *See* J. MITCHELL, WOMAN'S ESTATE 152–58 (1971). Such theories also range from loose notions that different institutions just happen to become liberalized at different times to beliefs that because the form of the family is determined by the market and the family exists to serve the market, the family will necessarily follow behind the market, as surely as a traditional Indian woman will follow two steps behind her husband. The important point here is not which of these explanations, if any, might be an accurate description of reality, nor even whether the lag theory is in general right or wrong, but rather the effect that the lag theory has upon our conception of market and family.

[66] For example, while the lag theory encourages reform of the family, it also reinforces our image of the family as a backward institution and sustains its devalued position. From the perspective of the lag theory, the market provides a model for improving the family.

[67] *See* R. SOUTHERN, THE MAKING OF THE MIDDLE AGES 98–117 (1953) (describing class structure in feudal society).

ful. Everyone was considered to have an interest in keeping inferiors and superiors in their places. The laws that reflected and maintained this hierarchy were not thought to undermine freedom. Law stood in opposition not to liberty but to will;[68] the higher one rose toward liberty, the more one was governed by law rather than by the arbitrary will of one's superiors. "High and low alike sought liberty by insisting on enlarging the number of rules under which they lived."[69]

During this period there was no dichotomy between the state and civil society. The state was not seen to intervene in society, because it was not defined as something separate from society. Even when it became meaningful to talk about the state and society as independent entities, "state intervention" posed no special problem as long as the state reflected the hierarchy chosen by God. To the extent that the law accurately reflected the hierarchy and this hierarchy was considered legitimate, the law itself would be deemed legitimate.[70]

This situation changed with the rise of the free market. Social and economic relationships lost their direct political character, and the state became something standing in opposition to civil society. Freedom came to be seen not as a condition dependent on laws,[71] but rather as a quality inherent in man.[72] The rules governing the hierarchy in society, which had protected people from the arbitrary will of their superiors, came to be considered "strangleholds on liberty."[73] Gradually these strangleholds were loosened, and the state seemed to withdraw from the marketplace. The primary role of law was then regarded to be protection of the rights of man, rights said to be shared equally by all.[74]

Of course, juridical equality did not result in social or economic equality, and the state never completely left the

---

[68] *See id.* at 107–08.

[69] *Id.* at 108.

[70] *See* Kennedy, *Form and Substance*, *supra* note 19, at 1725.

[71] *See* R. SOUTHERN, *supra* note 67, at 108.

[72] For a discussion of the extent to which this ideology included women and of the ways in which early liberal thought understood gender distinctions, see S. OKIN, WOMEN IN WESTERN POLITICAL THOUGHT 99–105, 197–230 (1979); *see also id.* at 106–94 (examining in detail Rousseau's ideas about women).

[73] R. SOUTHERN, *supra* note 67, at 108 (describing period before the "tedious gradations and irksome rules" of society came to be seen as "so many strangleholds on liberty").

[74] Slaves, women, children, and sometimes unpropertied men were excluded from the category "all." Often their exclusion was taken for granted and ignored, but some authors endeavored to justify, deny, or condemn it. *See, e.g.*, J. LOCKE, THE SECOND TREATISE OF GOVERNMENT 13–14 (J. Gough ed. 1952) (1st ed. London 1690) (justifying exclusion of slaves); *id.* at 30–44 (justifying exclusion of children); J. STEPHEN, LIBERTY, EQUALITY, FRATERNITY 188–210 (2d ed. 1874, 1967 printing) (justifying exclusion of women).

marketplace. The changes, however, were important. When men were said to be born equal, their subsequent inequality had to be explained or denied. Laissez-faire ideology either denied the inequality or particularized and privatized it. That some men were wealthier than others was attributable to their own efforts and to the laws of supply and demand. This explanation tended to place the onus of inequality upon its victims. Thus, the mode of legitimation shifted from a direct acknowledgment of pervasive hierarchy to an indirect justification of gross inequality among juridical equals.

The third stage of the market, which I will refer to as the welfare state, is characterized by the acknowledgment of state regulation of economic activity, including such legislative reforms as wage and hour laws, antitrust regulation, consumer protection provisions, and establishment of a national system of monetary control.[75] While the free market system was based on the idea that all men are equal and should be treated identically by the state, the welfare legislation of the late nineteenth century frequently singled out categories of people for special treatment. The relation of employer and employee, for example, was said to create certain noncontractual obligations on the part of the employer to protect his employees. Thus, statuses gave rise to various obligations that might be considered altruistic in that a particular relation would require forms of interaction not based on prospects for immediate individual gain.

Propagandists for the welfare state might suggest the following distinction: in the nineteenth century, men were treated as equals yet allowed to remain grossly unequal; in the twentieth century, the actual inequality was recognized, and through this recognition it became possible to design laws that tended to make people more equal in fact. Opponents of the welfare state have argued, however, that it is wrong to treat people unequally. Early in this century, for example, they claimed that the law demeaned workers by treating them as inferior beings unable to make labor contracts that would require them to work more than ten hours a day[76] or would prohibit them from joining a union.[77]

In the welfare state, the way that actual inequality and oppression are justified and legitimated differs somewhat from

---

[75] I am not using the term "welfare state" in its narrow, modern sense to refer to a system of bureaucratized cash transfer payments from the government to needy individuals. Rather, by welfare state I mean the market system that replaced the free market of the 19th century. *See* K. POLANYI, THE GREAT TRANSFORMATION 223–36 (1944).

[76] *See* Lochner v. New York, 198 U.S. 45, 57 (1905).

[77] *See* Coppage v. Kansas, 236 U.S. 1 (1915).

the way they were by laissez-faire theory. The state is still seen as something standing in stark opposition to the individual, but now its role is more than just to legalize or moderate the individual's interaction with others. The state is also seen to have a redistributive function and to protect individuals against severe adversity. The legitimacy of the state is in part dependent upon the belief that the state has provided all the protection necessary and has carried out as much redistribution as it can without causing more harm than good.[78]

Thus, unlike the free market, the welfare state rejects non-intervention and enacts remedial legislation that takes account of people's economic stations. Unlike the feudal system, the welfare state rejects explicit hierarchy and envisions the state regulating society to promote equality.

2. *Stages of the Family.* — Just as the feudal state was not perceived to be clearly separate from civil society, the feudal family was not perceived to be separate from the rest of economic life;[79] there was no dichotomy between the market and the family. The hierarchical family was an integral part of hierarchical society. Family life was highly regulated by a complex system of rules and laws,[80] many of which continued to operate as civil society was separated from the state and as the family was separated from the market. Well into the nineteenth century, the family was still openly and juridically hierarchical.

In the next stage of the family's development, the notion of separate spheres for men and women provided a kind of middle ground between traditional hierarchy and juridical equality. Women were said to be different, not inferior. During this stage, women began to gain greater juridical equality. The woman's sphere was gradually expanded to include in some cases the "external relations" of the family, which had previously been assigned to men. Around the middle of the nineteenth century, states began enacting married women's property acts, and mothers were sometimes said to have an equal right to the custody of children.[81]

---

78 *See* N. Furniss & T. Tilton, The Case for the Welfare State (1977).

79 *See* J. Flandrin, Families in Former Times 1–2 (1979).

80 Although we would consider much of this regulation of the family to be a product of the church rather than the state — in England, for example, most matters relating to the family were handled by the ecclesiastical courts until the 19th century — such a distinction would have been largely meaningless in the feudal period because of the integration of church and state. To the extent that a distinction could be drawn, however, the amount of regulation attributable to the state rather than the church was still considerable. *See* E. Shorter, The Making of the Modern Family 44–53 (1975).

81 *See* Miller v. Morrison, 43 Kan. 446, 23 P. 612 (1890) (holding that parents have equal and joint right to custody of child and asserting that tendency in state

The liberalization of the family was marked by shifts toward equal juridical rights and the withdrawal of the state. This trend has continued to the present, with the family coming to assume more of the characteristics associated with the free market. The juridical superiority of men over women and of parents over children has been steadily eroded. Moreover, state withdrawal from the family has continued in many areas. Restrictions on divorce have steadily decreased, and courts have been increasingly willing to allow parties to regulate their marriages by contract rather than have the state prescribe the incidents of the marriage relation.[82] Recent Supreme Court cases tend to remove the state from regulation of procreation decisions and of married people's sexual relations with each other or with third parties.[83]

As this liberalization has taken place, however, we have also entered the latest stage — the regulated family. As early as the nineteenth century, for example, courts began using the power to decide child custody cases[84] and to grant divorces[85] as a means of regulating the marital behavior of husbands and

---

had always been "toward an exact equality among [sic] the sexes under the law"); English v. English, 32 N.J. Eq. 738 (1880) (determining custody on basis of child's best interests, not superior common law rights of father); Commonwealth *ex rel.* Myers v. Myers, 18 Pa. C. 385 (1896) (applying state's equal guardianship statute); *cf.* Hewitt v. Long, 76 Ill. 399 (1875) (criticizing "arrogance" of the common law right of fatherhood and asserting that mothers' rights will not be disregarded); McShan v. McShan, 56 Miss. 413 (1879) (asserting that fathers' superior rights to custody are not absolute; court will look into entire circumstances).

[82] *See* Shultz, *Contractual Ordering of Marriage: A New Model for State Policy*, 70 CALIF. L. REV. 204, 280–86 (1982).

[83] *See, e.g.*, Carey v. Population Servs. Int'l, 431 U.S. 678 (1977) (striking down state bans on distribution of contraceptives by nonpharmacists and on advertising of contraceptives); Planned Parenthood v. Danforth, 428 U.S. 52 (1976) (limiting state power to regulate abortions); Roe v. Wade, 410 U.S. 113 (1973) (striking down state ban on abortions); Eisenstadt v. Baird, 405 U.S. 438 (1972) (striking down state ban on distribution of contraceptives to unmarried persons); Griswold v. Connecticut, 381 U.S. 479 (1965) (striking down state law forbidding use of contraceptives by married persons). *See generally Developments in the Law — The Constitution and the Family*, 93 HARV. L. REV. 1156, 1296–1308 (1980) (surveying decisions on procreative rights) [hereinafter cited as *Developments*]; Note, *On Privacy: Constitutional Protection for Personal Liberty*, 48 N.Y.U. L. REV. 670, 719–38 (1973) (surveying challenges to state interference with private sexual behavior).

[84] *See* Commonwealth v. Briggs, 33 Mass. 203 (1834) (ordering custody of child shifted from wife to husband to avoid "sanctioning" wife's unauthorized separation from husband); People *ex rel.* Brooks v. Brooks, 35 Barb. 85 (N.Y. App. Div. 1861) (refusing to apply equal parental guardianship statute when wife was found to have left husband without just cause); *cf.* Commonwealth *ex rel.* Myers v. Myers, 18 Pa. C. 385 (1896) (criticizing equal guardianship statute for removing from courts the power to use custody decision to control marital behavior of wife). *But see* Allen v. Affleck, 10 Daly 509 (N.Y. Ct. Common Pleas 1882) (arguing that custody law should not be used to coerce unwilling husband and wife to live together).

[85] This indirect regulation had both ideological and practical components. As a

wives. Near the beginning of the twentieth century,[86] child labor legislation and compulsory school laws significantly affected the control parents had over their children. In the latest stage of the family, as in the welfare state stage of the market, state policies commonly single out particular groups of people for special treatment. Regulation of the family continues to the present day, and legislation now offers protection to wives as well as children.[87] Many of the provisions that states have passed to deal with battered wives, for example, involve granting the wives remedial rights against their husbands, rights of a kind that would not be allowed against a third party.[88]

3. The Market as the Basis for a Critique of the Family. — The suffragists and other nineteenth century critics of family relations often looked to the progressive features of the contemporary market to garner material for their critique. The market ideology of equal rights and opportunity was turned against the structures and legal provisions that denied women juridical equality and offered them only limited opportunities. Elizabeth Cady Stanton told the New York legislature that "burning indignation" fills a woman's soul when she "turns over the pages of your statute books, and sees there how like feudal barons you freemen hold your women."[89] In the same way that serfs were subject to the arbitrary will of their masters, wives were all too subject to the arbitrary will of their husbands. Feminists demanded that wives be freed from such subordination. Stanton urged the legislature to stop treating marriage as "a kind of half-human, half-divine institution." If

---

practical matter, certain behavior could be deterred by allowing a divorce against the offending spouse. This was particularly significant for women (given that a wife might be denied alimony if a divorce were granted against her), as well as for spouses who wished to keep reluctant partners in the bonds of marriage for whatever reason. Ideologically, the inclusion of particular behavior as a ground for divorce was a societal statement of disapproval of the conduct. For example, making cruelty a ground for divorce was an important step beyond withdrawing explicit approval of a husband's disciplining of his wife.

86 Direct state regulation of poor families began much earlier than regulation of wealthy families. For example, in the 18th and 19th centuries, poor children could be and often were apprenticed out regardless of the wishes of their parents. *See* TenBroek, *California's Dual System of Family Law: Its Origin, Development, and Present Status* (pt. 1), 16 STAN. L. REV. 257, 271–81, 295 (1964).

87 *See* Note, *Domestic Violence: Legislative and Judicial Remedies*, 2 HARV. WOMEN'S L.J. 167, 169–73 (1979). For an example of such legislation, see MASS. GEN. LAWS ANN. ch. 209A (West Supp. 1983).

88 *See* People v. Cameron, 53 Cal. App. 3d 786, 790–97, 126 Cal. Rptr. 44, 46–51 (1975).

89 Address by Elizabeth Cady Stanton to the New York State Legislature (1860), *reprinted in* FEMINISM, *supra* note 56, at 115.

marriage was to be viewed as a civil contract, she urged, "let it be subject to the same laws which control all other contracts."[90]

In an essay published in 1851, Harriet Taylor Mill elaborated upon the notion that progress in family relations lags behind economic progress.[91] She argued that the world had just begun to "cast off injustice": "It is only now getting rid of monarchical despotism" and "hereditary feudal nobility."[92] She continued:

> Can we wonder that it has not yet done as much for women? As society was constituted until the last few generations, inequality was its very basis; association grounded on equal rights scarcely existed; to be equals was to be enemies; two persons could hardly co-operate in anything, or meet in any amicable relation, without the law's appointing that one of them should be the superior of the other. Mankind have outgrown this state, and all things now tend to substitute, as the general principle of human relations, a just equality, instead of the dominion of the strongest. But of all relations, that between men and women being the nearest and most intimate, and connected with the greatest number of strong emotions, was sure to be the last to throw off the old rule and receive the new . . . .[93]

In the twentieth century, feminists have continued to raise claims of individual freedom against more traditional "family" values. Feminist demands for emancipation have been channelled into assertions of the individual rights associated with the free market. The focus of liberal reforms on individualism and on the rights of women and children to pursue their self-interest has to some extent made family relations resemble market relations.[94]

Nineteenth century feminists attacked the feudal nature of the private family; similarly, an important strand in current feminist literature attacks the laissez-faire attitude toward the liberal family.[95] Juridical equality by itself is perceived to be inadequate to alleviate actual conditions of dominance and subordination. Much as the free operation of the market was

---

[90] *Id.*, *reprinted in* FEMINISM, *supra* note 56, at 113.

[91] *See* H.T. MILL, *Enfranchisement of Women*, in J.S. MILL & H.T. MILL, ESSAYS ON SEX EQUALITY 89, 99–100 (A. Rossi ed. 1970).

[92] *Id.* at 99.

[93] *Id.* at 99–100.

[94] For a complaint that the "economic rationality" of the capitalist market has pushed its way into family relations, see C. LASCH, HAVEN IN A HEARTLESS WORLD 36 (1977).

[95] *See* sources cited *supra* note 49.

said to lead to unacceptable results, so too the free operation of the family is said to lead to domination and oppression.[96] Many of the legislative proposals for employing state apparatuses to improve conditions for women are based on a legislative recognition of this actual inequality and may be said to involve treating men and women unequally. In short, the same kind of state intervention and special remedial legislation that moved the market toward a welfare state is called for by some feminist critics of the modern family. Furthermore, the free market ideal of the abstract, independent, equal individual is now coming under feminist attack,[97] just as it came under progressive attack by market reformers over half a century ago.

Thus, it could be said that during the nineteenth century the free market provided an ideological base from which to attack the family as "feudal," whereas in the twentieth century the welfare state provides a base from which to attack the family as asocial and in fact unequal. In the nineteenth century, efforts to support individualism and juridical equality in the family were considered progressive; in the twentieth century attacks similar to those made on the laissez-faire market over fifty years ago have pushed the family in the direction of becoming a welfare state institution. In both cases the market has provided a model, and one effect of the reform efforts has been state regulation tending to make the family more like the market.

D. *Alternative Picture: The Negation Theory*

1. The Radical Opposition of Market and Family. — A limitation of the lag theory is its failure to account for a different kind of relationship between the marketplace and the family — a relationship of negation. During the nineteenth century, when the marketplace and the family were both becoming "private," they were seen to exist in radical opposition to each other. The marketplace was considered competitive; the family, cooperative. The marketplace was the arena in which individuals were supposed to be most free to pursue their own interests without being responsible for the effects of their behavior on others. Indeed, an important tenet of liberal ideology was that self-interested behavior in the marketplace not only was acceptable, but also benefited society in general.

---

96 *See id.*

97 *See* Easton, *supra* note 49, at 29–34, *reprinted in* HERITAGE, *supra* note 49, at 571–75.

The marketplace was animated by an individualist ethic; to act selflessly was considered foolish as well as unnecessary.

In contrast, the family was based on the ethic of altruism. Marriage was seen as a decision to share a life together, and the common goals of family life were supposed to supersede the egoistic goals of individual members of the family. Neither husband nor wife was expected to pursue selfish interests over interests of the other. Sharing and self-sacrifice were considered appropriate family behavior.[98]

The opposite ethics of individualism and altruism were accompanied by opposite images of the proper role of the state in the market and in the family. The maintenance of the private marketplace was believed to require the state to limit and direct its own action in order to maximize the opportunity of individuals to enter into whatever contracts they might wish to form. The expression of the will of the contracting parties was supposed to define the terms of the parties' relations; the state was not to tamper with these terms but was to treat each individual as an abstract equal. At the same time, the state was expected to enforce relations that were considered to be voluntarily defined by individuals through their contracts. In this sense, the arena of the marketplace was fully legalized, and the terms dictated by the will of the parties were enforceable by the power of the state through the courts.[99] The coercive apparatus of the state could be called upon to protect each individual from the crimes, torts, and breaches of contract committed in the market.

Within the family, however, privatization meant delegalization. The state refused to give legal effect to any effort by the parties to define the rights, duties, and liabilities of their own marriage. Once a man and a woman were married, they could no longer enter enforceable contracts with each other.[100] Within the family, privatization created a limited "state of nature," in which the state refused to protect one family member from the harmful acts of any other family member. These

[98] For a classic view of this type of family, see L. ALCOTT, LITTLE WOMEN (Boston 1868).

[99] *See* Pound, *The End of Law as Developed In Juristic Thought* (pt. 2), 30 HARV. L. REV. 201, 203, 210 (1917) (discussing theory that law gradually progresses toward a system of individual liberty in which "rights, duties and liabilities flow from voluntary action").

[100] *See* H. CLARK, THE LAW OF DOMESTIC RELATIONS IN THE UNITED STATES § 7.1, at 220 (1968). Nor could they alter the terms of the marriage relationship by antenuptial agreement. *See, e.g.*, French v. McAnarney, 290 Mass. 544, 195 N.E. 714 (1935) (holding void as against public policy wife's contract to forego any provisions for her own support in return for husband's agreement to recognize their illegitimate child).

refusals were an important part of what it meant for the family to be private and for the state not to intervene in the family relationship. It was generally not considered state intrusion, however, when the state undertook to define the marriage relation and to enforce the roles it decided each family member would fill. The notion that the family was private did not mean that the members should determine their own roles and be able to rely on state enforcement of these roles. Rather, in the private family, the individual's only choice concerned whom to marry; individualism was then to be replaced with state-defined altruism.

Thus, the marketplace was said to be left alone by the state if courts blindly enforced contracts and refused to make any independent judgment of the equities in the existing relationship between the parties. In contrast, the family was said to be left alone by the state if courts flatly refused to enforce contracts between its members and insisted on authoritatively defining family relationships. Market legalization and family delegalization both avoided detailed state investigation and ad hoc readjustments, but they did so in opposite ways. As the market became "private," the state withdrew its controls over the individualism of that sphere. In contrast, the state treated the family as "private" by trusting to the altruistic principles thought to animate family life.

2. *Qualification of Radical Opposition.* — The image of an individualistic market opposed to an altruistic family was not, of course, a true picture of reality, and even the ideals of the marketplace and the family were more complex than this sketch would make them seem. Despite the claims of state withdrawal from the marketplace, there was an irreducible element of altruism in market relations; and despite claims of sharing within the family, there was always an irreducible element of self-interest in family relations.

The assumption that in the marketplace one should look only to one's own self-interest has always been qualified in practice. Market participants sometimes explain and justify their self-interested behavior as the unfortunate result of the pressures of the market; these claims of "altruism," whether believed or not, abound in the marketplace.[101] Moreover, the

[101] When an employer refuses a requested wage increase, he is more likely to point to competitive pressures than merely to assert that he will pay no more because he can get other workers for the lower price. The "altruism" that leads the employer to believe that he owes his workers an explanation for his actions can be considered simply a more enlightened version of self-interest. For an elaboration of the meaning of "altruism" as I am using the word, see Kennedy, *Form and Substance*, *supra* note 19, at 1717 & n.79.

very fact that the market is legalized — which is to say that the state enforces contract and tort law — requires that, although market relations are claimed to be defined solely by the autonomous wills of individuals, the courts will inevitably participate in the definition of market relations. Any such legalization is in an important sense altruistic.[102]

Similarly, the family was not really an altruistic institution of sharing and mutual sacrifice. Rather, it was patriarchal, and whatever sacrifice was made was often one sided. Women were said to be disinterested simply because they lacked the means for self-seeking.[103] They were economically dependent upon their husbands, and until the midcentury passage of married women's property acts, whatever property or earnings women received belonged to their husbands.[104] Men supported their wives and children but were free to decide how much support to provide beyond a bare subsistence level.[105]

Furthermore, the delegalized family was much like the marketplace. Women had to marry for economic security, and thus the very act of creating a new family was a kind of market transaction.[106] More basically, delegalization of the family carried with it the same internal contradiction from

---

[102] *See id.* at 1717–22. As Durkheim pointed out half a century ago, the recognition and guaranteeing of any rights among people is necessarily a form of solidarity; and this enforcement has an altruistic element that cannot be reduced to enlightened individualism. *See* E. DURKHEIM, THE DIVISION OF LABOR IN SOCIETY 121–22 (A. Simpson trans. 1933). The laws against theft can be seen as state protection for the owner who fails to act effectively in her own self-interest. Tort law similarly protects the victim who fails to look out for herself, and forces the actor to consider the losses his behavior may cause to his victim. Even the enforcement of a contract by the state protects the party who fails to provide her own protection against breach, and it forces the breaching party to compensate the victim for her losses.

[103] *See* N. COTT, *supra* note 4, at 20–21.

[104] This rule was modified by the equity courts, which enabled wealthy families to settle property upon their female members, but the modification did not affect the rule that the husband owned the wife's services and income. *See* H. CLARK, *supra* note 100, § 7.1, at 219–21.

[105] *See, e.g.*, McGuire v. McGuire, 157 Neb. 226, 238, 59 N.W.2d 336 (1953) ("As long as the home is maintained and the parties are living as husband and wife it may be said that the husband is legally supporting his wife.").

[106] Lucy Stone condemned the "horrible perversion of the marriage relation" caused by women's economic dependence. Extemporaneous remarks by Lucy Stone, National Woman's Rights Convention (1855), *reprinted in* FEMINISM, *supra* note 56, at 108.

Jane Austen's novels tried to create a morality that would comprehend the existence of a marriage market and prevent that market from corrupting the notions of love and affection. The women who advanced socially by marriage are deserving (Elizabeth and Jane Bennet in *Pride and Prejudice* and Jane Fairfax in *Emma*), and women who married for wealth without affection are condemned or pitied (Maria Bertram in *Mansfield Park* and Charlotte Lucas in *Pride and Prejudice*). *See* J. AUSTEN, EMMA (London 1816); J. AUSTEN, MANSFIELD PARK (London 1814); J. AUSTEN, PRIDE AND PREJUDICE (London 1813).

which legalization of the marketplace suffered. Delegalization creates only a limited "state of nature"; once the state undertakes to define the marriage relation, it is impossible for the state to refuse to engage in some enforcement of the individual will of the parties. Activities by the state necessarily encourage or discourage particular individual conduct that readjusts family relations in accordance with the self-interested behavior of the parties. For example, the state might refrain from hearing tort complaints between members of a family and might decriminalize most intrafamilial behavior, but it has never been willing to carry "nonintervention" to the point of providing a spousal exemption from the murder laws.[107]

3. Interdependency of Market and Family. — Although people considered the market and family to be in radical opposition to each other, they also believed that the strength of each sphere was dependent upon the existence of the other and that each sphere gained legitimacy from the presence of the other. The marketplace was acceptable in part because it was not the only sphere; there was also the family. The ideology of the private family provided reassurance that certain traditional human values would not be lost to society when they were banished from the market. The family offered men an altruistic motive and justification for carrying on their individualistic struggles in the marketplace. It also offered men compensation for their suffering in the debasing world[108] and thus reduced resistance to the increasing dehumanization of the market.

The existence of the free market made the constraints of family life more acceptable to both men and women. The marketplace provided images of freedom and of danger. The images of danger made the marketplace a fearsome alternative to the home and thus tended to reconcile women to being consigned to their own sphere. Further, such images provided men with a chivalrous justification for excluding women from the male sphere. At the same time, the freedom of the marketplace, whether actual or imaginary, made it easier for men to tolerate the confining aspects of family life.

4. Using the Family to Critique the Market. — In addition to questioning the possibility and reality of a laissez-faire system, critics of the market used the altruistic values of the

---

[107] Spousal status has, however, been relevant: the murder of a husband used to be punished with particular severity as a form of treason, whereas the murder of an adulterous wife was allowed under particular circumstances, either by written law or by the law as it was enforced.

[108] *See* J. MITCHELL, *supra* note 65, at 154.

family to attack market values.[109] Cooperation was urged against competition, and community against individualism. The self-interested individual was not considered a whole person, much less an ideal. Because it was said that in the marketplace the public good was neglected for the sake of private gain, some observers argued that the state had to regulate the private rights of stronger actors in order to prevent them from dominating weaker actors. Without state regulation, they warned, the market would undermine human values even while it appeared to promote freedom and individual rights.

As well as providing a basis for a direct critique of the market, images from the family were used within the marketplace to improve inhumane market conditions — or at least to appear to do so. Among the best-known attempts to appropriate the ideology of the family for the market was the project undertaken by George Pullman at his sleeping-car factory in Illinois. Pullman built a company town for his workers and tried to fashion it into a stable patriarchal community with himself as the authority figure.[110] The literature on the project stressed family values, and Pullman adopted an openly paternalistic attitude toward his workers. Regardless of their success or failure,[111] such experiments are significant as efforts to appropriate to the marketplace the values and images of the family.

5. The Private Family and the Welfare State Distinguished from Feudalism. — Although the private family of the nineteenth century could seem "feudal," it was also an important element of liberal society. The market and the family together created a complex structure in which each influenced and defined the other. The appropriation to the market of values and images from the family may similarly seem "feudal," but

---

[109] While the lag theory focuses on the market as a model for the family, *see supra* pp. 1513–20 & n.66, the negation theory sees the market and family as each providing a model for the other. To the extent that the family has provided the basis for a critique of the market, the lag theory by itself inadequately captures our understanding of the relation between the market and the family.

[110] *See* S. LENS, THE LABOR WARS 80, 86–87 (1973). Another well known effort to appropriate the values of the family to the market came to be known as the "Lowell Factory System." It was established in the 1820's when textile mill owners recruited the daughters of New England farmers to operate the mills. *See* H. ROBINSON, LOOM AND SPINDLE 7 (1898). The owners established an atmosphere of propriety by requiring the young females to live in special boarding houses staffed by mature Christian women, and tried in general to "exercise a paternal influence over the lives of their operatives." *Id.* at 7, 79–80.

[111] *See* R. SENNETT, AUTHORITY 62–74 (1980) (describing the failure of Pullman's plans); Addams, *A Modern Lear*, 29 SURV. MAG. 131 (1912) (describing Pullman's failures and comparing him to King Lear), *quoted in* R. SENNETT, *supra*, at 67–69.

once again, the situation is more complicated. The paternalistic or group-based ideals that find expression in the social provisions of the welfare state do represent the penetration of family ideals into the marketplace[112] and cannot adequately be explained as a kind of return to feudalism; they are not just residual feudal values that were preserved in the family.

It is quite true that conservative social reformers often appealed to the values of feudalism in their attacks upon industrial capitalism. Feudal society was sometimes used as a model for criticizing the narrow self-interest and lack of social responsibility ascribed to early industrialists and blamed upon the system of capitalism. Members of "Young England" — the renegade Tories led by Disraeli during Sir Robert Peel's ministry — are said to have "preached a kind of revivified and spiritualized feudalism."[113]

Similarly, Roscoe Pound described the welfare state of 1930 as a "new feudal system."[114] He suggested that the kind of relational society characteristic of feudalism had replaced or was in the process of replacing the individualistic society that had characterized the early period of local economic self-sufficiency in America. The typical laborer or businessman was not an isolated individual who freely competed; rather, he worked for a corporation to which he owed services and from which he received protection. Individual businesses were merging into ever-larger corporations and bringing about what Pound referred to as a "feudal organization of businesses."[115] Society increasingly was ordered not around isolated competing individuals and their rights, but rather around relations involving reciprocal duties of service and protection.

The ideology of the welfare state, however, cannot be reduced to feudalism. Pound himself recognized that we would never "exactly" return to a feudal organization of society.[116] In contrast with feudal society, the welfare state is based on government control and espouses an ideology of equality. The state undertakes to regulate the market and justifies this regulation primarily on the ground that it will protect the citizenry and promote equality. In feudalism it could not be imagined that the state might reform civil society, because the state was not seen to be separate from civil society. Furthermore, feu-

---

[112] Lag and negation are not competing theories. Each is an important way of understanding how we think about the family and the market, although neither completely captures our ideas.

[113] P. SMITH, DISRAELIAN CONSERVATISM AND SOCIAL REFORM 8 (1967).

[114] Pound, *The New Feudal System*, 35 COMM. L.J. 397, 397 (1930).

[115] *Id.* at 402.

[116] *See id.* at 403.

dalism was intentionally hierarchical; feudal society did not subscribe to the belief that people were or should be equal.

These two differences are particularly important with respect to the dichotomy between state and civil society. Although state and civil society might seem to have interpenetrated each other in the welfare state, the distinction between the two is as great as or greater than ever. Some conservatives complain that the state has taken over the market, whereas certain revisionists argue that the welfare state was created by powerful entrepreneurs who already controlled the market and who captured the apparatus of the state and utilized it to regulate the market in their private interests.[117] Nevertheless, the dichotomy between the state and the market (civil society) remains and plays a vital justificatory role in maintaining the status quo.

In the same way that free market ideology tended to legitimate the status quo by asserting the juridical equality of all individuals, welfare state ideology legitimates the status quo by claiming to promote the maximum equality consistent with the general welfare of society.[118] A crucial element of welfare state ideology is the limit placed upon the state's activities. Civil society is never swallowed up or overcome by the state; the state always stops short of public ownership of the means of production or public control of investment decisions.

E. Summary

With the decline of feudalism there arose the dichotomies between the state and civil society and between the market and the family. The free market combined an egalitarian ideology with an individualistic ethic. The private family com-

---

[117] *See, e.g.*, G. Kolko, The Triumph of Conservatism 2–10 (1963) ("[R]egulation . . . was invariably controlled by leaders of the regulated industry, and directed toward ends they deemed acceptable or desirable.").

[118] The critique of the reality and coherence of the free market has had two distinct and somewhat incompatible elements. *See supra* pp. 1508–09. The first is the claim that the state cannot be independent from civil society but is deeply implicated in the domination and hierarchies that characterize civil society. This element of the critique is subversive of the dichotomy between state and civil society. The second element, which supports the dichotomy, is the assertion that the state is not in fact neutral but rather favors entrepreneurs over workers.

It is the second element of the critique, and only the second element, that is addressed by the welfare state. Certain of the inequalities of civil society are said to be addressed by the state and to be moderated by it. For example, the welfare state claims to reverse the bias that existed against workers, through legislation that specifically protects workers against the exploitation possible in the free market.

bined a hierarchical ideology with an altruistic ethic. In both the market and the family, state activity has tended to moderate these characteristics. Welfare state reforms in the market have reduced individualism while promoting a new kind of hierarchy. Regulation of the family has undermined the hierarchical ideology and at the same time promoted individualism.

The market and the family reflect a parallel development with respect to the dichotomy between state and civil society. The ideologies of both the free market and the family tried to legitimate actual inequality by emphasizing the equality of all with respect to the state. Inequality was said to result from the private relations among people and was thus a natural attribute of civil society rather than the responsibility of the state. It is currently asserted that the state is promoting as much equality as it reasonably can in both the family and the marketplace and that any remaining inequality is a private or particularized matter.

The market and the family also relate to each other inversely. While the values of the market provide the basis for a critique of the family, the values of the family provide the basis for a critique of the market. The state intervenes in the market to make it more like the family, and in the family to make it more like the market.

Viewed from a perspective that favors democratic, intersubjective relations, these state interventions have two distinct effects. Intervention in the market is desirable insofar as it promotes altruism, but is undesirable insofar as it takes the form of the family hierarchy and legitimates and particularizes inequality instead of eliminating it. The state steps in to protect workers; the workers do not assert their own control through local organization and consolidation of power.[119] Similarly, intervention in the family is desirable insofar as it promotes women's claims for greater power and tends to undermine formal family hierarchy; it is undesirable insofar as it promotes individualism and particularizes and legitimates hierarchy rather than eliminates it. Intervention exposes family members to market exploitation. Further, it entails the state's stepping in to equalize the results of family interaction; it does not democratize the family.

[119] The family offered the model for safe, contained reform of the market system. Radical proposals would have abolished the dichotomy between state and civil society; a reformist program was developed that kept this dichotomy in place by utilizing the dichotomy between market and family. In very important ways, the welfare state is paternalistic rather than democratic.

Part III
Controversies within Feminist Legal Theory

Women's Voices

[7]

The 1984 James McCormick Mitchell Lecture

Feminist Discourse, Moral Values, and the Law—A Conversation*

Isabel Marcus,[1] Paul J. Spiegelman[2]—Moderators

Ellen C. DuBois,[3] Mary C. Dunlap,[4] Carol J. Gilligan,[5] Catharine A. MacKinnon,[6] Carrie J. Menkel-Meadow[7]—Conversants

Spiegelman: In my two years as chairperson of the lecture committee, I have tried to open the law school community to new voices. I am particularly excited about today's program because we have never had a woman before as a James McCormick Mitchell lecturer. Today, five women share that honor. I firmly believe a program of this sort is not a women's program in the sense that it is "for women only." I think feminism is at the cutting edge of positive social change in this country. Accordingly, this is to be a program in which we all will be challenged by new ideas and provoked to reevaluate old ones.

Marcus: I want to tell you a very small story about the origin of this whole enterprise. Two years ago, Carol Gilligan came to this campus during the summer and gave a community lecture. Marjorie Girth and I were sitting next to each other. As Carol began to talk, I turned to Marjorie and said: "Now I understand at a new level why I felt so uncomfortable in law school." At that point, I had the strong impulse to run up to Carol Gilligan and

---

* This Article is an edited transcript of the discussion held on October 19, 1984 at the law school of the State University of New York in Buffalo as part of the James McCormick Mitchell Lecture Series.

1. Associate Professor of Law, State University of New York at Buffalo. Visiting Professor, 1984-1985, City University of New York Law School.
2. Associate Professor of Law, State University of New York at Buffalo.
3. Associate Professor of History, State University of New York at Buffalo. Visiting Professor, 1984-1985, Department of History, University of Wisconsin.
4. Member, California Bar. Founder, Equal Rights Advocates.
5. Associate Professor of Education, Harvard University.
6. Associate Professor of Law, University of Minnesota.
7. Professor of Law, University of California at Los Angeles.

say: "Please come back, please come back during the academic year to talk in the law school. Your work demonstrates that you have something terribly important to say about legal education." As I began to think about a discussion concerning the law, and feminism, and politics, and moral values, and consulted with Paul, our horizons expanded. Paul and I began to think that rather than simply have one lecturer in a formal mode, and in a very traditional format, that it would be appropriate to have a series of conversations. Feminist discourse has moved away from the simple, formal presentation of papers. There are very complicated and sophisticated and explosive issues that need to be discussed. There are people who feel very strongly, and are very brave and courageous, on all sides of the issues that feminism has raised. Rather than have a single presentation, it would be more appropriate at this time to have a conversation which would raise some of the complicated issues of equality and difference and would explore the connection between theory and practice.

One of the reasons I have great hopes for this morning's conversation is that we have two people who have been engaged both as theoreticians and in the world of practice. We have Mary Dunlap, coming in from California, who has taught in law schools, and who, as a practitioner, is a founder of one of the first feminist public interest law firms in the United States: Equal Rights Advocates. And we have Catharine MacKinnon, whose official affiliation is with the University of Minnesota Law School. Not only has she written significant pieces of feminist jurisprudential theory, she also has been involved in the drafting of legislation and litigation.

Dunlap: I am delighted to go first. I am delighted to be here at all. I am thrilled by the energy that Paul, Isabel, and others have put into coming together today, and by the devotion of this lecture series to feminist issues. It's exciting. It's exciting to be able to address these issues, and to differ openly about them—which we will be doing today—to air our disagreements, to learn from them, to move on from them, and to work together from them.

The title of this morning's conversation, "Feminist Discourse, Moral Values, and the Law," raises a sundry set of definitional problems which I am going to completely skip over. You have to watch out for that—that's the prerogative of the self-proclaimed practitioner; when things get really tough in this type of forum they say, "Well, I'm a practitioner." That's one way of standing the heat. The fact of the matter is that while I am a practitioner, I am just absolutely opposed to the distinction between theory and practice that historically has enabled practitioners and theoreticians to hide from each other. I hope that my theories (to the extent that I have them) and my themes will have some integrity in terms of the theoretical models that we will try to work with. But I am not going to spend a lot of time defining them. It raises a question for me: Are there moral values that emerge from or can be defined in the confluence of feminism and law? Are there ways of analyzing the feminist contribution to justice that define themselves morally? And in order to figure out whether there are, I tried to break up or describe the areas in which feminists have been most active in law as a means of trying to determine what is behind that activism, what is beneath it, what is within it, and what part of it is distinctively or even tangentially moral in its content or in its resolve. It seems as if (this is my impression based on about fifteen years of watching and being involved in it) feminist legal activity clusters around certain issues. I'm going to propose four clusters. You will immediately see that these are very fluid walls and that any of the things I put into one of these clusters could readily be attached to another. I offer them not because they are some kind of hard and fast way of analyzing the contribution of feminism in law or of pulling out moral values, but rather as a convenient and descriptive way of (1) taking into account what we have done, and (2) seeing what our priorities are—moral, political, ethical, and personal priorities.

The first cluster I identify is a "physical health" cluster. That cluster would include all of the work that feminists have done and are doing in relation to bodily choices—choices about sexuality and sexual orientation and family and personal partnerships. I did not have to put all that under physical health; I could have as readily put it in one of the following clusters.

Next is the "money" cluster. The money cluster involves feminists' work in matters of equal pay, comparable worth, property, benefits of employment, ownership, and control of the material means to equal opportunity.

Still, that is not enough. These clusters, as sloppy as they are, as capacious as they are, are not yet sufficient; they do not yet take into account everything we have done. So we add the "violence-empowerment" cluster. I would suggest that to the extent this cluster overlaps with the physical health cluster, it also includes domestic battery, rape, sexual harassment, incest, homicide, and self defense.

Still, we cannot stop there. That is not yet descriptive of all the work the feminists in theory and practice have been doing and are doing and are continuing to do in the name of feminist values, moral and otherwise. So I have a fourth cluster, a "creativity" cluster. (Any resemblance to the miscellaneous docket of the Supreme Court should be set aside because inclusion in that category has always been kind of a "put-down"; if you're in the miscellaneous docket, you do not "fit anywhere else.") This fourth category is as difficult to define as it is because I think all of these issues that I am about to identify sometimes get neglected for one reason or another—issues of educational opportunity, athletics, women in art, women in religion, women in philosophy. Lawyers have to do a little with everything and do everything with a little knowledge, we are told. As one reads, or as one perceives, feminist involvement in law as an agenda, it is plain that such an agenda encompasses every realm of our lives, every aspect of who we are, who we are becoming, and what our experiences are.

Having offered that description, I pondered: "Well, have I helped myself at all in trying to isolate or express or define the moral values that operate in relation to feminist work?" I think I have, but there are some problems, so I want to offer those. Then we are going to come back to what these categories seem to suggest or in some cases spell out about the operating world values.

If you pose the question as, "What have feminists done with, or in, or through law?," right away a tremendous relativity attaches. There are those whose answer is: "Well, isn't Sandra Day O'Connor on the U.S. Supreme Court?" That is their full and sufficient answer. I think such an answer is founded on two erroneous premises—maybe more, but let me offer two. One error is that all women are feminists. Although one would love for that to be true, regrettably it is not. The second error is that to measure the progress of feminists in law one should count how many women rise to the top. I suggest that some of the more popular measures of what feminists have done with and through law are not going to be very useful to us. Some (including people with a more informed position on the "feminism" of Sandra Day O'Connor) have gone so far as to measure the progress of feminism by the number of women enrolled in law school. I submit that the most telling measure of how feminists have done in law and what we have done in law is how women are treated in the legal system. What happens to the woman client, plaintiff, or criminal defendant? What is the experience of a woman in the court, in the legislature, in those political functions that are related to the creation and perpetuation of law? When I offer that definition of law I think of Aaron Burr. Aaron Burr offered a definition of law that is very hard to get around. He said that law is that which is boldly asserted and plausibly maintained. So with that definition of law in mind, it seems to me that the most satisfactory question for measuring the progress of feminists, and feminism, and feminist values in law is: "What is *happening* to women in law?"

Now, let us go back to these "clusters." I cannot possibly pretend, in the time that I have, to assess, to describe, or for that matter to evaluate, morally or otherwise, all of the changes, progress, regression, and differences between then and now. I cannot pretend to say everything that feminists have done in each of these areas and then say *how* we have done. Instead, I am going to offer some observations about what I believe the operating moral themes are. Then I am going to come back to a few specifics that I think will be illustrative, although not necessarily fully descriptive.

There are moral themes in the physical-health cluster that appear again in the violence-empowerment cluster. It seems to me that at the heart or at least part of the heart of those clusters is the idea that harm and pain and hurt that are gender-correlated must end, must be prevented, must be remedied. For a woman to live in this society is for her to be in danger on account of her sex, in danger from deprivation of procreative choice, in danger from rape, in danger from those environmental hazards that are sex-correlated, whether they be lead battery plants or any other thing. Those kinds of sex-correlated violence, thoughtful and thoughtless alike, must end. That is a moral value. That, I would also suggest, is a moral imperative and it characterizes much of the work that has been done in some of these areas. And another moral value is the idea or notion of equalizing opportunity. (I propose it as a moral value although it is many other things as well.)

It is bitter but it is not embittering that the term "equality" shall have been misused so much and so often in such a way as to mislead and to suggest that a woman who is not being treated equally at work ought to *think* she is being treated equally at work and that happens—and it happens a lot. Nevertheless, I do not think it is sensible to abandon the equality principle. I want to talk about the equality principle as a source of moral directions, if not of moral values, a little bit later on.

Let me go back and say something about numbers. I said rather harshly before that counting heads seemed to be a rather inadequate measure of the progress of feminism and the effects of feminism in law and in life. At the same time, it's clear that our ambitions as feminists in law are very much affected by the realization that a little bit less than ten years ago the enrollment of women in law schools began to increase in a measurable way. In the 1960s, less than two percent of the licensed legal profession was female. When it came to judges, you could divide that percentage in half; when it came to the law professors and legal scholars, you could divide it in thirds. You would find two or three people out there, and you would attach yourself to them; they would be mentors (or womentors). But again, the measure of the progress of feminism is not the number of women in traditionally male fields. However, although not every woman is necessarily a feminist, *there is a substantial correlation*; similarly, and furthermore (and this is more painful), although not every man is a sexist, there is an overwhelming correlation. And, in another way, every man *is* a sexist—in the same way every white person, every Caucasian is a racist. And in that respect I think we have to stay tuned to the proposition that there is going to be another layer of evaluation here. We must not look to the experiences of women in the courts—rather, we must look to the legal system in general (a hang-up of mine is to overlook the fact that the legal system extends far beyond the courts)—to have them describe for us what they have experienced and how they have not been treated equally, and how their suffering with sex related violence has not been prevented, remedied, or otherwise treated. Along with that, we have to do something a little different in evaluation. I propose that we have to suspend the idea that the woman's account of her experiences must be corroborated. If I stand up in any group that is trained in Western objectivity and discuss a woman who has described to me that she got "fucked over" in court, the reaction will be: "Well, what do you think?" or "Well, what does so-and-so think?" or "Well, what did the judge think?" But let us put all that aside for a moment (although it is important); let us just listen to *her*. When we do that, we discover that in the last fifteen years, in all these areas or clusters that I have described, we have both succeeded and failed—succeeded and failed, that is, by the measure of the voices of the women who have gone through it, who are going through it, and who are subject to it. In every one of these realms, for every glowing account of a positive experience in the use of the legal system, we certainly (if we are honest) can array many descriptions by women of negative experiences.

If the measure is not equal opportunity, to prevent and remedy the sex-correlated harms, then what have we accomplished? Can we be proud of attaching our sense of our life-worth, our definitions of ourselves to feminism in law? Or is it a contradiction in terms as some propose? Well, I do not accept that, because it would make me so sad to accept it, and I will say that honestly.

There is another reason that I don't accept it. I teach a class at Golden Gate in San Francisco in gay and lesbian rights. We are in about the seventh week of it, and I find that I have brought in all this material and immersed my students in one truly indescribably depressing result after another: criminalization as a norm, the deprivation of every right from thought to breathing. I looked up at them and I said: "I'm doing a lousy job of teaching. You know why? Because I'm telling you everything that is happening out there and I'm conveying it all to you, but there are two things I am not doing. One is I am not pointing out any reason why you should not stay depressed and give up—and there are some. The other is that we are not together trying to figure out how to do something about this. This course is not sufficiently practical."

In the same way, I am going to be dealing with some of that frustration here. I do intend to give and not to mitigate all the bad news. At the same time, I think we have to look, if only to maintain momentum, at the parts of what we have done with feminism in law that have moved us forward. One is that we are here. This is a first that I am really glad to be a part of. I am only sorry that it did not happen a whole lot earlier. That is the bitter side of firsts.

Just the fact that we have prioritized and gotten as far as we have, just the fact that there is so much vital activity in each of these clusters, just the fact that women are in court and are being heard—sometimes, at least—in a different voice makes a difference. It makes a difference in the same way that I told the students in my gay rights class: "Just the fact that we are here matters." The fight to get that course in that, or any other, law school was phenomenal. Along with being ruthlessly critical of ourselves (as I think we must be), I think we also have to step back and say we are here and we are asking these questions and we are unlikely to treat the issues that we are raising in the same callous, disregarding way that the system historically, and most men historically, have treated issues of sex and sexuality.

Now, I want to take a position here, clear the air, get the morning going—"jump in." All the rest of this may be seen as very soft, but now it's going to get hard. Here is my position. I have to find it in my notes. [Laughter.] No matter how strongly held it is, I want to say it right. It has to do with these clusters, and with enjoying equality in opportunity, ending sexist violence, healing, being freer, and having opportunities that are sometimes not even imagined. Like the Olympics. When you watched the men's events, did you, from time to time, think that women could be doing that, too? And you sort of said: "Hey, it's neat watching the Olympics, but what's this?" Or maybe you even had a World Series wrecked for you by thinking that thought. Maybe somebody sat next to you in front of the television and said: "Well, that's very fine, a World Series—but where are the women?"

What I want to say is that when we consider redistributing the power and the resources and the strength (materially, physically, spiritually, and every other way you can redistribute resources), there are several options. One is the option of erring in favor of equality over other approaches. One (and a very common option it is) is keeping the status quo, because changing it seems all too hard. Underlying that is the belief which is, if not widespread, at least common enough that it rears its ugly head with some regularity: the belief that men are better. "Tough luck, honey. That's the way it is, because men are better. Men are stronger, men are smarter, men are this, men are that. Yes, women are this, and let's say some nice compensatory things about the girls, but society is the way it is because men are better." That is another response to the question of redistribution of resources. It is very real, and I suggest to you that, although we do not like to think so, it has a lot of adherents, both casual and die-hard.

So there is the equality approach to redistribution and there is the "men-are-better" approach. Let me suggest to you that there is the "women-are-better" approach. The "women-are-better" approach commends itself to those of us who want to believe that we are better. This is something we want to think when we look at the stuff that we identify as being correlated with men—and I can talk from cruise missiles on up and down. But people tune us out if we say: "Everything we see tells us women are better. We do not want equal distribution of the resources, we want to be in charge. We merely want our turf. O.K.?"

Now, it's crucial to remember that whether or not one is loyal to the principle of equality does not necessarily depend on one's beliefs. Lots of men buy the status quo because they believe they're better. Other men say in the backs or fronts of their minds: "Well, she is really not going to do that well, but we will give her a chance." What I am saying is that when all else fails, we should try at least to equalize opportunity. Let us see if we can reduce those instances of wrong that are correlated with gender. This, I suggest, is an integral part of the equality model. And that process is not necessarily precluded by one's belief that one gender or another is "better."

I want to offer an illustration. A very popular stereotype is that women are compassionate healers, that we are the ones to fix things and nurture. Now the temptation is to discard the stereotypes. How sad. Some of those very same values—nurturing and compassion and healing—are precisely what is making feminism have its best and greatest impact in a long time. We cannot afford to defy the patriarchy in the same way that one defies an abusive parent—"*everything* you say or do is wrong," and "everything we have said and done that makes you think we are a certain way is wrong." We cannot permit this. As to the operation of moral values through feminism, I suggest that we, those of us who are feminists, men and women alike, are challenged to choose, from all of the imagery, that which is closest to what we believe, care about, and can move forward through our minds and hearts and everything we have to offer. It is terribly important not to get caught in the categorizations in either direction. Categorizations are whipsaws. "Oh, women are more emotional than men." This one I always love. The last time I heard somebody say that seriously, the person was a male law professor ripping the microphone cord out of the wall while it was malfunctioning. The problem with that is, if you get offended by it, you are getting offended by emotions. Do not get offended by emotions—we need them all. We need the full range of emotion. In court we need anger (wow, do we need it). We need compassion. We need tenderness. We need all the things that make the legal system, or could make the legal system, more of a healer and less of a slayer. And those values I suggest are feminist. They are not necessarily female, but they are feminist—and I think that the challenge is not to live up or down to anybody's stereotypes. That is a very real challenge.

So I have taken my position on that. I am in favor of equality; I do not favor supremacy even as sweet as the vengeance would seem. No! I confess that. I favor equality because I think it's going to move us all toward a better place for people—for women, who are my first priority, and for men, who are my other priority.

MacKinnon: I am really glad to be here to have what is openly billed as a dialogue within feminism, particularly as it is clearly premised on a rather unusual assumption: All women are not the same.

I want to talk about the terrain of feminism, which has to do with relations between the sexes. I want to speak in particular about this principle of equality that Mary alluded to, and make reference to some particular legal applications in the doctrinal area of sex discrimination, which is (supposedly, at least) one area of law where the equality principle is fielded.

One question that feminism poses is: "What is the gender question a question of?" I see two answers. The first answer has historically been the politically dominant, legally and conceptually: The gender question is a question of difference. There are two options under it. The first option I call the "male standard": Women can be the *same* as men. In law, it is called gender neutrality. The other option I call the "female standard": You can be *different* from men. In law, it is called special protection. These bear a remarkable parallel resemblance to the masculine and the feminine.

The other answer to the question, a dissident view from the

dominant mainstream legal and political position and discourse, is that gender is a question of dominance. In this answer, the issue of discrimination or inequality is not centrally one of accurate categorization, as it is in the first. It is one of hierarchy, the top and the bottom of a hierarchy are different all right, but that is hardly all. One part of the distinction is dominant, and the other part of the distinction is subordinate.

From this second standpoint—which is my answer to the gender question—we see that the two standards in the first answer are two different versions of the male standard. If you see gender as a hierarchy—in which some people have power and some people are powerless, relatively speaking—you realize that the options of either being the same as men or being different from men are just two ways of having men as your standard. Men are set up as a standard for women by saying either: "You can be the same as men, and *then* you will be equal," or, "You can be different from men, and then you will be *women*."

This runs right through sex discrimination law, with a parallel in race discrimination. Just as men set both of those standards according to a standard of masculinity, and just as that standard is the standard of power and the standard of human, as well as the ruling definition of equal treatment (which is to say, "sameness," "same as," suppresses the fact that the referent for the "same as" is *men*), white culture sets the standard of racial equality according to a standard of whiteness. That standard too, supresses its referent; to define racial equality as based on "sameness" is, in a white supremacist society, to establish white as the standard by which one is assessed the "same" or not. Due to the political struggle of Black Americans in this country, people are more used to thinking about equality in terms of race. With race you also either have an implicit sameness standard or you understand that what you are dealing with is white supremacy. Similarly, with sex we either have a difference/sameness approach or we understand that what we are dealing with is male supremacy.

In my opinion, to take the differences approach is to take a moral approach, whereas to criticize hierarchy is to take a political approach. To take a differences view is also to take a liberal view (although that view, of course, includes conservatism as well), and to take the view that we are dealing with a hierarchy is to take a radical approach. I also think that to make issues of gender turn on the so-called gender difference is, ultimately, to take a male perspective. I therefore call the differences approach masculinist. The position that gender is first a political hierarchy of power is, in my opinion, a feminist position.

Now I am going to talk in some detail about the differences approach: the question of gender as a question of difference. The problem it targets is actually very important—having been entirely hard on it so far. I think its problem is how to value what women are, have been, have achieved, have become—while also demanding that we should get access to everything that we have been excluded from becoming, being, and having. The way this approach works in law is by conforming normative rules to empirical reality. In other words, you try to make your rules track a gender line which is accurate and real in the world. When it asks that we make categorizations that are fair, it means that we should treat likes alike and unlikes unlike. You will hear echoes of Aristotle in both the mainstream Supreme Court sex discrimination doctrines and in the work of most feminists. (In this I include, for instance, Wendy Williams' work. I also think it is a perspective implicit in some of the things Mary has said, although I do not mean to imply that she is necessarily going to want to defend it when I am done.) Legally, this standard runs under the rubric of gender neutrality. The real impulse behind it is: We're as good as you. Whatever you can do, we can do. Just let us do it. I have to say I really feel a lot of affection for this, the impulse behind the single standard. Set your standard; let us meet it. This view expresses a fundamental motive force behind most feminism, particularly in law: Just let us be persons. In athletics, it's: just let us compete. In academic and professional areas, it's: you define what merit is, we will meet it. In non-traditional jobs, in which I include lawyers and blue-collar workers, it's: you want thirty pounds lifted; watch us do it. You see it in the firefighting cases, the police cases, and so on.

This approach also underlies one side of the debate about the draft. Implicit in, "We can fight too," is, "What's the matter—don't you want us to learn to kill?" You see how much women just want to be members of this society when you try these cases. In my practice it really is moving to realize how much women just want to do the work. The draft issue is similar: wanting to pay the full price of citizenship. Imagine having to fight for that. To be against the draft means going to jail, too; why shouldn't the consequences of my choices count like yours count?

The first drawback of this view has been that it does not deal with what are taken to be real differences. There *are* some. For instance, pregnancy, an ability which some women have and all men do not. They lack it. What this means is that if one enters a world in which the standard is already constructed according to an implicit but suppressed male referent, you have a marketplace structured according to a male biography, a male-based series of social expectations, wherein only those women who are the most like that are the same as that, and therefore have a right to be treated equally by this definition of equality. There is no critique of the standard itself as gender based. Only women who are most *like* the male norm are advanced or advantaged by this notion of equality—as women of the right have tried to point out to those who have been willing to listen. Another disadvantage of the sameness approach, which I will articulate in expressly feminist terms, is that what we get in these cases—the athletic cases, the academic cases, and so on—is the right to pay the price of admission that men are supposed to pay but often do not, simply because they are benefited by that affirmative action plan for white men otherwise known as American society.

There is, however, a deeper critique of this standard: we can play with the boys but we cannot question competition as a measure of merit. We can think but we are not allowed to question objectivity as the measure of what we know. We are allowed to compete but we are not allowed to question competition as the test of accomplishment. Nor do we get to criticize conflict as a peculiarly ejaculatory means of conflict resolution.

I have talked about the sameness standard—what it gets us, what it does not, what we (or I, anyway) feel moved by in it, where it lets us down. When I read women's accounts of struggling with the decision of whether or not to have an abortion, I see how the sameness standard has let women down because there is no moral equivalent to abortion in the life of a man. The sameness standard has also let women down with regard to comparable worth. That is why we are having such trouble with it: There are no men around to compare with. They have other alternatives. How do we determine what equal treatment is if there are no men around to be made equal with? In the comparable worth cases, the struggle is to find men to be comparable with, when, because of sex segregation, men do other things, better things.

The other alternative the differences approach gives you is to ground equality claims *in* difference: "We are different from you." We want this difference equally accommodated. Legally, this has been codified as the special protection rule in sex discrimination law. It does not have to be limited to that. That is what it has meant, however, in men's hands. Women say: "We want to be taken on our own terms." Male-supremacist logic transforms that to: "You want to be treated as a woman," and men define what a woman is.

Having said what the single standard does for us, I would like to say a couple of things about what the double standard has done for us. Well, there were those protective laws that said all those things we could not do and all those stools we had to have to sit on, and how our reproductive organs would be abused if we were to work X number of hours.

Dunlap: Much less, if we were to run free.

MacKinnon: Yes, much less to actually run. But not corsets—not to mention what those did to our reproductive organs—or those shoes. The double standard, however, has obtained three more years for us to work for advancement in the military hierarchy before we had to be booted out or advanced up. It obtained for those women who were able to inherit money from men, in the state of Georgia, a certain percentage tax break to the tune of Justice Douglas waxing eloquent about economic discrimination against all women. In the past it has gotten us the maternal preference in custody of children—no small thing, children being one of the few "things" women have ever taken away from men, from the time when children, with women, were regarded as male property. It got us exclusion from contact prison guard jobs in male-only prisons because we might be raped. I call that looking at women from the standpoint of the reasonable rapist—adopting *that* as the standard for women's employment, as equal protection of the laws.

"Slippery slopes" work if you are liberals and you are in the position of being able to push people down them, right? When something would help us, they say, "You can't have that; that's the start of a slide down the slippery slope." I think women have already slid all the way to the bottom and are trying to crawl up.

The fertility protection gambit is a way to protect women *out of* jobs by making the potential interest of a possible fetus and the fact that that fetus might be legally real enough to sue them, might have some legal rights later, a reason for recognizing no legal rights to jobs for women *now*. This is the kind of thing that the double standard has gotten us. It has helped us, essentially, either to protection or to exclusion, which have amounted to the same thing. We've found out that this protection is a protection racket in which the "protectors" can violate us at will. And exclusion means that the minute you say, "I would appreciate it if you would take my particularities into account," they are very happy to take them into account by making sure that your particularities are nowhere around them.

The double standard is rather beautifully articulated in Carol Gilligan's book, *In a Different Voice*. Again, I do not mean that the only way one can accommodate the perspective that women have something distinctive to offer social life is by a double standard under discrimination law. The importance of the recognition that women are different has had to do with valuing women's experience—not only the experience of relatedness, responsibility, and care virtues, but also the experience reflected in the following insight, which is the impulse behind the discipline of women's history in many respects: "Wait a second. You may have defined history as wars, empires, governments, and so on, but we were there, too." This insight is effective only if you count what we were there *for* and what we were *doing* there, and only if you can see that other things are going on in society besides those things that men have measured as valuable. Women make history. Quilts are art. Those gardens are expression and creativity. A shorthand way of saying this is that, men notwithstanding, man is *not* "the measure of all things."

Up to now I've been talking about one answer to the equality question—the "difference" answer. I have not talked about who has power over whom, although there has been a sensitivity as to who sets the standards. In the view I have just characterized, we saw gender as a *difference* first and as an *inequality* second. In this second view I am suggesting, gender is a question of inequality first. The question is not so much how to make rules fit reality, but rather how to change reality. This perspective, this dissident view, criticizes the empirical world and the standards that are part of it. It criticizes the standards that set us up to be either the same as men or different from men; it criticizes the requirement that we have to define ourselves in terms of men. Its agenda is one of explaining and criticizing what women have had little choice to become, in order to change it.

Here I should quickly supply some facts. Consider that thirty-eight percent of young girls are sexually abused as children by older men in their dominant family unit with whom they are close. That is true for ten percent of boys. (Gender comparisons of little kids are about the only ones that make sense.) About forty to forty-four percent of women are either raped—in the usual legal sense of the word, not including marital rape—or are victims of an attempted rape. Around eighty-five percent of all women are, or have been, sexually harassed in the workforce at some point.

DuBois: Could you please cite your source?

MacKinnon: The bibliography appears in volume one of *Law and Inequality: A Journal of Theory and Practice*,[8] my debate with Phyllis Schlafly. One source that does not appear there is Diana Russell's latest article on child sexual abuse, in which she found that thirty-eight percent of all girls are victims of child sexual abuse.[9] The battery figure for women is between one-fourth and one-third. As for prostitution—as far as we can tell (statistics are hard to get a hold of, for reasons that are obvious)—apparently about twelve to fifteen percent of all American women are, or have been, prostitutes, by which is meant they make or have made their living more-or-less exclusively through the sale of their sexuality. The data on economics is also well known: a woman makes fifty-nine cents for every dollar a man makes, and that gap is widening. The segregation on jobs, too, is well known. And, the pornography industry, an excellent example of the dominance model, makes the sex difference sexy to the tune of $8 billion a year in entertainment. One manifestation of being a member of a degraded group must be that people call your torture and humiliation entertainment and pay a lot of money to enjoy it.

Few people, I have found, even Phyllis Schlafly, are interested

8. MacKinnon, *Excerpts from MacKinnon/Schlafly Debate*, L. & INEQUALITY: J. OF THEORY & PRAC. 341, 351-53 (1983).

9. Russell, *The Incidence and Prevalence of Intrafamilial and Extrafamilial Sexual Abuse of Female Children*, 7 CHILD ABUSE & NEGLECT 137 (1983).

in calling this picture the sex difference. Is it the sex difference to be targeted for rape, to be sexually molested, to be set up to be bought and sold, and then to be trivialized and humiliated, passed around, patted, put in place, and told to smile about it? None of these issues are traditionally seen as equality issues. Isn't that interesting? I think that is partly because, when these issues are seen at all, they are seen as issues of force, and sex inequality is *not* seen as an issue of force. Racial inequality, by contrast, *is* seen as a question of force, not just as a question of racial differences.

What this all means is that women are a subordinate group. And nothing is being done about it. Really, nothing. This abuse is passing unacknowledged as the sex difference, while the issues that are litigated as sex discrimination issues are seen as differentiation problems against a reality which is fundamentally equal. The practices I just described are that reality. Dominance and submission made into sex, made into the gender difference, constitute the suppressed social content of the gender definitions of men and women.

When you look at that, it makes a lot of sense that women might have a somewhat distinctive perspective on social life. We may or may not speak in a different voice—I think that the voice that we have been said to speak in is in fact in large part the "feminine" voice, the voice of the victim speaking without consciousness. But when we understand that women are forced into this situation of inequality, it makes a lot of sense that we should want to negotiate, since we lose conflicts. It makes a lot of sense that we should want to urge values of care, because it is what we have been valued for. We have had little choice but to be valued this way. It sure would be nice if somebody would care for *us*. Women of the right speak particularly strongly about values of responsibility. They are responsible; it would be nice if men would live up to their end of the bargain. It makes a lot of sense that women should claim our identity in relationships because we have not been allowed to have a social identity on our own terms. As to whether these values are women's, possessive, voice, I think that women's silence—and, for the same reasons, the damage to women's sexuality—goes deeper than the absence of words; it is the absence of life, of the ability to live in security or wholeness—hence, the inability to articulate or to express. This prior absence does affect questions of morality. If the first problem of inequality is the problem of the subordination of women and not the inaccurate differentiation between people on the basis of sex, it is inappropriate to discuss the reality or proposition of treating women as sub-human as a matter of good versus evil. Appropriate, instead, is an argument and a discussion about empowerment, about power. Gender then becomes a question of how people who do not have power are going to get some, and how people who do not have a voice are going to be able to speak in anything other than a male voice in a higher register. It is about how this romance with gender, elaborately played out as either sameness or difference, is going to be turned into something that is *not* going to look like our freedom to be feminine, which keeps us where we have been placed, but rather like something which values us for what we are without keeping us there; *not* our freedom to be masculine, but our right to have access to everything men have always kept for themselves whether we do with it what they have done with it, or not.

The freedom we have is so small compared to the kind of freedom that we could have if we transformed this society, if we were able to get this foot off our necks. If somebody has got their foot on your neck, what do you do? I don't think you negotiate. I don't think you compromise. I don't think you even address the foot on your neck in your own voice, such as it is, and attempt to persuade it to move off. You try to figure out how to get it up off of you so that you can, among other things, have something to say.

Marcus: We have two choices here: We can have the present conversation continue or we can bring in new people. I would like to be able to carry on a conversation among all of us. Now, in doing that, what I am going to ask is that we talk *with* each other, rather than ask questions simply to expand, increase, or create polarities. I'm not suggesting that we can't debate, but I am asking that questions be asked to *expand* the discourse.

Question from audience: I was really thrilled by the focus of looking at gender as hierarchy. It struck me that there might be a difference between lawyers and other people. What feminism discovered was a way to discuss hierarchy. If we looked at hierarchy in the past, we had to first make analysis between social classes, and then we had to make analysis of minority groups, then nations. Only after we analyzed all the other forms of hierarchy did we get to talk about gender hierarchy. I felt it was very clearly stated. It put us where we should be. But then I was surprised at the narrowing down of the focus to primarily issues of sex. It seems to me that sexuality is an area of both power for, as well as victimization of, women. I feel also that, at least for many women, the experience of hierarchy is not simply an issue of violence. There are other areas—look at *Good Housekeeping* or *Vogue*—that are as violent to me as the issues that are discussed in the areas of pornography and rape. Every time we deal with hierarchy, must we deal with violence and then right away tie that violence to sexual expression? In my mind, there are problems doing this because I think sexuality can be power for women, though I also think it gets us into trouble. I wondered whether you—since you've narrowed it down so simply—can help us redirect the focus. I'm concerned about this because I think in the long run it represents a very conservative element for the women's movement.

MacKinnon: I don't think that I did exactly the narrowing that you said I did, although in the data that I cited, which is about reality, I did select indications of sexual violence. I think that those indications are not episodic. They are data that structure a world in which women live with the constant possibilities of sexual violence. By violence I mean both the narrow form and the broader form of violation involved in essentially being defined in terms of sex all the time. And so, yes, I did mean to narrow the focus, but I did not mean to make it seem as though the only events that are relevant to the construction of a subordinated gender status have to do with those particular moments in which we can see that delivered in its most forcible form. Consider the data on lynching. The percentages are one thing, but the fact that Black people walk through life knowing that at any point that can happen to them—and that nothing will be done about it—is as crucial and as central a point. It is how racism works as terrorism. All women are also targeted as women. Women deal with this in a lot of different ways. Among the ways that women deal with this is denial—just in order to get through the day. Another way women deal with it is to eroticize it. In fact, one not very pleasant way of looking at what is often described as women's sexuality or female sexuality all the way through the masochism tradition is to suggest that it is the eroticized response to our subordinate status. In other words, it suggests that part of women's stake in gender is our own sexual pleasure, as that has been socially constructed in us. What if sexually oppressed people sexualize our oppression? I mean to say it that way in order to extend it into its softer forms. And I do think of myself as a feminist first and a lawyer second.

Dunlap: A couple of things. I appreciated your observations, particularly about gender as a hierarchy. The last time that someone attributed the sameness position to me was in a debate with Phyllis Schlafly. Ironically, I have never taken the position, and I believe Wendy Williams has not either, although she can defend herself. (Can she ever!) I have never taken the position that men should define merit and that we then should equal it. Pardon me, but that's crap. I take the position that the values that we are conveying and pursuing are related to gender and at the same time deeper than gender.

Let me see if I can give you an example. One that comes to mind is our relationships with children. Kitty MacKinnon's statistics on child abuse are interesting. Thirty-eight percent of female children are abused and ten percent of males. That by itself ought to tell us that sexist violence does not necessarily focus upon women. Men are raped (I can speak to this, coming from San Francisco and being close to a gay male community that has a facet of violence that goes well beyond rape), men are beaten in the street, called "fags," and killed. This is frequent all over the country. If that is not sexist violence, then I am not quite sure what it is. If the bond among women is based primarily upon opposition to men and a belief that it is only women who can be raped, then, I think, we have missed the boat.

I want to read a couple of quotes that crystallized for me my position with relation to this question about sexuality and the eroticization of exploitive sexuality. The first is from a book called *Understanding Women: A Feminist Psychoanalytic Approach* by Susie Orbach and Luise Eichenbaum. The authors are talking about seeing the future in terms of women and men in relationships: gay, lesbian, heterosexual, bisexual, and friendships. They say about friendships between women: "In friendship perhaps all women will be able to achieve what has begun to be achieved as a result of the women's movement: honest, loving relationships, built not on fear, betrayal, competition, or envy, and not on solidarity in opposition to men, but on sharing contact between equals, and support for autonomy."[10]

On the specific question of the eroticization of exploitive sexuality or exploitive sexual behavior, I offer a little piece of an introduction to a book that I found tremendously inspiring and well written: *Powers of Desire: The Politics of Sexuality*, edited by Snitow, Stansell, and Thompson. The introduction is I think *apropos* of not just the pornography issue, but, more broadly, the issue of whether we posit narrowly or broadly our reactions to this tremendous factual reality of assault. Do we take care of women as a response? Do we fight back and defend ourselves as a response? Do we make law that affords remedies and options and voices, for example, to victims of incest now seeking restitution and compensation? Do we legislate about pornography? On that subject, or at least anticipating that subject, about a year and a half ago, the editors of this book wrote:

> Those who created the modern women's movement could choose sex because it did not carry the same punitive consequences that it carried for previous generations of women, and we *have*, by and large, chosen sex. This is a victory, one both furthered and truncated by historical circumstance but one, certainly, that we grasped for ourselves, not out of false consciousness but out of desire and the impulse for freedom. This is not to imply that sexual violence does not continue to limit and shape our possibilities. But it is to affirm, at the same time, women's potential for autonomy and power. We need to do this at every level of feminism, in grassroots organizing as well as in intellectual work. We are on a long march. . .elevating one set of sexual practices over others—from whatever position on the feminist spectrum—as more correct, more fulfilling, or even more sexy only retards this process.[11]

Here is where I had a concrete problem with Kitty's position on rape and its relationship to heterosexual sexuality. As I read the articles, and I may have misread them, they take the position (and I see in the pornography ordinances a position close to this) that heterosexual sexuality is most of the time rape, that rape is male, that being raped is female, that women do not rape, men do, and that women are raped and men are not.

The position is then taken (paraphrasing from the "View-

10. S. Orbach & L. Eichenbaum, Understanding Women: A Feminist Psychoanalytic Approach 197 (1983).

11. Powers of Desire: The Politics of Sexuality 41-42 (A. Snitow, C. Stansell & S. Thompson eds. 1983).

point" article[12]) that, like heterosexuality, in relation to the crime of rape, penetration is not what is wrong with rape. It is not penetration that makes it rape. It is the inequality that goes with the situation that precludes consent that makes it rape. Thus, penetration is not definitive. I then look in the pornography ordinance at the operating definition of pornography and I discover that penetration is at the heart of the definition. Again we may be misattributing views to one another.

Andrea Dworkin has taken the position that the penis is the problem. I want to say something about *The Politics of Desire*, because I don't believe the penis is the problem. I believe that it is very often the source of many problems, but I do not believe the penis is the problem. The phrasing is more than just a semantical problem. Here is an essay entitled "My Mother Liked to Fuck" by Joan Nesley, an activist lesbian. Nesley found herself one afternoon at a workshop on pornography and was thinking of her deceased mother, who loved to fuck:

> As Andrea Dworkin's litany against the penis rang out that afternoon, I saw my mother's small figure with her ink-stained calloused hands never without a cigarette held out towards me, I saw her face with a slight smile, so Joan, is this the world you wanted for me, the world you wanted me to have where I should feel shame and guilt for what I like, and what I did for all the years of my life? I fought the rapist and the batterer and I did not give up my knowledge of what I liked. Do not scream penis at me, but help to change the world so no woman feels shame or fear because she likes to fuck, because she likes to fuck men, women, herself, in private, as an adult, (with consent, those are my restrictions).[13]

I agree emphatically with the latter part of what you said. When we narrow our response to these horrendous, hair-raising, important factual descriptions of reality (I will not even contest the percentages—I think, if anything, they are low) to a symbolic attack upon a body of literature and media (some of which is just as sickening as anything can be, some of which is erotic, and not all of which is either), what we do is take on a symbolic situation in which we are by definition *not* directly, taking care of the men and the women who are victims of these phenomena.

Comment from audience: It seems to me that the men that you

---

12. MacKinnon, *Feminism, Marxism, Method, and the State: An Agenda For Theory* (pts. 1 & 2), 7 SIGNS 515 (1982), 8 SIGNS 635, 647 (1983).

13. J. Nesley, *My Mother Liked to Fuck*, in POWERS OF DESIRE, *supra* note 11, at 468-70.

refer to, that were getting raped, were mostly gay men. It seems to me that the issue there is power again—force violence—and that the basis of the inequality in that case may not be gender, but sexual orientation. And, furthermore I suppose that there is a small percentage of straight men that are raped, but then I think we have to ask ourselves who is raping them. If you were to cite statistics that say that the majority of straight men that are raped are raped by women, then I would think we have a problem; but if we can identify that it is straight men that are doing the raping, then I think that the crux of the problem is still the same.

Another comment from audience: More often than not I find myself in a position, at least emotionally, of thinking: "What could be so wrong with female supremacy?" If we are all interested in equality, it seems to me to be really equal, given that men have had power for so many hundreds of thousands of years, that it should be our turn now—let us have our shot at the helm, and then we can talk about equality. For a second "academic" question, which is a little more attuned to the passion that I feel about this issue, I would like to ask Catharine MacKinnon: What do you espouse or what would you advocate in terms of a feminist standard for addressing these inequalities in the law? Are you advocating *one* standard, granting that we have different values, that we have different measures that would obviously characterize the problems at this point? And if you are, are we not going to run into the same sort of problems?

MacKinnon: Some women talk about female supremacy. It is not my position. One of the things you learn by being on the bottom is something that you do not forget: what it feels like to be kicked. So long as your alternatives are only kicking or getting kicked, if you remember what getting kicked was like, kicking may make you sick or it may make you turned on, or you may choose it over the alternative.

I will answer your question, the last one, and I will also talk a little bit about the pornography ordinance which Andrea Dworkin and I wrote and which Mary has taken the occasion to attack. I do urge—as a litigation strategy, as a way of doing briefs, and as a deep implicit as well as explicit argument—that the equality principle can mean that no group should be subordinated to another group on the basis of sex. We could use the term "subordination" *that* way, leaving the gender neutrality glossed the way I just did.

The other possibility is to say straightforwardly (in a sort of "thirteenth amendment" version of what an ERA could look like): "The subordination of women is hereby abolished." In other words, here we are in this legal system that, essentially, makes differences out of everything, abstract rules out of every substantive thing that it is given. It is an abstraction machine; it splits up and fractures anything. So, for instance, you say to it: "The subordination of women is hereby abolished." You put it in such affirmative terms that it means *whenever and wherever* such subordination is encountered, something should be done about it; you use the truly forbidden word, the truly obscene word, "women," in your law. This is not gender-neutral in the abstract sense, for it says the gender-specific word "women." The initial danger is that it will be interpreted in a way that applies to everything else that looks abstractly like it, raising the question: "If you do anything substantive, how do you keep control?" But we haven't kept control of the abstract strategies either, and *all* women have gotten very little out of them.

I want to talk now about our pornography ordinance. We made the choice to write a law to give women the ability to take legal action against pornography. It does not empower the state in the direct way that an obscenity law does. In that sense our law does not pose an issue of the state against the people, the way the ACLU would have you believe. It instead concerns people against other people. It attempts to give some people—women in particular, but men, too, who are hurt by pornography on the basis of their sex—a cause of action against the people whom they can prove hurt them. An amazing notion: if there is an injury, there should be a remedy. We decided to define pornography for what it is: something which *subordinates* women. Penetration is not at the heart of the definition, nor is the penis. Pornography is defined as the sexually explicit subordination of women through pictures or words. One of a list of concrete things also has to be there: women finding pleasure in rape, in pain, being humiliated, in postures of submission or display, being tortured or hurt—a long list of particulars. The only reference to penetration actually in there is that of being penetrated by objects or animals. One must also add, however, sexually explicit subordination. This is the pornographers' definition of pornography. They know what has to be there for it to work. We just described it.

The second part of the definition spells out that men, children, or transsexuals who are used in the place of women also have a cause of action, so that what is made through their use is pornography. This design is actually a new legal approach to the question of inequality in general, and of sexual inequality in particular. It is both sex-specific and gender-neutral. It is sex-specific because it defines pornography as pornography is. It defines pornography in terms of what it does to women, but it acknowledges that what pornography does is make inequality sexy—it reflects an understanding that *whoever* is on the bottom is *the girl*, regardless of whether that person be a woman, a man, a transsexual, or a child. If you look at what happens in gay male rape and talk to those male victims, they know that they have been treated like women. It is part of the insult. If you look at what happens with rape in prison, you know that the one who gets repeatedly raped is the *girl*. You understand that what it is to be female is to be targeted and stigmatized on the basis of your sexuality; you can tell it is a stigma and not just your identity by the fact that when it is transferred to somebody who does not share your biology everybody knows it is an insult. So, the law we drafted defines the harm sex specifically and then says: "If you treat other people that way, that is also an injury."

I think that anything that functions socially, on an on-going basis, to make inequality sexy can not be dismissed as mere symbolism. To say that this is merely a symbolic attack is to ignore the abuse of women that is directly tied to it. There is nothing symbolic about this abuse or our law's confrontation of it. People are coerced into pornography and assaulted because of it. Pornography is directly forced on people. If the people are children, they develop the same symptoms in later life as if they had had the sex forced on them. To reduce pornography to symbol ignores the documented facts that connect pornography with rape, battery, forced prostitution, child sexual abuse, and sexual harassment. This is not to say that all those things would automatically go away if pornography were eliminated. It is clear we are in a system that needs all of those things and that they are all mutually supportive. But few argue that we should do nothing about rape because it is just symbolic of women's status, and besides it is too hard to distinguish from intercourse, just as pornography is too hard to distinguish from erotica. That is, by the way, the same line, except with pornography it is easier because you have the real stuff in front of you. With rape, women have to be believed and nobody believes our story about rape because it looks like a story about intercourse. And that is partly because people have been looking at pornography.

Spiegelman: We are now going to have a second conversation between Carol Gilligan and Carrie Menkel-Meadow. It is a great personal pleasure for me to moderate this panel because Carol's research has informed my own work as well as Carrie's. I believe Carol's careful documentation of a different moral voice in the decision-making processes of the individual has profound implications for all of us concerned with the way people relate to each other, to the law, and to society. It gives new meaning to the feminist slogan "the personal is political" because it locates in women's personal experience a morality of care and concern for others which has the potential to transform our polity and its underlying assumptions from the alienated world of atomistic competition to an interconnected world of mutual cooperation.

As the conversation between Carol and Carrie will illustrate, that transformation can begin with a style of discourse different from the adversarial mode which seems to dominate much of our academic and political communication. One of the most illuminating aspects of the interaction between Carol and Carrie is the contrast between its cooperative mode and the more common combative one. Often lost in the heat of conflict and hostile analysis are the opportunities for synthesis generated by the kind of supportive, responsive interchange which characterizes the conversation which follows.

Gilligan: Carrie and I talked about how we wanted to proceed this afternoon, and we thought that we really wanted to have a conversation about the legal implications of different ways of constructing and thinking about resolving conflict situations, moral problems, and so forth. There is a real advantage here for me: My work was not done from a legal perspective, although the law was very present at the beginning stages of my work and raised a question for me which has persisted throughout it. We thought it would be a good idea if I began by presenting a summary of the work that I have done as a psychologist, including recent work which has not been published. We will then have a discussion, in which Carrie (since she is a lawyer) will be centrally involved, about some of the legal implications of the issues on which I have worked.

I wanted to say at the outset that all of my research in a sense was indebted to the Supreme Court and its 1973 abortion decision. I was a psychologist interested initially in the question of the relationship between judgment and action. I thought that a field that studied conflict—and, specifically, moral conflict—by looking at how people resolve hypothetical dilemmas was fooling itself and that we had to look at how people dealt with real situations of conflict and choice, where people had to live with the consequences of their decisions. It is easy to say what someone should do in some hypothetical place; it is very different if you are *in* the place *at the time*. I was looking for a situation where people were faced with a decision which could have moral implications.

I began by studying Harvard students in the early 1970s who were going to face the Vietnam draft. Then—this should give you an idea of how research goes—Nixon ended the draft. There went my study. I was back at square one waiting for another setting in which to do a study of judgment and action. Then, in 1973, the Supreme Court legalized abortion. The last thing on my mind at the time was the fact that this would bring me into contact with a population of women. Though that question was not at the center of my work at the time, I am certain that my own thinking was very influenced by the resurgence of the women's movement. I began to interview women who were pregnant and for one reason or another were deciding whether or not to have abortions. I did not make any assumptions about whether this was a moral problem or about what the moral problem was, and this was absolutely key to the findings of my work. I did not say, "Well, here you are facing a decision between liberty and life—how do you resolve it?" or, "When do you think life begins and how does that affect your thinking about the morality of your decision?" I simply asked the women: "How did you get pregnant and how have you been thinking about it so far?" As women began to talk about their decision, I picked up moral language. Spontaneously, words appeared like "should," "ought," "right," "wrong," "good," and "bad." And I asked: "When you say, 'This would be the better thing to do,' or when you say, 'This would be wrong,' what do you mean?" As I began to follow the moral language which spontaneously appeared in women's narratives about decisions that they were actually making, I began to trace the construction of morality implied in this use of moral language. I ended up (I'm shortcutting several steps) calling this "a different voice." I deliberately called it a different voice; I did not call it a woman's voice. I am going to talk later about the whole issue of gender difference as it came into my work and as it appears in the current analysis of findings that my research group has done.

I called the construction of morality I heard a different voice because I was not comparing women with men. Rather, as indicated by my book's[14] subtitle—"Psychological Theory and Women's Development"—I was comparing women with theory. I said this voice is different from the voice that has been described in the psychology of moral development, in moral philosophy, and in the legal and political system which was sitting all around my work. The way in which women were talking about the moral problem in abortion did not fit the public discussion of abortion in this country. In other words, it was *not* construed as an adversary fight between the mother and the fetus. In fact, the whole dilemma arose from the very connection between them. Women perceived that there were two lives that were in fact interconnected. Women who were pregnant talked about the fact that if they took drugs they would hurt the fetus. Here, therefore, were two lives which were by definition interdependent, and connected physically for about nine months. You might ask how long the lives were connected *psychically*. The women sometimes said eighteen years, sometimes twenty years, sometimes forever. They asked, in effect, whether it is responsible or irresponsible, moral or immoral, to sustain and deepen an attachment under circumstances in which you cannot be, for whatever reason, responsible, and in which you cannot exercise care? Where they decided it was not, they sometimes then concluded that abortion might be the better thing to do—it would not necessarily be a good thing to do, nor the right thing to do. There was seen no "right" thing to do in this situation. It might be, however—and I quote from women just picked at random—"the lesser of two evils," "the better of two things," "the more responsible thing." If you are interested in all the kinds of ways in which that has meaning, I provide

14. C. GILLIGAN, IN A DIFFERENT VOICE—PSYCHOLOGICAL THEORY AND WOMEN'S DEVELOPMENT (1982).

a lot of examples in my book of how that construction was worked out and how it changed over time, and of the various things that women meant when they said "care" and "responsibility." But the main point was that the assumptions that underlie the "justice" approach or the "rights" approach were not being made, and in fact were being seen as a distortion and a deformation of the situation. Women realized that to say that they thought pregnancy meant a life, developing through time—if nothing intervened, accident or biology—into a child, meant that you could not bring the issue into the legal system. To enter the legal system, therefore, women had to act as though they did not know things that they felt they knew, and that they did not in a sense understand issues of connection which could not be represented within the adversarial-rights model which pitted one life against the other. I was therefore talking about a voice literally different from the voice represented in psychology, from the voice represented in moral philosophy (that psychology was wedding itself to), and from the voice that was represented in the legal system. I began to say: "Let us explore this difference." At this point I noticed that women had been left out of the psychology research samples; the interesting thing is not just the absence but also the fact that neither I nor so many others had noticed it before. It is such an enormous design flaw. How can organizations such as the National Institute of Mental Health and the National Institute of Child Health that pride themselves on reviewing research, have funded, year after year and for incredible amounts of money, studies that had all-male samples and never have seen this as a design problem? While we might not be able to say whether a study *concept* is good or bad, we certainly can identify a bad study *design*. Since I was in the middle of this, I became very interested. I wondered whether the representation of human development within psychology as well as in philosophy and law (since these disciplines are closely related to psychology) was not a distortion of female experience. I wondered further whether it was a distortion of male experience as well; was it a distortion of human experience—a very destructive distortion? When women wanted to speak about what they thought of as the dilemmas presented by a problematic pregnancy, they could not even represent what they wanted to say within these systems. It was negated. Its validity was negated and the system began to shake the reality.

I therefore began to look and notice instances of anomaly—where familiar stories were told with a new slant, or where words were being used in ways that were at odds with their usual meanings. Examples of this are taken from a study of high school kids. In 1980, the *Handbook of Adolescent Psychology* came out. The editor, Joseph Adelson, reported that he had asked a leading scholar to write a chapter on female adolescent development. But when she surveyed the literature, she concluded that there was not enough material available to write a chapter.[15] I came to tell you about my field, to warn you about its measures, its methods of assessment. I came to tell you that the standards of identity, standards of morality, notions about what is a "healthy" life are derived from research that has not looked at women's experience. It has just simply not looked. I thought I would like to look at adolescents to see what had been missed. I was particularly interested in adolescents because I had noticed that while girls at about ten or eleven years of age seemed to be quite outspoken and fairly sure of themselves, by nineteen they had developed an acute tendency toward self-doubt and self-questioning. There was a kind of hesitation among women, and even a kind of disbelief in their own ability to talk about reality, that was very troubling. I once interviewed a woman in her early twenties about a moral dilemma. She said: "Would you like to know what I think, or would you like to know what I *really* think?" I thought that this was very interesting; she had learned to "think" in a way that was very different from the way that she "really thought." I thought about that when I talked about secondary education and the failure of interpretive schemes to reflect women's experiences. I thought I would tell you about Amy and Jake, whom I wrote about in my book when they were eleven.[16] When they were interviewed again at the age of fifteen, the interview caught Amy at the moment where you could see the erosion of self-confidence starting to happen. During the re-interview, she was again asked about the Heinz dilemma, which is one of Kohlberg's standard dilemmas and one of the most frequently used instruments for assessing moral maturity.

In the Heinz dilemma there is a man, Heinz, who cannot af-

15. HANDBOOK OF ADOLESCENT PYSCHOLOGY 114 (J. Adelson ed. 1980).
16. *See* C. GILLIGAN, *supra* note 14, at 24-39.

ford to buy a drug that will save the life of his wife. The question is: Should he steal the drug? Amy said, "I hated these dilemmas last time as much as I do now," and she elaborated the same reasoning that she had given at eleven: "It all depends. What if the husband got caught? It would not help his wife. And anyway, from everything I know about cancer, it cannot be cured by a single treatment. And, where would this drug be, sitting out on the shelf of a drugstore? The whole situation is unreal."[17] She then said: "Like I had said last time [actually she had not], life comes before property. He should steal the drug."

That, by the way, is the "right" answer. She jumps a full stage in moral development, as measured by Kohlberg's scale—from eleven to fifteen years. But look what she has done now: She is learning that if she enters into a construction of reality which she has identified as unreal and problematic, she will advance in "moral development." In other words, if you equate moral development with justice reasoning, then, in a sense you render her more deeply uncertain, more susceptible to the tension between what she thinks and what she really thinks, less convinced that her voice will be heard.

I wanted to tell you about the re-interview of Jake at fifteen because that is very interesting, too. It tells us how psychological systems of assessment distort male as well as female thinking. Jake is the one who said at age eleven, that moral dilemmas are like "math problems with humans." Anyone who can do math can solve these problems and agree on what the right answer is: that is, that life comes before property. At fifteen, he says (beginning the same way he did at eleven): "Money comes and goes but human life only comes once, so therefore the wife's claim to her life takes precedence over the druggist's claim to his property." But then Jake is asked to comment about the fact that the druggist feels strongly about his profit. Jake responds: "He's got the wrong set of priorities." That's the approach that says there is one logical way to answer and that if you disagree it is because you do not understand or because you have the wrong set of priorities. We say in psychology that it is because you are at a lower stage. But then Jake says something else which is extremely interesting.

17. The comments of Jake and Amy are not direct quotations, but are a summary of the argument presented using the language of the transcribed interview.

He starts to consider the situation and the feelings that would be evoked both by theft and by death and he says: "I think that what the druggist is going to experience is some sorrow and some anger over losing his money, and it is a shame that he has to feel that." Look what Jake is doing now: he is not detaching himself from the druggist. Instead he is moving very close to the druggist to consider how a druggist would feel in that situation. But, he says: "It is not as deplorable a thing as the idea of Heinz—with his wife dying and him having to deal with his wife's dying."

The point I want to make is that, when measured by Kohlberg's scale of moral development, Jake does not show any evidence of moral development between eleven and fifteen because his justice reasoning has not changed. Thus, these interpretative schemes encourage Amy to become more deeply uncertain and Jake to become more simply dogmatic—to take the position that anyone who does not agree with him has "the wrong set of priorities." I want, for the sake of time, simply to talk about the implications of this. Three anomalies can be described very quickly: a new way of looking at an old story; a different way of looking at a familiar word; and two ways of using the word "responsibility" that have very different implications and that create a systematic process of misunderstanding and mistranslation.

A new way of looking at an old story: I am doing research at a girls high school. Because of the study, one of the teachers who was teaching a course called "From Innocence to Experience" noticed that the four books in this class—*Billy Budd, Lord of The Flies, A Separate Peace*, and *Othello*—had almost no female characters. She raised this issue with the class. First they read *Member of the Wedding*, but the students did not like it. So the next year she started to have them write essays entitled: "If I were Captain Vere (in *Billy Budd*)," or "If I were Abraham in the Abraham and Isaac story." This is an in-class example of these essays. One girl wrote:

> *Were I in Abraham's position, in a position of choosing between disobedience to God and sacrificing my son, my choice would clearly be disobedience to God. The reason for this is that if God is said to represent such things as love, and life, and truth, [and if God] were to give a command involving killing and making necessary lying . . . as Abraham does to his son, I would not wish to obey him and defy the qualities that I hold as important.*

In other words, it is not simply the command involving killing that is problematic; it is also the *necessity for lying*, meaning the necessity for Abraham's detachment from Isaac. The moral problem identified in this story is one of *detachment*, and the lying, as the sign of detachment, becomes the harbinger of violence. Emphasis on detachment as morally problematic rather than the moral ideal also appears at the end of the essay as the student does not detach herself from Abraham. Note also the vulnerability of this position. Its strength becomes its vulnerability. Look at the final move she makes:

> *This answer, however, is from a person who probably cannot even understand "fear of God" and who is treating it, the question, symbolically instead of literally. Perhaps if I had lived at the time and felt God's actual power and wrath my decision would be one of obedience.*

She locates herself in time, she defines herself as having a perspective, she says there are limits on how much she can understand, and so forth. You see the point.

A different way of looking at a familiar word: A girl is asked how she wants to improve herself, change in the future, and what she might like to change about herself. She says: "I'd like to improve or expand on my compassion." She continues: "I'm sometimes not very understanding. I have a habit of putting myself in another person's place which I have found is not fair." When I talk about anomaly, I talk about saying that what is defined as the essence of fairness is not fair. The girl writes that putting herself in other persons' shoes is not fair. Watch her reasoning. This is the kind of place where girls learn that their answers are "wrong": "That is not what we mean by 'fairness' "; "This is not what we call a 'moral problem' "—that kind of thing.

I have been looking at specifically discrepant data, data that are discrepant with the interpretive schemes. People use these words in ways that seem "wrong", and I ask from what perspective the usage is "right." For example, they feel that things are not "fair" when they would do things differently and think in a different way:

> *If they get angry I would say: "All right, how can I understand that?" I will put myself in her place, and I will say: "I would not become angry at that; that does not help very much."*

Look at the criteria—it is unfair because it does not really *help* very much. Help with what? Help with compassion? Help with understanding? Thus you see that detachment and objectivity, which are usually valued as ways of solving dilemmas, are now identified as the *problem*, the impediment to working out the problem. You see two modes of thinking that are not just "different," that are not just alternative, but are in fundamental tension. What is valued by one—detachment, impartiality, the ability to stand back, the figure of blind justice—is defined by the other perspective as "the problem."

So you have two ways of "looking" that are in essential tension with each other, a tension that does not resolve itself. Where does this tension come from developmentally in the life cycle? Let me tell you about what happens when you then go back and look at many women trying to see through this double set of lenses. When you have these two ways of seeing, focusing, and highlighting, in a sense revealing the same thing in a different light, you experience a constant blur—almost like astigmatism.

Two ways of using the word "responsibility": One high school girl says: "Responsibility means making a commitment and sticking to it." This is what we usually mean by responsibility: personal commitment and contractual obligation.

Another girl's answer to the same question:

> *Responsibility is when you are aware of others and you are aware of their feelings. Responsibility is taking charge of yourself by looking at others around you and seeing what they need and seeing what you need, and taking the "initiative," taking the initiative to respond to your perceptions of your own and their needs.*

Responsibility in this context means response. The concept of autonomy remains, but it is conveyed by the seemingly paradoxical conjunction of "taking charge of yourself by looking at others around you." It does not mean taking charge of yourself by separating yourself. Rather, it means taking charge of yourself by looking at others around you, seeing what you need, seeing what they need, and taking the initiative to respond. Doing something once you have seen it.

This is what I mean by two voices, two ways of speaking. One voice speaks about equality, reciprocity, fairness, rights; one voice speaks about connection, not hurting, care, and response. My point is that these voices are in tension with each other. In my work I have attempted to ask, "What does it mean to include both voices in defining the domain of morality, of humanity, and so forth?" I want to give one example that illustrates well what I think it means, and what this inclusion implies. I do not think it implies a simple addition, a kind of separate-but-equal thing or an androgynous solution. I think it implies a transformation in thinking.

The best way I can illustrate this is through an example provided by two four-year-olds who were playing together and wanted to play different games. The girl said: "Let's play next-door neighbors." The boy said: "I want to play pirates." "Okay," said the girl, "then you can be the pirate who lives next door." She has reached what I would call *an inclusive solution* rather than *a fair solution*—the fair solution would be to take turns and play each game for an equal period. "First we will play pirates for ten minutes and then we will play neighbors for ten minutes." Each child would enter the other's imaginative world. The girl would learn about the world of pirates and the boy would learn about the world of neighbors. It is a kind of tourism on a four-year-old's level. Really, it's simple. But the interesting thing is that neither game would change—the pirate game would stay the pirate game, and the neighbor game would stay the neighbor game. Both children would learn both games, hopefully for an equal period of time. It is what is called "androgyny."

Now look what happens in the other solution, what I would call *the inclusive solution*. By bringing a pirate into the neighborhood, both the pirate game and the neighbor game change. In addition, the pirate-neighbor game, the combined game, is a game that *neither* child had separately imagined. In other words, a new game arises through the relationship.

That is basically my point: The inclusion of two voices in moral discourse, in thinking about conflicts, and in making choices, transforms the discourse. It is no longer either simply about justice or simply about caring; rather, it is about bringing them together to transform the domain. We are into a new game whose parameters have not been spelled out, whose values are not very well known. We are at the beginning of a process of inquiry, in which the methods themselves will have to be re-examined because the old methods are from the old game.

I want now to tell you very quickly what you see when you look at both male and female thinking through these lenses. Immediately two things change—two equations that have prevailed and have formed a self-enclosed system.

The first is the equation of human with male. No longer can

we know about human development by studying men. All our definitions of identity, morality, power, and health that have been derived from studies of men's lives are suddenly held in question—they seem to be highly tentative and possibly problematic. We can not even know how problematic they are. We now begin to take the time to look at those lives we have never looked at in defining "power," "identity," "morality," "health," "well-being,"—you name it. There is a sense that once you see and take seriously this problem, everything else becomes provisional—all the categories of judgment and assessment.

The second equation, which has sustained the first, is the equation of virtue for women, or caring by women, with self-sacrifice. Look at how neatly that perpetuates the system. "Human" is male and female virtue or "care" is self-sacrifice. So the good woman who values care would sacrifice herself rather than challenge the equation of human with male. In a sense it is brilliant. That is why women in the name of morality have cooperated with these all-male systems. In psychology women have said: "Let us help you, in the name of care, to build this portrait, of human development"—a portrait, which I will now demonstrate, distorts male experience as well as female experience.

Now to the last part of this presentation: findings. We asked: "What do we learn from looking at women?" What did we learn? The abortion study was the first study that drew moral categories from the analysis of women's language and thought. The first study *ever*. So we said: "Let's take the categories that we have drawn from this—how women in fact empirically define the moral domain, by looking at women's use of moral language." And everybody said: "That's not a moral problem." We said: "Well, we don't know. How can you have a definition of moral problem that excludes this language?" In essence, this language contained a realization that people's lives are interdependent. Therefore, the notion that life is a zero-sum game, that one is egoistic or altruistic, is based on a false premise. It denies the reality of interdependence. If one asks instead, "How does one act with responsibility and care toward oneself and toward others,?" the moral problem changes.

Now I will go back to the question of gender differences. A student working with me found that you could systematically differentiate the two voices and the way in which people—(this is absolutely crucial)—*defined* a "moral" problem. In other words, the voices were manifest in the very definition of the problem, because the definition of the problem sets the answer. (We all say that, but we do not actually think about what it means.) We asked people to describe an experience of moral conflict, a situation in which they had to make a decision when they were not sure what was the "right" thing to do. They would describe the situation and then we asked: "What was the conflict for you in that situation?" We could thus see how the person constructed the conflict. Finally, we asked: "In thinking about what to do, what did you consider? What did you do? Do you think it was the right thing to do? Right just for you, or for anyone?"

You can identify the presence of justice reasoning and care reasoning in the construction, resolution, and evaluation of the problem. What did we find from this analysis? Across six studies, most people, male and female, represent both voices in defining and resolving moral problems. This was true with regard to an average of sixty-five percent, and in no sample less than fifty percent, of the approximately two hundred people in the study, including medical students, college students, high school students, and adults across the life cycle. Of the two hundred people, seventy percent were women, a percentage we thought to be appropriate, given our focus on women's experience. Nevertheless, most people, both men and women (the percentages were not different) represent both voices in defining moral problems.

The unexpected finding of the study was that there is a very strong tendency to focus on one voice or the other. Let me make this very clear. The presence of both voices suggests that most people know about both inequality and detachment as moral problems. Most people use both voices. As a developmental psychologist, I would argue that this results from the fact that inequality is not just a social event but rather is a life cycle phenomenon. Everyone has been a child, everyone has experienced inequality, everyone knows what it's like to be less powerful than someone who is more powerful. Since inequality is a fact in the human life cycle, the idea of justice will recur over and over again across every generation. But there is another fact in the human life cycle: that no human child survives unless an adult attaches to that child. What characterizes the human species is its long period of dependence. And attachment has a different dynamic and a different set of moral implications. By virtue of making an attachment to someone, we become vulnerable to him or her. And not only the parent but also the child is powerful: she or he is able to have an effect on others through the attachment. One is not powerless in a situation of attachment, but the nature of the power is different from the power one holds by virtue of inequality. It has nothing to do with domination. Rather, it has to do with efficacy, the ability to move, to have an effect on another person, to elicit a response from others and to respond to them.

Everybody knows about attachment and everybody knows about inequality; my findings basically represent that fact. Everybody thinks that inequality and detachment are moral problems. That notion is built into the life cycle and then of course is constructed in the social context.

The next finding is that most people who use both orientations focus on one orientation and minimally represent the other. About seventy percent of people who use both orientations focus on one, and this finding holds across orientation and gender. This is very key for people in the law. The adversarial system can not easily accommodate two perspectives which are in a fundamental tension with each other. There is a wish to resolve or reduce ambiguity, to arrive at certainty, and that is done by eliminating one perspective or the other.

What is the nature of the focus phenomenon? There is in these samples of advantaged Americans an overwhelming tendency in men to focus on justice and only minimally to represent caring. Only three men from a total of sixty demonstrated a care focus. Among these advantaged American women, some focused on justice, and some on care (about sixty percent). Look at what happens if you start, as psychology did, with samples of men. You will come empirically to the position that moral reasoning is justice reasoning. In a sense you can now hear through these findings the empirical basis for such statements of psychologists as Freud's observations that women have less sense of justice than men and that women have less tendency to focus on justice issues in resolving moral problems or Piaget's observation that girls are less concerned with the elaboration of rules and are "deficient in the legal sense." If you start with all male samples, the inclusion of women becomes problematic because it challenges the very definition of the problem. You have this group that focuses on care and cannot be accounted for by a theory that equates morality with justice reasoning. The question shifts by virtue of the observation that *both* men and women in fact represent both justice and care considerations in defining moral problems. The question shifts from, "Why are women confusing morality with care or interpersonal relationships?" to, "Why are men not representing in their formal decision-making procedures what in fact is present in their thinking—the realization that there is another dimension to moral problems, a dimension which has to do with issues of care, responsibility, and interdependence?" The question thus really shifts in some ways away from women and toward men, toward a phenemenon within male psychology which permits what is known, seen, and present to be lost or unrepresented. This work (which initially started with taking seriously the discrepant data on women) thus leads to a change in the question.

I want to say one final thing. If you want to support what has been in the Western tradition since Plato—that is, the notion of a unitary truth, that virtue is one, that its name is justice, that it is part of the sense of one right answer upon which we all, in the end, can agree—then you will select an all-male sample. It is a very interesting thing. The inclusion of women will challenge this tradition and make it impossible to sustain a unitary view. In that sense this inclusion brings in the question of difference, of two perspectives. It offers the possibility of a more adequate representation of human experience by including what formerly was ruled out by definition and then sustained by a major flaw in research.

Menkel-Meadow: Let me start by telling you a little bit about how Carol's work related to work that I was doing as a lawyer. As feminists have said, the personal is the political. So let me start with my personal story so that you can see how it has been affected on many different levels by some of the things that Carol has just been speaking to us about. As a practicing lawyer, for some years engaged in quite difficult battles, I was struck by a number of ways in which I felt that I didn't belong in that particular structure or system. There were disturbing things about it. I was unable to explain to myself and to others what in particular caused me to have some difficulty with it.

The first level from which I approach this is my individual, personalistic, experiential level. This level, I think, represents another element of the feminist contribution to law. Our individual experience has something to tell us about the way in which we know the world and the way in which we know the law. When I came to be a law teacher, I had to begin to explain this world with which I had some difficulties to other people. I had increasing difficulty describing the structure of what I saw in a way in which I felt comfortable. I increasingly wanted to bring people into it as I started to talk about what I did not like about it. So as a teacher, I was struck by the fact that I was speaking in two voices: the voice that I *had* to speak in, in order to be a teacher in a predominantly male institution, and the voice which attempted to tell my students what I really thought. This latter voice attempted to convey that there were a number of values or possibilities in the legal system that were not expressed in the world as I knew it, both in practice and in law school. On a third level, I began as a scholar to look at what it is that creates the legal structure in which I had this difficulty. Just as I finished a major piece of work on what is problematic about legal negotiations as I perceived it, I read about Amy and Jake.

I would like to do a speculative meditation on Amy and Jake, if I might, and use Carol's example to tell you what Amy and Jake said to me about the legal system. I'd like to use that example to explore further how we might look at the legal system with that double lens or double vision Carol describes. First, let's look at Amy and Jake when they were originally studied, at eleven years of age, and then maybe we'll have a few words to say about them at fifteen. One of the interesting things about the Amy and Jake description is the different way in which they approach the problem. As Carol says, the way in which the problem is defined frequently suggests the solution.

One of the things that Amy does that might be of interest to law students is typical of a "bad" law student: Amy "fought the hypo." When asked whether or not Heinz should steal the drug, Amy asked a lot of questions about the situation. At fifteen, she is still fighting the hypo. "Look," she says to the researchers, "you have given me a totally silly situation that I do not think really exists in the world. Or if it did, I would know a whole lot more about it." She asks for what has come to be known in academic circles as "a greater feeling for the context." Law students, when faced with hypotheticals that seem to be missing something (perhaps facts about the particular people in the situation, or about the political context in which the case is found, or—to use the legal realist phrase—about what the judge had for breakfast that morning), usually behave the same way Amy did. They feel that the problems are disembodied and disemboweled from the way in which they occur in the world.

When I thought about Amy's response, I thought that we in the legal system may be focusing our problems too narrowly. Through her use of a different voice, Amy tells us that we may need to know a great deal more about facts and about situations before we can make decisions about them. What would those other facts be? What else would we want to know about the Heinz dilemma before we would be satisfied, as law students and lawyers, that we could solve the problem? Take that a step further. Amy not only fights the hypo, she approaches it in a different way. As Carol has pointed out in her book and this afternoon, Jake saw the problem as an algebraic equation with people; there is the druggist, and there is Heinz with Heinz's wife. How do we balance those equities? How do we decide between those two people? Jake "gets it right." He says: "Life is more important than property, so life wins." Amy says: "I see two people with a problem here: the druggist, whose goal in life is to make a profit; and Heinz, who would like to save his wife's life. Is there not some way of holding the needs of both of those parties constant, and trying to work out another solution?" Like the "pirate-next-door game," Amy begins to think about other sorts of solutions to the problem. She does not say (at least in that earlier part of the study): "I think Heinz should or should not necessarily steal the drug." Have Heinz and the druggist talked about some other ways to solve this problem? How about an installment contract? How about payments over time? Has Heinz explored other ways to raise the money? Has the druggist thought about ways of providing a drug and perhaps getting payment in some other way?

Amy doesn't see the problem as presenting, by necessity, a bipolar choice. Amy's approach to the problem is in direct contradiction, I think, to the way we typically solve problems in the legal system: in a bipolar, win-lose way. The drug is either stolen or it is not, and it is either right or wrong to steal. Thus, if Heinz steals the drug, and is later prosecuted for it, he will be exonerated if he can come up with a series of legally recognized justifications for stealing it. Amy tells us that if we learn more facts and we take the needs of the parties and hold them constant, perhaps we can come up with some other solutions—solutions, as Carol pointed out, which might not have been thought about if we looked at the problem from the perspective of only one party in the problem, either Heinz or the druggist. Amy is trying to remember everybody as she tries to solve the problem.

Amy then does another thing with the problem. She asks, as Carol reports in her book,[18] whether Heinz and the druggist ever sit down and talk about this. She wants to know why *she* has to solve the problem. She uses "I" as a third person looking at this problem from the outside. Maybe, she muses, if they sat down and talked to each other, they would come up with yet a whole bunch of other solutions that I, sitting here as a third person, could not think about. Perhaps the act of dialogue itself might produce some other solutions. Amy thus suggests not only different kinds of substantive solutions, she also thinks of a whole different sort of process: dialogue between the parties. Now, I think that has obvious implications for our adversary culture and our adversary system. Our Anglo-American culture and adversary system require, for the most part, that two parties talk to a judge. Amy and Jake are asked to play judge for Heinz and the druggist; they are asked to decide whether Heinz is right to steal the drug or not. Perhaps there are other forms that might encourage the parties to come up with other solutions.

I want to come back to yet another dimension of how Amy and Jake reform the way in which we might look at legal decision making and problem solving. This is something that is evident during both of Amy's interviews. She says: "Well, suppose Heinz steals the drug and then he goes to jail. That is not going to do his wife any good because in addition to the drug she also needs the relationship with her husband to get her through this difficult time of what may turn out to be terminal cancer." Amy is thus concerned with preserving the relationship of the parties and looking at the situation in which they are imbedded. She looks both at the past and at the future, considering the effect on the parties of a certain decision.

Maybe I have taken too much out of the Amy and Jake problem. It is, nevertheless, an interesting meditation on the legal sys-

18. *See* C. Gilligan, *supra* note 14, at 29.

tem because what we see in Jake's description is pretty much how the Heinz dilemma would get solved if it wound up either in court or if the parties attempted to negotiate something between themselves. It was from that work, in looking at how to be a practicing lawyer—in a courtroom, as a negotiator, or as a legal problem solver—that I began to rethink the theory of legal structure. My re-examination could well have been inspired by how Amy looked at the problem.

I should add here that I have noticed, as did Carol in psychology, how many of our conceptions of what the legal system ought to be and ought to do were derived exclusively from male practitioners and male scholars. The law may thus represent an embodiment of Jake's voice, the male voice. As a double footnote,[19] I, like Carol, want to say that although I am speaking of male and female voices, I am simply using those terms as a code for what she observed to exist empirically in those two genders. All of us have elements of both of those voices. Those men who see themselves fitting the description of the female voice should know that that is probably who they are, and vice versa for women. I use that as an easy way to talk about this material, but one that is not necessarily accurate for each one of you individually.

What would the legal system look like if Amy had devised it, either alone or with Jake's help? As I said, Amy might use different forms or different processes. To do this, let's look at the way the Anglo-American court system is in fact structured. We have basically a one-way communication, adverse parties talking to a judge. There may be a witness or, in more complicated form, a jury. But all of this communication is directed at somebody else. There is very little direct communication between the parties. Picking up on Amy's process notion that the parties might talk to each other, we can imagine a structure in which the parties might be asked to sit down and talk about whether the drug should be stolen or financed in some other way. One form that is beginning to emerge, which in some sense is a reaction to this adversary structure, is alternative dispute resolution or mediation.

I do not have time today to talk about a number of other important problems which may arise out of that alternative form, which attempts to get parties talking to one another. I think, how-

19. *See supra* p.27.

ever, that it is no accident that that particular form of dispute resolution is arising in the legal culture at this time. It comes with the kind of dissatisfaction that we see with that one-way communication and with the requirement that somebody outside of the problem must make the decision for the people who are in it.

If the parties are not in accord, they will do what most parties do when they are in dispute—they will probably arrive at a solution by negotiation. Typically, a plaintiff and a defendant—Heinz and the druggist—will start arguing with each other. Heinz might say: "I can't pay you anything." The druggist would respond: "I want one hundred dollars." At some point, they will split the difference, settling on paying perhaps half of what the druggist wanted.

What's wrong with that? What's wrong, according to some people, is that it reflects one form of the female voice—it is compromise, it is a combination, it is meeting somewhere in the middle, and it may leave both parties unhappy. What Amy was trying to do was to hold both parties' needs constant and to meet both sets of needs at the same time. Having the parties meet each other's needs does not necessarily result in compromise or accommodation, which is the way in which the female voice is frequently and inaccurately seen—as conciliatory, accommodating, giving up. As Carol's example of the "pirate-neighbor" game illustrates, by searching for other solutions we might meet both parties' needs without having to compromise. A new synergistic solution might emerge simply from having them talk to each other directly about their needs. If we learn to listen to the "Amys" of the world, we might begin to imagine different kinds of constructions and different ways of looking at our legal system in solving our legal problems.

That is just a very brief introduction to the kinds of things that you can do with this. One thing I always like to tell my "Jake" students is to try to think of themselves as "Amys." Similarly, "Amys" ought to look at the world from a "Jake" perspective; there is, after all, great value in the current system. The key, as Carol has indicated, is to try to imagine a legal system that might include both.

What are some other implications of this? I liked another

character in Carol's book, Hilary,[20] very much. Hilary was a subject of one of the studies, and, interestingly for our purposes, Hilary was a lawyer. Hilary talked about one of the dilemmas of the courtroom which most trial lawyers occasionally encounter. She perceived that the opposing lawyer had failed to make use of a document that would have been helpful to that lawyer's case. Hilary sat there and thought: "What should I do? The lawyer is doing a lousy job." Hilary is faced with the dilemma of the two voices, of the two ways in which she has been trained. That ethic of care which is within her prompts her to see the needs of the other lawyer's client, and some part of her wants to reach out and help. The more traditional critique of that problem is to point out that our legal system suppresses the truth and that Hilary wants the truth to come out so that a better decision can be reached. But I think that Hilary takes it a step further. It is not just the truth that matters to her. It is the fact that she experiences some care for the plight of the party on the other side. She is imprisoned in the role of an advocate who has been told that her role is to be a zealous advocate for her client and that she would be stepping beyond that role if she were to reach out and help the party on the other side by either telling the lawyer about that document or herself submitting the document. Hilary, if I remember correctly, decides to listen to the lawyer's voice. She says nothing about the document.

Hilary's account led me to speculate on what our code of ethics as lawyers might look like if Hilary herself had created it. Would Hilary have something to say about the way in which we construct our ethical rules, which represent the lawyer's effort to cope with moral problems by embodying principles for their resolution in an increasingly conflicting and confusing set of rules? Here's where we might begin to see the kind of things that Carol talked about: response with a sense of autonomy, concern, care for the other side, coupled with some appreciation of the fact that the parties may have different interests and that there might be a need for some rules. But I wonder whether the rules would be as protective of the profession as they currently are, or whether they might pay a little bit more attention to the relationship, not of lawyer-to-client or lawyer-to-lawyer, but rather client-to-client and

20. *See* C. GILLIGAN, *supra* note 14, at 134-35.

perhaps lawyer-to-other-client.

These are some of the kinds of questions that you can think about as you speculate—those of you who are going to be Amys and Hilarys in our legislature someday—as to how you might build a legal system with that voice. It is very clear to me that certain ethics or rules of behavior or notions of what is morally and ethically correct behavior are derived from a male image of what is appropriate within the legal system.

It is no accident, it seems to me, that that little drawing I put up there to illustrate the structure of legal negotiation looks like a football field. It is no accident, I think, that our court imagery is frequently described in battle terms. "Well, on this motion we won the battle, but who knows how the war will go?" We have a conception, as we frequently do in war, that one party must win and the other party must lose. The court is very limited in the remedies that it can award, and people begin to think in those kinds of limited, winless ways.

What would the practice of law look like if Amy and Hilary had a greater voice?[21] On this question, I think it is important to take note of at least one of the issues that Mary alluded to this morning: the numbers of women in a profession. As a lot of sociological research tells us, to the extent that women are tokens in a profession, and to the extent to which Amy and Hilary live in a world in which they are surrounded by people speaking in different voices and looking through different lenses, they may not feel free to express alternative ways of practicing law or looking at the legal system. It is, therefore, important to look at the numbers of both men and women who have this different voice and have begun to develop some support for expressing it and different ways of being able to practice law.

When I was speaking to a group of practicing lawyers about some of these subjects a few months ago in Los Angeles, a very experienced district attorney began to talk to the audience about how she viewed the trial process as one of creating a relationship with the other participants in the courtroom. She had been trained, as most of us are, in the ethic of persuasion and argument and intimidation of the decisionmaker (especially if the deci-

21. *See* Menkel-Meadow, *Portia in a Different Voice: Speculations On A Women's Lawyering Process*, to be published in 1 Berkely W.L.J. (1985).

sionmaker is a jury of lay people as opposed to a judge). Like me, when she began to operate in that mode, it did not feel comfortable to her; it did not feel like "who she was" or "what she wanted to express." Over time she began to express herself as who she *really* was in the trial court. She realized that she set a completely different tone in the courtroom. Her goal was not to persuade the jurors or judge to see it her way, but to have a quiet conversation with them that created an intimate relationship in which she would ask them to examine their own views and values and sense of the facts in a way that she thought attempted to appreciate their reality as well as her own. At least from her reports, she has been no more or less successful than anybody using the other mode. One might take heart from Carol's work, realizing that the different voice might inform the way in which one both thinks about solving legal problems and practicing law.

One final thing before I close. Kitty made reference this morning to the fact that much of this notion of "how we see ourselves in gender terms" is socially and politically constructed for us. One view that someone might have of all this is that all I have just described as "the woman's way of being" is not indigenous to women. This has occurred because it has developed in the shadow of the man's world. We have needed to develop our sense of relationship because historically the only way a woman has amounted to anything in this world has been through her relationship to some man. My own view on that topic is that while others look at the origins of these differences and begin to unpack the social and political constructs in which they originated, the differences reflect reality at the present time. Furthermore, I think it is useful to ask—even if one's sense of care and of relationship has developed out of the necessity for survival in the world in which one has been powerless—if those values are intrinsically important and have something to say about the way in which we look at ourselves. I think it is important to use them as a way of reconstructing all the institutions in which we live at the same time that we reconstruct ourselves. It seems to me that one of the wonderful things that feminist discourse has done to the law has been to make us look at the *method* by which we make a new world at the same time that we argue about the *substance* of what that new world should be. I hope that some day there will be unity between the substance and the method.

Gilligan: I would like to take a couple of the things that Carrie just said a step further. What really is so interesting to me is that the concept of gender has three dimensions: a biological, a psychological, and a cultural dimension. Also, the concept of gender does not fit the assumption that the opposite of the one is the many, since there is neither one nor many genders, but rather two.

Gender is a dimension of physiology, but it is also a dimension of identity—a psychological construct. We define ourselves as gendered. We cannot speak this language and use its pronouns without identifying ourselves as either male or female. Children, by the age of three, identify themselves as either male or female. With very few exceptions, gender identity remains constant across the life cycle. It's one of the few things that do. Identity can change in all kinds of other ways, but gender tends to remain constant. Gender is thus a component of biology and it is a component of identity; it has a physiological and it has a psychological dimension.

But gender also has a cultural dimension. It is socially constructed. We have gender-based norms and gender values. My sense is that it is like the nature-nurture argument—it is absurd to reduce it in either direction. Human personality and experiences are shaped neither simply by nature nor simply by nurture. In fact, that dichotomy ignores completely the psychological dimension—the dimension of identity and interpretation.

Gender, obviously, is a dimension of biology. It is also a dimension of identity and a dimension of social roles and values. But the experiences of inequality and attachment are not cultural constructions, although in different cultures they may take on different meanings. Inequality and attachment are facts of the human life cycle. Every person in this room has experienced inequality by virtue of having been a small child. Everyone has experienced attachment; if someone had not taken care of you, you would not be here. As I indicated before, there have been social deformations of both equality and attachment. The deformation of equality appears in the equation of human with male, and the deformation of attachment in the equation of care with self-sacrifice. And this equation leads to the sense that caring is the same as pleasing others or effacing oneself. Thus, both moral ideals, justice and care, basically have been deformed. Both have to be reconstructed in different ways. That, it seems, is what's so forward-looking about the subject of today's debate. How do we reform it? What is the nature of the transformations?

I think two of my findings are helpful for this discussion. One is the presence of both orientations in most people—probably in all people. Everybody knows about inequality and thinks oppression is a moral problem, and everybody knows about attachment and thinks that detachment is morally problematic, the turning away from someone in need. The other useful finding is the "focus phenomenon": that people tend to focus on justice or care in defining and resolving moral problems. All the men in our sample except three focused on justice. Thus, men who knew about care and detachment as morally problematic turned away from this knowledge when describing an actual problem. I think a lot of history demonstrates this. It may be a vicious cycle; forgetting has been encouraged and celebrated in terms of stereotypes of masculinity.

Among the women, the focus was divided. Some focused on justice, some on care. In a sense, we saw that with Amy. I think of these as "the women." Carrie, your reading of Amy is not exaggerated. It is very well supported by the text. At fifteen, Amy can now see in both ways; she can see these two ways of thinking. How could she not? Justice reasoning *must* correlate with educational attainment in society. The problem is that if one voice is celebrated, Amy is going to let go of the other one, at least as an articulated public voice. She will learn to speak in the voice which everybody hears and understands. These two findings seem to be in tension, but it is important not to simplify them.

Let me tell you two lawyers' responses to questions about moral conflicts in legal practice. They're interesting. Watch how these lawyers portray two ways of looking at a single image—the image of the game. (This picks up on Carrie's way of saying: "Look at this, does this not look like a football game?") The lawyer who focuses on the justice orientation resolves the dilemmas he faces by saying: "I have moral dilemmas all the time but I usually have no problems solving them." You would not have a problem solving them *if* you took the "algebraic" approach because everyone would agree.

He says: "I usually resolve the dilemmas according to my internal morality. The more important, publicly, your office is, the more important it is that you play by the rules." I want to focus on this: the game imagery. "You play by the rules because society hangs together by these rules. And, in my view, if you cheat on them, even for a laudatory purpose, eventually you break down the rules because it is impossible to draw fine lines."

Contrast this view with the view of a lawyer who focuses on care: "I have to preside over these decisions and I try to make them as non-disastrous as possible for the people who are most vulnerable. The fewer games you play, the better." Same image, turned around. We are really dealing with issues that are the very basis of people's day-to-day well-being: people's feelings, people's children, people's potential for growth. One should do everything in one's power to protect vulnerability and avoid hurt.

Statement from the justice-oriented male lawyer: "Once you, as an attorney, step out of the role of adversary, which is what you do if you start helping the other side,"—we are talking now about Hilary's dilemma—"then you are not being true to your role. You are changing your function, and that destroys the system."

The care orientation, on the same issue: "I am dealing with a legal system and dealing with something it does not know how to deal with very well. I become very distressed because it is hard for me to put together exactly what my role is supposed to be. You are presiding over some pretty emotional moments in people's lives and I never know whether I should say, 'Here is the law book,' and not do anything, or try to give whatever kind of counseling, whatever kind of support, one might provide for people without costing them a fortune. I think people need something like this."

Spiegelman: I would like to ask two questions. First, is "the different voice" a "better voice"—are you saying that things would be better if all people heard and acted on that voice? Second, what happens when people start articulating those feelings within the legal system? Does the legal system turn the feminine voice into a masculine voice, or would the feminine voice transform the legal system? To put it another way, what happens when Jake negotiates with Amy?

Gilligan: Both are very good questions. "Isn't the 'different voice' the better voice?" It is better than not representing it. To think about issues of care and responsibility is much better than to ignore them. To see detachment as morally problematic is better than not to see it as problematic at all. There is no question in my mind about that. "Is it a better voice than the voice that speaks about inequality?" I do not think that is the right question. I do not think highly of inequality. I think inequality is the condition for oppression. I think inequality is the condition for violence. I think that detachment also leads to violence. I say that if you include both voices you will transform the very nature of the conversation. The problems of detachment and attachment will be seen in a different way. One can trace this empirically by looking at male and female development over time. It tends to start from different premises and have different emphases. Women come to understand that the conventions of feminine care in this society involve the silencing of women. "Whatever you want, I will do it for you. I have no needs." That is neither a relationship, nor care, nor attachment.

If you bring the two voices together, you transform your understanding of what attachment is. It's not these empty hollow social forms. "I have this wonderful relationship, family, and children, yet I feel totally alone, isolated, out of touch with everybody because I do everything for everybody else and I have no needs. I have no life." Who wouldn't feel isolated and depressed in this situation? The key to the way out for women is to say: "This is no relationship." It's called "relationship" according to the conventions of this society, but it isn't a real relationship. It doesn't come out of females' life experiences—of girls' experiences with their mothers and with their female friends.

This transforms the definition of equality. In terms of equality, you start to look at what has been the celebration of detachment in the name of fairness, at what has allowed the equation of "human" with "male." It's mind-boggling what has been sustained under the name of "equality." My argument, therefore, about better voice/different voice, is that you really are going to have a new understanding of both attachment *and* equality. They're both vitally important. Attachment and inequality will always be with us. They're built into human experience. The way this society has constructed them has been a deformation of both equality and attachment. The two have played into each other in a sort of ongoing cycle, where equality is defined as "human is male" (and women are invited in if they want) and care is defined as "self-sacrifice." People then ask: "Why aren't you happy in your relationships?" It evolves into our identity: self, care, attachment, equality—all across the board. I really think that's precise. That's why I think this is a forward-looking moment.

Menkel-Meadow: I would like to pick up on the second question, the one that is always asked. "What happens when Amy negotiates with Jake?" Let me play "Amy" for that one. If Amy and Jake were negotiating just alone, the two of them, not embedded in the society, my hope would be that they could have the kind of transformative conversation that Carol is talking about. Chances are, at age fifteen, they will not be able to because of what Carol just told us. Amy is beginning to realize that she has got to be bilingual to exist in this world and that the male voice—or the Jake voice—will predominate. My concern is that Amy's voice will not be heard by Jake. If their negotiation doesn't work, they'll have to then go back within the larger system—and in that case Jake's voice will prevail. That's why the question of Amy and Jake has to be looked at in its contextual complexity—as a sign of the political environment in which it's located. That's why Amy's voice needs to get stronger: so that Amy and Jake can have the kind of conversation that will then transform the whole negotiation dialogue.

Gilligan: I think the other point to add is that there is a differential-vulnerability theory. If Jake chooses not to listen to Amy, he can win. Consider the way in which a high school girl answered the question, "What's the worst thing that can happen in a relationship?": "That people are on different levels and don't communicate at all." She then elaborated: "If one person doesn't want to listen to the other, they can block them out totally and achieve their objective. They'll win. They simply won't listen." I think that is where the power issue comes in. If you have power, you can opt not to listen. And you do so with impunity. On the other hand, the notion that you can go through the world not listening to Amy's voice and still maintain a sense of psychic well-being is a sham. The notion that men, in a society that silences women, live in a state of contentment, security, and psychological well-being is absurd. In my own work, I became attuned to the cost of not listening when I asked about moral conflicts in people's lives. I heard it a lot from men who described how relationships fell apart suddenly, in ways that were totally unexpected, totally unexplained. They had no sense that anything was wrong, because they had not been listening.

Spiegelman: Is it "not listening," Carol, or is it just that the words are different?

Gilligan: It's not listening. I think this is where the "power trip" comes in. I think this was Kitty's point this morning. The subservient individual is more likely to listen. In other words, if you have an unequal power situation, the people with greater power know less. Secretaries know more about their bosses than bosses know about their secretaries. That's my point. That's clearly true. On the other hand, if you think that you are going to be the boss, you may never develop the skills to listen because you think you will go through the world never having to listen. But then you feel very isolated and lonely. In this society at this moment, it's not clear who has the edge on psychic well-being.

There is, however, a differential vulnerability. The vulnerability for Amy is that no one will ever bother to listen to her, or to figure out what she needs or to recognize that her way of talking is not so weird. I wrote my book in part to amplify and explicate this voice. No one had been listening to it. Everyone dismissed it as naive, irrelevant, underdeveloped, sick, and so forth. But the vulnerability on Jake's part is that at fifteen, he is attuned to *and* listening to that other voice. At fifteen, both of these kids are bilingual—although their respective "second languages" seem to be different. Imagine them in an educational system that explores the implications of this dialogue, representing both sides, moving away from a simple "right" answer or an easy consensus. Jake no longer would be so likely to say that anyone who disagreed with him had the wrong set of priorities. I want to emphasize what Jake was saying: "I am going to enter into the druggist's situation. How would a man feel? He would feel sorrow and he would feel anger if someone came into his store and took his property." That's exactly the refusal of detachment. It's knowing "how a man would feel if his wife was dying and he had to watch her dying and then he had to deal with her dying." In this situation, they lead Jake to the same conclusions so he does not have a problem. But we can imagine situations in which these two ways of thinking would lead to opposite conclusions. Are we training ourselves and our children to look at this conflict? The answer is no.

Marcus: We thought we'd invite a new person to join our conversation: Ellen DuBois, a professor of history at Buffalo. Her specialty is women's history. She has written several important works on the history of women's suffrage and the women's movement at the turn of the century. We felt very strongly that there should be a historical dimension. All too often we talk about our experiences in contemporary terms; the trained eyes and ears of historians are lost to us. The historian can suggest the patterns and identify the re-emergence of issues which may have been cast in a slightly different form in the past.

I have asked Ellen to talk about two issues. First, does she hear the themes of the past in this discourse? Second, does she have any predictions for the future?

DuBois: This disarray of papers before me suggests the lack of clarity of my thought at this moment. I think that there is an almost religious faith in the ability of history to make everything coherent. I understand that my role here is to give a background in the history of nineteenth-century feminism to two themes at the core of today's presentations: the debate as to the similarity versus the difference between the sexes; and the kind of sexual politics that comes out of feminism. I'm going to try and do that. But I'm going to leave it to other people to suggest the link between the two. I'm also going to try to put in historical perspective a third element, beyond the similarity/difference question and the sexuality questions: the role of politics in establishing the status of women. As an historian of the women's suffrage movement, my understanding is that nineteenth-century feminism was brought into existence as a social movement to effect the entry of women as a class into the realms of political power. That was the way to emancipation.

There has been a change in the emphasis of feminist thought. In the last ten or fifteen years, modern feminist thought began by identifying the problem as one of overemphasis in social, political, and economic life on distinctions of gender; it defined the liberation of women as the elimination of gender as a social structure. This emphasis was followed by its "reverse": an increasing emphasis on discovering what women's true powers might be, thus, not eliminating gender but winning for women the power to elaborate and articulate gender freely.

From the late eighteenth century on, in the early decades of feminism, there were two distinct arguments for women's emancipation which sort of parallel these two modern approaches. One I call the "egalitarian-feminist argument." This premises women's emancipation on the belief that men and women basically have the same human character, and that the denial to women of their common humanity with men has kept them out of various privileges and resources monopolized by men. The other position was one which historians have called the "domestic-feminist position." This argued for elevating women not on the basis of their common humanity with men, but rather on the basis of what distinguishes them from men. In other words, women needed rights because they were *different* from men, because men could not, in fact, represent women. The domestic-feminist position also held that the introduction of women into political and social areas from which they had been excluded would change those areas because women would inject them with different characteristics. Although individual thinkers often drew on both positions, they remained fairly distinct. Let me read, for instance, a quote from Elizabeth Cady Stanton, who was the foremost American representative of egalitarian feminism. She believed that the best future for women lay in narrowing the distinction between them and men. In a debate with Stanton in 1853, another feminist, Antoinette Brown Blackwell, took the domestic-feminist position. Blackwell argued that as soon as you insist on women being the same as men, then inevitably they keep on being regarded as inferior versions of men. She argued that it was far better for women to admit the irreducible difference of sex and not try to compare the two categories. Stanton defended the egalitarian-feminist position:

> Man eats and drinks and sleeps and so does woman. He runs and walks, laughs and cries, feels joy and sorrow, pleasure and pain, and so does woman. He loves, hates, is angry, sorry, impatient, unreasonable, tyrannical, and so is woman. He is religious, penitent, prayerful, dependent, and so is woman. He is ambitious, loves glory, fame, power, and so does woman. He loves to think, reason, write, speak, debate, declaim, and so does woman. In fact what has man ever done, that woman has not done also—what does he like, that she does not like too? Are not our hopes and fears for time and eternity the same?[22]

Let me try to clarify one element in the thought of this great egalitarian feminist. I think that what Stanton was pushing for in arguing that men and women are "the same" was to free us all to be individuals and to be different! By calling for the elimination of

22. Stanton, *Rev. Sydney Smith v. Rev. Antoinette L. Brown*, 3 THE UNA 69, 69 (1855).

the categorical difference of gender, she imagined a world of infinite difference, not one of no difference. She imagined a world in which people are no longer held to the two possibilities of masculine and feminine but are open to an infinity of possibilities. This seems to me to be a particularly important issue when it comes to sexuality because sexual expression has the potential for infinite individual variation.

Until about 1860 or 1870 the egalitarian position was advocated by the most radical feminists. Its representatives not only included Stanton but also Mary Wollstonecraft.[23] The demands that came out of egalitarian feminism focused on equality of rights, especially in the public sphere: equality of education, equality of suffrage, equality of political participation. Later, the domestic-feminist position—I'd be happy to use any other term, such as woman-centered—became ascendent in the Anglo-American feminist movement, and continued to dominate the women's movement up to the victory of the vote. Indeed, the predominant arguments for getting the vote after 1900 had to do with the different values that women would bring into the political arena. Jane Addams argued that women had to be enfranchised because they would do what she called "municipal housekeeping." She was saying that women would bring to the political arena the same kind of orderly sanitary values that they bring to their homes.

I want to point out a couple of the programmatic consequences of that position. Let me say first that the ascendancy of this woman-centered feminist approach has a lot to do with feminism becoming a mass women's movement around the turn of the century. The earlier egalitarian-feminist line helped to bring forth feminism's most spectacular break-through insights. It challenged the whole structure of what we call gender and what the nineteenth century called sexual spheres. But once feminism began to be a mass women's movement, the distinction of sex which the movement originally called into question now became its avenue for affecting history. The way that feminism was going to affect

23. Wollstonecraft was born in London in 1759. A pioneer of the women's rights movement, she published her first book, *Thoughts on the Education of Daughters*, in 1787. In 1792 her most noted work, *A Vindication of the Rights of Women*, was published. In it, she proposed opening the professions up to women. The underlying theme of all her work was that the male-female relationship should be a "rational fellowship" rather than a relationship of "slavish obedience." Wollstonecraft died in 1797, immediately after giving birth.

history was by becoming a mass movement and this involved increasing the identity of women with their sex. Feminism increased women's awareness of gender and may well have exaggerated the differences between the sexes in some areas. The sexual program that grew out of this late nineteenth and early twentieth century woman-centered feminism bears certain similarities to the anti-pornography feminist politics of today. I am a critic of both, in part, because of the hindsight history allows us. The early twentieth-century feminist movement concentrated on raising the age of consent for girls from between four and eight where it was in the nineteenth century, to sixteen or eighteen or twenty-one as it is now. That victory was a very mixed bag. Age-of-consent laws are the same as statutory-rape laws. Consent laws—a feminist program—made it legally impossible for young women to consent to sexual intercourse. On the one hand, these laws protect children from sexual assault. On the other hand, they have resulted in an increased number of young women going to jail for sex crimes. A six-year old may not be able to consent but can the same be said of an eighteen, a seventeen, a sixteen, a fifteen, or a fourteen-year old?

The late nineteenth-century women's movement also began a campaign against obscene literature. The Women's Christian Temperance Union, which was the largest late-nineteenth century feminist organization, had a department of obscene literature. It gave political support to Anthony Comstock,[24] the author of the basic obscenity laws in the United States. The major impact of Anthony Comstock on American women's history is that the laws he developed explicitly prohibited the spread of contraceptive knowledge and devices. Margaret Sanger[25] was indicted under the Comstock laws.

24. Anthony Comstock (1844-1915) was a New York postal inspector and a leading member of the New York Society for the Suppression of Vice. In these capacities he was able to initiate the successful prosecutions of 3,670 violators of the obscenity laws and destroy 160 tons of "obscene" literature and pictures. He was also the author of several books on vice, including *Frauds Exposed* (1880), *Gambling Outrages* (1887), *Morals and Art* (1888), and *Traps for the Young* (1890).

25. Margaret Sanger was born in Corning, New York in 1883. For her efforts to remove legal barriers to dissemination of information about contraception, she is credited with founding the birth control movement in the United States. Though she never went to jail under an obscenity statute, she was indicted in 1914 for mailing pamphlets which advocated birth control (her case was dismissed in 1916), and in 1917 she served 30 days in a workhouse for operating a birth control clinic in Brooklyn.

This early-twentieth-century feminist movement also took a position *against* divorce law reform on the ground that divorce was something that men used against women. There was an argument to be made for its position, but it was an historically shortsighted one. In fact, it was not true. In the long run freedom of divorce benefited women at least as much as it benefited men.

I also want to talk about some other programs which flowed from this late-nineteenth century woman-centered feminist politics, for instance, protective labor legislation. I really feel I have to correct Kitty on this. Protective labor legislation, the labor legislation that dates from the early twentieth century and specifies that women cannot work night work, cannot work certain jobs, cannot work certain hours, cannot lift certain stuff, was a *feminist* program.

MacKinnon: I did not say it was not.

DuBois: Well, you called it a male program.

MacKinnon: What I meant to suggest is that it comes out of precisely what you are saying it comes out of: the affirmation of differences, which produces special benefits, rules, protectionism, for women.

DuBois: Right. I think you have a tautological definition of male and female in there. What does it mean to call protective labor legislation "male"? It was a program put forward by a movement that by any historical measurement you would have to call "feminist." It was put forward by progressive women pushing for women's suffrage who saw that women's motherhood and their role in the labor force were coming into conflict. The problem wasn't that it was "male." It was that it took an historically backward perspective on how to solve that problem.

At the turn of the century there was a kind of natural political identity among women based on their common femaleness. The organized women's movement believed that the female political perspective was an obvious one. At the core of this was the common conviction among feminists that women were naturally more pacifistic than men. This was an illusion and a delusion which the first world war exploded. As soon as the first world war developed, the women's movement—like every other political movement of the time—split right down the middle. I think this helps to explain why the massive women's movement that won the vote could go no further—because the premise of female unity on which it had been won was historically exploded: the idea that women by virtue of being women automatically had the same politics.

I came here to talk about a similar movement from a focus on obliteration of gender to an elaboration of gender in modern feminist thought. Instead I want to say something else. I was struck by something in both MacKinnon's and Gilligan's presentations. The essence of what each had to say was reminiscent of the first revelations of feminism a decade and a half ago. Catharine presented this in her exposition of the rage that discovering women's abused and degraded status initially produces. For me, that was the way radical feminism appeared to me when I first found it in 1969. Carol presented this in her scholarly indignation that women had been in fact totally ignored by scholars and that the ignoring of women distorted all subsequent intellectual discoveries. Both are first premises of modern feminism. However, we are not now at the beginning of feminism; we are right in the thick of it. In fact, as this panel suggests, there are by this time many feminisms. Women are no longer ignored in the political scene. *Au contraire*, the issues that the women's movement has raised are at the very center of this historical moment. I am talking about abortion, and I am talking about the question of a female vice president. I could never have imagined that these issues would have reached the level of historical significance that they have with the rapidity that they did.

This raises the question about where, in fact, historical change in the condition of women is going to come from. In some ways Carol Gilligan is too optimistic about change and Catharine MacKinnon is too pessimistic about it.

MacKinnon: That's why I'm doing this work on pornography, right?

DuBois: I think that I am more convinced that Catharine MacKinnon is too pessimistic than I am that Carol Gilligan is too optimistic. What Carol Gilligan is saying is that the introduction of women and the recognition of them is going to change the moral discourse. We have to face the existence of Sandra Day O'Connor—I mean, there are women, and there are women. Do not get me wrong: she is going to change the political discourse. I just do not want it to change in the direction that she is going to change it. I guess this leads to my second point: I see a tautology in Catharine MacKinnon's insistence (which I certainly do not disagree with and I do not think any substantial feminist would disagree with) that the issue is subordination and domination. The question is: What constitutes subordination and domination? Hers is a circular definition. To be dominant is to be male and to be subordinate is to be female. Who is a male? Anyone who is dominant. What is dominance? Whatever males do. So it goes around in circles. Consider "lesbian sadomasochism." If there's a woman on top, she is a male—she functions as if she were a male. That seems to me to be circular.

At one point MacKinnon talked about how male domination is an *almost* metaphysically perfect system. It seems to me what she presents *is* a metaphysically perfect system and therefore one that is unreal. By definition, it defines women as having no power, and if by definition women are those without power, then go home and lock the door because there is no possibility for change. It seems to me that history proves that is not the case. That, it seems to me, is what Mary was trying to say when she said, "Look, we are sitting here talking about gay and lesbian rights in a law school." Something has *happened*.

The basic discovery of the discipline of women's history is that women *act* in history: They create history and that includes their own oppression as well as their own liberation. If they don't create history, then there is no possibility for change in their position.

Marcus: I would like to open up the conversation again and ask the audience to participate.

Question from audience: Could you explain what you mean when you say that women create their own oppression?

DuBois: Women are not just the objects of historical action which only men make. I gave you some examples. An organized women's movement was basically responsible for protective labor legislation and for age-of-consent laws. Whatever the intent, which I am not calling into question, the historical result was a new kind of oppression of women. I think that when we act in history we basically have very little control over the impact of our actions. Women act in order to remedy those oppressions which they experience, and as a result they sometimes contribute to the creation of new forms of oppression. That is sort of the nature of history. You remedy one inequality and sometimes as a result you help to create a new form.

MacKinnon: I think that people who are powerless have particularly little control over the consequences of their own actions, but that people seeking to act in history with a consciousness of the past, together with what little power we have (if any), have a choice. We can either say: "All right, we cannot do anything about this because as a matter of fact nearly every attempt that women have made in history to change our status has not done so." Women in fact *have* fought against our status in the entire history that we know about and in point of fact we are still subordinate . . .

DuBois: But our status is not the same; for instance, we are enfranchised now.

MacKinnon: Yes, but what I am saying is that the fact that there are changes is not to me the crucial thing to look at, at this point. You can look at all the modifications in the status of women—and it really does mean something different to be a woman now than it has meant in other times, just as it means a different thing to be a woman of a different race or class now or sexual preference now. The varieties do matter. It means a different thing to be a feudal slave than to be a wage slave, right? There have been alterations in that and I am not saying there have not. But if you look at instead whether women have ever not been subordinate to men, putting aside those few examples (that people like to make the most of, and which I myself am not convinced by) that suggest either a female supremacist situation or one of "relative" inequality, as I see it, if bottom is bottom then look on the bottom, and there is where women will be.

I do not agree with the parallel being made here between the anti-pornography legislation proposed by Andrea Dworkin and me, and the four specific examples that were laid out, which come out of what I take to be, and criticize as, the "differences" approach. I do not agree that what we are doing is like statutory rape laws and raising the age of consent. I think that giving children power to do something about people who abuse them might be more like what we are doing; we're not having the state act as "daddy." I don't agree that what we are doing is like the W.C.T.U.'s department of obscene literature. However, I would really like to see somebody look at what they *were* trying to do in light of what we *are* trying to do, and see if there are some commonalities that have been obscured by historians looking to see if what they and we are doing is "moralistic." I also do not agree with the parallel to the protective labor legislation. All three of those examples empower the state. We are looking to empower women. We have the audacity to think that we might be able to use the state to help do it. It is either going to do something real for us or it is not. We can decide that the state is not an arena to use; we can also decide that it is not an arena to use in this case. Or, we can decide that there is nothing that we can do, because really we're trying to turn straw into gold; you know, turn powerlessness into power. If we are looking for an Archimedian point, a place to stand outside the world of sex inequality to put a lever to move it, I think our search is futile. There is no such place for the status of women. People who are looking at women's current situation and calling it "power" are looking for that, and it is not there.

DuBois: I am just struck that although you see a kind of seamless historical unity in the oppression of women, so much so that there is no significant change, you see absolutely no historical unity in the efforts to combat that oppression.

MacKinnon: I do not agree with your characterization of my position. I also think that "change/no-change" is a really sterile way to construct the problem we face.

DuBois: I believe that I was accurately repeating what you said. You said that if you look at the past of women, there has been no change in women's status. I said that there *has been* change: for instance women have become enfranchised. You see a kind of endless historical background to women's oppression, but not a single historical antecedent of our own efforts to change.

Comment from audience: This seems to be an example to me of part of the problem in the history and the present-day development of how women divide among themselves and therefore cannot go forward in a position of strength and unity to progress and indeed to come to power and change their world.

DuBois: I *do* think that women divide among themselves; that is the inevitable consequence of empowering and moving us ahead. We are different. We have different politics. There are right-wing women and left-wing women; Republican women and Democrat women and anarchist women.

Comment from audience: And feminist women!

DuBois: And feminists—exactly. That's the dilemma. When we get a voice, we don't all say the same thing. And then we have to fight among ourselves to discover what position we will unify behind; it is not automatic. And we have reached that point of struggling in history.

MacKinnon: I do see some basis in the past for change, and I see a basis throughout the society for it now. Women fight against subordination. What I particularly see, though, is that when women fight against sexual force through law, they are interpreted essentially as trying to engage the state in repression or to get special protection by the use of state power. I feel a lot in common with feminists of the past, and also with women who are not identified as feminist, who have fought against sexual subordination. However, my standard for change is really rather major. That is the reason that I do not see that past changes have been all that significant. Consider rape: No more rape. That, to me, would be a significant change, change dealing with the context of sexual force. Rape has been a constant condition in that it is and has been *de facto* legitimized and allowed. Granted, if lunatics were to still commit rape on occasion even after this change, I would still say there had been change. As it is now, rape can occur at any time and nothing is done about it. We're walking targets for it. Until this changes, I say we are in a subordinate circumstance.

Question from audience: What do you think about the discovery and elaboration of the women's voice as a different voice (as articulated by Carol Gilligan in psychology) as a political development? She seems to imply that we are going to start to talk to each other differently now that we understand this voice, and that this will force a change.

MacKinnon: I didn't think she predicted that that would happen. Rather, I thought she said that *if* the voice were listened to, the discourse would be transformed. I am—it will shock you to hear—ambivalent about it. On the one hand, I feel excited by the strong and elegant sensitivity in the work. There is something deeply feminist there: the impulse to listen to women. I also think the data is right. I don't think the attributes she advanced are biological but I do think that accurate social regularities were found—and for me gender is a social regularity. On the other hand, what is infuriating about it (which is a very heavy thing to say about a book that is so cool and graceful and gentle in its emotional touch), and this is a political infuriation, is that it neglects the explanatory level. *Why* do women become these people, more than men, who represent *these* values? This is really very important. For me, the answer is clear: the answer is the subordination of women. That does not mean that I throw out those values. Those are nice values; everyone should have them. I'm not saying that taking these values seriously would not transform discourse, which would be a good thing under any circumstance of gender. She also has found the voice of the victim—yes, women are a victimized group. The articulation of the voice of the victim is crucial because laws about victimization typically are made by people with power, and come from the perspective with power. I think the interjection of that perspective has important possibilities.

What bothers me is identifying women with it. I'm not saying that Carol does this expressly in her book. But I am troubled by the possibility of women identifying with what is a positively valued feminine stereotype. It is "the feminine." It is actually called "the feminine" in the middle chapter of the book. Given existing male dominance, those values amount to a set-up to be shafted. I am particularly worried about the legal impact of this. Take what Carrie said. If Jake and Amy converse, what happens? Well, we heard if Jake does not listen to Amy, he wins. There is something gendered about that. What happens if Amy doesn't listen to Jake? She loses. You see what I mean? The reason I put it out like that is because I think the power issues are crucial and unignorable. If it is male dominance which has created people in these images, then *recognizing that* really matters for the applications. So I think the explanation part is crucial on its own, but also for the applications. Power is socially constructed such that if Jake simply chooses not to listen to Amy, he wins; but if Amy simply chooses not to listen to Jake, she loses. In other words, Jake still wins because that is the system. And I am trying to work out how to change that system, not just how to make people be more fully human within it.

Gilligan: Your definition of power is his definition.

MacKinnon: That is because the society *is* that way, it operates on his definition, and I am trying to change it.

Gilligan: To have her definition come in?

MacKinnon: That would be part of it, but more to have a definition that she would articulate that she cannot now, because his foot is on her throat.

Gilligan: She's saying it.

MacKinnon: I know, but she is articulating the feminine. And you are calling it hers. That's what I find infuriating.

Gilligan: No, I am saying she is articulating a set of values which are very positive.

MacKinnon: Right, and I am saying they are feminine. And calling them hers is infuriating to me because we have never had the power to develop what ours really would be.

Dunlap: I am speaking out of turn. I am also standing, which I am told by some is a male thing to do. But I am still a woman—standing.

I am not subordinate to any man! I find myself very often contesting efforts at my subordination—both standing and lying down and sitting and in various other positions—but I am not subordinate to any man! And I have been told by Kitty MacKinnon that women have never *not* been subordinate to men. So I stand here an exception and invite all other women here to be an exception and stand.

Everyone who believes it is true that we have never *not* been subordinate to men, remain seated. Everyone who believes that you do not have to be subordinate to men, stand if you can.

Today we have been subordinated to a definition of who is radical, who is feminist, what sex is good, and who gets to talk. I think all those things are very subordinating and also very male. I also think such things happen in these kinds of environments and I'm not going to make a big deal out of it. I want to say something more positive. I want to talk about soccer. The most priceless thing I have done lately is play soccer with women. Very few of us have ever played before; thank goodness we have a female coach who did. We differ all the time about whether the purpose of the team is to win or to get to play. I have come to be fully sure that both are true and that something else is true. There is a woman, a friend of one of the women on the team, who cannot play because she is disabled. She cannot play—there is no equal opportunity for her, indeed no opportunity for her. She said to us at the game last week: "Just being out here with you, getting to watch you, lets me play." Now, as a disabled person, she is subordinate to everyone who gets to play soccer. And she has done something with that subordination which has turned it into a kind of love that gets her past that reality. I do not submit, by that example, that her disability in its immutability is like gender, which I believe is mutable in many ways, our self-definitions being part of it. What I am trying to say is that the idea that any of us here, or any of you there, should decide for all of us who is a good feminist, who is a good radical, what sex is good, and who gets to talk is taking advantage of the rest of us. I am not going to take such advantage of people.[26]

Question from audience (to Gilligan): If instead of breaking your subjects down into male and female, you had broken them into rich and poor, white and black, children of employed and unemployed parents, would you have found different things?

Gilligan: That is a terrific question. That is exactly my question and that is what I am doing now. I started my work on adolescents in a girls' school, of advantaged girls, and now I am working in the inner city so that I *can* answer your question. But let me give you some preliminary information; let me tell you why I did what I did and some preliminary answers that suggest it is not that simple, that you cannot assimilate the discussion of gender into the discussion of social inequality. There are elements and dimensions to questions of gender that do not fit that model. Basically, I am in disagreement with Kitty MacKinnon. Trying to make gender fit the inequality model is the most traditional way to deal with gender, and it will not work. Gender is not exactly like social class. It is not simply a matter of dominance and subordination. There is no way to envision gender disappearing as one envisions, in utopian visions of society, class disappearing or race becoming a difference that makes no difference. The fact that gender is a difference that one cannot envision disappearing is why it makes so many people so angry. It does not fit their schemes of analysis. It is always a thorn in their side.

Let me present one of my most interesting, intriguing, "findings in process." I have black women in my studies. I did not explain that explicitly in my book; I realize that was a serious omission: since I said nothing, everybody assumed my subjects were all white, which is a reasonable assumption. If you are not told the gender of subjects of psychological research and you assume they

26. Catharine A. MacKinnon had to leave at this point, by pre-arrangement, to catch a plane.

are male, you're probably right. If I had said to people that there were black women in my studies, people would assume, because of the way blacks have been portrayed in the social science literature, that the black women exemplify the lower stages of the various kinds of care that I wrote about in the middle chapters of my book. (There I focused on how women are what Kitty calls "the feminine"; I studied different ways that women conceptualize femininity—from oppressive ways to nonoppressive ways.) In fact, the opposite is true. Without having any particular criterion, I just picked women. I found that I was using the voices of black women to represent the integration of justice and care. I can explain that in my own terms by noting that black women are exactly in a position to know most acutely about both inequality and attachment—both experiences have been heightened for them in this racist society. I was thus very intrigued that the voices I picked to best illustrate the struggle to integrate justice and caring belong to black women.

I then did a study of medical students. I found a group of women within that study who seemed to be atypical of the rest of the women in the strength of their justice focus. They were black women. And these women were different from black women in my other studies, so I didn't even have a uniform finding about "black women vs. white women." I began to wonder: What was it about the medical school context that was heightening this issue? I then noticed that this group of black women, the medical students, had been interviewed by a white male. I realized it would certainly heighten all the elements of inequality, to have a white man interviewing black female medical students—there is a whole dominance issue right there. The strongest justice-focus women in my study were the black female medical students. One might think that the doubly oppressed groups should speak doubly strongly about care. It is not so simple. Perhaps the victims of violence are the proponents of care. Still, the victims of violence, most often male, are the perpetrators of violence.

It's a complicated set of problems. My own sense is that we shouldn't reach for all the familiar categories of analysis which have never been able to deal very well with these problems. I see an opening now. The source of my optimism is that opening. I don't think oppression will miraculously end and that things will change, but I see at this moment an opening. I think this opening is enlarged by the increasing presence of women in positions of some influence and power—this discussion is an example. I think there's a possibility for change. That is all.

In the next phase of my own work, working with adolescents in the inner city, I hope to begin to look at the interplay between social class and gender, between different cultures and gender. I hope to begin to see, but I am a big skeptic. The social class literature indicates that there is a correlation between high moral development and high social class. But ask yourself: If that's true, how come the people in power are perpetrating inequality or making wars?

Question from audience: I'd like to focus on pornography and, in general, on the implications of the speakers' ideas about sexuality. Why is this issue so important and so divisive within the women's movement and between the women's movement and the gay and lesbian activists in this country?

Menkel-Meadow: I'd like to answer that question in part because I find myself in the middle of this issue frequently. That is (to use all the labels Mary alluded to), I always like to think of myself as a radical feminist—until someone out-radicalizes me, and then I find myself sitting on the liberal fence again. Let me try to answer the question by saying that the problem is very complicated. One reason that the tension develops around it is that in the effort to unify, we keep seeking some basic principle that will bring us all together. Every time we think we have found one of those, we discover some of the exceptions to it and some people attach themselves to the exceptions and we become very troubled and very sad that we cannot get behind a particular principle. The first time I heard Kitty talking about her notion that what unifies us all as women is that we are oppressed, that we are oppressed by the particular condition that men view us primarily and exclusively as sexual objects, I thought: That has a tremendous ring of truth to it. But the more I thought about it, the more I thought that although I could get behind that principle, I could probably formulate some other principles that would also attempt to unify people.

I think that if you take a look at any male stereotypic statement of who women are, it includes not only the sexual-object notion but the mother notion also. We are also the mother of their children and we are their mothers when they are children. There has been a lot of important work in psychology about how men's perception of women is influenced by the way in which they have been mothered by women. I suspect there are several other people out there in the audience who can pick other principles that might explain the difference between men and women in efforts to unify all women behind them.

The truth of the matter is, as Carol mentioned in her work, all of these relationships are very complicated. Being viewed as a sexual object may be the most important one, but I prefer to be agnostic on that at the moment, in part because I think there are other principles that may have just as much explanatory force. The hard thing, the thing that tears us apart in meetings like this, is that we keep seeking a reductionist explanation behind which we can all unify. However, I think we are beginning to grasp the human complexity of it all.

I am pleased by and I will support Kitty's efforts at trying to get the pornography statute passed despite the fact that as a lawyer I see a whole lot of first amendment problems with it. I think it is an important field to be laboring in, though for me it is not the only field. It is important that we have many other voices up here trying to explore a lot of different fields.

I want to react to something Ellen said earlier as another effort to somehow reduce those variables that explain ourselves to each other and to the outside world. Whenever we have these discussions, there is much talk about whether they are sufficiently political or not. At the risk of yet another redundancy in our arguments, let me say that one of the powers of feminism is that the political arena, as we commonly conceive of it, is not the only place to be having these arguments and discussions. Talking about women in psychology is important, as is talking about domestic history, talking about women in architecture, looking at women in medicine, women in law, women at home, and in quilting (to use the image from this morning)—all of these things are different aspects of life. What the feminist movement has done has been to bring different spheres of the way we live into the discourse. That makes it far more complicated, because then we cannot agree on any one sphere as being the one that explains it all.

DuBois: I think it's a very hard question. Dorothy McCarrick[27]

27. Lecturer in Law, State University of New York at Buffalo.

made an historical analogy with which I agree. The way that the issue of protective labor legislation versus the ERA was unresolvable in 1920 and splintered the women's movement, has certain analogies to the question of pornography in feminism today. Most feminists I know are in the position you, Carrie, are; they kind of sit on one seat and then they have to go over and sit on the other one because they cannot take one side or the other.

I cannot say why pornography has become the brick wall up against which feminism has come. One thing I would point out is that it is a sexual issue. Much of the feelings people have about it have to do with the fact that it is sexual. I actually think that there is a kind of pornophobia; in some ways we are more afraid of pornography than we need to be. I want to read an article by Lisa Duggan. She answers this question in this way:

> Pornography is made to stand for all misogyny, all discrimination, all exploitation of women, in the view of the feminist anti-pornography campaign. It not only causes but constitutes the subordination of women. The commodification and objectification of women's bodies is believed to reside more centrally in pornography than in mainstream media. This society's cultural violence against women is said to radiate from, rather than be reflected in, pornography. The campaign against pornography is thus a symbolic substitute for more diffuse but more necessary campaign against the myriad forms of male domination in economic life and political life and sexual life. Pornography serves as a condensed metaphor for female degradation.[28]

Pornography is far easier to fight politically than other feminist issues in the conservative climate of the Reagan years. I think that's extremely important. I am not implying any motive, but the political context of the pornography issue cannot be ignored. It is an issue which, I believe the right wing has controlled. That cannot just be ignored or considered incidental. While the issue of pornography is more complicated than simply the fact that it is a right-wing issue, we cannot ignore that it is a central tenet of the right-wing program. I find it disturbing that at this time in history we should focus on the issue of pornography instead of the issue of, say, abortion, which is the issue that is going to be determined politically and is directly related to the lives and deaths of women. I don't know why pornography draws fire.

---

28. Duggan, *Censorship in the Name of Feminism*, Village Voice, Oct. 16, 1984, at 11 (one in a series of three articles in a symposium on feminism and the first amendment entitled *Forbidden Fantasies: A Special Issue on Pornography*).

Dunlap: I am going to try to be very brief. Keeping a close mind to human reality—the reality for women particularly—and considering the statistics that Kitty MacKinnon presented this morning about incest, child abuse, rape, sexual harassment, and all of the sexist violence, I find the anti-pornography approach very distracting, very diffusing. I work as a lawyer, among other things, representing people in novel causes of action. More often than not, I represent women. I represent, in a case that is as yet unfiled and anonymous, a woman who is the victim of tremendous, repeated, frequent, phenomenal—phenomenal in the sense that she survived—sexual and physical victimization by her father. I know that her anger is indispensable to her recovery. I also know that her anger is insufficient—in the same way I know that our anger about pornography, and all of our differences about it, is very valuable yet insufficient to respond to the needs of that client. Where are the attorneys in court representing the victims in rape cases? There is a problem of priorities, there is a problem of finitude of resources.

Here we have a ballot; let us vote on what things we are going to put our bodies, monies, minds, and anything else we have to offer, behind. I will not personally check on that ballot anti-pornography campaigns because I know how desperate the needs of women who are survivors of various crimes of sexual violence are—for attorneys in various stages, for psychologists, for therapists, for scholars, for you, for all of us. For me it is a question of priorities. I do take a position. I do not care if I am called liberal, radical, or whatever. I have been called everything and it really does not matter to me.

What I want (and this is not self-sacrificing—it's caring; that's a crucial distinction) is to be able to make the difference that Kitty MacKinnon also wants to be able to make. Let us end rape. I know that that is not "just going to happen." I also think that if we take on pornography as the image of rape, and we destroy it, we will have destroyed, I suspect, nothing more than the image of rape. I don't believe this as a sociological conclusion; I don't buy the idea that pornography is a primary cause of sexist violence. I do believe that it is very much reflective of it, and that it can lend an atmosphere of permission of violence, sexist or otherwise. I nevertheless don't buy that pornography is a primary cause of sexist violence.

My problem is thus prioritizing. My response is to prioritize boldly, whatever mistakes are involved. To go forward and not, having said that, to put down what is being done by others. However, I do want to put down a part of it, and I want to be clear about this. I have read, in these articles and elsewhere, that many people ask: "What is so good about the first amendment? Who needs it? This primacy of the first amendment is really male." *But wait a minute*! When you say that, you're overlooking ninety-seven percent of all the human rights movements—call it anti-nuke, call it pro-labor, call it pro-victims of McCarthyism. There's a lot more to expression than pornography. As soon as we cast out and throw aside first amendment protections in favor of vanquishing what I believe is primarily the image of sexist violence (and I am not excusing poronography; it makes me sick), as soon as we toss aside the right of expression in favor of that, we are going to lose. Speaking concretely, the U.S. Supreme Court took an appeal two weeks ago in a case called *National Gay Task Force v. Oklahoma City Board of Education*.[29] The issue is whether Oklahoma can, in effect, ban anyone who supports gay rights from teaching in the Oklahoma schools. But they have written it very cleverly. When you read that statute, you think what it has to do with is public sex acts for which people are criminalized and arrested. You think: All they are doing is getting rid of any teacher who has that particular crime record. That passes muster with a lot of people. But in fact what they are doing in that ordinance, and what they tried to do with the Briggs Initiative in California,[30] is to say: "Certain kinds of communication about sex are unacceptable and we are going to ban them." Does that sound familiar? There is a frightening parallel here. There is a parallel at least as frightening as the authors in the *Village Voice* article say.[31] The parallel is be-

29. 729 F.2d 1270 (10th Cir. 1984), *aff'd mem.* 105 S. Ct. 1858 (1985).

30. The Briggs Initiative was a referendum to prohibit school teachers from publicly giving their views on homosexuality. Specifically, the initiative provided for the filing of charges against teachers, teachers' aides, school administrators, or counselors either for advocating, promoting, encouraging, or soliciting private or public homosexual activities in a manner likely to come to the attention of other employees or students, or for publicly and indiscreetly engaging in such actions. *See* N.Y. Times, Aug. 30, 1978, at 107 (supplementary material). The referendum was defeated. Herben, *Tax Limits Passed in Several States*, N.Y. Times, Nov. 8,, 1978, at A1, col. 1, A19, col.3.

31. *See generally* Duggan, *supra* note 28; Hentoff, *Is the First Amendment Dangerous to Women?*, Village Voice, Oct. 16, 1984, at 14; Goldstein, *Pornography and Its Discontents*, Village Voice, Oct. 16, 1984, at 19.

tween saying, "The only kind of sex that is good is the kind that I say is good, and my name is Kitty MacKinnon," and "The only sex that is good is the kind that I say is good, and my name is Jerry Falwell." I am sorry, but there is a terribly frightening parallel there. With all that I have in common with *her* that I will never have in common with *him*, that parallel frightens me.

DuBois: Let me say one other thing about why pornography becomes so central. At this point in history feminism and the oppression of women have an ambivalent relationship to the question of sexuality: that we have had too much of it not under our own control and not enough of it under our own control. Pornography captures that. We have both been the victims—having sexuality impressed on us against our will—and we have been deprived of our own sexual expression. The debate over pornography gets caught in that.

Question from audience: I would like to go back to the central proposals that were made by the speakers throughout the course of the day. We seem to be heading in a somewhat anti-feminist direction. My reasons, briefly, for feeling this way: First of all, Carol Gilligan did not spend a lot of time elaborating on her assertion that an androgynous ideal is not out of the question as a long range goal of feminist strategies and reforms. Mary Dunlap seems to have suggested that she would back the ideal of equality, which even the softest feminist might agree is flawed by what male domination has done to the contents of that notion. We are told by Ellen DuBois that the whole notion of moralism can be somewhat of a co-opting trap for feminism. I guess that I am troubled by attempts, on a theoretical level, to characterize a largely more powerful and exciting movement, attempts that have led to the articulation of feminist theory. The tragedy is that such attempts really could be total dead-ends for feminism. I do not see androgyny as being an ideal that I am particularly interested in, but until "feminist values" (whatever those are) have been looked at a lot more carefully, I cannot back the ideal of equality. Nor can I do so until I see, in more detail, just what that ideal can produce for men rather than for women.

My real problem is that while everybody is happy to dump on Catharine MacKinnon's campaign against pornography, at the same time they ignore her very clearly stated position that the state is now a tool of patriarchal oppression. They seem to be holding her accountable for the problems that women experience at the hands of the state and trashing her for attempting to get around that. They are, in fact, misrepresenting her statement, so I do not really expect a complete answer to that. I would, however, like to raise the possibility that the trend in feminist thought is very much an anti-feminist one—if one looks back to the literature of the late sixties and early seventies.

Menkel-Meadow: Would you help me by defining what you mean by "anti-feminist" in that context?

Response from questioner: Setting up a set of tactics which are more likely to place you in the hands of male hegemony than continuing the line of analysis that Catharine MacKinnnon, for example, has tried to take. Trying to identify those sources of oppression and come up with specific tactics which deal with particular kinds of problems instead of trying to sketch out theoretical norms like equality or androgyny.

Gilligan: I just want to say one thing: I held up the androgyny solution in using the pirate-and-the-neighbor game as the solution that I rejected—the implication that we can have two games that can fit happily alongside each other. When I gave the example, using that as the shorthand illustration of the combination of the games, it was not an illustration of androgyny. It was precisely the opposite. It was an illustration of how to listen seriously and take seriously women's experience. It implied a transformation, a change, in both old games, in both the old masculine game and the old feminine game. I then illustrated exactly what I meant because the old masculine game had said "equality" for (you can correct me about how many years) a hundred years while sustaining inequality. The old feminine game had said "attachment and care" while silencing women. I was really suggesting that the androgyny model sustains both that definition of equality and that definition of attachment or care, both of which I reject. It also suggested that, in fact, if you include women's experience (my definition of feminism is to see in women's experience human experience) if you take it seriously, attend to it, explore it, that would be transformative.

Question from audience: I guess that I did not hear the example of what you described as being transformative.

Gilligan: You do not think that is a new notion of care—a notion that is not destructive to women? Or a new notion of equality that does not co-exist with, as Kitty said, fifty-nine cents to the dollar? What does the word "equality" mean?

Comment from audience: Getting back to the point on androgyny: I interpreted the resolution which the children arrived at as more a recognition that even at the age of four years, the young woman in the scenario knew quite well that she would not be able to influence the pirate's game and had decided instead to settle for as much of her own space as possible. This was to simply say: "Well, let's be neighbors."

Gilligan: That is very interesting and very illuminating because you assume there are two choices: either she dominates or she is subordinate. I say that her solution is transformative because it creates a game that is neither the neighbor game nor the pirate game but a new game—the pirate-neighbor game—which is different from the one that either imagined. How it works out in practice is one thing. But one sees this, as a matter of fact, in studies of small children. They do not resort to aggression as their first means of resolving conflict. Contrary to the image psychologists have created, they in fact play out solutions that are creative and cooperative, like the solution of a pirate-neighbor game. She says, basically: "Instead of my losing and your winning, let's invent a new game." I identify that as the creative solution.

Comment from audience: I guess I would be interested in the cultural content in the game of the four-year-old girl.

Gilligan: That's a very good question. If you observe the pirate-neighbor game, is it a concealed form of domination and subordination or is it in fact a kind of creative adventure for both kids?

DuBois: To return to I cannot see any purpose in calling any position in the debate between different feminist positions "anti-feminist." We often face clear and unambiguous anti-feminist opposition. These anti-feminists are easy to pick out. We are also at a point at which feminists have no political unity. We are at a crucial point. But I cannot understand why in the world we should call dissenting feminisms "anti-feminist." Do you mean to obscure the difference between feminists who disagree on that position and Phyllis Schlafly or Ronald Reagan?

Response from audience: No, but I do want to draw out connections between some of the more disparaging aspects of the analysis. I think that there are connections which could become disempowering to the women's movement. That is what concerns me. We ourselves, by our own theorizing, by the structure of our theorizing, might be too easily co-opted into reconstructing male methods of analysis or male forms which could make us abandon the kinds of positions that Catharine MacKinnon, for example, has been arguing.

Menkel-Meadow: I do not think it is that simple. I think a lot of what we are doing is really part of a much larger dialectical process where we begin with a reform, be it liberal, radical, or in some cases even conservative, and some of us unite behind it while others do not. We then watch it played out like protective labor legislation, which was a very good thing when it happened. The same thing is true of a lot of the concrete issues that we are talking about.

I would like to respond to another part of your earlier question, regarding the way I and others view the state. It is simplistic to the point of being incorrect to say that we want to avoid using the state at all costs to fight our battles. The use of the state in fighting feminist battles has been a mixed bag. In that bag have come some very good things. Feminists have fought very hard for laws that protect battered women and a number of other things. For those who have not read it, I recommmend Fran Olsen's article in the *Harvard Law Review*,[32] in which she outlines beautifully and exhaustively the mixed-bag nature of reforms that have occurred through law and through the use of the state to try to ameliorate some of these problems. It would be incorrect for us all to abandon the state, as it would be for us to totally embrace the state. There are times that it helps us and times that it hurts us. We are not going to find an answer today that will settle these questions for ever and for always. We have to keep working. When something turns out not to be helpful to us, we try to change it.

Marcus: I think that is precisely one of the reasons for my raising that question this morning and thank you for addressing it. The extent to which the state can be used to further feminist goals obviously is an issue that surfaces in the pornography debate. I am sorry that Kitty had to leave early. In her *Signs* arti-

32. Olsen, *The Family and the Market: A Study of Ideology and Legal Reform*, 96 HARV. L. REV. 1497 (1983).

cle,[33] she identifies the state with male domination, and yet the prescription is that feminists, who are concerned about images of sexual violence, try to use the state in order to eliminate or supress those images.[34]

One theme which emerges in these conversations is anger. What else are we besides our anger? Another theme which emerges is frustration. We have no way of knowing in advance whether the use of the state for a particular program over time will not lead to a reform being turned on its head. Perhaps the best example of that may be what has happened in the abortion debate. To hear the major presidential and vice-presidential candidates in 1984 talking about issues which we all thought were resolved in 1972 leaves one with the most extraordinary sense of anger and frustration. What we have heard in this conversation, the pitch of which rose at times, is a reflection of how complex we perceive the issues to be and how emotionally engaged we are.

I hope this will inspire you to continue the conversation.

33. MacKinnon, *supra* note 12.

34. At the request of the *Buffalo Law Review*, MacKinnon responded to this statement. In *Signs*, the state was analyzed as "male," not in its eternal essence (in the liberal mode), but in the interests it embodies and expresses. The point of the analysis is, therefore, not passively to contemplate the nature of the state, or to resignedly acquiesce in its operation but actively to criticize it, in order to develop a strategy for change. Both the *Signs* analysis and the pornography ordinances are parts of that theory and practice for change.

Sameness and Difference

[8]

Equality and Difference:
The Case of Pregnancy

Herma Hill Kay†

INTRODUCTION

Women and men in the United States are entitled to the equal protection of the laws,[1] and to freedom from discrimination in employment because of sex.[2] Beginning in the 1970s,[3] the United States Supreme Court has applied the laws that guarantee these rights so as to enable both women and men to gain access to positions and privileges formerly dominated by the other sex. The resulting exchange of power between the sexes reflected in Supreme Court litigation has not been equal, nor has the process of exchange been completed.[4] Men, who hold and historically have held most of the power in American society, have been called upon to concede their exclusive authority in the economically dominant public sphere, while women have been asked to relinquish their priority

---

† Professor of Law, University of California, Berkeley. B.A., 1956, Southern Methodist University; J.D., 1959, University of Chicago. I am grateful to my research assistant, Mark D. Greenberg, for his help during the preparation of this paper, and to Katherine Bartlett, Jesse Choper, Ruth Bader Ginsburg, Christine Littleton, Andrea Peterson, Robert Post, Deborah Rhode, and Karen Tokarz for commenting on an earlier draft of this paper. The views expressed here are my own.

1 U.S. CONST. amend. XIV.

2 Title VII of the Civil Rights Act, 42 U.S.C. § 2000e *et seq.* (1964); *see also* the Equal Pay Act, 29 U.S.C. § 206(d) (1963).

3 The Supreme Court first construed the provisions of Title VII in a sex discrimination case in Phillips v. Martin Marietta Corp., 400 U.S. 542 (1971); it first invalidated a sex-based classification on constitutional grounds in Reed v. Reed, 404 U.S. 71 (1971).

4 Wendy Williams has identified the roles that our culture associates most closely with a particular sex as the military combat role for men and the maternal role for women. *See* Williams, *The Equality Crisis: Some Reflections on Culture, Courts, and Feminism*, 7 WOMEN'S RIGHTS L. REP. 175, 182-183, 190 (1982). The Supreme Court has refused either to compel men to yield to women their exclusive responsibility for combat, *see* Rostker v. Goldberg, 453 U.S. 57 (1981) (upholding compulsory registration for males but not females on the theory that a draft would be necessary only to procure males as combat troops), or to deprive unwed mothers of newborns of their primary responsibility for decisions affecting infants, *see* Caban v. Mohammed, 441 U.S. 380, 392 n.11 (1979) (holding that the mother of an illegitimate child with whom the father had formed a family relationship must share with him her right to decide whether the child will be adopted, but declining to consider whether its holding extends to the adoption of newborns). *See also* Lehr v. Robertson, 463 U.S. 248, 265-68 (1983) (father who had not established a custodial relationship with his illegitimate child is not denied equal protection when mother is given the sole right to consent to a step-parent adoption).

in the less highly valued private sphere. But I have identified elsewhere[5] a pattern of dual access characteristic of the Supreme Court sex discrimination cases that suggests a mutual desire on the part of both women and men to transcend traditional sex lines.

In ruling upon the legal aspects of this exchange of power, the Supreme Court has attempted to use an assimilationist model of equality drawn from earlier cases challenging race discrimination.[6] I have argued that a model of cross-sex assimilation is useful in those many situations in which women and men share the relevant characteristics that are compared for purposes of measurement.[7] In those few situations where the biological reproductive differences that define the sexes are directly involved,[8] however, I have concluded that the assimilationist model is not useful in achieving legal equality between women and men, and that a different model must be developed.[9] This paper represents a beginning effort to develop an alternative model for thinking about the reproductive difference that has been used to justify the existence of a separate sphere for women: pregnancy. Part I of this paper will examine two recent cases that raise the question of whether pregnancy, a condition that only women experience, may be treated differently in the employment setting from other physical conditions that all workers may experience. Part II will offer a new analytical approach to conceptualizing the legal significance of biological reproductive conduct, which I call "episodic analysis." My thesis is that episodic analysis will help us to avoid penalizing women as the result of their reproductive behavior and thus permit us to accommodate pregnancy within a legal and philosophical framework that affirms the equality of women and men.

I. Pregnancy at Work: The Disability Cases

A. Background: *LaFleur, Geduldig*, and *Gilbert*

Litigation over the treatment of pregnancy at work appeared on the

---

[5] *See* Kay, *Models of Equality*, 1985 U. ILL. L. REV. 39 (1985).

[6] *Id.* at 48-77.

[7] *Id.* at 77-78. The Court's use of an assimilationist model is limited by its failure to apply that model free of stereotypical notions about the proper roles of women and men. *See supra* note 4; *see also* Freedman, *Sex Equality, Sex Differences, and the Supreme Court*, 92 YALE L.J. 913 (1983).

[8] Biological reproductive differences comprise the female's capacity to menstruate, become pregnant, and lactate, and the male's capacity to produce and ejaculate sperm. I do not examine, in this paper, assertions that more generalized sex differences support varying legal treatment of men and women. *Compare* Browne, *Biology, Equality, and the Law: The Legal Significance of Biological Sex Differences*, 38 SW. L.J. 617 (1984), *with* Darrough, *Biological Differences and Economic Equality: Race and Sex*, in BIOLOGICAL DIFFERENCES AND SOCIAL EQUALITY (M. Darrough & R. Blank eds. 1983); and Jaggar, *Human Biology in Feminist Theory: Sexual Equality Reconsidered*, in BEYOND DOMINATION: NEW PERSPECTIVES ON WOMEN AND PHILOSOPHY (C. Gould ed. 1983).

[9] Kay, *supra* note 5, at 78-87. *See also* Law, *Rethinking Sex and the Constitution*, 132 U. PA. L. REV. 955, 963-69 (1984).

Supreme Court's docket early in its consideration of the meaning of legal equality between the sexes. The first cases, consolidated under the name *Cleveland Board of Education v. LaFleur*,[10] involved mandatory maternity leave policies that excluded pregnant teachers from the classroom, even though they were able and willing to continue working.[11] Plaintiffs challenged the policies as violations of both due process and equal protection.[12]

The Courts of Appeal gave the equal protection claim a mixed response. In *LaFleur*, a Sixth Circuit majority accepted plaintiff's argument that a mandatory maternity leave rule based on pregnancy was a classification based on sex. Judge Edwards compared the treatment accorded to pregnant teachers with that applied to male teachers suffering from other illnesses or disabilities and held that the pregnant teachers had been denied equal protection.[13] In *Cohen v. Chesterfield County School Board*,[14] the Fourth Circuit split over whether a classification based on pregnancy constituted sex-based discrimination at all. Chief Judge Haynsworth was of the view that no sex discrimination was involved because the regulation "does not apply to women in an area in which they may compete with men."[15] Judge Winter, in dissent, made

---

10 414 U.S. 632 (1974). The *LaFleur* opinion also resolved another case reported below as Cohen v. Chesterfield County School Bd., 474 F.2d 395 (4th Cir. 1973), *rev'd sub nom.* Cleveland Bd. of Educ. v. LaFleur, 414 U.S. 632 (1974). These cases were the first to be reviewed on the merits. The Court had earlier denied review in one case involving a policy prohibiting pregnant women from working later than two months before the expected date of delivery, *see* Schattman v. Texas Employment Comm'n, 459 F.2d 32 (5th Cir. 1972), *cert. denied*, 409 U.S. 1107, *rehearing denied*, 410 U.S. 959 (1973), and had vacated and remanded another case involving pregnant servicewomen, *see* Struck v. Secretary of Defense, 460 F.2d 1372 (9th Cir. 1972), *cert. granted*, 409 U.S. 947, *vacated and remanded*, 409 U.S. 1071 (1972).

11 The pregnant teachers in *LaFleur* were required to take a maternity leave without pay, beginning five months before the expected date of birth. A teacher on maternity leave was not promised re-employment following delivery, but she was given priority in reassignment. At any event, she was not permitted to resume teaching until the beginning of the regular school semester which followed the date upon which her child attained the age of three months. In *Cohen*, a teacher was required to leave work four months prior to the expected date of birth, and was guaranteed re-employment no later than the first day of the school year following the date on which a physician certified in writing that she was physically fit for work, if she could assure the Board that care of the child would cause only minimal interference with her job responsibilities. *LaFleur*, 414 U.S. at 634-37.

12 *LaFleur* and *Cohen* were filed prior to March 24, 1972, the date on which Title VII was extended to cover state agencies and educational institutions, *see* Pub. L. 92-261, 86 Stat. 103 (1972), amending former 42 U.S.C. §§ 2000e-1 and 2000e(b), and were brought under 42 U.S.C. § 1983.

13 LaFleur v. Cleveland Bd. of Educ., 465 F.2d 1184, 1188 (6th Cir. 1972), *aff'd on other grounds*, 414 U.S. 632 (1974). Chief Judge Phillips dissented from that part of the majority opinion striking down the mandatory maternity leave prior to delivery. 465 F.2d at 1189.

14 474 F.2d 395 (4th Cir. 1973) (en banc), *rev'd sub nom.* Cleveland Bd. of Educ. v. LaFleur, 414 U.S. 632 (1974).

15 *Id.* 474 F.2d at 397. Chief Judge Haynsworth elaborated this point at length, *see* 474 F.2d at 397-98, finding it helpful to invoke in aid of his argument the observation of Anatole France that "the law, in its majestic equality, forbids the rich as well as the poor to sleep under bridges, to beg in the streets, and to steal bread," and concluded that "[p]regnancy and maternity are *sui generis*, and a governmental employer's notice of them is not an invidious classification by sex." 474 F.2d at 398.

two points. He argued first that a rule applicable to pregnant teachers affected only women, barring them from working because of their sex.[16] Second, he contended that such a rule treated pregnant women differently from other employees, both male and female, who were absent from work because of elective surgical procedures.[17] The Courts of Appeal thus disagreed over which groups were being compared for purposes of the equal protection analysis. Chief Judge Haynsworth was clear that the two comparison groups could not be men and women, since "only women become pregnant."[18] Neither Judge Winter nor Judge Edwards clearly affirmed that the two comparison groups were men and women. Instead, both compared women excluded from work because of pregnancy to a group of employees composed of women and men who were absent from work because of other medical conditions. Because both groups contain women, their analysis left open the possibility that the defect in the classification was the exclusion of pregnancy as a covered disability, rather than the exclusion of women because of their sex. An equal protection analysis, however, scrutinizes discriminations based on sex. In the absence of a demonstration that a discrimination based on pregnancy constitutes a discrimination based on sex, the equal protection argument is technically incomplete. One would have thought that the missing connection between pregnancy and sex could easily be supplied. But events proved that assumption to be mistaken.

Justice Stewart, writing for the Supreme Court majority in *LaFleur*, did not resolve the conflict between the Fourth and Sixth Circuits over

---

[16] *Id.* 474 F.2d at 400-01. Judge Winter's citation, 474 F.2d at 401, to Chief Judge Brown's telling point, made while dissenting from the denial of rehearing en banc in Phillips v. Martin-Marietta Corp., 416 F.2d 1257, 1259 (5th Cir. 1969), *rev'd*, 400 U.S. 542 (1971), that an employer's refusal to hire mothers of pre-school age children but not fathers of pre-school age children is a discrimination based on sex because "[n]obody . . . has yet seen a male mother," does not refute Judge Haynsworth's argument, spurious as it is. The relevant comparison groups in *Phillips* were mothers and fathers of young children, not mothers and non-parents, regardless of sex. Once a child is born, both male and female parents can be compared to determine whether their child care responsibilities are likely to interfere with their job performance. An employer could decline, consistently with Title VII, to hire any parent of young children. Haynsworth would presumably argue, however, that a rule excluding a pregnant woman from the work force would not constitute a sex-based discrimination because it would not admit a similarly-situated man. There are no pregnant males whose work routines may be disrupted by pregnancy. Judge Winter's subsequent citation, 474 F.2d at 401, to Judge Wisdom's reasoning, dissenting in *Schattman*, 459 F.2d 32 at 42, that since "[f]emale employees are the only employees . . . who become pregnant[,] it follows that they are provisionally dismissed from work on account of their sex," does advance the argument that a rule regulating pregnancy affects only women. This point still does not show, however, that if equal protection analysis requires a comparison between two similarly situated groups, one of which is disadvantaged by a rule in comparison to the other, that a rule regulating pregnancy disadvantages women in comparison to men. The rule more precisely compares pregnant women to a group composed of those women who are not pregnant and all men, who cannot become pregnant. This alignment of the groups being compared, however, seemingly rules out the argument that the classification is facially based on sex, and requires a showing that the policy has a disparate impact on women. *See infra* text at notes 27-35. The analysis suggested in this paper may help to solve this conceptual difficulty. *See infra* text following note 153.

[17] *Cohen*, 474 F.2d at 401.

[18] *Id.* at 397.

whether a classification based on pregnancy constituted a discrimination based on sex for purposes of the equal protection clause. Instead, he invalidated the school board policies on due process grounds, using an analysis that focused on whether the policies embodied an irrebuttable presumption of physical incapacity to work that unduly penalized the teacher's constitutionally-protected decision to bear a child.[19] Justice Powell, concurring in the result, thought that "equal protection analysis is the appropriate frame of reference,"[20] but added in a footnote that he did not reach the question "whether these regulations involve sex classifications at all."[21] In his view, the conclusion that the regulations did not rationally further any legitimate state interest was sufficient to decide the case.[22]

Five months later, in *Geduldig v. Aiello*,[23] Justice Stewart confronted the question of the fit between a pregnancy-based classification and equal protection analysis in the context of a state disability insurance program that excluded from coverage disabilities accompanying normal pregnancy and childbirth.[24] He did not discuss in the text of his opinion for the majority whether a classification based on pregnancy constituted a discrimination based on sex. Instead, he compared the condition of pregnancy to other excluded disabilities, primarily short-term disabilities of less than eight days' duration.[25] He concluded that the state could rationally distinguish between those two types of excluded disabilities and covered disabilities in order to preserve the self-supporting nature of the program, its low cost to employees, and the adequacy of its coverage.[26] Justice Stewart examined in a footnote[27] the impact of the state's choice of covered risks on women employees. He denied that the exclusion of pregnancy as a covered disability classified employees by sex. Rather, he asserted, "[t]he program divides potential recipients into two

---

[19] 414 U.S. at 644-48. Tribe catalogues the "irrebuttable presumption" approach as a technique of intermediate review in the context of equal protection analysis, *see* L. TRIBE, AMERICAN CONSTITUTIONAL LAW § 16-30 (1978), and defends its use as "a modest addition to the set of intermediate remedies where the alternative, in its absence, might have been a more dramatic form of invalidation." *Id.* § 16-32 at 1096. In the context of *LaFleur*, this point suggests that the School Boards could regulate pregnancy in ways more closely related to the goals of classroom continuity and safety, rather than that pregnancy could not be regulated at all. This suggestion is confirmed by Justice Stewart's footnoted qualifications of the holding in the case. *See* 414 U.S. at 647, nn.13 & 14.

[20] 414 U.S. at 651 (concurring opinion of Justice Powell).

[21] *Id.* at 653 n.2.

[22] *Id.*

[23] 417 U.S. 484 (1974).

[24] The California statute had originally excluded all disabilities arising in connection with pregnancy. But a California court construed the statute to cover disabilities resulting from medical complications arising during pregnancy. Rentzer v. Unemployment Ins. Appeals Bd., 32 Cal. App. 3d 604, 108 Cal. Rptr. 336 (1973).

[25] 417 U.S. at 495. Short-term disabilities were covered if the employee was hospitalized. 417 U.S. at 488.

[26] *Id.* at 495-96.

[27] *Id.* at 496 n.20.

groups—pregnant women and nonpregnant persons."[28] Based on this characterization of the groups being compared, Stewart drew the conclusion that neither Winter nor Edwards had expressed: "[w]hile the first group is exclusively female, the second includes members of both sexes."[29] It followed, seemingly inexorably, that the classification did not involve a "discrimination based upon gender as such."[30]

Justice Brennan, in dissent,[31] did not challenge the majority's logic directly. Instead, he argued that the exclusion of pregnancy created one set of rules for males and another for females: "a limitation is imposed upon the disabilities for which women workers may recover, while men receive full compensation for all disabilities suffered, including those that affect only or primarily their sex, such as prostatectomies, circumcision, hemophilia and gout."[32] Justice Stewart's implicit response to this criticism invoked still more formal logic. "There is no risk," he said, "from which men are protected and women are not."[33] True, for men do not risk pregnancy. "Likewise," he added, "there is no risk from which women are protected and men are not."[34] True again, for women are not protected against loss of work due to pregnancy. The suspicion that Justice Stewart saw only the trees, while ignoring the forest, is implicit in the criticism of one commentator who charged that "[t]he conclusion that pregnancy-based classifications are not in themselves sex-based suggests an exceedingly formalistic view of the problem."[35]

Justice Stewart's view that a classification based on pregnancy is not discrimination based on sex was extended from the context of equal protection analysis to an interpretation of Title VII's prohibition against sex discrimination in employment in *General Electric Co. v. Gilbert.*[36] General Electric's disability plan included benefits for nonoccupational sickness and accidents but excluded disabilities arising during pregnancy. Justice Rehnquist, speaking for the majority, explained that "[s]ince it is a finding of sex-based discrimination that must trigger, in a case such as this, the finding of an unlawful employment practice under [the statute], *Geduldig* is precisely in point in its holding that an exclusion of preg-

---

28 *Id.*

29 *Id.*

30 *Id.*

31 *Id.* at 500-01 (dissenting opinion of Justices Brennan, Douglas and Marshall). Justice Brennan's dissent uses the strict scrutiny standard of judicial review that he and three other members of the Court had applied to classifications based on sex challenged on equal protection grounds in Frontiero v. Richardson, 411 U.S. 677, 688 (1973) (plurality opinion of Justices Brennan, Douglas, White and Marshall), but the standard of review chosen does not affect the definition of the classes to be compared.

32 *Id.* at 501 (dissenting opinion of Justices Brennan, Douglas and Marshall).

33 *Id.* at 496-97.

34 *Id.* at 497.

35 *The Supreme Court, 1976 Term*, 91 HARV. L. REV. 1, 244 (1977). The criticism is directed at the *Geduldig* reasoning as it reappeared in General Electric Co. v. Gilbert, 429 U.S. 125 (1976). *See infra* text at notes 37-38.

36 429 U.S. 125 (1976).

nancy from a disability-benefits plan providing general coverage is not a gender-based discrimination at all."[37] He offered Justice Stewart's characterization of the relevant comparison groups as "pregnant women and nonpregnant persons,"[38] this time in the text of the opinion as the centerpiece of the Court's interpretation of Title VII.

Justice Brennan, in dissent, again responded indirectly to the Court's reasoning. He did not confront the Court's denial that the omission of pregnancy was necessarily a discrimination against women because of their sex. Rather, he challenged the Court's assumption that General Electric's plan represented a gender-free actuarial decision about which risks to include,[39] arguing instead that General Electric had a history of past practices that were designed to and did disadvantage pregnant women employees.[40]

Justice Stevens undertook the task of refuting the Court's characterization of the two groups being compared. He rose to the challenge, pointing out in a footnote that

> [i]t is not accurate to describe the program as dividing "potential recipients into two groups—pregnant women and non-pregnant persons." Insurance programs, company policies, and employment contracts all deal with future *risks* rather than historic facts. The classification is between persons who face a risk of pregnancy and those who do not.[41]

Stevens concluded from his characterization that the relevant comparison groups were indeed women and men. "By definition," he pointed out, "such a rule discriminates on account of sex; for it is the capacity to become pregnant which primarily differentiates the female from the male."[42]

Justice Stevens's characterization of the groups being compared provides one possible solution to the logical dilemma posed for traditional equal protection analysis by the absence of a matching male group for pregnant women. His classification does not, however, demonstrate that the respective classes are divided exclusively by sex. While all persons who face a risk of pregnancy are female, the group of those who do not includes women who are infertile and who have been surgically sterilized, as well as men.[43] Moreover, the first group is defined too broadly to be

---

[37] *Id.* at 136.

[38] *Id.* at 135 (quoting Geduldig v. Aiello, 417 U.S. 484, at 496-97, n.20).

[39] *Id.* at 147-48 (dissenting opinion of Justices Brennan and Marshall).

[40] *Id.* at 149-50 (dissenting opinion of Justices Brennan and Marshall).

[41] *Id.* at 161 n.5 (dissenting opinion of Justice Stevens) (emphasis in original).

[42] *Id.* at 161-62 (dissenting opinion of Justice Stevens).

[43] This distinction takes on practical significance in the context of toxic work sites. *See* Oil, Chemical & Atomic Workers v. Cyanamid Co., 741 F.2d 444, 450 (D.C. Cir. 1984) (holding that the company's fetus protection policy did not constitute a "hazard" within the meaning of the Occupational Safety and Health Act, 29 U.S.C. § 654(a)(1) (1983)). The fetus protection policy excluded women of childbearing age from holding jobs that exposed them to toxic substances at levels considered unsafe for fetuses. Women who could show that they had been surgically sterilized were exempted from the policy. 741 F.2d at 445. A related suit, challeng-

useful in all situations. Thus, the requirement imposed in *LaFleur* of a mandatory maternity leave prior to delivery affected only pregnant teachers, not all teachers who faced the risk of pregnancy. Stevens's characterization, with its emphasis on future risk, is helpful in the context of insurance, but it does not solve the entire range of actual problems associated with reproduction that confront working women.

The Supreme Court's analysis in *Gilbert* rejected the contrary view of Title VII's coverage that had been adopted in the wake of *Geduldig* by six Courts of Appeal.[44] Pregnant women and their allies, thwarted in their attempt to obtain judicial protection against the exclusion of pregnancy from employer disability programs, turned to Congress for relief.

B. The Congressional Response to *Gilbert*: The Pregnancy Discrimination Act of 1978

A coalition of more than three hundred groups, including labor unions, feminist groups and some church groups, lobbied for Congressional repeal of *Gilbert*.[45] In response, Congress amended Title VII by enacting the Pregnancy Discrimination Act[46] (PDA) which defined the statutory term "sex" to include "pregnancy." Commentators[47] pointed out that the PDA was intended to overrule the Supreme Court's decision in *Gilbert*. The Court, in *Newport News Shipbuilding & Dry Dock Co. v. EEOC*,[48] acknowledged that the PDA had rejected both the result and the reasoning in *Gilbert*. For statutory purposes,[49] after 1978, the Court conceded that "discrimination based on a woman's pregnancy is, on its

---

ing the fetus protection policy as a discrimination against women under Title VII, was settled. 741 F.2d at 450 n.1.

44 *See* cases cited in *Gilbert*, 429 U.S. at 147 (dissenting opinion of Justice Brennan).

45 J. GELB & M. PALLEY, WOMEN AND PUBLIC POLICIES 159-60 (1982).

46 Pregnancy Discrimination Act of 1978. The Act provides:

> The terms "because of sex" or "on the basis of sex" include, but are not limited to, because of or on the basis of pregnancy, childbirth, or related medical conditions; and women affected by pregnancy, childbirth, or related medical conditions shall be treated the same for all employment-related purposes, including receipt of benefits under fringe benefit programs, as other persons not so affected but similar in their ability or inability to work, and nothing in section 2000e-2(h) of this title shall be interpreted to permit otherwise. This subsection shall not require an employer to pay for health insurance benefits for abortion, except where the life of the mother would be endangered if the fetus were carried to term, or except where medical complications have arisen from an abortion: *Provided*, That nothing herein shall preclude an employer from providing abortion benefits or otherwise affect bargaining agreements in regard to abortion.

42 U.S.C. § 2000(e)(k) (1982).

47 *See, e.g.*, Williams, *supra* note 4, at 193; Note, *Sexual Equality Under the Pregnancy Discrimination Act*, 83 COLUM. L. REV. 690, 691-93 (1983) [hereinafter cited as Note, *Sexual Equality*].

48 462 U.S. 669 (1983) (holding that an employer that had amended its health insurance plan in response to the PDA to provide hospitalization benefits to female employees but had not at the same time extended such hospitalization benefits to the wives of male employees discriminated against men on the basis of their sex).

49 The PDA did not affect the Court's constitutional holding in *Geduldig*.

face, discrimination because of her sex."[50]

Many feminist lawyers active in the repeal effort interpreted the PDA as mandating that pregnant women be treated the same as other workers.[51] Other observers pointed out, however, that although the PDA ensures that pregnant women workers are equally entitled to any disability coverage the employer may provide for other workers, "[l]ess clear . . . is what the PDA requires of an employer who currently offers no disability programs at all, and who refuses to grant pregnancy benefits on the ground that to do so would be to treat pregnancy differently than other disabilities."[52] Specifically, the questions left open are whether Title VII, as amended by the PDA, forbids neutral employment practices with a disparate impact on pregnant women, and whether the PDA permits states to require employers to provide job-related incentives to retain pregnant women in the labor force if similar benefits are not mandated for other workers.[53] Such incentives may include, for example, the availability of a reasonable, non-mandatory leave during pregnancy, work-place accommodations, such as facilities for lying down during rest breaks, and the right to return to work following delivery.[54] Two recent

---

[50] *Newport News*, 462 U.S. at 684.

[51] *See, e.g.*, Williams, *supra* note 4, at 193-94:

> At the time the PDA was passed, all feminist groups supported it. Special treatment of pregnancy in the workplace had always been synonymous with unfavorable treatment; the rules generally had the effect of forcing women out of the work force and back into the home when they became pregnant. By treating pregnancy discrimination as sex discrimination, the PDA required that pregnant women be treated as well as other wage earners who became disabled. The degree to which this assisted women depended on the generosity of their particular employers' sick leave or disability policy, but anything at all was better than what most pregnant women had had before. (Footnotes omitted).

[52] *See* Note, *Sexual Equality*, *supra* note 47, at 693.

[53] Larson notes that "the character of the maternity leave issue changes markedly" in cases where the employer has no sick leave or temporary disability program. Since there is no class of employees composed of men and women who receive more generous benefits than those accorded to pregnant women, the PDA's comparative approach may be interpreted to require that pregnant women similarly receive no benefits. He offers the following illustration:

> Postulate a person (man or woman) disabled for four weeks by a broken arm. The employer gives such a person no sick leave. The ability or inability of that person to work is similar to that of a female employee during the late pregnancy and childbirth period. Read mechanically, the statute says that the pregnant employee shall be treated *the same* as the employee with the broken arm, which is to say, shall be given no leave.
>
> Obviously this amendment, consecrated to improving the lot of pregnant employees, never intended such a result, and, given half a chance, courts will undoubtedly find some way of preserving the pre-amendment rule.

1 A. LARSON, EMPLOYMENT DISCRIMINATION § 38.22, at 8-34—8-35 (1985) (emphasis in original). It seems fairly clear, however, that feminists who interpret the PDA as designed to achieve what they see as "equal treatment" of men and women accept the "mechanical" reading Larson identifies as a necessary by-product of their position, at least in the absence of a judicial or legislative willingness to extend what they see as "special" benefits designed for pregnant women to all disabled workers. *See infra* text and accompanying notes 88-91. Larson's view that, in this context, identical treatment does not constitute equal treatment is discussed *infra*, at note 99.

[54] *See* Chavkin, *Walking a Tightrope: Pregnancy, Parenting, and Work*, in DOUBLE EXPOSURE: WOMEN'S HEALTH HAZARDS ON THE JOB AND AT HOME, 196 (W. Chavkin, ed. 1984). *Cf.*

cases, discussed in the next section, raise the potential conflict between state and federal law when state statutes impose a duty upon employers to provide a reasonable leave to pregnant employees without regard to whether leaves are available to employees disabled for other reasons, and to provide re-employment after delivery. If such laws are not preempted by Title VII, the further question remains whether they violate any relevant state or federal constitutional provisions.

C. *Miller-Wohl* and *California Federal*: An Acknowledgement of Difference

1. *Miller-Wohl*

In 1972, Montana adopted an equal rights amendment to its state constitution.[55] In 1974, the Montana legislature created an interim study group and charged its members with the responsibility of studying existing Montana laws distinguishing between persons on the basis of sex, and determining "what changes should be made in these laws to achieve true legal equality of the sexes while preserving for all the people of Montana those essential protections which orderly government provides for its citizens."[56] In responding to this charge, the subcommittee noted its awareness of "the most common criticism of equal rights legislation: that equal rights for men and women would destroy the family and bring chaos to an orderly society and government."[57] The subcommittee sought to meet this criticism by harmonizing the potentially divisive pursuit of equality with the preservation of traditional family life. To that end, it proposed legislation which it believed "would accomplish real sexual equality while encouraging stable and workable family and societal relationships."[58] This approach, applied to the situation of pregnant working women, produced a bill that, as redrafted, was enacted in 1975 as the Montana Maternity Leave Act.[59] The Act enabled pregnant women to choose to continue working during pregnancy; to have a reasonable pregnancy leave; to collect any appropriate and available disabil-

---

Burns v. Rohr Corp., 346 F. Supp. 994, 996-98 (S.D. Cal. 1972) (invalidating under Title VII a state statute requiring rest periods for women only). Under the analysis suggested here, a more narrowly drawn statute authorizing, but not requiring, rest periods for pregnant workers only might survive a Title VII challenge.

55 Mont. Const. art. II, § 4 provides in part that "[n]either the state nor any person, firm, corporation, or institution shall discriminate against any person in the exercise of his civil or political rights on account of race, color, sex, culture, social origin or condition, or political or religious ideas."

56 1974 Mont. Laws, S.J. Res. No. 68. The study group issued an interim report recommending specific legislation, including a provision that ultimately became the Montana Maternity Leave Act. *See* Equality of the Sexes, Appendix 1-11 (Interim Study by the Montana Subcommittee on Judiciary, December, 1974).

57 Equality of the Sexes, *supra* note 56, at 3.

58 *Id.*

59 Mont. Code Ann. §§ 49-2-310—49-2-311 (1983). The Act reads in part as follows:

ity benefits; to return to work after delivery; and to be free of retaliation for filing a complaint against an employer who violated the Act.[60] The Montana law thus pre-dated the enactment of the PDA. Indeed, the House Committee Report accompanying the PDA cited Montana, along with five other states, as jurisdictions that "specifically include pregnancy in their Fair Employment Practices Laws."[61] Once the PDA became effective, on October 31, 1978, however, the stage was set for a potential conflict between the two laws.

The facts that provided the legal basis for a challenge to the Montana law based on the PDA occurred less than a year after the enactment of the federal provision. On August 1, 1979, the Miller-Wohl Company hired Tamara L. Buley to work as a salesperson in its clothing store in Great Falls, Montana. She missed two-and-a-half days of work during her first week of employment. She thought she had contracted the flu. Instead, as she learned two weeks later, she was pregnant. In its opinion in *Miller-Wohl Co. v. Commissioner of Labor and Industry*,[62] the Montana Supreme Court thus described her condition:

> During the next two weeks she suffered from "morning sickness." She felt nauseated and faint, and as a result missed time from work, had to leave the selling floor for breaks, and spent considerable time in the store bathroom vomiting, and was sent home early on occasion.[63]

Miller-Wohl fired Buley on August 27, 1979. The Montana Supreme Court observed that the employer took this action "undoubtedly because

---

§ 49-2-310. Maternity Leave—unlawful acts of employers. It shall be unlawful for an employer or his agent to:

(1) terminate a woman's employment because of her pregnancy;

(2) refuse to grant to the employee a reasonable leave of absence for such pregnancy;

(3) deny to the employee who is disabled as a result of pregnancy any compensation to which she is entitled as a result of the accumulation of disability or leave benefits accrued pursuant to plans maintained by her employer, provided that the employer may require disability as a result of pregnancy to be verfied by medical certification that the employee is not able to perform her employment duties; or

(4) require that an employee take a mandatory maternity leave for an unreasonable length of time.

§ 49-2-311. Reinstatement to job following pregnancy-related leave of absence. Upon signifying her intent to return at the end of her leave of absence, such employee shall be reinstated to her original job or to an equivalent position with equivalent pay and accumulated seniority, retirement, fringe benefits, and other service credits, unless, in the case of a private employer, the employer's circumstances have so changed as to make it impossible or unreasonable to do so.

[60] *Id.* Section 49-2-310(4) was not part of the subcommittee proposal. *See* EQUALITY OF THE SEXES, *supra* note 56, at 157-60. As originally enacted in 1975, the Act also contained § 39-7-203(4) which declared that it was unlawful for an employer to "retaliate against any employee who files a complaint with the commissioner under the provisions of this part." A 1983 amendment deleted subsection (4).

[61] H.R. REP. No. 948, 95th Cong., 2d Sess. 11, *reprinted in* 1978 U.S. CODE CONG. & AD. NEWS 4749, 4759. The other five states mentioned were Alaska, Connecticut, Maryland, Minnesota and Oregon.

[62] 692 P.2d 1243 (Mont. 1984), *appeal docketed*, 53 U.S.L.W. 3718 (U.S. April 9, 1985) (No. 84-1545).

[63] *Id.* at 1245.

her pregnancy diminished her effectiveness as a sales clerk."[64]

Buley filed a complaint on August 6, 1980, with the Montana Commissioner of Labor and Industry. The Commissioner found that Miller-Wohl had violated the Montana Maternity Leave Act. It ordered Miller-Wohl to reinstate Buley as an employee and provide her with back pay plus penalty of $6,573.60.[65] Miller-Wohl, which had earlier commenced a declaratory judgment complaint in the federal district court, then pressed that court for a determination that Title VII preempted the Montana law. The federal district court ruled against preemption,[66] but its judgment was vacated by the Ninth Circuit for lack of subject matter jurisdiction.[67]

Miller-Wohl then turned to the Montana state courts, petitioning for a review of the Commissioner's decision. A lower state court reversed the Commissioner's order.[68] Buley and the Commissioner appealed that judgment to the Montana Supreme Court, which reversed, reinstating the Commissioner's order.

2. *California Federal* (*Cal Fed*)

The California legislature amended the California Fair Employment Practice Act in 1978 to define as an unfair labor practice an employer's refusal to allow a female employee to take a leave for a reasonable period of time, not to exceed four months, on account of pregnancy.[69] Unlike the Montana Maternity Leave Act, which had been proposed in response

---

64 *Id.*

65 *Id.*

66 Miller-Wohl Co. v. Comm'r of Labor & Industry, 515 F. Supp. 1264 (D. Mont. 1981), *vacated*, 685 F.2d 1088 (9th Cir. 1982). Judge Hatfield reasoned that Miller-Wohl could comply with both state and federal law by amending its leave policy to grant reasonable sickness and disability leaves to all first year employees in its Montana stores. 515 F. Supp. at 1267. The Montana Supreme Court subsequently approved his reasoning supporting the view that the Montana statute did not violate the equal protection clause. *See infra* text and accompanying notes 97-98.

67 Miller-Wohl Co. v. Comm'r of Labor & Industry, 685 F.2d 1088, 1090-91 (9th Cir. 1982) (holding that the federal claims raised in Miller-Wohl's declaratory judgment complaint were defenses to Buley's state claim, and failed to create the requisite federal question).

68 *Miller-Wohl*, 692 P.2d at 1246.

69 1978 Cal. Stat. 4320 § 1, adding CAL. LAB. CODE § 1420.35 to the California Fair Employment Practice Act, former CAL. LAB. CODE §§ 1410-33. The FEPA was rechaptered and retitled as the Fair Employment and Housing Act in 1980. The provisions of CAL. LAB. CODE § 1420.35 were incorporated into the FEHA as CAL. GOV'T CODE § 12945. The language of CAL. GOV'T CODE § 12945(b)(2) is the same as that earlier contained in former CAL. LAB. CODE § 1420.35(b)(2). As § 12945(e) makes plain, only § 12945(b)(2) applies to employers subject to Title VII. The other provisions are limited to employers governed by state law only. CAL. GOV'T CODE. § 12945 (Deering 1982) reads in its entirety as follows:

> It shall be an unlawful employment practice unless based upon a bona fide occupational qualification:
>
> (a) For any employer, because of the pregnancy, childbirth, or related medical condition of any female employee, to refuse to promote her, or to refuse to select her for a training program leading to promotion, provided she is able to complete the training program at least three months prior to the anticipated date of departure for her pregnancy leave, or to discharge her from employment or from a training program leading

to a charge to implement the Montana Equal Rights Amendment,[70] the California statute was enacted in response to the Supreme Court's decision in *Gilbert*.[71] The amendment broadened the coverage of an existing provision that made it unlawful for governing boards of school districts to discriminate against females because of their pregnancy, or to terminate any employee whose temporary disability could not be accommodated because of an employment policy that provided no leave or insufficient leave, if the policy had a disparate impact on employees of one sex and was not justified by business necessity.[72] The Attorney Gen-

---

to promotion, or to discriminate against her in compensation or in terms, conditions, or privileges of employment.

(b) For any employer to refuse to allow a female employee affected by pregnancy, childbirth, or related medical conditions either:

(1) To receive the same benefits or privileges of employment granted by that employer to other persons not so affected who are similar in their ability or inability to work, including to take disability or sick leave or any other accrued leave which is made available by the employer to temporarily disabled employees. For purposes of this section, pregnancy, childbirth, and related medical conditions are treated as any other temporary disability. However, no employer shall be required to provide a female employee disability leave on account of normal pregnancy, childbirth, or related medical condition for a period exceeding six weeks. Nothing in this section shall be construed to require an employer to provide his or her employees with health insurance coverage for the medical costs of pregnancy, childbirth, or related medical conditions. The inclusion in any such health insurance coverage of any provisions or coverage relating to medical costs of pregnancy, childbirth, or related medical conditions shall not be construed to require the inclusion of any other provisions or coverage, nor shall coverage of any related medical conditions be required by virtue of coverage of any medical costs of pregnancy, childbirth, or other related medical conditions.

(2) To take a leave on account of pregnancy for a reasonable period of time; provided, such period shall not exceed four months. Such employee shall be entitled to utilize any accrued vacation leave during this period of time. Reasonable period of time means that period during which the female employee is disabled on account of pregnancy, childbirth, or related medical conditions. Nothing herein shall be construed to limit the provisions of paragraph (1) of subdivision (b).

An employer may require any employee who plans to take a leave pursuant to this subdivision to give the employer reasonable notice of the date such leave shall commence and the estimated duration of such leave.

(c)(1) For an employer who has a policy, practice, or collective-bargaining agreement requiring or authorizing the transfer of temporarily disabled employees to less strenuous or hazardous positions for the duration of the disability to refuse to transfer a pregnant female employee who so requests.

(2) For any employer to refuse to temporarily transfer a pregnant female employee to a less strenuous or hazardous position for the duration of her pregnancy if she so requests, with the advice of her physician, where such transfer can be reasonably accommodated, provided, however, that no employer shall be required by this section to create additional employment which the employer would not otherwise have created, nor shall such employer be required to discharge any employee, transfer any employee with more seniority, or promote any employee who is not qualified to perform the job.

(d) This section shall not be construed to affect any other provision of law relating to sex discrimination or pregnancy.

(e) The provisions of this section, except paragraph (2) of subdivision (b), shall be inapplicable to any employer subject to Title VII of the federal Civil Rights Act of 1964.

[70] *See supra* text at notes 55-58.

[71] *See Review of Selected 1978 California Legislation*, 10 PAC. L.J. 247, 463 (1979).

[72] CAL. LAB. CODE § 1420.2, added by 1975 Cal. Stat. 2018, § 3, rechaptered as CAL. GOV'T CODE § 12943 (1980).

eral of California argued in a brief filed before a federal district court that the legislative intent underlying the amendment "was aimed at broadening employee protection against adverse impact on the basis of pregnancy."[73]

As in the case of the Montana law, an employer charged with violating the state law challenged the California statute as being in conflict with Title VII. Lillian B. Garland, who worked as a receptionist and PBX operator for California Federal Savings and Loan Association in Los Angeles, took a pregnancy/childbirth disability leave beginning around January 18, 1982.[74] Her baby was born on February 12, 1982.[75] She notified the company on or about April 20, 1982, that she was able to return to work. The personnel department informed her that no receptionist position or similar job openings were then available. After waiting for seven months,[76] Lillian Garland returned to work at Cal Fed as a receptionist on November 22, 1982.

Garland contacted the California Department of Fair Employment and Housing for advice. The Department served an accusation on Cal Fed on May 2, 1983, alleging that it was in violation of California law. A hearing on the charge was scheduled for September 15-16, 1983. On August 1, 1983, Cal Fed filed a suit for declaratory and injunctive relief in the federal district court, contending that the California pregnancy leave provision was preempted by federal law.[77] The federal court

---

73 Defendants' Notice of Motion and Motion for Summary Judgment; Memorandum of Points and Authorities in Support of Motion for Summary Judgment at 23, California Federal Savings & Loan Ass'n v. Guerra, 34 Fair Empl. Prac. Cas. (BNA) 562 (C.D. Cal. 1984), *rev'd* 758 F.2d 390 (9th Cir. 1985) [hereafter cited as *Cal Fed*]. The legislation as enacted may have gone further than some of its sponsors and supporters intended, if they thought that a purely comparative approach extending already existing benefits to pregnant workers was envisioned. *See* Brief of National Organization for Women as *amicus curiae* at 36-41, California Federal Savings & Loan Ass'n v. Guerra, 758 F.2d 390 (9th Cir. 1985) [hereinafter cited as Brief of NOW].

74 *Id.* Defendants' Notice of Motion and Motion for Summary Judgment, *supra* note 73, at 5, 6. The parties entered into stipulated findings of fact, *id.* at 6, n.2. Except where indicated, the facts of the case stated in the text are based on this stipulation.

75 *See* Lewin, *Maternity Leave: Is It Leave, Indeed?* New York Times, July 22, 1984, at F1, col. 5.

76 Lewin reports that during that seven month period, "[t]hings got worse for Miss Garland . . . : Lacking income, she was evicted from her apartment, and had to sleep on a woman friend's couch. Without resources to care for the baby, she lost custody to the child's father." Lewin, *supra* note 75, at col. 6.

77 The federal court enjoined the Department from holding the scheduled hearing. Judge Real also rejected the Department's motion to dismiss for lack of subject matter jurisdiction. *Cal Fed*, 34 Fair Empl. Prac. Cas. (BNA) at 567. Subsequent to the Ninth Circuit's holding in *Miller-Wohl* that a defense based on federal law to a state claim was not sufficient to confer subject matter jurisdiction on a federal court, *see supra* text and accompanying note 67, the United States Supreme Court arguably undercut that holding. In Shaw v. Delta Air Lines, Inc., 463 U.S. 85, 96 n.14 (1983), the Court distinguished its holdings in Franchise Tax Board v. Construction Laborers Vacation Trust, 463 U.S. 1 (1983), that the federal courts lacked subject matter jurisdiction over an action seeking a declaration that state laws were not pre-empted by federal law. The Court pointed out that in *Shaw*, by contrast, "companies subject to ERISA [Employee Retirement Income Security Act] regulation seek injunctions against enforcement of state laws they claim *are* pre-empted by ERISA, as well as declarations that

entered its order on March 21, 1984, granting Cal Fed's motion for summary judgment.[78] The Department appealed the judgment to the Ninth Circuit, which reversed.[79]

3. Arguments By the Parties in *Miller-Wohl* and *Cal Fed*

The employers in *Miller-Wohl* and *Cal Fed* made broadly similar statutory arguments. Both characterized the respective state statutes as requiring that they violate Title VII by treating pregnant women more favorably than they treated other disabled employees.[80] Miller-Wohl, but not Cal Fed, also claimed that the state law violated the due process and equal protection clauses of the federal constitution.[81]

The state defendants in the two cases took essentially similar positions. The Montana Commissioner contended that the Maternity Leave Act was supplemental, rather than contradictory, to Title VII.[82] In addition, the Commissioner sought to uphold the statute against constitutional attack by characterizing it as an affirmative action measure designed to enable women to contribute to society according to their fullest possible potential.[83] The California state defendants argued that the state statute was fully consistent with the goals and objectives of Title

---

those laws are pre-empted." *Id.* 463 U.S. at 96 n.14 (emphasis in original). The Court went on to point out that

> It is beyond dispute that federal courts have jurisdiction over suits to enjoin state officials from interfering with federal rights. See *Ex parte Young*, 209 U.S. 123, 160-162, 28 S. Ct. 441, 454-455, 52 L.Ed. 714 (1908). A plaintiff who seeks injunctive relief from state regulation, on the ground that such regulation is pre-empted by a federal statute which, by virtue of the Supremacy Clause of the Constitution, must prevail, thus presents a federal question which the federal courts have jurisdiction under 28 U.S.C. § 1331 to resolve. [Citations and further text omitted.]

Id. The jurisdictional question was not briefed or argued in *Shaw*, but the Department accepted *Shaw* as controlling on this point in *Cal Fed*. Lillian Garland's subsequent motion to intervene as of right before the Ninth Circuit on the issue of subject matter jurisdiction was rejected by that court in an unpublished memorandum filed simultaneously with its opinion on the merits. *Cal Fed*, 758 F.2d at 393.

78 *Cal Fed*, 34 Fair Empl. Prac. Cas. (BNA) 562 (C.D. Cal. 1984), *rev'd*, 758 F.2d 390 (9th Cir. 1985).

79 *Cal Fed*, 758 F.2d 390 (9th Cir. 1985).

80 Complaint of Miller-Wohl Co. at 7, Miller-Wohl Co. v. Comm'r of Labor & Industry, Etc., 515 F. Supp. 1264 (D. Mont. 1981), *vacated*, 685 F.2d 1088 (9th Cir. 1982); Complaint of California Federal Savings & Loan Ass'n at 11, *Cal Fed*, 34 Fair Empl. Prac. Cas. (BNA) 562 (C.D. Cal. 1984), *rev'd* 758 F.2d 390 (9th Cir. 1985). Miller-Wohl also asserted that the Montana law required it to give "preference to females without equal or similar treatment to males." Complaint of Miller-Wohl Co. at 9. Cal Fed's additional claim that the California statute was preempted by the federal Employee Retirement Income Security Act of 1974 (ERISA), 88 Stat. 829, as amended, 29 U.S.C. § 1001 *et seq.* (1976 ed. and Supp. V), Complaint of Cal Fed at 13-15, was subsequently dropped. *Cal Fed*, 758 F.2d at 393 n.5.

81 Complaint of Miller-Wohl, *supra* note 80, at 7. Miller-Wohl refrained from claiming, however, that the Montana Maternity Leave Act violated the state constitutional Equal Rights Amendment that it was designed to implement.

82 Brief of the Commissioner of Labor and Industry at 1-14, Miller-Wohl Co. v. Comm'r of Labor & Industry, Etc., 515 F. Supp. 1264 (D. Mont. 1981), *vacated*, 685 F. 2d 1088 (9th Cir. 1982).

83 *Id.* at 15-17.

VII. In their view, the state statute was designed to assure equal employment opportunity for women by protecting female employees affected by pregnancy, childbirth, and related medical conditions from the adverse impact of employment policies that provide insufficient disability leave, or fail to assure that women who take disability leave on account of pregnancy have the right to return to the same or similar job within a reasonable period of time.[84] The California defendants relied on *Abraham v. Graphic Arts International Union*,[85] in which the Court of Appeals for the District of Columbia Circuit had held in a case arising prior to the enactment of the PDA that an employer's ten-day maximum leave policy violated Title VII because of its adverse impact on women who became pregnant. In addition, they pointed to passages in the legislative history of the PDA that they interpreted as evidencing Congressional approval of the Montana statute and other similar statutes dealing with pregnancy.[86] The California defendants broadly summarized this part of their argument:

> [W]hile the legislative history of the PDA reflects Congress' intent that women affected by pregnancy, childbirth or related medical conditions not receive less favorable treatment than similarly situated coworkers, plaintiffs have pointed to nothing in the legislative history which supports their assertion that in enacting the PDA it was Congress' intent to foreclose state legislation which provides pregnant workers with additional protection in order to ensure equality of employment opportunity.[87]

4. Arguments of *Amici Curiae* in *Miller-Wohl* and *Cal Fed*

Feminist and civil rights groups split over the question of statutory interpretation posed in *Miller-Wohl* and *Cal Fed*. Briefs filed in *Miller-Wohl* by a consortium of groups led by the American Civil Liberties Union[88] and in *Cal Fed* by a consortium of groups and individuals led by the National Organization for Women[89] argued that state legislative

---

[84] Defendants' Notice of Motion and Motion for Summary Judgment, *Cal Fed*, *supra* note 73, at 23-26.

[85] 660 F.2d 811 (D.C. Cir. 1981). *See* Defendants' Notice of Motion and Motion for Summary Judgment, *Cal Fed*, *supra* note 73, at 27-28.

[86] Defendants' Notice of Motion and Motion for Summary Judgment, *Cal Fed*, *supra* note 73, at 34-35 and 34 n.12.

[87] Defendants' Memorandum in Response to Plaintiffs' Motion for Summary Judgment at 12, *Cal Fed*, 34 Fair Empl. Prac. Cas. 562 (C.D. Cal. 1984), *rev'd* 758 F.2d 390 (9th Cir. 1985).

[88] Brief of American Civil Liberties Union as *Amicus Curiae*, Miller-Wohl Co. v. Comm'r of Labor & Industry, 692 P.2d 1243 (Mont. 1984) [hereinafter cited as Brief of ACLU]. Other groups joining the ACLU brief were the ACLU of Montana, the National Organization for Women, Montana State NOW, the NOW Legal Defense and Education Fund, the League of Women Voters of the United States, the League of Women Voters of Montana, the National Women's Law Center, and the Women's Legal Defense Fund. Three other Montana groups filed separate *amicus curiae* briefs in support of the Montana statute: the Women's Law Section of the State Bar of Montana, the Montana Human Rights Commission, and the Montana Education Association.

[89] Brief of NOW, *supra* note 73. NOW was joined by the NOW Legal Defense and Education Fund, the National Women's Political Caucus, the League of Women Voters of the United

efforts to provide special benefits to pregnant workers constituted "protective" legislation that was adverse to the long-range interests of women in equal treatment with men.[90] The state statutes were thus *prima facie* in conflict with the provisions of the PDA, which mandated equal treatment; but the courts could interpret those statutes so as to make their terms consistent with Title VII by ordering that their benefits be extended to all disabled workers.[91]

The California Department of Fair Employment and Housing, a defendant in *Cal Fed*, joined by two other groups, filed an *amicus curiae* brief[92] before the Ninth Circuit in *Miller-Wohl*. One of those groups, Equal Rights Advocates, Inc., appeared as *amicus curiae* in *Cal Fed* as well.[93] Both briefs argued that the restrictive leave policies maintained by the employers in the two cases violated Title VII because of their adverse impact on pregnant women.[94] Moreover, the state laws were consistent with the PDA in that both state and federal laws were designed to provide equal employment opportunities to pregnant women.[95]

Despite their theoretical disagreement, the two sets of *amici* were divided only narrowly in their proposed outcome in both cases. Each sought to sustain the state statutes against a claim of federal preemption. The ACLU and NOW briefs insisted, however, that the benefits provided by the state statutes must be judicially construed to extend to all workers, not merely to pregnant women. Benefits limited to pregnant workers, they contended, would be preempted by Title VII. Equal Rights Advocates and its allies believed that the PDA left the states free to enact additional measures to place pregnant workers on an equal basis with all other workers.

5. The Courts Decide

The Montana Supreme Court held that Miller-Wohl violated both the Montana law and Title VII when it fired Tamara Buley because of her pregnancy.[96] It rejected, however, the argument that the PDA pre-

---

States, the Women's Legal Defense Fund, the National Women's Law Center, the Women's Law Project, the Coal Employment Project, and by Ann E. Freedman, Eleanor Holmes Norton, Susan Deller Ross, Nadine Taub, and Wendy Webster Williams.

90 Brief of ACLU, *supra* note 88, at 9-16; Brief of NOW, *supra* note 73, at 12-16.

91 Brief of ACLU, *supra* note 88, at 27-29; Brief of NOW, *supra* note 73, at 29-45.

92 Brief of California Department of Fair Employment and Housing, Miller-Wohl Co. v. Comm'r of Labor & Industry, 685 F.2d 1088 (9th Cir. 1982). The other two groups were the Employment Law Center and Equal Rights Advocates, Inc.

93 Brief of Equal Rights Advocates, Inc., *Cal Fed*, 758 F.2d 390 (9th Cir. 1985).

94 Brief of California Department for Fair Employment and Housing, *supra* note 92, at 22-30; Brief of Equal Rights Advocates, Inc., *supra* note 93, at 20-29.

95 Brief of California Department of Fair Employment and Housing, *supra* note 92, at 31-39; Brief of Equal Rights Advocates, Inc., *supra* note 93, at 30-34.

96 *Miller-Wohl*, 692 P.2d at 1251-52. In holding that Miller-Wohl violated Title VII, the Montana Supreme Court seemed to rely both on disparate treatment (*see* McDonnell Douglas Co.

empted state law. Instead, it adopted Judge Hatfield's reasoning, which he had offered to rebut the equal protection argument in the subsequently-vacated federal district court judgment in *Miller-Wohl*.[97] Hatfield had argued that the Montana statute did not treat men and women unequally by providing benefits limited to pregnancy. He continued:

> Rather, by removing pregnancy-related disabilities as a legal grounds for discharge from employment, the MMLA places men and women on more equal terms. All workers, male or female, disabled for any reason other than pregnancy are still treated identically. Whether the disability or sickness is one that members of either sex could suffer—such as a broken leg, or hepatitis—or is one that members of only one sex could suffer—such as an ovarian cyst or prostatitis—the MMLA still permits plaintiff to treat workers under its leave policy with equal severity. The MMLA merely makes it illegal for an employer such as plaintiff [Miller-Wohl] ". . . to burden female employees in such a way as to deprive them of employment opportunities because of their different role." *National Gas Company v. Satty*, 434 U.S. 136, 142 (1977).[98]

The Montana Supreme Court thus recognized that the differentness of pregnancy cannot be adequately accommodated in the workplace by treating women the same as men. Its holding is consistent with the view taken in this paper, and developed more fully below, that equality between men and women requires compensating for biological reproductive sex differences that would otherwise handicap women and impede their realization of equal employment opportunity.[99]

---

v. Green, 411 U.S. 792, 802 (1972)) and disparate impact (*see* Griggs v. Duke Power Co., 401 U.S. 424, 430 (1971)) theories of Title VII violation. Thus, the court pointed out that "[t]he discharged pregnant woman is not treated the same for all employment-related purposes as all other persons not so affected, obviously, because men cannot be discharged for the same reason." *Id.* at 1251. This sentence, and the passage from which it is taken, equates pregnancy with sex and suggests that, after the PDA had amended Title VII, an employer's decision to fire a pregnant woman is a *per se* violation of Title VII. *Cf.* Phillips v. Martin Marietta Co., 400 U.S. 542 (1971) (holding that an employer's refusal to hire mothers, but not fathers, of pre-school aged children, constituted a *per se* violation of Title VII). The Montana court went on to hold that Miller-Wohl's no-leave policy violated Title VII because of its disparate impact on women who become pregnant, citing Abraham v. Graphic Arts Int'l Union, 660 F.2d 811 (D.C. Cir. 1981) (invalidating ten-day ceiling on disability leave because of its disparate impact on pregnant workers). *Id.* at 1252.

[97] Miller-Wohl Co. v. Comm'r of Labor & Industry, Etc., 515 F. Supp. 1264 (D. Mont. 1981), *vacated*, 685 F.2d 1088 (9th Cir. 1982).

[98] Miller-Wohl Co. v. Comm'r of Labor & Industry, 692 P.2d 1243, 1254 (Mont. 1984) (quoting *Miller-Wohl*, 515 F. Supp. at 1266).

[99] Other commentators support the view taken in this paper as well. Thus, Larson recognizes that cases like *Miller-Wohl*, where the employer has no available sick leave or temporary disability program, present problems for an analysis based on formal equality:

> We have here an example of the kind of case in which an "equality" issue cannot be disposed of by decreeing that the sexes shall be treated exactly alike. Instead, we must build upon a quite different premise: when the two sexes are *dissimilar* in that one sex exclusively possesses a trait which the other, without exception, does not possess, and when that trait has a bearing upon employability, it is a differentiation based on sex to treat the two sexes *similarly* as to that trait. Clearly, if an employer says, "All pregnant employees will be fired," there is sex differentiation. It is really no different in effect to say, "No maternity leaves will be granted." . . . [D]ischarge for pregnancy is

The Montana Supreme Court went on to point out that extension to all workers of the benefits provided by the Montana law only to pregnant workers would end any argument that the state law violated Title VII. The court recommended to the Montana legislature that it consider appropriate language to extend the Act's coverage.[100]

The Ninth Circuit also rejected the claim of federal preemption in *Cal Fed*. It disposed of Judge Real's assertion that the California statute discriminated against men on the basis of pregnancy as a conclusion that "defies common sense, misinterprets case law, and flouts Title VII and the PDA."[101] Judge Ferguson, writing for the court, characterized the preemption inquiry as a narrow one: the court must decide only whether the pregnancy leave provided by the California statute was "permissible"[102] under Title VII. In an effective rebuttal to those who fear that any judicial recognition of the uniqueness of pregnancy might lead to the uncritical acceptance of other differences as well, to the ultimate disadvantage of women,[103] Judge Ferguson made plain the limits of the holding:

> [B]ecause § 12945(b)(2) deals with a condition that is unique to women—pregnancy disability rather than, say, parenting—our decision has no bearing on the lawfulness of state statutes or employment practices that classify on the basis of purportedly sex-linked factors that are actually less biological than stereotypical.[104]

The Ninth Circuit's interpretation of the PDA recognizes that its two clauses are to be read independently.[105] It reasoned that the first

---

> sex differentiation unless accompanied by the alternative of maternity leave. This in turn leads inexorably to the statement of the proposition that exposes the apparent paradox of requiring inequality to produce equality: it is sex differentiation *not* to offer to women a benefit denied to men—maternity leave. The reason is that this "inequality" is necessary to provide substantial equality of employment opportunity.

1 A. LARSON, *supra* note 53, § 38.22, at 8-31—8-32 (emphasis in original).

See also Note, *Employment Equality Under the Pregnancy Discrimination Act of 1978*, 94 YALE L.J. 929 (1985) (arguing that the "parity of treatment" standard advanced by Wendy Williams and others for interpreting the PDA is based on a strictly formal definition of equality rather than a broader view that would permit the recognition of pregnancy as a condition specific to women) [hereinafter cited as Note, *Employment Equality*]. For a discussion of Williams's views, see *infra* text at notes 161-181. *See generally* Krieger & Cooney, *The* Miller-Wohl *Controversy: Equal Treatment, Positive Action and the Meaning of Women's Equality*, 13 GOLDEN GATE U.L. REV. 513 (1983); Scales, *Towards A Feminist Jurisprudence*, 56 IND. L.J. 375 (1981).

100 *Miller-Wohl*, 692 P.2d at 1255. The Montana legislature has not, at the date of this writing, amended the MMLA.

101 *Cal Fed*, 758 F.2d at 393 (9th Cir. 1985). The Court pointed out that Judge Real's reliance on *Newport News* for his conclusion was misplaced, since that case had required the extension to male employees' wives of pregnancy benefits available to female employees and their husbands. Cal Fed, on the contrary, sought to limit the pregnancy benefit provided by the state. *Id.* at 393-94.

102 *Id.* 758 F.2d at 394.

103 *See* Brief of NOW, *supra* note 73, at 12-16.

104 *Cal Fed*, 758 F.2d at 395.

105 A similar interpretation was advanced initially in Note, *Sexual Equality*, *supra* note 47, at 695-96, and more recently in Note, *Employment Equality*, *supra* note 99, at 934-40. *See supra* note 46 for the text of the PDA.

clause made the term "pregnancy" a substitute for the term "sex" in Title VII's antidiscrimination mandate, thus enabling Congress to procure "for pregnancy that which it had already procured for sex: a guarantee against discrimination of all varieties, including facially neutral policies with a disparate impact."[106] Contrary to Cal Fed's argument, however, the court refused to read the second clause of the PDA as demanding "pregnancy-neutral policies at all times."[107] Instead, it reasoned that Congress had intended to require at a minimum that pregnant women be treated as well as other employees, but not to prevent the states from requiring more complete maximum coverage.[108]

The Ninth Circuit's view of how pregnancy fits within the framework of an analysis based on equality between men and women is consistent with the approach taken in this paper. Judge Ferguson put the argument concisely and well in the following passage:

> The PDA does not require states to ignore pregnancy. It requires that women be treated equally. As the preceding discussion shows, the PDA also provides a common-sense test of whether a policy—or a statute—affords equal treatment to women who are pregnant. The measure is whether the policy furthers "Title VII's prophylactic purpose of achieving 'equality of employment opportunities.'" *EEOC v. Puget Sound Log Scaling & Grading Bureau*, 752 F.2d 1389, 1392 (9th Cir. 1985) (quoting *Griggs v. Duke Power Co.*, 401 U.S. 424, 429 (1971)). Thus, equality under the PDA must be measured in employment opportunity, not necessarily in amounts of money expended—or in amounts of days of disability leave expended. Equality in the disability context compares coverage to actual need, not coverage to hypothetical identical needs.[109]

The ultimate authority to interpret an Act of Congress rests, of course, with the United States Supreme Court. Litigants in both cases have invoked the Court's power to interpret the PDA.[110] The remaining task of this paper, in anticipation of that interpretation, is to show how the differentness of pregnancy can be recognized and accommodated within a legal and philosophical framework that affirms the equality of women and men.

---

[106] *Cal Fed*, 758 F.2d at 396. Despite the language quoted in the text, the Ninth Circuit indicated at an earlier point in its opinion that "[w]e need not determine, as the litigants would have us do, whether Title VII compels employers to grant reasonable pregnancy disability leave to protect women from the potentially disparate impact of facially neutral, but inadequate, disability leave policies; we need only decide whether section 12945(b)(2) is permissible under Title VII." *Id.* at 394. For an argument that the PDA should be interpreted to permit a disparate impact claim of pregnancy discrimination, see Note, *Employment Equality, supra* note 99, at 940-49.

[107] *Cal Fed*, 758 F.2d at 396.

[108] *Id.*

[109] *Id.*

[110] Miller-Wohl Co. v. Comm'r of Labor & Industry, 692 P.2d 1243 (Mont. 1984), *appeal docketed*, 53 U.S.L.W. 3718 (U.S. Apr. 9, 1985) (No. 84-1545); California Federal Savings & Loan Ass'n v. Guerra, 758 F.2d 390 (9th Cir. 1985), *cert. granted*, 54 U.S.L.W. 3460 (U.S. Jan. 14, 1986) (No. 85-494).

II. Equality and Difference

A. An Episodic Analysis of Biological Reproductive Sex Differences

The philosophical claim that all men—or all women—are equal is commonly challenged by the existence of such inequalities as those of intelligence, ability, merit, physical condition, wealth, status, or power. Some philosophers have chosen to respond to challenges of this sort by invoking a generalized ideal of equality that transcends inequalities stemming from the specific differences of the human condition, such as equality of respect owed to all humans,[111] equality of opportunity,[112] or equality of consideration of interests.[113] Others have sought to justify some forms of social and economic inequalities within a theory of justice.[114] With rare exceptions,[115] these philosophical discussions of equality have been phrased in terms of equality among men, with the term "man" being used in its generic sense to include "woman." When the specific question is raised about what equality between women and men might mean,[116] the debate focuses on a particular set of differences: the biological differences that define the two classes of male and female. The question then becomes: Given that biological reproductive sex differences exist and may be expected to persist, how can it be argued that men and women are equal?[117]

---

111 *See* B. Williams, *The Idea of Equality*, in Problems of the Self 230, 234-39 (1973) (discussing and refining Kant's view of the respect owed to each man as a rational moral agent). Nancy Hauserman has used the concept of equality of respect to defend equality between men and women. *See* Hauserman, *Sexual Equality: An Essay on the Importance of Recognizing Difference*, 7 ALSA Forum 251 (Special Double Issue on Women and Law, 1983).

112 *See* Frankel, *Equality of Opportunity*, 81 Ethics 191 (1971). *Compare* Simon, *The Liberal Conception of Equal Opportunity and Its Egalitarian Critics* in M. Darrogh & R. Blank, *supra* note 8, at 95-98, *with* Schaar, *Equality of Opportunity, and Beyond*, in Nomos IX: Equality 228, 233-36 (1967).

113 *See* Benn, *Egalitarianism and the Equal Consideration of Interests*, in Nomos IX: Equality 61 (1967).

114 *See, e.g.*, J. Rawls, A Theory of Justice 60 (1971) (justifying certain social and economic inequalitites provided that they are arranged so that they are both "(a) reasonably expected to be to everyone's advantage, and (b) attached to positions and offices open to all"). See, for an application of Rawls's difference principle to sexual justice, J. Radcliffe Richards, The Skeptical Feminist 90-120 (1980).

115 *See* Mill, *On the Subjection of Women* in Essays on Sex Equality 123 (A. Rossi ed. 1970). *See also* Annas, *Mill and the Subjection of Women*, 52 Philosophy 179 (1977). See, for reviews of the treatment of women in Western political thought, J. Elshtain, Public Man, Private Woman 19-197 (1981); S. Okin, Women In Western Political Thought 15-230 (1979). See also, for a refutation of the frequently-asserted belief that Plato was the first feminist, Annas, *Plato's Republic and Feminism*, 51 Phil. 307 (1976). *Compare* Saxonhouse, *The Philosopher and the Female in the Political Thought of Plato*, 4 Political Theory 195 (1976), giving an interpretation of why Socrates introduces women into his discussion in Plato's Republic.

116 *See* Gould, *The Woman Question: Philosophy of Liberation and the Liberation of Philosophy*, in Women and Philosophy: Toward A Theory of Liberation 5 (C. Gould & M. Wartofsky eds. 1980).

117 *See* Lucas, *'Because You Are A Woman'*, 48 Phil. 161 (1973) (arguing that sex-based differences exist, and may, in some instances, be the basis for differences in treatment). Lucas's arguments are criticized in Govier, *Woman's Place*, 49 Phil. 303 (1974); Bhattacharya, *Because He Is A Man*, 49 Phil. 96 (1974); and Haack, *On the Moral Relevance of Sex*, 49 Phil. 90 (1974). Lucas responds in *Vive La Difference*, 53 Phil. 363 (1978); rejoinders appear

At least two approaches to this question have been taken. The significance of biological reproductive sex differences can be minimized, or it can be exalted. The first approach holds that, although differences of this sort may be acknowledged, no public consequence should turn on whether a person is male or female.[118] Equality between men and women is achieved by removing sex as a consideration of consequence; that is, by making the sexes morally, if not physically, indistinguishable.[119] A second approach identifies biological reproductive sex differences as the basis of sexual identity and uses that identity, in turn, as the foundation for social differences that establish separate sex roles for women and men.[120] This approach would abandon egalitarian models in favor of a bivalent concept of the interests of women and men,[121] to create a sort of "separate but equal" social model for the sexes. Adherents of the first position generally support a vision of the good society in which cross-sex assimilation is the norm and difference is limited as narrowly as possible.[122] Those holding to the second position may support a range of social arrangements, from traditional ones in which women and men occupy separate spheres,[123] to more modern views of an androgynous society in which the spheres converge, preserving the best characteristics of both sexes.[124]

I wish to propose a third, alternative, approach: that we take account of biological reproductive sex differences and treat them as legally significant only when they are being utilized for reproductive purposes. I suggest that biological reproductive sex differences should be recognized as a functional attribute, rather than an inherent characteristic, of sexual identity, and as one that may or may not be exercised. A woman may be distinguished from a man by her capacity for pregnancy, childbirth, and lactation; but she may choose never to utilize that capac-

---

in Belsey & Belsey, *Sex, Equality and Mr. Lucas*, 55 PHIL. 386 (1980), and Yudkin, *Difference Be Damned*, 55 PHIL. 392 (1980). Lucas's objections to equality between women and men appear to be a specific instance of his general criticism of egalitarianism. *See* Lucas, *Against Equality*, 40 PHIL. 296 (1965).

118 This position is defended by Alison Jaggar and Richard Wasserstrom. *See* Wasserstrom, *Racism, Sexism, and Preferential Treatment: An Approach to the Topics*, 24 UCLA L. REV. 581, 605-15 (1977); Jaggar, *On Sexual Equality*, 84 ETHICS 275 (1974).

119 Thus, Jaggar denies "that it is either a conceptual or a moral truth that all persons are either female or male." Jaggar, *supra* note 118, at 279.

120 This position is defended by Elizabeth Wolgast. *See* E. WOLGAST, EQUALITY AND THE RIGHTS OF WOMEN 25-30, 103-37 (1980). Reviewers have criticized Wolgast for her failure to distinguish adequately between childbearing, a function that can be performed only by women, and childrearing, which can be carried out by either parent. *See, e.g.*, Pierce, Book Review, 93 THE PHIL. REV. 93 (1984); Keohane, Review Essay, 93 ETHICS 102, 108-111 (1982); Beggs, Recent Publications, 17 HARV. C.R.-C.L. L. REV. 287, 288-89 (1982).

121 WOLGAST, *supra* note 120, at 16.

122 *See, e.g.*, Wasserstrom, *supra* note 118, at 612-14.

123 *See, e.g.*, De Marco, *Men and Women, Their Difference and Its Importance*, 56 THOUGHT 449 (1981); Browne, *supra* note 8.

124 *See, e.g.*, Rossi, *Gender and Parenthood*, 49 AM. SOC. REV. 1 (1984).

ity.[125] Is she any less female? A man has the unique capacity to produce and ejaculate sperm. But if he fathers no children, he is still a man.[126] Infertile women and men retain their sexual identity,[127] if not their distinguishing sexual capacity. In our society salient distinctions are based on sexuality rather than reproductive behavior.[128] Women and men do not exercise their different biological reproductive capacities when they conform to social norms of appropriate interaction,[129] nor do they necessarily do so when they engage in sexual intercourse. Those differences

---

125 The model of equality I propose is furthered by, but is not conditioned upon, a woman's having the legal right and the effective power to control her reproductive capacity. If a woman cannot choose whether to utilize her reproductive capacity, she is not a free moral agent, let alone the equal of a man. The Supreme Court has recognized that procreation is a fundamental right that extends to both sexes regardless of marital status. *See* Carey v. Population Servs. Int'l, 431 U.S. 678, 687-88 (1977) (distribution of non-prescription contraceptives); Eisenstadt v. Baird, 405 U.S. 438, 452-53 (1972) (availability of contraceptives to unmarried persons); Griswold v. Connecticut, 381 U.S. 479, 485-86 (1965) (use of contraceptives by married persons); Skinner v. Oklahoma, 316 U.S. 535, 541-42 (1942) (compulsory sterilization). Once the reproductive cycle has been initiated, a woman's right to privacy encompasses her right to choose whether or not to terminate her pregnancy through induced abortion, *see* Roe v. Wade, 410 U.S. 113, 153 (1973). Moreover, the Court has recognized that a woman's unique physical experience of pregnancy justifies allowing her to make a unilateral choice to terminate her pregnancy through induced abortion despite her husband's objections, *see* Planned Parenthood of Central Missouri v. Danforth, 428 U.S. 52, 71 (1976).

The recognition of these fundamental rights facilitates an episodic analysis of biological reproductive sex differences by enabling a woman to control her reproductive capacity as freely as a man is able to control his, thus placing both sexes on an equal footing. But even if these rights were not recognized, or if that specific to women—namely, the decision to choose whether to continue a pregnancy to term or to terminate it through induced abortion—were sharply restricted, episodic analysis would still apply to the reproductive function. That is, a woman who finds herself pregnant, even if against her will and despite her wish to terminate the pregnancy, will still occupy a different position from that of a man as a result of procreation. The argument advanced in the text at notes 140-141, *infra*, based on the social policy favoring equality between men and women in employment will still apply to a pregnant worker whose pregnancy is unwanted. Indeed, she may have a stronger claim to be free of disadvantages at work than the woman whose pregnancy is desired: but for the hypothetical restriction against her decision to terminate the pregnancy, she could avoid the disadvantages.

Menstruation provides an example of an involuntary biological function associated with the female reproductive cycle. I agree with Wasserstrom that social institutions need not be built around this difference, *see* Wasserstrom, *supra* note 118, at 612-13, especially in view of the heavy cultural overlay that impedes even medical analysis of its characteristics. *See* Birke & Best, *Changing Minds: Women, Biology and the Menstrual Cycle*, in BIOLOGICAL WOMAN—THE CONVENIENT MYTH 161, 163-74 (R. Hubbard, M. Henifin & B. Fried, eds. 1982). Moreover, many women who are diagnosed as having premenstrual syndrome, a condition defined as "the recurrence of symptoms in the premenstruum with absence of symptoms in the postmenstruum," in a severe degree so that their normal working capacity and lifestyles are disrupted by the symptoms, are said to respond well to treatment with hormones. *See* K. DALTON, THE PREMENSTRUAL SYNDROME AND PROGESTERONE THERAPY 141 (2d ed. 1984).

126 The National Urban League's current campaign aimed at teaching young men to distinguish between manhood and fatherhood provides an apt example. The "male responsibility" campaign, using posters and spot radio announcements, carries the message "[d]on't make a baby if you can't be a father." New York Times, April 21, 1985, Sec. 4 at 20, col. 1.

127 *See generally*, Goffman, *The Arrangement Between the Sexes*, 4 THEORY & SOCIETY 301 (1977) (arguing that gender identity is a social, rather than a biological, phenomenon); *see also* Holmstrom, *Do Women Have A Distinct Nature?*, 14 PHIL. FORUM 25 (1982) (arguing that, if so, its determinants are social, rather than biological).

128 *See* MacKinnon, *Feminism, Marxism, Method, and the State: An Agenda For Theory*, 7 SIGNS 515, 516 (1982).

129 *See* Goffman, *supra* note 127, at 313-25, discussing examples of institutional reflexivity—

appear only when the reproductive function is manifested through a pregnancy that resulted from the reproductive behavior of both sexes.[130]

This way of looking at reproductive behavior permits us to examine biological reproductive sex differences in a new light. It becomes clearer that reproductive behavior is episodic and temporary. Male reproductive behavior is quite brief in duration; that of females occupies approximately nine months, but its cycle is complete following childbirth. Men and women who are parents are not functionally distinguishable by sex in their capacity to care for the newborn infant, except where breast-feeding is utilized as the method of choice for providing nourishment.[131] Some have argued that a cultural preference for females over males in the role of primary nurturing parent produces psychological differences based on sex in children that in turn reinforce existing social patterns of male domination, and have proposed that the recurrent cycle be broken by having males join females in caring for children.[132] Such arguments rest on the assumption that no innate biological traits prevent men from forming primary bonds with infants.

The relevance of this episodic analysis of biological reproductive sex differences for a theoretical model of equality between women and men is that it recognizes that those differences exist, but regards them as inconsequential except during the specific occasions on which they are utilized. Upon those occasions, as the result of the union between sperm and egg, pregnant women experience a complex of needs that are different from those of men and, indeed, of non-pregnant women. Pregnant women

---

defined as institutional practices which transform social sanctions into scenes for the performance of gender identity by both sexes.

130 Some pregnancies are the planned-for result of heterosexual intercourse, artificial insemination, or in vitro fertilization. Others are the presumably unanticipated consequence of recreational heterosexual intercourse. Still others are the product of rape or incest. Whether the pregnancy is desired by both participants, unanticipated, or even unwanted by one or both, does not affect the analysis presented in this paper. I do not undertake here an examination of the possible impact of modern reproductive technologies on my analysis. *See generally* G. Corea, The Mother Machine (1985); Test-Tube Women (R. Arditti, R. Klein & S. Minden eds. 1984).

131 Rossi, in a review of the literature, concludes that gender differences in parenting styles are of the same kind that emerge in psychological research: "greater empathy, affiliation, sensitivity to nonverbal cues and social skills in women, greater emphasis on skill mastery, autonomy and cognitive achievement in men." Rossi, *supra* note 124, at 8. She rejects the idea, however, that these different parenting styles arise as a result of pregnancy and birthing, relying instead on "gender differences that are in place long before a first pregnancy." *Id.* at 9. She identifies those differences as the result of both social and biological processes. *Id.* at 11. A recent study of the nurturing styles of fathers offers as one of its conclusions, however, the finding that "[t]he father's nurturing style is a distillate of selected identifications and disidentifications with the important objects in his own life. Such nurturing capacities do not, therefore, seem to be wholly determined by genetic endowment or gender identity." Pruett, *Infants of Primary Nurturing Fathers*, in 38 The Psychoanalytic Study of the Child 257, 274 (A. Solnit, R. Eissler & P. Neubauer, eds. 1983).

132 *See generally*, N. Chodorow, The Reproduction of Mothering: Psychoanalysis and the Sociology of Gender (1978); D. Dinnerstein, The Mermaid and the Minotaur: Sexual Arrangements and Human Malaise (1976).

may be advised to follow a certain diet,[133] to abstain from ingesting particular substances,[134] to avoid identified toxic environments,[135] and to engage in or refrain from specified conduct [136] in order to maximize their chances of delivering a healthy child. And, as a consequence of their changing physical condition, pregnant women may be temporarily disabled from work.[137]

The necessary result of a woman's reproductive behavior is that, for a limited time and in ways that may vary widely among pregnant women, her condition will be different from that of other persons of both sexes. Is she therefore unequal to those other persons? In particular, is she unequal to a man who has also engaged in reproductive conduct?

---

[133] *See, e.g.*, P. SIMKIN, J. WHALLEY & A. KEPPLER, PREGNANCY, CHILDBIRTH AND THE NEWBORN 51-58 (1984) [hereinafter cited as P. SIMKIN].

[134] *Id.* at 66-71 (discussing alcohol, tobacco, marijuana, caffeine, herbal teas, and medicines). The Surgeon-General has concluded that smoking is especially harmful to pregnant women, and warnings directed at them have been placed on cigarette packages. *See* New York Times, Sept. 27, 1984, at A1, col. 5. For a discussion of whether an unwilling mother could be compelled to undergo forced bodily intrusion in order to protect the fetus, see Robertson, *The Right to Procreate and In Utero Fetal Therapy*, 3 J. LEG. MED. 333, 353-61 (1982).

[135] Scientific evidence confirms the existence of a link between toxic work environments and fetal harm. *See* Furnish, *Prenatal Exposure to Fetally Toxic Work Environments: The Dilemma of the 1978 Pregnancy Amendment to Title VII of the Civil Rights Act of 1964*, 66 IOWA L. REV. 63, 119-29 (1980) (summarizing in an Appendix then existing scientific data). Toxic environments pose risk for the male reproductive system as well. *See* Hatch, *Mother, Father, Worker: Men and Women and Reproductive Risks of Work*, in W. Chavkin, *supra* note 54, at 161, 166.

[136] Bed rest may become necessary; exercise may be recommended. *See* P. SIMKIN, *supra* note 133, at 75-90.

[137] Dr. John A. Kerner, Clinical Professor of Obstetrics and Gynecology at the University of California, San Francisco, has provided me with a list of nonpathologic problems in pregnancy which might interfere with a woman's ability to work. These include, during the first trimester, nausea and vomiting; distraction caused by knowledge of the possibility of spontaneous abortion resulting from strenuous work, or concern about danger to the fetus from its exposure to toxic substances; and a work situation that might interfere with proper nutrition.

During the second trimester, the danger of fetal exposure to toxic substances continues, but spontaneous abortion is less likely.

During the third trimester, the woman's increasing size interferes with her ability to do certain sorts of work (e.g., work as a waitress or a coal miner who must get into confined spaces). Premature labor can be caused by strenuous work. The woman loses her ability to move quickly in an emergency (e.g., affecting her work as an airline cabin flight attendant or her performance in nontraditional occupations such as a police officer on patrol duty and some military jobs). The woman becomes unable to lift heavy objects or persons (e.g., affecting her ability to do some mechanical work, or to work as a firefighter). There is a danger that the onset of labor may occur far from the place of planned confinement (e.g., this may pose a problem in jobs requiring travel). She will be less able to stand or sit for long periods of time because of edema generated; and she may experience low back discomfort. Sleep disturbances cause loss of energy and sometimes produce loss of emotional control (such sleep disturbances can be mechanical or related to fetal motion, or stem from an emotional basis). A woman may experience disturbance in her emotional stability at any time during pregnancy. Letter from Dr. John A. Kerner to Professor Herma Hill Kay (June 24, 1985) (on file at Professor Kay's office—edited, and with some parenthetical material identifying specific jobs added, by Professor Kay). *See also* P. SIMKIN, *supra* note 133, at 36-39, setting out a "calendar of pregnancy" detailing physical and emotional changes in the mother during pregnancy. Non-pregnant workers may also, of course, become temporarily disabled from work and need to take disability leave without fear of job reprisal. I believe that all workers should be protected against disability at work. One of the burdens of this paper, however, is to show that it is not unfair to provide such work-place accommodations for pregnancy without first having provided similar relief for all other disabling conditions. *See infra* text and accompanying footnotes 176-184.

I think it is clear that if a woman who is not pregnant is assumed to be equal to a man on some such measure as, say, equality of respect or equality of consideration of interests, her reproductive behavior does not remove or detract in any way from her claim to that sort of equality. A woman may, however, unlike a man who engages in reproductive behavior, be placed at a temporary disadvantage with respect to equality of opportunity. In order to bear a child, she may be temporarily disabled from pursuing her own self-interests. If she becomes pregnant more than once, she may face recurrent disadvantages. It appears unjust to place the consequential disadvantages of reproductive conduct only upon women. This unjust result need not follow, however, for a philosophical basis exists for alleviating the temporary disadvantages of pregnancy within a framework of equality.

Philosophers recognize that, just as the concept of equality requires that equals be treated equally, so it requires that unequals be treated differently.[138] To treat persons who are different alike is to treat them unequally. The concept of formal equality, however, contains no independent justification for making unequals equal.[139] A different concept, that of equality of opportunity, offers a theoretical basis for making unequals equal in the limited sense of removing barriers which prevent individuals from performing according to their abilities.[140] The notion is that the perceived inequality does not stem from an innate difference in ability, but rather from a condition or circumstance that prevents certain uses or developments of that ability. As applied to reproductive behavior, the suggestion would be that women in general are not different from men in innate ability. During the temporary episode of a woman's pregnancy, however, she may become unable to utilize her abilities in the same way she had done prior to her reproductive conduct. Since a man's abilities are not similarly impaired as a result of his reproductive behavior, equality of opportunity implies that the woman should not be disadvantaged as a result of that sex-specific variation.

As applied to the employment context, the concept of equality of opportunity takes on the following form. Let us postulate two workers,

---

[138] The point seems to have been made originally by Aristotle. *See* NICHMACHEAN ETHICS v.3. 1113a-13b (W. Ross trans. 1925) ("Equality in morals means this: things that are alike should be treated alike, while things that are unalike should be treated unalike in proportion to their unalikeness."). Others have observed that this formula leads to a purely formal equality that is itself lacking in content. *See, e.g.*, Westen, *The Empty Idea of Equality*, 95 HARV. L. REV. 537, 542-48 (1982); Frankel, *supra* note 112, at 193-94.

[139] *See* Westen, *supra* note 138, at 551-56.

[140] *See* Frankel, *supra* note 112, at 204, advancing a conception of "educational" equality of opportunity, which I have adapted here to fit the case of pregnancy. Frankel's formulation is as follows:

> Equality of opportunity means that men shall not be limited except by their abilities; the advocate of the 'educational' conception of equality of opportunity holds that we cannot have real equality of opportunity unless we successfully modify those aspects of the individual's situation which prevent him from performing up to the level of his natural abilities.

one female, the other male, who respectively engage in reproductive conduct. Assume as well that prior to this activity, both were roughly equal in their ability to perform their similar jobs. The consequence of their having engaged in reproductive behavior will be vastly different. The man's ability to perform on the job will be largely unaffected.[141] The woman's ability to work, measured against her prior performance, may vary with the physical and emotional changes she experiences during pregnancy. At times, her ability to work may be unaffected by the pregnancy; at other times, she may be temporarily incapacitated by it. Ultimately, she may require medical care to recover from miscarriage, or to complete her pregnancy by delivery, or to terminate it earlier by induced abortion. In order to maintain the woman's equality of opportunity during her pregnancy, we should modify as far as reasonably possible those aspects of her work where her job performance is adversely affected by the pregnancy. Unless we do so, she will experience employment disadvantages arising from her reproductive activity that are not encountered by her male co-worker.

I will explore some of the legal implications of this theoretical position in the sections that follow. Here, I note a possible objection: the cost of compliance. Cost, however, is a function of social value. As the enactment of Title VII demonstrates, our society has made equality between women and men in the workplace a high priority. At the same time, it has accorded to individual decisions concerning procreation the status of a constitutionally-protected fundamental right.[142] Men do not experience a conflict between their right to engage in reproductive conduct and their right to be free of discrimination based on sex at work. Women, however, have experienced such a conflict, and will continue to do so unless pregnant workers are safeguarded from the loss of employ-

---

141 Some men experience pregnancy-like symptoms, such as nausea, vomiting, variations in appetite, toothache, some form of indigestion, and, occasionally, abdominal swelling, during their mate's pregnancy. This condition, known as the couvade syndrome, disappears upon or shortly after delivery. See generally, for an overview, Trethowan, *The Couvade Syndrome* in MODERN PERSPECTIVES IN PSYCHO-OBSTETRICS 68 (J. Howells ed. 1972) (discussing clinical symptoms at 74-79). Clinton and her co-investigators, in a study comparing the discomfort symptoms of 147 men living in the Milwaukee area, 88 of whom were expectant fathers and 66 of whom were non-expectant men, found that their daily diaries showed that expectant fathers did experience discomfort on a greater number of days during the end of pregnancy and the early postpartum period compared to non-expectant men. In response to their symptoms, the expectant fathers reduced their activities outside the home, such as leisure sports and social events, but they did not disrupt their employment at a greater rate than non-expectant men. Hours lost from work attributed to discomfort did not differ between the two study groups at any point during the pregnancy or the immediate postpartum period. The sample was largely composed of salaried, rather than hourly, employees. Mean salary loss in dollars for expectant fathers ranged from $0.00 to $15.46 in a typical month, compared to $0.00 to $14.98 for non-expectant men. J.F. Clinton, Final Report For Couvade: Patterns and Predictors 113-16 (May 1985) (technical report to the U.S. Public Health Service, Bureau of Professions, Health Resources and Services Administration, Division of Nursing) (on file at Professor Kay's office). Clinton's data are consistent with the view taken in this paper that men do not suffer work-related disadvantages as the result of engaging in reproductive conduct.

142 *See supra* note 125.

ment opportunities during pregnancy. The social value of accommodating reproduction and employment opportunities so that women remain free to engage in both activities on an equal basis with men justifies the additional cost of enabling working women to cope with the differential physical and emotional changes associated with pregnancy.[143]

B. Application of Episodic Analysis to Title VII

The episodic analysis of biological reproductive sex differences, particularly pregnancy, suggested in this paper is consistent with the interpretation of Title VII offered by Judge Ferguson for the Ninth Circuit in *Cal Fed*.[144] Under that interpretation, both "sex" and "pregnancy" are covered by Title VII's prohibition against discrimination, and the test of pregnancy discrimination consists of whether a challenged policy or statute affords the pregnant woman equality of employment opportunity.[145] The analysis offered here shows that pregnancy differs from sex, however, in that pregnancy is an episodic occurrence, rather than an immutable trait. The category of pregnant persons is a sub-class within the larger category of women. To some extent, the statutory prohibitions are the same for both groups. Neither women nor pregnant persons may be rejected for employment or fired[146] because of their sex or their pregnancy. *Per se* discrimination based on either sex or pregnancy may be justified, however, by a showing that the statutory bona fide occupational qualification defense[147] applies. If justified by that defense, pregnant

[143] Judge Ferguson recognized in *Cal Fed* that accommodating pregnancy in the work place might entail increased costs. In his view, however, Congress accepted this consequence when it enacted the PDA. *Cal Fed*, 758 F.2d at 395. ("In fact, the PDA's enactment showed that Congress sanctioned the expenditure of more dollars on medical coverage for female employees than for male in order to achieve equally complete health benefits for both. When the Supreme Court in *Newport News* extended to the wives of male employees medical coverage for pregnancy, it recognized that '[t]he cost of providing complete health insurance coverage for the dependents of male employees, including pregnant wives, might exceed the cost of providing such coverage for the dependents of female employees.' 103 S. Ct. at 2632 n.26. It extended pregnancy coverage anyway.") This analysis suggests that the increased cost of accommodating pregnancy in the work setting will be attributable to both male and female employees.

[144] *See supra* text and accompanying footnotes 101-09. Episodic analysis is also consistent with the result in *Miller-Wohl*. *See supra* text and accompanying footnotes 96-99.

[145] *Cal Fed*, 758 F.2d at 396. The term "sex" is expressly part of the language of Title VII, *see* 42 U.S.C.A. § 2000e-2(a); the term "pregnancy" is brought within the language by the PDA, which defines discrimination based on sex as including discrimination based on pregnancy. *See supra* note 46.

[146] *See, e.g.*, Hayes v. Shelby Memorial Hosp., 726 F.2d 1543, *reh'g denied*, 732 F.2d 944 (11th Cir. 1984) (hospital violated Title VII by firing pregnant x-ray technician).

[147] 42 U.S.C.A. § 2000e-2(e). The BFOQ exception applies to religion, sex and national origin, but not to race or color. Since the PDA defined "sex" to include "pregnancy," it follows that the BFOQ defense is potentially applicable to discrimination based on pregnancy. This view has been adopted by several courts. *See, e.g.*, *Hayes*, 726 F.2d at 1548-49; Harriss v. Pan Am. World Airways, Inc., 649 F.2d 670, 676 (9th Cir. 1980) (challenge to employer's policy of grounding pregnant flight attendants). *Per se* discrimination based on sex or pregnancy is justifiable only by the statutory BFOQ defense; the business necessity defense, which was judi-

workers who cannot perform their jobs may be temporarily removed from hazardous work sites,[148] or from jobs where the woman's pregnancy may prevent her from assuring the safety of customers.[149] Employers must take those measures that may be reasonably necessary to permit pregnant workers to continue working until delivery, in order to avoid discrimination against them.[150] Women returning from pregnancy leave must be allowed to resume their former status as workers.[151] An episodic view of pregnancy requires that any benefits extended to pregnant workers or restrictions imposed on them be tailored to actual medical need resulting from the pregnancy, and not be triggered by stereotypical notions of what pregnant women should or should not do.[152]

This interpretation of Title VII based on an episodic analysis of biological reproductive sex differences will permit pregnancy to be recognized as the normal consequence of reproductive behavior that can and should be accommodated in the workplace. Pregnancy is not itself a dis-

---

cially-created in the context of disparate impact race discrimination cases, *see* Griggs v. Duke Power Co., 401 U.S. 424 (1971), does not apply to *per se* discrimination.

[148] The removal must be based, however, on the pregnant woman's inability to perform the job, not on any perceived danger to the fetus. *See Hayes*, 726 F.2d at 1549. *But see* Wright v. Olin Corp., 697 F.2d 1172, 1182-92 (4th Cir. 1982) (characterizing an employer's "fetal vulnerability plan" as having a disparate impact on pregnant women and remanding to permit employer to attempt to make out a defense of business necessity). On remand, the district court held that Olin had established that its fetal vulnerability policy was a business necessity. Wright v. Olin Corp., 585 F. Supp. 1447, 1453 (W.D.N.C. 1984). I think a better analysis of the *Wright* problem would have been that it involved *per se* discrimination based on pregnancy to which only the BFOQ exception could provide a defense. *See* Note, *Employment Discrimination—* Wright v. Olin Corp.: *Title VII and the Exclusion of Women From the Fetally Toxic Workplace*, 62 N.C.L. REV. 1068, 1082-84 (1984). Furnish, who argues that none of the Title VII defenses is fully satisfactory when applied to an employer's effort to exclude a pregnant woman from a toxic work environment hazardous to the fetus, *see* Furnish, *supra* note 135, at 92-102, proposes instead that the PDA be amended to permit both a limited defense to employers in such cases and a right for pregnant women to request removal from the work site in order to minimize the hazards to the fetus. *Id.* at 115-18. *But see* Williams, *Firing the Woman to Protect the Fetus: The Reconciliation of Fetal Protection with Employment Opportunity Goals Under Title VII*, 69 GEO. L.J. 641, 703 (1981) (arguing that employers must adopt facially neutral fetal protection policies, must inform themselves of hazards to the reproductive systems of both men and women; and must apply those policies in a nondiscriminatory way). The Eleventh Circuit adopted Williams's approach in *Hayes*, 726 F.2d at 1549-50, and used it to fashion a remedy applicable to all workers whose offspring may be threatened by toxic hazards in the workplace.

[149] *See, e.g., Harriss*, 649 F.2d at 676-77 (upholding under the BFOQ exception an airline's policy of grounding pregnant flight attendants as soon as the pregnancy was known); Condit v. United Airlines, 558 F.2d 1176 (4th Cir. 1977), *cert. denied*, 435 U.S. 934 (1978) (same). *But see* Burwell v. Eastern Air Lines, 633 F.2d 361 (4th Cir. 1980) (en banc), *cert. denied*, 450 U.S. 965 (1981) (mandatory grounding permissible after first trimester of pregnancy).

[150] *See Miller-Wohl* and *Cal Fed*, discussed *supra* in text and accompanying notes 96-109. *See also* A. LARSON, *supra* notes 53 & 99; Note, *Employment Equality*, *supra* note 99, at 940-43.

[151] *Cf.* Nashville Gas Co. v. Satty, 434 U.S. 136, 138-43 (1977) (invalidating employer policy that women returning from pregnancy leave lost accumulated seniority, even though other workers returning from disability leave did not). *Cal Fed* means that this result would follow even if all other workers lost their seniority following a disability leave.

[152] *See, e.g.*, Note, *Pink Collar Blues: Potential Hazards of Video Display Terminal Radiation*, 57 S. CALIF. L. REV. 139, 152-57 (1983) (urging a gender neutral approach to VDT regulation, rather than assuming a special danger to pregnant workers not justified by then-available scientific evidence).

ability, although an individual pregnant woman may experience disabling symptoms and may require medical care. If she is temporarily impaired from performing at work up to her normal level of ability, the concept of equal employment opportunity embodied in Title VII requires not only that she remain free of resulting job reprisals, but also that she secure compensatory benefits to offset any potential work-related disadvantage. Under this analysis, women will be equal to men in their ability to work and to make reproductive choices.

C. Application of Episodic Analysis to the Constitution

After the effective date of the PDA, discrimination against pregnant persons was illegal in the employment context, but it was not unconstitutional. *Geduldig* remains the governing interpretation of the equal protection clause, and it stands for the proposition that a classification drawn on the basis of pregnancy is not a discrimination based on sex.[153]

An episodic analysis of pregnancy demonstrates the fallacy in the *Geduldig* classification between pregnant women and non-pregnant persons. The legal issue in *Geduldig* was how one consequence of reproductive conduct—pregnancy—should be treated in the workplace for purposes of an employer's disability plan. The Court took as its reference point a group composed of all persons who worked for the employer. But that is not the relevant reference group. Instead, the group should be limited to those persons who have engaged in reproductive behavior while continuing to work. That group is divided into two sub-groups, persons who will require medical care and who may at times be temporarily disabled as a result of that reproductive conduct and persons who will not. The first group of persons is exclusively female, while the second is entirely male. Men and women who have not engaged in reproductive behavior are not similarly situated with respect to the work-related consequences of that conduct to persons who have so acted, and so are not properly part of the equal protection equation. The *Geduldig* classification was overly-broad, because it included within the category of "non-pregnant persons" both women and men who had not chosen to initiate a reproductive episode as well as men who had so chosen.

Moreover, the *Geduldig* line was drawn at the wrong point in the reproductive cycle. By focusing on the consequence of reproductive conduct—pregnancy—the Court ignored the male role in reproduction. Properly rephrased in light of an episodic analysis of biological reproductive sex differences, the legal question in *Geduldig* is whether two persons of the opposite sex who have engaged in reproductive behavior and wish to continue working may be treated differently for purposes of disability

[153] *See supra* text and accompanying notes 23-35.

coverage. Since the man will not be disabled from work as the result of that conduct, equal protection for the woman requires that she not be penalized if she does become disabled. It follows not only that the pregnant woman must be covered by any existing disability plan applicable to workers generally, but also that she must be protected against disability resulting from pregnancy even in the absence of a general disability plan. *Geduldig* results in unequal treatment of similarly situated women and men who have engaged respectively in reproductive conduct. It should be overruled.[154]

It follows from this analysis that, for constitutional purposes as well as statutory coverage under Title VII, a discrimination against a woman based on pregnancy is a facial discrimination against her because of her sex. The same intermediate standard of judicial review developed for equal protection sex discrimination cases[155] can be adapted for use in pregnancy discrimination cases. The analysis will, however, be different in pregnancy discrimination cases, because there is no matching group of pregnant males to use for purposes of comparison. Instead, the constitutional test must be applied so as to assure pregnant women equality of opportunity to the same extent as that available to males who have engaged in reproductive conduct. Thus, pregnant women may be treated differently from such males if the result is to prevent a disadvantage that might otherwise follow from their condition.[156] For example, a reasonable leave provided by a state employer to pregnant workers is not only constitutional, it is constitutionally compelled to avoid discrimination by the state against pregnant workers.[157]

---

154 Despite the analysis offered in the text, however, the Court may decline to change its constitutional approach to pregnancy classifications established in *Geduldig*. If so, it may be worth considering whether the text of the proposed Equal Rights Amendment should be altered to include a specific reference to "pregnancy" as well as to "sex." Section 1 of the proposed amendment might, for example, be redrafted to read as follows: "Equality of rights under the law shall not be denied or abridged by the United States or by any State on account of sex or pregnancy." It does not appear necessary to use facially neutral language such as "sex or reproductive conduct." The Court has had no occasion to consider whether a discrimination based on the male capacity for the production and ejaculation of sperm would constitute a discrimination based on sex. Moreover, men do not appear to be disadvantaged by that capacity. Finally, such language might be read to afford constitutional protection to rape, a possibility best avoided.

155 *See, e.g.*, Mississippi Univ. for Women v. Hogan, 458 U.S. 718, 723-26 (1982); Kay, *supra* note 5, at 63-67. For a critique of the Court's application of the middle-tier standard in sex discrimination cases, see Freedman, *supra* note 7; *see also* Wildman, *The Legitimation of Sex Discrimination: A Critical Response to Supreme Court Jurisprudence*, 63 ORE. L. REV. 265 (1984).

156 Similar arguments were offered by the three-judge federal district court in Aiello v. Hansen, 359 F. Supp. 792, 796 (N.D. Cal. 1973), *rev'd sub nom.* Geduldig v. Aiello, 417 U.S. 496 (1974), and, in the context of Title VII, by the district court in Gilbert v. General Electric Co., 375 F. Supp. 367, 383 (E.D. Va. 1974), *rev'd*, 429 U.S. 125 (1976). Other commentators have elaborated these arguments. *See* Comment, *Sex Discrimination and Insurance Planning: The Rights of Pregnant Men and Women Under* General Electric Co. v. Gilbert, 22 ST. LOUIS U. L.J. 101, 131-36 (1978); Comment, Geduldig v. Aiello: *Pregnancy Classifications and the Definition of Sex Discrimination*, 75 COLUM. L. REV. 441, 479 (1975).

157 Preferential treatment based on pregnancy is not subject to claims of over-inclusiveness leveled

An employer's policy, however, may not be facially directed against pregnant workers but may have a disparate impact on them, such as a no-leave or inadequate leave policy. Present equal protection doctrine established in *Washington v. Davis*[158] does not restrict such policies unless the discrimination is intentional. But the very uniqueness of the condition of pregnancy may ameliorate the impact of *Washington v. Davis* in light of a recent modification of its procedural implications. The Court has made clear that "[o]nce racial discrimination is shown to have been a 'substantial' or 'motivating' factor behind enactment of the law, the burden shifts to the law's defenders to demonstrate that the law would have been enacted without this factor."[159] This holding should be extended to sex and pregnancy discrimination cases. In pregnancy discrimination cases, it may not be difficult to show, for example, that a state employer's inadequate or no-leave policy was motivated in part by a desire to reduce the cost of pregnancy leave coverage, if only because the practice of differential coverage for pregnancy at work was so widespread before the enactment of the PDA.[160] If such a showing is sufficient to shift the burden on the issue of intent to the employer, the impact of *Washington v. Davis* on pregnancy discrimination cases may be minimized.

D. Episodic Analysis and the "Equal Treatment/Special Treatment" Debate

The episodic analysis as applied to pregnancy may serve as a basis for harmonizing some of the views of the opposing participants in the so-

---

against preferential treatment accorded to women or members of racial minority groups who are not themselves identifiable victims of discrimination. *See* Firefighters Local Union No. 1784 v. Stotts, 104 S. Ct. 2576, 2588-90 (1984). A classification based on pregnancy will always be precisely limited to those persons exhibiting the condition in question. In my view, this difference in treatment is not unfair to other disabled persons. *See infra* text and accompanying notes 176-184.

Moreover, I am not suggesting, for example, that non-pregnant persons be displaced to make employment opportunities available to pregnant workers who request alternative work sites during pregnancy. *Compare* CAL. GOV'T CODE § 12945(c)(1)-(2), quoted *supra* note 69 (these provisions are expressly not applicable to employers covered by Title VII; *id.* at § 12945(e)). If no alternative sites are available, leave with pay would be an acceptable option. This approach may, indeed, make it more expensive to hire women who intend to exercise their reproductive capacities while remaining in the work force. The Ninth Circuit, however, rejected cost as a defense of the employer's postion in *Cal Fed*. *See supra* note 143. The cost differential is, at any event, likely to be brief in duration. The Supreme Court has already made clear that pregnancy benefits granted to women employees and their dependents must be extended to male employees and their dependents in order to avoid discrimination against men because of their sex. *See Newport News*, 462 U.S. at 682-85.

158 426 U.S. 229 (1976). *See generally* Segal, *Sexual Equality, The Equal Protection Clause, and the ERA*, 33 BUFFALO L. REV. 85, 114-30 (1984) (arguing that the *Washington v. Davis* standard, as applied to sex discrimination in Personnel Adm'r of Mass. v. Feeney, 446 U.S. 256 (1979), sanctions discriminatory policies by equating equality with facial neutrality).

159 Hunter v. Underwood, 105 S. Ct. 1916, 1920 (1985).

160 *See* Koontz, *Childbirth and Childrearing Leave: Job-Related Benefits*, 17 N.Y.L.J. 480, 482-87 (1971).

called "equal treatment/special treatment" debate.[161] For example, episodic analysis highlights how narrowly the dispute is limited. In her excellent defense of the "equal treatment" model, Wendy Williams identifies two propositions as essential to the theoretical framework within which that model was developed.[162] They are, first, "that sex-based generalizations are generally impermissible whether derived from physical differences such as size and strength, from cultural role assignments such as breadwinner or homemaker, or from some combination of innate and ascribed characteristics, such as the greater longevity of the average woman compared to the average man";[163] and second, "that laws and rules which do not overtly classify on the basis of sex, but which have a disproportionately negative effect upon one sex, warrant, under appropriate circumstances, placing a burden of justification upon the party defending the law or rule in court."[164] Neither of these propositions is in conflict with the episodic analysis of biological reproductive sex differences offered in this paper. I agree with Williams that, taken together, these two propositions form the basis of a legal doctrine of equality between women and men that has served both sexes well in breaking down "the legal barriers that restricted each sex to its predefined role and created a hierarchy based on gender."[165] As I have shown elsewhere, this assimilationist view of equality has worked well as a tool against both race discrimination and sex discrimination, where the two groups being compared are not different in any relevant way.[166]

Episodic analysis departs from the "equal treatment" model, however, at the point where Williams claims that her "general framework applies, with minor alteration, to laws or rules based on physical characteristics unique to one sex."[167] In my view, biological reproductive sex differences are not comparable to other traits or characteristics that are shared by both sexes, and cannot adequately be analyzed within a framework that turns on differential treatment of two comparable groups.[168] Instead, episodic analysis recognizes that biological reproductive sex differences exist, but confines their legal significance to the brief period during which they are utilized. I take it that Williams and I agree that women and men should be deemed equals prior to the time either engages in reproductive behavior. At the moment of conception, sperm and egg play equally important roles. Following childbirth, we both would place equal responsibility for childrearing on men and women

---

161 *See* Williams, *Equality's Riddle: Pregnancy and the Equal Treatment/Special Treatment Debate*, 13 N.Y.U. Rev. L. & Soc. Change 325 (1984-85).
162 *Id.* at 329-31.
163 *Id.* at 329.
164 *Id.* at 330.
165 *Id.* at 331.
166 *See* Kay, *supra* note 5, at 77-78.
167 Williams, *supra* note 161, at 331.
168 *See* Kay, *supra* note 5, at 78-87.

who are parents. But, unlike Williams, I insist that during the episode of pregnancy itself the woman's body functions in a unique way. We must recognize that unique function in order to prevent penalizing the woman who exercises it. If confined in this way, the recognition of pregnancy as "unique"[169] will enable the law to treat women differently than men during a limited period when their needs may be greater than those of men as a way of ensuring that women will be equal to men with respect to their overall employment opportunities.

The narrow difference between my approach and that taken by Williams is also emphasized by another consideration. One of the major arguments of proponents of the equal treatment model has been strategic, rather than theoretical. It is that ultimately women will be more successful in escaping traditional stereotypical roles if they refrain from seeking special treatment for the uniquely female condition of pregnancy and rely primarily on demands for benefits that can be pressed in common with all workers.[170] Thus, Williams points out that the equal treatment model "separates pregnancy and childrearing and insists that each be independently analyzed,"[171] so that the workplace can be restructured to accommodate parenting as the joint responsibility of working fathers and mothers.

As I have noted above, my analysis, like that of Williams, makes clear that the woman's reproductive cycle ends with childbirth. In those cases where two parents are available to care for the child, episodic analysis carries no implications for how they should assign between themselves the ensuing stage of childrearing.[172] My analysis envisions a bright line between pregnancy and child care that requires the provision of any available childrearing leave to both parents.[173] More fundamentally, episodic analysis is consistent with a model of equality that acknowledges

---

169 Katherine Bartlett accurately identified the danger to working women posed by treating pregnancy as a unique condition without carefully scrutinizing the stereotypical assumptions that often accompany such a characterization:

> With childbearing came the duties of childraising and taking care of the home, and the skill and habit which resulted from practice fed stereotypes that women prefer to stay at home and have children; that they make better parents than their husbands; that they don't want to do real work anyway.

Bartlett, *Pregnancy and the Constitution: The Uniqueness Trap*, 62 CALIF. L. REV. 1532, 1533 (1974).

But she also recognized that "[i]f the unique features of pregnancy truly justify differential treatment in a particular case, equal protection analysis, especially under an 'intermediate' standard of review where the outcome is not predetermined by the attachment of labels, should support that conclusion." *Id.* at 1560 (footnote omitted). As I have suggested earlier, episodic analysis offers a way of bringing classifications based on pregnancy within the intermediate standard of equal protection review presently afforded to sex-based classifications. *See supra* text and accompanying notes 153-155.

170 *See* Williams, *supra* note 4, at 196-98. This position was reflected in the *amicus* briefs filed in *Miller-Wohl* by the American Civil Liberties Union and in *Cal Fed* by the National Organization for Women. *See supra* text and accompanying notes 88-90.

171 Williams, *supra* note 161, at 354.

172 *See supra* text and accompanying notes 131-32.

173 Like Williams, I therefore prefer the Swedish model of parental caretaking to the ILO model

the reproductive conduct of both men and women, while allowing a woman's pregnancy to be recognized and provided for on its own terms.[174] It is thus consistent with the view of proponents of the "special treatment" approach that the best way to enable women to compete on an equal basis with men is to assure them that pregnancy will not hinder their achievements.[175]

Williams has questioned the fairness of a differential approach to pregnancy, using the *Miller-Wohl* case as a vehicle. She asks: "[o]n what basis can we fairly assert, for example, that the pregnant woman fired by Miller-Wohl deserved to keep her job when any other worker who got sick for any other reason did not?"[176] The short answer to this question is that no male worker who had exercised his reproductive capacity lost his job as a result. Episodic analysis supports that brief response, and also provides a more complete justification. The point at which that longer justification begins, however, is not when Miller-Wohl was thinking of firing Tamara Buley, but rather when she was thinking of going to work. Planned pregnancy, unlike other medical conditions, is an episode that is intended to culminate in the birth of a child. A woman who plans

---

which limits child care benefits following delivery to mothers. *See* Williams, *supra* note 161, at 376-78.

174 The episodic analysis of pregnancy does not extend without qualification to a woman's capacity to lactate. Lactation is a biological sex difference associated with reproduction which becomes functional following delivery. Lactation makes possible the choice of breastfeeding as one method of providing nutrition to the child, and it has valuable health consequences for the mother as well. *See* P. SIMKIN, *supra* note 133 at 237 (discussing some factors to consider when deciding whether to breastfeed). Breastfeeding declined in the United States during the 1940s and 1960s to a low of fewer than a quarter of babies being breastfed; breastfeeding grew in popularity in the mid-1970s through the 1980s, when more than sixty percent of American mothers breastfeed. *Id.* at 236. In addition, in developing countries, breastfeeding appears to be a primary determinant of birth spacing. *See* Smith, *Breast-feeding, Contraception, and Birth Intervals in Developing Countries*, 16 STUDIES IN FAM. PLANNING 154 (1985).

Unlike pregnancy, however, breastfeeding is not an unavoidable consequence of reproductive conduct. After childbirth, in two-parent families, either parent can feed the child. Single mothers may be able to call on friends or relatives for help if necessary. Mothers can express milk and refrigerate it for use within 24 hours or freeze it for longer periods, if appropriate. *See* P. SIMKIN, *supra* note 133, at 255-57.

It follows that the constitutional arguments advanced in support of preventing disadvantages to women resulting from pregnancy, *see supra* text and accompanying notes 153-158, do not apply with the same force to breastfeeding mothers. On the other hand, lactation is similar to pregnancy in that it is a sex-specific trait, and it is stimulated by childbirth. One court has held that breastfeeding is a constitutionally-protected liberty. *See* Dike v. School Bd. of Orange County, Fla., 650 F.2d 783, 785-87 (5th Cir. 1981). For Title VII purposes, the logic that equates discrimination based on pregnancy with discrimination based on sex may be sufficiently strong to extend to lactation. If so, an employer could not fire, or refuse to hire or promote, a breastfeeding woman. If an employer allowed flextime policies, parents could use those policies for childcare purposes, including breastfeeding. A state statute that mandated extra time off for breastfeeding only for working mothers, however, would probably be preempted by Title VII.

175 *See* Note, *Employment Equality*, *supra* note 99, at 952-55; Note, *Equality in the Workplace: Is That Enough For Pregnant Workers?*, 23 J. FAM. L. 401 (1984-85); Johnston, *Pregnancy Leave*, in 1984 YEARBOOK 8, 9 (California Women Lawyers 1984-85); Krieger & Cooney, *supra* note 99, at 515-17; Scales, *supra* note 99 at 435-42; Carey, *Pregnancy Without Penalty*, 1 CIV. LIB. REV. 31 (Fall 1973).

176 Williams, *supra* note 4, at 196.

both to work and to have children must take account of how she will manage her pregnancy at work. If she knows that her employer has in place a program that will accommodate her pregnancy-related needs, she will be able to enter the workforce without fear of encountering obstacles to her decision to bear a child.[177] Such employer programs will encourage women to enter and remain in the job market by mitigating the disadvantages to women caused by pregnancy.[178] Not being fired, of course, is an important part of such a program of accommodation. An employer disability policy that limits the amount of sick leave to very short periods,[179] or that has long probationary periods,[180] cannot provide the necessary assurance to women that they will not be penalized at work if they become pregnant. Such provisions are, therefore, inadequate for pregnant workers, although they may be justifiable—even if undesirable—when applied to fortuitous sickness or injury suffered by other workers. Although employers and their insurers can predict statistically how many workers will be injured or disabled while at work, individual workers themselves normally do not plan for such disabling events.[181] Therefore, they are not deterred from entering the workforce by the anticipation of such risks.

Ruth Bader Ginsburg put the point nicely, although I do not claim that she shares my views on this specific issue. Commenting on some of the pregnancy cases decided prior to the enactment of the PDA,[182] she observed:

> The likelihood that childbirth will occur nowadays normally twice in a working woman's life, and the cost generated by insurance coverage for pregnancy-related physical disability no doubt influenced the Court's decisions—its meandering course and its current position that discrimination based on pregnancy is unlawful "sometimes." If Congress is genuinely committed to eradication of sex-based discrimination and promotion of equal opportunity for women, it will respond to the uneven pattern of adjudication by providing firm legislative direction assuring job security, health insurance coverage, and income maintenance for childbearing

[177] *See* Chavkin, *supra* note 54, at 197-202 (discussing work hazards and the physical changes of pregnancy).

[178] *See* Comment, *Love's Labors Lost: New Conceptions of Maternity Leaves*, 7 HARV. C.R.-C.L. L. REV. 260, 261-62 (1972).

[179] *See, e.g.*, Abraham v. Graphic Arts Int'l Union, 660 F.2d 811 (D.C. Cir. 1981) (ten-day ceiling on sick leave).

[180] *See, e.g.*, Miller-Wohl v. Comm'r of Labor & Industry, 692 P.2d 1243, 1250 (Mont. 1984), (no leave for any disabled employee with less than one year seniority) *appeal docketed*, 53 U.S.L.W. 3718 (U.S. Apr. 9, 1985) (No. 84-1545).

[181] Workers can, of course, and typically do, bargain collectively through unions for adequate health and disability plans to protect themselves and their families against those statistical possibilities.

[182] Ginsburg discussed, in addition to *LaFleur*, *Geduldig*, and *Gilbert*, all cited *supra* text and accompanying notes 10-44, *supra*, Turner v. Department of Employment Sec., 423 U.S. 44 (1975) (invalidating a Utah statute that made pregnant women ineligible for unemployment benefits for a period extending from twelve weeks prior to the expected date of childbirth until a date six weeks after delivery).

> women. Women will remain more restricted than men in their options so long as this problem is brushed under the rug by the nation's lawmakers.[183]

I do not believe that enactment of the PDA, unless it is interpreted to permit employers to provide coverage for pregnant workers regardless of whether other workers are covered for other conditions, has responded satisfactorily to Ginsburg's argument. Such an interpretation would be consistent with the Congressional goal of ending discrimination against working women because of their pregnancy. If such an approach is adopted, feminists on both sides of the "equal treatment/special treatment" debate will be free to pursue our common goal of eradicating the pervasive prejudice against working mothers.[184]

CONCLUSION

The biological fact that only women have the capacity to become pregnant has been used historically to define women as different from men along social, psychological, and emotional dimensions. Those asserted differences, in turn, have served to justify the legal, political, and economic exclusion of women from men's public world. Even now, when the barriers that separate women and men in the work force are breaking down, the uniqueness of pregnancy remains an obstacle to equal opportunity for women.

The nadir of this isolation of pregnancy was reached in modern times by the Supreme Court's distinction in *Geduldig* between pregnant women and non-pregnant persons, an overly-broad characterization properly condemned as artificial and demeaning. Yet the Court's flawed perception of the relevant comparison groups contained an element of factual truth, albeit one from which the Court drew the wrong conclusion. Episodic analysis allows us to reclaim the accurate biological fact of sexual reproductive difference, and to draw the appropriate legal conclusion that difference requires. The Court's false conclusion was that pregnant persons are not women. That conclusion led to the improper legal result that women were protected against sex discrimination only when they are like men—that is, when they are not pregnant. Episodic analysis reveals the right conclusion: that both men and women engage in reproductive conduct, and that women are pregnant persons only for brief and self-contained periods. That insight can give rise to the proper legal result that women continue to be women even when pregnant, and

---

183 Ginsburg, *Some Thoughts on Benign Classification in the Context of Sex*, 10 CONN. L. REV. 813, 826-27 (1978).

184 *See generally* Frug, *Securing Job Market Equality For Women: Labor Market Hostility to Working Mothers*, 59 B.U.L. REV. 55 (1979); Project, *Law Firms and Lawyers With Children: An Empirical Analysis of Family/Work Conflict*, 34 STAN. L. REV. 1263 (1982). *See also* Brill, *The Woman Problem*, AM. LAW., Feb., 1983, at 1, col. 1.

should be provided with legal redress against discrimination based either on their sex or their pregnancy. On both legal and philosophical grounds, the temporary inequality that stems from the condition of pregnancy can and should be accommodated within a framework of equal opportunity for both sexes.

[9]

DECONSTRUCTING EQUALITY-VERSUS-DIFFERENCE: OR, THE USES OF POSTSTRUCTURALIST THEORY FOR FEMINISM

JOAN W. SCOTT

That feminism needs theory goes without saying (perhaps because it has been said so often). What is not always clear is what that theory will do, although there are certain common assumptions I think we can find in a wide range of feminist writings. We need theory that can analyze the workings of patriarchy in all its manifestations—ideological, institutional, organizational, subjective—accounting not only for continuities but also for change over time. We need theory that will let us think in terms of pluralities and diversities rather than of unities and universals. We need theory that will break the conceptual hold, at least, of those long traditions of (Western) philosophy that have systematically and repeatedly construed the world hierarchically in terms of masculine universals and feminine specificities. We need theory that will enable us to articulate alternative ways of thinking about (and thus acting upon) gender without either simply reversing the old hierarchies or confirming them. And we need theory that will be useful and relevant for political practice.

It seems to me that the body of theory referred to as poststructuralism best meets all these requirements. It is not by any means the only theory nor are its positions and formulations unique. In my own case, however, it was reading poststructuralist theory and arguing with literary scholars that provided the elements of clarification for which I was looking. I found a new way of analyzing constructions of meaning and relationships of power that called unitary, universal categories into question and historicized

Feminist Studies 14, no. 1 (Spring 1988). © 1988 by Feminist Studies, Inc.

concepts otherwise treated as natural (such as man/woman) or absolute (such as equality or justice). In addition, what attracted me was the historical connection between the two movements. Poststructuralism and contemporary feminism are late-twentieth-century movements that share a certain self-conscious critical relationship to established philosophical and political traditions. It thus seemed worthwhile for feminist scholars to exploit that relationship for their own ends.[1]

This article will not discuss the history of these various "exploitations" or elaborate on all the reasons a historian might look to this theory to organize her inquiry.[2] What seems most useful here is to give a short list of some major theoretical points and then devote most of my effort to a specific illustration. The first part of this article is a brief discussion of concepts used by poststructuralists that are also useful for feminists. The second part applies some of these concepts to one of the hotly contested issues among contemporary (U.S.) feminists—the "equality-versus-difference" debate.

Among the useful terms feminists have appropriated from poststructuralism are language, discourse, difference, and deconstruction.

Language. Following the work of structuralist linguistics and anthropology, the term is used to mean not simply words or even a vocabulary and set of grammatical rules but, rather, a meaning-constituting system: that is, any system—strictly verbal or other—through which meaning is constructed and cultural practices organized and by which, accordingly, people represent and understand their world, including who they are and how they relate to others. "Language," so conceived, is a central focus of poststructuralist analysis.

Language is not assumed to be a representation of ideas that either cause material relations or from which such relations follow; indeed, the idealist/materialist opposition is a false one to impose on this approach. Rather, the analysis of language provides a crucial point of entry, a starting point for understanding how social relations are conceived, and therefore—because understanding how they are conceived means understanding how they work—how institutions are organized, how relations of production are experienced, and how collective identity is established.

Without attention to language and the processes by which meanings and categories are constituted, one only imposes oversimplified models on the world, models that perpetuate conventional understandings rather than open up new interpretive possibilities.

The point is to find ways to analyze specific "texts"—not only books and documents but also utterances of any kind and in any medium, including cultural practices—in terms of specific historical and contextual meanings. Poststructuralists insist that words and texts have no fixed or intrinsic meanings, that there is no transparent or self-evident relationship between them and either ideas or things, no basic or ultimate correspondence between language and the world. The questions that must be answered in such an analysis, then, are how, in what specific contexts, among which specific communities of people, and by what textual and social processes has meaning been acquired? More generally, the questions are: How do meanings change? How have some meanings emerged as normative and others have been eclipsed or disappeared? What do these processes reveal about how power is constituted and operates?

Discourse. Some of the answers to these questions are offered in the concept of discourse, especially as it has been developed in the work of Michel Foucault. A discourse is not a language or a text but a historically, socially, and institutionally specific structure of statements, terms, categories, and beliefs. Foucault suggests that the elaboration of meaning involves conflict and power, that meanings are locally contested within discursive "fields of force," that (at least since the Enlightenment) the power to control a particular field resides in claims to (scientific) knowledge embodied not only in writing but also in disciplinary and professional organizations, in institutions (hospitals, prisons, schools, factories), and in social relationships (doctor/patient, teacher/student, employer/worker, parent/child, husband/wife). Discourse is thus contained or expressed in organizations and institutions as well as in words; all of these constitute texts or documents to be read.[3]

Discursive fields overlap, influence, and compete with one another; they appeal to one another's "truths" for authority and legitimation. These truths are assumed to be outside human invention, either already known and self-evident or discoverable through scientific inquiry. Precisely because they are assigned the status of objective knowledge, they seem to be beyond dispute and thus serve a powerful legitimating function. Darwinian theories of natural selection are one example of such legitimating truths; biological theories about sexual difference are another. The power of these "truths" comes from the way they function as givens or first premises for both sides in an argument, so that conflicts within discursive fields are framed to follow from rather than question them. The brilliance of so much of Foucault's work has been to illuminate the shared assumptions of what seemed to be sharply different arguments, thus exposing the limits of radical criticism and the extent of the power of dominant ideologies or epistemologies.

In addition, Foucault has shown how badly even challenges to fundamental assumptions often fared. They have been marginalized or silenced, forced to underplay their most radical claims in order to win a short-term goal, or completely absorbed into an existing framework. Yet the fact of change is crucial to Foucault's notion of "archaeology," to the way in which he uses contrasts from different historical periods to present his arguments. Exactly how the process happens is not spelled out to the satisfaction of many historians, some of whom want a more explicit causal model. But when causal theories are highly general, we are often drawn into the assumptions of the very discourse we ought to question. (If we are to question those assumptions, it may be necessary to forgo existing standards of historical inquiry.) Although some have read Foucault as an argument about the futility of human agency in the struggle for social change, I think that he is more appropriately taken as warning against simple solutions to difficult problems, as advising human actors to think strategically and more self-consciously about the philosophical and political implications and meanings of the programs they endorse. From this perspective, Foucault's work provides an important way of thinking differently (and perhaps more creatively) about the politics of the contextual construction of social meanings, about such organizing principles for political action as "equality" and "difference."

Difference. An important dimension of poststructuralist analyses of language has to do with the concept of difference, the notion (following Ferdinand de Saussure's structuralist linguistics) that meaning is made through implicit or explicit contrast, that a positive definition rests on the negation or repression of something represented as antithetical to it. Thus, any unitary concept in fact contains repressed or negated material; it is established in explicit opposition to another term. Any analysis of meaning involves teasing out these negations and oppositions, figuring out how (and whether) they are operating in specific contexts. Oppositions rest on metaphors and cross-references, and often in patriarchal discourse, sexual difference (the contrast masculine/feminine) serves to encode or establish meanings that are literally unrelated to gender or the body. In that way, the meanings of gender become tied to many kinds of cultural representations, and these in turn establish terms by which relations between women and men are organized and understood. The possibilities of this kind of analysis have, for obvious reasons, drawn the interest and attention of feminist scholars.

Fixed oppositions conceal the extent to which things presented as oppositional are, in fact, interdependent—that is, they derive their meaning from a particularly established contrast rather than from some inherent or pure antithesis. Furthermore, according to Jacques Derrida, the interdependence is hierarchical with one term dominant or prior, the opposite term subordinate and secondary. The Western philosophical tradition, he argues, rests on binary oppositions: unity/diversity, identity/difference, presence/absence, and universality/specificity. The leading terms are accorded primacy; their partners are represented as weaker or derivative. Yet the first terms depend on and derive their meaning from the second to such an extent that the secondary terms can be seen as generative of the definition of the first terms.[4] If binary oppositions provide insight into the way meaning is constructed, and if they operate as Derrida suggests, then analyses of meaning cannot take binary oppositions at face value but rather must "deconstruct" them for the processes they embody.

Deconstruction. Although this term is used loosely among scholars—often to refer to a dismantling or destructive enterprise—it also has a precise definition in the work of Derrida and his followers. Deconstruction involves analyzing the operations of difference in texts, the ways in which meanings are made to work. The method consists of two related steps: the reversal and displacement of binary oppositions. This double process reveals the interdependence of seemingly dichotomous terms and their meaning relative to a particular history. It shows them to be not natural but constructed oppositions, constructed for particular purposes in particular contexts.[5] The literary critic Barbara Johnson describes deconstruction as crucially dependent on difference.

> The starting point is often a binary difference that is subsequently shown to be an illusion created by the working of differences much harder to pin down. The differences *between* entities . . . are shown to be based on a repression of differences *within* entities, ways in which an entity differs from itself. . . . The "deconstruction" of a binary opposition is thus not an annihilation of all values or differences; it is an attempt to follow the subtle, powerful effects of differences already at work within the illusion of a binary opposition.[6]

Deconstruction is, then, an important exercise, for it allows us to be critical of the way in which ideas we want to use are ordinarily expressed, exhibited in patterns of meaning that may undercut the ends we seek to attain. A case in point – of meaning expressed in a politically self-defeating way – is the "equality-versus-difference" debate among feminists. Here a binary opposition has been created to offer a choice to feminists, of either endorsing "equality" or its presumed antithesis "difference." In fact, the antithesis itself hides the interdependence of the two terms, for equality is not the elimination of difference, and difference does not preclude equality.

In the past few years, "equality-versus-difference" has been used as a shorthand to characterize conflicting feminist positions and political strategies.[7] Those who argue that sexual difference ought to be an irrelevant consideration in schools, employment, the courts, and the legislature are put in the equality category. Those who insist that appeals on behalf of women ought to be made in terms of the needs, interests, and characteristics common to women as a group are placed in the difference category. In the clashes over the superiority of one or another of these strategies, feminists have invoked history, philosophy, and morality and have devised new classificatory labels: cultural feminism, liberal feminism, feminist separatism, and so on.[8] Most recently, the debate about equality and difference has been used to analyze the Sears case, the sex discrimination suit brought against the retailing giant by the Equal Employment Opportunities Commission (EEOC) in 1979, in which historians Alice Kessler-Harris and Rosalind Rosenberg testified on opposite sides.

There have been many articles written on the Sears case, among them a recent one by Ruth Milkman. Milkman insists that we attend to the political context of seemingly timeless principles: "We ignore the political dimensions of the equality-versus-difference debate at our peril, especially in a period of conservative resurgence like the present." She concludes:

> As long as this is the political context in which we find ourselves, feminist scholars must be aware of the real danger that arguments about "difference" or "women's culture" will be put to uses other than those for which they were originally developed. That does not mean we must abandon these arguments or the intellectual terrain they have opened up; it does mean that we must be self-conscious in our formulations, keeping firmly in view the ways in which our work can be exploited politically.[9]

Milkman's carefully nuanced formulation implies that equality is our safest course, but she is also reluctant to reject difference entirely. She feels a need to choose a side, but which side is the problem. Milkman's ambivalence is an example of what the legal theorist Martha Minow has labeled in another context "the difference dilemma." Ignoring difference in the case of subordinated groups, Minow points out, "leaves in place a faulty neutrality," but focusing on difference can underscore the stigma of deviance. "Both focusing on and ignoring difference risk recreating it. This is the dilemma of difference."[10] What is required, Minow suggests, is a new way of thinking about difference, and this involves rejecting the idea that equality-versus-difference constitutes an opposition. Instead of framing analyses and strategies as if such binary pairs were timeless and true, we need to ask how the dichotomous pairing of equality and difference itself works. Instead of remaining within the terms of existing political discourse, we need to subject those terms to critical examination. Until we understand how the concepts work to constrain and construct specific meanings, we cannot make them work for us.

A close look at the evidence in the Sears case suggests that equality-versus-difference may not accurately depict the opposing sides in the Sears case. During testimony, most of the arguments against equality and for difference were, in fact, made by the Sears lawyers or by Rosalind Rosenberg. They constructed an opponent against whom they asserted that women and men differed, that "fundamental differences"—the result of culture or long-standing patterns of socialization—led to women's presumed lack of interest in commission sales jobs. In order to make their own claim that sexual difference and not discrimination could explain the hiring patterns of Sears, the Sears defense attributed to EEOC an assumption that no one had made in those terms—that women and men had identical interests.[11] Alice Kessler-Harris did not argue that women were the same as men; instead, she used a variety of strategies to challenge Rosenberg's assertions. First, she argued that historical evidence suggested far more variety in the jobs women actually took than Rosenberg assumed. Second, she maintained that economic considerations usually offset the effects of socialization in women's attitudes to employment. And, third, she pointed out that, historically, job segregation by sex was the consequence of employer preferences, not employee choices. The question of women's choices could not be resolved, Kessler-Harris maintained, when the hiring process itself predetermined the outcome, imposing generalized gendered criteria that were not necessarily relevant to the work at hand. The debate joined then not around equality-versus-difference but around the relevance of general ideas of sexual difference in a specific context.[12]

To make the case for employer discrimination, EEOC lawyers cited obviously biased job applicant questionnaires and statements by personnel officers, but they had no individuals to testify that they had experienced discrimination. Kessler-Harris referred to past patterns of sexual segregation in the job market as the product of employer choices, but mostly she invoked history to break down Rosenberg's contention that women as a group differed consistently in the details of their behavior from men, instead insisting that variety characterized female job choices (as it did male job choices), that it made no sense in this case to talk about women as a uniform group. She defined equality to mean a presumption that women and men might have an equal interest in sales commission jobs. She did not claim that women and men, by definition, had such an equal interest. Rather, Kessler-Harris and the EEOC called into question the relevance for hiring decisions of generalizations about the necessarily antithetical behaviors of women and men. EEOC argued that Sears's hiring practices reflected inaccurate and inapplicable notions of sexual difference; Sears argued that "fundamental" differences between the sexes (and not its own actions) explained the gender imbalances in its labor force.

The Sears case was complicated by the fact that almost all the evidence offered was statistical. The testimony of the historians, therefore, could only be inferential at best. Each of them sought to explain small statistical disparities by reference to gross generalizations about the entire history of working women; furthermore, neither historian had much information about what had actually happened at Sears. They were forced, instead, to swear to the truth or falsehood of interpretive generalizations developed for purposes other than legal contestation, and they were forced to treat their interpretive premises as matters of fact. Reading the cross-examination of Kessler-Harris is revealing in this respect. Each of her carefully nuanced explanations of women's work history was forced into a reductive assertion by the Sears lawyers' insistence that she answer questions only by saying yes or no. Similarly, Rosalind Rosenberg's rebuttal to Alice Kessler-Harris eschewed the historian's subtle contextual reading of evidence and sought instead to impose a test of absolute consistency. She juxtaposed Kessler-Harris's testimony in the trial to her earlier published work (in which Kessler-Harris stressed differences between female and male workers in their approaches to work, arguing that women were more domestically oriented and less individualistic than men) in an effort to show that Kessler-Harris had misled the court.[13] Outside the courtroom, however, the disparities of the Kessler-Harris argument could also be explained in other ways. In relationship to a labor history that had typically excluded women, it might make sense to overgeneralize about women's experience, emphasizing difference in order to demonstrate that the universal term "worker" was really a male reference that could not account for all aspects of women's job experiences. In relationship to an employer who sought to justify discrimination by reference to sexual difference, it made more sense to deny the totalizing effects of difference by stressing instead the diversity and complexity of women's behavior and motivation. In the first case, difference served a positive function, unveiling the inequity hidden in a presumably neutral term; in the second case, difference served a negative purpose, justifying what Kessler-Harris believed to be unequal treatment. Although the inconsistency might have been avoided with a more self-conscious analysis of the "difference dilemma," Kessler-Harris's different positions were quite legitimately different emphases for different contexts; only in a courtroom could they be taken as proof of bad faith.[14]

The exacting demands of the courtroom for consistency and "truth" also point out the profound difficulties of arguing about difference. Although the testimony of the historians had to explain only a relatively small statistical disparity in the numbers of women and men hired for full-time commission sales jobs, the explanations that were preferred were totalizing and categorical.[15] In cross-examination, Kessler-Harris's multiple interpretations were found to be contradictory and confusing, although the judge praised Rosenberg for her coherence and lucidity.[16] In part, that was because Rosenberg held to a tight model that unproblematically linked socialization to individual choice; in part it was because her descriptions of gender differences accorded with prevailing normative views. In contrast, Kessler-Harris had trouble finding a simple model that would at once acknowledge difference *and* refuse it as an acceptable explanation for the employment pattern of Sears. So she fell into great difficulty maintaining her case in the face of hostile questioning. On the one hand, she was accused of assuming that economic opportunism equally affected women and men (and thus of believing that women and men were the same). How, then, could she explain the differences her own work had identified? On the other hand, she was tarred (by Rosenberg) with the brush of subversion, for implying that all employers might have some interest in sex typing the labor force, for deducing from her own (presumably Marxist) theory, a "conspiratorial" conclusion about the behavior of Sears.[17] If the patterns of discrimination that Kessler-Harris alluded to were real, after all, one of their effects might well be the kind of difference Rosenberg pointed out. Caught within the framework of Rosenberg's use of historical evidence, Kessler-Harris and her lawyers relied on an essentially negative strategy, offering details designed to complicate and undercut Rosenberg's assertions. Kessler-Harris did not directly challenge the theoretical shortcomings of Rosenberg's socialization model, nor did she offer an alternative model of her own. That would have required, I think, either fully developing the case for employer discrimination or insisting more completely on the "differences" line of argument by exposing the "equality-versus-difference" formulation as an illusion.

In the end, the most nuanced arguments of Kessler-Harris were rejected as contradictory or inapplicable, and the judge decided in Sears's favor, repeating the defense argument that an assumption of equal interest was "unfounded" because of the differences between women and men.[18] Not only was EEOC's position rejected, but the hiring policies of Sears were implicitly endorsed. According to the judge, because difference was real and fundamental, it could explain statistical variations in Sears's hiring. Discrimination was redefined as simply the recognition of "natural" difference (however culturally or historically produced), fitting in nicely with the logic of Reagan conservatism. Difference was substituted for inequality, the appropriate antithesis of equality, becoming inequality's explanation and legitimation. The judge's decision illustrates a process literary scholar Naomi Schor has described in another context: it "essentializes difference and naturalizes social inequity."[19]

The Sears case offers a sobering lesson in the operation of a discursive, that is a political field. Analysis of language here provides insight not only into the manipulation of concepts and definitions but also into the implementation and justification of institutional and political power. References to categorical differences between women and men set the terms within which Sears defended its policies *and* EEOC challenged them. Equality-versus-difference was the intellectual trap within which historians argued not about tiny disparities in Sears's employment practices, but about the normative behaviors of women and men. Although we might conclude that the balance of power was against EEOC by the time the case was heard and that, therefore, its outcome was inevitable (part of the Reagan plan to reverse affirmative action programs of the 1970s), we still need to articulate a critique of what happened that can inform the next round of political encounter. How should that position be conceptualized?

When equality and difference are paired dichotomously, they structure an impossible choice. If one opts for equality, one is forced to accept the notion that difference is antithetical to it. If one opts for difference, one admits that equality is unattainable. That, in a sense, is the dilemma apparent in Milkman's conclusion cited above. Feminists cannot give up "difference"; it has been our most creative analytic tool. We cannot give up equality, at least as long as we want to speak to the principles and values of our political system. But it makes no sense for the feminist movement to let its arguments be forced into preexisting categories and its political disputes to be characterized by a dichotomy we did not invent. How then do we recognize and use notions of sexual difference and yet make arguments for equality? The only response is a double one: the unmasking of the power relationship constructed by posing equality as the antithesis of difference and the refusal of its consequent dichotomous construction of political choices.

Equality-versus-difference cannot structure choices for feminist politics; the oppositional pairing misrepresents the relationship of both terms. Equality, in the political theory of rights that lies behind the claims of excluded groups for justice, means the ignoring of differences between individuals for a particular purpose or in a particular context. Michael Walzer puts it this way: "The root meaning of equality is negative; egalitarianism in its origins is an abolitionist politics. It aims at eliminating not all differences, but a particular set of differences, and a different set in different times and places."[20] This presumes a social agreement to consider obviously different people as equivalent (not identical) for a stated purpose. In this usage, the opposite of equality is inequality or inequivalence, the noncommensurability of individuals or groups in certain circumstances, for certain purposes. Thus, for purposes of democratic citizenship, the measure of equivalence has been, at different times, independence or ownership of property or race or sex. The political notion of equality thus includes, indeed depends on, an acknowledgment of the existence of difference. Demands for equality have rested on implicit and usually unrecognized arguments from difference; if individuals or groups were identical or the same there would be no need to ask for equality. Equality might well be defined as deliberate indifference to specified differences.

The antithesis of difference in most usages is sameness or identity. But even here the contrast and the context must be specified. There is nothing self-evident or transcendent about difference, even if the fact of difference—sexual difference, for example—seems apparent to the naked eye. The questions always ought to be, What qualities or aspects are being compared? What is the nature of the comparison? How is the meaning of difference being constructed? Yet in the Sears testimony and in some debates among feminists (sexual) difference is assumed to be an immutable fact, its meaning inherent in the categories female and male. The lawyers for Sears put it this way: "The reasonableness of the EEOC's *a priori* assumptions of male/female sameness with respect to preferences, interests, and qualifications is . . . the crux of the issue."[21] The point of the EEOC challenge, however, was never sameness but the irrelevance of categorical differences.

The opposition men/women, as Rosenberg employed it, asserted the incomparability of the sexes, and although history and socialization were the explanatory factors, these resonated with categorical distinctions inferred from the facts of bodily difference. When the opposition men/women is invoked, as it was in the Sears case, it refers a specific issue (the small statistical discrepancy between women and men hired for commission sales jobs) back to a general principle (the "fundamental" differences between women and men). The differences within each group that might apply to this particular situation – the fact, for example, that some women might choose "aggressive" or "risk-taking" jobs or that some women might prefer high- to low-paying positions – were excluded by definition in the antithesis between the groups. The irony is, of course, that the statistical case required only a small percentage of women's behaviors to be explained. Yet the historical testimony argued categorically about "women." It thus became impossible to argue (as EEOC and Kessler-Harris tried to) that within the female category, women typically exhibit and participate in all sorts of "male" behaviors, that socialization is a complex process that does not yield uniform choices. To make the argument would have required a direct attack on categorical thinking about gender. For the generalized opposition male/female serves to obscure the differences among women in behavior, character, desire, subjectivity, sexuality, gender identification, and historical experience. In the light of Rosenberg's insistence on the primacy of sexual difference, Kessler-Harris's insistence on the specificity (and historically variable aspect) of women's actions could be dismissed as an unreasonable and trivial claim.

The alternative to the binary construction of sexual difference is not sameness, identity, or androgyny. By subsuming women into a general "human" identity, we lose the specificity of female diversity and women's experiences; we are back, in other words, to the days when "Man's" story was supposed to be everyone's story, when women were "hidden from history," when the feminine served as the negative counterpoint, the "Other," for the construction of positive masculine identity. It is not sameness *or* identity between women and men that we want to claim but a more complicated historically variable diversity than is permitted by the opposition male/female, a diversity that is also differently expressed for different purposes in different contexts. In effect, the duality this opposition creates draws one line of difference, invests it with biological explanations, and then treats each side of the opposition as a unitary phenomenon. Everything in each category (male/female) is assumed to be the same; hence, differences within either category are suppressed. In contrast, our goal is to see not only differences between the sexes but also the way these work to repress differences within gender groups. The sameness constructed on each side of the binary opposition hides the multiple play of differences and maintains their irrelevance and invisibility.

Placing equality and difference in antithetical relationship has, then, a double effect. It denies the way in which difference has long figured in political notions of equality and it suggests that sameness is the only ground on which equality can be claimed. It thus puts feminists in an impossible position, for as long as we argue within the terms of a discourse set up by this opposition we grant the current conservative premise that because women cannot be identical to men in all respects, we cannot expect to be equal to them. The only alternative, it seems to me, is to refuse to oppose equality to difference and insist continually on differences—differences as the condition of individual and collective identities, differences as the constant challenge to the fixing of those identities, history as the repeated illustration of the play of differences, differences as the very meaning of equality itself.

Alice Kessler-Harris's experience in the Sears case shows, however, that the assertion of differences in the face of gender categories is not a sufficient strategy. What is required in addition is an analysis of fixed gender categories as normative statements that organize cultural understandings of sexual difference. This means that we must open to scrutiny the terms women and men as they are used to define one another in particular contexts—workplaces, for example. The history of women's work needs to be retold from this perspective as part of the story of the creation of a gendered workforce. In the nineteenth century, for example, certain concepts of male skill rested on a contrast with female labor (by definition unskilled). The organization and reorganization of work processes was accomplished by reference to the gender attributes of workers, rather than to issues of training, education, or social class. And wage differentials between the sexes were attributed to fundamentally different family roles that preceded (rather than followed from) employment arrangements. In all these processes the meaning of "worker" was established through a contrast between the presumably natural qualities of women and men. If we write the history of women's work by gathering data that describes the activities, needs, interests, and culture of "women workers," we leave in place the naturalized contrast and reify a fixed categorical difference between women and men. We start the story, in other words, too late, by uncritically accepting a gendered category (the "woman worker") that itself needs investigation because its meaning is relative to its history.

If in our histories we relativize the categories woman and man, it means, of course, that we must also recognize the contingent and specific nature of our political claims. Political strategies then will rest on analyses of the utility of certain arguments in certain discursive contexts, without, however, invoking absolute qualities for women or men. There are moments when it makes sense for mothers to demand consideration for their social role, and contexts within which motherhood is irrelevant to women's behavior; but to maintain that womanhood is motherhood is to obscure the differences that make choice possible. There are moments when it makes sense to demand a reevaluation of the status of what has been socially constructed as women's work ("comparable worth" strategies are the current example) and contexts within which it makes much more sense to prepare women for entry into "non-traditional" jobs. But to maintain that femininity predisposes women to certain (nurturing) jobs or (collaborative) styles of work is to naturalize complex economic and social processes and, once again, to obscure the differences that have characterized women's occupational histories. An insistence on differences undercuts the tendency to absolutist, and in the case of sexual difference, essentialist categories. It does not deny the existence of gender difference, but it does suggest that its meanings are always relative to particular constructions in specified contexts. In contrast, absolutist categorizations of difference end up always enforcing normative rules.

It is surely not easy to formulate a "deconstructive" political strategy in the face of powerful tendencies that construct the world in binary terms. Yet there seems to me no other choice. Perhaps as we learn to think this way solutions will become more readily apparent. Perhaps the theoretical and historical work we do can prepare the ground. Certainly we can take heart from the history of feminism, which is full of illustrations of refusals of simple dichotomies and attempts instead to demonstrate that equality requires the recognition and inclusion of differences. Indeed, one way historians could contribute to a genuine rethinking of these concepts, is to stop writing the history of feminisms as a story of oscillations between demands for equality and affirmations of difference. This approach inadvertently strengthens the hold of the binary construction, establishing it as inevitable by giving it a long history. When looked at closely, in fact, the historical arguments of feminists do not usually fall into these neat compartments; they are instead attempts to reconcile theories of equal rights with cultural concepts of sexual difference, to question the validity of normative constructions of gender in the light of the existence of behaviors and qualities that contradict the rules, to point up rather than resolve conditions of contradiction, to articulate a political identity for women without conforming to existing stereotypes about them.

In histories of feminism and in feminist political strategies there needs to be at once attention to the operations of difference and an insistence on differences, but not a simple substitution of multiple for binary difference for it is not a happy pluralism we ought to invoke. The resolution of the "difference dilemma" comes neither from ignoring nor embracing difference as it is normatively constituted. Instead, it seems to me that the critical feminist position must always involve *two* moves. The first is the systematic criticism of the operations of categorical difference, the exposure of the kinds of exclusions and inclusions – the hierarchies – it constructs, and a refusal of their ultimate "truth." A refusal, however, not in the name of an equality that implies sameness or identity, but rather (and this is the second move) in the name of an equality that rests on differences – differences that confound, disrupt, and render ambiguous the meaning of any fixed binary opposition. To do anything else is to buy into the political argument that sameness is a requirement for equality, an untenable position for feminists (and historians) who know that power is constructed on and so must be challenged from the ground of difference.

NOTES

I am extremely grateful to William Connolly, Sanford Levinson, Andrew Pickering, Barbara Herrnstein Smith, and Elizabeth Weed for their thoughtful suggestions, which sharpened and improved my argument.

1. On the problem of appropriating poststructuralism for feminism, see Biddy Martin, "Feminism, Criticism, Foucault," *New German Critique* 27 (Fall 1982): 3-30.
2. Joan W. Scott, "Gender: A Useful Category of Historical Analysis," *American Historical Review* 91 (December 1986): 1053-75; Donna Haraway, "A Manifesto for Cyborgs: Science, Technology, and Socialist Feminism in the 1980s," *Socialist Review* 15 (March-April 1985): 65-107.
3. Examples of Michel Foucault's work include *The Archaeology of Knowledge* (New York: Harper & Row, 1976), *The History of Sexuality,* vol. 1, *An Introduction* (New York: Vintage, 1980), and *Power/Knowledge: Selected Interviews and Other Writings, 1972-1977* (New York: Pantheon, 1980). See also Hubert L. Dreyfus and Paul Rabinow, *Michel Foucault: Beyond Structuralism and Hermeneutics* (Chicago: University of Chicago Press, 1983).
4. The Australian philosopher Elizabeth Gross puts it this way: "What Derrida attempts to show is that within these binary couples, the primary or dominant term derives its privilege from a curtailment or suppression of its opposite. Sameness or identity, presence, speech, the origin, mind, etc. are all privileged in relation to their opposites, which are regarded as debased, impure variants of the primary term. Difference, for example, is the lack of identity or sameness; absence is the lack of presence; writing is the supplement of speech, and so on." See her "Derrida, Irigaray, and Deconstruction," *Leftwright, Intervention* (Sydney, Australia): 20 (1986): 73. See also Jacques Derrida, *Of Grammatology* (Baltimore: Johns Hopkins University Press, 1976); and Jonathan Culler, *On Deconstruction: Theory and Criticism after Structuralism* (Ithaca: Cornell University Press, 1982).
5. Again, to cite Elizabeth Gross's formulation: "Taken together, reversal and its useful displacement show the necessary but unfounded function of these terms in Western thought. One must both reverse the dichotomy and the values attached to the two terms, as well as displace the excluded term, placing it beyond its oppositional role, as the internal condition of the dominant term. This move makes clear the violence of the hierarchy and the debt the dominant term owes to the subordinate one. It also demonstrates that there are other ways of conceiving these terms than dichotomously. If these terms were only or necessarily dichotomies, the process of displacement would not be possible. Although historically necessary, the terms are not logically necessary." See Gross, 74.
6. Barbara Johnson, *The Critical Difference: Essays in the Contemporary Rhetoric of Reading* (Baltimore: Johns Hopkins University Press, 1980): x-xi.
7. Most recently, attention has been focused on the issue of pregnancy benefits. See, for example, Lucinda M. Finley, "Transcending Equality Theory: A Way Out of the Maternity and the Workplace Debate," *Columbia Law Review* 86 (October 1986): 1118-83. See Sylvia A. Law, "Rethinking Sex and the Constitution," *University of Pennsylvania Law Review* 132 (June 1984): 955-1040.
8. Recently, historians have begun to cast feminist history in terms of the equality-versus-difference debate. Rather than accept it as an accurate characterization of antithetical positions, however, I think we need to look more closely at how feminists used these arguments. A close reading of nineteenth-century French feminist texts, for

example, leads me to conclude that they are far less easily categorized into difference or equality positions than one would have supposed. I think it is a mistake for feminist historians to write this debate uncritically into history for it reifies an "antithesis" that may not actually have existed. We need instead to "deconstruct" feminist arguments and read them in their discursive contexts, all as explorations of "the difference dilemma."

9. Ruth Milkman, "Women's History and the Sears Case," *Feminist Studies* 12 (Summer 1986): 394-95. In my discussion of the Sears case, I have drawn heavily on this careful and intelligent article, the best so far of the many that have been written on the subject.

10. Martha Minow,"Learning to Live with the Dilemma of Difference: Bilingual and Special Education," *Law and Contemporary Problems* 48, no. 2 (1984): 157-211; quotation is from p. 160; see also pp. 202-6.

11. There is a difference, it seems to me, between arguing that women and men have identical interests and arguing that one should presume such identity in all aspects of the hiring process. The second position is the only strategic way of not building into the hiring process prejudice or the wrong presumptions about differences of interest.

12. Rosenberg's "Offer of Proof" and Kessler-Harris's "Written Testimony" appeared in *Signs* 11 (Summer 1986): 757-79. The "Written Rebuttal Testimony of Dr. Rosalind Rosenberg" is part of the official transcript of the case, U.S. District Court for the Northern District of Illinois, Eastern Division, *EEOC vs Sears,* Civil Action No. 79-C-4373. (I am grateful to Sanford Levinson for sharing the trial documents with me and for our many conversations about them.)

13. Appendix to the "Written Rebuttal Testimony of Dr. Rosalind Rosenberg," 1-12.

14. On the limits imposed by courtrooms and the pitfalls expert witnesses may encounter, see Nadine Taub, "Thinking about Testifying," *Perspectives* (American Historical Association Newsletter) 24 (November 1986): 10-11.

15. On this point, Taub asks a useful question: "Is there a danger in discrimination cases that historical or other expert testimony not grounded in the particular facts of the case will reinforce the idea that it is acceptable to make generalizations about particular groups?" (p. 11).

16. See the cross-examination of Kessler-Harris, *EEOC vs Sears,* 16376-619.

17. The Rosenberg "Rebuttal" is particularly vehement on this question: "This assumption that all employers discriminate is prominent in her [Kessler-Harris's] work. . . . In a 1979 article, she wrote hopefully that women harbor values, attitudes, and behavior patterns potentially subversive to capitalism" (p. 11). "There are, of course, documented instances of employers limiting the opportunities of women. But the fact that some employers have discriminated does not prove that all do" (p. 19). The rebuttal raises another issue about the political and ideological limits of a courtroom or, perhaps it is better to say, about the way the courtroom reproduces dominant ideologies. The general notion that employers discriminate was unacceptable (but the general notion that women prefer certain jobs was not). This unacceptability was underscored by linking it to subversion and Marxism, positions intolerable in U.S. political discourse. Rosenberg's innuendos attempted to discredit Kessler-Harris on two counts – first, by suggesting she was making a ridiculous generalization and, second, by suggesting that only people outside acceptable politics could even entertain that generalization.

18. Milkman, 391.

19. Naomi Schor, "Reading Double: Sand's Difference," in *The Poetics of Gender,* ed. Nancy K. Miller (New York: Columbia University Press, 1986), 256.

20. Michael Walzer, *Spheres of Justice: A Defense of Pluralism and Equality* (New York: Basic Books, 1983), xii. See also Minow, 202-3.

21. Milkman, 384.

Abortion: Privacy or Equality

[10]

ESSAY

SOME THOUGHTS ON AUTONOMY AND EQUALITY IN RELATION TO *ROE V. WADE*†

RUTH BADER GINSBURG‡

The 1973 United States Supreme Court decision in Roe v. Wade *sparked a legal and political controversy that continues to this day. Judge Ginsburg suggests that the* Roe *opinion would have been more acceptable if it had not gone beyond a ruling on the extreme statute involved in the case. She agrees with commentary maintaining that the Court should have adverted specifically to sex equality considerations. Such an approach might have muted the criticism of the* Roe *decision. The breadth and detail of the* Roe *opinion ironically may have stimulated, rather than discouraged, antiabortion measures, particularly with respect to public funding of abortion.*

These remarks contrast two related areas of constitutional adjudication: gender-based classification and reproductive autonomy. In both areas, the Burger Court, in contrast to the Warren Court, has been uncommonly active. The two areas are intimately related in this practical sense: the law's response to questions subsumed under these headings bears pervasively on the situation of women in society. Inevitably, the shape of the law on gender-based classification and reproductive autonomy indicates and influences the opportunity women will have to participate as men's full partners in the nation's social, political, and economic life.[1]

Doctrine in the two areas, however, has evolved in discrete compartments. The High Court has analyzed classification by gender under an equal

---

† This Essay was delivered as the William T. Joyner Lecture on Constitutional Law at the University of North Carolina School of Law on April 6, 1984.

‡ United States Circuit Judge, United States Court of Appeals for the District of Columbia Circuit. The author acknowledges with appreciation the assistance of her 1983-1984 law clerk, Michael Klarman, in the composition of this Essay.

1. *See* Karst, *Foreword: Equal Citizenship Under the Fourteenth Amendment*, 91 HARV. L. REV. 1, 53-59 (1977). In composing this presentation, I have been stimulated, particularly, by the more encompassing and trenchant work of Professor Sylvia Law of New York University Law School, Law, *Rethinking Sex and the Constitution*, 132 U. PA. L. REV. 955 (1984), and Professor Wendy Williams of Georgetown University Law Center, W. Williams, Equality Riddle: Pregnancy and the Equal Treatment/Special Treatment Debate (Mar. 1984) (unpublished manuscript); W. Williams, Pregnancy: Special Treatment vs. Equal Treatment (Mar. 7, 1982) (unpublished manuscript); W. Williams, The Equality Crisis: Some Reflections on Culture, Courts and Feminism (1982) (unpublished manuscript). I owe both of them special appreciation for sharing their draft manuscripts and ideas with me. For the vulnerabilities readers find in this discussion of tense issues, however, I bear sole responsibility.

protection/sex discrimination rubric; it has treated reproductive autonomy under a substantive due process/personal autonomy headline not expressly linked to discrimination against women. The Court's gender classification decisions overturning state and federal legislation, in the main, have not provoked large controversy; the Court's initial 1973 abortion decision, *Roe v. Wade*,[2] on the other hand, became and remains a storm center. *Roe v. Wade* sparked public opposition and academic criticism,[3] in part, I believe, because the Court ventured too far in the change it ordered and presented an incomplete justification for its action. I will attempt to explain these twin perspectives on *Roe* later in this Essay.

Preliminarily, I will relate why an invitation to speak at Chapel Hill on any topic relating to constitutional law led me to think about gender-based classification coupled with *Roe* and its aftermath. In 1971, just before the Supreme Court's turning-point gender-classification decision in *Reed v. Reed*,[4] and over a year before *Roe v. Wade*, I visited a neighboring institution to participate in a conference on women and the law. I spoke then of the utility of litigation attacking official line-drawing by sex. My comments focused on the chance in the 1970s that courts, through constitutional adjudication, would aid in evening out the rights, responsibilities, and opportunities of women and men.[5] I did not mention the abortion cases then on the dockets of several lower courts—I was not at that time or any other time thereafter personally engaged in reproductive-autonomy litigation. Nonetheless, the most heated questions I received concerned abortion.

The questions were pressed by black men. The suggestion, not thinly veiled, was that legislative reform and litigation regarding abortion might have less to do with individual autonomy or discrimination against women than with restricting population growth among oppressed minorities.[6] The

---

2. 410 U.S. 113 (1973).

3. *See, e.g.*, Ely, *The Wages of Crying Wolf: A Comment on* Roe v. Wade, 82 YALE L.J. 920 (1973); Epstein, *Substantive Due Process by Any Other Name: The Abortion Cases*, 1973 SUP. CT. REV. 159.

4. 404 U.S. 71 (1971) (statutory preference for males as estate administrators held unconstitutional).

5. *See* Ginsburg, *Sex and Unequal Protection: Men and Women as Victims*, 11 J. FAM. L. 347 (1971) (presenting text of October 1, 1971 remarks made at the Southern Regional Conference of the National Conference of Law Women, held at Duke University Law School).

6. Law journal commentary around that time discussed population control measures that the government might order. *See, e.g.*, Note, *Legal Analysis and Population Control: The Problem of Coercion*, 84 HARV. L. REV. 1856 (1971). Some commentators explicitly noted links between the abortion and population explosion issues. *See, e.g.*, Leavy & Kummer, *Abortion and the Population Crisis; Therapeutic Abortion and the Law; Some New Approaches*, 27 OHIO ST. L.J. 647, 652 (1966) ("[T]he subject of abortion is riding the wave of the grand dialogue over the population explosion and the need for birth control programs."); Note, *Abortion Reform: History, Status, and Prognosis*, 21 CASE W. RES. L. REV. 521, 523 (1970) ("[T]hose countries that have sanctioned abortion on demand have been rewarded with consequent alleviation of dire overpopulation . . . ."); *see also Survey Finds 50% Back Liberalization of Abortion Policy*, N.Y. Times, Oct. 28, 1971, at A1, col. 1 ("General concern over population growth has become so intense . . . that half the public now favors liberalization of restrictions on abortion."). As the text indicates, blacks—and in particular, black men—also noted the coincidence of rising population with the liberalization of abortion laws, and sometimes were strongly suspicious of the implications. *See, e.g.*, *City Blacks Get Most Abortions*, N.Y. Times, Dec. 6, 1973, at 94, col. 3 (remarking upon "[t]raditional

strong word "genocide" was uttered more than once. It is a notable irony that, as constitutional law in this domain has unfolded, women who are not poor have achieved access to abortion with relative ease; for poor women, however, a group in which minorities are disproportionately represented, access to abortion is not markedly different from what it was in pre-*Roe* days.

I will summarize first the Supreme Court's performance in cases challenging explicit gender-based classification—a development that has encountered no significant backlash—and then turn to the far more turbulent reproductive autonomy area.

The Warren Court uncabined the equal protection guarantee in diverse settings,[7] but line drawing by sex was a quarter in which no change occurred in the 1950s and 1960s. From the 1860s until 1971, the record remained unbroken: the Supreme Court rejected virtually every effort to overturn sex-based classification by law. Without offense to the Constitution, for example, women could be kept off juries[8] and could be barred from occupations ranging from lawyer to bartender.[9]

In the 1970s overt sex-based classification fell prey to the Burger Court's intervention. Men could not be preferred to women for estate administration purposes, the Court declared in the pivotal *Reed v. Reed*[10] decision. Married women in the military could not be denied fringe benefits—family housing and health care allowances—accorded married men in military service, the High Court held in *Frontiero v. Richardson.*[11] Social security benefits, welfare assistance, and workers' compensation secured by a male's employment must be secured, to the same extent, by a female's employment, the Supreme Court ruled in a progression of cases: *Weinberger v. Wiesenfeld,*[12] *Califano v. Goldfarb,*[13] *Califano v. Westcott,*[14] and *Wengler v. Druggists Mutual Insurance Co.*[15] Girls are entitled to the same parental support as boys, the Supreme Court stated in *Stanton v. Stanton.*[16] Evidencing its neutrality, the Court declared in

. . . black male resistance to abortion" and the view of the "militant [black] movement" that abortion is "genocide").

7. *See* Shapiro v. Thompson, 394 U.S. 618 (1969) (interstate travel); Levy v. Louisiana, 391 U.S. 68 (1968) (discrimination on the basis of out-of-wedlock birth); Harper v. Virginia Bd. of Elections, 383 U.S. 663 (1966) (access to ballot); Reynolds v. Sims, 377 U.S. 533 (1964) (apportionment); Griffin v. Illinois, 351 U.S. 12 (1956) (access to court); Brown v. Board of Educ., 347 U.S. 483 (1954) (race discrimination).

8. *See* Hoyt v. Florida, 368 U.S. 57 (1961) (upholding state statute requiring that, to serve on juries, women, but not men, must volunteer affirmatively for service); Fay v. New York, 332 U.S. 261 (1947) (upholding state's "blue ribbon" jury scheme despite gross disparity between numbers of women and men selected to serve); Strauder v. West Virginia, 100 U.S. 303, 310 (1879) (stating in dictum that states may "confine [juror] selection to males").

9. *See* Goesaert v. Cleary, 335 U.S. 464 (1948) (bartender) (decision "disapproved" in Craig v. Boren, 429 U.S. 190, 210 (1976)); Bradwell v. Illinois, 83 U.S. (16 Wall.) 130 (1872) (lawyer). *See generally* Ginsburg, *Sex Equality and the Constitution*, 52 TUL. L. REV. 451, 451-57 (1978).

10. 404 U.S. 71 (1971).

11. 411 U.S. 677 (1973).

12. 420 U.S. 636 (1975) (social security).

13. 430 U.S. 199 (1977) (social security).

14. 443 U.S. 76 (1979) (aid to families with dependent children).

15. 446 U.S. 142 (1980) (workers' compensation).

16. 421 U.S. 7 (1975).

Craig v. Boren[17] that boys must be permitted to buy 3.2 percent beer at the same age as girls and, in *Orr v. Orr*,[18] that alimony could not be retained as a one-way street: a state could compel able men to make payments to women in need only if it also held women of means accountable for payments to men unable to fend for themselves. Louisiana's rule, derived from Napoleon's Civil Code, designating husband head and master of the household, was held in *Kirchberg v. Feenstra*[19] to be offensive to the evolving sex equality principle.

However sensible—and noncontroversial—these results, the decisions had a spectacular aspect. The race cases that trooped before the Warren Court could be viewed as moving the federal judiciary onto the course set by the Reconstruction Congress a century earlier in the post-Civil War amendments. No similar foundation, set deliberately by actors in the political arena, can account for the Burger Court sex discrimination decisions.[20] Perhaps for that reason, the Court has proceeded cautiously. It has taken no giant step. In its most recent decision, *Mississippi University for Women v. Hogan*,[21] the High Court recognized the right of men to a nursing school education at an institution maintained by the state for women only. But it earlier had declined to condemn a state property tax advantage reserved for widows,[22] a state statutory rape law penalizing males but not females,[23] and draft registration limited to males.[24] It has formally reserved judgment on the question whether, absent ratification of an equal rights amendment, sex, like race, should rank as a suspect classification.[25]

The Court's gender-based classification precedent impelled acknowledgment of a middle-tier equal protection standard of review, a level of judicial scrutiny demanding more than minimal rationality but less than a near-perfect fit between legislative ends and means. This movement away from the empty-cupboard interpretation of the equal protection principle in relation to sex equality claims largely trailed and mirrored changing patterns in society—most conspicuously, the emergence of the two-career family. The Court's decisions provoked no outraged opposition in legislative chambers. On the contrary, in a key area in which the Court rejected claims of impermissible sex-

---

17. 429 U.S. 190 (1976).

18. 440 U.S. 268 (1979).

19. 450 U.S. 455 (1981). The Louisiana legislation at issue provided specifically that a husband had a unilateral right to dispose of jointly owned property without his wife's consent. *Id.* at 456.

20. The Court once observed that the 19th amendment gave women the vote but only that. *See* Fay v. New York, 332 U.S. 261, 290 (1947).

21. 458 U.S. 718 (1982).

22. Kahn v. Shevin, 416 U.S. 351 (1974).

23. Michael M. v. Superior Court, 450 U.S. 464 (1981).

24. Rostker v. Goldberg, 453 U.S. 57 (1981).

25. *See* Mississippi Univ. for Women v. Hogan, 458 U.S. 718, 724 n.9 (1982); Frontiero v. Richardson, 411 U.S. 677, 691-92 (1973) (Powell, J., concurring).

For a more detailed review of the Burger Court's sex discrimination rulings, see Ginsburg, *The Burger Court's Grapplings with Sex Discrimination*, THE BURGER COURT: THE COUNTER-REVOLUTION THAT WASN'T 132 (V. Blasi ed. 1983) [hereinafter cited as THE BURGER COURT].

based classification, Congress indicated a different view, one more sensitive to discrimination against women.

That area, significantly in view of the Court's approach to reproductive choice, was pregnancy. In 1974 the Court decided an issue pressed by pregnant school teachers forced to terminate their employment, or take unpaid maternity leave, months before the anticipated birth date.[26] Policies singling out pregnant women for disadvantageous treatment discriminated invidiously on the basis of sex, the teachers argued. The Court bypassed that argument; instead, the Court rested its decision holding mandatory maternity leaves unconstitutional on due process/conclusive presumption reasoning.[27] Some weeks later, the Court held that a state-operated disability income protection plan could exclude normal pregnancy without offense to the equal protection principle.[28] In a statutory setting as well, under Title VII, the Court later ruled, as it earlier had held in a constitutional context, that women unable to work due to pregnancy or childbirth could be excluded from disability coverage.[29] The classifications in these disability cases, according to the Court, were not gender-based on their face, and were not shown to have any sex-discriminatory effect. All "nonpregnant persons," women along with men, the Court pointed out, were treated alike.[30]

With respect to Title VII, Congress prospectively overruled the Court in 1978. It amended the statute to state explicitly that classification on the basis of sex includes classification on the basis of pregnancy.[31] That congressional definition is not controlling in constitutional adjudication, but it might stimulate the Court one day to revise its position that regulation governing "pregnant persons" is not sex-based.

Roe v. Wade, in contrast to decisions involving explicit male/female classification, has occasioned searing criticism of the Court, over a decade of demonstrations, a stream of vituperative mail addressed to Justice Blackmun (the author of the opinion), annual proposals for overruling *Roe* by constitutional amendment,[32] and a variety of measures in Congress and state legislatures to contain or curtail the decision.[33] In 1973, when *Roe* issued, abortion law was in a state of change across the nation. There was a distinct trend in the states,

26. Cleveland Bd. of Educ. v. LaFleur, 414 U.S. 632 (1974).

27. *Id.* at 639-50. The irrebuttable or conclusive presumption mode of analysis has lost favor with the Court in other contexts. *See* Weinberger v. Salfi, 422 U.S. 749, 771-72 (1975).

28. Geduldig v. Aiello, 417 U.S. 484 (1974).

29. General Elec. Co. v. Gilbert, 429 U.S. 125 (1976).

30. *Id.* at 135.

31. Act of Oct. 31, 1978, Pub. L. No. 95-555, 92 Stat. 2076 (amending 42 U.S.C. § 2000e (1976)).

32. *See, e.g.*, Destro, *Abortion and the Constitution: The Need for a Life-Protective Amendment*, 63 CALIF. L. REV. 1250, 1319-25 (1975) (discussing proposed amendments).

33. *See, e.g.*, Hyde, *The Human Life Bill: Some Issues and Answers*, 27 N.Y.L. SCH. L. REV. 1077 (1982) (congressional response); Witherspoon, *The New Pro-Life Legislation: Patterns and Recommendations*, 7 ST. MARY'S L.J. 637 (1976) (state response); Note, *Implications of the Abortion Decisions: Post* Roe *and* Doe *Litigation and Legislation*, 74 COLUM. L. REV. 237 (1974) (state response); *see also infra* notes 50-52 and accompanying text.

noted by the Court, "toward liberalization of abortion statutes."[34] Several states had adopted the American Law Institute's Model Penal Code approach setting out grounds on which abortion could be justified at any stage of pregnancy; most significantly, the Code included as a permissible ground preservation of the woman's physical or mental health.[35] Four states—New York, Washington, Alaska, and Hawaii—permitted physicians to perform first-trimester abortions with virtually no restrictions. This movement in legislative arenas bore some resemblance to the law revision activity that eventually swept through the states establishing no-fault divorce as the national pattern.[36]

The Texas law at issue in *Roe* made it a crime to "procure an abortion" except "by medical advice for the purpose of saving the life of the mother."[37] It was the most extreme prohibition extant. The Court had in close view two pathmarking opinions on reproductive autonomy: first, a 1965 precedent, *Griswold v. Connecticut*,[38] holding inconsistent with personal privacy, somehow sheltered by due process, a state ban on the use of contraceptives even by married couples; second, a 1972 decision, *Eisenstadt v. Baird*,[39] extending *Griswold* to strike down a state prohibition on sales of contraceptives except to married persons by prescription. The Court had already decided *Reed v. Reed*,[40] recognizing the arbitrariness in the 1970s of a once traditional gender-based classification, but it did not further pursue that avenue in *Roe*.

The decision in *Roe* appeared to be a stunning victory for the plaintiffs. The Court declared that a woman, guided by the medical judgment of her physician, had a "fundamental"[41] right to abort a pregnancy, a right the Court

34. *Roe*, 410 U.S. at 140; *see also infra* note 81.

35. MODEL PENAL CODE § 230.3 (1980).

36. On the transition from fault to no-fault divorce, see Raphael, Frank & Wilder, *Divorce in America: The Erosion of Fault*, 81 DICK. L. REV. 719, 728 (1976-1977) ("For the past three decades there has been a strong trend away from the traditional notion that one spouse must be guilty of some injury to the other before a divorce may be granted."); Note, *Untying the Knot: The Course and Patterns of Divorce Reform*, 57 CORNELL L. REV. 649 (1972). Long before no-fault divorce legislation became the norm in this country, persons with the financial resources to do so could travel to certain states or outside the country to end their marriages. *See, e.g.*, Friedman & Percival, *Who Sues for Divorce? From Fault Through Fiction to Freedom*, 5 J. LEGAL STUD. 61, 68 (1976) (before the sudden burst of no-fault divorce legislation in early 1970s, "divorce on demand had been available in many states, but at a stiff price"); Wash. Post, Feb. 1, 1972, at A18, col. 1 ("[S]omething is wrong when people who have $400 and a plane ticket can get quickie divorces and those who don't can't."), *quoted in* Zuckman, *Recent Developments in American Divorce Legislation*, 35 JURIST 6, 12 (1975). Similarly, before *Roe*, women of means could end their pregnancies by traveling to states or foreign nations with less restrictive abortion laws. *See* Burt, *The Burger Court and the Family*, THE BURGER COURT, *supra* note 25, at 92, 107-08 (for practical purposes, the availability of abortions in some states undermined the more restrictive regimes); Karst, *supra* note 1, at 59 ("Even before *Roe v. Wade*, wealthy women . . . could obtain abortions by traveling."); *Abortion for Whom*, NEW REPUBLIC, Oct. 25, 1969, at 12 ("The rich have always been able to get abortions by going abroad. The poor cannot travel . . . ."). For example, in 1971, the second year New York's liberalized abortion law was in effect, 60% of the women having abortions in New York were nonresidents. *See Light on Abortion*, N.Y. Times, Sept. 4, 1972, at A14, col. 2.

37. *Roe*, 410 U.S. at 117-18 (citing TEX. PENAL CODE ANN. §§ 1191, 1196 (Vernon 1961)).

38. 381 U.S. 479 (1965). Earlier, in Skinner v. Oklahoma *ex rel.* Williamson, 316 U.S. 535, 541 (1942), the Court had referred to an individual's right to procreate as "a basic liberty."

39. 405 U.S. 438 (1972).

40. 404 U.S. 71 (1971).

41. *See Roe*, 410 U.S. at 152, 155.

anchored to a concept of personal autonomy derived from the due process guarantee. The Court then proceeded to define with precision the state regulation of abortion henceforth permissible. The rulings in *Roe*, and in a companion case decided the same day, *Doe v. Bolton*,[42] were stunning in this sense: they called into question the criminal abortion statutes of every state, even those with the least restrictive provisions.

Roe announced a trimester approach Professor Archibald Cox has described as "read[ing] like a set of hospital rules and regulations."[43] During the first trimester, "the abortion decision and its effectuation must be left to the medical judgment of the pregnant woman's attending physician";[44] in the next, roughly three-month stage, the state may, if it chooses, require other measures protective of the woman's health.[45] During the final months, "the stage subsequent to viability," the state also may concern itself with an emerging interest, the "potentiality of human life"; at that stage, the state "may, if it chooses, regulate, and even proscribe, abortion except where it is necessary, in appropriate medical judgment, for the preservation of the life or health of the mother."[46]

Justice O'Connor, ten years after *Roe*, described the trimester approach as "on a collision course with itself."[47] Advances in medical technology would continue to move *forward* the point at which regulation could be justified as protective of a woman's health, and to move *backward* the point of viability, when the state could proscribe abortions unnecessary to preserve the patient's life or health. The approach, she thought, impelled legislatures to remain *au courant* with changing medical practices and called upon courts to examine legislative judgments, not as jurists applying "neutral principles," but as "science review boards."[48]

I earlier observed that, in my judgment, *Roe* ventured too far in the change it ordered. The sweep and detail of the opinion stimulated the mobilization of a right-to-life movement and an attendant reaction in Congress and state legislatures. In place of the trend "toward liberalization of abortion statutes" noted in *Roe*,[49] legislatures adopted measures aimed at minimizing the impact of the 1973 rulings, including notification and consent requirements,[50]

---

42. 410 U.S. 179 (1973).

43. A. COX, THE ROLE OF THE SUPREME COURT IN AMERICAN GOVERNMENT 113 (1976).

44. *Roe*, 410 U.S. at 164.

45. *Id.*

46. *Id.* at 164-65. The Model Penal Code provision, on which several states had patterned abortion legislation reform, *see Special Project, Survey of Abortion Law*, 1980 ARIZ. ST. L.J. 67, 109 & nn.229-31, contained no limitation as to the stage of pregnancy at which an abortion could be obtained. *See* MODEL PENAL CODE § 230.3(2) (1980).

47. City of Akron v. Akron Center for Reproductive Health, Inc., 103 S. Ct. 2481, 2507 (1983) (O'Connor, J., dissenting).

48. *Id.*

49. *Roe*, 410 U.S. at 140; *see also infra* note 81.

50. *See* City of Akron v. Akron Center for Reproductive Health, Inc., 103 S. Ct. 2481, 2497-99 (1983) (parental and court consent); H.L. v. Matheson, 450 U.S. 398 (1981) (parental notification); Planned Parenthood v. Danforth, 428 U.S. 52, 67-75 (1976) (spousal and parental consent).

prescriptions for the protection of fetal life,[51] and bans on public expenditures for poor women's abortions.[52]

Professor Paul Freund explained where he thought the Court went astray in *Roe*, and I agree with his statement. The Court properly invalidated the Texas proscription, he indicated, because "[a] law that absolutely made criminal all kinds and forms of abortion could not stand up; it is not a reasonable accommodation of interests."[53] If *Roe* had left off at that point and not adopted what Professor Freund called a "medical approach,"[54] physicians might have been less pleased with the decision, but the legislative trend might have continued in the direction in which it was headed in the early 1970s. "[S]ome of the bitter debate on the issue might have been averted," Professor Freund believed; "[t]he animus against the Court might at least have been diverted to the legislative halls."[55] Overall, he thought that the *Roe* distinctions turning on trimesters and viability of the fetus illustrated a troublesome tendency of the modern Supreme Court under Chief Justices Burger and Warren "to specify by a kind of legislative code the one alternative pattern that will satisfy the Constitution."[56]

I commented at the outset that I believe the Court presented an incomplete justification for its action. Academic criticism of *Roe*, charging the Court with reading its own values into the due process clause, might have been less pointed had the Court placed the woman alone, rather than the woman tied to her physician, at the center of its attention. Professor Karst's commentary is indicative of the perspective not developed in the High Court's opinion; he solidly linked abortion prohibitions with discrimination against women.[57] The issue in *Roe*, he wrote, deeply touched and concerned "women's position in society in relation to men."[58]

It is not a sufficient answer to charge it all to women's anatomy—a natural, not man-made, phenomenon. Society, not anatomy, "places a greater stigma on unmarried women who become pregnant than on the men who father their children."[59] Society expects, but nature does not command, that "women take the major responsibility . . . for child care"[60] and that they will

51. *See* Planned Parenthood Ass'n v. Ashcroft, 103 S. Ct. 2517, 2521-22 (1983); Planned Parenthood v. Danforth, 428 U.S. 52, 81-84 (1976).

52. *See* Harris v. McRae, 448 U.S. 297 (1980) ("Hyde Amendment" to Title XIX of Social Security Act); Maher v. Roe, 432 U.S. 464 (1977) (state Medicaid regulations).

53. Freund, *Storms over the Supreme Court*, 69 A.B.A. J. 1474, 1480 (1983) (adapted from inaugural Harold Leventhal Lecture at Columbia Law School).

54. *Id.*

55. *Id.*; *cf.* Burt, *supra* note 36, at 107-09 (arguing that *Roe* was "unnecessary" because "majoritarian institutions" were not "unfairly disregard[ing]" interests of "proponents of free abortion"); *infra* note 81.

56. Freund, *supra* note 53, at 1480.

57. Karst, *supra* note 1, at 58; *cf.* M. CAPPELLETTI & W. COHEN, COMPARATIVE CONSTITUTIONAL LAW 614-15 (1979) (observing that Italian Constitutional Court ruling on abortion statutes also avoided treating the matter as a women's rights issue).

58. Karst, *supra* note 1, at 58.

59. *Id.* at 57.

60. *Id.*

stay with their children, bearing nurture and support burdens alone, when fathers deny paternity or otherwise refuse to provide care or financial support for unwanted offspring.

I do not pretend that, if the Court had added a distinct sex discrimination theme to its medically oriented opinion, the storm *Roe* generated would have been less furious. I appreciate the intense divisions of opinion on the moral question and recognize that abortion today cannot fairly be described as nothing more than birth control delayed. The conflict, however, is not simply one between a fetus' interests and a woman's interests, narrowly conceived, nor is the overriding issue state versus private control of a woman's body for a span of nine months.[61] Also in the balance is a woman's autonomous charge of her full life's course—as Professor Karst put it, her ability to stand in relation to man, society, and the state as an independent, self-sustaining, equal citizen.[62]

On several occasions since *Roe* the Court has confronted legislative responses to the decision. With the notable exception of the public funding cases, the Court typically has applied *Roe* to overturn or limit efforts to impede access to abortion. I will not survey in the brief compass of this Essay the Court's series of opinions addressing: regulation of the abortion decisionmaking process; specifications regarding personnel, facilities, and medical procedures; and parental notification and consent requirements in the case of minors.[63] Instead, I will simply highlight the Court's statement last year reaffirming *Roe*'s "basic principle that a woman has a fundamental right to make the highly personal choice whether or not to terminate her pregnancy."[64] In *City of Akron v. Akron Center for Reproductive Health, Inc.*,[65] the Court acknowledged arguments it continues to hear that *Roe* "erred in interpreting the Constitution."[66] Nonetheless, the Court declared it would adhere to *Roe* because "*stare decisis*, while perhaps never entirely persuasive on a constitutional question, is a doctrine that demands respect in a society governed by the rule of law."[67]

I turn, finally, to the plight of the woman who lacks resources to finance privately implementation of her personal choice to terminate her pregnancy. The hostile reaction to *Roe* has trained largely on her.

Some observers speculated that the seven-two judgment in *Roe* was motivated at least in part by pragmatic considerations—population control concerns, the specter of coat hanger abortions, and concerns about unwanted children born to impoverished women. I recalled earlier the view that the

61. *But cf.* Regan, *Rewriting* Roe v. Wade, 77 MICH. L. REV. 1569 (1979) (contending that even when the parent-child relationship is involved our law generally does not require a person to submit to a bodily invasion or the imposition of physical pain to save the life of another).

62. Karst, *supra* note 1, at 57-59.

63. The Court's 1975-1981 decisions are listed in City of Akron v. Akron Center for Reproductive Health, Inc., 103 S. Ct. 2481, 2487 n.1 (1983).

64. *Id.*

65. 103 S. Ct. 2481 (1983).

66. *Id.* at 2487.

67. *Id.*

demand for open access to abortions had as its real purpose suppressing minorities.[68] In a set of 1977 decisions, however, the Court upheld state denial of medical expense reimbursement or hospital facilities for abortions sought by indigent women.[69] Moreover, in a 1980 decision, *Harris v. McRae*,[70] the Court found no constitutional infirmity in the Hyde Amendment, which excluded even medically necessary abortions from Medicaid coverage.[71] After these decisions, the Court was accused of sensitivity only to the Justices' own social milieu—"of creating a middle-class right to abortion."[72]

The argument for constitutionally mandated public assistance to effectuate the poor woman's choice ran along these lines. Accepting that our Constitution's Bill of Rights places restraints, not affirmative obligations, on government,[73] counsel for the impoverished women stressed that childbirth was publicly subsidized. As long as the government paid for childbirth, the argument proceeded, public funding could not be denied for abortion, often a safer and always a far less expensive course, short and long run. By paying for childbirth but not abortion, the complainants maintained, government increased spending and intruded upon or steered a choice *Roe* had ranked as a woman's "fundamental" right.[74]

The Court responded that, like other individual rights secured by the Constitution, the right to abortion is indeed a negative right. Government could not intervene by blocking a woman's utilization of her own resources to effectuate her decision. It could not " 'impose its will by force of law.' "[75] But *Roe* did not demand government neutrality, the Court reasoned; it left room for substantive government control to this extent: Action "deemed in the public interest"[76]—in this instance, protection of the potential life of the fetus—could be promoted by encouraging childbirth in preference to abortion.[77]

Financial need alone, under the Court's jurisprudence, does not identify a class of persons whose complaints of disadvantageous treatment attract close scrutiny.[78] Generally, constitutional claims to government benefits on behalf

---

68. *See supra* text accompanying notes 5-6.

69. Poelker v. Doe, 432 U.S. 519 (1977) (per curiam) (equal protection clause does not require public hospitals to perform abortions simply because they provide publicly financed hospital services for childbirth); Maher v. Roe, 432 U.S. 464 (1977) (equal protection clause does not require state participating in Medicaid program to pay expenses incident to nontherapeutic abortions for indigent women simply because it pays expenses incident to childbirth); Beal v. Doe, 432 U.S. 438 (1977) (same ruling under Social Security Act).

70. 448 U.S. 297 (1980).

71. *Id.* at 326-27. *But see* Fischer v. Department of Pub. Welfare, 475 A.2d 873 (Pa. Commw. Ct. 1984) (state denial of Medical Assistance funds to indigent women seeking medically necessary abortions violates equal protection clause of, and equal rights amendment to, state constitution).

72. Shapiro, *Fathers and Sons: The Court, The Commentators, and the Search for Values*, THE BURGER COURT, *supra* note 25, at 218, 229; *see* Karst, *supra* note 1, at 59.

73. *See* Henkin, *Rights: Here and There*, 81 COLUM. L. REV. 1582 (1981); Henkin, *Rights: American and Human*, 79 COLUM. L. REV. 403 (1979).

74. *See Harris*, 448 U.S. at 329 (Brennan, J., dissenting).

75. *Id.* at 315 (quoting Maher v. Roe, 432 U.S. 464, 476 (1977)).

76. *Id.*

77. *Id.*

78. San Antonio Indep. School Dist. v. Rodriguez, 411 U.S. 1 (1973).

of the poor have prevailed only when tied to another bark—a right to travel interstate, discrimination because of out-of-wedlock birth, or gender-based discrimination.[79] If the Court had acknowledged a woman's equality aspect, not simply a patient-physician autonomy constitutional dimension to the abortion issue, a majority perhaps might have seen the public assistance cases as instances in which, borrowing a phrase from Justice Stevens, the sovereign had violated its "duty to govern impartially."[80]

I have tried to discuss some features of constitutional adjudication concerning sex equality, in relation to the autonomy and equal-regard values involved in cases on abortion. I have done so tentatively and with trepidation. *Roe v. Wade* is a decision I approached gingerly in prior comment; until now I have limited my remarks to a brief description of what others have said. While I claim no original contribution, I have endeavored here to state my own reflections and concerns.

Roe, I believe, would have been more acceptable as a judicial decision if it had not gone beyond a ruling on the extreme statute before the Court. The political process was moving in the early 1970s, not swiftly enough for advocates of quick, complete change, but majoritarian institutions were listening and acting.[81] Heavy-handed judicial intervention was difficult to justify and

---

79. *See* Bennett, *The Burger Court and the Poor*, THE BURGER COURT, *supra* note 25, at 46, 52-53.

80. *Harris*, 448 U.S. at 357 (Stevens, J., dissenting).

81. *See, e.g.*, *Abortion Backers Hopeful of Gains*, N.Y. Times, Oct. 9, 1972, at A9, col. 1 ("Pro-abortion forces believe they are on the verge of major victories that will soon make abortion on request available throughout much of the country."); *Abortion Laws Gaining Favor as New Statutes Spur Debate*, N.Y. Times, Nov. 29, 1970, at A13, col. 2 ("Senator Robert W. Packwood, Republican of Oregon, predicted . . . that most states would abolish laws against abortion within the next 'one to three years.' "). Polls taken prior to the 1970s indicated that substantial majorities of Americans had opposed liberalization of abortion laws. *See Survey Finds 50% Back Liberalization of Abortion Policy*, *supra* note 6, at A1, col. 1 (1965—91% oppose liberalized abortion policy; 1968—85%; 1969—79%; 1971—50%); *see also Survey Finds Majority, In Shift, Now Favors Liberalized Laws*, N.Y. Times, Aug. 25, 1972, at A1, col. 3 (noting same statistics, and adding to them a 1972 poll revealing that 64% of public believe abortion decision should be left to woman and her doctor).

Testifying to the "superiority of the legislative solution," Second Circuit Judge Henry J. Friendly described what happened in 1970 when New York reformed its law:

> I can speak with feeling because I was to have presided over a three-judge court before which the constitutionality of the old law was being challenged. Although we had not yet heard argument, I could perceive not merely how soul wrenching but how politically disturbing—and I use "politically" in the highest sense—decision either way would be. If we upheld the old law, we would be disappointing the expectations of many high-minded citizens, deeply concerned over the human misery it was creating, its discriminatory effects, its consequences for the population explosion, and the hopes of the least privileged elements in the community. These people would never understand that if we held the law constitutional, we would not be finding it good. Indeed, some opponents of reform would have claimed we had done precisely that. If we were to decide the other way, many adherents of a deeply respected religion would consider we had taken unto ourselves a role that belonged to their elected representatives and that we had done what the latter, after full consideration, had refused. If they asked what specific provision of the Constitution was violated by this law of more than a century's standing, we would have had to concede that there was none and that we were drawing on what the Supreme Court has euphemistically termed "penumbras" to construct a new "fundamental" right. How much better that the issue was settled by the legislature! I do not mean that everyone is happy; presumably those who opposed the reform have not changed their views.

appears to have provoked, not resolved, conflict.[82]

The public funding of abortion decisions appear incongruous following so soon after the intrepid 1973 rulings. The Court did not adequately explain why the "fundamental" choice principle and trimester approach embraced in *Roe* did not bar the sovereign, at least at the previability stage of pregnancy, from taking sides.[83]

Overall, the Court's *Roe* position is weakened, I believe, by the opinion's concentration on a medically approved autonomy idea, to the exclusion of a constitutionally based sex-equality perspective. I understand the view that for political reasons the reproductive autonomy controversy should be isolated from the general debate on equal rights, responsibilities, and opportunities for women and men. I expect, however, that organized and determined opposing efforts to inform and persuade the public on the abortion issue will continue through the 1980s. In that process there will be opportunities for elaborating in public forums the equal-regard conception of women's claims to reproductive choice uncoerced and unsteered by government.

> But the result is acceptable in the sense that it was reached by the democratic process and thus will be accepted, even though many will not regard it as right.

H. Friendly, Some Equal Protection Problems of the 1970's 14-15 (NYU School of Law 1970) (available at North Carolina Law Review office).

82. *See* Burt, *supra* note 36, at 107-09; *cf.* Blasi, *The Rootless Activism of the Burger Court*, THE BURGER COURT, *supra* note 25, at 198, 212. (*Roe* was "[g]rounded not on principle," but on an "ad hoc comparison of . . . interests"). One pair of commentators observed:

> In many respects the abortion controversy of the 1970s is similar to the busing disputes of the late 1960s and early 1970s. Both the pro-life and anti-busing movements began in reaction to decisions of the Supreme Court. Both activated many people who previously had been at the periphery of . . . politics. The two movements each caught on quickly and developed a strong national base.

Uslaner & Weber, *Public Support for Pro-Choice Abortion Policies in the Nation and States: Changes and Stability After the* Roe *and* Doe *Decisions*, 77 MICH. L. REV. 1772, 1787-88 (1979); *see also id.* at 1785.

83. *Cf.* Bennett, *supra* note 79, at 52 (arguing that *Harris* (upholding denial of Medicaid funds for abortion) is inconsistent with Shapiro v. Thompson, 394 U.S. 618 (1969) (declaring inconsistent with equal protection denial of welfare benefits to new residents)).

[11]

BOOK REVIEW

TRIBAL CONFLICT OVER ABORTION

ABORTION: THE CLASH OF ABSOLUTES. By Laurence H. Tribe.* New York: W.W. Norton & Company, 1990. Pp. 270. $19.95.

*Jean Braucher***

I. LONGING FOR COMPROMISE, OBSCURING THE ISSUES

In *Abortion: The Clash of Absolutes*,[1] Laurence Tribe joins the hot competition for the middle ground in the abortion debate.[2] What makes this battle especially difficult to wage is the problem that there is no "compromise" or "middle position" on the legality of abortion.[3] Certain questions require a yes or no answer. Either a pregnant woman who does not wish to carry a fetus to term may abort it legally or she may not. Either abortion is a decision to be

---

* Ralph S. Tyler, Jr., Professor of Constitutional Law, Harvard Law School.

** Kraft W. Eidman Centennial Visiting Professor of Law, University of Texas School of Law (1990-91), Professor of Law, University of Cincinnati College of Law. I wish to thank John Applegate, Joseph P. Tomain and David R. Wohl for useful comments on earlier drafts of this essay and Tara Hanneken for research assistance.

[1] L. TRIBE, ABORTION: THE CLASH OF ABSOLUTES (1990) [hereinafter L. TRIBE, ABORTION].

[2] Two other recent instances of attempts to find compromises on abortion are M. GLENDON, ABORTION AND DIVORCE IN WESTERN LAW (1987), and Colker, *Feminism, Theology, and Abortion: Toward Love, Compassion, and Wisdom*, 77 CALIF. L. REV. 1011 (1989).

[3] This point has been demonstrated repeatedly in United States politics. *See* Weisberg, *Abortion Olympics*, THE NEW REPUBLIC, Feb. 12, 1990, at 12 (humorous account of politicians' attempts to avoid picking a side). Weisberg writes:

> Abortion is a fine test of a politician's skill. Because it is a question of conscience with two clear, opposing positions, there's hardly a hedge to hide behind. Basically, you're on one side or the other. Even George Bush hasn't found a good way to split the difference on this one yet.

Id. at 12-13. The American experience has recently been replicated in Germany, where those negotiating for unification were unable to find a compromise between the restrictiveness of West German abortion law and the legal access in East Germany and thus deferred a decision on the issue. Simons, *A Divisive Issue of German Unity: How to Reconcile Abortion Laws*, N.Y. Times, July 19, 1990, at 1 (nat'l ed.).

made by the individual pregnant woman or it is a collective one, to be regulated by law, however ineffectively.

It does not count as a compromise to deviate slightly from a legal position of either "permit all abortions" or "permit no abortions." For example, limiting legal abortion only after fetal viability is a pro-choice[4] position. Such abortions are in any event rare.[5] On the other hand, prohibiting abortion except in certain extreme cases, such as cases in which the life of the woman is at risk or in which the pregnancy is the result of rape, is a pro-life[6] position, one that would prohibit most abortions now performed. In the absence of any real compromise position, the only way to wage the battle for the center is to mobilize the committed and to persuade people who are wavering or uncommitted to one's side.

Tribe resists this conclusion about the nature of the controversy. He longs for common ground and compromise.[7] Although he ends up taking a pro-choice legal and policy position, he does so with great heaves of moral doubt, in a manner that gives ammunition to the other side.

This tone of inner conflict is all the odder because, although Tribe makes concessions in tone and in rationale, he makes none in result.[8] His bottom line is to favor constitutional protection of

---

[4] In this book review, I adopt the style of referring to the two sides of the debate according to the labels they themselves have chosen.

[5] Only one hundredth of one percent of abortions (about 100 per year) occur in the third trimester. Brief of Amici Curiae, American Medical Association, in Support of Appellees, at 5, Webster v. Reproductive Health Servs., 109 S. Ct. 3040 (1989) (No. 88-605) [hereinafter AMA Brief].

[6] *See supra* note 4.

[7] L. Tribe, Abortion, *supra* note 1, at 8, 197, 229.

[8] Other scholars who have advocated compromise have given some substantive ground. Mary Ann Glendon, from a pro-life perspective, praises European approaches, particularly that of France, where early abortion is legal but pro-life rhetoric is used and counseling and a waiting-period are required. M. Glendon, *supra* note 2, at 18-21. She writes:

> In contrast to the current American legal situation, it is worth noting that the French statute *names* the underlying problem as one involving human life, not as a conflict involving a woman's individual liberty or privacy and a non-person. While showing great concern for the pregnant woman, it tries, through legal provisions [requiring that the woman have a counseling session and that information be given about the public benefits and programs that are guaranteed to mothers and children and about the possibilities of adoption and requiring a waiting period of a week] of a type that have been struck down in a series of American cases, to make her aware of alternatives without either frightening or unduly burdening her.

Id. at 19. But the French requirements—especially the week's waiting period—may be quite

women's unlimited access to abortion prior to fetal viability.[9] He also supports public funding of abortion, although he bases this position primarily on fairness and never clearly states whether he believes funding for the poor who want abortions should be a matter of constitutional right.[10] In addition, he opposes various restrictions that have been suggested by pro-lifers, such as requiring parental notification or limiting permitted reasons for abortion.[11]

His supposed "compromise" is to support programs to reduce abortion by improving contraception and the social support for families with children.[12] This is no compromise at all, however, to a core group of pro-life activists. Their commitment to this cause is part of a world view in which traditional gender roles are the natu-

---

burdensome (for example, in the case of a teenager from a rural area who has to travel a long distance to get an abortion). Also, the French law makes it very difficult to get an abortion after ten weeks of pregnancy (two doctors must certify that the woman's health is seriously endangered or that there is a strong possibility of serious incurable disease or condition in the fetus, *id.* at 17), thereby creating an arbitrary time-limit that, in the American context, would make illegal many abortions now permitted. Finally, the French law requires a woman who wants an abortion to declare that she is "in distress," a rhetorical approach that seems to suggest that the woman must declare herself a victim rather than a moral agent. *See* Ashe, *Conversation and Abortion* (Book Review), 82 Nw. U.L. Rev. 387, 395 (1988) (review of M. Glendon, *supra* note 2).

Tribe criticizes the French approach praised by Glendon on the ground that it "seems to teach mostly hypocrisy" by using life-affirming rhetoric but not backing it up with legal enforcement. L. Tribe, Abortion, *supra* note 1, at 73-74. This is a terribly American reaction; the French approach may in part reflect a conclusion that prohibition involves hypocritical posturing because it leads only to large numbers of illegal abortions. Assuming the French approach is hypocritical, however, Tribe's rationale for legal abortion involves callous individualism, not necessarily a more attractive teaching. *See infra* notes 96-132 and accompanying text.

Ruth Colker, from a pro-choice perspective, makes a minor substantive concession: she favors requiring health care providers to offer counseling sessions to pregnant women and their partners to discuss the implications of raising a child or of having an abortion and the meaning or value of the fetus' life. Colker, *supra* note 2, at 1067. Most pro-choice advocates would probably applaud this requirement. Colker also makes concessions in the constitutional rationale for abortion rights. She recognizes a compelling state interest in ensuring the valuation of fetal life but argues criminal sanctions are unconstitutional because they are not necessary to serve that goal (for example, because a woman who chooses an abortion may value fetal life). *Id.* at 1058.

[9] L. Tribe, Abortion, *supra* note 1, at 128-29, 138.

[10] *Id.* at 206-07.

[11] He rejects, as cruel and false compromises, parental or father's consent or notification requirements, waiting periods, limiting the reasons for abortion, restrictions on clinics and earlier cutoff dates, such as somewhere between four and fourteen weeks from conception. L. Tribe, Abortion, *supra* note 1, at 197-208.

[12] *Id.* at 211-14, 228.

ral order of things.[13] As Kristin Luker has documented, these activists tend to oppose sexual intercourse outside of marriage and tend to believe that contraception even within marriage profanes sex, interferes with a divine plan and elevates material considerations over transcendent principles.[14] They also tend to oppose social welfare programs, which they see as state interference in the family.[15]

This pro-life world view is anti-pluralistic on gender roles and sexual and reproductive morality. Thus, it rejects basic values of the world view of pro-choice activists. These values include recognizing that women need to be able to control reproduction to achieve greater social participation, that the value of sex is not tied to procreation, that practicing contraception is responsible behavior to be fostered and promoted and that, ideally, people should plan parenthood to best meet the myriad needs of their children.[16]

Tribe's book shows glimmers of understanding that the abortion question must be situated within our system of gender roles and sexual politics,[17] but he fails to come to terms with the way this system constructs views of morality and legal duty. He seems, at least in places in this book, to cling to a belief in one ultimate, ahistorical, core morality on abortion—a morality that is external to social conditions and the power structure.[18] In this morality, abortion is a "horror"[19] and a "wrong."[20] He never explores an alternative moral view—that abortion can be the right way for a woman, given her historical and social situation, to resolve a complex moral dilemma. Even if he does not personally accept this moral view, he should have explained it in order to make the case for moral pluralism. What is missing from his book is a picture of

---

[13] K. LUKER, ABORTION AND THE POLITICS OF MOTHERHOOD 159-75 (1984) [hereinafter K. LUKER, MOTHERHOOD].

[14] *Id.* at 162-66, 170-74.

[15] *Id.* at 173.

[16] *Id.* at 175-85.

[17] For example, he refers to abortion as a problem at the "crossroads of power and sex" and to restrictions on abortion as reflecting in part a willingness "to enforce traditional sex roles upon women and to impose upon them an unequal and harsh sexual morality." L. TRIBE, ABORTION, *supra* note 1, at 228, 237. He also notes that abortion laws directly burden women alone and pose "an obvious danger of majoritarian oppression and enduring subjugation . . . ." *Id.* at 105.

[18] *See infra* notes 85-95, 111-12 & 121-32 and accompanying text.

[19] L. TRIBE, ABORTION, *supra* note 1, at 230.

[20] *Id.* at 53.

women as moral agents, deciding to have abortions for reasons of conscience. The closest Tribe gets to this crucial point is to write, "Women who make that choice [abortion] to end a pregnancy ordinarily recognize the gravity of what they are doing."[21]

He presents the law of abortion in terms of a woman's right to control her own body in order to protect her liberty and autonomy.[22] The trouble with this rationale is that it leaves out significant elements of the moral reasoning of many women who have abortions. Women have abortions because of the conditions and responsibilities of their lives, not primarily as a vindication of an atomistic individualism.[23] Women give multiple reasons for having abortions, usually some combination of the following: they are too young, too poor, too sick, too isolated; they do not feel ready; they have not finished their formal education; they have too many children to provide for and nurture already; they are unmarried or having difficulty in a marriage; they lack a social network.[24] These women are concerned with relationships and responsibilities.[25]

Using analogies from tort law concerning the absence of a general duty to help, Tribe argues that, even if a fetus is considered a person, a woman should not be required to continue a pregnancy to sustain it.[26] This rationale should be rejected by the pro-choice side. It is based on highly individualistic thinking—the very antithesis of a relational approach—and it does not explain the pro-choice position best. A humane and authentic moral rationale con-

---

[21] *Id.* at 211.

[22] *Id.* at 114, 135.

[23] *See* Jaggar, *Abortion and A Woman's Right to Decide*, 5 PHIL. F. 347 (1974) (arguing that a woman's right to decide whether to have an abortion depends on contingent features of her social situation).

[24] In narratives of women's abortion decisions reported by Carol Gilligan, a consistent theme was a moral concern about bringing children into the world in conditions of financial need and social isolation. C. GILLIGAN, IN A DIFFERENT VOICE 111-12, 116-17, 120 (1982). In a 1987 survey of 1900 women concerning their reasons for having abortions, "yes" answers were given to the following questions in the indicated percentages:

> —"because having a baby would dramatically change your life in ways you are not ready for?" (76%)
>
> —"because you cannot afford a baby now?" (68%)
>
> —"because you don't want to be a single mother or because of problems with your relationship with your husband or partner?" (51%)

Torres & Forrest, *Why Do Women Have Abortions?*, 20 FAM. PLAN. PERSP. 169, 170-71 (1988).

[25] C. GILLIGAN, *supra* note 24, at 17.

[26] L. TRIBE, ABORTION, *supra* note 1, at 130-35.

cerning the nature of a fetus and a pregnant woman's responsibility to it has already evolved among pro-choice activists.[27] The moral pluralism that best supports the pro-choice position needs to recognize this view, which takes a "gradualist" approach to human life and its personhood and views parenthood as a major commitment.[28]

In the gradualist view, ova and sperm are human life, and the same is true of fertilized eggs. Tribe does note the scientific estimate that two-thirds of fertilized eggs never implant (and thus die within about two weeks). He adds: "And who among us really believes that we are now faced with a tragedy in which two-thirds of the people who have *ever come into existence* have been lost through this normal feature of human reproduction?"[29] In the moral scheme that the pro-choice position recognizes, ova, sperm, single-cell zygotes (fertilized eggs) and multi-celled blastocysts prior to implantation—although biologically they are early human life—have little or no claim to personhood. Therefore, spermicides and methods of birth control such as birth control pills, intrauterine devices (IUD) and "morning after" pills, all of which may sometimes act as abortifacients by preventing or disrupting implantation, are not at all objectionable.[30] Furthermore, in this moral scheme, an implanted blastocyst and an embryo (the correct biological name for the developing organism from three to eight weeks) have little more claim to personhood, especially when compared to the fully realized personhood of the pregnant woman, with her social history, commitments and responsibilities. Still, if abortion is to occur, the earlier it occurs, the better. As the fetus ages,[31] its moral claim increases, and viability is a possibility for a logical point at which legal restrictions to protect it should begin. A fetus should never be viewed as having an equal claim to personhood with the pregnant woman, but, out of respect for its potential for personhood, even very early human life should not be trivialized. These views explain why many pro-choice people *are*

---

[27] K. Luker, Motherhood, *supra* note 13, at 180.

[28] *Id.*

[29] L. Tribe, Abortion, *supra* note 1, at 123-24.

[30] For short descriptions of the biology of human reproduction and birth control, see R. Goldstein, Mother-Love and Abortion 7-9, 16-17 (1988).

[31] Hereafter, I use this term to refer to every stage of pre-birth human development after fertilization.

troubled by multiple abortions by repeat contraceptive risk-takers.[32]

The pro-choice position also best rests on recognition of a morality involving very high aspirations for what parents and society should provide for children in the way of emotional, social and financial resources. Given this recognition, planning parenthood is usually the best course. In this view, it is not illogical to think of a "right" of some fetuses "not to be born"[33] and of a woman's having an abortion in a spirit of love for the fetus and the persons in her life.[34]

The pro-choice position is most powerfully explained and defended from a perspective in which the abortion question is part of a choice between, on one hand, gender role pluralism and pluralism on sexual and reproductive morality and, on the other, a commitment to perpetuating traditional roles and related morality (with the aid of the criminal law).[35] Compromise between these two positions is not possible, and Tribe's unsuccessful attempt to find one muddies the waters. Pluralism and anti-pluralism cannot coexist.

---

[32] K. Luker, Motherhood, *supra* note 13, at 180-81. For a discussion concerning the problem of the nonuse of contraceptives, see *infra* notes 155-60 and accompanying text.

[33] K. Luker, Motherhood, *supra* note 13, at 182 (quoting a pro-choice activist).

[34] *Id.* at 185.

[35] A weaker defense of legal abortion can be based on the assessment that legal restrictions have unacceptably brutal and unfair consequences that are not justified by the gains (if any) in terms of fetal life; these consequences warrant legalized abortions despite the fact that abortion is "wrong." In this view, the legalization of abortion is a lesser evil than its prohibition. Tribe relies on this sort of argument in places. L. Tribe, Abortion, *supra* note 1, at 197-210. Even so, he should have explored and explained the view, held by many people, that abortion can be a morally correct course of action. The prevalence of this view helps to explain why legal restrictions lead to so many unsafe, degrading illegal abortions. Thus, abortion is the only humane solution in our heterogeneous society.

Governor Mario Cuomo of New York has noted that criminal laws against abortion "would be Prohibition revisited," because even those who supposedly believe abortion is a sin have abortions:

> Despite the teaching in our homes and schools and pulpits, despite the sermons and pleadings of parents and priests and prelates, despite all the effort at defining our opposition to the sin of abortion, collectively we Catholics apparently believe—and perhaps act—little differently from those who don't share our commitment.
>
> Are we asking government to make criminal what we believe to be sinful because we ourselves can't stop committing the sin?

Cuomo, *Religious Belief and Public Morality: A Catholic Governor's Perspective*, in Abortion and Catholicism 202, 212-13 (1988).

II. Stereotyping the Sides, Questioning Their Honesty

To whom is Tribe trying to appeal and on what basis? Has he gauged well the tenor of his presentation for his intended audience? The answers are not easy, except for the simple observation that the book is written for a general readership rather than an exclusively academic audience. For example, two of its ten chapters are digests of other scholars' research into the history of abortion in America[36] and the treatment of abortion in other cultures.[37] Another two chapters give a shrewd account of the political battles over abortion from 1973, when *Roe v. Wade*[38] was decided, through early 1990.[39] Somewhat harder going for the general reader will be the three chapters describing the constitutional law applicable to the abortion issue,[40] but Tribe has made this subject matter accessible to nonexperts and nonlawyers.[41] The last two chapters present his ideas about compromise.[42]

The book does not make a sustained argument. Tribe's position eventually emerges, but it is defended haphazardly and equivocally. Although he repeatedly refers to the influence of social context on views of abortion, he does not develop a thesis broadly grounded in this context.[43]

Tribe professes to be interested in appealing to both sides in the abortion debate, as well as to those who have not made up their minds and those "with no thought of taking sides."[44] He calls for those on both sides to strive for humility, to listen to each other with respect and to re-examine their own positions in a search for common ground or at least political reconciliation.[45] Tribe is not

---

[36] L. Tribe, Abortion, *supra* note 1, at 27-51.

[37] *Id.* at 52-76.

[38] 410 U.S. 113 (1973).

[39] L. Tribe, Abortion, *supra* note 1, at 139-96.

[40] *Id.* at 10-26, 77-138.

[41] Tribe tries to spice up this material with personal descriptions (all flattering ones) of the Justices: Blackmun is "extraordinarily kind," *id.* at 11, Rehnquist is "remarkably talented," *id.* at 12, and Powell is a "gracious Southerner," *id.* at 13, and "the likable Antonin Scalia," *id.* at 168, "has a brilliant and incisive conservative mind," *id.* at 18. Justices O'Connor, Kennedy, Burger, Marshall, Stevens and Brennan and Judges Bork and Ginsburg, although discussed or mentioned, *id.* at 18-20, 167-70, get no similar "handles" of praise (or of criticism).

[42] *Id.* at 197-242.

[43] *See, e.g.*, *id.* at 27, 52, 76.

[44] *Id.* at 8-9.

[45] *Id.* at 8-9, 238-42.

good at following his own advice. He treats those who share his position even more contemptuously than he treats his opponents. By obscuring the nature and the strength of the commitments of both sides, he also obscures the gender politics that underlie the controversy.

Tribe stereotypes the sides as well as the arguments in the abortion debate. This is an indication that, despite his introductory appeal to a broad audience,[46] he is not really trying to get activists or the committed to re-examine their own views. He presents the controversy as a debate between two unreasonable sides, each of which threatens to upset American politics with single-issue fervor.[47] This presentation serves as another indication that he is not really addressing the people who are already committed to the pro-choice or pro-life position. In addition, because he gets the gist of both sides' views wrong (particularly if he has in mind the well-developed positions of the leadership of the pro-life and pro-choice movements), he cannot achieve his professed goal of giving each side a view of how the other side thinks.[48]

He uses demographic information from public opinion polls to describe the sides. This reliance would be harmless if he also probed the commitments of each side. Tribe describes pro-lifers as less educated[49] and drawn from recent immigrant and lower-status religious groups.[50] Going beyond demographics, he portrays pro-lifers as lacking tolerance,[51] but he does not consider why. Their movement is described as dominated by the hierarchy of the Roman Catholic Church, and this leadership, in turn, is seen as willing to sell out its pursuit of social justice in an unholy alliance with

---

[46] *Id.* at 8.

[47] Tribe writes:

> The debate is unending. None of its participants ever seems even mildly persuaded by the arguments of the other side. As the apparently irresistible force of the pro-life movement bears down on the seemingly immovable object of abortion rights, local politics may at times be overwhelmed by the kind of single-issue campaigning that has already distorted the face of national elections. If this happens, the losers will be the democratic process and the American people.

Id. at 6-7.

[48] *Id.* at 9.

[49] *Id.* at 196, 238.

[50] *Id.* at 238.

[51] Pro-lifers, Tribe writes, "rarely claim to be especially tolerant of diversity." *Id.* at 239.

the New Right.[52] Again, he does not attempt to explain why this might be so. Because Tribe fails to appreciate pro-lifers' values or experiences, he cannot fathom how they could be acting in good faith.

In Tribe's description, pro-choicers come from "various privileged elites, the 'upper echelons' of American society: scientists, intellectuals . . . the working press, much of the publishing industry, and all those 'pointy-headed' types whom George Wallace loved to hate."[53] They are "contemptuous" of pro-lifers,[54] Tribe writes, and subscribe to a predictable cluster of positions, including:

> abortion rights, more vigorous enforcement of laws protecting racial minorities, unrestricted speech and artistic expression, tighter control of police brutality, opposition to the death penalty, stronger environmental protection, stricter gun control, gay rights, and so forth. The very fact that both this listing and its mirror image are so familiar and so predictable suggests either that a remarkable moral logic ties all these views together or, far more plausibly, that much of what *each* of us believes about all these matters says more about who we are and where we come from than about our depth of vision or about the ultimate truth.[55]

Tribe thus gives us Archie Bunker versus Archibald Cox.[56] In his picture of pro-choicers, is he being self-deprecatory? Is this a self-portrait? And where does Tribe think these stereotypes get us? He seems to be buying into the anti-limousine liberal imagery of Peggy Noonan, the Ronald Reagan speech writer.[57] Tribe's carica-

---

[52] *Id.* at 143-50, 159-60, 165-67.

[53] *Id.* at 238.

[54] *Id.* at 239.

[55] *Id.* at 239-40.

[56] These stereotypes should give us pause: for example, Cox has been critical of *Roe v. Wade*. A. Cox, The Role of the Supreme Court in American Government 51-55, 114 (1976).

[57] *See* P. Noonan, What I Saw At the Revolution: A Political Life in the Reagan Era (1990). Noonan writes:

> Up on the Hill or at the White House the young rough-looking guy from a state school is probably either a Republican or a conservative, and the snooty sniffy guy with a THANK YOU FOR NOT SMOKING sign on his tidy little desk is a Democrat . . . . It was all changing (and the cliches hadn't begun to catch up!)

ture of his allies (or himself?) may appeal to some pro-life readers by evoking the stereotypes of the pro-choicers they love to hate. But will Tribe's tone get these readers in a mood to rethink their views and attempt to find common ground? I doubt it. With this scorn, will he get anyone to understand the pro-choice position better? Again, I doubt it.

Tribe stereotypes the arguments as well as the people on both sides. In his view, on the surface the debate involves the "clash of absolutes" of the title: life versus liberty.[58] Setting up the debate in this oversimplified way contributes to his basic error, one that impairs his ability to understand the opposing positions: he questions both sides' honesty. He writes:

> So it is that a close look at the clash of absolutes may in the end reveal a sliver of light in a world of shadow. For if, in *a moment of honesty* with ourselves, we recognize—on either side of the question—that what is at stake is not really the absolute in whose name the battle has been fought, then we may get beyond our once intractable dispute about the question of abortion.[59]

He suggests that the position of pro-lifers grows "at least in part, out of a reflexive willingness to enforce traditional sex roles upon women and to impose upon them an unequal and harsh sexual morality."[60] As a basis for this observation, he uses an analysis of polling results:

> Support of a rape exception makes plain that most people's opposition to abortion, unlike their opposition to murder, can be overridden. It therefore suggests that anti-abortion sentiment is not *entirely* rooted in a belief

Id. at 102.

It is worth noting Wilfred Sheed's retort to Noonan:

> (In fact, the cliches caught up so long ago that the Republicans have based their last five campaigns on them—a tactic which might account for at least some of those rough-looking Republicans.) There may be something to be said for keeping your eye on the enemy when the alternative is looking at friends like the Reagans.

Sheed, *His Sentiments Exactly*, N.Y. Times, Feb. 4, 1990, § 7 (Book Review), at 1.

[58] L. Tribe, Abortion, *supra* note 1, at 3.

[59] *Id.* at 242 (emphasis added).

[60] *Id.* at 237.

that abortion constitutes the killing of an innocent human being.[61]

Tribe's point that honesty on the pro-life side will lead to a confession that an absolute belief in sacredness of fetal life is not really what is at stake thus confuses unarticulated, perhaps self-contradictory positions suggested by polling data with the position of pro-life activists. Tribe does not clearly distinguish between those who give pro-life or pro-choice answers to pollsters and the leadership of the movements. Most people may not have thought through their position on all aspects of abortion and related social issues; their answers to pollsters' questions are gut reactions that do not easily make up a coherent statement.[62] In contrast, activists are likely to have fully developed positions.

Most activists involved with the National Right to Life Committee, for example, would hardly be devastated by the charge that they want to perpetuate traditional gender roles and traditional sexual morality. Of course they do![63] But this does not undercut the sincerity of their belief in the sacredness of fetal life. It is quite possible—in fact much easier—to believe in *both* the sacredness of fetal life *and* in traditional gender roles as the natural order of things.

And what is the basis for the charge that honesty on the part of pro-choicers will reveal that an absolute allegiance to liberty is not what is really at stake? The only answer suggested by Tribe is that many abortion rights supporters reflexively add that item to their list of politically correct positions: "stronger environmental protection, stricter gun control, gay rights, and so forth."[64] Tribe seems to think people support abortion rights to be among the liberal chic.

Where to begin to unpack the errors in this picture of pro-choice views? Two points are crucial. First, whether the focus is on pro-

---

[61] *Id.* at 232.

[62] Tribe quotes the analysis in the New York Times that "one of every six Americans says simultaneously that abortion is murder and that it is sometimes the best course." L. TRIBE, ABORTION, *supra* note 1, at 231. Of course, most people do not necessarily use the words "kill" and "murder" precisely. Even the English version of the biblical commandment, "Thou shalt not kill," seems to confuse these terms. Abortion involves killing a living thing, but it is murder only if that thing is a person and the killing is not excused or justified.

[63] K. LUKER, MOTHERHOOD, *supra* note 13, at 159-75.

[64] L. TRIBE, ABORTION, *supra* note 1, at 240.

choice activists or the larger group of people who hold pro-choice opinions, the importance of access to safe, legal abortion is often felt very personally. This is true even for many men, whose personal experiences with wives, daughters and girlfriends have given rise to their opinions. For pro-choice activists, values central to their lives are at stake. Although he cites *Abortion and the Politics of Motherhood*, Tribe seems to reject Kristin Luker's point that the great majority of activists in *both* camps are fighting for their deeply felt values.[65]

Second, Tribe's choice of "liberty" as the universal central value of pro-choicers (other than the desire to be trendy) is questionable. Certainly the rhetoric of liberty is used in mainstream debate. For many women, however, this may be a matter of shoe-horning their concerns and experiences into male-gendered conceptual categories that do not fit well.[66] Women's experiences and values are left out of Tribe's account.[67] His description of pro-choicers fails to capture the commitment of activists to take seriously women's situations, subjective experiences, aspirations and values.

A general-audience book such as Tribe's is an opportunity to reach the reading public in many walks of life. This book is especially disappointing because it missed the opportunity to present a clear explanation to an audience receptive to the pro-choice side of the abortion controversy in its social context. Such an audience exists, and it is probably ahead of Tribe in resolving ambivalence about legal abortion. One bit of evidence for this proposition is a recent study showing strong pro-choice attitudes among American elites. Two-thirds of 1843 persons from leadership groups strongly agreed with the following statement: "A woman has the right to choose whether or not she should have an abortion"; another sixteen percent somewhat agreed.[68] The strongly pro-choice position was taken by very high percentages in "new class" elite subgroups: directors and producers of popular films (ninety-three percent), creators of prime-time television (ninety-one percent), public in-

---

65 K. LUKER, MOTHERHOOD, *supra* note 13, at 158-91.

66 *See* Finley, *Breaking Women's Silence in Law: The Dilemma of the Gendered Nature of Legal Reasoning*, 64 NOTRE DAME L. REV. 886 (1989) (analyzing whether legal concepts constructed largely by men can encompass women's experiences of harm).

67 *See supra* notes 23-25 & 27-34 and accompanying text.

68 Lerner, Nagai & Rothman, *Abortion and Social Change in America*, SOC'Y, Jan.-Feb. 1990, at 8, 11.

terest group leaders (eighty-two percent) and the media elite (seventy-nine percent).[69] Even among more traditional leadership groups, high percentages were strongly pro-choice: almost seventy-five percent of corporate lawyers, sixty-eight percent of those at the top of the federal civil service, sixty-four percent of federal judges, sixty-two percent of business leaders and fifty-nine percent of congressional aides.[70] Even half of the military elite were strongly pro-choice.[71]

The ideology explaining these strongly pro-choice views among elites is a combination of individualism, moral pluralism and the rejection of the traditional, with an emphasis on exploration of experience.[72] This ideology, which has been called "expressive individualism," helps to explain, for example, a high correlation between pro-choice opinions and tolerance of homosexuality.[73] This is a different and more complex individualism than Tribe's version. A book that included the experiences and the moral views of women who have abortions would have tapped into this contemporary consciousness.

III. Attempting to Compromise on Rationale but Not on Result

Tribe casts himself as mediator, the reasonable man in the middle: "This book challenges the inevitability of permanent conflict on that question [abortion policy] and tries to lay the groundwork for moving on."[74] In this role, he comes up with a two-part position, one part constitutional law and one part social legislation. First, as constitutional law expert he argues forcefully for constitutional protection of abortion rights. The constitutional argument has two steps: (1) a fundamental right of the pregnant woman is at stake;[75] and (2) even if the fetus is considered a person, that characterization does not justify compelling the woman to use her body to save the fetus' life.[76] In the legislative part of his position, dis-

---

[69] *Id.* at 12.
[70] *Id.*
[71] *Id.*
[72] *Id.* at 9, 14.
[73] *Id.* at 11.
[74] L. Tribe, Abortion, *supra* note 1, at 7.
[75] *Id.* at 104.
[76] *Id.* at 130-35. Tribe first referred to this idea in Tribe, *The Supreme Court, 1972*

cussed in the next section of this essay, he supports social programs to reduce unwanted pregnancy and thus to reduce abortion.[77]

If *any* unenumerated liberty interests are protected by the fourteenth amendment as fundamental ones, Tribe argues, then it is not even fairly debatable whether the right to abortion—involving women's bodily integrity—implicates a fundamental liberty that cannot be infringed without a compelling reason.[78] He backs up this argument with an equal protection argument, not used in *Roe*, grounded in the fact that laws restricting abortion directly burden only women.[79] In a revealing section of his argument on the fundamental liberty point, headed "What's at Stake?," he writes:

> Why is it so important whether the abortion right, although nowhere mentioned in the Constitution by name, is a fundamental right protected by that document so that any governmental restriction of the right requires special justification? The answer is that much more is at stake in this battle, a battle being fought out in the Supreme Court today, than abortion rights alone.[80]

He thus fails to appreciate how personally many people take the question of abortion access. For many people, the answer to the question why is it so important that abortion access be constitutionally protected is obvious: "Because I or someone I care about may desperately need one, and the vagaries of electoral politics do not guarantee access." Tribe is addressing people who do not feel personally affected. He puts the argument in terms of other liberties that might be next if access to safe, legal abortion is taken away, liberties that might directly affect "us," that is, Tribe himself or the audience for whom he is writing:

Term—Foreword: Toward a Model of Roles in the Due Process of Life and Law, 87 HARV. L. REV. 1, 32-33 n.144 (1973), where he said that there is a justification for treating nonviable fetuses, whether or not persons, differently than infants because "their destruction can be prevented only at the cost of a vastly greater imposition on other persons (*i.e.*, the women who carry them) than is required for the protection of infants."

[77] *See infra* notes 133-64 and accompanying text.

[78] L. TRIBE, ABORTION, *supra* note 1, at 104.

[79] *Id.* at 105.

[80] *Id.* at 111.

> And if women may be forced to use *their* bodies to develop and nurture children against *their* will without even a compelling public justification, who can guess what other bodily invasions and indignities could be imposed upon any of *us* without any special showing of necessity? The threat of such invasions is as real as the history of the twentieth century.[81]

Women, in this text, are others. Impositions on "their" bodies and "their" will are only an indirect threat to the liberty of "us."

The second part of Tribe's constitutional argument addresses whether laws against abortion are justified on the basis of a compelling state interest in the protection of human life.[82] At this point, he makes a major concession in rationale. He argues that even if the fetus is a person, women's interest in autonomy requires abortion rights.[83] This argument indicates that Tribe's legal rationale is constructed on the assumption that the fetus is a legal person.[84]

The use of this "even if" argument originates in moral doubt. Tribe expresses doubt both about the morality of the *Roe v. Wade* decision, despite its constitutional defensibility,[85] and the morality of abortion itself. He writes: "Something akin to horror must be felt by everyone involved in the question of abortion who has not become anesthetized to the reality of what is at stake."[86] It is simply false to say that *everyone* feels horror about abortion, particu-

---

[81] *Id.* at 112 (emphasis added).

[82] *Id.* at 114.

[83] *Id.* at 129-35.

[84] Although he uses a rationale that assumes fetuses are persons, he dismisses the argument that the fetus could be a "person" as that word is used in the Constitution because that argument would carry with it "consequences for which no one seems willing to argue." *Id.* at 125. These consequences would include arguing that fetuses cannot be treated differently from any other child under the fourteenth amendment's equal protection clause. *Id.* at 124. Moreover, a logical extension of the argument is that fetuses must be treated as equivalent to the pregnant woman in analyzing whether a woman may abort when pregnancy presents a high risk of causing her death. *Id.* at 122.

By resorting to the Good Samaritan doctrine, however, Tribe concedes that the constitutional rationale for abortion rights should be based on the assumption that fetuses are legal persons, though not the "persons" referred to in the Constitution.

[85] He writes, "On the view explained here, the ultimate moral rightness of *Roe*'s result seems considerably less clear than does its defensibility as a constitutional matter." *Id.* at 129.

[86] *Id.* at 230.

larly partly abortifacient methods of birth control or early abortions.[87] Is Tribe saying everyone should feel horror? Assuming for the moment it is a horror, why does he focus on this horror, rather than on others? For example, in a passage remarkably parallel to the one just quoted, Donald Regan has written:

> For a start, anyone who attempts simply to deny that there is an intrinsic horror to unwanted pregnancy lacks either imagination or compassion. . . . [L]aws forbidding abortion involve the requisitioning of the woman's body by the state. . . . [so that she is] relegated to the status of a broodmare (for this is how the pregnant woman may well view the matter). . . .[88]

Other horrors Tribe might have highlighted are the conditions of objectification in too many women's lives that lead to so many unwanted pregnancies or the unmet needs of millions of American children who live in poverty or in worse conditions—disease, abuse or abandonment to institutions. The pro-choice side needs to have its morality articulated, an effort Tribe does not aid.

Rather, after reviewing views of abortion in other cultures across history, his sweeping conclusion is: "Whether or not abortion is justified in some situations, it appears generally in most cultures to be considered a 'wrong.' "[89] He does not even acknowledge the view—one he should be aware of because it is held by people who share his legal and policy position in his own time and country—that women usually have abortions for *moral* reasons that are grounded in their values and sense of obligation to others, including the fetus, and to themselves. For example, an amicus brief filed

---

[87] The drug RU486 may further blur the line between abortifacient birth control and abortion. *See* Ricks, *The New French Abortion Pill: The Moral Property of Women*, 1 YALE J.L. & FEMINISM 75 (1989). This drug, effective up to the seventh week of pregnancy, causes the lining of the uterus, as in normal menstruation, to break down and be expelled, along with a fertilized egg or the multi-celled blastocyst that has evolved from it, if any is present. *Id.* at 79. The drug's effect may not be markedly different from how the IUD sometimes works. *Id.* at 80. The IUD usually prevents fertilization but sometimes may prevent implantation. Brief of Amicus Curiae, Association of Reproductive Health Professionals, in Support of Appellees, Webster v. Reproductive Health Servs., 109 S. Ct. 3040 (1989) (No. 88-605).

[88] Regan, *Rewriting* Roe v. Wade, 77 MICH. L. REV. 1569, 1617 (1979).

[89] L. TRIBE, ABORTION, *supra* note 1, at 53.

in *Webster v. Reproductive Health Services*[90] on behalf of 2887 women who have had abortions stated: "We are among the millions of American women who have faced an unplanned or problematic pregnancy and decided that having an abortion, legal or illegal, was the *right* choice for us, our loved ones and our lives."[91] Tribe fails to explore the view that a woman's decision to have an abortion is usually a "conscientious choice"[92] and a resolution of a "complicated moral dilemma."[93] David Richards has written:

> [T]he prohibitions on abortion encumber what many now reasonably regard as a highly conscientious choice by women regarding their bodies, their sexuality and gender, and the nature and place of pregnancy, birth, and child rearing in their personal and ethical lives. The traditional condemnation of abortion fails, at a deep ethical level, to take seriously the moral independence of women as free and rational persons, lending force of law to theological ideas of biological naturalness and gender hierarchy that degrade the constructive moral powers of women themselves to establish the meaning of their sexual and reproductive life histories.[94]

Richards' point that moral views of abortion are frequently driven by particular theological views is confirmed by survey evidence indicating that Jews and those with no current religious affiliation are most strongly pro-choice.[95]

The cause of Tribe's horror at abortion is not clear, but that hor-

---

[90] 109 S. Ct. 3040 (1989).

[91] Brief for Amici Curiae, Women Who Have Had Abortions, and Friends of Amici Curiae, in Support of Appellees at 1, Webster v. Reproductive Health Servs., 109 S. Ct. 3040 (1989) (No. 88-605) (emphasis added).

[92] D. Richards, Toleration and the Constitution 268 (1986).

[93] This is Kristin Luker's characterization of how pro-choice activists tend to think of abortion decisions. K. Luker, Motherhood, *supra* note 13, at 244.

[94] D. Richards, *supra* note 92, at 268.

[95] In a study of the views of elites on abortion, a strongly pro-choice position was taken by the following religious groups in the percentages indicated in parentheses: Jews (85%), those with no current religious affiliation (84%), Protestants (67%) and Roman Catholics (approximately 50%). Lerner, Nagai & Rothman, *supra* note 67, at 12. Polling data from the general public also confirms a connection between religion and abortion views. In one poll of the general public, the percentages favoring legal abortion for any reason, according to religion, were as follows: Jews (75%), those with no current religious affiliation (69%), Protestants (35%) and Roman Catholics (21%). *Id.* at 13.

ror seems to be what leads him to use a rationale that justifies abortion rights even if the fetus is a person. He defends abortion rights by drawing upon the "Good Samaritan doctrine" in Anglo-American law—the absence of a general duty to give of oneself in order to rescue another person.[96] He draws upon this idea to argue that, even if a fetus is a person, the state's interest in life does not justify compelling the profound connection and physical risks associated with pregnancy and childbirth.[97] Tribe points out that a father cannot be legally compelled to give a part of his liver or one kidney to his child, even if he is the only potential donor with compatible tissue.[98]

One reason that Tribe likes the Good Samaritan rationale is because it avoids the need to resolve whether a fetus is a person—he assumes it is—and thus avoids what he sees as a problem with the reasoning of *Roe v. Wade*:

> [P]erhaps the Supreme Court's opinion in *Roe*, by gratuitously insisting that the fetus *cannot* be deemed a "person," needlessly insulted and alienated those for whom the view that the fetus is a person represents a fundamental article of faith or a bedrock personal commitment.[99]

Even if the fetus is treated as a person, he argues, the pregnant woman does not have to save it by continuing an unwanted pregnancy.[100] Although Tribe's change of rationale from that in *Roe* does not change the result that compelled pregnancy is constitutionally impermissible, he appears to think his concession will be satisfying to pro-lifers.[101] This seems unlikely.

Tribe's rationale should be rejected by the pro-choice side for two reasons. First, the Good Samaritan doctrine is a slender reed on which to hang abortion rights. Second, the radical individualism involved in applying this doctrine in the abortion context is not consistent with the way in which many women make the moral decision to have an abortion. Each of these points requires

---

[96] L. TRIBE, ABORTION, *supra* note 1, at 130-33.
[97] *Id.* at 103, 129-30.
[98] *Id.* at 133, 210.
[99] *Id.* at 135.
[100] *Id.*
[101] *Id.*

elaboration.

In his constitutional law treatise,[102] although not in this book, Tribe does refer to two difficulties with analogies between the law of abortion and Good Samaritan principles in tort law, difficulties that have been fully explored by Regan.[103] One difficulty is that the common law has made a distinction between acts and omissions.[104] To use the no-duty-to-help doctrine, having an abortion has to be characterized as an omission, a refusal to help, rather than as an act causing harm.[105] Some may view the act-omission distinction as formal, but people certainly feel very differently about, for example, a decision to hook up a person to life-supporting medical technology and a decision to pull the plug. A second difficulty with the Good Samaritan rationale is that the common law has developed exceptions, creating a duty to help in certain circumstances, based on (1) a relationship of dependence and power, (2) a breach of a duty undertaken or (3) a "special relationship," including that of parent and child.[106] All of the situations that give rise to exceptions to the no-duty-to-help principle are arguably analogous to that of a pregnant woman and a fetus. (Although, if forced to use the no-duty-to-help rationale for abortion access, I would probably not agree that the exceptions are analogous.)[107] A third difficulty is that the lack of a duty to help under the common law is questionable policy—the common-law doctrine on this point has been repeatedly criticized.[108] In particular, from a feminist perspective, it has most recently been criticized as failing to incorporate relational morality and an ethic of care.[109] Ironi-

---

[102] L. Tribe, American Constitutional Law 1354-57 (2d ed. 1988).

[103] Regan, *supra* note 88, at 1573-79.

[104] *Id.* at 1573. Tribe also refers to the problem of the act-omission distinction in L. Tribe, Constitutional Choices 244-45 (1985).

[105] Regan, *supra* note 88, at 1573-79.

[106] W. Prosser & W. Keeton, The Law of Torts 373-77 (5th ed. 1984).

[107] If the Good Samaritan doctrine is employed as a rationale for legal abortion, one can make use of the fact that ordinarily when there is a duty to help, the duty only requires persons to take actions that do not involve serious inconvenience or possibility of harm to themselves. M. Shapo, The Duty to Act: Tort Law, Power and Public Policy 69 (1977).

[108] *See, e.g.*, *id.* at xii-xiii, 70-73 (analyzing failures to act in terms of power to give aid); Kelman, *Choice and Utility*, 1979 Wis. L. Rev. 769, 790-93 (arguing that distinguishing "harm" from "failure to help" depends on "political attitudes and empirical guesses" and that deciding when there should be a duty to help depends on where one stands on the libertarian-to-communitarian spectrum).

[109] Bender, *A Lawyer's Primer on Feminist Theory and Tort*, 38 J. Legal Educ. 3, 33-36

cally, given Tribe's search for common ground, he never considers a very general point on which many pro-choice and pro-life advocates *could* agree—that we need a more relational view of the morality of abortion.[110]

Examining the common law concerning obligations to help reminds us that in general the law reflects and is part of the social construction of obligation or no obligation in various circumstances. Ultimately, however, argument by analogy cannot resolve the question whether a pregnant woman should have a legal obligation to continue the pregnancy to sustain the fetus. Tribe refers to Frances Olsen's point that the value of fetal life cannot be discovered; it is culturally created and rests upon social meaning and sexual politics.[111] After quoting her statement that " 'fetal life has value when people with power value it,' " Tribe comments, "Nicely put, but . . . . *[t]hat doesn't make it right.*"[112] He then mistakenly equates Olsen's position with a moral code of "might makes right."[113] This surely would be a losing proposition for any feminist.

Rather, Olsen argues that the pregnant woman should be the one to decide the value of the fetus.[114] She bases this position not on a "might makes right" basis, but on an evaluation of the relative social harms that would result from the pro-choice as opposed to the pro-life legal approach.[115] She notes that some well-meaning people oppose abortion because they fear that it will lead to devaluation of human life, but they fail to realize that forbidding abortion is itself brutal and dehumanizing and involves devaluing

---

(1988).

[110] *See* Smolin, *Why Abortion Rights Are Not Justified by Reference to Gender Equality: A Response to Professor Tribe*, 23 J. MARSHALL L. REV. 621 (1990) (critiquing Tribe's book from a pro-life perspective). Smolin argues that Tribe "accepts an unattractive, raw version of male sexuality" in seeing equality for women in terms of autonomy from a fetus. *Id.* at 638-39. Smolin, however, seems to elevate a pregnant woman's physical connection to a fetus above all her other relations and commitments. As a result, he does not see the brutality of imposing his hierarchy of values on a woman whose commitments are different from those he would choose for her and whose social situation may be a bleak environment in which to undertake motherhood.

[111] L. TRIBE, ABORTION, *supra* note 1, at 119 (citing Olsen, *Unraveling Compromise*, 103 HARV. L. REV. 105, 128 (1989)).

[112] *Id.* at 119 (quoting Olsen, *supra* note 111, at 128), 119-20.

[113] *Id.* at 120.

[114] Olsen, *supra* note 111, at 131.

[115] *Id.* at 131-32.

human life.[116] Thus, "[i]n opposing abortion, one cooperates with the devaluation of women's lives and paves the way for further devaluation of life."[117] For example, she notes that the Nazis and the repressive regime that fell in Romania in 1989 had repressive abortion policies.[118] Under current social conditions, fetal life can only be valued as fully, rather than potentially, human if women are treated as sub-human. Olsen explains:

> The possibility of valuing fetal life from an early stage exists because of the systematic undervaluation of women's lives. If women were taken seriously, early fetal life would not be valued by society at large unless and until the woman carrying the fetus valued it.[119]

She argues further that, if women were not devalued, people would not conceptualize a fetus as a baby or as a person with interests separate from and potentially hostile to those of the pregnant woman.[120]

In contrast to Olsen's perspective that views about abortion are a result of women's subordination, Tribe repeatedly refers to abortion restrictions as a cause of women's subordination.[121] He fails to see that it is the other way around: the subordination is prior, and abortion restrictions and views about the immorality of abortion—especially early abortion—result from this subordination (and also perpetuate it). Tribe's lack of perception on this point is related to his only partially articulated view that the immorality of abortion is part of an ahistorical core morality. Although he refers to the cultural basis of ideas about abortion,[122] he concludes that abortion is cross-culturally "a wrong."[123] On the abortion question,

---

[116] *Id.* at 132.

[117] *Id.*

[118] *Id.* at 108 n.15, 132.

[119] *Id.* at 128.

[120] *Id.* at 126.

[121] He writes: "If someone thinks the Constitution should be amended to endow all fetuses with the status of persons, there may be no way to convince that individual that such an amendment would be morally wrong because it *would subordinate* women." L. TRIBE, ABORTION, *supra* note 1, at 128 (emphasis added). And again, he writes: "[A] ban on abortion imposes truly burdensome duties *only* on women. Such a ban *thus places* women, by accident of their biology, in a permanently and irrevocably subordinate position to men." *Id.* at 132 (emphasis added to "thus places").

[122] *Id.* at 76.

[123] *Id.* at 53.

he thinks in terms of "ultimate moral rightness,"[124] "ultimate truth"[125] and whether a position is "wrong."[126] He writes: "We must be able to import into the law some moral view from a perspective external to that of those with power . . . ."[127] Feminists, in order to hope for an eventual end to women's subordination, must agree, but they agree for different reasons than Tribe suggests. He has in mind the moral claims of the powerless "unborn,"[128] rather than the idea that morality about abortion results from power structures that have excluded and devalued women.

How can there be any morality other than "might makes right" if the powerful create and enforce social views of morality? The way out of this box, the solution to this dilemma, is in the hope (perhaps a forlorn one) that the powerful can act disinterestedly or perhaps out of enlightened self-interest, so as not to oppress those without power. In other words, the powerful should cede some power. (I hear Arthur Leff's voice: "Sez who?" Leff notes, "It looks as if we are all we have," in the way of resources for creating a moral order. He adds, "Given what we know about ourselves and each other, this is an extraordinarily unappetizing prospect . . . .")[129]

Tribe seems to believe that there is a discoverable truth about the nature of the fetus, and he is troubled by the hunch that it is a human being.[130] As has been discussed, he likes the Good Samaritan rationale because it involves assuming that the fetus is a person, thus avoiding the need to decide that question.[131] Another reason Tribe likes the Good Samaritan rationale seems to be that it evades the question of the social contingency of morality, but of course it fails to do that. To use the Good Samaritan doctrine in the abortion context, Tribe must subscribe to a very individualistic credo, an artifact of people with power in our time. This credo is not consistent with the kind of relational moral thinking that has

---

[124] *Id.* at 129.
[125] *Id.* at 240.
[126] *Id.* at 120.
[127] *Id.*
[128] *Id.*
[129] Leff, *Unspeakable Ethics, Unnatural Law*, 1979 DUKE L.J. 1229, 1249.
[130] Leff described the method used by Tribe to fill in the Constitution, when it is silent on a question, as "substantive intuition." *Id.* at 1248-49.
[131] *See supra* notes 96-101 and accompanying text.

been found to be characteristic of many women's abortion decisions, which are grounded in feelings of social responsibility.[132] Thus, his rationale does not give an authentic account of many women's moral decisions to have abortions.

The pro-choice side should insist that, as a matter of law, a fetus is *not* a person; it is for the individual pregnant woman to decide its moral status. This is the moral pluralism of the strongest pro-choice position. Rhetoric is very important because it helps us to understand our individual and social choices. Characterizing an early fetus as a child makes the pregnant woman the child's mother, even if she is unwilling or unable to play that role. Tribe's rationale allows a mother, on the basis of her interest in autonomy, to refuse life-saving help to her child. This rationale does not accurately reflect many women's moral decisions to have abortions, and it certainly does not explain why women should be allowed to make those decisions. It does not recognize women's relational morality or affirm women's moral agency. The pro-choice side should not concede or assume that a fetus is a legal person; it should stress that there is more than one acceptable moral view in our country on the nature of a fetus and on a pregnant woman's responsibility to it. Those who believe fetuses are persons should not have the power to restrict women who do not share their moral views.

IV. Broadening the Perspective—Not a Compromise, but Good Advocacy

Tribe's substantive "compromise" is to support programs to reduce abortion by improving contraception and the social support for families with children.[133] He writes:

> If advocates on both sides of the abortion debate would just pause, they would recognize at least one broadly shared interest, that of working toward a world of only

[132] C. Gilligan, *supra* note 24, at 111-12, 115-17, 120; *see also* West, *The Supreme Court, 1989 Term—Foreword: Taking Freedom Seriously*, 104 Harv. L. Rev. 43 (1990). West argues that abortion rights should be viewed in a context of reproductive responsibility and of societal failures, *id.* at 79-85, and that women deserve abortion rights because an abortion decision "typically rests not on a desire to destroy life but on a responsible and moral desire to ensure that a new life will be borne only if it will be nurtured and loved." *Id.* at 83.

[133] L. Tribe, Abortion, *supra* note 1, at 211-14, 228.

> wanted pregnancies. Better education, the provision of contraception, indeed the creation of a society in which the burden of raising a child is lighter, are all achievable goals that are lost in the shouting about abortion.[134]

The progams Tribe supports include improving sex education and access to birth control, supporting research into better methods of contraception and establishing programs to support families (especially mothers) with children.[135]

To many pro-life activists, however, this is decidedly not a compromise. As Kristin Luker has so powerfully demonstrated, among pro-life activists, opposition to abortion is part of a world view based on traditional sex roles and sexual morality and based on the primacy of the family.[136] Some of the beliefs associated with this world view are that motherhood is women's natural destiny,[137] contraception profanes sex[138] and the state should avoid "intrusions" into the family (such as free school lunches, day care, extra nutrition for pregnant women and anti-child-abuse programs).[139] Pro-life activists even reject the phrase "unwanted pregnancy," preferring the term, "surprise pregnancy."[140] They tend to think of exact planning of the number and timing of children as elevating material considerations over the intangible benefits of children.[141] As Luker puts it, "pro-life people object to every step of the pro-choice logic."[142]

It is hard to believe that Tribe really thinks he is offering a compromise. The two chapters of the book that recount the political story of abortion from *Roe v. Wade* through early 1990 display the talents of a shrewd political observer.[143] Compromise is stymied by the fundamental difference in the world views underlying well-defined pro-choice and pro-life positions, most significantly those concerning gender and related morality. Pro-choice activists take a

---

[134] *Id.* at 228.
[135] *Id.* at 211-13.
[136] K. LUKER, MOTHERHOOD, *supra* note 13, at 159-75.
[137] *Id.* at 168.
[138] *Id.* at 163-67.
[139] *Id.* at 173.
[140] *Id.* at 198.
[141] *Id.* at 170-71.
[142] *Id.* at 171.
[143] L. TRIBE, ABORTION, *supra* note 1, at 139-96.

pluralistic position on the roles for men and women and on the moral issues involved in abortion decisions.[144] They recognize that some women (although probably a gradually declining number) will continue to play the exclusive homemaker-mother role throughout their adult lives. Pro-choicers insist, however, upon legal abortion as one of the essentials for those women who have sexual intercourse *and* who want to be able to attempt roles other than or in addition to that of mother.[145] Given the current state of contraceptive technology and the social conditions surrounding its availability and use (or lack thereof), abortion becomes necessary for many women at some time during their reproductive years.[146] Even those who never have abortions are aided in making life plans by knowing abortion is available in the event of, for example, contraceptive failure or serious genetic defect in a fetus.

In contrast to pro-choicers' pluralism on gender roles and related sexual and reproductive morality, pro-life activists seek to preserve women's traditional role of mother and homemaker by making motherhood potentially mandatory for women who have intercourse.[147] They also tend to have a rigid moral code which supports their views on sex, contraception and abortion.[148] Pro-lifers who wish to preserve traditional gender roles are probably correct in opposing gender role pluralism, which, on the surface, looks like a compromise. Their opposition reflects the intuition—probably correct—that traditional roles cannot thrive, and perhaps even long survive, in a climate where they are not enforced and socially supported. Understanding of this point on the part of pro-choicers may make them more tolerant of intolerance on the part of pro-lifers, who are fighting for their way of life. But this recognition

---

[144] K. LUKER, MOTHERHOOD, *supra* note 13, at 175-85.

[145] *Id.*

[146] According to the AMA Brief in *Webster*: "Among women age 15-44, more than 21% have had an abortion; if current abortion rates continue, 46% of all American women will have had an abortion by the time they are 45." AMA Brief, *supra* note 5, at 5 (citing Forrest, *Unintended Pregnancy Among American Women*, 19 FAM. PLAN. PERSP. 76, 76-77 (1987)).

[147] K. LUKER, MOTHERHOOD, *supra* note 13, at 159-70. Some pro-life activists became involved in the movement in part because of their feelings of being undervalued in their traditional roles. *Id.* I have no doubt that there is good cause for these feelings—that women in traditional roles receive strong cultural messages that they are not valued, but the solution is not enforced motherhood.

[148] *Id.* at 174-75.

does not suggest that compromise is possible—quite the contrary.

The abortion issue is particularly divisive and intractable because it is currently the main battleground in America on the question of the appropriate role or roles for women. The problem with pluralism in work-family gender roles—involving a diversity that I would like to see survive (with different work and family roles open to men, too)—is that this system needs social support from a bread-winner who earns enough for the whole family, from various communities and from the state. This system of social support is eroding. Women who work exclusively (without wages, of course) as mothers and homemakers and their families feel under seige in America, and this feeling motivates some of these women to become pro-life activists.[149] The more common it is for women with children—even very small children[150]—to work outside the home, the harder it is to marshal backing for private- or public-sector mechanisms to support families in which the mother—or in a non-sexist world, one parent—has no paid employment. Thus, arguments for a family-wage and for employer-paid medical benefits for the whole family and arguments against expectations that welfare mothers should work have lost much of their appeal. What Tribe thinks of as a substantive compromise, his call to address the conditions that lead to so many unwanted pregnancies, is really something very different. It involves broadening the perspective on the abortion question, which is good advocacy for the pro-choice position. It also means supporting programs that have value independent of their effects, if any, on abortion.

The birth control part of Tribe's program ought to be the most economically and politically feasible, surely more so than the family support part. Contraception and birth control such as the pill and the IUD, which may be partly abortifacient, are much to be preferred to abortion. These methods of birth control spare women difficult decisions and the regret some women feel about abortions[151] and avoid the risk of trivializing the value of human life.

---

[149] *Id.* at 162-63, 170.

[150] Half, or 11,200,000, of all American preschool-age children are now living in families where no parent is available to care for them on a full-time basis. Hernandez & Myers, *Family Composition, Parents' Work and the Need for Child Care Among Preschool Children*, paper presented at the annual meeting of the Population Association of America, New Orleans (Apr. 21-23, 1988) (findings reported in 20 FAM. PLAN. PERSP. 181 (1988)).

[151] Most women, however, primarily feel relief after abortions and regret tends to be

Because these methods are more widely accepted than abortion,[152] marshalling political support for birth control programs should be possible. We should not underestimate, however, the difficulties of implementing programs that require the political leadership and the electorate to come to terms with teenage sex and extramarital sex generally.[153] In the summer of 1990, for example, the Bush Administration reportedly rejected the idea of supporting expanded family planning services, in particular in-school clinics in high-poverty areas with high rates of "out-of-wedlock" births, on the grounds that it would cost money, would be seen as encouraging promiscuity and might cause political problems with groups opposed to birth control.[154]

Furthermore, even when birth control methods are easily available and the mechanics of using them are known, they are not always used. A world in which men and women use birth control universally except when they intend to procreate may be a utopian dream that would require a feminist transformation of society. Kristin Luker's study of contraceptive risk-taking revealed the subtle, pervasive effects of gender roles and gender hierarchy in this area of life.[155] For example, part of the "costs" of contraceptive use to women—especially for methods that remain in place such as birth control pills and the IUD—are the implication of sexual availability and consequent loss of status and bargaining position with men.[156] Part of the "benefits" of a pregnancy—even one that ends in abortion—can be to prompt discussion of marriage and to test commitment, including within marriages.[157] Emphasiz-

short-lived. AMA Brief, *supra* note 5, at 20-21.

[152] Among women aged 15-44 who have ever had intercourse, 95% have used one or more contraceptive methods. Kaeser, *Contraceptive Development: Why the Snail's Pace?*, 22 FAM. PLAN. PERSP. 131 (1990).

[153] *See id.*; Rosoff, *The Politics of Birth Control*, 20 FAM. PLAN. PERSP. 312 (1988).

[154] Pear, *Bush Administration Rejects Proposal For New Anti-Poverty Programs*, N.Y. Times, July 6, 1990, at A1, A9 (nat'l ed.).

[155] K. LUKER, TAKING CHANCES—ABORTION AND THE DECISION NOT TO CONTRACEPT (1975) [hereinafter, K. LUKER, TAKING CHANCES].

[156] *Id.* at 46-49.

[157] *Id.* 81-85. Marriage is economically desirable for most women because it gives them access to the higher income-earning power of men. *Id.* at 115-19. Marriage also tends to be more fundamental to women's self-identity than it is for men. *Id.* at 119-23.

Lack of opportunity can also make having a baby look appealing to those who are ill-equipped to be parents. Leon Dash has written of how low achievement and self-esteem lead some teenage girls to view having a baby as "a tangible achievement in an otherwise dreary

ing the dynamics of dominance in male-female relations, Catherine MacKinnon has discussed the inability of some women to interrupt intercourse to use birth control or even to refuse intercourse because of lack of desire.[158] She concluded that "socially, women's bodies have not been ours."[159]

These points about the effects of gender hierarchy on contraceptive use and nonuse are tricky and perhaps dangerous to employ in mainstream debate. To an unsympathetic audience, the point may seem to be that people—especially women—are irresponsible, rather than that too many women live in horrifying conditions of objectification in their intimate relationships and have too few options in their lives.[160] For those who are willing to see these conditions, however, it becomes clearer that the need for abortion is in significant part a result of women's subordination.[161] The irony is that women's subordination also tends to produce restrictions on abortion.[162] The result can be no way out.

Calling for improved social benefits to ease the burdens on women and their families from bearing and rearing children also can be a way to emphasize the link between the need for abortion and women's subordination. It is highly unlikely that there will be sufficient political support any time soon to improve social benefits enough to reduce abortion,[163] but these benefits are desirable in

---

and empty future." L. Dash, When Children Want Children 9 (1989).

[158] C. MacKinnon, Feminism Unmodified 95 (1987).

[159] *Id.* at 98.

[160] In Kristin Luker's view, the solutions to contraceptive risk-taking are complex. Among other strategies, she advocates taking steps to help women to understand why they take such risks in order to help them stop taking them. K. Luker, Taking Chances, *supra* note 155, at 110. This effort would require professionals involved in providing contraceptive and abortion services to abandon the view that women act irrationally when they fail to use contraception. Luker develops the theory that women use a cost-benefit logic of which they are often only dimly aware. She thinks women should be counseled to become aware of this logic and its fallacies. *Id.* at 78-111.

[161] *See* Olsen, *supra* note 111, at 123-24: "The antiabortion movement puts women into the position of having to fight for something they need rather than want. . . . The abortion debate keeps women off-balance and less able to struggle against the unreasonable conditions that make unwanted pregnancy so common an occurrence."

[162] *See id.* at 128, 131-32.

[163] Legal sociologist Heleen F.P. Ietswaart, writing about Mary Ann Glendon's favorable reaction to the superior maternity and child grant benefits available in various European countries, questioned whether social benefits play a major role in the decision to have or not to have a child. Ietswaart, *Incomplete Stories* (Book Review), 69 B.U.L. Rev. 257, 265 (1989) (reviewing M. Glendon, *supra* note 2). Specifically, Ietswaart noted: "French pregnant

themselves (if you are a social democrat). Raising this issue in the abortion debate emphasizes the costs of child-rearing and makes the point that those who seek to compel pregnant women to complete all or nearly all pregnancies are usually unwilling to bear any of the financial burden and certainly unwilling to bear the other burdens.[164] It also shifts the focus from abstract "life," to the crying, unmet needs of millions of children in our country. Concern about individual and social planning to meet the needs of children is part of the morality behind the pro-choice position. To show our respect for the value of life, we have plenty of work to do on behalf of lives already in being.

---

women without resources, especially without an employed male companion, know that transfer payments barely provide a decent standard of living. Moreover, young unmarried women are not the only group seeking abortions." *Id.* at 265-66.

[164] Tribe makes a similar point that, if costly artificial wombs were available, we might be forced to confront the unexamined costs placed on women by compelling them to complete pregnancies. L. TRIBE, ABORTION, *supra* note 1, at 225-27.

Sexual Expression and Pornography

[12]

AGAINST THE MALE FLOOD: CENSORSHIP, PORNOGRAPHY, AND EQUALITY

ANDREA DWORKIN*

To say what one thought—that was my little problem—against the prodigious Current; to find a sentence that could hold its own against the male flood. —VIRGINIA WOOLF

I want to say right here, that those well-meaning friends on the outside who say that we have suffered these horrors of prison, of hunger strikes and forcible feeding, because we desired to martyrise ourselves for the cause, are absolutely and entirely mistaken. We never went to prison in order to be martyrs. We went there in order that we might obtain the rights of citizenship.

 Andrea Dworkin is a radical feminist writer.

I thank all of the women who talked to me about how pornography has been used on them over all the years when there was nothing we could do. I thank Jeanne Barkey in particular for her stunning work in organizing the first Minneapolis hearings on pornography; and Charlee Hoyt, for being the driving force behind getting the legislation written and enacted. I thank Van White for co-sponsoring the bill and conducting the hearings. I thank everyone who testified in behalf of the legislation at the first hearings and later in subsequent hearings, and also those who talked to the press about sexual abuse at great cost to themselves. I thank the people who organized and now run the Pornography Resource Center in Minneapolis, especially for their work in organizing victims. I especially thank Therese Stanton for her extraordinary personal courage in testifying at the first Minneapolis hearings and for her untiring work in behalf of victims. I thank Steve Jevning for his tenacity, courage, and astuteness in working for the legislation, and for initiating the political process that led to both the legislation and a new kind of grassroots organizing. I especially thank my colleague, Catharine MacKinnon, for the honor of the intellectual and political dialogue we have had in conceiving and drafting the legislation, and for her indomitable will to stop the pornographers from hurting women. I thank John Stoltenberg for his many contributions to the politics of equality on which the legislation and this essay are built. All of these people contributed in both knowledge and faith to the writing of this essay. I dedicate this essay to all those resolute and brave people who worked to accomplish the passage of the first Minneapolis anti-pornography civil rights bill. Thank you.

We were willing to break laws that we might force men to give us the right to make laws. —EMMELINE PANKHURST

I. CENSORSHIP

Censorship is a real thing, not an abstract idea or a word that can be used to mean anything at all.

In ancient Rome, a censor was a magistrate who took the census (a count of the male population and an evaluation of property for the purpose of taxation done every fifth year), assessed taxes, and inspected morals and conduct. His power over conduct came from his power to tax. For instance, in 403 B.C., the censors Camillus and Postimius heavily fined elderly bachelors for not marrying. The power to tax, then as now, was the power to destroy. The censor, using the police and judicial powers of the state, regulated social behavior.

At its origins, then, censorship had nothing to do with striking down ideas as such; it had to do with acts. In my view, real state censorship still does. In South Africa and the Soviet Union, for instance, writing is treated entirely as an act, and writers are viewed as persons who engage in an act (writing) that by its very nature is dangerous to the continued existence of the state. The police in these countries do not try to suppress ideas. They are more specific, more concrete, more realistic. They go after books and manuscripts (writing) and destroy them. They go after writers as persons who have done something that they will do again and they persecute, punish, or kill them. They do not worry about what people think—not, at least, as we use the word *think*: a mental event, entirely internal, abstract. They worry about what people do: and writing, speaking, even as evidence that thinking is going on, are seen as things people *do*. There is a quality of immediacy and reality in what writing is taken to be. Where police power is used against writers systematically, writers are seen as people who by writing do something socially real and significant, not contemplative or dithering. Therefore, writing is never peripheral or beside the point. It is serious and easily seditious. I am offering no brief for police states when I say that virtually all great writers, crossculturally and transhistorically, share this view of what writing is. In countries like ours, controlled by a bourgeoisie to whom the police are accountable, writing is easier to do and valued less. It has less impact. It is more abundant and cheaper. Less is at stake for reader and writer both. The writer may hold writing to be a life-or-death matter, but the police and society do not. Writing is seen to be a personal choice, not a social, political, or esthetic necessity fraught with danger and meaning. The general view in these pleasant places* is that writers think up ideas or words and then other people read them and all this happens in the head, a vast cavern somewhere north of the eyes. It is all air, except for the paper and ink, which are simply banal. Nothing happens.

Police in police states and most great writers throughout time see writing as act, not air—as act, not idea; concrete, specific, real, not insubstantial blather on a dead page. Censorship goes after the act and the actor: the book and the writer. It needs to destroy both. The cost in human lives is staggering, and it is perhaps essential to say that human lives destroyed must count more in the weighing of horror than books burned. This is my personal view, and I love books more than I love people.

Censorship is deeply misunderstood in the United States, because the fairly spoiled, privileged, frivolous people who are the literate citizens of this country think that censorship is some foggy effort to suppress ideas. For them, censorship is not something in itself—an act of police power with discernible consequences to hunted people; instead, it is about something abstract—the suppressing or controlling of ideas. Censorship, like writing itself, is no longer an act. Because it is no longer the blatant exercise of police power against writers or books because of what they do, what they accomplish in the real world, it becomes vague, hard to find, except perhaps as an attitude. It gets used to mean unpleasant, even angry frowns of disapproval or critiques delivered in harsh tones; it means social disapproval or small retaliations by outraged citizens where the book is still available and the writer is entirely unharmed, even if insulted. It

* "Well, you know, it amazes me . . . ." says dissident South African writer Nadine Gordimer in an interview. "I come to America, I go to England, I go to France . . . nobody's at risk. They're afraid of getting cancer, losing a lover, losing their jobs, being insecure . . . . It's only in my own country that I find people who voluntarily choose to put everything at risk—in their personal life." *Nadine Gordimer*, WRITERS AT WORK: THE PARIS REVIEW INTERVIEWS 261 (G. Plimpton ed. 6th ser. 1984).

hangs in the air, ominous, like the threat of drizzle. It gets to be, in silly countries like this one, whatever people say it is, separate from any material definition, separate from police power, separate from state repression (jail, banning, exile, death), separate from devastating consequences to real people (jail, banning, exile, death). It is something that people who eat fine food and wear fine clothes worry about frenetically, trying to find it, anticipating it with great anxiety, arguing it down as if—if it were real—an argument would make it go away; not knowing that it has a clear, simple, unavoidable momentum and meaning in a cruel world of police power that their privilege cannot comprehend.

II. OBSCENITY

In the nineteenth and twentieth centuries, in most of Western Europe, England, and the United States, more often than not (time-out for Franco, for instance), writing has been most consistently viewed as an act warranting prosecution when the writing is construed to be obscene.

The republics, democracies, and constitutional monarchies of the West, now and then, do not smother writers in police violence; they prefer to pick off writers who annoy and irritate selectively with fairly token prosecutions. The list of writers so harassed is elegant, white, male (therefore the pronoun "he" is used throughout this discussion), and remarkably small. Being among them is more than a ceremonial honor. As Flaubert wrote his brother in 1857:

> My persecution has brought me widespread sympathy. If my book is bad, that will serve to make it seem better. If, on the other hand, it has lasting qualities, that will build a foundation for it. There you are!
>
> I am hourly awaiting the official document which will name the day when I am to take my seat (for the crime of having written in French) in the dock in the company of thieves and homosexuals.[1]

[1] G. Flaubert, Letters 94 (J.M. Cohen trans. 1950).

A few months later that same year, Baudelaire was fined 300 francs for publishing six obscene poems. They also had to be removed from future editions of his book. In harder, earlier days, Jean-Jacques Rousseau spent eight years as a fugitive after his *Émile* was banned and a warrant was issued for his arrest. English censors criminally prosecuted Swinburne's *Poems and Ballads* in 1866. They were particularly piqued at Zola, even in translation, so his English publisher, seventy years old, went to jail for three months. In 1898, a bookseller was arrested for selling Havelock Ellis' work and received a suspended sentence. This list is representative, not exhaustive. While prosecutions of writers under obscenity laws have created great difficulties for writers already plagued with them (as most writers are), criminal prosecutions under obscenity law in Europe and the United States are notable for how narrowly they reach writers, how sanguine writers tend to be about the consequences to themselves, and how little is paid in the writer's life-blood to what D.H. Lawrence (who paid more than most modern Western writers) called the "censor-moron."[2] In South Africa, one would hardly be so flip. In our world, the writer gets harassed, as Lawrence did; the writer may be poor or not—the injury is considerably worse if he is; but the writer is not terrorized or tortured, and writers do not live under a reign of terror as writers, because of what they *do*. The potshot application of criminal law for writing is not good, nice, or right; but it is important to recognize the relatively narrow scope and marginal character of criminal prosecution under obscenity law in particular—especially compared with the scope and character of police-state censorship. Resisting obscenity law does not require hyperbolic renderings of what it is and how it has been used. It can be fought or repudiated on its own terms.

The use of obscenity laws against writers, however haphazard or insistent, is censorship and it does hold writing to be an act. This is a unique perception of what writing is, taking place, as it does, in a liberal context in which writing is held to be ideas. It is the obscene quality of the writing, the obscenity itself, that is seen to turn writing from idea into act. Writing of any kind or

[2] Letter from D.H. Lawrence to Morris Ernst, *quoted in* H. Moore, *Introduction* to D.H. LAWRENCE, SEX, LITERATURE AND CENSORSHIP 9 (1959).

quality is idea, except for obscene writing, which is act. Writing is censored, even in our own happy little land of Oz, as act, not idea.

What is obscenity, such that it turns writing, when obscene, into something that actually happens—changes it from internal wind somewhere in the elevated mind into a genuinely offensive and utterly real fart, noticed, rude, occasioning pinched fingers on the nose?

There is the legal answer and the artistic answer. Artists have been consistently pushing on the boundaries of obscenity because great writers see writing as an act, and in liberal culture, only obscene writing has that social standing, that quality of dynamism and heroism. Great writers tend to experience writing as an intense and disruptive act; in the West, it is only recognized as such when the writing itself is experienced as obscene. In liberal culture, the writer has needed obscenity to be perceived as socially real.

What is it that obscenity does? The writer uses what the society deems to be obscene because the society then reacts to the writing the way the writer values the writing: as if it does something. But obscenity itself is socially constructed; the writer does not invent it or in any sense originate it. He finds it, knowing that it is what society hides. He looks under rocks and in dark corners.

There are two possible derivations of the word *obscenity*: the discredited one, *what is concealed*; and the accepted one, *filth*. Animals bury their filth, hide it, cover it, leave it behind, separate it from themselves: so do we, going way way back. Filth is excrement: from down there. We bury it or hide it; also, we hide where it comes from. Under male rule, menstrual blood is also filth, so women are twice dirty. Filth is where the sexual organs are and because women are seen primarily as sex, existing to provide sex, women have to be covered: our naked bodies being obscene.

Obscenity law uses both possible root meanings of *obscene* intertwined: it typically condemns nudity, public display, lewd exhibition, exposed genitals or buttocks or pubic areas, sodomy, masturbation, sexual intercourse, excretion. Obscenity law is applied to pictures and words: the artifact itself exposes what should be hidden; it shows dirt. The human body and all sex and excretory acts are the domain of obscenity law.

But being in the domain of obscenity law is not enough. One must feel alive there. To be obscene, the representations must arouse prurient interest. *Prurient* means *itching* or *itch*; it is related to the Sanskrit for *he burns*. It means sexual arousal. Judges, lawmakers, and juries have been, until very recently, entirely male: empirically, *prurient* means *causes erection*. Theologians have called this same quality of obscenity "venereal pleasure," holding that

> if a work is to be called obscene it must, of its nature, be such as actually to arouse or calculated to arouse in the viewer or reader such venereal pleasure. If the work is *not* of such a kind, it may, indeed, be vulgar, disgusting, crude, unpleasant, what you will—but it will *not* be, in the strict sense which Canon Law obliges us to apply, obscene.[3]

A secular philosopher of pornography isolated the same quality when he wrote: "Obscenity is our name for the uneasiness which upsets the physical state associated with self-possession . . . ."[4]

Throughout history, the male has been the standard for obscenity law: erection is his venereal pleasure or the uneasiness which upsets the physical state associated with his self-possession. It is not surprising, then, that in the same period when women became jurors, lawyers, and judges—but especially jurors, women having been summarily excluded from most juries until perhaps a decade ago—obscenity law fell into disuse and disregard. In order for obscenity law to have retained social and legal coherence, it would have had to recognize as part of its standard women's sexual arousal, a more subjective standard than erection. It would also have had to use the standard of penile erection in a social environment that was no longer sex-segregated, an environment in which male sexual arousal would be subjected to female scrutiny. In my view, the presence of women in the public sphere of legal decision-making has done

---

[3] H. GARDINER, CATHOLIC VIEWPOINT ON CENSORSHIP 65 (1958).
[4] G. BATAILLE, DEATH AND SENSUALITY 12 (1969).

more to undermine the efficacy of obscenity law than any self-conscious movement against it.

The act that obscenity recognizes is erection, and whatever writing produces erection is seen to be obscene—act, not idea—because of what it makes happen. The male sexual response is seen to be involuntary, so there is no experientially explicable division between the material that causes erection and the erection itself. That is the logic of obscenity law used against important writers who have pushed against the borders of the socially defined obscene, because they wanted writing to have that very quality of being a socially recognized act. They wanted the inevitability of the response—the social response. The erection makes the writing socially real from the society's point of view, not from the writer's. What the writer needs is to be taken seriously, by any means necessary. In liberal societies, only obscenity law comprehends writing as an act. It defines the nature and quality of the act narrowly—not writing itself, but producing erections. Flaubert apparently did produce them; so did Baudelaire, Zola, Rousseau, Lawrence, Joyce, and Nabokov. It's that simple.

What is at stake in obscenity law is always erection: under what conditions, in what circumstances, how, by whom, by what materials men want it produced in themselves. Men have made this public policy. Why they want to regulate their own erections through law is a question of endless interest and importance to feminists. Nevertheless, that they do persist in this regulation is simple fact. There are civil and social conflicts over how best to regulate erection through law, especially when caused by words or pictures. Arguments among men notwithstanding, high culture is phallocentric. It is also, using the civilized criteria of jurisprudence, not infrequently obscene.

Most important writers have insisted that their own uses of the obscene as socially defined are not pornography. As D.H. Lawrence wrote: "But even I would censor genuine pornography, rigorously. It would not be very difficult . . . . [Y]ou can recognize it by the insult it offers, invariably, to sex, and to the human spirit."[5] It was also, he pointed out, produced by the underworld. Nabokov saw in pornography "mediocrity, commercialism, and certain strict rules of narration . . . . [A]ction has to be limited

[5] D.H. Lawrence, *supra* note 2, at 69.

to the copulation of clichés. Style, structure, imagery should never distract the reader from his tepid lust."[6] They knew that what they did was different from pornography, but they did not entirely know what the difference was. They missed the heart of an empirical distinction because writing was indeed real to them but women were not.

The insult pornography offers, invariably, to sex is accomplished in the active subordination of women: the creation of a sexual dynamic in which the putting-down of women, the suppression of women, and ultimately the brutalization of women, *is* what sex is taken to be. Obscenity in law, and in what it does socially, is erection. Law recognizes the act in this. Pornography, however, is a broader, more comprehensive act, because it crushes a whole class of people through violence and subjugation: and sex is the vehicle that does the crushing. The penis is not the test, as it is in obscenity. Instead, the status of women is the issue. Erection is implicated in the subordinating, but who it reaches and how are the pressing legal and social questions. Pornography, unlike obscenity, is a discrete, identifiable system of sexual exploitation that hurts women as a class by creating inequality and abuse. This is a new legal idea, but it is the recognition and naming of an old and cruel injury to a dispossessed and coerced underclass. It is the sound of women's words breaking the longest silence.

III. PORNOGRAPHY

In the United States, it is an $8-billion trade in sexual exploitation.

It is women turned into subhumans, beaver, pussy, body parts, genitals exposed, buttocks, breasts, mouths opened and throats penetrated, covered in semen, pissed on, shitted on, hung from light fixtures, tortured, maimed, bleeding, disemboweled, killed.

It is some creature called female, used.

It is scissors poised at the vagina and objects stuck in it, a smile on the woman's face, her tongue hanging out.

[6] V. Nabokov, *Afterword* to Lolita 284 (1977).

It is a woman being fucked by dogs, horses, snakes.

It is every torture in every prison cell in the world, done to women and sold as sexual entertainment.

It is rape and gang rape and anal rape and throat rape: and it is the woman raped, asking for more.

It is the woman in the picture to whom it is really happening and the women against whom the picture is used, to make them do what the woman in the picture is doing.

It is the power men have over women turned into sexual acts men do to women, because pornography is the power and the act.

It is the conditioning of erection and orgasm in men to the powerlessness of women: our inferiority, humiliation, pain, torment; to us as objects, things, or commodities for use in sex as servants.

It sexualizes inequality and in doing so creates discrimination as a sex-based practice.

It permeates the political condition of women in society by being the substance of our inequality however located—in jobs, in education, in marriage, *in life*.

It is women, kept a sexual underclass, kept available for rape and battery and incest and prostitution.

It is what we are under male domination; it is what we are for under male domination.

It is the heretofore hidden (from us) system of subordination that women have been told is just life.

Under male supremacy, it is the synonym for what being a woman is.

It is access to our bodies as a birthright to men: the grant, the gift, the permission, the license, the proof, the promise, the method, how-to; it is us accessible, no matter what the law pretends to say, no matter what we pretend to say.

It is physical injury and physical humiliation and physical pain: to the women against whom it is used after it is made; to the women used to make it.

As words alone, or words and pictures, moving or still, it creates systematic harm to women in the form of discrimination and physical hurt. It creates harm inevitably by its nature because of what it is and what it does. The harm will occur as long as it is made and used. The name of the next victim is unknown, but everything else is known.

Because of it—because it is the subordination of women perfectly achieved—the abuse done to us by any human standard is perceived as using us for what we are by nature: women are whores; women want to be raped; she provoked it; women like to be hurt; she says no but means yes because she wants to be taken against her will which is not really her will because what she wants underneath is to have anything done to her that violates or humiliates or hurts her; she wants it, because she is a woman, no matter what it is, because she is a woman; that is how women are, what women are, what women are for. This view is institutionally expressed in law. So much for equal protection.

If it were being done to human beings, it would be reckoned an atrocity. It is being done to women. It is reckoned fun, pleasure, entertainment, sex, somebody's (not something's) civil liberty no less.

What do you want to be when you grow up? *Doggie Girl*? *Gestapo Sex Slave*? *Black Bitch in Bondage*? Pet, bunny, beaver? In dreams begin responsibilities,[7] whether one is the dreamer or the dreamed.

IV. PORNOGRAPHERS

Most of them are small-time pimps or big-time pimps. They sell women: the real flesh-and-blood women in the pictures. They like the excitement of domination; they are greedy for profit; they are sadistic in their exploitation of women; they hate women, and the pornography they make is the distillation of that hate. The photographs are what they have created live, for themselves, for their own enjoyment. The exchanges of women among them are part of the fun, too: so that the fictional creature "Linda Lovelace," who was the real woman Linda Marchiano, was forced to "deep-throat" every pornographer her owner-pornographer wanted to impress. Of course, it was the woman,

---

[7] The actual line is "In dreams begins responsibility," quoted by Yeats as an epigram to a collection of his poetry. W.B. YEATS, RESPONSIBILITIES AND OTHER POEMS (1916).

not the fiction, who had to be hypnotized so that the men could penetrate to the bottom of her throat, and who had to be beaten and terrorized to get her compliance at all. The finding of new and terrible things to do to women is part of the challenge of the vocation: so the inventor of "Linda Lovelace" and "deep-throating" is a genius in the field, a pioneer. Or, as Al Goldstein, a colleague, referred to him in an interview with him in *Screw* several years ago: a pimp's pimp.

Even with written pornography, there has never been the distinction between making pornography and the sexual abuse of live women that is taken as a truism by those who approach pornography as if it were an intellectual phenomenon. The Marquis de Sade, as the world's foremost literary pornographer, is archetypal. His sexual practice was the persistent sexual abuse of women and girls, with occasional excursions into the abuse of boys. As an aristocrat in a feudal society, he preyed with near impunity on prostitutes and servants. The pornography he wrote was an urgent part of the sexual abuse he practiced: not only because he did what he wrote, but also because the intense hatred of women that fueled the one also fueled the other: not two separate engines, but one engine running on the same tank. The acts of pornography and the acts of rape were waves on the same sea: that sea, becoming for its victims however it reached them, a tidal wave of destruction. Pornographers who use words know that what they are doing is both aggressive and destructive: sometimes they philosophize about how sex inevitably ends in death, the death of a woman being a thing of sexual beauty as well as excitement. Pornography, even when written, is sex because of the dynamism of the sexual hatred in it; and for pornographers, the sexual abuse of women as commonly understood and pornography are both acts of sexual predation, which is how they live.

One reason that stopping pornographers and pornography is not censorship is that pornographers are more like the police in police states than they are like the writers in police states. They are the instruments of terror, not its victims. What police do to the powerless in police states is what pornographers do to women, except that it is entertainment for the masses, not dignified as political. Writers do not do what pornographers do. Secret police do. Torturers do. What pornographers do to women is more like what police do to political prisoners than it is like anything else: except for the fact that it is watched with so much pleasure by so many. Intervening in a system of terror where it is vulnerable to public scrutiny to stop it is not censorship; it is the system of terror that stops speech and creates abuse and despair. The pornographers are the secret police of male supremacy: keeping women subordinate through intimidation and assault.

V. SUBORDINATION

In the amendment to the Human Rights Ordinance of the City of Minneapolis written by Catharine A. MacKinnon and myself,* pornography is defined as the graphic, sexually explicit subordination of women whether in pictures or in words that also includes one or more of the following: women are presented dehumanized as sexual objects, things or commodities; or women are presented as sexual objects who enjoy pain or humiliation; or women are presented as sexual objects who experience sexual pleasure in being raped; or women are presented as sexual objects tied up or cut up or mutilated or bruised or physically hurt; or women are presented in postures of sexual submission; or women's body parts are exhibited, such that women are reduced to those parts; or women are presented being penetrated by objects or animals; or women are presented in scenarios of deg-

---

* *Editor's note:* The first anti-pornography law drafted by Dworkin and MacKinnon was proposed as an amendment to Minneapolis, Minn., Code of Ordinances Relating to Civil Rights tit. 7, chs. 139 & 141. Extensive hearings on the proposed bill, which included testimony from expert witnesses and victims of sexual abuse, were held on December 12 and 13, 1983. The Minneapolis City Council passed the ordinance on December 30, 1983; Mayor Donald Fraser vetoed it on January 5, 1984. The City Council, with several newly elected members, passed a slightly revised form of the bill on July 13, 1984, and Mayor Fraser again vetoed it.

The Indianapolis City Council passed a similar bill on April 23, 1984; it was signed into law by Mayor William H. Hudnut, III. Gen'l Ordinance No. 24 (May 1, 1984) (amending Indianapolis & Marion County, Ind., Code ch. 16). The ordinance was later amended by Gen'l Ordinance No. 35 (June 15, 1984), to bring it into closer conformity with the Minneapolis prototype.

The Indianapolis ordinance was immediately challenged on first amendment grounds by media trade groups with support from civil liberties organizations. On November 19, 1984, Judge Sarah Evans Barker held the ordinance unconstitutional. *See* American Booksellers Ass'n, Inc. v. Hudnut, 598 F. Supp. 1316 (S.D. Ind. 1984), *appeal docketed*, No. 84-3147 (7th Cir. Dec. 21, 1984).

radation, injury, abasement, torture, shown as filthy or inferior, bleeding, bruised, or hurt in a context that makes these conditions sexual.

This statutory definition is an objectively accurate definition of what pornography is, based on an analysis of the material produced by the $8-billion-a-year industry, and also on extensive study of the whole range of pornography extant from other eras and other cultures. Given the fact that women's oppression has an ahistorical character—a sameness across time and cultures expressed in rape, battery, incest, and prostitution—it is no surprise that pornography, a central phenomenon in that oppression, has precisely that quality of sameness. It does not significantly change in what it is, what it does, what is in it, or how it works, whether it is, for instance, classical or feudal or modern, Western or Asian; whether the method of manufacture is words, photographs, or video. What has changed is the public availability of pornography and the numbers of live women used in it because of new technologies: not its nature. Many people note what seems to them a qualitative change in pornography—that it has gotten more violent, even grotesquely violent, over the last two decades. The change is only in what is publicly visible: not in the range or preponderance of violent pornography (*e.g.*, the place of rape in pornography stays constant and central, no matter where, when, or how the pornography is produced); not in the character, quality, or content of what the pornographers actually produce; not in the harm caused; not in the valuation of women in it, or the metaphysical definition of what women are; not in the sexual abuse promoted, including rape, battery, and incest; not in the centrality of its role in subordinating women. Until recently, pornography operated in private, where most abuse of women takes place.

The oppression of women occurs through sexual subordination. It is the use of sex as the medium of oppression that makes the subordination of women so distinct from racism or prejudice against a group based on religion or national origin. Social inequality is created in many different ways. In my view, the radical responsibility is to isolate the material means of creating the inequality so that material remedies can be found for it.

This is particularly difficult with respect to women's inequality because that inequality is achieved through sex. Sex as desired by the class that dominates women is held by that class to be elemental, urgent, necessary, even if or even though it appears to *require* the repudiation of any claim women might have to full human standing. In the subordination of women, inequality itself is sexualized: made into the experience of sexual pleasure, essential to sexual desire. Pornography is the material means of sexualizing inequality; and that is why pornography is a central practice in the subordination of women.

Subordination itself is a broad, deep, systematic dynamic discernible in any persecution based on race or sex. Social subordination has four main parts. First, there is *hierarchy*, a group on top and a group on the bottom. For women, this hierarchy is experienced both socially and sexually, publicly and privately. Women are physically integrated into the society in which we are held to be inferior, and our low status is both put in place and maintained in the sexual usage of us by men; and so women's experience of hierarchy is incredibly intimate and wounding.

Second, subordination is *objectification*. Objectification occurs when a human being, through social means, is made less than human, turned into a thing or commodity, bought and sold. When objectification occurs, a person is depersonalized, so that no individuality or integrity is available socially or in what is an extremely circumscribed privacy (because those who dominate determine its boundaries). Objectification is an injury right at the heart of discrimination: those who can be used as if they are not fully human are no longer fully human in social terms; their humanity is hurt by being diminished.

Third, subordination is *submission*. A person is at the bottom of a hierarchy because of a condition of birth; a person on the bottom is dehumanized, an object or commodity; inevitably, the situation of that person requires obedience and compliance. That diminished person is expected to be submissive; there is no longer any right to self-determination, because there is no basis in equality for any such right to exist. In a condition of inferiority and objectification, submission is usually essential for survival. Oppressed groups are known for their abilities to anticipate the orders and desires of those who have power over them, to comply with an obsequiousness that is then used by the dominant group to justify its own dominance: the master, not able to imagine a human like himself in such degrading servility, thinks the servility is proof that the hierarchy is natural and that the objectification simply amounts to seeing these lesser creatures for what they are. The submission forced on inferior, objectified groups precisely by hierarchy and objectification is taken to be the proof of inherent inferiority and subhuman capacities.

Fourth, subordination is *violence*. The violence is systematic, endemic enough to be unremarkable and normative, usually taken as an implicit right of the one committing the violence. In my view, hierarchy, objectification, and submission are the preconditions for systematic social violence against any group targeted because of a condition of birth. If violence against a group is both socially pervasive and socially normal, then hierarchy, objectification, and submission are already solidly in place.

The role of violence in subordinating women has one special characteristic congruent with sex as the instrumentality of subordination: the violence is supposed to be sex for the woman too—what women want and like as part of our sexual nature; it is supposed to give women pleasure (as in rape); it is supposed to mean love to a woman from her point of view (as in battery). The violence against women is seen to be done not just in accord with something compliant in women, but in response to something active in and basic to women's nature.

Pornography uses each component of social subordination. Its particular medium is sex. Hierarchy, objectification, submission, and violence all become alive with sexual energy and sexual meaning. A hierarchy, for instance, can have a static quality; but pornography, by sexualizing it, makes it dynamic, almost carnivorous, so that men keep imposing it for the sake of their own sexual pleasure—for the sexual pleasure it gives them to impose it. In pornography, each element of subordination is conveyed through the sexually explicit usage of women: pornography in fact is what women are and what women are for and how women are used in a society premised on the inferiority of women. It is a metaphysics of women's subjugation: our existence delineated in a definition of our nature; our status in society predetermined by the uses to which we are put. The woman's body is what is materially subordinated. Sex is the material means through which the subordination is accomplished. Pornography is the institution of male dominance that sexualizes hierarchy, objectification, submission, and violence. As such, pornography creates inequality, not as artifact but as a system of social reality; it creates the necessity for and the actual behaviors that constitute sex inequality.

VI. SPEECH

Subordination can be so deep that those who are hurt by it are utterly silent. Subordination can create a silence quieter than death. The women flattened out on the page are deathly still, except for *hurt me*. *Hurt me* is not women's speech. It is the speech imposed on women by pimps to cover the awful, condemning silence. The Three Marias of Portugal went to jail for writing this: "Let no one tell me that silence gives consent, because whoever is silent dissents."[8] The women say the pimp's words: the language is another element of the rape; the language is part of the humiliation; the language is part of the forced sex. Real silence might signify dissent, for those reared to understand its sad discourse. The pimps cannot tolerate literal silence—it is too eloquent as testimony—so they force the words out of the woman's mouth. The women say pimp's words: which is worse than silence. The silence of the women not in the picture, outside the pages, hurt but silent, used but silent, is staggering in how deep and wide it goes. It is a silence over centuries: an exile into speechlessness. One is shut up by the inferiority and the abuse. One is shut up by the threat and the injury. In her memoir of the Stalin period, *Hope Against Hope*, Nadezha Mandelstam wrote that screaming

> is a man's way of leaving a trace, of telling people how he lived and died. By his screams he asserts his right to live, sends a message to the outside world demanding help and calling for resistance. If nothing else is left, one must scream. Silence is the real crime against humanity.[9]

Screaming is a man's way of leaving a trace. The scream of a man is never misunderstood as a scream of pleasure by passers-

[8] M.I. Barreno, M.T. Horta & M. Velho da Costa, The Three Marias: New Portuguese Letters 291 (H.R. Lane trans. 1976).

[9] N. Mandelstam, Hope Against Hope 42–43 (M. Hayward trans. 1978).

by or politicians or historians, nor by the tormentor. A man's scream is a call for resistance. A man's scream asserts his right to live, sends a message; he leaves a trace. A woman's scream is the sound of her female will and her female pleasure in doing what the pornographers say she is for. Her scream is a sound of celebration to those who overhear. Women's way of leaving a trace is the silence, centuries' worth: the entirely inhuman silence that surely one day will be noticed, someone will say that something is wrong, some sound is missing, some voice is lost; the entirely inhuman silence that will be a clue to human hope denied, a shard of evidence that a crime has occurred, the crime that created the silence; the entirely inhuman silence that is a cold, cold condemnation of hurt sustained in speechlessness, a cold, cold condemnation of what those who speak have done to those who do not.

But there is more than the *hurt me* forced out of us, and the silence in which it lies. The pornographers actually use our bodies as their language. Our bodies are the building blocks of their sentences. What they do to us, called speech, is not unlike what Kafka's Harrow machine—"'The needles are set in like the teeth of a harrow and the whole thing works something like a harrow, although its action is limited to one place and contrived with much more artistic skill'"[10]—did to the condemned in *In the Penal Colony*:

> "Our sentence does not sound severe. Whatever commandment the prisoner has disobeyed is written upon his body by the Harrow. This prisoner, for instance"—the officer indicated the man—"will have written on his body: HONOR THY SUPERIORS!"[11]
>
> . . .
>
> ". . . The Harrow is beginning to write; when it finishes the first draft of the inscription on the man's back, the layer of cotton wool begins to roll and slowly turns the body over, to give the Harrow fresh space for writing . . . . So it keeps on writing deeper and deeper . . . ."[12]

---

[10] F. Kafka, *In the Penal Colony*, in The Penal Colony 194 (W. Muir & E. Muir trans. 1965).

[11] *Id.* at 197.

[12] *Id.* at 203.

Asked if the prisoner knows his sentence, the officer replies: "'There would be no point in telling him. He'll learn it on his body.'"[13]

This is the so-called speech of the pornographers, protected now by law.

Protecting what they "say" means protecting what they do to us, how they do it. It means protecting their sadism on our bodies, because that is how they write: not like a writer at all; like a torturer. Protecting what they "say" means protecting sexual exploitation, because they cannot "say" anything without diminishing, hurting, or destroying us. Their rights of speech express their rights over us. Their rights of speech require our inferiority: and that we be powerless in relation to them. Their rights of speech mean that *hurt me* is accepted as the real speech of women, not speech forced on us as part of the sex forced on us but originating with us because we are what the pornographers "say" we are.

If what we want to say is not *hurt me*, we have the real social power only to use silence as eloquent dissent. Silence is what women have instead of speech. Silence is our dissent during rape unless the rapist, like the pornographer, prefers *hurt me*, in which case we have no dissent. Silence is our moving, persuasive dissent during battery unless the batterer, like the pornographer, prefers *hurt me*. Silence is a fine dissent during incest and for all the long years after.

Silence is not speech. We have silence, not speech. We fight rape, battery, incest, and prostitution with it. We lose. But someday someone will notice: that people called women were buried in a long silence that meant dissent and that the pornographers—with needles set in like the teeth of a harrow—chattered on.

VII. EQUALITY

To get that word, male, out of the Constitution, cost the women of this country fifty-two years of pauseless campaign; 56 state referendum campaigns; 480 legislative campaigns to get state

[13] *Id.* at 197.

suffrage amendments submitted; 47 state constitutional convention campaigns; 277 state party convention campaigns; 30 national party convention campaigns to get suffrage planks in the party platforms; 19 campaigns with 19 successive Congresses to get the federal amendment submitted, and the final ratification campaign.

Millions of dollars were raised, mostly in small sums, and spent with economic care. Hundreds of women gave the accumulated possibilities of an entire lifetime, thousands gave years of their lives, hundreds of thousands gave constant interest and such aid as they could. It was a continuous and seemingly endless chain of activity. Young suffragists who helped forge the last links of that chain were not born when it began. Old suffragists who helped forge the first links were dead when it ended.

—CARRIE CHAPMAN CATT

Feminists have wanted equality. Radicals and reformists have different ideas of what equality would be, but it has been the wisdom of feminism to value equality as a political goal with social integrity and complex meaning. The Jacobins also wanted equality, and the French Revolution was fought to accomplish it. Conservatism as a modern political movement actually developed to resist social and political movements for equality, beginning with the egalitarian imperatives of the French Revolution.

Women have had to prove human status, before having any claim to equality. But equality has been impossible to achieve, perhaps because, really, women have not been able to prove human status. The burden of proof is on the victim.

Not one inch of change has been easy or cheap. We have fought so hard and so long for so little. The vote did not change the status of women. The changes in women's lives that we can see on the surface do not change the status of women. By the year 2000, women are expected to be one hundred percent of this nation's poor.* We are raped, battered, and prostituted: these acts against us are in the fabric of social life. As children, we are

* For a comprehensive analysis of how the feminization of poverty brutally impacts on people of color in the United States, see *The Coming Gynocide*, in A. DWORKIN, RIGHT-WING WOMEN 147, 162–73 (1983).

raped, physically abused, and prostituted. The country enjoys the injuries done to us, and spends $8 billion a year on the pleasure of watching us being hurt (exploitation as well as torture constituting substantive harm). The subordination gets deeper: we keep getting pushed down further. Rape is an entertainment. The contempt for us in that fact is immeasurable: yet we live under the weight of it. Discrimination is a euphemism for what happens to us.

It has plagued us to try to understand why the status of women does not change. Those who hate the politics of equality say they know: we are biologically destined for rape; God made us to be submissive unto our husbands. We change, but our status does not change. Laws change, but our status stays fixed. We move into the marketplace, only to face there classic sexual exploitation, now called sexual harassment. Rape, battery, prostitution, and incest stay the same in that they keep happening to us as part of what life is: even though we name the crimes against us as such and try to keep the victims from being destroyed by what we cannot stop from happening to them. And the silence stays in place too, however much we try to dislodge it with our truths. We say what has happened to us, but newspapers, governments, the culture that excludes us as fully human participants, wipe us out, wipe out our speech: by refusing to hear it. We are the tree falling in the desert. Should it matter: they are the desert.

The cost of trying to shatter the silence is astonishing to those who do it: the women, raped, battered, prostituted, who have something to say and say it. They stand there, even as they are erased. Governments turn from them; courts ignore them; this country disavows and dispossesses them. Men ridicule, threaten, or hurt them. Women jeopardized by them—silence being safer than speech—betray them. It is ugly to watch the complacent destroy the brave. It is horrible to watch power win.

Still, equality is what we want, and we are going to get it. What we understand about it now is that it cannot be proclaimed; it must be created. It has to take the place of subordination in human experience: physically replace it. Equality does not co-exist with subordination, as if it were a little pocket located somewhere within it. Equality has to win. Subordination has to lose. The subordination of women has not even been knocked loose, and equality has not materially advanced, at least in part because the pornography has been creating sexualized inequality in hiding, in private, where the abuses occur on a massive scale.

Equality for women requires material remedies for pornography, whether pornography is central to the inequality of women or only one cause of it. Pornography's antagonism to civil equality, integrity, and self-determination for women is absolute; and it is effective in making that antagonism socially real and socially determining.

The law that Catharine A. MacKinnon and I wrote making pornography a violation of women's civil rights recognizes the injury that pornography does: how it hurts women's rights of citizenship through sexual exploitation and sexual torture both.

The civil rights law empowers women by allowing women to civilly sue those who hurt us through pornography by trafficking in it, coercing people into it, forcing it on people, and assaulting people directly because of a specific piece of it.

The civil rights law does not force the pornography back underground. There is no prior restraint or police power to make arrests, which would then result in a revivified black market. This respects the reach of the first amendment, but it also keeps the pornography from getting sexier—hidden, forbidden, dirty, happily back in the land of the obscene, sexy slime oozing on great books. Wanting to cover the pornography up, hide it, is the first response of those who need pornography to the civil rights law. If pornography is hidden, it is still accessible to men as a male right of access to women; its injuries to the status of women are safe and secure in those hidden rooms, behind those opaque covers; the abuses of women are sustained as a private right supported by public policy. The civil rights law puts a flood of light on the pornography, what it is, how it is used, what it does, those who are hurt by it.

The civil rights law changes the power relationship between pornographers and women: it stops the pornographers from producing discrimination with the total impunity they now enjoy, and gives women a legal standing resembling equality from which to repudiate the subordination itself. The secret-police power of the pornographers suddenly has to confront a modest amount of due process.

The civil rights law undermines the subordination of women in society by confronting the pornography, which is the systematic sexualization of that subordination. Pornography is inequality. The civil rights law would allow women to advance equality by removing this concrete discrimination and hurting economically those who make, sell, distribute, or exhibit it. The pornography, being power, has a right to exist that we are not allowed to challenge under this system of law. After it hurts us by being what it is and doing what it does, the civil rights law would allow us to hurt it back. Women, not being power, do not have a right to exist equal to the right the pornography has. If we did, the pornographers would be precluded from exercising their rights at the expense of ours, and since they cannot exercise them any other way, they would be precluded period. We come to the legal system beggars: though in the public dialogue around the passage of this civil rights law we have the satisfaction of being regarded as thieves.

The civil rights law is women's speech. It defines an injury to us from our point of view. It is premised on a repudiation of sexual subordination which is born of our experience of it. It breaks the silence. It is a sentence that can hold its own against the male flood. It is a sentence on which we can build a paragraph, then a page.

It is my view, learned largely from Catharine MacKinnon, that women have a right to be effective. The pornographers, of course, do not think so, nor do other male supremacists; and it is hard for women to think so. We have been told to educate people on the evils of pornography: before the development of this civil rights law, we were told just to keep quiet about pornography altogether; but now that we have a law we want to use, we are encouraged to educate and stop there. Law educates. This law educates. It also allows women to *do* something. In hurting the pornography back, we gain ground in making equality more likely, more possible—someday it will be real. We have a means to fight the pornographers' trade in women. We have a means to get at the torture and the terror. We have a means with which to challenge the pornography's efficacy in making exploitation and inferiority the bedrock of women's social status. The civil rights law introduces into the public consciousness an analysis: of what pornography is, what sexual subordination is, what equality might be. The civil rights law introduces a new legal standard: these things are not done to citizens of this country. The civil rights law introduces a new political standard: these things are not done to human beings. The civil rights law provides a new mode of action for women through which we can pursue equality and because of which *our* speech will have social meaning. The civil rights law gives us back what the pornographers have taken from us: hope rooted in real possibility.

APPENDIX A
MODEL ANTI-PORNOGRAPHY LAW

Section 1. STATEMENT OF POLICY

Pornography is sex discrimination. It exists in [PLACE], posing a substantial threat to the health, safety, peace, welfare, and equality of citizens in the community. Existing [state and] federal laws are inadequate to solve these problems in [PLACE].

Pornography is a systematic practice of exploitation and subordination based on sex that differentially harms women. The harm of pornography includes dehumanization, sexual exploitation, forced sex, forced prostitution, physical injury, and social and sexual terrorism and inferiority presented as entertainment. The bigotry and contempt it promotes, with the acts of aggression it fosters, diminish opportunities for equality of rights in employment, education, property, public accommodations and public services; create public and private harassment, persecution and denigration; promote injury and degradation such as rape, battery, child sexual abuse, and prostitution and inhibit just enforcement of laws against these acts; contribute significantly to restricting women in particular from full exercise of citizenship and participation in public life, including in neighborhoods; damage relations between the sexes; and undermine women's equal exercise of rights to speech and action guaranteed to all citizens under the Constitutions and laws of the United States and [PLACE, INCLUDING STATE].

Section 2. DEFINITIONS

1. *Pornography* is the graphic sexually explicit subordination of women through pictures and/or words that also includes one or more of the following: (i) women are presented dehumanized as sexual objects, things, or commodities; or (ii) women are presented as sexual objects who enjoy pain or humiliation; or (iii) women are presented as sexual objects who experience sexual pleasure in being raped; or (iv) women are presented as sexual objects tied up or cut up or mutilated or bruised or physically hurt; or (v) women are presented in postures or positions of sexual submission, servility, or display; or (vi) women's body parts—including but not limited to vaginas, breasts, or buttocks—are exhibited such that women are reduced to those parts; or (vii) women are presented as whores by nature; or (viii) women are presented being penetrated by objects or animals; or (ix) women are presented in scenarios of degradation, injury, torture, shown as filthy or inferior, bleeding, bruised, or hurt in a context that makes these conditions sexual.

2. The use of men, children, or transsexuals in the place of women in (1) above is pornography for purposes of this law.

Section 3. UNLAWFUL PRACTICES

1. *Coercion into pornography*: It shall be sex discrimination to coerce, intimidate, or fraudulently induce (hereafter, "coerce") any person, including transsexual, into performing for pornography, which injury may date from any appearance or sale of any product(s) of such performance(s). The maker(s), seller(s), exhibitor(s), and/or distributor(s) of said pornography may be sued for damages and for an injunction, including to eliminate the product(s) of the performance(s) from the public view.

Proof of one or more of the following facts or conditions shall not, without more, negate a finding of coercion: (i) that the person is a woman; or (ii) that the person is or has been a prostitute; or (iii) that the person has attained the age of majority; or (iv) that the person is connected by blood or marriage to anyone involved in or related to the making of the pornography; or (v) that the person has previously had, or been thought to have had, sexual relations with anyone, including anyone involved in or related to the making of the pornography; or (vi) that the person has previously posed for sexually explicit pictures with or for anyone, including anyone involved in or related to the making of the pornography at issue; or (vii) that anyone else, including a spouse or other relative, has given permission on the person's behalf; or (viii) that the person actually consented to a use of the performance that is changed into pornography; or (ix) that the person knew that the purpose of the acts or events in question was to make pornography; or (x) that the person showed no resistance or appeared to cooperate actively in the photographic sessions or in the events that produced the pornography; or (xi) that the person signed a contract, or made statements affirming a willingness to cooperate in the production of pornography; or (xii) that no physical force, threats, or weapons were used in the making of the pornography; or (xiii) that the person was paid or otherwise compensated.

2. *Trafficking in pornography*: It shall be sex discrimination to produce, sell, exhibit, or distribute pornography, including through private clubs.

(i) City, state, and federally funded public libraries or private and public university and college libraries in which pornography is available for study, including on open shelves but excluding special display presentations, shall not be construed to be trafficking in pornography.

(ii) Isolated passages or isolated parts shall not be actionable under this section.

(iii) Any woman has a claim hereunder as a woman acting against the subordination of women. Any man, child, or transsexual who alleges injury by pornography in the way women are injured by it also has a claim.

3. *Forcing pornography on a person*: It shall be sex discrimination to force pornography on a person, including a child or transsexual, in any place of employment, education, home, or public place. Only the perpetrator of the force or responsible institution may be sued.

4. *Assault of physical attack due to pornography*: It shall be sex discrimination to assault, physically attack, or injure any person, including child or transsexual, in a way that is directly caused by specific pornography. The perpetrator of the assault or attack may be sued for damages and enjoined where appropriate. The maker(s), distributor(s), seller(s), and/or exhibitor(s)

may also be sued for damages and for an injunction against the specific pornography's further exhibition, distribution, or sale.

Section 4. DEFENSES

1. It shall not be a defense that the defendant in an action under this law did not know or intend that the materials were pornography or sex discrimination.

2. No damages or compensation for losses shall be recoverable under Sec. 3(2) or other than against the perpetrator of the assault or attack in Sec. 3(4) unless the defendant knew or had reason to know that the materials were pornography.

3. In actions under Sec. 3(2) or other than against the perpetrator of the assault or attack in Sec. 3(4), no damages or compensation for losses shall be recoverable against maker(s) for pornography made, against distributor(s) for pornography distributed, against seller(s) for pornography sold, or against exhibitor(s) for pornography exhibited, prior to the effective date of this law.

Section 5. ENFORCEMENT*

1. *Civil action*: Any person aggrieved by violations of this law may enforce its provisions by means of a civil action. No criminal penalties shall attach for any violation of the provisions of this law. Relief for violation of this act may include reasonable attorney's fees.

2. *Injunction*: Any person who violates this law may be enjoined except that:

(i) In actions under Sec. 3(2), and other than against the perpetrator of the assault or attack under Sec. 3(4), no temporary or permanent injunction shall issue prior to a final judicial determination that the challenged activities constitute a violation of this law.

(ii) No temporary or permanent injunction shall extend beyond such material(s) that, having been described with reasonable

* In the event that this law is amended to a preexisting human-rights law, the complaint would first be made to a Civil Rights Commission. Any injunction issued under Sec. 3(2), the trafficking provision, would require trial *de novo* (a full court trial after the administrative hearing).

specificity by the injunction, have been determined to be validly proscribed under this law.

Section 6. SEVERABILITY

Should any part(s) of this law be found legally invalid, the remaining part(s) remains valid. A judicial declaration that any part(s) of this law cannot be applied validly in a particular manner or to a particular case or category of cases shall not affect the validity of that part(s) as otherwise applied, unless such other application would clearly frustrate the [LEGISLATIVE BODY'S] intent in adopting this law.

Section 7. LIMITATION OF ACTION

Actions under this law must be filed within one year of the alleged discriminatory acts.

APPENDIX B
SELECTED BIBLIOGRAPHY

Able-Peterson, Trudee. Children of the Evening (1981).
Armstrong, Louise. Kiss Daddy Goodnight (1982).
Barry, Kathleen. Female Sexual Slavery (1981).
Blakely, Mary Kay. *Who Were the Men?*, Ms. (July 1983).
Bogdanovitch, Peter. The Killing of the Unicorn: Dorothy Stratton, 1960–1980 (1984).
Brady, Katherine. Father's Days: A True Story of Incest (1981).
Brownmiller, Susan. Against Our Will: Men, Women, and Rape (1976).
Daly, Mary. Gyn/Ecology (1979).
Dworkin, Andrea. *The Root Cause*, in Our Blood: Prophecies and Discourses on Sexual Politics (1976).
———. Pornography: Men Possessing Women (1981).
———. Woman Hating (1974).
Griffin, Susan. Pornography and Silence (1981).
Hite, Shere. The Hite Report on Male Sexuality (1982).
Lederer, Laura, ed. Take Back the Night (1980).
Linden, Robin Ruth, et al., eds. Against Sadomasochism (1981).
Lovelace, Linda with Mike McGrady. Ordeal (1983).

MacKinnon, Catharine. Sexual Harassment of Working Women (1979).

Morgan, Robin. *The Stake in the Heart*, in The Anatomy of Freedom (1984).

Steinem, Gloria. *Erotica vs. Pornography*, in Outrageous Acts and Everyday Rebellions (1983).

———. *I Was a Playboy Bunny, id.*

———. *The Real Linda Lovelace, id.*

[13]

Theory into Practice? Pornography and the Public/Private Dichotomy

NICOLA LACEY *

'The feminist total critique of the liberal opposition of private and public still awaits its philosopher'.[1] So concluded Carole Pateman in an important article written a decade ago. During the intervening years, there has been an explosion of feminist literature reflecting upon issues raised by public/private dichotomies in social and political thought, much of it concerned with legal analysis or questions of legal policy and reform. Yet, notwithstanding this theoretical development, questions around public/private dichotomies have lost little of their power to bewilder, as each confidently asserted critique raises further questions of theory and strategy. Indeed, it sometimes seems that the more we criticize the public/private dichotomy, the more we get trapped within its conceptual framework.

In this paper, I want to return to this well-worked terrain with two purposes in mind. First, I want to distinguish several different concerns which have informed feminist preoccupation with the public/private dichotomy. Drawing on feminist political and social theory, I shall explore how each of the different concerns I identify feeds into questions of legal policy. Secondly, I shall turn my attention to one concrete area, namely pornography, in which feminist activism – including that directed to law reform – has been informed by the public/private critique. Pornography is an issue which, perhaps above all others, has been controversial *within* feminist thought, and in which issues of theory and strategy connect particularly closely. I hope to shed some light on why the pornography debate has been such a problematic one for contemporary feminism by looking at it again in the light of a more differentiated appreciation of the public/private critique. In particular, I shall try to identify the negative consequences which unjustified inferences from the public/private critique have had on feminist politics around pornography.

DISENTANGLING PUBLIC/PRIVATE DICHOTOMIES

The idea that 'the personal is political' has been a central tenet of the

**Fellow in Law, New College, Oxford OX1 3BN, England*

I would like to thank Susanne Baer, Joanne Conaghan, and Katherine O'Donovan for giving me useful comments on an earlier draft of this paper.

contemporary women's movement, though its precise meaning is less than clear. At its broadest, the idea has issued in a thorough-going reassessment of the traditional conception of what is properly within the realm of public debate and critique, by unearthing and making visible issues of gender which have been ignored in political theory and practice. One particular theoretical ploy has been to focus on a supposed liberal division of the world into public and private spheres: a strictly limited public sphere is appropriate for the enforcement of justice, whilst the state leaves relations and distributions in the private sphere untouched.[2] But though the idea of privacy as an essential constituent of individual autonomy has been central to the liberal tradition, public/private divisions are not confined to liberal or libertarian thought. The delineation of a 'private' sphere beyond the scope of politics is a feature of Marxist thought too: the sphere of reproduction within the family does not form the object of revolutionary critique or practice except in specifically feminist versions of Marxist theory.[3] Feminists have pointed out that, since women's lives have in many societies been lived to a greater extent than men's within the so-called private sphere, the implication of the public/private division has meant that fundamental sources of women's oppression politically invisible and hence ignored. But both the arguments on which the feminist critique focuses and the critique itself have been obscured by the difficulty of identifying precisely what is meant by the public/private divide. In what follows, therefore, I shall try to distinguish between a number of different issues which are relevant to the debate.

1. Public and Private Spheres: Normative and Descriptive Arguments

The claim most commonly associated with public/private ideology, that the world divides into public and private *spheres*, presents two immediate questions. First, what are these spheres – what do public and private denote in this context? Secondly, is this a descriptive or a normative claim? I shall look at each in turn.

As far as the identification of public and private spheres is concerned, two basic accounts have been influential. In the first, the division is between the state and civil society. Particularly in nineteenth-century *laissez-faire* versions of liberalism, a central idea was that the role of the state should be strictly limited, with the market governing relations other than family relations in civil society. The continuing influence of such ideas is reflected in the ideology of recent governments in the United Kingdom and the United States of America. In the second account, the division is between the state and/or the market on the one hand and the family on the other. The family is constructed as the quintessentially private sphere in which human relations must be allowed to develop away from the scrutiny let alone intervention of state or market institutions. In each case, the ideas of 'public' and 'private' roughly correspond to 'regulated' and 'unregulated', and the claim is offered variously as descriptive and as normative. On one level, the idea of a division between state and civil society or between the market or state and the family is offered as a characterization of the world. At another, it is connected with substantive political arguments about the appropriateness of regulation in the relevant areas.[4] Clearly, this means that we need to assess the various kinds of public/private sphere claims in terms of different criteria.

First, let us examine the descriptive version of the public/private dichotomy. To what extent is it sensible to see our social world as divided into spheres corresponding to state/civil society, market/family? Obviously, these categories have a certain degree of institutional validity. But, at the level of political and sociological analysis, taking these categories as a starting-point would be very crude. 'The' state consists of many interlocking institutions and practices, as does 'the' market; 'families' can be defined in different ways and come in a variety of forms. Nor does this three-tier institutional characterization seem an adequate starting-point for social theory. For modern capitalist societies also develop a 'public sphere' or set of 'publics' which constitute not only the state or state institutions but also non-state fora for public, political debate – social movements, trades unions, pressure groups and so on.[5] Here, too, politics, in the broad sense of 'the critical activity of raising issues and deciding how institutional and social relations should be organized',[6] goes on.

What of the specific attempt to understand social institutions as public or private in the sense of their being (at least predominantly) regulated or unregulated by state power? Historically, it could fairly be said that in, for example, mid-nineteenth century Britain the operation of the market and contractual relations were relatively unregulated by the state, or that in mid-twentieth-century Britain legal regulation was not applied to some significant aspects of family life and relations. But we are talking here of *relativities* rather than clear divisions. Indeed, the very institution of contract law always, in some sense, regulates market transactions, even though the degree to which the state controls the terms on which parties may contract with each other has steadily increased. Similarly, in spite of a great deal of rhetoric about privacy in the family sphere, a moment's thought reveals that many aspects of family life are hedged around with legal regulation – marriage, divorce, child custody, social welfare rules, to name but the most obviously relevant areas of law. Moreover, it would be wrong to see direct *legal* regulation as the touchstone for state involvement. In all sorts of indirect ways – economic, administrative, and political – state institutions have a crucial and often deliberate impact on the conduct of family life.[7] Indeed, it might be argued that in late twentieth-century Britain we have seen an increasing willingness to regulate the family, whilst *laissez-faire* attitudes to the market (not always realized in political practice as opposed to rhetoric) have experienced a revival. As for the non-state 'publics' referred to above, the question of regulation or non-regulation seems inappropriate, yet their importance to the conduct of social life further blurs any supposed division between public and private spheres. We may be able to make relative judgements, and draw crude distinctions between family, market, and state at an institutional level. But the search for the public/private division in terms of the presence or absence of state-directed or state-sponsored regulation is as hopeless as the analysis of society merely in terms of state, market, and family is inadequate.

This conclusion becomes even clearer when we take into account the difficulty in attaching any general significance to a distinction between regulation and non-regulation, or between intervention and abstention. In any given case it can be unclear analytically whether to characterize the state's position as one of regulation or non-regulation.[8] For example, the exemption of married men from charges of rape of their wives which persists in many jurisdictions is generally seen in terms of non-regulation. Yet it discloses a certain view of the marriage relationship which is positively inscribed in law. In such cases, abstention amounts to a form of regulation. And even where a regulation/non-regulation distinction can be drawn analytically, its significance is called into question by the fact that decisions *not* to regulate made by state or other institutions with the power to do so are every bit as much *political* decisions as are decisions to regulate. Clearly, both within and beyond liberal theory, the shape of arguments for regulation and non-regulation cannot be taken to be identical. But the strong liberal presumption in favour of non-regulation which proceeds from the commitment of some of the most influential versions of modern liberalism to a *negative* conception of freedom – freedom as the absence of constraint – has obscured the way in which state decisions not to regulate are themselves political and call for justification.[9]

Another problematic feature of the characterization of family or civil society as private in the sense of unregulated has to do with what such a characterization presupposes about the regulator. This is generally conceived in simple terms as 'the state'. But, as I have already observed, the state is not monolithic; it is rather a set of diverse institutions. This gives rise to further complexities in identifying regulation or non-regulation. What are we to say of issues such as wife-battering – always 'regulated' in the sense of being within the purview of criminal law, but frequently 'unregulated' because of the decisions of law enforcement agencies? The picture is fragmented, even leaving aside the operation of powerful regulation which cannot be identified with 'the state'. Once we incorporate non-state power, and acknowledge the difficulty of distinguishing between state and non-state bodies in a world where 'public' and 'private' power are inextricably linked with each other, the picture threatens to disintegrate.[10] The very idea of power as something which is deliberately exercised by identifiable agents, as opposed to, or at least also, subsisting in discourses and practices spreading throughout the social body – including those other 'publics' ignored by the traditional public/private distinction – misses important aspects of how subjects' positions are constituted and maintained in the social world.[11] Finally, the descriptive association of women with 'the private sphere', particularly in the sense of the family, is itself problematic. For whilst it is both true and highly significant that women still bear a disproportionate responsibility for domestic labour, the converse suggestion that women have lived their lives exclusively or even mainly in the private sphere of the family is quite unsustainable. Working-class women in particular have worked outside the home to a far greater degree than the public/private critique has tended to acknowledge. At a descriptive level, the idea of a private, unregulated family simply collapses when subjected to scrutiny.

Now let us move from the descriptive to the normative. The idea that the state's use of coercive force to curtail citizens' behaviour calls for special justification lies at the heart of liberal political philosophy. In Mill's famous formulation, the only justification for state intervention to curtail individual freedom lies in the prevention of harm to others.[12] Individual freedom is the paramount liberal value. State power threatens that freedom in a peculiarly dangerous way, and must be strictly limited. Leaving aside for the moment Mill's unitary conception of state power, the implications of his argument depend on how freedom is conceived. To the extent that we recognize that genuine freedom depends not only on being left alone – not interfered with, regulated, or scrutinized – but also on being provided with certain positive goods and facilities, we will be alert to the freedom-enhancing as well as the freedom-threatening potential of state or state-sponsored action. This, certainly, was a position to which Mill was sympathetic, and it has come to be known as the idea of *positive freedom*. However, in modern debates about the proper limits of state action, the tendency has been to focus on *negative freedom* – freedom as being left in peace.[13] On this view, a conceptually neat and rhetorically powerful way of realizing the argument for human freedom is in terms of the delineation of a 'private sphere' – famously described in the Wolfenden Report as that which is 'in brief and crude terms, not the law's business'.[14] The central thrust of feminist critique has borne upon this normative interpretation of liberal theory. For, it has been argued, the practical consequence of non-regulation is the consolidation of the *status quo*: the *de facto* support of pre-existing power relations and distributions of goods within the 'private' sphere. In effect, if not explicitly, much of the feminist critique espouses a positive conception of freedom. It exposes the way in which the ideology of the public/private dichotomy allows government to clean its hands of any *responsibility* for the state of the 'private' world and *depoliticizes* the disadvantages which inevitably spill over the alleged divide by affecting the position of the 'privately' disadvantaged in the 'public' world.

The feminist critique, then, is a direct attack on the idea of public and private spheres, which it sees as a politically and ethically inadequate realization of liberal arguments about individual freedom and the proper role of the state. The attack consists in both a normative argument about positive freedom and an analytical argument about the interdependence of regulated and unregulated spheres. Liberal theory which depends on the public/private distinction is self-defeating in that the guarantees of justice and equality held out to citizens in the 'public' sphere are worth systematically less to those who are pre-politically disadvantaged. The limits of the scope of politics and justice asserted by liberals such as Rawls, in other words, are inconsistent with the realization of the general values which they claim to espouse.[15] Also notable from a critical point of view is a tendency to couch the normative argument in superficially descriptive terms, in a way which is at once intellectually indefensible and rhetorically powerful. As we saw above, the project of delineating public and private spheres at a descriptive level is fraught with difficulty. Yet the substantively normative argument often proceeds by simply announcing a particular issue to fall 'within the private sphere' and 'hence' to be inappropriate for regulation. The statement of the Wolfenden Committee quoted above is an excellent example: the labels 'public' and 'private' are used in question-begging ways which *suppress* the normative arguments which they actually presuppose so that the debate sounds common-sensical rather than politically controversial. One of the main successes of feminist critique has been to expose the *politics* – the 'power-laden' character[16] – of 'privatization' of this kind. It ought to go without saying that this repoliticization of attributions of 'privacy' is quite different from an argument for the propriety let alone the efficacy of state regulation: to say that what has been thought of as private is within the scope of political *critique* is not to say that it must necessarily be *regulated*. Unfortunately, as we shall see, this crucial distinction has not always been observed.

2. Public and Private Values

At an explicit level, most of the debate around public/private dichotomies has centred on the idea of public and private spheres. But just below the surface has been another equally important set of ideas to do with the place of the public/private opposition within a set of dichotomies which structure Western thought. Other dualisms include objectivity and subjectivity, reason and passion, self and other, culture and nature, and, crucially for feminist thinking, male and female. Many feminist theorists have argued that the male/female opposition maps onto these other dichotomies, identifying, for example, femaleness with emotion, passivity, subjectivity, nature; male with reason, objectivity, activity, culture.[17] They have also observed that in Western culture one half of each pair is valued above the other, and that the halves with which women and femaleness are associated are the less valued. This kind of analysis in turn maps onto the public/private dichotomy. For, it is argued, what we need to focus on is not so much empirical (and highly problematic) claims about women's lives being lived disproportionately in the private sphere but rather *cultural associations* between femaleness, the private and under-recognized values and attributes. On this view, the importance of the public/private dichotomy lies in the fact that the cultural construction of the public sphere as the sphere in which universal reason holds sway implicitly marginalizes or is inhospitable to women, because reason and hence the public, are culturally associated with the masculine, whereas the private, conversely, is associated with the feminine – with particularity, emotion, the body, *otherness*. The task of feminist critique, then, is to expose the gendered nature of the concepts in terms of which our notions of 'the public sphere' are constructed, and to offer alternative conceptions which would render the 'public' genuinely accessible not just to women as well as men, but also to all those whose 'particularity' currently marks them as 'different' and hence as excluded from the unity of the public.[18]

Another aspect of this feminist argument relates to the very nature of public/private and the other dualisms as *dichotomies*. Here feminist thought participates in a broad project of exposing and challenging ways in which our thinking is structured around pairs of ideas which are opposed in the sense that the attribution of one excludes the other: that which is public cannot be private; that which is male cannot be female, and so on. By showing how each side of each dualism depends on the other for its own meaning – subjectivity can only be understood by differentiating itself from objectivity, maleness takes its meaning from femaleness, and so on – this 'deconstruction' shows how the less valued half acts as a 'dangerous supplement' to the other. Each member of the pair refers to the other at the same time as it suppresses it. Thus, the self-sufficiency of the more powerful side of the dichotomy is fragile, being undermined in the very moment in which it is expressed. This kind of deconstruction proceeds on the assumption that we need to erode the power of hierarchically ordered dichotomies as part of a liberating political programme. For the fact that one side of the dualisms has cultural status helps to invest people related to those attributes or values with greater power. Hierarchically dichotomized thinking operates by way of suppressing the implied reference to the 'other'; by marginalizing that 'other', it forms an important part of the politics of the powerful as realized through language.

As always, it is easier to identify the problem here than to find a way of resolving it. Some deconstructionists affirm the inevitability of working *within* the dichotomies: since they are part of our cultural and linguistic heritage, they cannot be left behind by an act of political will. There must therefore be a phase – for some deconstructionists it is a phase which will never end – in which we work to unearth the 'dangerous supplement', to effect a revaluation of that which has been suppressed.[19] Since gender neutrality is unrealizable, the only possible immediate goal is to attack gender hierarchy – to expose the contingency (and hence the *politics*) of the current cultural hierarchy. This is disappointing, for to the extent that we stay within the dichotomized categories, our only political option seems to be to change the position of particular groups within those structures – merely substituting one oppressed, marginalized group for another.[20] The hope of a genuinely radical politics would be to escape oppression altogether, and this, in the view of many critical theorists, entails transcending the dichotomies rather than reversing them. But how is such a project to be effected; how is the logic of binary oppositions, in which deconstruction itself seems to participate, to be escaped? Two possibilities (they are not mutually exclusive) have been suggested. The first is exemplified by Cornell's feminist reading of Derrida. Whilst Cornell acknowledges the need to 'take off' from within the dichotomies, the openness of language, particularly as realized through devices such as metaphor and metonymy, opens a utopian moment within deconstruction. Different meanings and possibilities can be glimpsed or imagined which may gradually allow us to transcend the oppressive social relations expressed in the current dichotomies.[21] In the work of other theorists such as Young, in which deconstruction plays a less central role, the possibility of transcending the dichotomies proceeds from a decided rejection of the idea that the world must be understood in terms of their binary straitjacket. Rather, it is argued, we can move to a realization of difference as multiple and relational, hence undermining the dichotomized construction/understanding of the world and rejecting the limited political options that its either/or analysis seemed to force upon us.[22] Each of these strategies needs to be borne in mind in considering feminist critique of public/private dichotomies.

3. The Value of Privacy

One final aspect of the debate about public and private needs to be distinguished. This is the argument about what, if any, value should be ascribed to privacy. Clearly, the idea that privacy in the sense of a space around the individual or a particular association from which she or it is entitled to exclude others, connects closely with liberal notions of individual freedom, contributing to liberal arguments about the desirability of an unregulated private sphere, particularly the family. But a commitment to the idea that privacy can be of value and should sometimes be respected does not entail a commitment to a private *sphere* in any of the senses generally understood by that term. Evidently, the value of privacy is contextual – it depends on the particular area of life we are thinking of, and the circumstances which prevail. This means that an approach to protecting privacy which operates by delineating a relatively concrete *sphere* seems inappropriate. But, from a feminist point of view, it is far from clear that a critique of the public/private dichotomy should bring with it a total rejection of the notion that privacy can be valuable and ought sometimes to be protected by the state and other powerful institutions.[23] Indeed, given the double burden inherent in current social arrangements, privacy is one of the many things which women tend to lack. This needs to be emphasized because some feminist critiques have been taken (not always without justification) to imply that privacy is a value which has nothing to recommend it to women.[24]

PROBLEMS FOR THE PUBLIC/PRIVATE CRITIQUE

Now that we have a clearer view of the different aspects of the public/private dichotomy and the critique which it has generated, we can begin to focus on some of the specific difficulties which the critique has encountered. The main problems associated with the division between public and private spheres can be summarized as follows. In its 'descriptive' guise, it inappropriately 'reifies' spheres which cannot be clearly identified by means of careful concrete sociological analysis. The construction of public and private spheres as analytical categories exaggerates the extent of actual institutional divisions, suppresses the ways in which women's as well as men's lives are lived across 'public and private spheres', and gives insufficient attention to concrete social practices and historical changes. Secondly, the analytical categories are applied to particular areas and practices as if descriptively, but with normative conclusions being drawn from the 'descriptive' denotation of publicity or privacy. The premises on which these conclusions are based are hence obscured and protected from critical scrutiny. Thirdly, the assumption that the world can be divided into separate spheres obscures the interdependence of those spheres and the spill-over from oppression in one sphere to subordination in another. Finally, the analysis is crude in its focus on 'the state' and 'state intervention' as the touchstones of 'the public' and of regulation, when in fact both the state and the means of regulation are multiple rather than unitary. Many different modes of regulation exist – overt and covert, legal and administrative, more or less coercive – operated by a variety of state institutions. Indeed, the very idea of state as opposed to non-state agencies (yet another form of public/private dichotomy) is inappropriate in a world where 'public' and 'private' power are inextricably linked. The critique of the public/private dichotomy questions the common assumption that politics has to do exclusively or at least primarily with the state. It also suggests that we should reject the idea that power can be understood exclusively in terms of sovereignty: rather than seeing power as something which is wielded by particular persons or agencies in a conscious or overt way, we must also attend to the operations of power in a diversity of state and non-state institutions, practices, and discourses.

Unfortunately, however, the critique of the division between public and private spheres which has generated these insights has itself not always escaped the problems it has identified. The difficulty lies in the fact that once one engages in a critique of the division, one gets sucked into the very categorization one is attempting to undermine. One good example is provided by the last two chapters of Katherine O'Donovan's *Sexual Divisions in Law* (1985). This book, which broke new ground in feminist legal scholarship in the United Kingdom, devoted much of its argument to a critique of the public/private dichotomy. Yet O'Donovan's models of reform essentially consist in turning the values which characterize one side of the dichotomy against practices on the other. In doing so, O'Donovan elides two aspects of the public/private divide which we have distinguished: public versus private *spheres* and the sexualization of the public/private dichotomy at the level of *values*. Evidently, the idea of 'making a man more like a woman', and the public more like the private, precisely does not transcend the dichotomy it critiques, for it speaks in the unreconstructed terms of the dichotomy itself. And, despite her vision of transcending the dichotomy via a world of reds and greens and blues, Frances Olsen's sophisticated analysis too makes little progress in this transformative direction. In 'The Family and the Market',[25] most of her argument, like O'Donovan's, consists of an analysis of the way law reform has mapped the values associated with the private onto the public, and vice versa. Because the critique of the ideological power which the public/private dichotomy has as part of a sexualized and hierarchical cultural discourse is mapped back on to a division between public and private spheres which has effectively been exploded as a myth, the argument reaches a kind of deadlock in which the promise of genuine transformation cannot be made good. In Olsen's metaphor we begin to escape the binary and the dichotomized, but the utopian vision opened up by deconstruction is glimpsed rather than developed.

Another way of looking at this problem is to think of the public/private critique as operating at several different levels. At one level, the dichotomy is criticized as being impossibly indeterminate or even analytically incoherent; as being an inaccurate description of the world; and as implying an unattractive prescription for social organization. At a different level, the critique focuses not on the dichotomy itself but on the power which that dichotomy, incoherent, inaccurate, unattractive though it may be, has actually had in constructing or consolidating certain features of women's oppression. In spite of all its glaring defects, in other words, its discursive power in our culture is acknowledged. This involves the feminist critique in a delicate balancing act, and one which can all too easily appear to lose its equilibrium. It can seem as though our theoretical critique of the public/private distinction undermines our critique of its power: if the division is so hopelessly indeterminate, to what concrete political practices is the normative liberal argument and, more importantly, the feminist critique of it, meant to relate? It is extremely difficult, in other words, to engage in critique of the public/private dichotomy or its effects without speaking as if it had an analytic and empirical validity which the critique denies. The way out of this impasse lies in seeing that the dichotomy has operated, and continues to operate, ideologically – and ideological power does not necessarily depend upon empirical validation or logical coherence. This suggests that the critique may have focused to too great an extent on the idea of public and private *spheres*. For the ideological role of the dichotomy can be – and has been – played *without* necessarily being realized in any empirically identifiable separation of institutions, activities, or areas of life, or indeed in articulated policy.

A final problem encountered by the critique has to do with the conclusions which are to be drawn from it. All too often, feminist theorists have made the assumption that a critique of the depoliticization of the private should go hand in hand with change in the form of greater legal regulation. Consider the assumption tucked away in Alison Jaggar's otherwise careful analysis: 'By defining sexual and family relations as private . . . liberal theorists provide grounds for arguing that these assaults are no business of the law *and so* for allowing them to continue'[26] (my emphasis). It is perhaps unfair to attribute to Jaggar a general view on the basis of a particular example in which law is arguably a rather obviously apt response. Nonetheless, the passage makes a strong assumption both about the appropriateness of legal intervention as a remedy for the ills of privatized wrongs and about the efficacy of such legal intervention. Both of these assumptions call for much more argument, fleshed out in particular contexts.

Whilst feminist lawyers have widely debated the strategic implications of legal regulation, the normative arguments have been less fully developed. This is perhaps because of a pervasive and understandable scepticism in feminist thought about the utility of normative theories which pretend to a politically dubious universalism and fail to articulate the position from which they speak. Nonetheless, feminists should address the underlying substantive political and ethical issues which have been skated over by both public/private dichotomized discourse and its critique. This must be part of a larger feminist enterprise of reconstructing concepts such as autonomy and privacy.[27] The kind of enterprise I have in mind is well illustrated by the following passage from feminist philosopher Iris Marion Young:

> Instead of defining the private as what the public excludes, I suggest, the private should be defined, as in one strain of liberal theory, as that aspect of his or her life and activity that any person has a right to exclude others from. The private in this sense is not what public institutions exclude, but what the individual chooses to withdraw from public view. With the growth of both state and non-state bureaucracies, the protection of privacy has become a burning public issue. In welfare capitalist society, the defence of personal privacy has become not merely a matter of keeping the state out of certain affairs, but of calling for positive state regulation to ensure that both its own agencies and non-state organizations, such as corporations, respect the claims of individuals to privacy.
>
> This manner of formulating the concepts of public and private, which is inspired by feminist confrontations with traditional political theory, does not deny their distinction. It does deny, however, a social division between public and private spheres, each with different kinds of institutions, activities and human attributes.[28]

This passage captures the importance of reconstructing an adequate distinction between public and private – a distinction which is neither dichotomous nor mapped onto separate spheres – and shows how this connects with central ethical considerations. It also implies that adequate notions of public and private do not automatically map on to conclusions about regulation and non-regulation. I shall now move on to consider these theoretical points in the context of the concrete issue of pornography.

PORNOGRAPHY AND THE PUBLIC/PRIVATE DICHOTOMY

Feminist concern with pornography is certainly not new, but it has taken a particular shape and gained a new intensity over the last twenty years. In a period of reflection upon the implications for women of the sexual 'liberation' of the 1960s, many women began to be concerned with the proliferation of readily available pornography, asking questions not just about the relationship between pornography and sexual violence, or about the exploitation of women involved in the production of pornography, but also about the broader cultural implications of the spread of pornography for the status and citizenship of women. In Andrea Dworkin's work, for example, pornography is seen as central to the maintenance of women's oppression: heterosexuality constructs women as the sexual objects of men, and this objectification finds its most graphic as well as one of its most powerful expressions in pornographic material.[29] On this view, sexuality is the fundamental site of women's oppression, and pornography, along with rape, wife-beating, sexual harassment, and other forms of sexually specific violence, represent the social practices which both express and cause women's subordination and powerlessness. This analysis of pornography emphasizes its implicit or explicit violence, its dehumanization of its objects – mostly women or children, disproportionately often black women – by representing them in positions of servility, as enjoying pain or humiliation, by reducing them to particular body parts. A somewhat different account has emphasized the ways in which the proliferation of pornography has affected other areas of life. Pornography, on this view, is a regime of representation through which we see the world. Once widely available as a genre, the regime of representation which pornography engenders is not restricted to the viewing of pornographic materials themselves. It affects the way in which consumers of pornography look at other genres – advertising, novels, and so on.[30] Moreover, the question of whether or not pornography contributes to actual sexual violence is not the exclusive or even the central concern. The point is that the profusion of the pornographic regime of representation inevitably affects the social constitution of femininity – affects the ways in which women can be represented and can represent ourselves across all social practices – and hence directly and adversely, albeit intangibly, affects the status of women.

My concern here is not to engage in further analysis of pornography but rather to focus specifically on the contribution which the critique of the public/private dichotomy has made to feminist analyses of pornography. In the first place, pornography in liberal society has largely been constructed as a matter of private consumption, and hence as outside the ambit of political critique or action. Without any proof of the contribution of pornography to overt acts of violence, and without any overt violence or coercion in its production, pornography has been taken to be either an instance of expression or a form of sexual practice and hence within the sphere of individuals' privacy. Feminist critique has brought pornography into the sphere of the public and has insisted upon its political relevance. This is both because of the interdependence argument – the argument that private oppression inevitably leads to public disadvantage – and because the traditional denomination of pornography as private can itself be shown to be disingenuous. The liberal analysis which constructs pornography as a matter of private sexual preference in one breath constructs it as a matter of public rights to free expression in the next. In what might be called a 'no-lose situation' for the producers and consumers of pornography, the production of pornography is seen as a matter of public right, and hence protected, whilst its consumption is constructed as a matter of private interest, and also protected. Both public and private sides of the dichotomy are manipulated in ways which exclude anti-pornography arguments. Another twist to the conundrum comes from the ways in which the public right to pornographic expression has often been limited to the private sphere: legal regulation of pornography tends to focus on public manifestations which cause offence. This policy compromise may be functional to the meaning of pornography by in effect making pornography easily available whilst maintaining the illusion of illicitness which forms part of the power of pornography to arouse.[31]

In many senses, then, issues of public and private suffuse the feminist analysis and critique of the traditional construction of pornography: the private consumption of pornography inevitably impacts on the public status of women - on women's citizenship. However, in the work of several feminist lawyers, the critique of the privatization of pornography has been developed in the form of inferences from critique to practice, and to practice in a very specific legal reformist guise. I want to consider this specific attempt at reform, because I think it illustrates some of the theoretical problems I have identified, as well as some of the pitfalls of making simple inferences from theory to strategy. In response to a local grassroots movement in Minneapolis, Andrea Dworkin and Catharine MacKinnon were invited to draft an anti-pornography ordinance.[32] The political process included lengthy hearings in which many women gave painful and appalling evidence about the effect of pornography on their lives. The hearings helped to produce a political atmosphere in which pornography was widely acknowledged to be a serious social harm with a differential impact upon women. The ordinance which Dworkin and MacKinnon drafted enunciated a very broad definition of pornography as the 'graphic, sexually explicit subordination of women through pictures and/or words' which also exhibits one or more of a number of further features. These further features included the presentation of women as dehumanized sexual objects; as experiencing sexual pleasure in rape, incest, or other sexual assault; and, perhaps most controversially, in postures or positions of sexual submission, servility, or display. Pornography in these senses was conceptualized as sex discrimination – that is, as behaviour which exploits and differentially harms women. The ordinance went on to give civil causes of action for injunctions and/or damages to anyone coerced, intimidated, or fraudulently induced into performing pornography; to anyone on whom pornography is forced in a place of employment, education, home, or any public place, as against the person forcing it on them; to anyone assaulted, attacked, or injured in a way that is directly caused by specific pornography; to anyone defamed by the unauthorized use of pornography in their proper name, image, or recognizable likeness; and to any woman acting against the subordination of women or other person who alleges injury by pornography, against anyone who produces, sells, exhibits, or distributes pornography, including through private clubs.

In many respects, the ordinance represented an inspired piece of feminist legal politics. First, the conceptualization of pornography as sex discrimination placed at the heart of the legislation a feminist view of pornography. Moreover, by pitching one constitutional standard (free expression) against another (equal protection) it in effect forced the courts in the United States of America into a position where, if they were to hold the ordinance unconstitutional, they had to do so in terms which were easily interpreted as valuing an at best dubiously worthwhile form of expression over and above the removal of sex discrimination, and as valuing men's expression over the worth or even possibility of women's. Indeed, the United States Court of Appeals, which did find the ordinance to be unconstitutional, underlined these embarrassing implications of its decision by making it clear that it accepted the premises on which the ordinance was based.[33] Secondly, the reform process itself was a model of feminist political practice. The hearings gave a public voice to women whose suffering had been hidden and silenced; indeed, they constituted precisely the kind of civic forum which illustrates the inadequacy of the traditional public/private distinction and its focus on the state. Thirdly, the important choice of civil over criminal enforcement helped to some extent to defuse the accusation that the ordinance amounted to censorship. More significantly, the process of giving individual women rights of action was symbolically apt. It sought to empower women to use a legal process whose terms are generally constructed in ways which are inattentive or even hostile to the interests and needs which many women may wish to defend legally. Finally, by defining pornography *as* sex discrimination, causal links between pornography and harms to women were taken as already established. Hence the legal process was relieved from having to deal with intractable questions about the relationship between pornography and sexual violence: these would only arise legally in the specific cases where this was what the cause of action alleged.

As is well known, however, the ordinance also raised some very difficult questions for feminist politics, and generated a bitter controversy within the women's movement. At its heart, this controversy had to do with the basic shape of the feminist analysis on which the ordinance rested: in short, the claim that pornography is a *central* means of perpetuating women's oppression. Many feminists see pornography and sexual violence as epiphenomenal rather than as central: as the product of economic and other material means of subordination.[34] For the purposes of this discussion, I shall make an intermediate assumption: that is, that pornography in the forms which predominate in our culture, whilst not being a root cause of women's oppression, is a practice which does contribute to sex discrimination, not just in the sense of sexual violence but also in the sense of contributing to the low esteem in which women are held by men and, all too often, in which we hold ourselves. Pornography is by no means the only or even the most important means of degrading objectification to which women (and indeed men) are subjected in our society, but as one such form, it is of political relevance and concern. To this extent, bringing the *issue* of pornography into public debate, and the recognition of the interdependence between privately consumed pornography and the public status of women, is entirely progressive.

However, reflection on the instrumental and symbolic implications of legislation against pornography of the kind embodied in the ordinance gives serious pause for thought about how the public/private critique is to be realized in political practice. Such a legislative strategy exhibits two features which I have already suggested are among the failings of the feminist development of the critique. First, it participates in an over-concentration on the public/private *spheres* aspect of the critique at the expense of its ideological or discursive aspects. It recognizes the discursive power of pornography, but adopts a strategy which, though it has short-term attractions because of its concreteness, is likely to be discursively counter-productive in the medium term. The price of this way of constructing pornography as a public wrong is that it has to be fitted into the conceptual straitjacket of an already legally recognized harm: in the case of the ordinance, sex discrimination. But it is unlikely that all the important aspects of the feminist critique of pornography can be captured in terms of the individualized and relatively tangible harms to which both criminal and civil law have tended to address themselves and which the idea of sex discrimination evokes. Secondly and relatedly, a legislative strategy risks falling back into the assumptions made by the public/private dichotomy itself about the importance of the state as the main source of political/regulatory power. If the power which has kept in place the negative aspects of public/private thinking inheres in a wide variety of institutions and discursive practices, the resort to state/legal reform as a means of undermining public/private divisions looks less promising than the proponents of the legislative strategy have assumed.

Of course, the relative costs and benefits of pursuing a particular legal strategy as one aspect of feminist politics may vary in different jurisdictions. The virtually absolute constitutional protection of free speech in the United States of America presented Dworkin and MacKinnon with a very constraining legal and political framework. Conversely, the greater salience of litigation strategies as part of political life in the United States of America means that the gains to be expected of such a strategy may well have been greater than in the United Kingdom. Some of the most important problems presented by a legal reform strategy against pornography, however, would arise in most jurisdictions. For example, how many women could gather the resources, financial and otherwise, to bring cases against pornography? The experience in Britain and elsewhere of individual-initiated sex discrimination litigation is not encouraging. Even in the few cases where the best legal representation is available, and even where litigants have a very firm political commitment to their cause and a great deal of emotional and material support, research suggests that they may find it a disempowering experience rather than the reverse.[35] Strategic litigation funded by pressure groups may be a more realistic possibility, but the knock-on effects of local cases such as could have been brought under the ordinance can easily be overestimated, whilst the resources which would have to be devoted to litigation strategies, as some women's groups in Canada can attest as a result of their experience under the Charter of Rights and Freedoms, are enormous.[36] Conversely, we have to consider who might use the law in question. Given the breadth of the ordinance's definition, it cannot be doubted that such a law might be exploited by right-wing litigants to attack a wide range of sexually explicit art and literature including that evoking or expressing lesbian sexuality. These, of course, are forms which radical feminists would not see as coming within the ambit of the definition because of the background equality which may be argued to be possible in principle in homosexual but not heterosexual relations. It seems unlikely that judges would confine themselves to such an interpretation. A feminist conception of pornography, already moulded to fit a legal framework, could be further distorted in the interpretive process so as to push it towards a conservative conception inimical to the direction of feminist analysis.

Nor can we assume that a reasonable proportion of cases challenging pornographic material would succeed. Problems of proof – particularly of requirements such as being 'coerced' into pornography, 'forcing' pornography on a person, an attack or injury being 'directly caused by specific pornography' – give strong reason to think that cases would be fraught with practical difficulties, and that the success rate, as in other sex discrimination cases, would be low.[37] In any event, would the remedies envisaged by the ordinance be instrumentally effective? What level of awards of damages could be realistically expected in cases where the harm involved is intangible? How often would courts be willing to award injunctions, and how effectively would or could these be policed? If injunctions were to be awarded and enforced, the argument that the law is not a form of censorship would be hard to sustain. More importantly, what would be the impact on the working conditions in the pornography production industry? The ordinance focused on victims at the production stage only in so far as they have been coerced into performing. Such a law would have no bite against the social conditions which put women into the position where they are able to be so coerced, particularly where their performance for pornography is a rational way of making a living because of the poverty of their other options.[38] It seems unlikely that a broad interpretation of coercion such as would cohere with a feminist analysis of this issue would gain a secure foothold in legal practice.

A supporter of the legislative strategy against pornography could justly object that I have been assuming that legal reform intervenes only at a concrete, material level, underplaying the discursive aspects of law and exaggerating the difference between the discursive and the material. If power inheres to an important extent in discourses, as I have argued, then influential discourses such as law *are* material in constituting social relations, and legal interventions can deploy discursive power in seeking to change the world, as well as operating at the level of the concrete. We need, then, to look also at what are sometimes called the 'symbolic' aspects of this kind of law reform. Here again, several considerations suggest that a law such as the ordinance might be counter-productive. In the first place, if the instrumental arguments just rehearsed are correct, a symbolic message follows from them: the political meaning of having an unenforceable or unenforced law on the statute books is, at best, ambiguous and, at worst, suggests that legal policy is being used as a sop to political sentiment and as a way of avoiding the need for more effective political action. An interesting analogue here is the British (criminal) law on incitement to racial hatred – an offence which is sometimes suggested as a model for anti-pornography legislation.[39] The number of successful prosecutions since this offence was first introduced has been miniscule, and the law is widely regarded as a costless (for government) sop to concern about racism which merely serves to legitimate government's relative inaction in other more potentially fruitful areas.[40] In addition, each unsuccessful prosecution implies the *legitimacy* of the racist conduct thereby condoned. A second symbolic worry about this sort of anti-pornography law lies in its openness to use by litigants motivated by other than feminist concerns, and indeed in the need (realized in the political process in Indianapolis) to build political alliances with those on the (evangelical) right in order to enact and sustain the legislation.[41] In certain quarters the pornography debate in the United States of America has increased the image of feminism as moralistic and potentially repressive. Doubtless this is to some extent inevitable: the charge of moralism is one way of trying to marginalize a view with which one disagrees. But the feminist position has been made more vulnerable because of the quick inference from the theoretical reconstruction of pornography as public to the idea that *some* instrumental regulatory strategy must be appropriate, and hence by a failure to engage in a sufficient debate about not just the efficacy but also the ethics of legal control. At a discursive level, the implications of the legislative strategy seem at best, uncertain and at worst, damaging.

FEMINIST CRITIQUE AND FEMINIST STRATEGY: A FALSE DICHOTOMY?

I have suggested that the legal reform strategy encapsulated in the Dworkin/MacKinnon anti-pornography ordinance makes some unjustified inferences from the theory of the public/private critique to the political practice of regulation. The idea that rescuing an issue like pornography from the insulation from political critique implicit in its 'privacy' entails a regulative strategy, gets stuck within the very categories of public and private criticized earlier in this paper. For it buys into the idea of the private as the unregulated and the public as the regulated and to the idea that the relevant regulator is the state. It misses out on, or gives insufficient emphasis to, the substantive normative arguments underlying attributions of public and private which I argued earlier were a useful part of the public/private critique. It also assumes that feminist critique is in some sense deficient unless accompanied by feminist strategic action. This entails a strong dichotomy between critique and action which is questionable, not least in the light of feminist emphasis on forms of consciousness-raising as a political practice. It underestimates the importance of undermining the discursive power of attributions of public and private by reconstructing conceptions of private and public adequate to the explication and defence of feminist politics. This is a project which has to be realized through a diversity of political practices – debates, boycotts, counter-propaganda, pickets, and so on. Of course, the publicity which tends to be given to legal fora means that a court-centred strategy may have positive secondary effects for these extra-legal politics. But the risks attendant on legal strategies are acute where we try to use new legal regulation instrumentally, to realise values which command little acceptance among those who will administer the laws in question.[42]

The idea that feminist critique must always engender reformist regulatory practice is, however, one which has often recommended itself to feminist lawyers. Since in my view the elision is an unfortunate one, I want to try to unsettle it by sketching the kind of feminist politics which an adequate reconceptualization of public and private would produce. To do so, I want to return to Young's conception of the public as openness to political debate and dialogue and the (legitimate) private as that area of life from which people have the right to exclude others. This conception of public and private is entirely consonant with the idea expressed earlier in the paper that human autonomy – the value *allegedly* respected by the traditional public/private divide – may require not, or not only, non-intervention, but also positive regulation, the provision of goods and facilities, education, and so on.[43] Feminist critique has exposed the ways in which sexuality, an area of life traditionally constructed as private, impacts upon women's lives in an adverse way which should not be beyond the sphere of politics. It has argued for, *and has actually engendered*, a *public*, political debate about sexuality, and about pornography in particular. Feminist arguments are perfectly consistent with the idea that sexual practices are among those from which people have the right to exclude others and the state, but point out that the range of seriously autonomy-reducing sexual practices which call for political critique and, sometimes, action go beyond those, such as rape, traditionally acknowledged to be harmful. Thus, feminist critique has put *women's* autonomy as well as men's on the political agenda.[44] By making the link between sexual subordination and citizenship status, and by pointing out the impact of oppressive sexual practices on the value of women's speech, Dworkin, MacKinnon, and others have already begun to effect a process of social re-education, consciousness-raising, and change. Their political critique has itself undermined the traditional public/private divide in that it *constitutes* a form of political action – a discursive intervention in the production of dominant meanings, albeit one which still has an uneven hold. Unless we were to believe that a legal reform strategy was likely to be very effective in furthering this discursive and educational process, a less formalized process of campaigning and consciousness-raising in regional and national political fora seems a more sensible feminist strategy.

In short, the inference from the reconstruction of pornography as a political issue to the strategy of legislating against it seems to me to be unjustified. First, it takes an unduly narrow view of the power and role of feminist critique conceived as a form of political practice. Secondly, it falls into the trap of thinking that as feminist lawyers we have to be lawyers first and feminists second – in other words, that we have to find legal solutions to all the problems identified by feminist critique. As a general assumption this is dangerous, for questions about law reform are essentially strategic and have to be assessed carefully in the context of particular reform possibilities. At least in the United Kingdom, such an assessment in the case of pornography leads, I have argued, to the conclusion that legal reform of the kind attempted in Minneapolis is likely to be a counter-productive feminist strategy. Finally, the history of the pornography debate illustrates the importance of distinguishing between different aspects of the public/private dichotomy and its deconstruction in feminist theory. The critique of public/private divisions in social, political, and legal thought cannot of itself recommend particular political strategies. What it can do, properly differentiated, is to give us a broader conception of the political and a sense of the questions we have to confront. In their work on not only pornography but also a range of other issues – abortion, sexual harassment, rape, and so on – radical feminist lawyers have made an invaluable contribution to feminist politics, irrespective of their activities around law reform. To regard legislative reform as the invariable core of feminist legal politics is to exaggerate the power of such reform and to undervalue the power of legal critique.

NOTES AND REFERENCES

1 C. Pateman, 'Feminist Critiques of the Public/Private Dichotomy', in *The Disorder of Women* (1989) 118 at 136, originally published in *Public and Private in Social Life*, eds. S. Benn and G. Gaus (1983).

2 See S. Moller Okin, *Justice, Gender, and the Family* (1989); 'Gender, the Public and the Private' in *Political Theory Today*, ed. D. Held (1985); F. Olsen, 'The Family and the Market: A Study of Ideology and Legal Reform' (1983) 96 *Harvard Law Rev.* 1497.

3 See A. M. Jaggar, *Feminist Politics and Human Nature* (1983) 207–215.

4 Jaggar suggests that the state/civil society division is an analytical feature of liberal economics whilst the market/family division is an explicitly normative feature of liberal theory (id., pp. 143–8). I do not dissent from this, but believe that the state/civil society dichotomy also has a normative dimension, whilst the market/family dichotomy is sometimes presented as descriptive.

5 J. Habermas, *The Theory of Communicative Action* (1981) Vols. 1 and 2 (transl. T. McCarthy) (1984 and 1987). For a feminist commentary on Habermas's social theory, see N. Fraser, 'What's Critical about Critical Theory? The Case of Habermas and Gender' in her *Unruly Practices: Power, Discourse, and Gender in Contemporary Social Theory* (1989) 113. On the idea of 'civic publics', see I. M. Young. *Throwing Like a Girl and Other Essays in Feminist Philosophy and Social Theory* (1990) ch. 7; *Justice and the Politics of Difference* (1990) ch. 3, 4, and 6.

6 I. M. Young, *Justice and the Politics of Difference* (1990) 240; see also Fraser, op. cit., n. 5, pp. 166–171. The importance of this kind of public sphere to social theory is shown by the way in which writers like Arendt and Habermas have been preoccupied, in various ways, with a reduction in the vigour and richness of debate in non-state fora, and with the importance of 'communicatively achieved action contexts'. The idea of the 'decline of the political' as a symptom of a worrying dilution of democracy identified by civic republican theory, is in stark contrast to the emphasis on the state which characterizes dichotomized public/private analysis.

7 J. Donzelot, *Policing the Family: Welfare Versus the State* (1979); N. Naffine, *Law and the Sexes* (1990) 69–71; C. Smart, *The Ties that Bind: Law, Marriage, and the Reproduction of Patriarchal Relations* (1984).

8 See F. Olsen, 'The Myth of State Intervention in the Family' (1985) 18 *Mich. J. Law Reform* 835.

9 On the distinction between negative and positive freedom, see below; see Berlin's influential *Four Essays on Liberty* (1989). The preference for negative as opposed to positive ideas of freedom does not characterize all forms of liberal thought: see, for example, J. S. Mill, *On Liberty* (1859); V. Haksar, *Liberty, Equality, and Perfectionism* (1979); J. Raz, *The Morality of Freedom* (1986). But the idea of freedom as non-intervention has continued to dominate liberal political theory.

10 See P. McAuslan and J. McEldowney (eds.), *Law, Legitimacy, and the Constitution* (1986).
11 The disciplinary theory of power derives from the work of Foucault; see in particular *Power/Knowledge: selected writings and interviews* (1980); *The History of Sexuality: Volume 1* (1976) 90ff. For discussion of the implications of this theory for debates around the public/private dichotomy, see N. Rose, 'Beyond the Public/Private Division: Law, Power, and the Family' (1987) 14 *J. Law and Society* 61.
12 Mill, op. cit., n. 9.
13 H. L. A. Hart, *Law, Liberty, and Morality* (1961).
14 Wolfenden, *Report of the Committee on Homosexual Offences and Prostitution* (1957).
15 For a particularly clear statement of this position, see Okin, op. cit., n. 2, ch. 1, 2, 5, 8. Much of her immanent critique in these chapters is directed to Rawls's *A Theory of Justice* (1971).
16 Fraser, op. cit., n. 5, p. 110, n. 24. Fraser's argument in this note accords closely with the general position I want to defend in this paper.
17 See, for example, G. Lloyd, *The Man of Reason: 'Male' and 'Female' in Western Philosophy* (1984).
18 See Young, op. cit., n. 6, ch. 4.
19 See D. Cornell, *Beyond Accommodation* (1991) 92–106, especially p. 95.
20 See, for example, the vision sketched in the final pages of Olsen, op. cit., n. 2.
21 Cornell, op. cit., n. 19, ch. 4.
22 Young, op. cit., n. 6, pp. 169ff. On the danger of deconstruction's re-erecting binary oppositions where our critical thought has begun to escape them, see M. J. Radin and F. Michelman, 'Pragmatist and Poststructuralist Critical Legal Practice' (1991) 139 *Univ. Pennsylvania Law Rev.* 1019, at 1053.
23 Privacy has, of course, been an important strategic counter in certain feminist legal arguments, most notably in the context of abortion rights in the United States of America: *Roe* v *Wade* 410 US 113 (1973). This is not to say that privacy was necessarily the most advantageous conceptual framework for the protection of abortion: see C. A. MacKinnon, *Toward a Feminist Theory of the State* (1989) ch. 10.
24 For a useful discussion of privacy in terms of personhood and in the context of a clear rejection of any public/private *separation*, see M. J. Radin, 'The Pragmatist and the Feminist'. and F. Michelman, 'Private Personal but not Split' (1990) 63 *Southern California Law Rev.* 1699 and 1783 respectively.
25 op. cit., n. 2.
26 op. cit., n. 3, p. 145.
27 See J. Nedelsky, 'Reconceiving Autonomy' (1989) 1 *Yale J. of Law and Feminism* 7.
28 Young, op. cit., n. 6, pp. 119–120.
29 A. Dworkin, *Pornography: Men Possessing Women* (1981). Similar analyses are to be found in C. A. MacKinnon, *Feminism Unmodified* (1987); S. Jeffreys, *Anticlimax* (1990).
30 See S. Kappeler, *The Pornography of Representation* (1986); R. Coward, *Female Desire* (1984). For an analysis of the differences between conceptions of pornography as violence and pornography as representation, see C. Smart, *Feminism and the Power of Law* (1989) ch. 6.
31 Coward, op. cit., n. 30; MacKinnon also makes this point: 'Feminism, Marxism, Method and the State: Toward Feminist Jurisprudence' (1983) 8 *Signs* 635, although in her later work her acceptance of it is less decisive (op. cit., n. 23, pp. 200–201).
32 See A. Dworkin and C. A McKinnon, *Pornography and Civil Rights: A New Day for Women's Equality*, Organizing Against Pornography, Minneapolis (1988). The text of the ordinance is also to be found in R. Graycar and J. Morgan, *The Hidden Gender of Law* (1990) and is discussed in MacKinnon, op. cit., n. 29, Part III. See also Smart, op. cit., n. 30, ch. 6.
33 See *American Booksellers Association, Inc et al.* v *Williams Hudnut III, Mayor, City of Indianapolis, et al.* 771 F 2d 323 (7th Cir 1985). The decision was summarily upheld by the Supreme Court: 475 US (1986).
34 For varied contributions to the debate, see D. Cameron and E. Frazer, *The Lust to Kill: A Feminist Investigation of Sexual Murder* (1987); Coward, op. cit., n. 30; Dworkin, op. cit., n. 29; Jeffreys, op. cit., n. 29; MacKinnon, op. cit., n. 29; A. Rich, *On Lies, Secrets and Silence*

(1977); L. Segal, *Is the Future Female? Troubled Thoughts on Contemporary Feminism* (1987) 105–116.

35 For an assessment of the strengths and weaknesses of the individual enforcement model in sex discrimination law, see K. O'Donovan and E. Szyszczak, *Equality and Sex Discrimination Law* (1988). The limitations of the individual enforcement model are certainly not confined to the United Kingdom; see M. Thornton, *The Liberal Promise: Legislation Against Sex Discrimination in Australia* (1990).

36 See J. Fudge, 'The Effect of Entrenching a Bill of Rights upon Political Discourse: Feminist Demands and Sexual Violence in Canada' (1989) 17 *Int. J. Sociology of Law* 445; J. Fudge and H. Glasbeek, 'The Politics of Rights: A Politics with Little Class' (1992) 1 *Social and Legal Studies* 45. For a contrasting view, see the bulletins of LEAF (Women's Legal Education and Action Fund): cf. *R* v *Butler* [1992] 1 S.C.R. 452.

37 See N. Lacey, 'Legislation Against Sex Discrimination: Questions from a Feminist Perspective' (1987) 14 *J. Law and Society* 410.

38 See N. Roberts, *The Front Line* (1986).

39 Graycar and Morgan, op. cit., n. 32, p. 398.

40 For comment see N. Lacey, C. Wells, and D. Meure, *Reconstructing Criminal Law*(1990) 118–120. See also P. Fitzpatrick, 'Racism and the Innocence of Law' (1987) 14 *J. Law and Society* 119.

41 See L. Segal, *Slow Motion: Changing Masculinities, Changing Men* (1990) 225.

42 In my view, the case of pornography can be distinguished from, for example, current court-centred debates around provocation, diminished responsibility. and 'battered women's syndrome'. Here, the burden of the feminist campaign has been the oppressive way in which the existing legal position fails to recognize arguments which have already attained a degree of acceptance outside the legal sphere. The issue to which the campaign addresses itself is already and unavoidably constituted in legal terms.

43 Young herself wants to draw a distinction between autonomy and empowerment, op. cit., n. 6, p. 251. Her distinction is blurred by my formulation, but the difference between us on this point does not, I believe, affect the way in which I have drawn on her views about public and private.

44 This is not to say that autonomy is the only value which should be of political concern. It is rather to address the influential liberal argument, and show it to be wanting, even in its own terms.

Scepticism or Embrace of Grand Theory

[14]

SYMPOSIUM ARTICLES

IDEOLOGY AND WOMEN'S CHOICES

*Kathryn Abrams**

The argument that women suffer from "false consciousness," or that their choices are unconsciously determined by gender ideology, has been a continuing source of controversy in feminist theory. The controversy has taken a new turn with a growing debate over how such claims are intended by their authors. Until recently, many commentators assumed that "false consciousness" or "ideological determination"[1] claims were offered solely for their truth value. When Catharine MacKinnon said that some women eroticize dominance, or want to believe that they "already have [consensual sex] more than they want to have it,"[2] commentators saw this as expressing an unqualified belief that women learn to view coercive sex as consensual. This view of ideological determination arguments made them immensely problematic, exposing their proponents to charges of reductionism, essentialism and the same pretensions to objectivity of which feminists had accused men.

More recently, however, some feminist theorists have advanced a

---

* Associate Professor, Boston University Law School. I was aided in my development of these arguments by conversations with Bill Kell and Cynthia Farina. I also want to thank Joan Williams, who was generous in discussing her ideas with me. She is not, of course, responsible for the characterizations of those ideas that appear below.

[1] In this Essay, I will use the term "ideological determination" to signify the claim that women's choices are shaped primarily or exclusively by gender ideology. I use this term, rather than the more popular term "false consciousness," because the reference to ideology gives it more descriptive power. Also, this term responds to the distinction some proponents draw between false consciousness claims, which assume an objective ground from which to assess the interests of the oppressed group, and ideological determination claims, which do not. In the last section of this Essay, I use the term "ideological influence" to describe arguments about women's choices which describe ideology as one of several factors shaping women's choices.

[2] *See* C. MacKinnon, Feminism Unmodified: Discourses on Life and Law 217 (1987) [hereinafter, C. MacKinnon, Feminism Unmodified].

different view of these claims. Scholars such as Frances Olsen[3] have argued that feminists do not offer "ideological determination" arguments because they reflect some aperspectival "truth" about certain women's experiences. Instead, proponents offer concededly partial views of women's experiences because they possess a strategic advantage. By describing the influence of ideology on women's choices in a particularly strong way, proponents expose the reach of gender inequality and prevent their arguments from being assimilated to conventional understandings. Because arguments such as Olsen's attempt primarily to explain the purpose of ideological determination claims, they do not ask whether viewing these claims as instruments of strategy renders them any less problematic. In this Essay, I take up this question. While my analysis does not yield a simple answer, it suggests that the strategic interpretation of "ideological determination" arguments does not completely ameliorate their substantial drawbacks.[4] Although the strategic view mutes some objections that go to the author's understanding, and raises the possibility of persuasive advantages, it also raises the specter of some potent strategic drawbacks. Ideological determination arguments may be particularly off-putting for women who have understood, or resisted, the pull of ideological influences; they may cast doubt on women's capacity for choice in contexts in which such doubts may be particularly costly; and they may, by presenting women's choices as determined by one socially diffuse influence, impede remedial inquiry into the complex array of factors that shape women's choices. In this Essay, I will highlight these drawbacks and will ask how feminist scholars might develop ways of examining women's choices that retain the capacity to pose a comprehensive challenge to existing gender relations, yet avoid these distinctive dangers.

---

[3] *See* Olsen, *Feminist Theory in Grand Style* (Book Review), 89 Col. L. Rev. 1147 (1989)(reviewing C. MacKinnon, Feminism Unmodified, *supra* note 2).

[4] There are some senses in which Olsen does ask and answer the question of whether viewing MacKinnon's ideological determination claims in this way makes them less problematic. Olsen's interpretation suggests that feminists making these arguments are somewhat less vulnerable to charges of reductionism: they do not hold unidimensional views, but simply emphasize simplified explanations when they believe their audiences require them. But Olsen's argument does not take on the question of whether viewing these claims as strategic responds to objections beyond reductionism, or whether the strategic advantages of these arguments exceed their strategic costs.

I. Ideological Determination and Feminist Theory

"False consciousness" claims have long been affiliated with radical critiques, finding their origins in the work of Engels and Marx.[5] The analogous claims in feminist theory are often distinguished on the ground that they do not assume an aperspectival position from which feminist scholars can determine women's "objective" interests. "Women's situation," as Catharine MacKinnon writes, "offers no outside to stand on or gaze at . . . . There is no Archimedean point—or, men are their own Archimedean point, which makes it not very Archimedean."[6] Yet these claims have several elements in common with false consciousness arguments. First, they purport to explain behavior through which an oppressed group contributes to or perpetuates the patterns of its own oppression. Second, they describe such actions as being the product of internalization, by the oppressed group, of essential elements of the dominant ideology. Third, they describe this internalization of and determination by ideology as occurring beyond the conscious comprehension of the oppressed group: members of the group may perceive their actions as freely chosen, or as influenced by a range of non-ideological factors.

The play of these characteristics is illustrated by perhaps the best known of ideological determination arguments: Catharine MacKinnon's claims regarding sexuality. MacKinnon's claims arise in the context of her central argument: that coercion is paradigmatic of heterosexual relations and constitutive of the social meaning of gender under gender inequality.[7] This argument points to the controversial conclusion that, by engaging in heterosexual relations, women may be contributing to their own subordination. This claim often prompts the challenge from MacKinnon's audiences that many women enjoy, and voluntarily choose to engage in, heterosexual sex. This choice and this experience cast doubt on the contention that forced sex is paradigmatic and on the possibility that women could be contributing to their own oppression.[8] MacK-

---

[5] *See* C. MacKinnon, Feminism Unmodified, *supra* note 2, at 60-61. *See also* C. MacKinnon, Toward a Feminist Theory of the State 13-35 (1989) [hereinafter C. MacKinnon, Toward a Feminist Theory] (describing origins of feminist thought in Marx and Engels).

[6] C. MacKinnon, Toward a Feminist Theory, *supra* note 5, at 117.

[7] *See generally* MacKinnon, *Feminism, Marxism, Method and the State: Toward Feminist Jurisprudence*, 8 Signs 65 (1983).

[8] *See* C. MacKinnon, Feminism Unmodified, *supra* note 2, at 217-18.

innon responds that both the choice and the enjoyment of sex may themselves be shaped by the practice and the ideology of male dominance.[9] Women are socialized to expectations of veiled (or not-so-veiled) force in sex; they come of age in a culture permeated with pornography's eroticization of violence. Women may believe that they are enjoying sex, or engaging in it by mutual consent, when in fact they are engaging in ritualized forms of domination which have become almost eerily familiar.[10] As MacKinnon explains:

> The deeper problem is that women are socialized to passive receptivity; may have or perceive no alternative to acquiescence; may prefer it to the escalated risk of injury and the humiliation of a lost fight; submit to survive. Also, force and desire are not mutually exclusive under male supremacy. So long as dominance is eroticized they never will be. Some women eroticize dominance and submission; it beats feeling forced.[11]

MacKinnon does not rule out the possibility that an individual woman may find herself within a crack in the system of gender inequality[12]—a rare experience which may transform her "choices"

---

[9] I understand MacKinnon to be making the claim that, because women's attitudes are shaped by an ideology that operates beyond their conscious comprehension, women may not accurately describe (or fully understand) their choices or experiences of sexuality. I do not understand her to be making the claim, which is a part of some ideological determination arguments, that women's ideologically influenced attitudes—in this case, women's eroticization of dominance—play a primary role in their subordination. In much of MacKinnon's work, discussions of dominance are sufficiently focused on male responsibility, that it would be difficult to reach the conclusion that she assigned women a leading role in their own subordination. In MacKinnon's oral presentations, such as those recounted in *Feminism Unmodified*, *supra* note 2, there seems to be greater attention given to the ideological determination of women's attitudes and choices, perhaps in part because MacKinnon is confronted with recurrent questions on this topic from her audiences. Her focus on this question in certain contexts and her tendency to amplify the effects of ideology on women's choices may give some readers or listeners the impression that she sees ideologically infused choices as contributing substantially to women's subordination. I do not understand this to be her point; although in keeping with her strategic purpose, MacKinnon might have taken greater pains to prevent this misimpression.

[10] *See generally* C. MacKinnon, Toward a Feminist Theory, *supra* note 5, at 172-83 (describing coercion and consent in sex).

[11] *Id.* at 177.

[12] "Sex feeling good," MacKinnon explains, "may mean that one is enjoying one's subordination; it would not be the first time. Or it may mean that one has glimpsed freedom, a rare and valuable and contradictory event. Under existing conditions, what else would free-

into choices and make her "consensual" sex consensual—yet this is rarely the way she responds to women's reports of such experiences. She is more likely to ask, for example, whether lesbians who engage in forms of behavior that resemble heterosexual relations "express the male supremacist structure or subvert it"[13] or to suggest that those people, including women, who report consensual sex "want to believe they already have this more than they want to have it."[14] Through such explanations, MacKinnon depicts women's purportedly unencumbered choices as ideologically infused acts which contribute to their own subordination, and suggests that women's perceptions of their experiences are less reliable than her own.

Not all ideological determination arguments, however, take the same form or involve equally expansive claims about the ideological coloration of women's attitudes. In her article, *Deconstructing Gender*, Joan Williams discusses women's decisions regarding the workplace in ways which often reflect greater subtlety in depicting constraints on women's choices, but ultimately seem to rest on assumptions similar to MacKinnon's.[15] *Deconstructing Gender* is directed toward feminists of difference, particularly those who take their bearings from the difference theory articulated by Carol Gilligan. Williams argues that Gilligan's description of gender differences constitutes an updated version of the Victorian ideology of domesticity.[16] Although this account contains, or implies, a critique of the possessive individualism that has shaped the workplace, it has not resulted in a restructuring of the workplace. It has been used instead to justify and celebrate the rejection of the workplace

---

dom be?" C. MACKINNON, FEMINISM UNMODIFIED, *supra* note 2, at 218.

[13] C. MACKINNON, TOWARD A FEMINIST THEORY, *supra* note 5, at 119.

[14] C. MACKINNON, FEMINISM UNMODIFIED, *supra* note 2, at 217.

[15] *See* Williams, *Deconstructing Gender*, 87 MICH. L. REV. 797 (1989) [hereinafter *Deconstructing Gender*].

[16] Williams notes that Gilligan's updating differs in certain respects from the original. She suggests that Gilligan is ambivalent about whether women's morality is of a "higher" order. She adds further that relational feminists "reclaim the compliments of Victorian gender ideology while rejecting its insults:"

> Thus relational feminists agree with the Victorians that women are more nurturing than men . . . , less tied to the questionable virtues of capitalism, and ultimately more moral than men. But they disagree with the Victorians' view that women are also more passive than men, less competent, more timid and naturally demure.

Williams, *Deconstructing Gender*, *supra* note 15, at 807.

by women who leave their jobs to care for their children. The modern ideology of domesticity paints such abdication as "virtue," facilitating the economic marginalization of women and short-circuiting workplace reform.

Although Williams' primary target is the ideology of domesticity itself, she also casts a critical gaze on the women who heed its siren song.[17] She describes the decision to leave the workplace as a "choice,"—a decision which is less free than the women making it suspect.[18] Williams' descriptions of this "choice" vary in the self-awareness she attributes to women and the role she ascribes to domestic ideology in shaping their decisions. In some sections, Williams seems to suggest that women's choices are not so much determined as constrained, that women are not so much unaware of the reasons for their choices as mixed in their motives. This is true, for example, when Williams invokes Gramsci's notion of "consent" to explain the concept of "choice":

> Gramsci painted a complex picture of how the dominant culture rules with the consent of the governed by shaping a "hegemony" of values, norms, perceptions, and beliefs that "helps mark the boundaries of permissible discourse, discourages the clarification of social alternatives, and makes it difficult for the dispossessed to locate the sources of their unease, let alone remedy it."
>
> . . . For Gramsci consent is a complex state fraught with ambiguities, a " 'contradictory consciousness' mixing approbation and apathy, resistance and resignation."[19]

---

[17] As my explanation here suggests, this claim constitutes only one portion of Williams' argument about the dangers of Gilliganesque domesticity. I do not regard my differences with Williams' characterization of women's choices here as implicating her larger argument that modern domesticity shaped the perspective of the court in *Sears*, *infra* note 18, and contributed to women's marginalization in the workplace and the economy.

[18] I suspect Williams also uses the term "choice" (meaning use of the word choice combined with the use of quotation marks) as an ironic commentary on the invocation of unencumbered choice by the court in EEOC v. Sears, 628 F. Supp. 1264 (N.D. Ill. 1986) (finding EEOC failed to establish a prima facie case of sex discrimination by Sears Roebuck & Co.), *aff'd*, 839 F.2d 302 (7th Cir. 1988).

[19] *See* Williams, *Deconstructing Gender*, *supra* note 15, at 829 (citations omitted) (quoting from Lears, *The Concept of Cultural Hegemony: Problems and Possibilities*, 90 Am. Hist. Rev. 567, 569-70 (1985)).

Yet in other portions of her discussion, Williams' focus is less on the struggle than on the self-congratulatory serenity produced by the ideology of domesticity; women's "contradictory consciousness" is not so much an ambivalent by-product of male hegemony as its surprisingly puissant partner. Williams notes that

> *Sears* showed how traditionalist judges can use women's culture against women. The more troubling question is the extent to which women use it against themselves, as they do every time a woman "chooses" to subordinate her career "for the good of her family" and congratulates herself on that choice as a mature assessment of her own "priorities."[20]

Or, in another passage, Williams argues that

> both discrimination against women and women's "choices" must be seen as elements of an integrated system of power relations that systematically disadvantages women . . . . Women's choices show how women perpetuate the gender system themselves; discrimination shows how others join them in policing the gender system.[21]

Taken in sum, Williams' depictions contain a descriptive precision and a thread of complexity that is not consistently present in MacKinnon's accounts; yet the two arguments contain important elements in common.[22] Like the women discussed by MacKinnon, Williams' subjects contribute to their own subordination (this

---

[20] *Id.* at 830. In a footnote to this argument, Williams offers the following qualification:

> I do not mean to imply that all women who take primary child care responsibility at the expense of their ability to be ideal workers do so because they are persuaded by domesticity's reassurance that their choice places them on a higher moral plane. Many no doubt settle for part-time work or make other trade-offs with the sense that they are making the best of a bad bargain through a temporary expedient not desirable but inevitable under the circumstances. Yet my sense is that the societal message that women are inherently more nurturing and self-sacrificing and less competitive and ambitious, often plays a role in helping persuade women that what is inevitable is also "natural" and desirable.

Id. at 830-31 n.144. See *infra* note 39, where I discuss the implication of this qualification.

[21] *Id.* at 826.

[22] This is perhaps not surprising, considering that Williams states that she begins from MacKinnon's central premise that "inequalities are the core feature of the gender system as we know it." Williams, *Deconstructing Gender*, *supra* note 15, at 822.

time, economic rather than sexual), with only limited understanding of the constraints on their choices and little sense of these choices as systematically self-destructive.

When ideological determination claims are regarded as unambiguous explanations of controversial choices made by women, they are vulnerable to a range of criticisms. They are vulnerable, first, to the claims of reductionism that haunt any "grand theory"[23] of oppression. Whether guided by post-structuralism or our complex, practical reconstructions of our own choices, many feminists are skeptical of theories which attribute entire categories of decisions to ideology or any single influence. The decision to leave the workplace, for example, seems to be a function of many things: the needs of the child, the inherent interest of the job, the financial needs of the family, the availability of childcare, the flexibility of the employer—as well as a variety of attitudes toward work and family that seem to vary palpably among women.[24] It is difficult to concur with an explanation which neglects the complex interaction of these influences. Moreover, even if ideological influence could be identified as primary in some choices—a subset of sexual encounters, for example—it is hard to imagine that it could be determinative of the choices of an entire group of people.[25]

This last question foreshadows the related though politically distinct charge of essentialism. By arguing that the social meanings ascribed to gender affect most women in the same (strong) ways, ideological determination arguments neglect the crucially diversifying influences of race, class and sexual orientation.[26] The nine-

---

[23] *See* Olsen, *supra* note 3, at 1168. Olsen explains that "MacKinnon's theory of gender oppression is a total or grand theory in that it attempts to explain a major portion of American social reality—gender—on the basis of a single powerful construct." *Id.*

[24] *See, e.g.*, A. Hochschild & A. Machung, The Second Shift: Working Parents and the Revolution at Home (1989) [hereinafter The Second Shift]; K. Abrams, Work/Family Conflict as a Paradigm for Gender Discrimination (unpublished manuscript on file with the author).

[25] *See generally The James McCormick Mitchell Lecture, Feminist Discourse, Moral Values, and the Law—a Conversation*, 34 Buffalo L. Rev. 11 (1985) [hereinafter *The James McCormick Mitchell Lecture*]. In this conversation, feminist scholar and activist Mary Dunlap argues that the extent to which sexuality is enjoyed and chosen and the extent to which it is colored by ideological influence varies among different groups of women. *Id.* at 30-32.

[26] *See, e.g.*, b. hooks, Ain't I a Woman: Black Women and Feminism (1981); E. Spelman, Inessential Woman: Problems of Exclusion in Feminist Thought (1988); Harris, *Race and Essentialism in Feminist Legal Theory*, 42 Stan. L. Rev. 581 (1990); Minow, *Feminist*

teenth century ideology of domesticity, for example, played little role in the socialization of black women,[27] suggesting that their response to its modern incarnation may differ from that of whites. In the area of sexuality, Angela Harris[28] and Elizabeth V. Spelman[29] have argued eloquently that the social construction of the sexuality of women of color has often differed radically from that of whites. Neglecting these powerful sources of differentiation, at best, duplicates the obscuring reification characteristic of the dominant ideology[30] and, at worst, presents as universal the specific experiences of white, middle-class, able-bodied heterosexual women.[31]

Perhaps the most potent claim against ideological determination arguments arises from the feminist critique of objectivity itself. If, as MacKinnon attests, experiential ways of knowing have led feminists to question the possibility of an aperspectival, objective position from which to assess the situation of women,[32] several features of these arguments seem problematic. It would seem more difficult than proponents assert to determine that a particular action chosen by women contributes to women's subordination.[33] And it

---

Reason: Getting It and Losing It, 38 J. OF LEGAL EDUC. 47 (1988) [hereinafter *Feminist Reason*]; Minow, *The Supreme Court, 1986 Term—Foreword: Justice Engendered*, 101 HARV. L. REV. 10 (1987).

[27] *See generally* b. hooks, *supra* note 26. Particularly applicable in this context is hooks' invocation of the historic speech of Sojourner Truth at the second annual convention of the women's rights movement in Akron, Ohio in 1852. Responding to screams of white women that she not be allowed to speak, and to the jeering challenge of one white man, "I don't believe you really are a woman," she replied:

> Dat man ober dar say dat women needs to be helped into carriages, and lifted ober ditches, and to have de best places . . . and ain't I a woman? Look at me! Look at my arm! . . . I have plowed, and planted, and gathered into barns, and no man could head me—and ain't I a woman? I could work as much as any man (when I could get it), and bear de lash as well—and ain't I a woman?

Id. at 160.

[28] *See* Harris, *supra* note 26.

[29] *See* E. SPELMAN, *supra* note 26.

[30] *See* Minow, *Feminist Reason*, *supra* note 26.

[31] *See* E. SPELMAN, *supra* note 26; Harris, *supra* note 26.

[32] *See* C. MACKINNON, TOWARD A FEMINIST THEORY, *supra* note 5, at 95-105 (describing evolution, through feminist consciousness raising, of new epistemological approach).

[33] Both MacKinnon and Williams might meet this argument by saying that gender discrimination is not simply a motive subjectively experienced by the perpetrator or an effect subjectively experienced by the victim, but a system whose features can be denominated and whose effects can be presented in verifiable, quantitative form. Thus, MacKinnon frequently begins her articles or presentations by quantifying the extent of sexual harassment, spousal abuse or rape, and Williams devotes a portion of *Deconstructing Gender* to the

would seem particularly problematic to claim that a woman does not understand the causes of her own actions or that a feminist scholar's explanations of her choices should be categorically preferred to the woman's own. When MacKinnon argues that women who claim to enjoy consensual sex eroticize dominance, or want to believe that they have attained mutuality more than they want to attain it, her arguments not only suggest a belief in the same kind of unsituated or objective knowledge she decries, but they also display a dismissive approach to women's accounts of their own experience that recalls the stance of the dominant ideology.[34]

Responding, perhaps, to the force of these objections, some feminist scholars have begun to view ideological determination arguments in a different light.[35] They argue that, in advancing such claims, proponents do not see themselves as presenting the unambiguous truth of all women's experience. Instead, proponents understand such perspectives to be partial. Yet they present them in particularly unambivalent ways, because such presentations offer strategic advantages. In discussing MacKinnon, for example, Frances Olsen describes as a strategic choice MacKinnon's decision to depict claims of consensual sex as the products of gendered ideology. MacKinnon does not, Olsen suggests, deny the possibility of mutual, consensual heterosexual sex. Yet she selects an argument or, as Olsen describes it, an emphasis, which presents such relations as a virtual impossibility, because that presentation offers certain advantages in conveying her dominance theory to an often-resistant audience. The uncompromising character of her claim

---

description and quantification of the feminization of poverty. If gender discrimination is not a perception but a system, victims' experiences are one but not the only route to its discovery. However, there is still the question of the extent to which a particular choice or set of choices contributes to this system. A feminist scholar who wishes to contest the victim's view of her choices as free or as not contributing to subordination, must still evaluate the contribution of those choices from some perspective outside that of the victim whose existence many feminist scholars have been reluctant to acknowledge. MacKinnon seems to argue that such a perspective is possible: a view that is neither "objective" nor "subjective." C. MacKinnon, Toward a Feminist Theory, *supra* note 5, at 116. This view emerges when women speak from their experience of victimization rather than their denial. *Id.* at 173. As I note and have noted elsewhere, I find the latter distinction difficult to draw in practice. *See infra* note 91.

[34] Katharine Bartlett makes this point in a concise and insightful review of *Feminism Unmodified*. *See* Bartlett, *MacKinnon's Feminism: Power on Whose Terms?* (Book Review), 75 Calif. L. Rev. 1559, 1564 (1987).

[35] *See* Olsen, *supra* note 3.

may jar many people into awareness who would be impervious to subtler claims of gender oppression.[36] The choice of an unqualified explanation over a more nuanced, fully-balanced treatment may prevent her understanding from being " 'rounded up' or 'rounded down,' "[37] that is, assimilated to less radical understandings of many groups in the larger population. An unqualified claim of ideological determination may also prevent MacKinnon's audience from focusing on any qualifications to the exclusion of her larger message.[38]

The strategic perspective blunts the force of some of the initial objections by suggesting that proponents of ideological determination arguments may be aware of the potential drawbacks of their strategic choice. Joan Williams, for example, does not believe that all departures from the workplace are caused by ideology.[39] She risks the charges of reductionism that may arise from her singular focus,[40] to prevent observers of the workplace from ignoring the central role of the new domestic ideology. Similarly, Catharine

---

[36] *Id.* at 1175.

[37] *Id.* at 1176.

[38] *Id.* at 1176 n.117. Olsen describes MacKinnon's response to an article in which Olsen had stated that there were "nooks and crannies in which the beginnings of a new sexuality could be discovered." *Id.* Olsen relates that "MacKinnon did not suggest that I was wrong, but warned that my statement about nooks and crannies might be the only thing people would quote from the article and that the force of my critique would be lost." *Id.*

[39] Williams acknowledges as much in a footnote described earlier. *See* Williams, *Deconstructing Gender*, *supra* note 20, at 830-31 n.144. The fact that Williams offers her reservations in a footnote, while presenting a less qualified version of her claim in the text is, to me, indicative of the strategic presentation of a concededly partial claim. She seeks to awaken her audience with the bold claim that women deploy women's culture against themselves "every time a woman 'chooses' to subordinate her career 'for the good of the family' and then congratulates herself on that choice as a mature assessment of her own priorities." *Id.* at 830. Yet she wants to assure those readers interested or careful enough to look "below the line" that she "do[es] not mean to imply that all women who take primary child-care responsibility at the expense of their ability to be ideal workers do so because they are persuaded by domesticity's reassurance that their choices places them on a higher moral plane." *Id.* at 830-31 n.144. By remarking on Williams' apparent strategy here, I do not mean to criticize her choice—I consider it preferable to add these qualifications in a footnote than not to—nor do I mean to take on the practice, altogether common in law review articles, of stating a general point in the text and offering elaborations or qualifications in footnotes. In the remainder of the article, however, I hope to suggest that there may be alternative ways of communicating both the possibility of ideological influence and the role of other contributing factors.

[40] It is interesting to note, however, that even when Williams acknowledges that all departures are not attributable to ideology, she does not elaborate on the other causal factors that may play a role in women's decisionmaking. *See id.* at 830-31 n.144.

MacKinnon risks the charges of pretending to objectivity, or devaluing women's accounts of their experience, in order to highlight certain accounts that she finds paradigmatic of, and essential to understanding, gender oppression. This interpretation strengthens the position of ideological determination arguments by presenting their drawbacks not as casual oversights, but as calculated decisions to undertake substantive and methodological risks in the interests of feminist strategy.

But this benefit does not, to my mind, conclude the matter. In fact, it reveals less about the value making of ideological determination claims than about the value of viewing those which are made strategically. The strategic interpretation makes sense because it explains how arguments with evident vulnerabilities can be offered by innovative and sophisticated feminist scholars. To say that there is a calculus that explains these arguments, however, does not tell us whether that calculus is correct. The strategic judgments which yield ideological determination claims might be better than oversight, but still be critically flawed. Consider, for example, the charge of race or class essentialism. We may judge it more intellectually subtle or politically sensitive to *risk universalizing* a portrait of white, middle-class, heterosexual response, than to *believe* that such a portrait really represents *all women*. Yet risking the erasure of the experience of lesbians or women of color remains a substantial cost of any theoretical approach. We need to know more about its comparative advantages and the availability of alternatives before we can judge whether such risks are justified. As this example suggests, viewing ideological determination claims as strategy does not provide answers to the quandaries these claims create, it simply substitutes a new set of questions. And the information we need to assess these questions is currently incomplete. If we are to evaluate these claims as calculated judgments about feminist strategy, it is not enough to know their potential benefits; we also have to know the range of potential costs.

Some of these costs—such as the risk of oversimplification or methodological inconsistency—are intellectual or reputational costs to the proponents of such arguments. Others are costs which are sustained primarily by subgroups whose experiences are obscured in the quest for a unitary portrait.[41] Still others are costs

[41] The exclusion of subgroups ought to redound to the disadvantage of the scholar or

which are paid out in the very currency in which proponents claim their advantage: practical progress in feminist persuasion and institutional reconstruction. Although ideological determination arguments may have advantages in awakening some audiences to gender discrimination, or facilitating analytic clarity under some circumstances, these advantages do not exist across the boards. Some audiences are likely to be less receptive to ideological determination claims; some are likely to embrace them in ways that impede feminist change. Under some circumstances these arguments are likely to create analytic confusion rather than clarity. These costs have not been thoroughly investigated in the literature assessing such arguments. In the following section I explore several of these tactical costs and then ask how they affect ideological determination arguments.

II. Strategy as a Vantage Point

Before considering the strategic costs of employing ideological determination arguments, it may be useful to consider how feminist legal scholars have come to focus on strategy and what specifically the term "strategy" might refer to in discussions such as Olsen's. The connection of even theoretical choices with political strategy is largely a product of the relations that feminist scholars have envisioned between theory and practice. Many forms of feminist theory arose coterminously with, or in response to, women's political struggle for gender equality. That connection has led many feminist scholars to contest the traditional distinction between theory and practice, and to argue instead for an integration, or a dialectical relationship that stressed their interrelation.[42] This perspective has reinforced the practical orientation of some feminist legal scholars, whose professional training has led them to ask what role legal institutions might play in producing social change. One feature of this orientation toward practice has been a concern

---

activist perpetrating it as well; yet, such exclusion is so pervasive that it frequently does not.

[42] The work of MacKinnon herself epitomizes this new understanding of the relationship between theory and practice. *See generally* Olsen, *supra* note 3, at 1171 n.93 (noting that C. MacKinnon, Feminism Unmodified, *supra* note 2, a collection of speeches, presents a unified theory of gender discrimination while producing an important organizing document for the feminist antipornography movement). *See also* Schneider, *The Dialectic of Rights and Politics: Perspectives from the Women's Movement*, 61 N.Y.U. L. Rev. 589 (1986) (describing dialectical relationship between rights theory and feminist practice).

with strategy: asking not simply what changes need to be made, but how such changes might be grounded, developed and presented in a political context which makes their introduction controversial. Some strategic questions, for example, concern the approach that is optimal for addressing a particular type of audience: an audience lacking any awareness of the problem, an audience whose awareness has sparked resistance to change, or an ambivalent or supportive audience. Others ask what choices should be made to facilitate a particular stage of reform: What arguments work best for mobilization? Which approaches help to explicate the complex origins of social or institutional discrimination? Which approaches contribute to remedial efforts? In identifying so broad a range of strategic concerns, feminist legal scholars assume that the work of feminist legal reform is dependent upon, and integrally connected with, the examination and reconstruction of understandings which have traditionally been viewed as more political than strictly legal in nature.[43]

Considered from this vantage point, it is evident that ideological determination arguments have strategic advantages not associated with their more qualified counterparts. For example, I suspect that Olsen's analysis only begins the list of the advantages that might flow from MacKinnon's choice. The amplified character of MacKinnon's claims may awaken an audience lulled by its immersion in the status quo, may focus her listeners on her argument rather than its exceptions and may prevent audiences from assimilating her radical claims to their more conventional understandings.[44] But her unqualified descriptions of women's choices regarding sexuality also require that her audiences take her message personally. MacKinnon explains:

> Many women in this country believe gender is a crushing reality from which no woman is exempt. They also believe, or rather act a belief on a daily basis, that they are or can be exempt. If every tacit "present company ex-

---

[43] MacKinnon's career and explicit arguments were among the first to highlight this interrelationship; but many feminists have been working from a method that begins with insights gleaned from feminist theory and epistemology, and uses these to reform legal method. *See* Abrams, *Feminist Lawyering and Legal Method*, 16 L. & Soc. Inq. (forthcoming 1991) [hereinafter Abrams, *Feminist Lawyering*].

[44] These are the primary advantages Olsen cites. *See* Olsen, *supra* note 3.

> cluded" exception I encountered on the road were excluded from the analysis, an analysis would remain that everyone accepts as generally true, but that almost no one—meaning nearly everyone—acknowledges applies to them in particular. Sexuality is like this with a vengeance.[45]

By declining to acknowledge the possibility that women's choices regarding sexuality might be free from ideological determination, MacKinnon prevents women from exempting themselves from her analysis. An analysis that omits the obligatory "present company excluded" challenges each woman to re-examine her own life and search out the ideological influence over her own choices.

Williams' argument, the amplification of which seems both subtler and more self-evidently strategic, also has advantages that a more qualified account would lack. Modern proponents of domesticity may present a more pointed danger even than women who claim to enjoy heterosexual relations. The former not only manifest a particular pattern of choice, but offer a rationale for preferring it—the claim of virtue. Williams' argument may be understood as an effort to counteract this influence by suggesting that departure from the workplace does not reflect virtue; in fact, it does not even reflect choice. It shows only the influence of a justificatory explanation which has been employed for decades to prevent women from claiming their social and economic equality. In this context, the powerful influence of the adversary seems to justify a maximally forceful iteration of the competing claim. If Williams were to give freer reign to the qualifications she occasionally acknowledges—if she were to describe domestic ideology as yet another factor encouraging women to abandon the workplace—she might never awaken women from the trance of self-affirmation induced by difference feminism. Additionally, Williams' argument contains the important reconstructive point that women whose critical view of possessive individualism might contribute to the reform of the workplace are being lost through family-related departures. Her reluctance to acknowledge the justifications—or even the agency—of those who depart, like MacKinnon's reluctance, forces women to take her message personally. It challenges them to

---

[45] C. MacKinnon, Feminism Unmodified, *supra* note 2, at 218.

consider her point that by declining to become part of the solution, they become part of the problem.

In other respects, however, ideological determination arguments carry disadvantages not associated with more qualified claims. MacKinnon and Williams seem, in varying ways, to posit an audience whose capacity to hear a feminist message is blocked by layers of ideology. Because the particular impediment suffered by this audience is a kind of auditory deadening or insulation, elements of presentation (such as the ideological determination claim) that "turn up the volume" on the feminist message offer a strategic advantage. For many people, however, a failure to embrace feminist arguments arises not simply from a failure to hear them, but from resistance that arises after they are heard and (mis)understood.[46] In many cases, this resistance may be fed by ideological determination arguments and the escalation of the "volume" they entail. Women socialized to the conception of the autonomous, self-determining individual perpetrated by liberal society may find incomprehensible or unpalatable the lack of agency which appears to be ascribed to them under these theories. Even those willing to acknowledge socially constructed impediments to autonomy may bridle at the premise that they do not understand the central motivating factors in their choices. Men who are initially opposed to equality for women may find in such arguments not a challenge to their beliefs, but support for their position that women lack the capacities for self-determination necessary to give them autonomous control over all spheres of their existence.

The same may be said of ideological determination arguments in relation to different phases of feminist reform. Arguments such as those above assume that we are at the very outset of a long struggle for gender equality, in which it is crucial to focus audiences on glimpsing the problem itself. They are, not surprisingly, most effective at mobilizing or raising the consciousness of potential activists. MacKinnon's claims about sexuality may penetrate the happy ignorance of the politically insulated, alert lukewarm feminists to

[46] Both MacKinnon and Williams, of course, understand this fully. In offering ideological determination claims, they either diverge from my view that these arguments will fuel resistance or make the judgment that winning those audiences who can be reached by such claims should take priority presently over reaching those audiences who cannot or who, indeed, might be put off by such claims.

the scope of the problem and challenge all women to reconsider their own sexuality. Similarly, Williams' forceful message about domesticity may shed new light on departures from the workplace that are sapping the energy and critical orientation necessary for change. These claims, however, may be less productive in addressing the task of remediation.[47] Claims that magnify the determining influence of a single factor in women's choices may limit inquiry into the many interacting factors, inquiry that is necessary to redirect choices and restructure the environments in which these choices occur. And arguments that magnify the effect of a diffuse socio-political influence such as ideology may short-circuit the inquiry into particularized institutional causation that can be important to legal remediation.

In the interests of beginning a broad evaluation of the strategic implication of ideological determination claims, I will consider three specific problems posed by such arguments. The first is their potential for distancing women who are able to hear the argument being offered, but unable to accept its implications. The second is the danger the arguments pose in contexts where women's agency is increasingly called into question. The third is the barriers these arguments create to remedial analyses which require decisionmakers to identify the range of factors that influence women's choices.

A. *Distancing Women*

There is little doubt that ideological determination claims are off-putting to many women.[48] Catharine MacKinnon reports that

---

[47] For MacKinnon, this may not be a critical drawback. Although she is the architect of several important remedial efforts—including the use of Title VII to address sexual harassment and the enactment of municipal ordinances to regulate pornography—MacKinnon has become well-known for her policy of promulgating no remedial strategy before its time. She resists invitations to speculate on the "endstate" toward which feminist theory is intended to produce and argues that focusing prematurely on remedy is not only unproductive but also may distort emerging understandings of the problem. *See* C. MacKinnon, Feminism Unmodified, *supra* note 2, at 219. But Williams, who spotlights the maternal exodus as a preliminary to restructuring the workplace, and other feminists, who believe that the task of remediation must go on despite incomplete social understanding, may regard it as problematic that arguments offered to expose the problem may complicate its remediation.

[48] There are probably some women, however, who find such claims affirmatively appealing. Carol Weisbrod explains, for example, that ideological determination arguments may be viewed by women as relieving them of responsibility for their choices, a result that might be applauded by women who look back with discomfort on choices made earlier in their lives.

women find dozens of ways to resist her hypotheses about "consensual" sexuality.[49] Women who stay home with their children bristle at the suggestion of working parents that they are reflexively following outdated patterns.[50] The academic furor over ideological determination arguments may reflect the alienation of many feminist scholars from the images of women implicit in these arguments. These responses, in and of themselves, do not justify abandoning such ideological determination claims. Resistance may simply signify—as it sometimes does with male audiences—that these arguments "hit too close to home": they describe a pattern that women dimly recognize but would prefer to ignore or one that seems too burdensome to change. Yet they justify a closer look at women's responses: there may be additional animating factors that cast ideological determination claims not as needed medicine but as flawed strategy.

Several factors explain a response on the part of women that moves beyond rejection toward indignation. Some women, many of whom would identify themselves as liberal feminists, resist ideological determination claims as part of a larger effort to judge the choices made by women. According to this group, the purpose of feminist reform is to make more important life choices available to women; what women do with these choices should be trusted to their own judgment and considered a question beyond the scope of feminist theory. Other women, more subliminally infused with certain liberal assumptions underlying our political society, resist ideological determination claims because they do not ascribe to women the powers of self-determination that presumably inhere in all human beings.[51] They may consequently be heard to complain that ideological determination arguments "demean women."[52] Still

---

Telephone conversation with Carol Weisbrod, Professor of Law, University of Connecticut (Sept. 13, 1990).

[49] *See* C. MacKinnon, Feminism Unmodified, *supra* note 2, at 217-18.

[50] For an interesting treatment of this issue in the popular media, see *Mommy v. Mommy*, Newsweek, June 4, 1990, at 64 [hereinafter *Mommy v. Mommy*].

[51] Women whose choices are "determined" by deeply embedded ideological influences they neither detect nor understand do not appear to be the autonomous, self-determining agents of liberal theory. Carol Weisbrod describes one version of this tension in her article in this symposium issue. *See* Weisbrod, *Practical Polyphony: Theories of the State and Feminist Jurisprudence*, 24 Ga. L. Rev. 985 (1990).

[52] MacKinnon describes this response in C. MacKinnon, Feminism Unmodified, *supra* note 2, at 220-21.

other women may support the critical scrutiny of women's choices and may concur in accounts which present women's autonomy as compromised by ideology; yet they resist these arguments as unacceptably facile in their depiction of gender ideology's effect on women's lives.

The first response offers little ground for dismissing ideological determination arguments as flawed strategy. This reaction seems more indicative of a division among feminists—between those who see the goal of feminism as securing more choices for women and those who believe that, to make those choices meaningful, feminism must provide a substantive critique of the institutional and attitudinal context in which those choices are made, a critique which may sometimes implicate women.[53] This division could be exacerbated by ideological determination arguments—feminists of the first category are likely to display less tolerance toward arguments which contest women's choices in categorical terms—but the effect is unlikely to be substantial. Feminists who seek primarily to create opportunities for women's choice are unlikely to view favorably any argument which critiques the exercise of those choices.

The second response is only slightly more suggestive of strategic drawbacks. In its strongest form, this argument is almost too extreme to credit—a *reductio ad absurdum* of liberal assumptions. It is remarkably difficult, in the face of contemporary findings on rape, sexual harassment, the wage gap or work/family conflict, to conclude that women enjoy, and should be represented by feminists as enjoying, uncompromised powers of self-determination.[54] It is also evident that arguments such as those made by MacKinnon and Williams do not present women as lacking in all features of

---

[53] It is my view that the former position has, in most areas, foundered on the gap between formal opportunities for choice and the practical consequences for women of exercising them, and that, increasingly, feminist scholars and activists offer variants of the latter position. *See generally* Abrams, *Gender Discrimination and the Transformation of Workplace Norms*, 42 VAND. L. REV. 1183 (1989)(discussing gender equality in the workplace).

[54] Nor do I believe that feminist scholarship has any obligation to present women as having such uncompromised powers of self-determination, in order to make women feel somehow empowered. To this extent, I agree with MacKinnon when she says, "Since when is politics therapy?" C. MACKINNON, FEMINISM UNMODIFIED, *supra* note 2, at 220. I do believe, however, that it is strategically advantageous for feminist scholars, in communicating with even vaguely receptive audiences, to avoid presenting women's powers of self-determination as largely or completely compromised where they are only partially compromised. Here, I suspect that MacKinnon and I part company.

agency or control over their lives. Yet, to the extent that female readers move from an argument that choices are being determined by ideological influences to a conclusion that women are being depicted as lacking in the attributes of agency, this suggests that ideological determination claims can be "rounded up" or "rounded down" as easily as their more conventional counterparts.

The third response is more indicative of strategic drawbacks. This response suggests, in short, that women are put off by ideological determination arguments because they present as simple or reflexive choices that women experience as complex, considered and painful. Arlie Hochschild provides support for this interpretation in her pathbreaking study of work/family conflict, *The Second Shift*.[55] Hochschild depicts a gender ideology which directs even working women to take primary responsibility for home and children, yet whose effects are modulated by family background, socioeconomic status and marital relationship. Moreover, her analysis makes clear that even decisions to acquiesce in an unequal allocation of responsibilities are not easily made, but often result from a long siege of struggle, resistance, emotional frustration, physical exhaustion and unsuccessful efforts at compromise. Interestingly, Hochschild points out that the ideological rhetoric which is sometimes taken to signal women's reflexive capitulation often appears only when a long struggle has reached its end. The exhausted woman seeks to protect herself from further antagonism by embracing rhetoric that enjoys broad cultural acceptance and that creates few social waves.

Hochschild tells, for example, the story of Nancy Holt, a self-identified feminist and social worker who battles unsuccessfully with her non-professional husband for a more equal allocation of household work. Confronted with his passivity in response to her requests for assistance, with his alternating forgetfulness and hostility in response to her creation of "work schedules," with his intimations that she is shirking her responsibilities and with his demand that she take a part-time job if she is unable to finish the housework, she realizes that her demands for equality will cost her her marriage. Unable to face the personal or economic consequences of that choice, she begins to acquiesce in a greater share of household responsibilities. It is only at this point of resignation

---

[55] THE SECOND SHIFT, *supra* note 24.

that she begins to justify her choice by reference to claims such as "[w]omen always adjust more, don't they?"[56] or "I was brought up to do the housework. Evan wasn't."[57]

Findings such as these highlight the potentially alienating characteristics of ideological determination claims. First, they seem to take as dispositive in a woman's decision ideological factors which play only a contributing role and which are mobilized rhetorically only when a decision has already been made. Second, these arguments seem to describe women, through their assimilation of gendered ideology, as playing a leading role in their own subordination, when closer scrutiny suggests that such ideology only hinders women in what is often a pitched battle with external adversaries—men and the institutions they create. Women may oppose these arguments not simply as reductionism, but as reductionism that conceals, on the one hand, women's acts of assertion on their own behalf[58] and, on the other, the depth and variety of the forces arrayed against them.

Finally, women may feel that such arguments conceal the affective component of their struggles. Ideological determination arguments describe a woman who operates reflexively or at worst resignedly, while many women's experiences are more indicative of the tension and anxiety that accompany hard choices. Joan Williams illustrates this point in a recent discussion of Carol Gilligan and her subjects.[59] Examining Gilligan's interviews of several

---

[56] *Id.* at 43.

[57] *Id.* at 55. Ironically, at this point, Nancy also begins to create a myth of more equal division than in fact exists, to hide from herself and others the full extent of her defeat.

Although Hochschild's point about the late appearance of rhetoric which might be labelled ideological does not necessarily conflict with Williams' argument about the importance of domestic ideology in influencing women's departures from the workplace, this point seems to suggest a view that the role of ideological arguments is less causative than justificatory. As I understand Williams' view, she also understands domestic ideology to play a prominent role in women's justifications for their choices, and would welcome its re-examination in that context as well. Telephone conversation with Joan Williams, Professor of Law, American University, Washington College of Law (Oct. 2, 1990).

[58] Ellen DuBois articulated a version of this view when responding to Catharine MacKinnon in *The James McCormick Mitchell Lecture*, *supra* note 25, at 72. DuBois stated, "I am just struck that although you see a kind of seamless historical unity in the oppression of women, so much so that there is no significant change, you see absolutely no historical unity in the efforts to combat that oppression." *Id.*

[59] *See* Williams, *Domesticity as a Dangerous Supplement of Liberalism* (forthcoming in J. WOMEN'S HIST.) [hereinafter Williams, *Dangerous Supplement*] (manuscript on file with the author).

young women who face a decision whether to abort a pregnancy, Williams criticizes Gilligan for highlighting their reflexive responses of nurturance and responsibility for others, when the interviews are, in fact, more expressive of tension and conflict. These women feel pulled between an ideology of "neutrality" that teaches them that if they apply themselves like their male counterparts, they can expect to enjoy the high-achieving career of the "ideal worker" and an ideology of domesticity that teaches them that this self-centered kind of career can take its toll on the lives of others. The affective impression communicated by these interviews is not of the automatic assimilation of the more nurturing point of view, but of the anguish of being pulled in two different directions. Hochschild's case histories also illustrate the anger, frustration, depression and physical illness that punctuate the efforts of women to negotiate a more equal arrangement. This emotional struggle sometimes persists indefinitely, and is almost always precedent to the numb acceptance which prevails in cases of insuperable resistance. By presenting women as having reflexively assimilated views that contribute to their own subordination, ideological determination arguments deny the tension and anguish that often replace, and at the very least precede, this numb acquiescence. This may make them unpalatable to many women.

Commentators such as Olsen might say that proponents of these arguments recognize women's struggles; they simply elect to mute these elements so as to call attention to the gender ideology that contributes to and cloaks women's defeat, and point up the fact that defeat remains pervasive, almost inevitable. My point here is not to contest this interpretation but to argue that, with a substantial group of women, it may have costs. Many women resent this choice as a decision to record women's defeats without honoring their struggles: the progress that even the will to struggle represents, the many adversaries whose opposition necessitates it, the varied forms it takes and the massive personal toll it exacts.[60]

---

[60] Joan Williams argues that the need for a more critical reassessment of the effects of a "women's culture" arises precisely from the fact that women's struggles have been depicted in terms that are too unremittingly celebratory. She notes:

> In their effort to do justice to the dignity of women, [women's historians and other feminists] resoundingly rejected the image of women as victims, and instead have celebrated women's "nearly inexhaustible resources for resistance." Now that this refusal to see women as victims has been transposed into a

Women may also resent such arguments for what they see as a misplaced emphasis: for spotlighting the limited role of women in perpetuating a system of gender inequality they did not create.[61]

These responses also shed light on the first two categories of resistance discussed above, which I first dismissed as too broad to be indicative of countervailing strategic considerations. While they may in fact be unnecessarily broad arguments based on distinct premises that are of little interest here, they may also be magnifications of the responses discussed above. Women may argue that judging women's choices is not the purpose of feminist theory because they find it difficult to reach conclusive judgments about women whose lives are inevitably complex and whose capitulations are not dictated by a single factor but are the products of many influences, some of which the observing women may not them-

---

> blame-the-victim argument through the rhetoric of choice, there is an acute need for a more balanced view of women's culture.

Williams, *Deconstructing Gender*, *supra* note 15, at 829 (citation omitted).

I concur in Williams' goal of creating a "more balanced view," but question whether her depiction of women as being eased into self-marginalization by the "compliments of domesticity" moves too far in the opposite direction. We need to honor women's struggles, even as we acknowledge their all-too-frequent defeats; and, as I argue below, I believe the best vehicles for communicating this are not celebratory encomia, but complex explanations revealing the many factors shaping women's choices and narrative accounts revealing the palpable diversity within the common threads of women's experiences. *See infra* text accompanying notes 93-99.

[61] The sensitivity many women feel about arguments that highlight their role in their own subordination is generated, in the first instance, not by scholarly articles which highlight women's role in perpetuating a complex, male-created system of gender inequality, but by popular presentations of women's struggles which perversely depict women as each other's worst enemies in their efforts to get ahead. A good example of an article in this genre is *Mommy v. Mommy*, *supra* note 50. It highlights the antagonism between women who work during the infancy of their children and women who stay home, focusing on the instances of mutual exclusion and social stigmatization that mark their increasingly infrequent interaction. At a time when many workplaces have made little effort to accommodate record numbers of working parents and when many parents unable to arrange childcare face the decision whether to leave jobs in favor of public assistance, one might legitimately question whether this is the most significant or newsworthy focus *Newsweek* could have chosen. One might also question why the authors of such articles so rarely attempt to put the internecine quarrels among women in their proper political context. *Newsweek* might, for example, have titled its article *Employers v. Mothers: Skirmishes Behind the Lines*, and explained that the gendered expectations of employers made working mothers uneasy about women who seem to give credence to those images and that the social devaluation of parenting, combined with the difficulty of obtaining accommodation at work, had made those mothers who had left the workplace resentful of those who remained.

selves have experienced.[62] Similarly, those who claim that these arguments depict women as devoid of agency actually may be objecting that these claims obscure what efforts at self-determination women have been able to mount on their own behalf and conceal the very real and identifiably human emotional repercussions of these efforts.[63]

So against the benefits of shaking into awareness a particularly impenetrable part of the population, feminists must balance the costs of alienating a more receptive portion of their audience. A second category of costs suggests that even with this "impenetrable" group, ideological determination arguments may not present a purely advantageous strategy.

B. *Women as Rational Decisionmakers*

Among the tangle of attitudes that generate discrimination against women is the belief that women are deficient in those faculties necessary to make important decisions.[64] This attitude not only fueled the exclusion of women from the jury and the franchise,[65] but also contributed, in the view of some scholars,[66] to

---

[62] Christine Littleton makes the point that to describe women's responses as appropriate, given a particular factual context, is distinct from, and to her mind preferable to, the liberal position that broadly validates all women's choices. *See* Littleton, *Women's Experience and the Problem of Transition: Perspectives on the Male Battering of Women*, 1989 U. CHI. LEGAL F. 23, 27. *See also* Bartlett, *Feminist Legal Methods*, 103 HARV. L. REV. 829, 880 (1990) (describing "positionality" as a stance which "acknowledges the existence of empirical truths, values, and knowledge, and also their contingency").

[63] It is interesting and ironic that, understood this way, female critics of ideological determination claims seem to be "turning up the volume" on their objections, just as Olsen argues that proponents of ideological determination claims are "turning up the volume" on arguments that women may be unconscious contributors to their own subordination.

[64] In *Deconstructing Gender*, Joan Williams traces several different incarnations of this view. Before the mid-eighteenth century, this view was expressed through the image of the "weaker vessel." Women were creatures of "intense sexuality and fundamental irrationality" who required guidance from men to prevent them from slipping into "collusion with evil." Williams, *Deconstructing Gender*, *supra* note 15, at 804. After the Enlightenment, philosophers began to celebrate logic and reason, and "women's intellectual inferiority came to be expressed as an inability to engage in rigorous, abstract thinking." *Id.*

[65] *See generally* S. EVANS, BORN TO LIBERTY (1989); Weisbrod, *Images of the Woman Juror*, 9 HARV. WOMEN'S L.J. 59 (1986). As authors such as Evans and Weisbrod note, arguments regarding women's "difference" were used both to oppose and to buttress women's demands to participate in public life. Opponents of women's inclusion argued that women were too delicate to take part in robust debate over public matters and lacked the judgment and understanding necessary to reach sound decisions. Advocates of inclusion sometimes simply claimed their "equal rights," but at other times argued that a distinctive female

the efforts of state officials to regulate reproductive experience. The persistence of this attitude among substantial groups in the population creates a volatile environment for the injection of ideological determination claims. These claims are not intended to suggest, nor does their careful interpretation lead to the conclusion, that women are not responsible decisionmakers. Because of their potential for misinterpretation by groups which hold the latter view, however, such claims may give unintended succor to efforts to restrict women's choices. While feminist advocates have been exquisitely sensitive to this danger in some areas, they have been less alert to it in others. I will explore this phenomenon by looking at feminists' responses to two sets of choices made by women: the choice whether to abort a fetus and the choice whether to leave (or substantially reduce one's commitment to) the workplace upon the birth or adoption of a child.[67] The reproductive choice is rarely, if ever, the subject of criticism or arguments of "ideological determination"; the work/family choice, on the other hand, has been subjected to increasing critical scrutiny. Not only is it the case that the decision to leave the workplace has been the subject of continual, practical second-guessing, but also some scholars have begun to analyze departure from the workplace as the product of gender ideology. By discussing the factors that have contributed to this difference in treatment, I hope to highlight another set of strategic dangers to the use of "ideological determination" claims.

---

morality would be useful in cleaning up corruption and would be suitable to the new nurturing or service-providing role of the state. *See* S. EVANS, *supra*, at 152-56.

[66] *See* Ashe, *Zig-Zag Stitching and the Seamless Web*, 13 NOVA L.J. 355 (1989). Both ordinary and extraordinary legal regulation of reproductive experience, Ashe argues, raise a series of common questions: "Who will be permitted to exercise the power of extinguishing certain forms of human life? May women be entrusted to exercise such power? Ought the choice of mortality by women—or the willing assumption of certain risks of death—be tolerated by law?" *Id.* at 372. Arguing for deregulation in such areas as abortion, home births and court-ordered caesarians, Ashe concludes, "I want a law that . . . recognizing the violence inherent in every regulation of female 'reproduction,' defines an area of non-regulation, within which we will make, each of us, our own 'mortal decisions.'" *Id.* at 383.

[67] My focus on the question of women's departures from the workplace in this section and the next should not suggest that my disagreements with *Deconstructing Gender* are greater in any way than my disagreements with *Feminism Unmodified* or other works involving ideological determination claims. In fact, as the above analysis suggests, I believe *Deconstructing Gender* is subtler and involves less amplification than some other examples of ideological determination arguments. I consider the question of women's departures from the workplace at length simply because my own work in the work/family area makes this question particularly interesting to me. *See* Abrams, *supra* note 53.

In the rhetoric and scholarship of pro-choice feminism, the right to choose is pre-eminent: there is little or no effort to judge the way that choice is exercised. This can be seen in the political campaigns waged to protect choice: the National Abortion Rights Action League "Silent No More" campaign publicized a range of stories by women who had obtained legal abortions, evincing a thoroughgoing neutrality toward the range of reasons revealed. This reluctance to judge women's choices is evident in the scholarly literature as well. Some scholars have criticized the process of investigating and deliberating through which women approach the choice to abort;[68] others have argued that certain ways of framing or describing the reproductive choice reflect the influence of ideology.[69] But few, if any, feminist scholars have made the claim that a decision to abort or to carry to term is the product of gendered ideology. MacKinnon, in an essay intensely critical of the privacy rationale inaugurated in *Roe*, argues that the decision to engage in (unprotected) sex is often the product of ideological determination, necessitating a right to abortion.[70] Yet even she stops short of arguing that the choice itself may be dictated by gendered ideology. This restraint contrasts markedly with the chorus of critical arguments that have erupted in the area of work/family choice.

What accounts for this difference in treatment? Surely not the fact that decisions regarding abortion are free from the influence of gender ideology. In my feminism seminar, I ask my students to read three fictional works relating to abortion: Alice Walker's short story "The Abortion,"[71] and excerpts from Meridel LeSuer's *The Girl*[72] and Gloria Naylor's *The Women of Brewster Place*.[73] In each of these stories, a woman approaches a reproductive choice strongly, and sometimes reflexively, influenced by the desires of the man with whom she is involved. In Walker's story, Imani aborts a pregnancy, notwithstanding her own palpable ambivalence, because her distracted husband fails to express a desire to

---

[68] *See* Colker, *Feminism, Theology and Abortion: Toward Love, Compassion and Wisdom*, 77 CALIF. L. REV. 1011 (1989).

[69] Williams, *Dangerous Supplement*, *supra* note 59.

[70] MacKinnon, Roe v. Wade*: A Study in Male Ideology*, in ABORTION: MORAL AND LEGAL PERSPECTIVES 45, 53 (1984) [hereinafter *A Study in Male Ideology*].

[71] Walker, *The Abortion*, in YOU CAN'T KEEP A GOOD WOMAN DOWN 64 (1981).

[72] M. LESUER, THE GIRL (1978).

[73] G. NAYLOR, THE WOMEN OF BREWSTER PLACE (1980).

raise the child. In *The Girl*, the narrator is driven by her lover's threats of violence to seek an abortion she does not want.[74] In *The Women of Brewster Place*, Ciel dejectedly obtains an abortion in an unsuccessful effort to hold her lover, who accuses her of being "good for nothing" but "babies and bills."[75] Though any of these women might defend their decisions as "choice," these decisions reflect a strong, intuitive response to the expressed preferences of the men in their lives—a response which ranges from fear of violence to desire for connection.

Nor are instances of such influence restricted to the pages of literature. Surveying a group of empirical studies on male and female responses to abortion,[76] John Stoltenberg concludes that male opposition is often a critical deterrent for women otherwise anxious to obtain abortions:

> Knowing that he can make her life miserable if she transgresses, if she crosses him in any way, she opts for a lesser misery. As she surrenders her will to his, it doesn't make a lot of difference whether she does so grudgingly, thinking, 'He's making me do this,' or whether she does so completely browbeaten, believing, 'This is what I wanted anyway.' What matters is that *he* gets his way. Often as not, she carries an unwanted pregnancy to term rather than provoke her male partner's threatening rage. It's easier, she imagines, to live with the screaming of a defenseless, unwanted child.[77]

Stoltenberg's argument suggests not only that an ideologically-instilled range of feelings from fear to deference may prompt the decision to continue an unwanted pregnancy, but that women sometimes manifest a response resembling "false consciousness": they

---

[74] Ultimately the narrator escapes from the home of the abortionist (and her coercive relationship) and proceeds to carry and deliver her baby. Interestingly, this story, in which the woman rebels against the pressure of male preference, is the only one of three stories in which the reproductive choice, and its relational consequences, appear to be satisfying to the woman in question. In *The Abortion*, *supra* note 71, Imani's growing resentment over her husband's casual disinterest in their potential child leads her to detach herself from her marriage; in *The Women of Brewster Place*, *supra* note 73, Ciel's sacrifice of a pregnancy she wanted does not prevent her lover from leaving her.

[75] G. NAYLOR, *supra* note 73, at 94.

[76] *See* J. STOLTENBERG, REFUSING TO BE A MAN: ESSAYS ON SEX AND JUSTICE 91-100 (1989).

[77] *Id.* at 95.

interpret a self-destructive decision as their choice when it is actually the product of ideological influence.

The avoidance of claims of "ideological determination" in the abortion area, then, stems not from the impossibility of making them, but rather from some decision that they are inappropriate or unwise. What might lead feminists to such a decision in the area of abortion, even as they reach a different verdict in the area of work/family choice? I see two possibilities. First, the abortion area is, with abundant reason, considered to be vulnerable, embattled ground. Even so uncompromising a critic as MacKinnon acknowledges, in rejecting a privacy ground for abortion, that "we have not been able to risk thinking about these issues on our own terms, because the terms have not been ours, either in sex, in life in general, or in court."[78] At a time when a woman's right to choose is afforded decreasing protection from the courts and is subject to curtailment or compromise at the hands of state legislatures, any argument which questions the ways in which women choose or impugns their capacities as rational decisionmakers seems unaccountably reckless. Ideological determination claims do not, in fact, prove what detractors allege—that women lack the faculties to perform the basic analysis of pros and cons necessary to reach an important decision. They do suggest, however, that women develop a tendency to value certain costs (such as male disapprobation) too highly or that they may not understand all the reasons behind the choices they make. These arguments, when offered by feminist advocates themselves, may be eagerly grasped as fodder for broader claims by detractors of women's choice.

A second explanation might attribute the difference in response to a difference in the nature of feminist goals in each area. For better or for worse, the purpose of feminist activism in the area of abortion is to protect women's opportunities for choice from governmental regulation. Some feminists support this goal as optimal, regarding the enhancement (but not the content) of women's choices as the primary object of feminist efforts. Many other feminists regard this goal not as optimal, but as inevitable—the unfortunate consequence of a flawed litigation strategy and a hostile judicial response. Both the initial decision to pursue a privacy

---

[78] *See* MacKinnon, *A Study in Male Ideology*, *supra* note 70, at 46.

rationale and subsequent cases such as *Harris v. McRae*[79] have undermined efforts to create an affirmative public role (such as funding or publicly-supported counseling) in reproductive choice. With efforts to reconstruct the public sphere either impossible or undesired, there seems little reason to look beyond the formal occasion for choice: there is little to be gained (and arguably much to be lost) by inquiry into the grounds of women's choices—including inquiries into ideological determination.

Those feminists who seek reform in the work/family area confront a different task. Neither chastened by judicial or legislative defeats nor restricted by liberal privacy rationale, these activists are less inclined to view the creation of opportunities for choice as their primary goal. They seek instead the comprehensive institutional change that makes it possible for women to exercise choice without financial cost or stigma. In this posture, it becomes essential to analyze the attitudes that fuel choices by both men and women in the workplace. By analyzing the attitudes of those men still largely responsible for shaping the workplace, feminists can identify the barriers that may prevent formal choices from being meaningful. By analyzing the choices of women who respond to work/family conflicts, feminists can better understand the ways in which contemporary workplaces thwart many women's (and some men's) ability to manage both roles. The scrutiny of women's decisions that was superfluous or harmful to the protection of choice in the area of abortion becomes central to facilitating choice in the work/family area. Criticizing and highlighting the elements of "ideological determination" in these decisions might be defended as part of that task.

To my mind, however, neither the need for caution in the abortion area nor the need for a substantive critique of participants' choices in the work/family area justifies the differential resort to "ideological determination" claims. First, it may be naive to assume that the practical threat which makes care prudent in the area of abortion is limited to that area. Doubts about the capacity of women to make critical choices, as I note above, have long played a role in the opposition to equality for women. The fact that these arguments no longer occupy the primary ground of po-

---

[79] 448 U.S. 297 (1980) (finding Hyde Act, which severely limits use of federal funds to reimburse cost of abortion under medicaid programs, constitutionally valid).

litical debate does not mean that they have been successfully banished; in some cases, they have lurked beneath the conversational surface, only to emerge in restrictive enactments. It may be no coincidence that many of the most popular forms of legislation restricting abortion require women to secure the consent of others, rather than allowing the reproductive choices to be made by the women by themselves. Moreover, two recent categories of enactments relating to work/family conflict reflect doubts about women's ability to make rational cost-benefit calculations in this area.

The most controversial example is the fetal protection policy. In this type of policy, pending now before the Supreme Court in *International Union, UAW v. Johnson Controls*,[80] employers have enacted a blanket exclusion of potentially fertile women from certain types of jobs, because they involve exposure to chemicals which pose a threat to the health of a fetus. This blanket exclusion in some cases replaces earlier policies which permitted women to evaluate for themselves the hazards of becoming pregnant in a potentially toxic environment. Such policies are based on an array of explicit rationales: they are necessary to protect employers from staggering liability for birth defects in children, which cannot be waived by their mothers; they are necessary to protect women who may not be aware that they are pregnant.[81] Yet the breadth of these prohibitions[82] and their choice over options which offer more autonomy to fertile women suggest at least an indifference to, and at most an abiding suspicion of, women's capacity for choice.[83] In his dissent in *Johnson Controls*, Judge Easterbrook highlighted the ways in which fetal protection policies impugn a woman's capacity to make rational choices about her work and family. He compared the policy to state laws which assume "that women are

[80] 886 F.2d 871 (7th Cir. 1989) (finding fetal protection policy precluding fertile women from working in high lead exposure position did not violate Title VII), *cert. granted* 110 S. Ct. 1522 (1990).

[81] *See id.* at 877-79.

[82] Johnson Controls' policy, for example, defines women of childbearing capacity as "[a]ll women except those whose inability to bear children is medically documented." Id. at 876 n.8.

[83] *See* Becker, *From* Muller v. Oregon *to Fetal Vulnerability Policies*, 53 U. Chi. L. Rev. 1219, 1241-43 (1986). Becker's article was, of course, written before *International Union*, but discusses earlier fetal vulnerability cases such as Oil, Chemical & Atomic Workers Internat'l Union v. American Cyanamid Co., 741 F.2d 444 (D.C. Cir. 1984).

less able than men to take the precautions essential for healthy children"[84] and concluded that "no legal or ethical principle compels or allows Johnson to assume that women are less able than men to make intelligent decisions about the welfare of the next generation . . . ."[85]

A similar assumption is reflected in the "alternative work schedules" currently being promulgated by some large law firms. These policies permit mothers (or, occasionally, parents) of small children to work a reduced schedule, but impose an unconditional requirement that they exit the partnership track upon so doing, with no guarantee of re-entry.[86] These policies signal to those within the firm that lawyers who commit substantial time to parenting are not "ideal workers"[87] (perhaps not even "serious" professionals); yet they also raise questions about the abilities of women attorneys to make rational decisions about their professional progress. By removing the decision whether to remain on partnership track from the hands of the women involved, these policies protect the firm from the inconvenience that might be perpetrated by women who misestimate the priority they will be able to place on their work. To assume that such misestimation would be so endemic as to create a problem that could not be handled on an individual basis—to assume, moreover, that it would be prevalent among women who would have every professional reason to be conservative in their estimations—is to raise substantial doubts about women's abilities to make work/family choices.

The doubts underlying these programs are not the same ones expressed by proponents of "ideological determination" claims. It is not clear that the architects of such programs are familiar with these claims, or that a careful reading would lead them to view

---

[84] *International Union*, 886 F.2d at 912 (Easterbrook, J., dissenting).

[85] *Id.* at 913.

[86] A thumbnail empirical survey I initiated in connection with an earlier article suggested that neither "alternative work schedules" nor the requirements imposed by some such programs of exit programs from the partnership track are regular features of law-related workplaces. Both the programs and the exit requirements, however, are appearing in numbers sufficient to warrant careful examination. Of approximately twenty legal employers surveyed (including law firms, investment banks, law schools and a municipal corporation counsel), six had "alternative work schedule" programs, and two of these required participants in such programs to exit the partnership track. *See* Abrams, *supra* note 53, at 1242 n.220.

[87] I take this phrase from Joan Williams. *See* Williams, *Deconstructing Gender*, *supra* note 15, at 823.

these claims as supportive of their efforts.[88] Yet to the extent these policies reveal a re-emergent suspicion of women's decisionmaking powers, they suggest the hazard of arguments that systematically amplify the uniformity, reflexivity or self-destructiveness of choices made by women. This circumstance does not demand the censorship of all arguments which impugn the judgment of women:[89] it would be pointless and misleading to deny that women make bad judgments or that ideology exerts some influence over their choices. But it does suggest the need for a middle path. We need ways of describing the influence of gender ideology on women that avoid amplifying its effect on their choices or women's confusion about their own motives.

C. *Ideological Determination and Remedial Efforts*

This is also the conclusion I reach by reflecting on the second factor that distinguishes the work/family area from that of abortion. The goal of reconstructing a workplace that is more receptive to women's choices makes it helpful, in fact necessary, to examine the choices of those within the workplace. Yet, it is not clear that arguments of ideological determination are the most useful instruments in that examination. Indeed, ideological determination arguments have a troubled relationship to efforts at reconstructive change that may be explained in several ways. In many cases, ideological determination arguments structure the feminist agenda in ways that do not give priority to reconstructive efforts. This may sometimes be intentional: proponents deliberately focus attention on the problem of women's ideological indoctrination, a focus

---

[88] Taken literally, the ideological determination arguments discussed in this Essay might even seem to run counter to the animating norms of these restrictive programs. The argument made by Joan Williams in *Deconstructing Gender*, for example, suggests that gender ideology causes women to neglect their professional interests in order to "take responsibility" for their families. The assumption of architects of fetal protection and alternative work-schedule policies appears to be that women will neglect the interests of their families in order to advance their careers. It is difficult, however, to be sure whether the architects of these programs would take such arguments literally or would use them more loosely as evidence of the inadequacy of women's decisionmaking capacities.

[89] To my mind, it does not even demand the rigid self-scrutiny which has characterized the area of abortion. I agree with those scholars who have argued that feminist analysis in this area has been circumscribed too strictly by the possibility of courting political danger. *See, e.g.*, Ashe, *supra* note 66; Colker, *supra* note 68; MacKinnon, *A Study in Male Ideology*, *supra* note 70.

which illuminates the scope, rather than the remediation, of the problem. It may also be unintentional: the controversy generated by ideological determination claims keeps these issues, rather than remedial questions, on the front burner.[90] Even where these arguments do not divert attention from remedial efforts, they may discourage women from undertaking them. Ideological determination claims present women's choices as determined by pervasive, diffuse influences which operate in many cases beyond their awareness or complete comprehension. If these claims are embraced by women, rather than resisted, they may suggest to some women that they are ill-equipped to judge the kinds of changes which are necessary.[91] More likely, they will suggest to women that the kinds of limited changes that could be most readily achieved are no match for the forces holding them in place.

More importantly, even where ideological determination arguments are offered to facilitate change by illuminating the influences operating on women, these arguments may be less useful than others which depict such influences as more numerous, more contingent and more heterogeneous. Most of these drawbacks concern the elaboration of causation. A complete understanding of causation can be important to remediation, not only because it can reveal the range of factors whose control may ameliorate the problem but also because it can reveal the role being played by institu-

---

[90] I find in teaching MacKinnon, for example, that students spend what I view as a disproportionate amount of time trying to decide whether she actually believes that women eroticize dominance or that much of what is conventionally considered to be intercourse is rape and whether this possible belief affects the credibility of her theory.

[91] I see this possibility as less likely, but I am not sure whether this is true because ideological determination claims are not, in fact, so debilitating or because, at some subconscious level, even women who try to take them seriously and personally continue to resist them.

Catharine MacKinnon would contest this possibility: in her view, the fact that women's choices may be determined by gender ideology does not necessarily make women's perspectives on the changes that need to be made less reliable. She argues that the same experience of domination that may give rise to ideological determination also gives women a singularly accurate perspective on gender inequality. *See, e.g.*, C. MACKINNON, TOWARD A FEMINIST THEORY, *supra* note 5, at 173 (describing as instrumental to legal change a "view [of rape] that derives most directly from victims' experiences, rather than from their denial"). I find the view, that women's perspective is both dominated and accurate, a paradox in MacKinnon's thought that is not fully explained; moreover, looking at the examples she gives, I find it difficult to distinguish women victims' "experiential" views from women victims' "denials," except by reference to MacKinnon's own perspective. *See* Abrams, *Feminist Lawyering*, *supra* note 43.

tions or actors who may be liable under law. Several features of ideological determination arguments have made them unhelpful or even counterproductive in efforts to illuminate causation. If we assume, as many readers have, that ideological influence operates independently of institutional or other causal factors, the strategic amplification of this influence is the root of the problem. "Turning up the volume" on ideological influence obscures the role of other factors whose identification may be important to remediation. If we assume, on the other hand, that the ideological coloration of women's views bears some relation to other causal factors, we encounter a different problem. The ways in which ideological determination is depicted by feminist scholars make this relation, which might be crucial to remediation, difficult to discern.

The ideological coloration of women's attitudes is often presented as a kind of a testament to the completeness of a system of gender inequality, something which emerges when all the other components of gender domination are in place. Inasmuch as we are encouraged to think at all about the etiology of this phenomenon, it seems to arise, as in MacKinnon, from the sum total of the structures of gender discrimination. Even those scholars such as Williams, who have spoken more precisely about its development, have focused on the exacerbating influence of scholarly arguments taken up by the public.[92] Little scholarship in this area has focused on the generation of these attitudes among women, or, perhaps more importantly, on the relationship between ideological influence and institutional patterns and practices.[93] This has meant

---

[92] I recognize that while my objection to the arguments of MacKinnon in this respect is based on a claim of imprecision in her work, my objection to the arguments of Williams may be based on a difference of opinion about historical causation, that is, about the comparative roles of institutions and ideas. It is not, however, a difference upon which I would lean too hard: as lawyers, we may be better equipped to address institutional causation; but as legal scholars and as activists, we need to know about the influence of ideas as well. Thus, beyond the claim that Williams focuses on the exacerbation of ideological influence, while I would like to see more inquiry into the generation of ideological influence, my difference with her focus exists only to the extent that its amplification of such influences as Gilligan's work obscures the possibility of an institutional contribution to the ideological coloration of women's attitudes.

[93] One exception is the work of Vicki Schultz. *See* Schultz, *Telling Stories about Women and Work: Judicial Interpretation of Sex Segregation in the Workplace in Title VII Cases Raising the Lack of Interest Argument*, 103 HARV. L. REV. 1749 (1990). In this article, Schultz considers the argument, raised in Title VII cases, that women lack interest in particular categories of jobs. She argues that both "liberal" decisions rejecting and "conservative" de-

that the generative or contributing role of institutions most readily subject to legal remediation—institutions such as workplaces, police forces or legislatures—has remained largely beyond the reach of reconstructive thought.

III. Talking About Women's Choices

These musings on the strategic consequences of ideological determination claims yield no easy solutions. Clearly, highlighting women's assimilation of gender ideology has important advantages. It communicates the important point that neither biological sex nor the experience of oppression makes one immune to the influence of a pervasive ideology. It points to the politically valuable conclusion that securing opportunities for women's choice can rarely be viewed as the alpha and omega of feminist reform. It challenges women to apply the unsparing scrutiny of feminist theory to their own lives. Yet making this point too strongly may also have the negative repercussions suggested above. These consequences suggest that feminists cannot restrict themselves to, or rely too heavily on, the strategy of "turning up the volume" epitomized in ideological determination claims. Feminist scholars and activists need alternative modes of discourse through which to analyze controversial choices made by women: forms of discourse that acknowledge the possibility that women may be influenced by the internalization of the very ideology that has subordinated them, yet avoid the claims of determination that alienate women, facilitate the misrepresentation of their decisionmaking capacities and impede the inquiry into contributing causal factors which may be more readily subject to remediation. We also need an ongoing debate over what circumstances make particular modes of discussion most advantageous or appropriate. Fortunately, the question of a suitable discourse for discussing women's choices has begun to be considered by feminists in several different contexts.[94] In these

cisions accepting the lack of interest argument have assumed that women's job preferences are formed outside the workplace. She argues that these approaches incorrectly focus judicial attention outside the workplace and therefore have only limited potential for transforming the workplace. Schultz advocates, instead, new explanations of women's choice which reveal the role the workplace plays in shaping women's preferences for particular jobs. These explanations, which Schultz finds to be supported by sociological evidence, will require deeper judicial scrutiny of the way employers have structured the workplace.

[94] *See, e.g.*, Bartlett, *supra* note 62; Littleton, *supra* note 62; Mahoney, *Legal Images of*

concluding thoughts, I will draw on some of this work to suggest the contours of an approach which holds out more strategic promise.

1. Complex or Multi-Causal Explanations. The first feature of an alternative discourse is a willingness to explore multi-causal explanations of controversial choices made by women. This approach would begin from the premise, articulated by Williams, MacKinnon and others, that it is possible for women to assimilate parts of a ideology that oppresses them. Given the pervasiveness of these norms in our society, it would indeed be surprising if women were able to avoid it. This approach would, however, avoid the claim that these assimilated norms *determine* the choices of *women as a group*—that they constitute a singular force which overshadows the impact of other factors and that they exert a comparable influence over diverse segments of the female population. It is from these premises that most strategic drawbacks of these arguments flow. The focus on ideology as a primary causal factor evokes resentment and impedes remediation among women: it suggests that their choices can be largely explained by forces that women neither fully understand nor credit and it obscures other influences that shape and constrain women's lives. The implied uniformity of this influence not only makes it less credible to women, but makes it vulnerable to abuse by those who would circumscribe women's choices.

One way of avoiding these drawbacks would be to offer ideological influence arguments not as conclusive or even primary explanations, but as elements of a more complex picture of women's choices. A woman leaving the workplace on the birth of a child, for example, might be described as responding to an ideologically inculcated belief that it was "virtuous" to "take responsibility" for the lives of her family; but she might simultaneously be described as having been thwarted by a workplace which refused her request for a job-sharing arrangement, frustrated by a husband who refused to share responsibility for night-time feedings and defeated by the collapse of her childcare arrangements. This approach would not deny the influence of ideological assimilation, but would present it as a part of the attitudinal backdrop against which relational or institutional impediments arose, and the woman's re-

Battered Women, 43 STAN. L. REV. (forthcoming 1990); Schultz, *supra* note 93.

sponse to them took shape. Another way of pursuing these goals would be to inquire more systematically into the development of ideological influence itself. We might attempt to identify discrete influences—specific cultural conventions or institutional practices—which contributed to the ideological coloration of women's opinions.[95] Such inquiries, if productive, could simultaneously connect ideological influence more closely to the system of gender discrimination and reduce its implication that women are somehow a primary source of their own subordination.

Although these approaches might "turn down the volume" on ideological influence claims, such de-escalation might make it easier for such claims to be heard. Ideological determination arguments often seem to involve a mismatch between the expectations of proponents who believe that such arguments cannot be heard unless singularly stressed and the response of many audiences whose defensiveness or sensitivity leads them to amplify any hint of "false consciousness" they hear in advocacy claims. Inclusion of these arguments in multi-causal explanations will make them less threatening to many audiences. It will assure women they are not being fingered with weighty responsibility for their subordination; it will assure men and women that the structural and institutional factors they regard as playing a role in women's choices are actually a part of the picture; and it will give those focused on the task of remediation a less diffuse and more appropriate set of starting points for their work. A less defensive response from audiences may make it more promising for feminist scholars and activists—even those who seek to jar their audiences from their complacency[96]—to try a more modulated mode of discourse.

---

[95] In her article, *Legal Images of Battered Women*, Martha Mahoney challenges feminists to look for ways in which the state may be implicated in some women's tendency to submit to their husband's assertions of control over their lives. She offers, for example, a story about a couple who went to a state office to obtain a marriage license; upon completion of the requisite forms, the woman (not the man) was presented with a packet containing detergents, cleansers and other household implements. Mahoney views this story as offering provocative suggestions, deserving of further inquiry, about the role of the state in fostering women's attitudes of subordination in the domestic sphere. *See* Mahoney, *supra* note 94.

[96] Some of these proponents may fear that multi-causal explanations of women's choices will bring in causal elements that are not related to gender. Although there are bound to be some such elements, I suspect this view neglects the complex character of gender discrimination—increasingly evident in both the area of sexuality and the area of work/family conflict. Multi-causal analysis can be a useful educational tool in this respect, because it shows us or reminds us of the numerous forms discrimination can take. *See* Littleton, *Equality*

2. *Narrative Accounts.* Communicating multi-causal explanations of women's choices can be a difficult enterprise. This is particularly true because the causal factors and the relationships among factors may vary among women or groups of women. General or categorical statements of explanation may not capture this variety, and even abstract descriptions of particular patterns (such as the one attempted above) may not convey the interplay among factors. Feminist scholars may be able to convey a better sense of this complex pattern of causation by offering narrative accounts of women's choices. Narratives have been used by many feminist scholars to supply the often-excluded perspectives produced by women's experience. Some early narrative accounts tended to highlight a single attribute or pattern in women's experience that had been excluded by mainstream legal arrangements or analysis. However, more recently, narrative scholars have offered more complex accounts to critique both mainstream legal solutions[97] and the singularity implicit in early feminist explanations.[98] A narrative detailing the attitudes, employer policies, spousal obstacles and logistical pressures that led a primary parent to leave her workplace would expose the range of factors contributing to her choice. It would also describe their interplay: the way that a "domestic ideology" conditioned not only the expectations of the woman but the leave policies of her husband's employer or the hours of her child-care center; the way that the lack of flex-time arrangements or the low esteem assigned to part-time work made it difficult to attend to a sick child; the way that the inflexibility of requirements for travel made her husband impatient and resentful or made her feel that she had failed in her "responsibility" for her family.

Narrative accounts also have several advantages that permit them to reap some of the benefits of ideological determination claims without risking the rigidity such arguments can entail. First, the inevitable particularity of narratives makes it possible to communicate the variety that exists even within similar choices or

---

and Feminist Legal Theory, 48 U. Pitt. L. Rev. 1043 (1987) (describing three distinct categories of gender discrimination).

[97] *See* Williams, *The Obliging Shell*, 87 Mich. L. Rev. 2128 (1989).

[98] An interesting example of such an effort is the work of Martha Mahoney on spousal abuse. *See* Mahoney, *supra* note 94. Mahoney uses narratives from the lives of battered women to suggest the need for a more complex account of the battering relationship than that provided by theories of "learned helplessness."

comparable patterns of behavior among women. All decisions to submit to aggressive sexual pressure, or to leave the workplace on the birth of a child, do not look the same when they are reported in close detail. Narratives may provide a way for readers to see the diversity in perception or response—if not in ultimate choice—that are attributable to race, class, sexual orientation, family background or other individual factors. Moreover, because narratives make it possible to examine a woman's response over time, they can communicate protracted resistance or a war among competing impulses in a way that simple description of the choice made or the justification offered cannot. Because of this quality, narratives become a vehicle for honoring women's struggles, as well as documenting their all-too-frequent defeats. Finally, the concreteness of narrative accounts makes it far easier for readers to take their message personally. It is one thing for a woman to exempt herself from a statistic or from a generalized pattern of behavior; it is quite another for her to insist on her difference from women whose spouses, jobs, desires or constraints seem tangibly similar to her own.

These benefits are manifest, for example, in Arlie Hochschild's *The Second Shift*.[99] Drawing on an exhaustive set of interviews, Hochschild tells the stories of ten two-career families who attempt to allocate the extra day's labor involved in the care of home and children. These stories are set in the context of a comprehensive sociological discussion of work/family conflict; they are communicated through a complex interweaving of narration and analysis, which highlights the causal influences and the relationships among them. The particularity of these accounts make vivid the numerous factors that can influence women's choices, even as the repetition of particular patterns bespeaks the persistence of ideological influence. Hochschild's ten families vary by race, socioeconomic status, family background, job descriptions and the arrangements they ultimately arrive at for allocating the labor of the second shift. Yet, the prevalence of gender differentiation in the tasks assigned and the persistence of gender stereotypes in the "myths" mobilized by both men and women to justify inequalities emerge as unmistakable themes. The patient detail in which these stories are elaborated also makes it possible for readers to appreciate the resistance these

---

[99] THE SECOND SHIFT, *supra* note 24.

women wage against a world of rigid employers and insensitive spouses, even as we steel ourselves for the virtual inevitability of their capitulation. Finally, the variety and concreteness of these accounts makes it difficult to evade their message. These women travel the road to compromised aspirations over so many different paths that it becomes virtually impossible to see oneself as exempt from the forces they face. These stories produce the same systematic accusation and the same call to self-scrutiny that is implicit in MacKinnon's approach. Yet they do so without erasing women's differences or undervaluing their struggles.

* * *

In elaborating these alternative forms of discourse, I do not suggest that they will be appropriate in all settings. A lack of background in one's audience may make multi-causal analysis a treacherous undertaking. Limitations of time or space or the need for a concise analysis may make multiple narrative accounts impossible. It may be that ideological determination claims will remain a useful instrument in some contexts, such as introducing gender inequality to the uninitiated. In exploring new ways of characterizing women's choices, I mean simply to suggest that feminists and other legal scholars have at our disposal a wider array of tools for expressing our situation and persuading each other than we sometimes suspect; and that we may come to useful insights about using them by considering their effects on our audience and on those tasks of reform of which our scholarship is a part.

In concluding her discussion of MacKinnon, Frances Olsen offers a telling analogy:

> A story about Clarence Darrow, perhaps apocryphal, describes the famous lawyer engaging in discussions of all sides of a variety of public questions with a young man who afterwards hears Darrow make simplistic, one-sided comments to the press on the same issues. Darrow's explanation, when confronted by the young man, was that the kind of complex, balanced statements he had presented in their earlier discussions would not have made news.[100]

---

[100] *See* Olsen, *supra* note 3, at 1176 (citing I. STONE, CLARENCE DARROW FOR THE DEFENSE 172-73 (1943)).

Darrow's seemingly instinctive strategic feat, in fact, rested on the development of multiple forms of discourse and carefully honed judgment about the situations that called for each. Feminist discourse about women's choices will benefit from committed attention to both of these questions.

Part IV
New Directions

[15]

ROBIN WEST, THE DIFFERENCE IN WOMEN'S HEDONIC LIVES: A PHENOMENOLOGICAL CRITIQUE OF FEMINIST LEGAL THEORY

3 Wis.Women's L.J. 81, 81–87, 90–99, 103–104, 108, 111–115, 119–122, 128–132, 134–142, 144–145 (1987).

Women's subjective, hedonic lives are different from men's. The quality of our suffering is different from that of men's, as is the nature of our joy. Furthermore, and of more direct concern to feminist lawyers, the quantity of pain and pleasure enjoyed or suffered by the two genders is different: women suffer more than men. The two points are related. One reason that women suffer more than men is that women often find painful the same objective event or condition that men find pleasurable. The introduction of oxymorons in our vocabulary, wrought by feminist victories, evidences this difference in women's and men's hedonic lives. The phrases "date-rape," for example and "sexual harassment," capture these different subjective experiences of shared social realities: For the man, the office pass was sex (and pleasurable), for the woman, it was harassment (and painful); for the man the evening was a date—perhaps not pleasant, but certainly not frightening—for the woman, it was a rape and very scary indeed. ... Women's distinctive, gender-specific injuries are now or have in the recent past been variously dismissed as trivial (sexual harassment on the street); consensual (sexual harassment on the job); humorous (non-violent marital rape); participatory, subconsciously wanted, or self-induced (father/daughter incest); natural or biological, and therefore inevitable (childbirth); sporadic, and conceptually continuous with gender-neutral pain (rape, viewed as a crime of violence); deserved or private (domestic violence); non-existent (pornography); incomprehensible (unpleasant and unwanted consensual sex) or legally predetermined (marital rape, in states with the marital exemption).

It is not so clear, though, *why* women's suffering is so pervasively dismissed or trivialized by legal culture, or more importantly what to do about it. As I will argue in a moment, feminist legal theorists do not typically frame the problem in the way I have just posed it. Nevertheless, it is not hard to construct two characteristic feminist explanations of the phenomenon, and the strategies they entail. The "liberal-legal feminist" would characterize the legal culture's discriminatory treatment of women's suffering as the reflection of a "perceptual error" committed by that culture. Women are in fact *the same as*—and therefore *equal to*—men, in the only sense which should matter to liberal legal theory. Women, like men, are autonomous individuals who, if free to do so, will choose among proffered alternatives so as to fashion their own "good life," and thereby create social value. However, the legal culture fails to see or acknowledge this central sameness—and hence equality—of women and men. Because we are not *perceived* as identical to men in this way, we are not treated as such. Our choices are differentially restricted, and as a result we disproportionately suffer. The liberal feminist's strategy is directly implied by her diagnosis: what we must do is prove that we are what we are—individualists and egoists, as are men—and then fight for the equal rights and respect that sameness demands. Equal respect will in turn ensure, through the logic of formal justice and the Equal Protection Clause of the Fourteenth Amendment, that our suffering will be alleviated by law—just as is men's suffering—through a liberating expansion of our opportunities for choice.

The radical legal feminist's explanation of this phenomenon is also not hard to construct. The blanket dismissal of women's suffering by the male legal culture is not a reflection of a misperception. Indeed the larger culture's perception is accurate: women are *not* as autonomous or individualistic as men. The liberal is wrong to insist that women and men are equal in this way. The reason the legal culture tends to dismiss women's gender-specific sufferings is that women don't matter. Those in power ignore women's suffering because they don't care about the suffering of the disempowered. Hierarchical power imbalances do that to people—they make the disempowered less than human, and they make the empowered ruthless. The radical feminist's strategy follows directly from her diagnosis: what we must do is dismantle the hierarchy. The Equal Protection Clause—at least if we can interpret it (and use it) as an "Equality Promotion Clause"—might help.

The recent explosion of feminist writings on the multitude of problems generated by women's "difference" prompts me to suggest a third explanation of this blanket dismissal by the legal culture of women's pain, and thus a third strategy. ... If the pain women feel is in fact discontinuous from—different than—what is experienced by men, then it is not really surprising that the injuries we sustain are trivialized or dismissed by the larger male culture. It is hard to empathize with the pain of another, when the nature of that pain is not understood. ... The strategic inference I draw is this: if we want to enlist the aid of the larger legal culture, the feel of our gender-specific pain must be described before we can ever hope to communicate its magnitude.

Focus on the "difference" of our hedonic lives also suggests a different way to address the related problem of "false consciousness." As feminists know all too well, it is not just the legal culture which trivializes women's suffering, women do so also. Again, if we focus on the distinctiveness of our pain, this becomes less surprising. An injury uniquely sustained by a disempowered group will lack a name, a history, and in general a linguistic reality. Consequently, the victim as well as the perpetrator will transform the pain into *something else*, such as, for example, punishment, or flattery, or transcendence, or unconscious pleasure. A victim's response to an injury which is perceived by the victim as deservedly punitive, consensual, natural, subconsciously desired, legally inevitable, or trivial will be very different from a response to an injury which is perceived as simply *painful*. We change our behavior in response to the threat of what we perceive as punishment; we diminish ourselves in response to injuries we perceive as trivial; we reconstruct our pasts in response to injuries we perceive as subconsciously desired; we negate our inner selves in response to injuries we perceive as consensual and we constrain our potentiality in response to injuries we perceive as inevitable. We respond to pain, on the other hand, by resisting the source of the pain. The strategic inference should be clear: we must give voice to the hurting self, even when that hurting self sounds like a child rather than an adult; even when that hurting self voices "trivial" complaints; even when the hurting self is ambivalent toward the harm and even when (especially when) the hurting self is talking a language not heard in public discourse. Only by so doing will we *ourselves* become aware of the meaning of the suffering in our lives, and its contingency in our history. Only when we understand the contingency of that pain, will we be free to address it and change the conditions which cause it through legal tools.

If my argument is correct, then it would seem that feminist legal theorists should be hard at work providing rich descriptions of women's subjective, hedonic lives, particularly the pain in those lives, and more particularly the pain in our lives which is different. And yet *we aren't,* by which I mean, feminist *legal theorists* aren't. ... [A]t least one reason—and perhaps the main reason—that feminist legal theorists have neglected the hedonic dimension of our difference—and the subject of this article—is ... the emerging logic of feminist legal theory itself. ... [F]eminist legal theorists have adopted *non-feminist* normative models of legal criticism, and then applied those models to women's problems. I have no objection to this strategy: there is no reason that feminist legal theorists should aim for relentless originality. I do object, though, to the *particular* models feminist legal theorists have adopted. The two major normative models of legal criticism which feminist legal theorists have thus far embraced—liberal legalism and radical legalism—*themselves* deny the normative significance of the subjective pleasure and suffering of our lives. Because of the normative models employed by modern legal feminists, the internal, phenomenological reality of women's hedonic lives—and its difference from men's—has become virtually irrelevant to feminist legal theory.

Thus, I will argue that *liberal-legal* feminist theorists—true to their liberalism—want women to have more choices, and that *radical-legal* feminist theorists—true to their radicalism—want women to have more power. Both models direct our critical attention *outward*—liberalism to the number of choices we have, radicalism to the amount of power. Neither model of legal criticism, and therefore, derivatively, of feminist legal criticism, posits subjective happiness as the direct goal of legal reform, or subjective suffering as the direct evil to be eradicated. Neither model directs our critical attention *inward.* Consequently, and unsurprisingly, neither liberal nor radical feminist legal critics have committed themselves to the task of determining the measure of women's happiness or suffering. ...

Liberal Feminism: Consent, Autonomy and the Giving Self

Perhaps the most widely held normative commitment of mainstream liberal legal theorists is that individuals should be free to choose their own style of life, and to exercise that freedom of choice in as many spheres as possible—economic, political and personal. The conception of the human and the relation between the individual and the state which implicitly motivates this commitment is relatively straightforward. According to the liberal vision, value is produced in our social world through satiation of the subjective desires and preferences of the individual. That satiation is in turn manifested and facilitated through the individual's voluntary choices. The individual's choice will reflect that individual's judgment of what will best satisfy that individual's own desires. It follows that whatever is freely consented to by an individual is what is good for that individual, and, if free of adverse effects on others, is good for society. The way to maximize value in the social world is therefore to maximize the opportunities for the exercise of choice through voluntary transactions between individuals. A law which either facilitates or mimics consensual transactions between freely choosing individuals is a good law on this model, while a law which frustrates such transactions is a bad law. Individual freedom is the ideal toward which law and legal reform ought press, and coercion or restraint on freedom is the evil.

The contribution of feminist liberal legalism has been to extend the umbrella of this normative vision to women as well as men. The liberal legal feminist insists that the depiction of the human embraced by liberal legalism—which I will sometimes refer to as the "liberal self"—is also true of women, and that therefore the relationship of the state to the individual must be the same for both women and men. What it means for women to be equal to men in the liberal feminist vision is basically that women and men are the same in the only sense that matters to the liberal legalist: women as well as men create value by satiating their subjective desires through consensual choices. Because women and men are equal in this way—because they share the same definitive human attribute—women should be equally free to choose their own life plans, and women should be equally entitled to the respect from the state that that freedom requires.

The liberal feminist legal strategy for dealing with women's suffering is directly entailed by her liberalism. Women, like men, consent to that which will minimize their own suffering and maximize their own felt happiness. Therefore, the way to deal with women's suffering is to increase women's sphere of consensual freedom. What we should do with law, then, is insure that women's sphere of consensual freedom is as large as possible, or at least as large as men's. Thus, the liberal feminist's central jurisprudential commitment tracks the liberal's: a law is a good law if it increases the freedom of women to enter into consensual transactions or if it equalizes that freedom with that enjoyed by men. A law is a bad law if it decreases that freedom.

Liberal feminist legal theory carries with it the same problems which now plague liberal legalism, but multiplied. Modern liberal legal feminists, like modern liberals generally, have failed to examine the essentially descriptive claims about the human being that underlie their normative model. The liberal claim that human beings consent to transactions in order to maximize their welfare may be false. If it is, then the liberal claim that social value is created through facilitating choice will be false as well. But furthermore, *women* may be "different" in precisely the way which would render the empirical assumptions regarding human motivation which underlie the liberal's commitment to the ethics of consent *more false for women than for men.* Thus, it may be that women generally *don't* consent to changes *so as to* increase our own pleasure or satisfy our own desires. It may be that women consent to changes so as to increase the pleasure or satisfy the desires of *others*. The descriptive account of the phenomenology of choice that underlies the liberal's conceptual defense of the moral primacy of consent may be wildly at odds with the way women phenomenologically experience the act of consent. If it is—if women "consent" to transactions not to increase our own welfare, but to increase the welfare of others—if women are "different" in this psychological way—then the liberal's ethic of consent, with its presumption of an essentially selfish human (male) actor and an essentially selfish consensual act, when even-handedly applied to both genders, will have disastrous implications for women. For if women consent to changes so as to increase the happiness of others rather than to increase our own happiness, then the ethic of consent, applied even-handedly, may indeed increase the amount of happiness in the world, but women will not be the beneficiaries.

And indeed, the liberal ethic of consent does, oftentimes, have less than happy consequences for women. ... That is, much of women's suffering is a product of a state of being which was *itself* brought into being through a transaction to which women unquestionably tendered consent. A woman's experience of marital sexuality, for example, may range from boring to irritating to invasive to intensely painful. Similarly, a female employee may experience the sexual advances of an employer as degrading. But the fact is that neither the wife nor the employee was brought to the altar in shackles or place of employment in chains. Put affirmatively, the conditions which create our misery—unwanted pregnancies, violent and abusive marriages, sexual harassment on the job—are often traceable to acts of consent. Women—somewhat uniquely—consent to their misery. ...

I ... suggest ... that many women, much of the time, consent to transactions, changes, or situations in the world so as to satisfy not their own desires or to maximize their own pleasure, as liberal legalism and liberal legal feminism both presume, but to maximize the pleasure and satiate the desires of others, and that they do so by virtue of conditions which only women experience. I will sometimes call the cluster of "other-regarding," other-pleasing motivations that rule these women's actions the "giving self," so as to distinguish it from the "liberal self": the cluster of self-regarding "rational" motivations presumed by liberal legalism. Thus my descriptive claim is that many women much of the time are giving selves rather than liberal selves. ...

I believe that women become giving rather than liberal selves for a range of reasons ... I will focus on only one causal hypothesis. ... [W]omen's lives are dangerous, and it is the acquisitive and potentially violent nature of male sexuality which is the cause of the danger. A fully justified fear of acquisitive and violent male sexuality consequently permeates many women's—perhaps all women's—sexual and emotional self-definition. Women respond to this fear by *re-constituting* themselves in a way that controls the danger and suppresses the fear. Thus: women define themselves as "giving selves" so as to obviate the threat, the danger, the pain, and the fear of being self-regarding selves from whom their sexuality is taken. ... Most simply, a woman will define herself as a "giving self" so that she will not be violated. She defines herself as a being who "gives" sex, so that she will not become a being *from whom sex is taken.* ... [S]he becomes a person who gives her consent *so as to ensure the other's happiness* (not her own), so as to satiate the *other's* desires (not her own), so as to promote the *other's* well-being (not her own), and ultimately so as *to obey the other's commands.* In other words, she embraces a self-definition and a motive for acting which is the direct antithesis of the internal motivational life presupposed by liberalism. The motivation of her consensual acts is the satisfaction of another's desires. She consents to serve the needs and satiate the desires of others.

I have no interest in arguing that all women are giving selves all of the time. I want to suggest in the next few subsections that enough women have lived with enough fear and danger in their lives as to justify the inference that significant numbers of women have defined themselves in a way that undercuts the commitment to the ethical primacy of consent which underlies liberal feminist legal theory. ...

Del Martin begins her book Battered Wives with the following Letter from a Battered Wife:

> I am in my thirties and so is my husband. I have a high school diploma and am presently attending a local college, trying to obtain the additional education I need. My husband is a college graduate and a professional in his field. We are both attractive and ... respected and well-liked. We have four children and live in a middle-class home with all the comforts we could possibly want.
>
> I have everything except life without fear.
>
> For most of my married life I have been periodically beaten by my husband. What do I mean by "beaten"? I mean that parts of my body have been hit violently and repeatedly, and that painful bruises, swelling, bleeding wounds, unconsciousness [sic], and combinations of these things have resulted.
>
> I have had glasses thrown at me. I have been kicked in the abdomen when I was visibly pregnant. I have been kicked off the bed and hit while lying on the floor—again, while I was pregnant. I have been whipped, kicked and thrown, picked up again and thrown down again. I have been punched and kicked in the head, chest, face and abdomen more times than I can count.
>
> Few people have ever seen my black and blue face or swollen lips because I have always stayed indoors afterwards, feeling ashamed. I was never able to drive following one of these beatings,

so I could not get myself to a hospital for care. I could never have left my young children alone, even if I could have driven a car.

Being beaten is a terrible thing; it is most terrible of all if you are not equipped to fight back. I recall an occasion when I tried to defend myself and actually tore my husband's shirt. Later, he showed it to a relative as proof that I had done something wrong. The fact that at that moment I had several raised spots on my head hidden by my hair, a swollen lip that was bleeding, and a severely damaged cheek with a blood clot that caused a permanent dimple didn't matter to him. What mattered was that I tore his shirt! That I tore it in self-defense didn't mean anything to him.

My situation is so untenable I would guess that anyone who has not experienced one like it would find it incomprehensible. I find it difficult to believe myself.

How do women respond to the total fear that accompanies the daily violence that characterizes an abusive domestic relationship? What does such fear *teach* you? A woman cannot live in a state of terror *every day* and what a battered woman learns in an abusive marriage is how to define herself in such a way that she can on occasion suppress the fear. Thus, what a violent intimate relationship taught me was to live *for the other.* I was—as these things go—relatively lucky, by which I mean the abuse I sustained was not nearly so extreme as that suffered by the woman quoted above. But I did learn in this relatively lucky environment of fists, slaps, bruises, threats, glares and terror the lesson of daily fear. Daily fear taught me to define myself as an object, the purpose of which was to buffer—and silence—another's violence. My purpose—my *only* reason for acting and my *only* motivation—was to serve *that* need of another. Fear taught me to view as literally incongruous the mere suggestion that I should expect to reap pleasure for myself from anything at all; surely not from sex, but nor from more ordinary sources, such as food, flowers, music, friendship or scenery. The notion that I would act—or *consent*—so as to further my own welfare or to create pleasure for myself was both inconceivable and unconceived: until circumstances and self-preservatory desperation inspired my exit, it never crossed my mind. Pleasures were for others. Sensuality was for others. "Personal welfare" was for others. Subjectivity was for others. I did not have, much less act on, preferences. I learned to view this as both natural and as naturally *inarticulable,* meaning I learned not just to lie, but to be a lie, to embody lying, to have no entitlement to either truth or language. I learned to be *for another's violence* and to view it as my reason for being, and I learned not to think about it much. ...

Almost all women, including those who have never experienced unwanted sex or battery, have experienced the fear of rape. ... [A] working paper on rape ... elaborates:

The fear of rape is always with us. It affects our lives in countless ways—not only in that we are afraid to walk the streets

> late at night, but in all our dealings with men, however superficial these might be. ... This makes us self-conscious about our bodies, the way we sit and stand and walk—when was the last time you saw a woman sit sprawled across a bus seat the way men do all the time? We keep our knees together, our legs crossed, our faces neutral. Somewhere in our minds we are always aware that any man—every man—can, if he wants to, use the weapon of rape against us.
>
> And men know it too. The man who mutters obscenities at us in the street knows it, the local greengrocer who insists on calling us love ... knows it, the wolf-whistling building workers know it, the man reading page three on the tube and grinning at us knows it. *At one point on Reclaim the Night in Soho, we were confronted by a large group of men shouting "We're on the rapist's side—we're with the rapist." They didn't really need to tell us. We already knew.*

One way that (some) women respond to the pervasive, silent, unspoken and invisible fear of rape in their lives is by giving their (sexual) selves to a consensual, protective, and monogamous relationship. This is widely denied—but it may be widely denied because it is so widely presumed. It is, after all, precisely what we are supposed to do. One woman describes her embrace of this option thusly:

> The brutality and coldness of (promiscuous heterosexual) experiences were largely instrumental in persuading me to have steady and secure relationships with men. I did not feel safe with lots of different ones. The threat of men's violence drove me into couple relationships. I feel ambivalent about these men. They were not unmitigated bastards and they did afford me protection. My mother would often mutter ominously about the world not being a safe place for women and my experiences could only confirm this. Being alone I felt, at times, besieged and up for grabs. Being with one man sheltered unwelcome attention from men in the streets, at parties, etc.

Women who give themselves to a monogamous relationship in order to avoid the danger of rape from others, often end up giving themselves *within* the monogamous relationship so as to avoid the danger of rape by their partner. ...

Women, ... and only women, live with ... [this] danger: women and only women must somehow ward off the threat of acquisitive and violent male sexuality. It should not be so hard to understand (*why* is it so hard to understand?) that women develop protective strategies for coping with this ... threat. The means with which we do so—primarily by learning to give ourselves to consensual, protective relationships, within which we then define ourselves as "giving"—are not the product of false consciousness or brain-washing. But nor are they value-creating voluntary and mutual relationships worthy of celebration. They are no less and no more than the product of our victimization: they are coherent, understandable responses to very real danger. Until we create a better world, they are also all we have. ...

Radical Feminism and the Ethical Primacy of Power and Equality

Radical feminist legal theory begins with a description of women which is diametrically opposed to that embraced by liberal feminists. Liberal feminists assume a definitional *equality*—a "sameness"—between the female and male experience of consensual choice, and then argue that the legal system should respect that fundamental, empirical equality. In sharp contrast, radical feminists assume a definitional *in*equality of women—women are *definitionally* the disempowered group—and urge the legal system to eradicate that disempowerment and thereby make women what they presently are not, and that is equal. Radical feminism thus begins with a denial of the liberal feminist's starting assumption. Women and men are *not* equally autonomous individuals. Women, unlike men, live in a world with two sovereigns—the state, and men—and this is true not just some of the time but all of the time. Women, unlike men, are definitionally submissive twice over; once vis-a-vis the state, and once vis-a-vis the superior power of men. A legal regime which ignores this central reality will simply perpetuate the fundamental, underlying inequality.

The cause of women's disempowerment, as well as its effect, is the expropriation of our sexuality. Women are the group, in Catharine MacKinnon's phrase, "from whom sexuality is expropriated." ... The threat of male violence and violent sexuality both defines the class *woman* and causes her disempowerment and the expropriation of her sexuality. ...

This much, radical feminist legal theory shares with radical feminism, and with this much I am in full agreement. Where radical feminist legal theory has departed from radical feminism, I believe, is in the normative argument it draws from the insight that women are, definitionally, the group from whom sexuality is expropriated. The argument, I believe, owes more to radical legalism than to radical feminism. ... [R]adical feminist legal theorists share with radical legalists a methodological insistence that the correlation between objective equality and subjective well-being is foundational and definitional; it is therefore *not* something that can be discredited by counter-example. Both groups of theorists accordingly refuse to credit the *phenomenological* evidence that the essentially descriptive claims that underlie the normative commitment to substantive equality may be false. Thus, to radical legalists generally, and to radical feminist legalists in particular, the extent to which the disempowered desire anything other than their own empowerment, and anything at odds with an equalitarian idea, is the extent to which the disempowered are victims of false consciousness. ...

The striking political contribution of radical *feminist* legal theory has been to extend the umbrella of the normative argument of radical legalism to include women as well as men, and thus to address hierarchies of gender as well as hierarchies dictated by class and race. If hierarchy is bad, then hierarchies and sexual hierarchies according to sex and gender are bad; if disempowerment is a prescription for misery, then women's disempowerment is a prescription for misery; and if expropriation is bad, then expropriation of our sexuality is bad. The radical feminist legalist's commitment to gender equality stems from her empirical insistence that in the only respect which should be of concern to radical legalists, women and men are *the same:* women, like men, *suffer* from relative disempowerment and inequality, and will therefore benefit from empowerment and equality. Women, like men, just are such that objective inequality will cause us subjective misery, and objective empowerment—and thus, equality—will be our script for salvation. The legal strategy is directly entailed. Women are made miserable by inequality and enlivened by equality. What we should do with law, then, if we mean to address the problem of women's suffering, is disable the objective hierarchies of gender that cause it. The scope and depth of women's power must be increased, and the sphere of disempowerment must be shrunk. Legal reform should therefore be directed toward a dismantling of gendered hierarchies. ...

Radical feminist legal theorists, true to their radicalism, refuse to consider whether or not the definitional implication it assumes between objective equality and subjective well-being resonates with women's desires and pleasures, and hence whether the conception of the human on which that implication is based is true of *women.* The radical feminist legal theorist—to the extent that she is a radical—will—must—deny that substantive equality in any sphere could ever be less than ideal or that empowerment of women could ever work to our disadvantage. Thus, to radical feminists, that women on occasion take pleasure in their own submissiveness, is simply a manifestation of their disempowered state, not a meaningful counter-example to the posited egalitarian ideal. ...

... The contours of the conflict between stated ideal and felt pleasure, and between method and theory with which radical feminism is now grappling, I believe, are starkly brought out in [Danish radical feminist Maria] Marcus's detailed, moving, and candid account of her own profoundly ambivalent reaction to The Story of O. The Story of O is, in Marcus's phrase, a "masochistic pipe-dream." Written pseudonymously in the mid-fifties, it is without question the unsurpassed, modern, masochistic text. It is a stunning piece of pornography. ... Marcus ... has an intensely empathic and sexual response to The Story of O:

> When I first read The Story of O, it filled me with a mixture of sexual excitement, horror, anxiety—and envy. I read it many times, each time with the same feelings. But gradually, as I had the good fortune to plunge to some extent into acting out an "Imitation of O," my envy, anyhow, lessened, because on one (sic) imitates O with overstepping a boundary into a state which is not particularly enviable.

> But I must still say that ... I understand O. I understand her pride in the weals from the whip ... He owns me. I'm worth owning. Look what he makes me put up with. Look how strong the man who loves me is. Look I'm valuable. I *exist.* I understand that O comes to feel an inner peace, strength, dignity, security and psychic energy in this particular way, an energy that is nothing like anything else I (O) know.

The Story of O, Marcus concludes, is *the* text with which radical feminists must concern themselves, and the magnitude of female readers' responsive, empathic and erotic response to the text is the issue with which radical feminism must come to grips.

Radical feminists have responded, I believe, to the conflict between pleasure and ideal posed by the undeniable female eroticization of sexual submission in three characteristic ways. First, some feminists claim that there is no conflict between stated ideal and felt pleasure because feminist consciousness-raising—properly understood—has revealed the falsity of these pleasures. Thus there is no contradiction between feminist methodology—consciousness raising—and feminist goal—sexual equality. What the methodology reveals is that the pleasure had in sexual submission is false. ...

The second response (which was, until very recently, the near-standard feminist response) is simply to abandon feminist methodology. One way of maintaining the ideals of freedom and equality is by abandoning whatever methodology brought you to the conclusion that you enjoy being a sexual slave. If that methodology is feminist consciousness-raising, then so much the worse for consciousness-raising. ...

The third possible response to the conflict between the pleasure we take in erotic domination and our equalitarian ideals is to put our ideals in abeyance—maybe they are what is false—and hold true to consciousness-raising. This is the position for which I will argue. ... [O]nly by understanding our felt pleasures will we achieve any meaningful understanding of our stated ideals. We cannot possibly give content to the substantive equality we seek until we understand the erotic appeal of submission. If we can identify what human needs are met through eroticized submission, perhaps we can better understand, and identify, the human needs which will be met or frustrated through political, legal and economic equality. ...

I believe that sexual submission has erotic *appeal* and *value* when it is an expression of *trust;* is damaging, injurious and painful when it is an expression of *fear;* and is *dangerous* because of its ambiguity: both others and we ourselves have difficulty in disentangling the two. Here, I want to emphasize—I hope not overemphasize—the value of sexual submission when it is an expression of trust, because that, I believe, is the source of the pleasure women find in voluntary and fantasized erotic submission, in all of its forms. Absolutely pliant obedience—the willingness to transform one's subjectivity into another's object—is sexually arousing (for some) when it enables the submissive subject to transcend her own selfhood, and thereby to abdicate her responsibility for her own action. That this total abdication of responsibility can be erotic, I think, reflects a genuine human truth and a deep human need. It can be pleasurable and exhilarating and sometimes so much so that it is sexually stimulating to forego authorship of one's actions. When we grant power to another to control—to author—our acts, that grant may, and I have argued often does, express a deep seated and forgotten (or not so forgotten) fear. But it might not. It *might* also express our total trust in that other. That "other" *might* be trustworthy. That placing trust in one who is stronger is felt by some to be intensely pleasurable, and that the fantasy of doing just that is felt by many more to be so, should teach us something. ...

Are the desires to "know and be known," to trust another, to blend in identity, at least sometimes expressed in the eroticization of submission and dominance, of any value, and do they express anything of value? Or are they soiled by their extremity, by their expression in forms which implicate "sweat and semen," whips and whip lashes, marks of obedience, and of objectification? *It's a close question. When* (if ever) and *why* (if ever) are these desires and the pleasure felt in their satiation beautiful? When are they *not* "muck we could well do without"? If they cannot, as I have argued they cannot, be entirely dismissed as false, can they be in any sense affirmed as truth? Do they express a political truth? Minimally, ... they remind us of the hedonistic limits—the limits of pleasure, pain and desire—upon the otherwise near-relentless quest by both feminists and non-feminists of the fruits of liberal individualism—of subjective autonomy, of severe differentiation, and ... of "discontinuity and rationality." That so many women and more than a few men undeniably take pleasure in controlled objectification may be testimony to the limit of the desirability of the pure subjectivism endorsed by virtually all forms of liberalism, including feminist liberal legalism. In a parallel fashion, the fact that many women and more than a few men take pleasure from sexual submission can be read as a critique of the absolutist commitment to substantive equality endorsed by radical legalism of all forms, including feminist radical legalism. The trust expressed by the submissive party *in a controlled* and unequal sexual encounter is such a high pleasure that it is erotic. That *fact*—that the trust felt by the submissive party in controlled inequality *is* pleasurable—should serve to remind us that to the extent that absolute equality comes at the cost of the trust of which human beings are capable, often expressed in the consensual abandonment of autonomy and relinquishment of control over oneself to another, that equality will come at a high cost.

The political lesson of the pleasure in eroticized submission is not that we should forsake either individualism or equality as ultimately "undesirable." But there is no discontinuity here: *nor* is it the case that the woman who enjoys fantasies of erotic domination would enjoy literal servitude, or for that matter thinks she woud. The lesson—the truth—of the erotic pleasure many feel in controlled submission may be this: while we crave liberal autonomy and radical equality, while we crave the freedom which the liberal feminist pursues and the equality the radical feminist envisions, *at least in this society as it is presently constituted, we also crave—because we also need—the capacity to trust one another, including those who are stronger than we are.* The weak and the strong are in fact interdependent in this society—we *aren't* equally autonomous individuals—and what that means is that the weak need to be able to depend on the strong. The capacity to safely depend on another, to look after one's own well-being, is a desirable state, and it is no great mystery that it is pursued as pleasure. When we test the limits of our capacity to trust, of our willingness to embrace absolute dependency, and when we discover erotic pleasure lurking at that limit, we give expression to our desire to be able to trust someone who is strong and trustworthy—which may be a fully human, and not just female, need.

Either trust or fear can prompt us to submit to the will of the other. Trust is enlivening, and fear is deadening. There is a difference. It is a subjective, internal, hedonic difference. It is the difference between the battered woman's consensual endurance—motivated by fear—of beatings, and the lover's consensual enjoyment—motivated by trust—of controlled submission. The first submission is deadening, the second (can be) enlivening. It is a difference we will only be able to *see*, much less understand, if we look at our *internal* lives. From an external perspective, this difference is muted. From an internal perspective, it is glaring.

There is—*of course*—a danger in this. The internal difference is not *inevitably* glaring, even to ourselves. And because it is not, there is a danger in the pleasure of submission just as there is a limit to the desirability in the non-sexual world of relationships of dependence and trust. . . .

As I said at the outset of this section, the radical feminist legal theorist's refusal to engage in phenomenological critique of the ideal she proposes—substantive equality—is usually benign, for the straightforward reason that generally there is no conflict between our felt pleasures—once we have correctly identified them—and radical feminist ideals of political and substantive equality. Occasionally, though, the radical legalist's refusal to check stated objective ideal against felt subjective pleasure will result in a misfire. The Indianapolis antipornography ordinance is a now notorious instance of just such a misfire. . . .

The ordinance and the theory behind it defines and targets pornography as the subordination of women through sexually explicit graphic or textual means. . . . [T]he ordinance rests on the clear normative premise that . . . submission . . . is . . . bad . . . because submission itself is bad, and . . . because equality is good, and equality is good because people, definitionally, simply are such that equality is good. Yet many women—including some feminists, and including some lesbians—don't *feel* sexual submission as bad. In fact, many women feel sexual submission as pleasurable, as so pleasurable as to be erotic, and as so erotic as to be orgasmic. And many women have come to this understanding of themselves and of their pleasure through consciousness-raising sessions. The anti-pornography ordinance has defined the depiction or expression of sexual submission as objectively bad, when for many women both the thing expressed and its expression is subjectively pleasurable. The ordinance raises the conflict between objective ideal and subjective pleasure, and the result has been chaos. ... [A]nti-pornography advocates urge that the evil of pornography is not that it causes *violence* against women, but that it *subordinates* women, on the theory, no doubt, that the former is symptom, the latter is root cause. The shift from "violence" to "subordination" has splintered the movement, for, I think, primarily the reason noted above—subordination is taken to be both reflected in and caused by sexual submission, and consensual, controlled, sexual submission, is hedonically, for many, pleasurable.

This is the lesson I draw: we might be able to re-build a consensus on pornography by focusing our attention on the harm we want to eradicate, rather than on the classification or description of the thing we want to prohibit. I suggest we go back for a moment to what we know of our own pleasure and pain and *trust* it. What we all know—and by "all" I mean, on some level, all women—to be undeniably painful is the expropriation of our sexuality which is motivated by *fear*—sexual submission under threat or memory of sexual compulsion—the ever-present threat of that expropriation, the fear which the threat engenders, the danger with which we consequently live, and the torture we endure when the fear proves to have been horrifically well-grounded. When we "give" ourselves because we have been taught to *and the teacher is fear,* the "giving" is *not pleasurable.* It is painful. The transaction is neither erotic, pleasurable nor valuable; it is damaging and deadening. Both the coercive *and the consensual* relinquishment of control expressed in sexual relationships, which is grounded in fear, is damaging, painful, unpleasant, deadening, and not at all erotic. Relinquishment of control over one's body that is motivated by fear is damaging *whether or not the external indicia of "consent" to the relationship or transfer are present.* Pornographic literature that facilitates by legitimating *either* the violent expropriation of our sexuality or fear-induced *giving* so as not to be one from whom sexuality is taken, hurts us. It damages us. It injures us. If pornography proximately causes that injury and the proximity is provable, it should be civilly actionable.

By contrast, the relinquishment of authority and responsibility expressed in masochistic sexual fantasy and controlled masochistic practice at least sometimes constitutes a willed sexual submission which is motivated by *trust,* not fear. When motivated by trust, that submission can be pleasurable, erotic, and therefore valuable. Erotic literature that facilitates sexual fantasies or consensual practices (or understanding of those fantasies) which express and give rise to the experience of trust, can, I think, be pleasurable, erotic, and of value regardless of the content of the fantasy or the practice.

There is no contradiction in holding both of these positions simultaneously. What they pose is a difficult causation question, but that's a far cry from being faced with a disabling *contradiction* between theory and method or ideal and pleasure. We need to know what pornography hurts us and endangers us and what pornography frees us or enlivens us. We need to know if there is no overlap (ideal), a great deal of overlap (worst case) or some overlap (most likely). This may be a very difficult factual question; it may be too difficult, but it does not give rise to a "contradiction." ...

I think the crisis in radical feminist legal theory which the pornography debate has engendered is false, for this reason. ... [I]t is at least possible that on this issue we can have it both ways. Many of us are debating the pornography issue without having looked at much of it. We have a "category" in mind that might not be a sensible category. If we *look* at what is presently and too broadly defined as pornography, we might discover that the pornography that hurts us—the pornography that contributes to the violent expropriation of our sexuality—is not so hard to distinguish from the pornography that doesn't hurt us and which might be pleasurable—the description of controlled erotic submission. For example, it may just be *true*—the Meese report suggests it is—that pictures are more prone to cause violence than words, and that violent pictures are more prone to cause violence than non-violent pictures. It may also be true—sales of pornography to women suggest it is—that *words* are erotic in the way described above while pictures of dominance and submission are not. The Story of O—unquestionably violent—is, as Marcus suggests, a "lyrical poem." Whatever else it is, it is *words*.

It also, of course, may not be true. The Story of O, no matter how erotic as text, might be proximately causing literally untold miseries—silenced, actual, fearful, terrifying enslavements—and *no woman wants that.* If it is, then we cannot have it both ways, and ... where we can't have it both ways we have to think carefully about which way we want to have it. In my own mind, I have no doubt—if The Story of O is being re-enacted in real life on some farm somewhere in the hills of Kentucky right through to the bitter end, then we can all live without The Story of O. For me, this is not a close question, although I know it may be for others. But again—this poses a choice, and even if it is a hard choice, that is a far cry from a disabling contradiction. Erotic energy—no less than clean, cheap nuclear energy—comes with a price, and the price of both energies may be too high. ...

Conclusion: Women's Difference, and an Alternative Standard for a Feminist Critique of Law

Although liberal and radical legalism are typically contrasted, as I contrasted them in the bulk of this paper, I want briefly to suggest in this conclusion that it is by virtue of an assumption that liberalism and radicalism *share* that their respective chosen proxies for well-being—choice and power—are so at odds with women's subjective, hedonic lives. Both liberal and radical legalism share a vision of the human being—and therefore of our subjective well-being—as "autonomous." The liberal insists that choice is necessary for the "true" exercise of that autonomy—and thus is an adequate proxy for subjective well-being—while the radical insists the same for power. But this strategic difference should not blind us to their commonality. Both the liberal and the radical legalist have accepted the Kantian assumption that *to be human* is to be in some sense autonomous—meaning, minimally, to be differentiated, or individuated, from the rest of social life.

Underlying and underscoring the poor fit between the proxies for subjective well-being endorsed by liberals and radicals—choice and power—and women's subjective, hedonic lives is the simple fact that women's lives—*because of our biological, reproductive role*—are drastically at odds with this fundamental vision of human life. Women's lives are *not* autonomous, they are profoundly relational. This is at least the biological reflection, if not the biological cause, of virtually all aspects, hedonic and otherwise, of our "difference." Women, and *only* women, and *most* women, transcend *physically* the differentiation or individuation of biological self from the rest of human life trumpeted as the norm by the entire Kantian tradition. When a woman is pregnant her biological life embraces the embryonic life of another. When she later nurtures children, her needs will embrace their needs. The experience of being human, for women, differentially from men, includes the counter-autonomous experience of a shared physical identity between woman and fetus, as well as the counter-autonomous experience of the emotional and psychological bond between mother and infant.

Our reproductive role renders us non-autonomous in a second, less obvious, but ultimately more far-reaching sense. Emotionally and morally women may benefit from the dependency of the fetus and the infant upon us. But *materially* we are more often burdened than enriched by that dependency. And because we are burdened, we differentially depend more heavily upon others, both for our own survival, and for the survival of the children who are part of us. Women, more than men, depend upon relationships with others, because the weakest of human beings—infants—depend upon us. ... If women's "difference" lies in the fact that our lives are relational rather than autonomous, and if autonomy is a necessary attribute of a human being, then women's difference rather abruptly implies that women are not human beings. Politics that are designed to benefit human beings—including liberal and radical legalism—will leave women out in the cold.

This is not a novel insight: that women are not human as human is now conceived has in a sense always been the dominant problem for feminism. But the two characteristic ways in which modern feminist legal theorists have responded to this dilemma are both, I think, flawed. The liberal feminist's solution is to deny it. The fact that women become pregnant, give birth, and nurse infants is a difference that *does not count.* It does not make us any less "autonomous" than men. ...

[T]his response does not work. ... If we embrace a false conception of our nature we can be sure of only one thing, and that is that legal reform based on such a conception will only occasionally—and then only incidentally—benefit real instead of hypothetical women.

The radical feminist's proposal is that we seek to *become* autonomous creatures. We are indeed not "autonomous," but what that reflects is our lack of power—our social, political and legal victimization—not our essential nature. To the extent that we become autonomous by gaining power, we will *become* the beneficiaries of the legal system designed to promote the well-being of just such people. This radical vision is at root deeply assimilationist—by gaining power, we become equal, as we become equal we become less "relational"—meaning less victimized—as we become less relational we become more autonomous, and as we become more autonomous we become more like "human beings"—more like men. Radical assimilation, though, has costs no less weighty (and no less familiar) than liberal denial. There is no guarantee that women can become autonomous "human beings," no guarantee that women want to, and at heart, no persuasive argument that women should.

A very new and third response, which does not fit easily (or at all) within the liberal and radical models described above, and which I think has great promise, is that feminists should insist on women's humanity—and thus on our entitlements—and on the wrongness of the dominant conception of what it means to be a "human being." We should insist, as Christine Littleton has argued, for an equal "acceptance of our difference." This third course is surely more promising—it has truth and candor on its side—but without hedonistic criticism it is insufficient: *which* differences are to be accepted? ... If "difference" includes our differential suffering, or our differential vulnerability to sexual assault, or our differential endurance of pain, or our differentially negative self-esteem, then "acceptance" of those differences will backfire. We need more than just acceptance of our differences; we need a vocabulary in which to articulate and then evaluate them, as well as the power to reject or affirm them. ...

Women must start speaking the truth about the quality of our internal lives. The pain women feel may be unique, but women and men (I believe) are alike in this way: both women and men resist pain when it is our own, and (most) women and (most) men will sympathetically resist pain suffered by others, when that pain is meaningfully communicated. And even if that is unduly optimistic, it is at least clear that *without* a clear articulation of the content and meaning of our pain, it will not be sympathetically resisted by men who do not share it. But more fundamentally, women will come to recognize the truth about our inner lives only when we start to speak it. Women's inner reality simply does not fit the Kantian conception of human nature that underlies so much of our liberal and radical legalist commitments. It is only by starting with our own experiences that we will be able to develop a description of human nature which is faithful to our lived reality, rather than one which ignores it. From that set of descriptions, and only from that set of descriptions, can we construct, or reconstruct, our own political ideals, whether they be autonomy, equality, freedom, fraternity, sisterhood, or something completely other, and as yet unnamed.

[16]

Demarginalizing the Intersection of Race and Sex: A Black Feminist Critique of Antidiscrimination Doctrine, Feminist Theory and Antiracist Politics

Kimberle Crenshaw†

One of the very few Black women's studies books is entitled *All the Women Are White, All the Blacks Are Men, But Some of Us are Brave.*[1] I have chosen this title as a point of departure in my efforts to develop a Black feminist criticism[2] because it sets forth a problematic consequence of the tendency to treat race and gender as mutually exclusive categories of experience and analysis.[3] In this talk, I want to examine how this tendency is perpetuated by a single-axis framework that is dominant in antidiscrimination law and that is also reflected in feminist theory and antiracist politics.

I will center Black women in this analysis in order to contrast the multidimensionality of Black women's experience with the single-axis analysis that distorts these experiences. Not only will this juxtaposition reveal how Black women are theoretically erased, it will also illustrate how this framework imports its own theoretical limitations that undermine efforts to broaden feminist and an-

---

† Acting Professor of Law, University of California, Los Angeles Law School.

[1] Gloria T. Hull, et al, eds (The Feminist Press, 1982).

[2] For other work setting forth a Black feminist perspective on law, see Judy Scales-Trent, *Black Women and the Constitution: Finding Our Place, Asserting Our Rights (Voices of Experience: New Responses to Gender Discourse)*, 24 Harv CR-CL L Rev 9 (1989); Regina Austin, *Sapphire-Bound!*, forthcoming in Wisc Women's L J (1989); Angela Harris, *Race and Essentialism in Feminist Legal Theory* (unpublished manuscript on file with author); and Paulette M. Caldwell, *A Hair Piece* (unpublished manuscript on file with author).

[3] The most common linguistic manifestation of this analytical dilemma is represented in the conventional usage of the term "Blacks and women." Although it may be true that some people mean to include Black women in either "Blacks" or "women," the context in which the term is used actually suggests that often Black women are not considered. See, for example, Elizabeth Spelman, *The Inessential Woman* 114-15 (Beacon Press, 1988) (discussing an article on Blacks and women in the military where "the racial identity of those identified as 'women' does not become explicit until reference is made to Black women, at which point it also becomes clear that the category of women excludes Black women"). It seems that if Black women were explicitly included, the preferred term would be either "Blacks and white women" or "Black men and all women."

tiracist analyses. With Black women as the starting point, it becomes more apparent how dominant conceptions of discrimination condition us to think about subordination as disadvantage occurring along a single categorical axis. I want to suggest further that this single-axis framework erases Black women in the conceptualization, identification and remediation of race and sex discrimination by limiting inquiry to the experiences of otherwise-privileged members of the group. In other words, in race discrimination cases, discrimination tends to be viewed in terms of sex- or class-privileged Blacks; in sex discrimination cases, the focus is on race- and class-privileged women.

This focus on the most privileged group members marginalizes those who are multiply-burdened and obscures claims that cannot be understood as resulting from discrete sources of discrimination. I suggest further that this focus on otherwise-privileged group members creates a distorted analysis of racism and sexism because the operative conceptions of race and sex become grounded in experiences that actually represent only a subset of a much more complex phenomenon.

After examining the doctrinal manifestations of this single-axis framework, I will discuss how it contributes to the marginalization of Black women in feminist theory and in antiracist politics. I argue that Black women are sometimes excluded from feminist theory and antiracist policy discourse because both are predicated on a discrete set of experiences that often does not accurately reflect the interaction of race and gender. These problems of exclusion cannot be solved simply by including Black women within an already established analytical structure. Because the intersectional experience is greater than the sum of racism and sexism, any analysis that does not take intersectionality into account cannot sufficiently address the particular manner in which Black women are subordinated. Thus, for feminist theory and antiracist policy discourse to embrace the experiences and concerns of Black women, the entire framework that has been used as a basis for translating "women's experience" or "the Black experience" into concrete policy demands must be rethought and recast.

As examples of theoretical and political developments that miss the mark with respect to Black women because of their failure to consider intersectionality, I will briefly discuss the feminist critique of rape and separate spheres ideology, and the public policy debates concerning female-headed households within the Black community.

I. The Antidiscrimination Framework

A. The Experience of Intersectionality and the Doctrinal Response

One way to approach the problem of intersectionality is to examine how courts frame and interpret the stories of Black women plaintiffs. While I cannot claim to know the circumstances underlying the cases that I will discuss, I nevertheless believe that the way courts interpret claims made by Black women is itself part of Black women's experience and, consequently, a cursory review of cases involving Black female plaintiffs is quite revealing. To illustrate the difficulties inherent in judicial treatment of intersectionality, I will consider three Title VII[4] cases: *DeGraffenreid v General Motors*,[5] *Moore v Hughes Helicopter*[6] and *Payne v Travenol*.[7]

1. *DeGraffenreid v General Motors*.

In *DeGraffenreid*, five Black women brought suit against General Motors, alleging that the employer's seniority system perpetuated the effects of past discrimination against Black women. Evidence adduced at trial revealed that General Motors simply did not hire Black women prior to 1964 and that all of the Black women hired after 1970 lost their jobs in a seniority-based layoff during a subsequent recession. The district court granted summary judgment for the defendant, rejecting the plaintiffs' attempt to bring a suit not on behalf of Blacks or women, but specifically on behalf of Black women. The court stated:

> [P]laintiffs have failed to cite any decisions which have stated that Black women are a special class to be protected from discrimination. The Court's own research has failed to disclose such a decision. The plaintiffs are clearly entitled to a remedy if they have been discriminated against. However, they should not be allowed to combine statutory remedies to create a new 'super-remedy' which would give them relief beyond what the drafters of the relevant statutes intended. Thus, this lawsuit must be examined to see if it states a cause of action for race discrimination, sex discrimination, or alternatively either, but not a combination of both.[8]

---

[4] Civil Rights Act of 1964, 42 USC § 2000e, et seq as amended (1982).

[5] 413 F Supp 142 (E D Mo 1976).

[6] 708 F2d 475 (9th Cir 1983).

[7] 673 F2d 798 (5th Cir 1982).

[8] *DeGraffenreid*, 413 F Supp at 143.

Although General Motors did not hire Black women prior to 1964, the court noted that "General Motors has hired . . . female employees for a number of years prior to the enactment of the Civil Rights Act of 1964."[9] Because General Motors did hire women—albeit *white women*—during the period that no Black women were hired, there was, in the court's view, no sex discrimination that the seniority system could conceivably have perpetuated.

After refusing to consider the plaintiffs' sex discrimination claim, the court dismissed the race discrimination complaint and recommended its consolidation with another case alleging race discrimination against the same employer.[10] The plaintiffs responded that such consolidation would defeat the purpose of their suit since theirs was not purely a race claim, but an action brought specifically on behalf of Black women alleging race *and* sex discrimination. The court, however, reasoned:

> The legislative history surrounding Title VII does not indicate that the goal of the statute was to create a new classification of 'black women' who would have greater standing than, for example, a black male. The prospect of the creation of new classes of protected minorities, governed only by the mathematical principles of permutation and combination, clearly raises the prospect of opening the hackneyed Pandora's box.[11]

Thus, the court apparently concluded that Congress either did not contemplate that Black women could be discriminated against as "Black women" or did not intend to protect them when such discrimination occurred.[12] The court's refusal in *DeGraffenreid* to

---

[9] Id at 144.

[10] Id at 145. In *Mosley v General Motors*, 497 F Supp 583 (E D Mo 1980), plaintiffs, alleging broad-based racial discrimination at General Motors' St. Louis facility, prevailed in a portion of their Title VII claim. The seniority system challenged in *DeGraffenreid*, however, was not considered in *Mosley*.

[11] Id at 145.

[12] Interestingly, no case has been discovered in which a court denied a white male's attempt to bring a reverse discrimination claim on similar grounds—that is, that sex and race claims cannot be combined because Congress did not intend to protect compound classes. White males in a typical reverse discrimination case are in no better position than the frustrated plaintiffs in *DeGraffenreid*: If they are required to made their claims separately, white males cannot prove race discrimination because white women are not discriminated against, and they cannot prove sex discrimination because Black males are not discriminated against. Yet it seems that courts do not acknowledge the compound nature of most reverse discrimination cases. That Black women's claims automatically raise the question of compound discrimination and white males' "reverse discrimination" cases do not suggest

acknowledge that Black women encounter combined race and sex discrimination implies that the boundaries of sex and race discrimination doctrine are defined respectively by white women's and Black men's experiences. Under this view, Black women are protected only to the extent that their experiences coincide with those of either of the two groups.[13] Where their experiences are distinct, Black women can expect little protection as long as approaches, such as that in *DeGraffenreid*, which completely obscure problems of intersectionality prevail.

2. *Moore v Hughes Helicopter, Inc.*.

Moore v Hughes Helicopters, Inc.[14] presents a different way in which courts fail to understand or recognize Black women's claims. *Moore* is typical of a number of cases in which courts refused to certify Black females as class representatives in race *and* sex discrimination actions.[15] In *Moore*, the plaintiff alleged that the employer, Hughes Helicopter, practiced race and sex discrimination in promotions to upper-level craft positions and to supervisory jobs. Moore introduced statistical evidence establishing a significant disparity between men and women, and somewhat less of a disparity between Black and white men in supervisory jobs.[16]

---

that the notion of compoundedness is somehow contingent upon an implicit norm that is not neutral but is white male. Thus, Black women are perceived as a compound class because they are two steps removed from a white male norm, while white males are apparently not perceived to be a compound class because they somehow represent the norm.

[13] I do not mean to imply that all courts that have grappled with this problem have adopted the *DeGraffenreid* approach. Indeed, other courts have concluded that Black women are protected by Title VII. See, for example, *Jefferies v Harris Community Action Ass'n.*, 615 F2d 1025 (5th Cir 1980). I do mean to suggest that the very fact that the Black women's claims are seen as aberrant suggests that sex discrimination doctrine is centered in the experiences of white women. Even those courts that have held that Black women are protected seem to accept that Black women's claims raise issues that the "standard" sex discrimination claims do not. See Elaine W. Shoben, *Compound Discrimination: The Interaction of Race and Sex in Employment Discrimination*, 55 NYU L Rev 793, 803-04 (1980) (criticizing the *Jefferies* use of a sex-plus analysis to create a subclass of Black women).

[14] 708 F2d 475.

[15] See also *Moore v National Association of Securities Dealers*, 27 EPD (CCH) ¶ 32,238 (D DC 1981); but see *Edmondson v Simon*, 86 FRD 375 (N D Ill 1980) (where the court was unwilling to hold as a matter of law that no Black female could represent without conflict the interests of both Blacks and females).

[16] 708 F2d at 479. Between January 1976 and June 1979, the three years in which Moore claimed that she was passed over for promotion, the percentage of white males occupying first-level supervisory positions ranged from 70.3 to 76.8%; Black males from 8.9 to 10.9%; white women from 1.8 to 3.3%; and Black females from 0 to 2.2%. The overall male/female ratio in the top five labor grades ranged from 100/0% in 1976 to 98/1.8% in 1979. The white/Black ratio was 85/3.3% in 1976 and 79.6/8% in 1979. The overall ratio of men to women in supervisory positions was 98.2 to 1.8% in 1976 to 93.4 to 6.6% in 1979; the Black to white ratio during the same time period was 78.6 to 8.9% and 73.6 to 13.1%

For promotions to the top five labor grades, the percentages were worse. Between 1976

Affirming the district court's refusal to certify Moore as the class representative in the sex discrimination complaint on behalf of all women at Hughes, the Ninth Circuit noted approvingly:

> . . . Moore had never claimed before the EEOC that she was discriminated against as a female, *but only* as a Black female . . . . [T]his raised serious doubts as to Moore's ability to adequately represent white female employees.[17]

The curious logic in *Moore* reveals not only the narrow scope of antidiscrimination doctrine and its failure to embrace intersectionality, but also the centrality of white female experiences in the conceptualization of gender discrimination. One inference that could be drawn from the court's statement that Moore's complaint did not entail a claim of discrimination "against females" is that discrimination against Black females is something less than discrimination against females. More than likely, however, the court meant to imply that Moore did not claim that *all* females were discriminated against *but only* Black females. But even thus recast, the court's rationale is problematic for Black women. The court rejected Moore's bid to represent all females apparently because her attempt to specify her race was seen as being at odds with the standard allegation that the employer simply discriminated "against females."

The court failed to see that the absence of a racial referent does not necessarily mean that the claim being made is a more inclusive one. A white woman claiming discrimination against females may be in no better position to represent all women than a Black woman who claims discrimination as a Black female and wants to represent all females. The court's preferred articulation of "against females" is not necessarily more inclusive—it just appears to be so because the racial contours of the claim are not specified.

The court's preference for "against females" rather than "against Black females" reveals the implicit grounding of white female experiences in the doctrinal conceptualization of sex discrimination. For white women, claiming sex discrimination is simply a statement that but for gender, they would not have been disadvantaged. For them there is no need to specify discrimination as *white*

and 1979, the percentage of white males in these positions ranged from 85.3 to 77.9%; Black males 3.3 to 8%; white females from 0 to 1.4%, and Black females from 0 to 0%. Overall, in 1979, 98.2% of the highest level employees were male; 1.8% were female.

[17] 708 F2d at 480 (emphasis added).

females because their race does not contribute to the disadvantage for which they seek redress. The view of discrimination that is derived from this grounding takes race privilege as a given.

Discrimination against a white female is thus the standard sex discrimination claim; claims that diverge from this standard appear to present some sort of hybrid claim. More significantly, because Black females' claims are seen as hybrid, they sometimes cannot represent those who may have "pure" claims of sex discrimination. The effect of this approach is that even though a challenged policy or practice may clearly discriminate against all females, the fact that it has particularly harsh consequences for Black females places Black female plaintiffs at odds with white females.

Moore illustrates one of the limitations of antidiscrimination law's remedial scope and normative vision. The refusal to allow a multiply-disadvantaged class to represent others who may be singularly-disadvantaged defeats efforts to restructure the distribution of opportunity and limits remedial relief to minor adjustments within an established hierarchy. Consequently, "bottom-up" approaches, those which combine all discriminatees in order to challenge an entire employment system, are foreclosed by the limited view of the wrong and the narrow scope of the available remedy. If such "bottom-up" intersectional representation were routinely permitted, employees might accept the possibility that there is more to gain by collectively challenging the hierarchy rather than by each discriminatee individually seeking to protect her source of privilege within the hierarchy. But as long as antidiscrimination doctrine proceeds from the premise that employment systems need only minor adjustments, opportunities for advancement by disadvantaged employees will be limited. Relatively privileged employees probably are better off guarding their advantage while jockeying against others to gain more. As a result, Black women—the class of employees which, because of its intersectionality, is best able to challenge all forms of discrimination—are essentially isolated and often required to fend for themselves.

In *Moore*, the court's denial of the plaintiff's bid to represent all Blacks and females left Moore with the task of supporting her race and sex discrimination claims with statistical evidence of discrimination against Black females alone.[18] Because she was unable to represent white women or Black men, she could not use overall

[18] Id at 484-86.

statistics on sex disparity at Hughes, nor could she use statistics on race. Proving her claim using statistics on Black women alone was no small task, due to the fact that she was bringing the suit under a disparate impact theory of discrimination.[19]

The court further limited the relevant statistical pool to include only Black women who it determined were qualified to fill the openings in upper-level labor jobs and in supervisory positions.[20] According to the court, Moore had not demonstrated that there were any qualified Black women within her bargaining unit or the general labor pool for either category of jobs.[21] Finally, the court stated that even if it accepted Moore's contention that the percentage of Black females in supervisory positions should equal the percentage of Black females in the employee pool, it still would not find discriminatory impact.[22] Because the promotion of only two Black women into supervisory positions would have achieved the expected mean distribution of Black women within that job category, the court was "unwilling to agree that a prima facie case of disparate impact ha[d] been proven."[23]

The court's rulings on Moore's sex and race claim left her with such a small statistical sample that even if she had proved that there were qualified Black women, she could not have shown discrimination under a disparate impact theory. *Moore* illustrates yet another way that antidiscrimination doctrine essentially erases Black women's distinct experiences and, as a result, deems their discrimination complaints groundless.

3. *Payne v Travenol.*

Black female plaintiffs have also encountered difficulty in

---

[19] Under the disparate impact theory that prevailed at the time, the plaintiff had to introduce statistics suggesting that a policy or procedure disparately affects the members of a protected group. The employer could rebut that evidence by showing that there was a business necessity supporting the rule. The plaintiff then countered the rebuttal by showing that there was a less discriminatory alternative. See, for example, *Griggs v Duke Power*, 401 US 424 (1971); *Connecticut v Teal*, 457 US 440 (1982).

A central issue in a disparate impact case is whether the impact proved is statistically significant. A related issue is how the protected group is defined. In many cases a Black female plaintiff would prefer to use statistics which include white women and/or Black men to indicate that the policy in question does in fact disparately affect the protected class. If, as in *Moore*, the plaintiff may use only statistics involving Black women, there may not be enough Black women employees to create a statistically significant sample.

[20] Id at 484.

[21] The court buttressed its finding with respect to the upper-level labor jobs with statistics for the Los Angeles Metropolitan Area which indicated the there were only 0.2% Black women within comparable job categories. Id at 485 n 9.

[22] Id at 486.

[23] Id.

their efforts to win certification as class representatives in some race discrimination actions. This problem typically arises in cases where statistics suggest significant disparities between Black and white workers and further disparities between Black men and Black women. Courts in some cases[24] have denied certification based on logic that mirrors the rationale in *Moore*: The sex disparities between Black men and Black women created such conflicting interests that Black women could not possibly represent Black men adequately. In one such case, *Payne v Travenol*,[25] two Black female plaintiffs alleging race discrimination brought a class action suit on behalf of all Black employees at a pharmaceutical plant.[26] The court refused, however, to allow the plaintiffs to represent Black males and granted the defendant's request to narrow the class to Black women only. Ultimately, the district court found that there had been extensive racial discrimination at the plant and awarded back pay and constructive seniority to the class of Black female employees. But, despite its finding of general race discrimination, the court refused to extend the remedy to Black men for fear that their conflicting interests would not be adequately addressed;[27] the Fifth Circuit affirmed.[28]

Notably, the plaintiffs in *Travenol* fared better than the similarly-situated plaintiff in *Moore*: They were not denied use of meaningful statistics showing an overall pattern of race discrimination simply because there were no men in their class. The plaintiffs' bid to represent all Black employees, however, like Moore's attempt to represent all women employees, failed as a consequence

---

[24] See *Strong v Arkansas Blue Cross & Blue Shield, Inc.*, 87 FRD 496 (E D Ark 1980); *Hammons v Folger Coffee Co.*, 87 FRD 600 (W D Mo 1980); *Edmondson v Simon*, 86 FRD 375 (N D Ill 1980); *Vuyanich v Republic National Bank of Dallas*, 82 FRD 420 (N D Tex 1979); *Colston v Maryland Cup Corp.*, 26 Fed Rules Serv 940 (D Md 1978).

[25] 416 F Supp 248 (N D Miss 1976).

[26] The suit commenced on March 2, 1972, with the filing of a complaint by three employees seeking to represent a class of persons allegedly subjected to racial discrimination at the hands of the defendants. Subsequently, the plaintiffs amended the complaint to add an allegation of sex discrimination. Of the original named plaintiffs, one was a Black male and two were Black females. In the course of the three-year period between the filing of the complaint and the trial, the only named male plaintiff received permission of the court to withdraw for religious reasons. Id at 250.

[27] As the dissent in *Travenol* pointed out, there was no reason to exclude Black males from the scope of the remedy *after* counsel had presented sufficient evidence to support a finding of discrimination against Black men. If the rationale for excluding Black males was the potential conflict between Black males and Black females, then "[i]n this case, to paraphrase an old adage, the proof of plaintiffs' ability to represent the interests of Black males was in the representation thereof." 673 F2d at 837-38.

[28] 673 F2d 798 (5th Cir 1982).

of the court's narrow view of class interest.

Even though *Travenol* was a partial victory for Black women, the case specifically illustrates how antidiscrimination doctrine generally creates a dilemma for Black women. It forces them to choose between specifically articulating the intersectional aspects of their subordination, thereby risking their ability to represent Black men, or ignoring intersectionality in order to state a claim that would not lead to the exclusion of Black men. When one considers the political consequences of this dilemma, there is little wonder that many people within the Black community view the specific articulation of Black women's interests as dangerously divisive.

In sum, several courts have proved unable to deal with intersectionality, although for contrasting reasons. In *DeGraffenreid*, the court refused to recognize the possibility of compound discrimination against Black women and analyzed their claim using the employment of white women as the historical base. As a consequence, the employment experiences of white women obscured the distinct discrimination that Black women experienced.

Conversely, in *Moore*, the court held that a Black woman could not use statistics reflecting the overall sex disparity in supervisory and upper-level labor jobs because she had not claimed discrimination as a woman, but "only" as a Black woman. The court would not entertain the notion that discrimination experienced by Black women is indeed sex discrimination—provable through disparate impact statistics on women.

Finally, courts, such as the one in *Travenol*, have held that Black women cannot represent an entire class of Blacks due to presumed class conflicts in cases where sex additionally disadvantaged Black women. As a result, in the few cases where Black women are allowed to use overall statistics indicating racially disparate treatment Black men may not be able to share in the remedy.

Perhaps it appears to some that I have offered inconsistent criticisms of how Black women are treated in antidiscrimination law: I seem to be saying that in one case, Black women's claims were rejected and their experiences obscured because the court refused to acknowledge that the employment experience of Black women can be distinct from that of white women, while in other cases, the interests of Black women were harmed because Black women's claims were viewed as so distinct from the claims of either white women or Black men that the court denied to Black females representation of the larger class. It seems that I have to say that Black women are the same and harmed by being treated differently, or that they are different and harmed by being treated the same. But I cannot say both.

This apparent contradiction is but another manifestation of the conceptual limitations of the single-issue analyses that intersectionality challenges. The point is that Black women can experience discrimination in any number of ways and that the contradiction arises from our assumptions that their claims of exclusion must be unidirectional. Consider an analogy to traffic in an intersection, coming and going in all four directions. Discrimination, like traffic through an intersection, may flow in one direction, and it may flow in another. If an accident happens in an intersection, it can be caused by cars traveling from any number of directions and, sometimes, from all of them. Similarly, if a Black woman is harmed because she is in the intersection, her injury could result from sex discrimination or race discrimination.

Judicial decisions which premise intersectional relief on a showing that Black women are specifically recognized as a class are analogous to a doctor's decision at the scene of an accident to treat an accident victim only if the injury is recognized by medical insurance. Similarly, providing legal relief only when Black women show that their claims are based on race or on sex is analogous to calling an ambulance for the victim only after the driver responsible for the injuries is identified. But it is not always easy to reconstruct an accident: Sometimes the skid marks and the injuries simply indicate that they occurred simultaneously, frustrating efforts to determine which driver caused the harm. In these cases the tendency seems to be that no driver is held responsible, no treatment is administered, and the involved parties simply get back in their cars and zoom away.

To bring this back to a non-metaphorical level, I am suggesting that Black women can experience discrimination in ways that are both similar to and different from those experienced by white women and Black men. Black women sometimes experience discrimination in ways similar to white women's experiences; sometimes they share very similar experiences with Black men. Yet often they experience double-discrimination—the combined effects of practices which discriminate on the basis of race, and on the basis of sex. And sometimes, they experience discrimination as Black women—not the sum of race and sex discrimination, but as Black women.

Black women's experiences are much broader than the general categories that discrimination discourse provides. Yet the continued insistence that Black women's demands and needs be filtered through categorical analyses that completely obscure their experiences guarantees that their needs will seldom be addressed.

B. The Significance of Doctrinal Treatment of Intersectionality

DeGraffenreid, *Moore* and *Travenol* are doctrinal manifestations of a common political and theoretical approach to discrimination which operates to marginalize Black women. Unable to grasp the importance of Black women's intersectional experiences, not only courts, but feminist and civil rights thinkers as well have treated Black women in ways that deny both the unique compoundedness of their situation and the centrality of their experiences to the larger classes of women and Blacks. Black women are regarded either as too much like women or Blacks and the compounded nature of their experience is absorbed into the collective experiences of either group or as too different, in which case Black women's Blackness or femaleness sometimes has placed their needs and perspectives at the margin of the feminist and Black liberationist agendas.

While it could be argued that this failure represents an absence of political will to include Black women, I believe that it reflects an uncritical and disturbing acceptance of dominant ways of thinking about discrimination. Consider first the definition of discrimination that seems to be operative in antidiscrimination law: Discrimination which is wrongful proceeds from the identification of a specific class or category; either a discriminator intentionally identifies this category, or a process is adopted which somehow disadvantages all members of this category.[29] According to the dominant view, a discriminator treats all people within a race or sex category similarly. Any significant experiential or statistical variation within this group suggests either that the group is not being discriminated against or that conflicting interests exist which de-

---

[29] In much of antidiscrimination doctrine, the presence of intent to discriminate distinguishes unlawful from lawful discrimination. See *Washington v Davis*, 426 US 229, 239-45 (1976) (proof of discriminatory purpose required to substantiate Equal Protection violation). Under Title VII, however, the Court has held that statistical data showing a disproportionate impact can suffice to support a finding of discrimination. See *Griggs*, 401 US at 432. Whether the distinction between the two analyses will survive is an open question. See *Wards Cove Packing Co., Inc. v Atonio*, 109 S Ct 2115, 2122-23 (1989) (plaintiffs must show more than mere disparity to support a prima facie case of disparate impact). For a discussion of the competing normative visions that underlie the intent and effects analyses, see Alan David Freeman, *Legitimizing Racial Discrimination Through Antidiscrimination Law: A Critical Review of Supreme Court Doctrine*, 62 Minn L Rev 1049 (1978).

feat any attempts to bring a common claim.[30] Consequently, one generally cannot combine these categories. Race and sex, moreover, become significant only when they operate to explicitly *disadvantage* the victims; because the *privileging* of whiteness or maleness is implicit, it is generally not perceived at all.

Underlying this conception of discrimination is a view that the wrong which antidiscrimination law addresses is the use of race or gender factors to interfere with decisions that would otherwise be fair or neutral. This process-based definition is not grounded in a bottom-up commitment to improve the substantive conditions for those who are victimized by the interplay of numerous factors. Instead, the dominant message of antidiscrimination law is that it will regulate only the limited extent to which race or sex interferes with the process of determining outcomes. This narrow objective is facilitated by the top-down strategy of using a singular "but for" analysis to ascertain the effects of race or sex. Because the scope of antidiscrimination law is so limited, sex and race discrimination have come to be defined in terms of the experiences of those who are privileged *but for* their racial or sexual characteristics. Put differently, the paradigm of sex discrimination tends to be based on the experiences of white women; the model of race discrimination tends to be based on the experiences of the most privileged Blacks. Notions of what constitutes race and sex discrimination are, as a result, narrowly tailored to embrace only a small set of circumstances, none of which include discrimination against Black women.

To the extent that this general description is accurate, the following analogy can be useful in describing how Black women are marginalized in the interface between antidiscrimination law and race and gender hierarchies: Imagine a basement which contains all people who are disadvantaged on the basis of race, sex, class, sexual preference, age and/or physical ability. These people are stacked—feet standing on shoulders—with those on the bottom being disadvantaged by the full array of factors, up to the very top, where the heads of all those disadvantaged by a singular factor brush up against the ceiling. Their ceiling is actually the floor above which only those who are *not* disadvantaged in any way reside. In efforts to correct some aspects of domination, those above the ceiling admit from the basement only those who can say that "but for" the ceiling, they too would be in the upper room. A hatch

30 See, for example, *Moore*, 708 F2d at 479.

is developed through which those placed immediately below can crawl. Yet this hatch is generally available only to those who—due to the singularity of their burden and their otherwise privileged position relative to those below—are in the position to crawl through. Those who are multiply-burdened are generally left below unless they can somehow pull themselves into the groups that are permitted to squeeze through the hatch.

As this analogy translates for Black women, the problem is that they can receive protection only to the extent that their experiences are recognizably similar to those whose experiences tend to be reflected in antidiscrimination doctrine. If Black women cannot conclusively say that "but for" their race or "but for" their gender they would be treated differently, they are not invited to climb through the hatch but told to wait in the unprotected margin until they can be absorbed into the broader, protected categories of race and sex.

Despite the narrow scope of this dominant conception of discrimination and its tendency to marginalize those whose experiences cannot be described within its tightly-drawn parameters, this approach has been regarded as the appropriate framework for addressing a range of problems. In much of feminist theory and, to some extent, in antiracist politics, this framework is reflected in the belief that sexism or racism can be meaningfully discussed without paying attention to the lives of those other than the race-, gender- or class-privileged. As a result, both feminist theory and antiracist politics have been organized, in part, around the equation of racism with what happens to the Black middle-class or to Black men, and the equation of sexism with what happens to white women.

Looking at historical and contemporary issues in both the feminist and the civil rights communities, one can find ample evidence of how both communities' acceptance of the dominant framework of discrimination has hindered the development of an adequate theory and praxis to address problems of intersectionality. This adoption of a single-issue framework for discrimination not only marginalizes Black women within the very movements that claim them as part of their constituency but it also makes the illusive goal of ending racism and patriarchy even more difficult to attain.

II. Feminism and Black Women: "Ain't We Women?"

Oddly, despite the relative inability of feminist politics and theory to address Black women substantively, feminist theory and tradition borrow considerably from Black women's history. For example, "Ain't I a Woman" has come to represent a standard refrain in feminist discourse.[31] Yet the lesson of this powerful oratory is not fully appreciated because the context of the delivery is seldom examined. I would like to tell part of the story because it establishes some themes that have characterized feminist treatment of race and illustrates the importance of including Black women's experiences as a rich source for the critique of patriarchy.

In 1851, Sojourner Truth declared "Ain't I a Woman?" and challenged the sexist imagery used by male critics to justify the disenfranchisement of women.[32] The scene was a Women's Rights Conference in Akron, Ohio; white male hecklers, invoking stereotypical images of "womanhood," argued that women were too frail and delicate to take on the responsibilities of political activity. When Sojourner Truth rose to speak, many white women urged that she be silenced, fearing that she would divert attention from women's suffrage to emancipation. Truth, once permitted to speak, recounted the horrors of slavery, and its particular impact on Black women:

> Look at my arm! I have ploughed and planted and gathered into barns, and no man could head me—and ain't I a woman? I could work as much and eat as much as a man—when I could get it—and bear the lash as well! And ain't I a woman? I have born thirteen children, and seen most of 'em sold into slavery, and when I cried out with my mother's grief, none but Jesus heard me—and ain't I a woman?[33]

By using her own life to reveal the contradiction between the ideological myths of womanhood and the reality of Black women's experience, Truth's oratory provided a powerful rebuttal to the claim that women were categorically weaker than men. Yet Truth's personal challenge to the coherence of the cult of true womanhood

---

[31] See Phyliss Palmer, *The Racial Feminization of Poverty: Women of Color as Portents of the Future for All Women*, Women's Studies Quarterly 11:3-4 (Fall 1983) (posing the question of why "white women in the women's movement had not created more effective and continuous alliances with Black women" when "simultaneously . . . Black women [have] become heroines for the women's movement, a position symbolized by the consistent use of Sojourner Truth and her famous words, "Ain't I a Woman?").

[32] See Paula Giddings, *When and Where I Enter: The Impact of Black Women on Race and Sex in America* 54 (William Morrow and Co, Inc, 1st ed 1984).

[33] Eleanor Flexner, *Century of Struggle: The Women's Rights Movement in the United States* 91 (Belknap Press of Harvard University Press, 1975). See also Bell Hooks, *Ain't I a Woman* 159-60 (South End Press, 1981).

was useful only to the extent that white women were willing to reject the racist attempts to rationalize the contradiction—that because Black women were something less than real women, their experiences had no bearing on true womanhood. Thus, this 19th-century Black feminist challenged not only patriarchy, but she also challenged white feminists wishing to embrace Black women's history to relinquish their vestedness in whiteness.

Contemporary white feminists inherit not the legacy of Truth's challenge to patriarchy but, instead, Truth's challenge to their forbearers. Even today, the difficulty that white women have traditionally experienced in sacrificing racial privilege to strengthen feminism renders them susceptible to Truth's critical question. When feminist theory and politics that claim to reflect *women's* experience and *women's* aspirations do not include or speak to Black women, Black women must ask: "Ain't *We* Women?" If this is so, how can the claims that "women are," "women believe" and "women need" be made when such claims are inapplicable or unresponsive to the needs, interests and experiences of Black women?

The value of feminist theory to Black women is diminished because it evolves from a white racial context that is seldom acknowledged. Not only are women of color in fact overlooked, but their exclusion is reinforced when *white* women speak for and as *women*. The authoritative universal voice—usually white male subjectivity masquerading as non-racial, non-gendered objectivity[34]—is merely transferred to those who, but for gender, share many of the same cultural, economic and social characteristics. When feminist theory attempts to describe women's experiences through analyzing patriarchy, sexuality, or separate spheres ideology, it often overlooks the role of race. Feminists thus ignore how their own race functions to mitigate some aspects of sexism and, moreover, how it often privileges them over and contributes to the domination of other women.[35] Consequently, feminist theory remains *white*, and its potential to broaden and deepen its analysis by addressing non-privileged women remains unrealized.

An example of how some feminist theories are narrowly con-

---

[34] "'Objectivity' is itself an example of the reification of white male thought." Hull et al, eds, *But Some of Us Are Brave* at XXV (cited in note 1).

[35] For example, many white females were able to gain entry into previously all white male enclaves not through bringing about a fundamental reordering of male versus female work, but in large part by shifting their "female" responsibilities to poor and minority women.

structed around white women's experiences is found in the separate spheres literature. The critique of how separate spheres ideology shapes and limits women's roles in the home and in public life is a central theme in feminist legal thought.[36] Feminists have attempted to expose and dismantle separate spheres ideology by identifying and criticizing the stereotypes that traditionally have justified the disparate societal roles assigned to men and women.[37] Yet this attempt to debunk ideological justifications for *women's* subordination offers little insight into the domination of *Black* women. Because the experiential base upon which many feminist insights are grounded is white, theoretical statements drawn from them are overgeneralized at best, and often wrong.[38] Statements such as "men and women are taught to see men as independent, capable, powerful; men and women are taught to see women as dependent, limited in abilities, and passive,"[39] are common within this literature. But this "observation" overlooks the anomalies created by crosscurrents of racism and sexism. Black men and women live in a society that creates sex-based norms and expectations which racism operates simultaneously to deny; Black men are not viewed as powerful, nor are Black women seen as passive. An effort to develop an ideological explanation of gender domination in the Black community should proceed from an understanding of how crosscutting forces establish gender norms and how the conditions

---

[36] Feminists often discuss how gender-based stereotypes and norms reinforce the subordination of women by justifying their exclusion from public life and glorifying their roles within the private sphere. Law has historically played a role in maintaining this subordination by enforcing the exclusion of women from public life and by limiting its reach into the private sphere. See, for example, Deborah L. Rhode, *Association and Assimilation*, 81 Nw U L Rev 106 (1986); Frances Olsen, *From False Paternalism to False Equality: Judicial Assaults on Feminist Community, Illinois 1869-95*, 84 Mich L Rev 1518 (1986); Martha Minow, *Foreword: Justice Engendered*, 101 Harv L Rev 10 (1987); Nadine Taub and Elizabeth M. Schneider, *Perspectives on Women's Subordination and the Role of Law*, in David Kairys, ed, *The Politics of Law* 117-39 (Pantheon Books, 1982).

[37] See works cited in note 36.

[38] This criticism is a discrete illustration of a more general claim that feminism has been premised on white middle-class women's experience. For example, early feminist texts such as Betty Friedan's *The Feminine Mystique* (W. W. Norton, 1963), placed white middle-class problems at the center of feminism and thus contributed to its rejection within the Black community. See Hooks, *Ain't I a Woman* at 185-96 (cited in note 33) (noting that feminism was eschewed by Black women because its white middle-class agenda ignored Black women's concerns).

[39] Richard A. Wasserstrom, *Racism, Sexism and Preferential Treatment: An Approach to the Topics*, 24 UCLA L Rev 581, 588 (1977). I chose this phrase not because it is typical of most feminist statements of separate spheres; indeed, most discussions are not as simplistic as the bold statement presented here. See, for example, Taub and Schneider, *Perspectives on Women's Subordination and the Role of Law* at 117-39 (cited in note 36).

of Black subordination wholly frustrate access to these norms. Given this understanding, perhaps we can begin to see why Black women have been dogged by the stereotype of the pathological matriarch[40] or why there have been those in the Black liberation movement who aspire to create institutions and to build traditions that are intentionally patriarchal.[41]

Because ideological and descriptive definitions of patriarchy are usually premised upon white female experiences, feminists and others informed by feminist literature may make the mistake of assuming that since the role of Black women in the family and in other Black institutions does not always resemble the familiar manifestations of patriarchy in the white community, Black women are somehow exempt from patriarchal norms. For example, Black women have traditionally worked outside the home in numbers far exceeding the labor participation rate of white women.[42] An analysis of patriarchy that highlights the history of white women's exclusion from the workplace might permit the inference that Black women have not been burdened by this particular gender-based expectation. Yet the very fact that Black women must work conflicts with norms that women should not, often creating personal, emotional and relationship problems in Black women's lives. Thus, Black women are burdened not only because they often have to take on responsibilities that are not traditionally feminine but, moreover, their assumption of these roles is sometimes interpreted within the Black community as either Black women's failure to live up to such norms or as another manifestation of racism's scourge upon the Black community.[43] This is one of the many aspects of intersectionality that cannot be understood

---

[40] For example, Black families have sometimes been cast as pathological largely because Black women's divergence from the white middle-class female norm. The most infamous rendition of this view is found in the Moynihan report which blamed many of the Black community's ills on a supposed pathological family structure. For a discussion of the report and its contemporary reincarnation, see pp 163-165.

[41] See Hooks, *Ain't I a Woman* at 94-99 (cited in note 33) (discussing the elevation of sexist imagery in the Black liberation movement during the 1960s).

[42] See generally Jacqueline Jones, *Labor of Love, Labor of Sorrow; Black Women, Work, and the Family from Slavery to the Present* (Basic Books, 1985); Angela Davis, *Women, Race and Class* (Random House, 1981).

[43] As Elizabeth Higginbotham noted, "women, who often fail to conform to 'appropriate' sex roles, have been pictured as, and made to feel, inadequate—even though as women, they possess traits recognized as positive when held by men in the wider society. Such women are stigmatized because their lack of adherence to expected gender roles is seen as a threat to the value system." Elizabeth Higginbotham, *Two Representative Issues in Contemporary Sociological Work on Black Women*, in Hull, et al, eds, *But Some of Us Are Brave* at 95 (cited in note 1).

through an analysis of patriarchy rooted in white experience.

Another example of how theory emanating from a white context obscures the multidimensionality of Black women's lives is found in feminist discourse on rape. A central political issue on the feminist agenda has been the pervasive problem of rape. Part of the intellectual and political effort to mobilize around this issue has involved the development of a historical critique of the role that law has played in establishing the bounds of normative sexuality and in regulating female sexual behavior.[44] Early carnal knowledge statutes and rape laws are understood within this discourse to illustrate that the objective of rape statutes traditionally has not been to protect women from coercive intimacy but to protect and maintain a property-like interest in female chastity.[45] Although feminists quite rightly criticize these objectives, to characterize rape law as reflecting male control over female sexuality is for Black women an oversimplified account and an ultimately inadequate account.

Rape statutes generally do not reflect *male* control over *female* sexuality, but *white* male regulation of *white* female sexuality.[46] Historically, there has been absolutely no institutional effort to regulate Black female chastity.[47] Courts in some states had gone so far as to instruct juries that, unlike white women, Black women were not presumed to be chaste.[48] Also, while it was true that the

---

[44] See generally Susan Brownmiller, *Against Our Will* (Simon and Schuster, 1975); Susan Estrich, *Real Rape* (Harvard University Press, 1987).

[45] See Brownmiller, *Against Our Will* at 17; see generally Estrich, *Real Rape*.

[46] One of the central theoretical dilemmas of feminism that is largely obscured by universalizing the white female experience is that experiences that are described as a manifestation of male control over females can be instead a manifestation of dominant group control over all subordinates. The significance is that other nondominant men may not share in, participate in or connect with the behavior, beliefs or actions at issue, and may be victimized themselves by "male" power. In other contexts, however, "male authority" might include nonwhite men, particularly in private sphere contexts. Efforts to think more clearly about when Black women are dominated as *women* and when they are dominated as *Black women* are directly related to the question of when power is *male* and when it is *white male*.

[47] See Note, *Rape, Racism and the Law*, 6 Harv Women's L J 103, 117-23 (1983) (discussing the historical and contemporary evidence suggesting that Black women are generally not thought to be chaste). See also Hooks, *Ain't I a Woman* at 54 (cited in note 33) (stating that stereotypical images of Black womanhood during slavery were based on the myth that "all black women were immoral and sexually loose"); Beverly Smith, *Black Women's Health: Notes for a Course*, in Hull et al, eds, *But Some of Us Are Brave* at 110 (cited in note 1) (noting that ". . . white men for centuries have justified their sexual abuse of Black women by claiming that we are licentious, always 'ready' for any sexual encounter").

[48] The following statement is probably unusual only in its candor: "What has been said by some of our courts about an unchaste female being a comparatively rare exception is no doubt true where the population is composed largely of the Caucasian race, but we would blind ourselves to actual conditions if we adopted this rule where another race that is largely

attempt to regulate the sexuality of white women placed unchaste women outside the law's protection, racism restored a fallen white woman's chastity where the alleged assailant was a Black man.[49] No such restoration was available to Black women.

The singular focus on rape as a manifestation of male power over female sexuality tends to eclipse the use of rape as a weapon of racial terror.[50] When Black women were raped by white males, they were being raped not as women generally, but as Black women specifically: Their femaleness made them sexually vulnerable to racist domination, while their Blackness effectively denied

---

immoral constitutes an appreciable part of the population." *Dallas v State*, 76 Fla 358, 79 So 690 (1918), quoted in Note, 6 Harv Women's L J at 121 (cited in note 47).

Espousing precisely this view, one commentator stated in 1902: "I sometimes hear of a virtuous Negro woman but the idea is so absolutely inconceivable to me . . . I cannot imagine such a creature as a virtuous Negro woman." Id at 82. Such images persist in popular culture. See Paul Grein, *Taking Stock of the Latest Pop Record Surprises*, LA Times § 6 at 1 (July 7, 1988) (recalling the controversy in the late 70s over a Rolling Stones recording which included the line "Black girls just wanna get fucked all night").

Opposition to such negative stereotypes has sometimes taken the form of sexual conservatism. "A desperate reaction to this slanderous myth is the attempt . . . to conform to the strictest versions of patriarchal morality." Smith, *Black Women's Health*, in Hull et al, eds, *But Some of Us Are Brave* at 111 (cited in note 1). Part of this reaction is reflected in the attitudes and policies of Black schools which have been notoriously strict in regulating the behavior of female students. See Gail Elizabeth Wyatt, *The Sexual Experience of Afro-American Women*, in Martha Kirkpatrick, ed, *Women's Sexual Experience: Exploration of the Dark Continent* 24 (Plenum, 1982) (noting "the differences between the predominantly Afro-American universities, where there was far more supervision regarding sexual behavior, and the majority of white colleges, where there were fewer curfews and restrictions placed on the resident"). Any attempt to understand and critique the emphasis on Black virtue without focusing on the racist ideology that places virtue beyond the reach of Black women would be incomplete and probably incorrect.

[49] Because of the way the legal system viewed chastity, Black women could not be victims of forcible rape. One commentator has noted that "[a]ccording to governing sterotypes [sic], chastity could not be possessed by Black women. Thus, Black women's rape charges were automatically discounted, and the issue of chastity was contested only in cases where the rape complainant was a white woman." Note, 6 Harv Women's L J at 126 (cited in note 47). Black women's claims of rape were not taken seriously regardless of the offender's race. A judge in 1912 said: "This court will never take the word of a nigger against the word of a white man [concerning rape]." Id at 120. On the other hand, lynching was considered an effective remedy for a Black man's rape of a white woman. Since rape of a white woman by a Black man was "a crime more horrible than death," the only way to assuage society's rage and to make the woman whole again was to brutally murder the Black man. Id at 125.

[50] See *The Rape of Black Women as a Weapon of Terror*, in Gerda Lerner, ed, *Black Women in White America* 172-93 (Pantheon Books, 1972). See also Brownmiller, *Against Our Will* (cited in note 44). Even where Brownmiller acknowledges the use of rape as racial terrorism, she resists making a "special case" for Black women by offering evidence that white women were raped by the Klan as well. Id at 139. Whether or not one considers the racist rape of Black women a "special case," such experiences are probably different. In any case, Brownmiller's treatment of the issue raises serious questions about the ability to sustain an analysis of patriarchy without understanding its multiple intersections with racism.

them any protection.[51] This white male power was reinforced by a judicial system in which the successful conviction of a white man for raping a Black woman was virtually unthinkable.[52]

In sum, sexist expectations of chastity and racist assumptions of sexual promiscuity combined to create a distinct set of issues confronting Black women.[53] These issues have seldom been explored in feminist literature nor are they prominent in antiracist politics. The lynching of Black males, the institutional practice that was legitimized by the regulation of white women's sexuality, has historically and contemporaneously occupied the Black agenda on sexuality and violence. Consequently, Black women are caught between a Black community that, perhaps understandably, views with suspicion attempts to litigate questions of sexual violence, and a feminist community that reinforces those suspicions by focusing on white female sexuality.[54] The suspicion is compounded

---

[51] Lerner, *Black Women in White America* at 173.

[52] See generally, Note, 6 Harv Women's L J at 103 (cited in note 47).

[53] Paula Giddings notes the combined effect of sexual and racial stereotypes: "Black women were seen having all of the inferior qualities of white women without any of their virtues." Giddings, *When and Where I Enter* at 82 (cited in note 32).

[54] Susan Brownmiller's treatment of the Emmett Till case illustrates why antirape politicization makes some African Americans uncomfortable. Despite Brownmiller's quite laudable efforts to discuss elsewhere the rape of Black women and the racism involved in much of the hysteria over the Black male threat, her analysis of the Till case places the sexuality of white women, rather than racial terrorism, at center stage. Brownmiller states: "Rarely has one single case exposed so clearly as Till's the underlying group-male antagonisms over access to women, for what began in Bryant's store should not be misconstrued as an innocent flirtation . . . . In concrete terms, the accessibility of all white women was on review." Brownmiller, *Against Our Will* at 272 (cited in note 44).

Later, Brownmiller argues:

> And what of the wolf whistle, Till's 'gesture of adolescent bravado'? We are rightly aghast that a whistle could be cause for murder but we must also accept that Emmett Till and J. W. Millam shared something in common. They both understood that the whistle was no small tweet of hubba-hubba or melodious approval for a well-turned ankle. Given the deteriorated situation . . . it was a deliberate insult just short of physical assault, a last reminder to Carolyn Bryant that this black boy, Till, had a mind to possess her.

Id at 273.

While Brownmiller seems to categorize the case as one that evidences a conflict over possession, it is regarded in African American history as a tragic dramatization of the South's pathological hatred and fear of African Americans. Till's body, mutilated beyond recognition, was viewed by thousands so that, in the words of Till's mother, "the world could see what they did to my boy." Juan Williams, *Standing for Justice*, in *Eyes on the Prize* 44 (Viking, 1987). The Till tragedy is also regarded as one of the historical events that bore directly on the emergence of the Civil Rights movement. "[W]ithout question it moved black America in a way the Supreme Court ruling on school desegregation could not match." Id. As Williams later observed, "the murder of Emmitt Till had a powerful impact on a generation of blacks. It was this generation, those who were adolescents when Till was killed, that would soon demand justice and freedom in a way unknown in America before."

by the historical fact that the protection of white female sexuality was often the pretext for terrorizing the Black community. Even today some fear that antirape agendas may undermine antiracist objectives. This is the paradigmatic political and theoretical dilemma created by the intersection of race and gender: Black women are caught between ideological and political currents that combine first to create and then to bury Black women's experiences.

III. When and Where I Enter: Integrating an Analysis of Sexism into Black Liberation Politics

Anna Julia Cooper, a 19th-century Black feminist, coined a phrase that has been useful in evaluating the need to incorporate an explicit analysis of patriarchy in any effort to address racial domination.[55] Cooper often criticized Black leaders and spokespersons for claiming to speak for the race, but failing to speak for Black women. Referring to one of Martin Delaney's public claims that where he was allowed to enter, the race entered with him, Cooper countered: "Only the Black Woman can say, when and where I enter . . . then and there the whole Negro race enters with me."[56]

Cooper's words bring to mind a personal experience involving two Black men with whom I had formed a study group during our first year of law school. One of our group members, a graduate from Harvard College, often told us stories about a prestigious and exclusive men's club that boasted memberships of several past United States presidents and other influential white males. He was one of its very few Black members. To celebrate completing our first-year exams, our friend invited us to join him at the club for drinks. Anxious to see this fabled place, we approached the large door and grasped the brass door ring to announce our arrival. But our grand entrance was cut short when our friend sheepishly slipped from behind the door and whispered that he had forgotten

---

Id at 57. Thus, while Brownmiller looks at the Till case and sees the vicious struggle over the possession of a white woman, African Americans see the case as a symbol of the insane degree to which whites were willing to suppress the Black race. While patriarchal attitudes toward women's sexuality played a supporting role, to place white women center stage in this tragedy is to manifest such confusion over racism as to make it difficult to imagine that the white antirape movement could be sensitive to more subtle racial tensions regarding Black women's participation in it.

[55] See Anna Julia Cooper, *A Voice from the South* (Negro Universities Press, 1969 reprint of the Aldine Printing House, Ohio, 1892).

[56] Id at 31.

a very important detail. My companion and I bristled, our training as Black people having taught us to expect yet another barrier to our inclusion; even an informal one-Black-person quota at the establishment was not unimaginable. The tension broke, however, when we learned that *we* would not be excluded because of our race, but that *I* would have to go around to the back door because I was a female. I entertained the idea of making a scene to dramatize the fact that my humiliation as a female was no less painful and my exclusion no more excusable than had we all been sent to the back door because we were Black. But, sensing no general assent to this proposition, and also being of the mind that due to our race a scene would in some way jeopardize all of us, I failed to stand my ground. After all, the Club was about to entertain its first Black guests—even though one would have to enter through the back door.[57]

Perhaps this story is not the best example of the Black community's failure to address problems related to Black women's intersectionality seriously. The story would be more apt if Black women, and only Black women, had to go around to the back door of the club and if the restriction came from within, and not from the outside of the Black community. Still this story does reflect a markedly decreased political and emotional vigilance toward barriers to Black women's enjoyment of privileges that have been won on the basis of race but continue to be denied on the basis of sex.[58]

The story also illustrates the ambivalence among Black women about the degree of political and social capital that ought to be expended toward challenging gender barriers, particularly when the challenges might conflict with the antiracism agenda. While there are a number of reasons—including antifeminist ones—why gender has not figured directly in analyses of the subordination of Black Americans, a central reason is that race is still seen by many as the primary oppositional force in Black lives.[59] If

---

[57] In all fairness, I must acknowledge that my companion accompanied me to the back door. I remain uncertain, however, as to whether the gesture was an expression of solidarity or an effort to quiet my anger.

[58] To this one could easily add class.

[59] An anecdote illustrates this point. A group of female law professors gathered to discuss "Isms in the Classroom." One exercise led by Pat Cain involved each participant listing the three primary factors that described herself. Almost without exception, white women in the room listed their gender either primarily or secondarily; none listed their race. All of the women of color listed their race first, and then their gender. This seems to suggest that identity descriptions seem to begin with the primary source of opposition with whatever the dominant norm is. See Pat Cain, *Feminist Jurisprudence: Grounding the Theories* 19-20 (unpublished manuscript on file with author) (explaining the exercise and noting that "no

one accepts that the social experience of race creates both a primary group identity as well as a shared sense of being under collective assault, some of the reasons that Black feminist theory and politics have not figured prominently in the Black political agenda may be better understood.[60]

The point is not that African Americans are simply involved in a more important struggle. Although some efforts to oppose Black feminism are based on this assumption, a fuller appreciation of the problems of the Black community will reveal that gender subordination does contribute significantly to the destitute conditions of so many African Americans and that it must therefore be addressed. Moreover, the foregoing critique of the single-issue framework renders problematic the claim that the struggle against racism is distinguishable from, much less prioritized over, the struggle against sexism. Yet it is also true that the politics of racial otherness that Black women experience along with Black men prevent Black feminist consciousness from patterning the development of white feminism. For white women, the creation of a consciousness that was distinct from and in opposition to that of white men figured prominently in the development of white feminist politics. Black women, like Black men, live in a community that has been defined and subordinated by color and culture.[61] Although patriarchy clearly operates within the Black community, presenting yet another source of domination to which Black women are vulnerable, the racial context in which Black women find themselves makes the creation of a political consciousness that is oppositional to Black men difficult.

Yet while it is true that the distinct experience of racial otherness militates against the development of an oppositional feminist consciousness, the assertion of racial community sometimes supports defensive priorities that marginalize Black women. Black

---

white woman ever mentions race, whereas every woman of color does" and that, similarly, "straight women do not include 'heterosexual' . . . whereas lesbians who are open always include 'lesbian' ").

[60] For a comparative discussion of Third World feminism paralleling this observation, see Kumari Jayawardena, *Feminism and Nationalism in the Third World* 1-24 (Zed Books Ltd, 1986). Jayawardena states that feminism in the Third World has been "accepted" only within the central struggle against international domination. Women's social and political status has improved most when advancement is necessary to the broader struggle against imperialism.

[61] For a discussion of how racial ideology creates a polarizing dynamic which subordinates Blacks and privileges whites, see Kimberle Crenshaw, *Race, Reform and Retrenchment: Transformation and Legitimation in Antidiscrimination Law*, 101 Harv L Rev 1331, 1371-76 (1988).

women's particular interests are thus relegated to the periphery in public policy discussions about the presumed needs of the Black community. The controversy over the movie *The Color Purple* is illustrative. The animating fear behind much of the publicized protest was that by portraying domestic abuse in a Black family, the movie confirmed the negative stereotypes of Black men.[62] The debate over the propriety of presenting such an image on the screen overshadowed the issue of sexism and patriarchy in the Black community. Even though it was sometimes acknowledged that the Black community was not immune from domestic violence and other manifestations of gender subordination, some nevertheless felt that in the absence of positive Black male images in the media, portraying such images merely reinforced racial stereotypes.[63] The struggle against racism seemed to compel the subordination of certain aspects of the Black female experience in order to ensure the security of the larger Black community.

The nature of this debate should sound familiar to anyone who recalls Daniel Moynihan's diagnosis of the ills of Black America.[64] Moynihan's report depicted a deteriorating Black family, foretold the destruction of the Black male householder and lamented the creation of the Black matriarch. His conclusions prompted a massive critique from liberal sociologists[65] and from civil rights leaders.[66] Surprisingly, while many critics characterized the report as racist for its blind use of white cultural norms as the standard for evaluating Black families, few pointed out the sexism apparent in Moynihan's labeling Black women as pathological for their "failure" to live up to a white female standard of motherhood.[67]

---

[62] Jack Matthews, *Three Color Purple Actresses Talk About Its Impact*, LA Times § 6 at 1 (Jan 31, 1986); Jack Matthews, *Some Blacks Critical of Spielberg's Purple*, LA Times § 6 at 1 (Dec 20, 1985). But see Gene Siskel, *Does Purple Hate Men?*, Chicago Tribune § 13 at 16 (Jan 5, 1986); Clarence Page, *Toward a New Black Cinema*, Chicago Tribune § 5 at 3 (Jan 12, 1986).

[63] A consistent problem with any negative portrayal of African Americans is that they are seldom balanced by positive images. On the other hand, most critics overlooked the positive transformation of the primary male character in *The Color Purple*.

[64] Daniel P. Moynihan, *The Negro Family: The Case for National Action* (Office of Policy Planning and Research, United States Department of Labor, 1965).

[65] See Lee Rainwater and William L. Yancey, *The Moynihan Report and the Politics of Controversy* 427-29 (MIT Press, 1967) (containing criticisms of the Moynihan Report by, among others, Charles E. Silberman, Christopher Jencks, William Ryan, Laura Carper, Frank Riessman and Herbert Gans).

[66] Id at 395-97 (critics included Martin Luther King, Jr., Benjamin Payton, James Farmer, Whitney Young, Jr. and Bayard Rustin).

[67] One of the notable exceptions is Jacquelyne Johnson Jackson, *Black Women in a*

The latest versions of a Moynihanesque analysis can be found in the Moyers televised special, *The Vanishing Black Family*,[68] and, to a lesser extent, in William Julius Wilson's *The Truly Disadvantaged*.[69] In *The Vanishing Black Family*, Moyers presented the problem of female-headed households as a problem of irresponsible sexuality, induced in part by government policies that encouraged family breakdown.[70] The theme of the report was that the welfare state reinforced the deterioration of the Black family by rendering the Black male's role obsolete. As the argument goes, because Black men know that someone will take care of their families, they are free to make babies and leave them. A corollary to the Moyers view is that welfare is also dysfunctional because it allows poor women to leave men upon whom they would otherwise be dependent.

Most commentators criticizing the program failed to pose challenges that might have revealed the patriarchal assumptions underlying much of the Moyers report. They instead focused on the dimension of the problem that was clearly recognizable as racist.[71] White feminists were equally culpable. There was little, if any, published response to the Moyers report from the white feminist community. Perhaps feminists were under the mistaken assumption that since the report focused on the Black community,

---

Racist Society, in *Racism and Mental Health* 185-86 (University of Pittsburgh Press, 1973).

[68] *The Vanishing Black Family* (PBS Television Broadcast, January 1986).

[69] William Julius Wilson, *The Truly Disadvantaged: The Inner City, The Underclass and Public Policy* (The University of Chicago Press, 1987).

[70] Columnist Mary McGrory, applauding the show, reported that Moyers found that sex was as common in the Black ghetto as a cup of coffee. McGrory, *Moynihan was Right 21 Years Ago*, The Washington Post B1 and B4 (Jan 26, 1986). George Will argued that oversexed Black men were more of a menace than Bull Conner, the Birmingham Police Chief who in 1968 achieved international notoriety by turning fire hoses on protesting school children. George Will, *Voting Rights Won't Fix It*, The Washington Post A23 (Jan 23, 1986).

My guess is that the program has influenced the debate about the so-called underclass by providing graphic support to pre-existing tendencies to attribute poverty to individual immorality. During a recent and memorable discussion on the public policy implications of poverty in the Black community, one student remarked that nothing can be done about Black poverty until Black men stop acting like "roving penises," Black women stop having babies "at the drop of a hat," and they all learn middle-class morality. The student cited the Moyers report as her source.

[71] Although the nearly exclusive focus on the racist aspects of the program poses both theoretical and political problems, it was entirely understandable given the racial nature of the subsequent comments that were sympathetic to the Moyers view. As is typical in discussions involving race, the dialogue regarding the Moyers program covered more than just the issue of Black families; some commentators took the opportunity to indict not only the Black underclass, but the Black civil rights leadership, the war on poverty, affirmative action and other race-based remedies. See, for example, Will, *Voting Rights Won't Fix It* at A23 (cited in note 70).

the problems highlighted were racial, not gender based. Whatever the reason, the result was that the ensuing debates over the future direction of welfare and family policy proceeded without significant feminist input. The absence of a strong feminist critique of the Moynihan/Moyers model not only impeded the interests of Black women, but it also compromised the interests of growing numbers of white women heads of household who find it difficult to make ends meet.[72]

William Julius Wilson's *The Truly Disadvantaged* modified much of the moralistic tone of this debate by reframing the issue in terms of a lack of marriageable Black men.[73] According to Wilson, the decline in Black marriages is not attributable to poor motivation, bad work habits or irresponsibility but instead is caused by structural economics which have forced Black unskilled labor out of the work force. Wilson's approach represents a significant move away from that of Moynihan/Moyers in that he rejects their attempt to center the analysis on the morals of the Black community. Yet, he too considers the proliferation of female-headed households as dysfunctional *per se* and fails to explain fully why such households are so much in peril. Because he incorporates no analysis of the way the structure of the economy and the workforce subordinates the interests of women, especially childbearing Black women, Wilson's suggested reform begins with finding ways to put Black men back in the family.[74] In Wilson's view, we must change the economic structure with an eye toward providing more Black jobs for Black men. Because he offers no critique of sexism, Wilson fails to consider economic or social reorganization that directly empowers and supports these single Black mothers.[75]

---

[72] Their difficulties can also be linked to the prevalence of an economic system and family policy that treat the nuclear family as the norm and other family units as aberrant and unworthy of societal accommodation.

[73] Wilson, *The Truly Disadvantaged* at 96 (cited in note 69).

[74] Id at 154 (suggestions include macroeconomic policies which promote balanced economic growth, a nationally-oriented labor market strategy, a child support assurance program, a child care strategy, and a family allowances program which would be both means tested and race specific).

[75] Nor does Wilson include an analysis of the impact of gender on changes in family patterns. Consequently, little attention is paid to the conflict that may result when gender-based expectations are frustrated by economic and demographic factors. This focus on demographic and structural explanations represent an effort to regain the high ground from the Moyers/Moynihan approach which is more psycho-social. Perhaps because psycho-social explanations have come dangerously close to victim-blaming, their prevalence is thought to threaten efforts to win policy directives that might effectively address deteriorating conditions within the working class and poor Black communities. See Kimberle Crenshaw, *A Comment on Gender, Difference, and Victim Ideology in the Study of the Black Family*, in

My criticism is not that providing Black men with jobs is undesirable; indeed, this is necessary not only for the Black men themselves, but for an entire community, depressed and subject to a host of sociological and economic ills that accompany massive rates of unemployment. But as long as we assume that the massive social reorganization Wilson calls for is possible, why not think about it in ways that maximize the choices of Black women?[76] A more complete theoretical and political agenda for the Black underclass must take into account the specific and particular concerns of Black women; their families occupy the bottom rung of the economic ladder, and it is only through placing them at the center of the analysis that their needs and the needs of their families will be directly addressed.[77]

IV. Expanding Feminist Theory and Antiracist Politics by Embracing the Intersection

If any real efforts are to be made to free Black people of the constraints and conditions that characterize racial subordination, then theories and strategies purporting to reflect the Black community's needs must include an analysis of sexism and patriarchy. Similarly, feminism must include an analysis of race if it hopes to express the aspirations of non-white women. Neither Black liberationist politics nor feminist theory can ignore the intersectional experiences of those whom the movements claim as their respective constituents. In order to include Black women, both movements must distance themselves from earlier approaches in which experiences are relevant only when they are related to certain clearly identifiable causes (for example, the oppression of Blacks is significant when based on race, of women when based on gender). The praxis of both should be centered on the life chances and life situations of people who should be cared about without regard to the source of their difficulties.

I have stated earlier that the failure to embrace the complexities of compoundedness is not simply a matter of political will, but

---

The Decline of Marriage Among African Americans: Causes, Consequences and Policy Implications (forthcoming 1989).

[76] For instance, Wilson only mentions in passing the need for day care and job training for single mothers. Wilson at 153 (cited in note 69). No mention at all is made of other practices and policies that are racist and sexist, and that contribute to the poor conditions under which nearly half of all Black women must live.

[77] Pauli Murray observes that the operation of sexism is at least the partial cause of social problems affecting Black women. See Murray, *The Liberation of Black Women*, in Jo Freeman, ed, *Women: A Feminist Perspective* 351-62 (Mayfield Publishing Co, 1975).

is also due to the influence of a way of thinking about discrimination which structures politics so that struggles are categorized as singular issues. Moreover, this structure imports a descriptive and normative view of society that reinforces the status quo.

It is somewhat ironic that those concerned with alleviating the ills of racism and sexism should adopt such a top-down approach to discrimination. If their efforts instead began with addressing the needs and problems of those who are most disadvantaged and with restructuring and remaking the world where necessary, then others who are singularly disadvantaged would also benefit. In addition, it seems that placing those who currently are marginalized in the center is the most effective way to resist efforts to compartmentalize experiences and undermine potential collective action.

It is not necessary to believe that a political consensus to focus on the lives of the most disadvantaged will happen tomorrow in order to recenter discrimination discourse at the intersection. It is enough, for now, that such an effort would encourage us to look beneath the prevailing conceptions of discrimination and to challenge the complacency that accompanies belief in the effectiveness of this framework. By so doing, we may develop language which is critical of the dominant view and which provides some basis for unifying activity. The goal of this activity should be to facilitate the inclusion of marginalized groups for whom it can be said: "When they enter, we all enter."

[17]

International Journal of the Sociology of Law 1990, **18**, 199–215

Feminism and Critical Legal Theory: An American Perspective

FRANCES OLSEN
School of Law, University of California at Los Angeles, U.S.A.

Liberal Dualisms

Since the rise of classical liberal thought, and perhaps since the time of Plato, most of us have structured our thinking around a complex series of dualisms, or opposing pairs: rational/irrational; active/passive; thought/feeling; reason/emotion; culture/nature; power/sensitivity; objective/subjective; abstract/contextualized; principled/personalized. These dualistic pairs divide things into contrasting spheres or polar opposites (Olsen, 1983: 1575–76; Frug, 1980: 1057).

This system of dualisms has three characteristics that are important to this discussion. First, the dualisms are sexualized. One half of each dualism is considered masculine, the other half feminine. Second, the terms of the dualism are not equal, but are thought to constitute a heirarchy. In each pair, the term identified as 'masculine' is privileged as superior, while the other is considered negative, corrupt, or inferior. And third, law is identified with the 'male' side of the dualisms.

Sexualization

The division between male and female has been crucial to this dualistic system of thought. Men have identified themselves with one side of the dualisms and have projected the other side upon women (Cixous, 1981: 90–91; Christ, 1980: 25; Olsen, 1983: 1570–76). I have listed each dualism in the same order, with the term associated with men on the left: rational, active, thought, reason, culture, power, objective, abstract, principled. The terms associated with women

A version of this essay will appear in *The Politics of Law*, edited by David Kairys, 2nd edition, 1991.

0194–6595/90/020199 + 17 $03.00/0

are on the right side: irrational, passive, feeling, emotion, nature, sensitivity, subjective, contextualized, personalized.

rational/irrational
active/passive
thought/feeling
reason/emotion
culture/nature
power/sensitivity
objective/subjective
abstract/contextualized
principled/personalized

The sexual identification of the dualisms has both a descriptive and a normative element. Sometimes it is said that men are rational, active, etc., and other times it will be said that men should be rational, active, etc. Similarly, the claim about women is sometimes considered to be descriptive; women simply are irrational, passive, etc. A lot of people used to believe that this was an inevitable, immutable fact about women—that women were unable to become rational, active, etc. Another kind of claim is that women should be irrational, passive, etc., or at least that they should *not* become rational, active, etc.—either because it is important that women remain different from men, or because irrational, passive, etc., are good traits *as applied to women.*

Hierarchization

The system of dualisms is hierarchized. The dualisms do not just divide the world between two terms; the two terms are arranged in a hierarchical order. Just as men dominate and define women, one side of the dualism dominates and defines the other. Irrational is the absence of rational; passive is the failure of active; thought is more important than feeling; reason takes precedence over emotion.

This hierarchy has been somewhat obscured by a complex and often insincere glorification of women and the feminine. While men have oppressed and exploited women in the real world, they have also placed women on a pedestal and treasured them in a fantasy world. And just as men simultaneously exalt and degrade women, so, too, do they simultaneously exalt and degrade the concepts on the 'feminine' side of the dualisms. Nature, for example, is glorified as something awesome, a worthy subject of conquest by male heroes, while it is simultaneously degraded as inert matter to be exploited and shaped to men's purpose. Irrational subjectivity and sensitivity are similarly treasured and denigrated at the same time. However much they might romanticize the womanly virtues, most men still believe that rational is better than irrational, objectivity is better than subjectivity, and being abstract and principled is better than being contextualized and personalized. It is more complicated than this, however, because no one would really want to *eliminate* irrational, passive, etc. from the world altogether. But men usually want to distance *themselves* from these traits; they want women to be irrational, passive, and so forth [1]. To women, this glorification of the 'feminine' side of the dualisms seems insincere.

Law as male

Law is identified with the heirarchically superior, 'masculine' sides of the dualisms. 'Justice' may be depicted as a woman, but, according to the dominant ideology, law is male, not female. Law is supposed to be rational, objective, abstract and principled (Unger, 1976: 52–54), like men; it is not supposed to be irrational, subjective, contextualized or personalized, like women [2].

The social, political and intellectual practices that constitute 'law' were for many years carried on almost exclusively by men. Given that women were long excluded from the practice of law (Olsen, 1986: 1523–31), it is not surprising that the traits associated with women are not greatly valued in law. Moreover, in a kind of vicious cycle, this presumed 'maleness' of law used to provide justification for excluding women from practicing law. While the number of women in law has been rapidly increasing [3], the field continues to be heavily male-dominated (Epstein, 1981: 13–22; Kanter, 1978). In a similar vicious cycle, law is considered rational and objective in part because it is highly valued, and it is highly valued in part because it is considered rational and objective.

The most interesting and promising challenges to this dominant system of thought are those made by feminists. Feminist critiques of law bear a close analogy to feminist critiques of male-dominance in general, and the several conflicting attitudes that various feminists have taken toward law can best be understood when viewed in this broader context. In Part II, I examine feminist critiques of male dominance in general—the attacks feminists have been making for years on the system of sexualized and hierarchized dualisms. Part III focuses specifically on feminist criticisms of law.

Feminist Strategies

Feminist strategies for attacking the dominant dualistic system of thought fall into three broad categories. The first category consists of strategies that oppose the sexualization of the dualisms and struggle to identify women with the favored side, with rational, active, and so forth. Strategies in the second category reject the hierarchy men have established between the two sides of the dualisms. This second category accepts the identification of women with irrational, passive, etc. but proclaims the value of these traits; they are as good as or better than rational, active, and so forth. The third category rejects both the sexualization and the hierarchization of the dualisms. Strategies in this third category question and disrupt the differences asserted between men and women, and they deny the hierarchy of rational, active, etc. over irrational, passive, and so forth. Rational, active, etc. and irrational, passive, etc. are not polar opposites, and they do not and cannot divide the world into contrasting spheres.

Reject sexualization

Strategies that reject the sexualization of the dualisms are like the dominant ideology in that they accept the hierarchy of rational over irrational, of active over passive, etc. They differ from the dominant ideology in that they reject the normative claim that women should be irrational, passive, etc. and for the most part they reject the descriptive assertion that women are irrational, passive, etc. They most strongly reject the idea that women cannot help but be irrational, passive, etc.

This strategy is illustrated by an essay written in 1851 by Harriet Taylor Mill (Mill, 1970: 89). She disputed the assertion that women were naturally or universally inferior to men and argued that each individual should be free to develop his or her own abilities to their fullest, "to prove his or her capacities . . . by trial." (Mill, 1970: 100–01.) "The proper sphere for all human beings is the largest and highest which they are able to attain to." (Mill, 1970: 100.)

Harriet Taylor Mill rejected the sexualization of the dualisms but accepted the hierarchy. She used "rational" as an honorific and "irrational" as a term of derision, and argued that "reason and principle," not "sentimentalities," offered the strongest support for women's emancipation (Mill, 1970: 120). She denied that women were inherently irrational, passive, etc. but believed that women's education and situation in life tended to make them so (Mill, 1970: 100) [4]. This was both "an injustice to the individual and a detriment to society." (Mill, 1970: 101.) To deny women the opportunity to develop their fullest potentials is an effective way to prevent them from being rational, active, etc. [5]. "[T]he qualities which are not permitted to be exercised shall not exist." (Mill, 1970: 110.) Harriet Taylor Mill dismissed as "nonsensical" (Mill, 1970: 120) the efforts of some feminists to challenge the hierarchy of rational, active, etc. over irrational, passive, etc. "What is wanted for women is equal rights, equal admission to all social privileges; not a position apart, a sort of sentimental priesthood." (Mill, 1970: 120.)

This attitude towards women's equality is widely held today. Many feminists and most liberals believe that sex roles should be a matter of individual choice. If women can act as rationally and reasonably as men, they should be treated like men. If women choose to be or to remain irrational, passive, etc., they cannot expect to be treated as well. Moreover, if women do not want to bear and raise children, they should not have to do so; and if men want to nurture children they should be free to make that choice.

There is more to this category than simple sex-blindness. One claim is that women have been trained to be irrational and passive and that this training should be reversed. Affirmative action for women, a departure from sex-blindness, may be justified and supported as a method to counteract years of teaching women to be irrational, passive, etc. A different claim is that women already are rational, active, etc., but are not recognized to be. Affirmative action may still be justified and supported as a technique for counteracting prejudiced, inaccurate views that women are irrational, passive, etc. (Olsen, 1983: 1549–50). The point of these strategies is not that gender must be ignored, but that women are or should become rational, active, etc.

Under these strategies, equal treatment for women is the eventual goal. Equal treatment for women is also the current norm, and gender-conscious policies are a limited departure from this norm—an exception that may be justified in order to counteract and correct inequality. [6] The result of these gender-conscious policies should be to secure to women the same power and prestige that men have, and to let women be, and be recognized to be, as rational, active, etc. as men are.

Reject hierarchization

The second set of strategies rejects the hierarchy but accepts the sexualization. These strategies are like the dominant ideology in that they accept in general the proposition that men and women are different—that men are rational, active, etc. and women irrational, passive, etc. They differ from the dominant ideology in that they reject the proposition that rational, active, etc. are superior to irrational, passive, etc. Also they tend to chose alternative adjectives that are a bit less value-laden, or value-laden in the opposite direction: rationalistic/spontaneous, aggressive/receptive, etc. [7].

During the nineteenth and early twentieth centuries, a major focus of the women's movement was the exclusion of women from the public arena and the denial to women of equal opportunities (Easton, 1979: 556, 557; Cott & Pleck, 1979: 11). These concerns were addressed primarily by strategies that rejected the sexualization of the dualisms, rather than by strategies that rejected the heirarchy. The main exception to this in the United States was the movement for social purity and other moral reforms.

For the most part, moral reform movements led by feminists rejected the hierarchization of the dualisms and accepted their sexualization. The reformers argued that women were morally superior to men and thus had a special mission to improve society (Melder, 1977: 53). Many of these reformers hoped that men would adopt more of the womanly virtues—especially sexual restraint (Walkowitz, 1980: 145)—but they basically accepted the dualisms, accepted women's identification with irrational, passive, etc., and were generally resigned to men not changing much. Their chief focus was not transforming men or abolishing the dualisms, but on forcing a reevaluation of irrational passive, etc.

Charlotte Perkins Gilman, although strongly critical of many of the character traits actually prevalent among turn-of-the-century women, wrote an eloquent endorsement of the devalued side of the dualisms. The novel *Herland* describes a feminist utopia established in a geographically isolated setting after all the men are killed in war. Gilman passed quickly over the expediency of an implausibly miraculous shift to asexual reproduction, to get to a description of how an all-female society might function. Although Gilman's women are stronger and more capable than the standard stereotype of the day would have allowed, and although there are some other androgynous overtones to the novel, the main message of the book is a disruption and partial reversal of the hierarchy of rational, active, etc. over irrational, passive, etc. (Gilman, 1901).

A group of modern feminists has continued this disruption and partial reversal of hierarchy. Talk of "women's psychology," (Gilligan, 1982) "women's imagination," (Spacks, 1975) and women's "common language" (Rich, 1978) has become quite popular in the United States. The distinction between the strategy of rejecting the hierarchization while accepting the sexualization of the dualisms, on one hand, and, on the other hand, the strategy of androgyny—rejecting the entire dualistic structure—has begun to break down.

To focus on women's experience and on women's culture, psychology, imagination, or language can be an effective way to recover what has been excluded or obscured by dominant culture; but it can also entail an acceptance of the sexualization of the dualisms. To reverse or invert the hierarchy between rational, active, etc. and irrational, passive, etc. may simply reinforce the dualisms and ultimately maintain dominant values. Alternately, it may be the most effective way to subvert the dualisms (Cornell & Thurschwell, 1986). Moreover, an author may intend her writing to serve one strategy and readers may use it to serve another. Although some authors articulate clear support for the maintenance of sex roles (e.g., Elshtain, 1981), in other cases the disruption of the hierarchy within the dualisms may or may not be intended to disrupt the sexualization of the dualisms and the dualisms themselves. When this is the intention, I would classify the strategy in the third category—androgyny.

Androgyny

The third strategy, androgyny, rejects both the sexualization of the dualisms and the hierarchy of rational, objective, etc. over irrational, subjective, etc. This third strategy also rejects the dualistic opposition between men and women and intends to disrupt conventional sex roles.

During the second half of the nineteenth century there was significant support for moderating sex role expectations for men and women. William Leach, in his study of nineteenth-century feminism in America, asserts that "[a]ll feminists believed that only strong, independent, but also tender men and women, who combined in their natures the best virtues of both sexes, could make good marital partners and parents." (Leach, 1980: 32.) Only "symmetrically developed men and women" were considered "whole human beings" (id.).

The rebirth of the women's movement has brought these ideas back into popular discourse (Olsen, 1983: 1569–78; Heilbrun, 1973; Kaplan & Bean, 1976; O'Flaherty, 1980; Cook, 1985). Some feminists argue that women are and must be both rational and irrational, objective and subjective, abstract and contextualized, and principled and personalized. This strategy also challenges the border between these concepts, problematizes the straightforward opposition between them, and denies their separateness. It is rational, to be irrational, and objectivity is necessarily subjective.

Feminist Critiques of Law

Feminists in the United States maintain three rather differing attitudes toward law. Feminist criticisms of law fall into three broad categories, corresponding to the categories of feminist strategies for attacking male domination in general. The dominant ideology maintains that law is rational, objective, abstract and principled and that rational, objective, etc. is better than irrational, subjective, etc. The first category consists of those critiques that attack the claim that law is rational, objective, abstract and principled, while agreeing that rational, objective, etc. is better than irrational, subjective, etc. These feminists argue that law should be rational, objective, and principled and struggle to improve the lot of women by trying to make law live up to its claims and actually be rational, objective, and principled. Criticisms in the second category accept that law is rational, objective, and principled but reject the hierarchization of the dualisms. Feminists holding this view characterize law as male and patriarchal, and thus ideologically oppressive to women. The third category of criticism rejects both the characterization of law as rational, objective, abstract and principled and the hierarchization of rational, objective, etc. over irrational, subjective, etc. Law is not and cannot be rational, objective, abstract and principled. Once again, according to these feminists, rational, active, etc. and irrational, passive, etc. are not polar opposites, and they do not and cannot divide the world into contrasting spheres.

Legal reformist

The first category of criticisms questions the accuracy of the assertion that law is rational, objective and principled. It accepts the notion that law should be rational, objective and principled, but points out the ways in which law fails to live up to this aspiration when it deals with women. In particular, reformist feminists condemn laws that deny women rights—or otherwise harm women—as irrational, subjective and unprincipled. This approach to law has been the single most important feminist legal strategy in the United States and is the theoretical underpinning of the American women's rights movement in law. It includes a broad range of arguments for reform, from a demand for sex-blindness to the argument that to be 'truly neutral' the law must take account of women's current subordination and devise rules carefully tailored to rectify and overcome this unfair inequality. Each of these arguments identifies a different aspect of law to condemn for failing to be rational, objective and principled.

Denial of formal equality. For many years feminists have complained that law draws irrational distinctions between men and women. These critics have argued that law should instead really be rational and objective, which in this context would mean treating women as being the same as men. This argument has often been successful, and American courts have overturned laws preferring male to female executors (*Reed v. Reed*, 1971), discharging parents' obligation to support daughters at a younger age than sons (*Stanton v. Stanton*, 1975), and prescribing different legal drinking ages for males and females (*Craig v. Boren*, 1976).

Feminists have also argued successfully that laws should forbid employers, schools, and other important private actors from discriminating against women. American anti-discrimination laws have been shaped and extended in part by feminist insistence that the law accord formal legal equality of treatment to men and women—that law really become rational, objective, and principled.

Denial of substantive equality. To achieve a substantive equality of outcome, it may be necessary for the law to take account of existing differences among people and to deny formal legal equality. Thus, in some cases there will be a conflict between feminists seeking formal equality for women—'equal treatment'—and those seeking substantive equality, sometimes through 'special treatment'. This 'equal treatment' versus 'special treatment' debate takes place *within* this same broad category of legal criticism. Both sides agree that the law should be rational, objective, and principled; they just disagree about what particular outcome these traits require in a given case. Feminists urging 'special treatment' claims to favor a truly neutral result and debunk certain instances of formal equality as 'pseudo-neutrality' (Olsen, 1985; Olsen, 1986; Olsen, 1989).

Operating on an assimilationist or 'male' model. Another basis for feminist charges that law is not truly rational, objective, and principled is that equality is at present judged by comparing women to men. To state a claim, a woman usually has to show that she has been treated worse than a man would have been. This means that sex discrimination law operates on an assimilationist or male model (MacKinnon, 1979). Sex discrimination law serves only to allow those women who choose to act as men do to receive the rewards men receive—that is, it facilitates the first feminist strategy, the strategy that denies the sexualization of the dualism. When the law chooses to support this feminist strategy instead of another one, it is not being rational and objective. Anti-discrimination law could require, for example, that jobs be structured so that workers can devote significant periods of time to child care without prejudice to their incomes or careers (Frug, 1979), or it could require that all jobs, including child care, be rewarded in accordance with the skill and responsibility they entail.

Exclusion of law from the domestic sphere. Feminists point out that "law has been conspicuously absent from the [domestic] sphere" and that this has contributed to women's subordination (Taub & Schneider, 1982: 117). On a practical level, it leaves wives without a remedy against domination by their husbands; and on an ideological level, it 'devalues women and their functions'. The important activities of our society are regulated by law; and when law maintains a hands-off posture, it implies "women simply are not sufficiently important to merit legal regulation." (id.). Thus, once again law has failed to be truly rational, objective, abstract and principled.

Law as patriarchy

The second category of feminist criticisms of law accepts the descriptive claims that law is rational, objective, abstract and principled but rejects the hierarchy of rational, objective, etc. over irrational, subjective, etc. These feminists identify law as part of the structure of male-domination; they characterize rational, objective, etc. as patriarchal and condemn law for being therefore ideologically oppressive to women. The legal system is said to have a "pervasive maleness." (Polan, 1982: 294.) "The whole structure of law—its hierarchical organization; its combative, adversarial format; and its undeviating bias in favor of rationality over all other values—defines it as a fundamentally patriarchal institution." (id.).

Janet Rifkin has asserted that law is "a paradigm of maleness," (Rifkin, 1980: 84) "the ultimate symbol of masculine authority in patriarchal society." (id. at 92). Catharine MacKinnon agrees that law is male. Objectivity is a male norm as well as law's image of itself (MacKinnon, 1983: 635.) Law therefore "not only reflects a society in which men rule women; it rules in a male way." (id. at 645).

This conception of law leads to a less than sanguine view of legal reform. MacKinnon writes that "law will most reinforce existing distributions of power when it most closely adheres to its own highest ideal of fairness." (id.). Diane Polan warns that to the extent women articulate their grievances in terms of "equal rights" and "equal opportunities" and confine their struggle to litigation and lobbying, they are giving tacit approval to the basic social order and "giving up the battle" for more radical challenges to society. (Polan, 1982: 300.) Litigation and other forms of law-making can be effective, Polan argues, only when "they are undertaken in the context of broader economic, social, and cultural changes." (id. at 302). Rifkin goes further. She argues that litigation "cannot lead to social changes, because in upholding and relying on the paradigm of law, the paradigm of patriarchy is upheld and reinforced." (Rifkin, 1980: 88). To eliminate patriarchy "the male power paradigm of law" must be "challenged and transformed." (id. at 87).

Critical legal theory

The third category of feminist criticisms of law rejects the heirarchy of rational, objective, etc. over irrational, subjective, etc. and denies that law is or could be rational, objective, abstract and principled. The feminists who endorse this third category agree in part and disagree in part with the first two categories of criticism [8].

These feminists do not belittle the benefits obtained by the legal reform feminists in the name of women's rights, but remain unconvinced by their claims about the role of abstract legal theory in obtaining these benefits. Legal reasoning and legal battles are not sharply distinguishable from moral and political reasoning and moral and political battles.

Similarly, feminists of the third category agree that law is often ideologically oppressive to women. They disagree, however, that law is male; law has no essence or immutable nature. Law is a form of human activity, a practice carried on by people—predominantly men. The men who carry on this activity make claims about what they are doing that are just not true and could not be true. While it is true that law has been dominated by men, the traits associated with women have been only obscured, not eliminated. Law is not male. Law is irrational, subjective, concrete and contextualized as it is rational, objective, abstract and principled.

Law is not all one side of the dualisms

Law is not now, and could not, consistent with what we believe, become principled, rational, and objective.

(*1*) *Law not principled.* The claim that law is principled is based upon the belief that law consists of a few rules or principles and that these general rules provide a principled basis for deciding individual cases. But instead of this, law is actually made up of an agglomeration of lots of specific rules and some very general standards.

The rules are too specific, definite, and contextualized to count as principles. The existence of these rules is what gives law the degree of predictability that it has—but the rules are too detailed and each rule covers too few cases to make the law *principled*. For example, in the United States there is at present a rule which allows for states to use gender-based statutory rape laws to try to reduce the incidence of teenage pregnancy, and there is another rule which states that age of majority for purposes of terminating parental support may not be gender-based. In *Michael M. v. Sonoma County* (1981), the United States Supreme Court let stand a gender-based statutory rape law that the California Supreme Court said was intended to reduce the incidence of teenage pregnancy. In *Stanton v. Stanton* (1975), the Supreme Court struck down a Utah law that required a parent to support his son until age 21 but allowed him to stop supporting his daughter at age 18. My point is not that these two rules conflict or that the cases cannot be reconciled with one another. Rather, each of these two rules apply in too few circumstances to provide any principled answer to the questions of when states may use gender-based laws.

The standards, on the other hand, are too vague and indeterminate to decide cases. In each interesting disputed case, you can find at least two different broad, general standards, that could apply to the case and that would lead to different results. For example, American courts have a long tradition of respecting family autonomy and not intervening in the family; they have an equally long tradition of protecting the welfare of children. Often, in particular cases, the standard of non-interference in the family will support one outcome, while the standard of protecting children will support the opposite outcome. Just as rules apply to too few cases, standards apply to too many. The legal system fluctuates between being based on rules and being based on standards, but its aspiration to be principled is not achieved. Law is no more abstract and principled than it is personalized and contextualized.

(2) *Law not rational.* Nor is law rational. The efforts by American feminists to work out a rational elaboration of equal rights of human beings in order to achieve rights for women has not worked and it will not work. The classic conflicts between equality of opportunity and equality of result, between natural rights and positive rights, and between rights-as-a-guarantee-of-security and rights-as-a-guarantee-of-freedom, render rights analysis incapable of settling any meaningful conflict (Singer, 1982; Kennedy, 1979; Olsen, 1984; Holmes, 1984). More specifically, if one outcome will protect the plaintiff's right to freedom of action, the opposite outcome will often protect the defendant's right to security. If one outcome will protect a woman's right to formal equality of treatment, her right to substantive equality of result may seem to require a different outcome. This conflict explains, for example, why American feminists argued opposite sides in *California Federal v. Guerra* (1987), in which the United States Supreme Court upheld a state maternity leave provision. Some feminists argued that formal equality requires that the law treat pregnancy just like any other temporary disability, while other feminists maintained that substantive equality requires that women be able to give birth to children without losing their jobs—even if no other temporary absence from work is

excused. Therefore some feminists argued that women should insist on formal equality and reject any form of special maternity leave; while other feminists argued that working women need adequate maternity leave, even if no similar leaves of absence are given to men or other people who are not pregnant. Law does not provide a *rational* basis for choosing which right to recognize and protect in any particular case. Rights analysis cannot settle these conflicts, but merely restates them in a new—at most somewhat obscured—form.

(*3*) *Law not objective.* Further, law is not objective. The idea that law is objective is refuted by the gradual recognition that *policy* issues appear everywhere. Every time a choice is made, every legal decision that is not obvious and uncontroversial, is a decision based on policy—which cannot be objective. Thus, it is simply a mistake to say that law is or could become rational, principled and objective. Law is not all one side of the dualisms.

Law cannot be segregated

Sometimes dominant legal theory recognizes that law is not principled, rational and objective. The dominant ideology does recognize the so-called 'female' traits—indeed it celebrates them—but only on the periphery, or in their own 'separate sphere'. For example, family law may be subjective, contextual and personalized, but commercial law is thought to be principled, rational and objective. It is important for feminists to correct this misperception, to dissolve the ghettos of law, and to show that you cannot exclude the personalized, irrational, and subjective from any part of law.

(*1*) *Dissolve law's irrational, subjective ghettos.* One way that dominant ideology makes law seem principled, rational, and objective is by banishing to the periphery of law those fields believed to be tainted by unruly, discretionary standards—fields such as family law, trust law, and the law of fiduciary obligation in general. The core subjects or the important fields of law are said to remain male. We can show, however, that in banishment, family law, trusts, and fiduciary obligations continue to influence the rest of law—including those fields that were supposed to be the bastion of the so-called 'male' principles of law. For example, the ideology of the market-place depends upon the ideology of the family, and commercial law can be understood adequately only by recognizing the interrelationship between it and family law (Olsen, 1983; Kennedy, 1983; Kennedy, 1975).

(*2*) *Reconceive the core and periphery.* Another technique by which the dominant ideology tries to make the law seem rational and objective is by separating each field between, on the one hand, a set of basic rules, or a 'male' core that is principled, rational and objective and, on the other hand, a periphery of exceptions that can contain irrational and subjective elements. For example, contract law is frequently conceptualized as a set of rational, consistent, individualistic rules, softened by somewhat subjective, variable, 'altruistic' exceptions, such as promissory estoppel. The basic core of contract law remains male. Feminists can disrupt this by showing that the conflict between the individualistic 'rule' and the altruistic 'exception' reappears in every doctrine. Every doctrine is a choice or compromise of sorts between the individualistic and altruistic impulses (Frug, 1985; Dalton, 1985; Kennedy, 1976; Unger, 1983). This feminist analysis also problematizes what should be considered the rule and what the exception. It is not possible to separate any field of law into a core and a periphery and the traits associated with women cannot be excluded from law.

Conclusion

As I have said, the feminist strategies for attacking legal theory are analogous to feminist strategies for attacking male dominance in general. The 'reject sexualization' position resonates with the 'legal reformist' position, the 'reject heirarchization' with the 'law as patriarchy' and the 'androgyny' with 'critical legal theory'. But I do not want to claim that the relationship is anything more than this—an analogy or a resonance. The sets of categories are not identical, and no strategy from one set requires or entails any strategy from the other set.

First there is no necessary relationship between a feminist's attitude towards the sexualization of the dualisms and her attitude toward the identification of law as rational, objective, and principled. Moreover, a feminist can accept the hierarchization for some purposes—for example, can believe that it is better for law to be rational, objective, and principled—but still reject the hierarchization in general. Some feminists support androgyny, but still claim that law is patriarchal. Similarly, one can support critical legal theory and still believe either that women are inherently or morally superior to men or that women should be rational, active, etc., like men.

My support for androgyny would not require me to support critical legal theory or vice versa, but both are related to my values and vision of the universe and both inform my political activity. Nothing in either theory will provide easy answers to concrete questions—such as 'Would women really benefit from more state regulation of the family?' or 'Could revised statutory rape laws protect young females without oppressing and demeaning them?' What I do hope is that by improving the theories upon which we operate we can understand better what is at stake in questions like these. I hope that by recognizing the impossibility of easy, logical answers we can free ourselves to think about the questions in a more constructive and imaginative manner. Law cannot be successfully separated from politics, morals, and the rest of human activities, but is an integral part of the web of social life.

Notes

1 Men also appear to want to control women and to control all the concepts on the right side of the dualisms. They may want to distance themselves as a way of controlling, or they may want to control in order to maintain their distance. Women seem to focus more on men's desire to control them, but men seem more inclined to see the control as secondary to the distancing.

2 Certain areas of law—for example child custody decisions—are considered to be somewhat irrational and necessarily subjective, as well as preferably contextualized and personalized. Child custody law, and more generally law relating to the internal life of families (Unger, 1976: 55), is for this reason considered less legalistic than most law, which is considered to be rational, objective, etc. Moreover, family law is associated with women and, like women, is devalued.

3 In 1920, there were 1738 women lawyers. In 1960, the number was up to 7543. In 1970, 13,000. By 1976, 38,000; and in 1980, 62,000 (Epstein, 1981: 4).

4 A male abolitionist wrote in a similar vein in 1836, "A mind whether deposited in a male or female body is equally valuable for all moral and intellectual purposes. Indeed, there is no station in life but what may be filled as ably and beneficially by woman as by man. The difference is made principally by education." He urged feminists to fight for abolition "to redeem your character and name from unjust reproach." Letter from Augustus Wattles to Betsy Cowles (9 Apr., 1836), quoted in Melder, 1977: 60.

5 Indeed, Mill even warned men that they would themselves lose "manliness" unless women acquired it. "Those who are associated in their lives, tend to become assimilated in character." (Mill, 1851: 110.) She noted "a progressive deterioration among men in what had hitherto been considered the masculine excellences," (*id.*), and warned that men were becoming "what they . . . decided that women should be— . . . falling into the feebleness which they have so long cultivated in their companions." (*Id.*) For similar views from a somewhat earlier period, see M. Wollstonecraft, at 49–92.

6 Pregnancy and childbirth present some conceptual difficulty, since they involve physical conditions unique to women. Because pregnancy was treated worse than disabilities shared by men and women (and indeed worse than medical conditions unique to men), many feminists decided to conceptualize pregnancy as a medical disability and insist it receive the same treatment (Williams, 1982).

It has been argued that military combat presents similar conceptual difficulties, but feminists have rejected this claim (Williams, at 183–85). While many feminists oppose the draft, they oppose it for men as well as for women (Olsen, 1983: 1557 n. 235). The possibility of drafting women has been used by anti-feminists to oppose equal rights for women.

7 For a marvellous list of positively and negatively connoted terms describing rules and standards respectively, see Kennedy, 1976: 1710–11.

8 In an interesting and provocative review of *The Politics of Law* (Kairys, 1982), Clare Dalton uses "reformist" as a subcategory within the critical legal studies movement (Dalton, 1983). She places in opposition to "reformist" the "irrationalist" position, which she supports. She differentiates these categories on the basis of their sense of the indeterminancy of legal doctrine and the nature of their programmatic suggestions. Her "reformist" position is similar to my category "legal reformist." Hers is

broader than mine in that she does not focus explicitly on feminist critiques of law, and it is narrower than mine in that it probably does not include feminist reform efforts that are not leftist and not identified with the critical legal studies movement. Here reformist position does focus on defining equal rights and making law live up to its claims, or making the state keep its promises. The position Dalton characterizes as "irrationalist" is closest to the category I refer to as "critical legal theory." It is not clear what Dalton would do with my "law as patriarchy" category. Dalton's "irrationalist" position is characterized by a deep commitment to the indeterminancy of legal doctrine. This would seem to be a clear statement that law is not and cannot become rational, objective, etc. She supports the idea of developing the irrational, subjective, etc. in law *as a way to reinforce* the recognition of the indeterminancy of doctrine. *Id.* at 246. She concludes the book review with an appeal to search for women's voices, to tap into social experiences, and to find or develop a "grounded" position "from which women might speak." *Id.* at 247–48. Dalton does not specify whether she would develop the "missing woman's voice," *id.* at 247, as a counter-vision or—like the motive for developing the irrational, subjective, etc. in law—as a way to reinforce the recognition of the indeterminancy of the male/female dualism itself.

Cases Cited

California Federal v. Guerra, 107 S. Ct. 683 (1987).
Craig v. Boren, 429 U.S. 190 (1976).
Michael M. v. Sonoma County, 450 U.S. 464 (1981).
Reed v. Reed, 404 U.S. 71 (1971).
Stanton v. Stanton, 421 U.S. 7 (1975).

References

Christ, C. (1980) *Diving Deep and Surfacing*. Beacon Press: Boston.
Cixous, H. (1981) Sorties. In *New French Feminisms* (Marks, E. & Courtivron, I., Eds). Schocken Books: New York, pp. 90–98.
Clegg, J. (1977) *The Structure of Plato's Philosophy*. Bucknell University Press: Lewisberg, Pennsylvania.
Cook, E. (1985) *Psychological Androgyny*. Pergamon Press: New York.
Cornell, D. & Thurschwell, A. (1986) Femininity, negativity, and intersubjectivity. *Praxis International* 5, 484–504.
Cott, N. & Pleck, N. (1979) Introduction. In *A Heritage of Her Own* (Cott, N. & Pleck, E., Eds). Simon & Schuster: New York, pp. 9–24.
Dalton, C. (1983) Book Review. *Harvard Women's Law Journal* **6**, 229.
Dalton, C. (1985) An essay in the deconstruction of contract doctrine. *The Yale Law Journal* **94**, 997–1114.
Derrida, J. (1981) *Dissemination* (Johnson, B., Trans.). The University of Chicago Press: Chicago.
Easton, B. (1979) Feminism and the contemporary family. In *A Heritage of Her Own* (Cott, N. & Pleck, E., Eds). Simon & Schuster: New York, pp. 555–77.
Elshtain, B. (1981) Against androgyny. *Telos* **47**, 5–21.

Epstein, C. (1981) *Women in Law*. Basic Books: New York.
Frug, G. (1980) The city as a legal concept. *Harvard Law Review* **93**, 1057–1154.
Frug, M. J. (1979) Securing job equality for women: labor market hostility to working mothers. *Boston University Law Review* **59**, 55–103.
Frug, M. J. (1985) Rereading contracts: a feminist analysis of a contracts casebook. *American University Law Review* **34**, 1065–1140.
Gilligan, C. (1982) *In a Different Voice*. Harvard University Press: Cambridge, Massachusetts.
Gilman, C. (1901) *Herland*. Panthem Books: New York, 1979.
Heilbrun, C. (1973) *Toward a Recognition of Androgyny*. Harper & Row: New York.
Holmes, O. W. (1984) Privilege, malice, and intent. *Harvard Law Review* **8**, 1–14.
Kairys, D. (Ed.) (1982) *The Politics of Law*, 1st edition. Pantheon: New York.
Kanter, M. (1978) Reflections on women and the legal profession: a sociological perspective. *Harvard Women's Law Journal* **1**, 1.
Kaplan, A. & Bean, J. (Eds) (1976) *Beyond Sex-Role Stereotypes: Readings Toward a Psychology of Androgyny*. Little, Brown & Company: Boston, Massachusetts.
Kennedy, D. (1975) The Rise and Fall of Classical Legal Thought. Unpublished manuscript.
Kennedy, D. (1976) Form and substance in private law adjudication. *Harvard Law Review* **89**, 1685.
Kennedy, D. (1979) The structure of Blackstone's Commentaries, *Buffalo Law Review* **28**, 205.
Kennedy, D. (1983) The political significance of the structure of the law school curriculum. *Seton Hall Law Review* **14**, 1.
Leach, W. (1980) *True Love and Perfect Union*. Basic Books: New York.
MacKinnon, C. (1979) *Sexual Harassment of Working Women: A Case of Sex Discrimination*. Yale University Press: New Haven, Connecticut.
MacKinnon, C. (1983) Feminism, marxism, method and the state: toward feminist jurisprudence. *Signs: Journal of Women in Culture and Society* **8**, 635–6.
Melder, K. (1977) *Beginnings of Sisterhood*. Schocken Books: New York.
Mill, H. T. (1851) Enfranchisement of women. In *John Stuart Mill and Harriet Taylor Mill: Essays on Sex Equality* (A. Rossi, Ed., 1970). The University of Chicago Press: Chicago, pp. 89–121.
O'Flaherty, W. (1980) *Women, Androgynes, and Other Mythical Beasts*. The University of Chicago Press: Chicago.
Olsen, F. (1983) The family and the market: a study of ideology and legal reform. *Harvard Law Review* **96**, 1497–1576.
Olsen, F. (1984) Statutory rape: a feminist critique of rights analysis. *Texas Law Review* **63**, 387–432.
Olsen, F. (1985) The myth of state intervention in the family. *Michigan Journal of Law Reform* **18**, 83.
Olsen, F. (1986) From false paternalism to false equality: judicial assaults on feminist community, Illinois 1869–1895. *Michigan Law Review* **84**, 1518–1541.
Olsen, F. (1989) Feminist theory in grand style. *Columbia Law Review* **89**, 1147–78.
Polan, D. (1982) Towards a theory of law and patriarchy. In *The Politics of Law* (Kairys, D., Ed.). Pantheon: New York, pp. 294–303.
Rich, A. (1978) Origins and history of consciousness. In *The Dream of a Common Language: Poems, 1974–1977*. Norton: New York, p. 7.

Rifkin, J. (1980) Toward a theory of law and patriarchy. *Harvard Women's Law Journal* **3**, 83.
Singer, J. (1982) The legal rights to debate in analytical jurisprudence from Bentham to Hohfeld. *Wisconsin Law Review* **1982**, 975–1059.
Spacks, P. (1975) *The Female Imagination.* Knopf, Random House: New York.
Taub, N. & Schneider, E. (1982) Perspectives on women's subordination and the role of law. In *The Politics of Law* (Kairys, D., Ed.). Pantheon; New York, pp. 117–139.
Unger, R. (1976) *Law in Modern Society.* The Free Press: New York.
Unger, R. (1983) The critical legal studies movement. *Harvard Law Review* **96**, 561–675.
Walkowitz, J. (1980) The politics of prostitution. *Signs: Journal of Women in Culture and Society* **6**. *Reprinted* in *Women: Sex and Sexuality* 145 (Stimpson, C. & Person, E. Eds).
Williams (1982) The equality crisis: Some reflections on culture, courts, and feminism. *The Women's Rights Law Reporter* **8**, 175.
Wollstonecraft, M. (1792) *A Vindication of the Rights of Women.* J. Johnson: London.

[18]

COMMENTARY

A POSTMODERN FEMINIST LEGAL MANIFESTO (AN UNFINISHED DRAFT)

*Mary Joe Frug**

The following Commentary is an unfinished work. Professor Frug was working on this Commentary when she was murdered on April 4, 1991. The Editors of the Harvard Law Review agreed that, under the circumstances, the preservation of Mary Joe Frug's voice outweighed strict adherence to traditional editorial policy. For this reason, neither stylistic nor organizational changes have been made, and footnotes have been expanded but not added.

To complete some of the thoughts that Professor Frug left unfinished and to continue the conversation about the relationship between feminism, postmodernism, and law reform, the Editors of the Law Review have solicited brief responses to "A Postmodern Feminist Legal Manifesto" from Professors Barbara Johnson, Ruth Colker, and Martha Minow.

I. PRELIMINARIES

I am worried about the title of this article.

Postmodernism may already be passe, for some readers. Like a shooting star or last night's popovers, its genius was the surprise of its appearance. Once that initial moment has passed, there's not much value in what's left over.

For other readers, postmodernism may refer to such an elaborate and demanding genre — within linguistics, psychoanalysis, literary theory, and philosophy — that claiming an affinity to "it" will quite properly invoke a flood of criticism regarding the omissions, misrepresentations, and mistakes that one paper will inevitably make.

The manifesto part may also be troublesome. The dictionary describes a manifesto as a statement of principles or intentions, while I have in mind a rather informal presentation; more of a discussion, say, in which the "principles" are somewhat contradictory and the "intentions" are loosely formulated goals that are qualified by an admission that they might not work. MacKinnon, of course, launched feminism into social theory orbit by drawing on Marxism to present her biting analysis.[1] Referring to one word in a Karl Marx title may

---

* Professor, New England School of Law, 1981–1991.

[1] *See* Catharine A. MacKinnon, *Feminism, Marxism, Method, and the State: An Agenda for Theory*, 7 SIGNS: J. WOMEN CULTURE & SOC'Y 515 (1982) [hereinafter MacKinnon, *Agenda for Theory*]; Catharine A. MacKinnon, *Feminism, Marxism, Method, and the State: Toward*

represent an acknowledgement of her work, an unconscious, copyKat gesture; but I don't want to get carried away. I am in favor of localized disruptions. I am against totalizing theory.

Sometimes the "PM"s that label my notes remind me of female troubles — of premenstrual and postmenopausal blues. Maybe I am destined to do exactly what my title prescribes; just note the discomfort and keep going.

One "Principle"

The liberal equality doctrine is often understood as an engine of liberation with respect to sex-specific rules. This imagery suggests the repressive function of law, a function that feminists have inventively sought to appropriate and exploit through critical scholarship, litigation, and legislative campaigns. Examples of these efforts include work seeking to strengthen domestic violence statutes, to enact a model anti-pornography ordinance, and to expand sexual harassment doctrine.

The postmodern position locating human experience as inescapably within language suggests that feminists should not overlook the constructive function of legal language as a critical frontier for feminist reforms. To put this "principle" more bluntly, legal discourse should be recognized as a site of political struggle over sex differences.

This is not a proposal that we try to promote a benevolent and fixed meaning for sex differences. (See the "principle" below.) Rather, the argument is that continuous interpretive struggles over the meaning of sex differences can have an impact on patriarchal legal power.

Another "Principle"

In their most vulgar, bootlegged versions, both radical and cultural legal feminisms depict male and female sexual identities as anatomically determined and psychologically predictable. This is inconsistent with the semiotic character of sex differences and the impact that historical specificity has on any individual identity. In postmodern jargon, this treatment of sexual identity is inconsistent with a decentered, polymorphous, contingent understanding of the subject.

Because sex differences are semiotic — that is, constituted by a system of signs that we produce and interpret — each of us inescapably produces herself within the gender meaning system, although the meaning of gender is indeterminate or undecidable. The dilemma of

---

Feminist Jurisprudence, 8 SIGNS: J. WOMEN CULTURE & SOC'Y 635 (1983) [hereinafter MacKinnon, *Toward Feminist Jurisprudence*].

difference, which the liberal equality guarantee seeks to avoid through neutrality, is unavoidable.

On Style

Style is important in postmodern work. The medium *is* the message, in some cases — although by no means all. When style is salient, it is characterized by irony and by wordplay that is often dazzlingly funny, smart, and irreverent. Things aren't just what they seem.

By arguing that legal rhetoric should not be dominated by masculine pronouns or by stereotypically masculine imagery, legal feminists have conceded the significance of style. But the postmodern tone sharply contrasts with the earnestness that almost universally characterizes feminist scholarship. "[T]he circumstances of women's lives [are] unbearable," Andrea Dworkin writes.[2] Legal feminists tend to agree. Hardly appropriate material for irony and play.

I do not underestimate the oppression of women as Andrea Dworkin describes it. I also appreciate what a hard time women have had communicating our situation. Reports from numerous state commissions on gender bias in the courts have concluded that one of the most significant problems of women in law is their lack of credibility. Dworkin puts this point more movingly:

> The accounts of rape, wife beating, forced childbearing, medical butchering, sex-motivated murder, forced prostitution, physical mutilation, sadistic psychological abuse, and other commonplaces of female experience that are excavated from the past or given by contemporary survivors should leave the heart seared, the mind in anguish, the conscience in upheaval. But they do not. No matter how often these stories are told, with whatever clarity or eloquence, bitterness or sorrow, they might as well have been whispered in wind or written in sand: they disappear, as if they were nothing. The tellers and the stories are ignored or ridiculed, threatened back into silence or destroyed, and the experience of female suffering is buried in cultural invisibility and contempt.[3]

Although the flip, condescending, and mocking tones that often characterize postmodernism may not capture the intensity and urgency that frequently motivate feminist legal scholarship, the postmodern style does not strike me as "politically incorrect." Indeed, the oppositional character of the style arguably coincides with the oppositional spirit of feminism. Irony, for example, is a stylistic method of acknowledging and challenging a dominant meaning, of saying some-

---

[2] ANDREA DWORKIN, LETTERS FROM A WAR ZONE 65 (1989).

[3] ANDREA DWORKIN, RIGHT-WING WOMEN 20 (1983).

thing and simultaneously denying it. Figures of speech invite ideas to break out of the linear argument of a text; they challenge singular, dominant interpretations.

I confess to having considerable performance anxiety about the postmodern style myself. It may require more art, more creativity and inspiration, than I can manage. But I don't think feminist legal activists need to adopt the postmodern medium in order to exploit the postmodern message; my point about the style is simply that it doesn't require us, strategically, to dismiss postmodernism as an influence on our work.

II. Applying Postmodern "Principles": Law and the Female Body

A. Introduction

Most feminists are committed to the position that however "natural" and common sex differences may seem, the differences between women and men are not biologically compelled; they are, rather, "socially constructed." Over the past two decades this conviction has fueled many efforts to change the ways in which law produces — or socially constructs — the differences and the hierarchies between the sexes. Feminists have reasoned, for example, that when women are uneducated for "men's work," or when they are sexually harassed in the men's work they do, they are not "naturally" more suited for "women's work"; they have been constructed to be that way. Although law is by no means the only factor that influences which jobs men and women prefer, how well they perform at work, or the intensity of their wage market commitment, outlawing employment discrimination can affect to some degree what women and men are "like" as workers. What law (at least in part) constructs, law reform projects can re-construct or alter.

Regardless of how commonplace the constructed character of sex differences may be, particular differences can seem quite deeply embedded within the sexes — so much so, in fact, that the social construction thesis is undermined. When applied to differences that seem especially entrenched — differences such as masculine aggression or feminine compassion, or differences related to the erotic and reproductive aspects of women's lives, social construction seems like a clichéd, improbable, and unconvincing account of experience, an explanation for sex differences that undervalues "reality." This reaction does not necessarily provoke a return to a "natural" explanation for sex differences; but it does radically stunt the liberatory potential of the social construction thesis. One's expectations for law reform projects are reduced; law might be able to mitigate the harsh impact of these embedded traits on women's lives, but law does not seem responsible for *constructing* them.

The subject of Part II is the role of law in the production of sex differences that seem "natural." One of my objectives is to explain and challenge the essentializing impulse that places particular sex differences outside the borders of legal responsibility. Another objective is to provide an analysis of the legal role in the production of gendered identity that will invigorate the liberatory potential of the social construction thesis.

I have chosen the relationship of law to the female body as my principal focus. I am convinced that law is more cunningly disguised but just as implicated in the production of apparently intractable sex-related traits as in those that seem more legally malleable. Since the anatomical distinctions between the sexes seem not only "natural" but fundamental to identity, proposing and describing the role of law in the production of the meaning of the female body seems like the most convincing subject with which to defend my case. In the following sections, I will argue that legal rules — like other cultural mechanisms — encode the female body with meanings. Legal discourse then explains and rationalizes these meanings by an appeal to the "natural" differences between the sexes, differences that the rules themselves help to produce. The formal norm of legal neutrality conceals the way in which legal rules participate in the construction of those meanings.

The proliferation of women's legal rights during the past two decades has liberated women from some of the restraining meanings of femininity. This liberation has been enhanced by the emergence of different feminisms over the past decade. These feminisms have made possible a stance of opposition toward a singular feminine identity; they have demonstrated that women stand in a multitude of places, depending on time and geographical location, on race, age, sexual preference, health, class status, religion, and other factors. Despite these significant changes, there remains a common residue of meaning that seems affixed, as if by nature, to the female body. Law participates in creating that meaning.

I will argue that there are at least three general claims that can be made about the relationship between legal rules and legal discourse and the meaning of the female body:

1. Legal rules permit and sometimes mandate the *terrorization* of the female body. This occurs by a combination of provisions that inadequately protect women against physical abuse and that encourage women to seek refuge against insecurity. One meaning of "female body," then, is a body that is "in terror," a body that has learned to

scurry, to cringe, and to submit. Legal discourse supports that meaning.

2. Legal rules permit and sometimes mandate the *maternalization* of the female body. This occurs with the use of provisions that reward women for singularly assuming responsibilities after childbirth and with those that penalize conduct — such as sexuality or labor market work — that conflicts with mothering. Maternalization also occurs through rules such as abortion restrictions that compel women to become mothers and by domestic relations rules that favor mothers over fathers as parents. Another meaning of "female body," then, is a body that is "for" maternity. Legal discourse supports that meaning.

3. Legal rules permit and sometimes mandate the *sexualization* of the female body. This occurs through provisions that criminalize individual sexual conduct, such as rules against commercial sex (prostitution) or same sex practices (homosexuality) and also through rules that legitimate and support institutions such as the pornography, advertising, and entertainment industries that eroticize the female body. Sexualization also occurs, paradoxically, in the application of rules such as rape and sexual harassment laws that are designed to protect women against sex-related injuries. These rules grant or deny women protection by interrogating their sexual promiscuity. The more sexually available or desiring a woman looks, the less protection these rules are likely to give her. Another meaning of "female body," then, is a body that is "for" sex with men, a body that is "desirable" and also rapable, that wants sex and wants raping. Legal discourse supports that meaning.

These groups of legal rules and discourse constitute a system that "constructs" or engenders the female body. The feminine figures the rules pose are naturalized within legal discourse by declaration — "women *are* (choose one) weak, nurturing, sexy" — and by a host of linguistic strategies that link women to particular images of the female body. By deploying these images, legal discourse rationalizes, explains, and renders authoritative the female body rule network. The impact of the rule network on women's reality in turn reacts back on the discourse, reinforcing the "truth" of these images.

Contractions of confidence in the thesis that sex differences are socially constructed have had a significant impact on women in law. Liberal jurists, for example, have been unwilling to extend the protection of the gender equality guarantee to anatomical distinctions between female and male bodies; these differences seem so basic to individual identity that law need not — or should not — be responsible for them. Feminist legal scholars have been unable to overcome this intransigence, partly because we ourselves sometimes find particular sex-related traits quite intransigent. Indeed, one way to understand the fracturing of law-related feminism into separate schools of thought over the past decade is by the sexual traits that are considered unsusceptible to legal transformation[4] and by the criticisms these analyses have provoked within our own ranks.[5]

The fracturing of feminist criticism has occurred partly because particular sex differences seem so powerfully fixed that feminists are as unable to resist their "naturalization" as liberal jurists. But feminists also cling to particular sex-related differences because of a strategic desire to protect the feminist legal agenda from sabotage. Many feminist critics have argued that the condition of "real" women makes it too early to be post-feminist. The social construction thesis is useful to feminists insofar as it informs and supports our efforts to improve the condition of women in law. If, or when, the social construction thesis seems about to deconstruct the basic category of woman, its usefulness to feminism is problematized. How can we build a political coalition to advance the position of women in law if the subject that drives our efforts is "indeterminate," "incoherent," or "contingent?"

I think this concern is based upon a misperception of where we are in the legal struggle against sexism. I think we are in danger of being politically immobilized by a system for the production of what sex means that makes particular sex differences seem "natural." If my assessment is right, then describing the mechanics of this system is potentially enabling rather than disempowering; it may reveal opportunities for resisting the legal role in producing the radical asymmetry between the sexes.

I also think this concern is based on a misperception about the impact of deconstruction. Skeptics tend to think, I believe, that the legal deconstruction of "woman" — in one paper or in many papers, say, written over the next decade — will entail the immediate destruc-

---

[4] For the radical feminist focus on male domination, see ANDREA DWORKIN, PORNOGRAPHY: MEN POSSESSING WOMEN 14–18, 53–56 (1989); DWORKIN, *supra* note 3, at 78–87; CATHARINE A. MACKINNON, FEMINISM UNMODIFIED 40–45, 171–74 (1987); MacKinnon, *Agenda for Theory*, *supra* note 1, at 530–34; and MacKinnon, *Toward Feminist Jurisprudence*, *supra* note 1, at 643. For the cultural feminist focus on the ethic of care, see CAROL GILLIGAN, IN A DIFFERENT VOICE: PSYCHOLOGICAL THEORY AND WOMEN'S DEVELOPMENT 64–105 (1982); and Leslie Bender, *A Lawyer's Primer on Feminist Theory and Tort*, 38 J. LEGAL EDUC. 3, 28–37 (1988) (suggesting the incorporation of Gilligan's ethic into tort law's standard of care).

[5] For a race-conscious critique of liberal, radical, and cultural feminism for overlooking minority women concerns, see Kimberlé Crenshaw, *Demarginalizing the Intersection of Race and Sex: A Black Feminist Critique of Antidiscrimination Doctrine, Feminist Theory and Antiracist Politics*, 1989 U. CHI. LEGAL F. 139, 140, 152–60; Angela P. Harris, *Race and Essentialism in Feminist Legal Theory*, 42 STAN. L. REV. 581, 585–86 (1990); and Marlee Kline, *Race, Racism, and Feminist Legal Theory*, 12 HARV. WOMEN'S L.J. 115, 120–23, 144–50 (1989). For the lesbian feminist critique of heterosexist assumptions in liberal, radical, and cultural feminisms, see AUDRE LORDE, SISTER OUTSIDER 114–23 (1984); Adrienne Rich, *Compulsory Heterosexuality and Lesbian Existence*, *in* POWERS OF DESIRE: THE POLITICS OF SEXUALITY 177, 178–82 (Ann Snitow, Christine Stansell & Sharon Thompson eds., 1983). For a class-conscious feminist critique of the class bias inherent in liberal, radical, and cultural feminisms, see KRISTIN LUKER, ABORTION AND THE POLITICS OF MOTHERHOOD 192–215 (1984).

tion of "women" as identifiable subjects who are affected by law reform projects. Despite the healthy, self-serving respect I have for the influence of legal scholarship and for the role of law as a significant cultural factor (among many) that contributes to the production of femininity, I think "women" cannot be eliminated from our lexicon very quickly. The question this paper addresses is not whether sex differences exist — they do — or how to transcend them — we can't — but the character of their treatment in law.

B. Sexualization, Terrorization and Maternalization: The Case of Prostitution

Since most anti-prostitution rules are gender neutral, let me explain, before going any further, how I can argue that they have a particular impact on the meaning of the female body. Like other rules regulating sexual conduct, anti-prostitution rules sexualize male as well as female bodies; they indicate that sex — unlike, say, laughing, sneezing, or making eye contact — is legally regulated. Regardless of whether one is male or female, the pleasures and the virtue of sex are produced, at least in part, by legal rules.[6] The gendered lopsidedness of this meaning system — which I describe below — occurs, quite simply, because most sex workers are women. Thus, even though anti-prostitution rules could, in theory, generate parallel meanings for male and female bodies, in practice they just don't. At least they don't right now.

The legal definition of prostitution as the unlawful sale of sex occurs in statutes that criminalize specific commercial sex practices and in decisional law, such as contract cases that hold that agreements for the sale of sexual services are legally unenforceable. By characterizing certain sexual practices as illegal, these rules sexualize the female body. They invite a sexual interrogation of every female body: is it for or against prostitution?

This sexualization of the female body explains an experience many women have: an insistent concern that this outfit, this pose, this gesture may send the wrong signal — a fear of looking like a whore. Sexy talking, sexy walking, sexy dressing seem sexy, at least in part, because they are the telltale signs of a sex worker plying her trade. This sexualization also explains the shadow many women feel when having sex for unromantic reasons — to comfort themselves, to avoid

---

[6] *Cf.* LOUIS ALTHUSSER, LENIN AND PHILOSOPHY AND OTHER ESSAYS (Ben Brewster trans., 1971) (demonstrating the role of ideology and social structure in shaping personality); MICHEL FOUCAULT, 1 THE HISTORY OF SEXUALITY 6–7 (Robert Hurley trans., 1978) (discussing the power-sex relationship in terms of affirmation).

a confrontation over some domestic issue, or to secure a favor — a fear of acting like a whore.[7]

This reading of the relationship between prostitution rules and the female body is aligned with but somewhat different from the radical feminist description of the relationship between prostitution and female subjectivity. Catharine MacKinnon's 1982 *Signs* piece describes the relationship this way:

> [Feminist] investigations reveal . . . [that] prostitution [is] not primarily [an] abuse[] of physical force, violence, authority, or economics. [It is an] abuse[] of sex. [It] need not and do[es] not rely for [its] coerciveness upon forms of enforcement other than the sexual . . . .
>
> . . . .
>
> . . . If women are socially defined such that female sexuality cannot be lived or spoken or felt or even somatically sensed apart from its enforced definition, so that it *is* its own lack, then there is no such thing as a woman as such, there are only walking embodiments of men's projected needs.[8]

MacKinnon's description of the impact of prostitution on women suggests that the sexual experience of all women may be, like sex work, the experience of having sex solely at the command of and for the pleasure of an other. This is a more extreme interpretation of the sexualized female body than mine and not one all women share.

> The feminists' point of view? Well, I would like to point out that they're missing a couple of things, because, you know, I may be dressing like the typical bimbo, whatever, but I'm in charge. You know. I'm in charge of my fantasies. I put myself in these situations with men, you know . . . . [A]ren't I in charge of my life?[9]

Although I believe Madonna's claim about herself, there are probably a number of people who don't. Anyone who looks as much like a sex worker as she does couldn't possibly be in charge of herself, they are likely to say; she is an example of exactly what MacKinnon

---

[7] Even sex workers who are "in the life" feel interrogated by the sexualization question; they too struggle against acting like whores. Consider, for example, one sex worker's description of the discomfort she experienced because she sexually responded to her customer during an act of prostitution. Her orgasm in those circumstances broke down a distinction she sought to maintain between her work and the sexual pleasure she obtained from her non-work-related sexual activity. *See* Judy Edelstein, *In the Massage Parlor*, *in* SEX WORK: WRITINGS BY WOMEN IN THE SEX INDUSTRY 62, 62–63 (Frédérique Delacoste & Priscilla Alexander eds., 1987) [hereinafter SEX WORK]. Consider also the many accounts of sex workers who feel degraded or angry about their work; this is an experience of sexual division, a fear that, in their work as whores, they are acting like whores. *See, e.g.*, Jean Johnston, *Speaking in Tongues*, *in* SEX WORK, *supra*, at 70, 70; Sharon Kaiser, *Coming Out of Denial*, *in* SEX WORK, *supra*, at 104, 104–05; Rosie Summers, *Prostitution*, *in* SEX WORK, *supra*, at 113, 114–15.

[8] MacKinnon, *Agenda for Theory*, *supra* note 1, at 533–34.

[9] *Nightline*: Interview with Madonna (ABC television broadcast, Dec. 3, 1990).

means by a "walking embodiment[] of men's projected needs."[10] Without going further into the cottage industry of Madonna interpretation, it seems indisputable that Madonna's version of the female sexualized body is radically more autonomous and self-serving than MacKinnon's interpretation, and significantly less troubled and doubled than mine.

Because sex differences are semiotic — because the female body is produced and interpreted through a system of signs — all three of these interpretations of the sexualized female body may be accurate. The truth of any particular meaning would depend on the circumstances in which it was asserted. Thus, the sexualized female body that is produced and sustained by the legal regulation of prostitution may have multiple meanings. Moreover, the meaning of the sexualized female body for an individual woman is also affected by other feminine images that the legal regulation of prostitution produces.

Anti-prostitution rules terrorize the female body. The regulation of prostitution is accomplished not only by rules that expressly repress or prohibit commercialized sex. Prostitution regulation also occurs through a network of cultural practices that endanger sex workers' lives and make their work terrifying. These practices include the random, demeaning, and sometimes brutal character of anti-prostitution law enforcement. They also include the symbiotic relationship between the illegal drug industry and sex work, the use of prostitutes in the production of certain forms of pornography, hotel compliance with sex work, inadequate police protection for crimes against sex workers, and unregulated bias against prostitutes and their children in housing, education, the health care system, and in domestic relations law. Legal rules support and facilitate these practices.

The legal terrorization of prostitutes forces many sex workers to rely on pimps for protection and security, an arrangement which in most cases is also terrorizing. Pimps control when sex workers work, what kind of sex they do for money, and how much they make for doing it; they often use sexual seduction and physical abuse to "manage" the women who work for them. The terrorization of sex workers affects women who are not sex workers by encouraging them to do whatever they can to avoid being asked if they are "for" illegal sex. Indeed, marriage can function as one of these avoidance mechanisms, in that, conventionally, marriage signals that a woman has chosen legal sex over illegal sex.

One might argue that the terrorized female body is not that much different from the sexualized female body. Both experiences of femininity often — some might say always — entail being dominated by a man. Regardless of whether a woman is terrorized or sexualized, there are social incentives to reduce the hardships of her position,

---

[10] MacKinnon, *Agenda for Theory*, *supra* note 1, at 534.

either by marrying or by aligning herself with a pimp. In both cases she typically becomes emotionally, financially, physically, and sexually dependent on and subordinate to a man.

If the terrorized and sexualized female bodies can be conflated and reduced to a dominated female body, then Madonna's claim that she's in charge, like the claims other women make that they experience sexual pleasure or autonomy in their relations with men, is suspect — perhaps, even, the product of false consciousness. But I argue that the dominated female body does not fully capture the impact of anti-prostitution rules on women. This is because anti-prostitution rules also maternalize the female body, by virtue of the interrelationship between anti-prostitution rules and legal rules that encourage women to bear and rear children. The maternalized female body triangulates the relationship between law and the meanings of the female body. It proposes a choice of roles for women.

The maternalization of the female body can be explained through the operation of the first and second postmodern "principles." That is, because we construct our identities in language and because the meaning of language is contextual and contingent, the relationship between anti-prostitution rules and the meaning of the female body is also affected by other legal rules and their relationship to the female body. The legal rules that criminalize prostitution are located in a legal system in which other legal rules legalize sex — rules, for example, that establish marriage as the legal site of sex and that link marital sex to reproduction by, for example, legitimating children born in marriage. As a result of this conjuncture, anti-prostitution rules maternalize the female body. They not only interrogate women with the question of whether they are for or against prostitution; they also raise the question of whether a woman is for illegal sex or whether she is for legal, maternalized sex.

The legal system maintains a shaky line between sex workers and other women. Anti-prostitution laws are erratically enforced; eager customers and obliging hotel services collaborate in the "crimes" prostitutes commit with relative impunity, and the legal, systemic devaluation of "women's work" sometimes makes prostitution more lucrative for women than legitimate wage labor. Anti-prostitution rules formally preserve the distinction between legal and illegal sexual activity. By preventing the line between sex workers and "mothers" from disappearing altogether, anti-prostitution rules reinforce the maternalized female body that other legal rules more directly support.

The legal discourse of anti-prostitution law explicitly deploys the image of maternalized femininity in order to contrast sex workers with women who are not sex workers. This can be observed in defamation cases involving women who are incorrectly identified or depicted as whores. In authorizing compensation for such women, courts typically appeal to maternal imagery to describe the woman who has been wrongly described; they justify their decisions by contrasting the images of two female bodies against each other, the virgin and the whore — madonna and bimbo. The discourse of these decisions maternalizes the female body.[11] The maternalized female body is responsible for her children. Madonna's bambino puts her in charge.

The conjunction and displacement of these alternative meanings of the female body are rationalized in legal discourse, where they are presented as both "natural" but also necessary, for reasons associated with liberalism. A Massachusetts case involving a rape prosecution[12] and feminist controversy regarding the decriminalization of prostitution provide two examples.

Sometime after three o'clock in the morning on a December night in Malden Square, a police cruiser entered a parking lot where police officers had heard screams. "Seeing the headlights of an approaching car," Judge Liacos wrote for the Supreme Judicial Court, a woman "naked and bleeding around the mouth, jumped from the defendant's car and ran toward [the police cruiser] screaming and waving her arms."[13] She claimed that she had been raped, that the defendant had forced her to perform oral sex and to engage in intercourse twice. After the defendant was convicted on charges of rape and commission of an unnatural and lascivious act, he appealed. He claimed that he had wrongfully been denied the opportunity to inform the jury that the complainant had twice been charged with prostitution. He argued that the complainant's allegation of rape, which he denied, "may have been motivated by her desire to avoid further prosecution."[14]

The trial court had prohibited the defendant from mentioning the complainant's arrests to the jury because of the Massachusetts rape-shield statute,[15] a rule that prohibits the admission of reputation evidence or of specific instances of a victim's sexual conduct in a rape trial. The purpose of the rule is to encourage victims to report rapes, to eliminate victim harassment at trial, and to support the assumption that reputation evidence is "only marginally, if at all, probative of

---

[11] *See, e.g.*, Veazy v. Blair, 86 Ga. App. 721, 726 (1952) (holding that a cause of action existed when the defendant had stated that "the plaintiff, a pure and chaste lady of unblemished character, was a 'public whore'"); Mullins v. Mutter, 151 S.W.2d 1047, 1048, 1051 (Ken. 1941) (upholding a large slander award when the defendant called the plaintiff a "damned whore"). In *Mullins*, the court noted that:

> In this case plaintiff is an orphaned girl, bearing — so far as the record discloses — a good reputation . . . . Up to the time complained of no breath of suspicion had been leveled against her chastity. But, so emphatically repeated charges by defendant was calculated to leave a scar upon her reputation that might follow her to her grave.

Id. at 1051.

[12] *See* Commonwealth v. Joyce, 415 N.E.2d 181 (Mass. 1981).

[13] *Id.* at 183.

[14] *Id.* at 184.

[15] *See* MASS. GEN. L. ch. 233, § 21B (1991).

consent."[16] Reasoning that a defendant's right to argue bias "may be the last refuge of an innocent defendant," the Supreme Judicial Court lifted the shield.[17]

> We emphasize that we do not depart from the long held view that prostitution is not relevant to credibility . . . . Nor do we depart from the policy of the statute in viewing prostitution or the lack of chastity as inadmissible on the issue of consent. Where, however, such facts are relevant to a showing of bias or motive to lie, the general evidentiary rule of exclusion must give way to the constitutionally based right of effective cross-examination.[18]

This interpretation of the rape-shield statute, broadly applied, denies sex workers who dare to complain of sexual violence the presumption of innocence. Because prostitution is unlawful, this ruling simultaneously terrorizes, sexualizes, and de-maternalizes sex workers. This triple whammy is accomplished by an appeal to fairness:

> [T]he defendant is entitled to present his own theory of the encounter to the jury . . . . The relevancy of testimony depends on whether it has a 'rational tendency to prove an issue in the case.' . . . Under the defendant's theory he and the complainant, previously strangers to each other, were in a car late at night parked in a vacant parking lot. Having just engaged in sexual acts, they were both naked. A police car was approaching. The defendant intended to show that the complainant, having been found in a similar situation on two prior occasions, had been arrested on each occasion and charged with prostitution. We cannot say that this evidence has no rational tendency to prove that the complainant was motivated falsely to accuse the defendant of rape by a desire to avoid further prosecution.[19]

Seems perfectly reasonable. Fair. If a guy can't explain a gal's reasons for misrepresenting a situation, that bleeding mouth might compromise *his* credibility.

It might seem obvious, at this point, that decriminalization of prostitution would be an appropriate strategy for feminist legal activists concerned about the physical security of sex workers. However, although the feminists I've read all agree that prostitution should be decriminalized, they disagree about *how* decriminalization should occur. The arguments in this dispute are another example of how legal discourse reproduces and is mired in the interpretations of the female body produced by legal rules.

Should the reform of prostitution law be restricted to the repeal of rules penalizing the sale of sex, or should other legally supported

---

16 *Joyce*, 415 N.E.2d at 186.

17 *Id.* at 186.

18 *Id.* at 187 (citations omitted).

19 *Id.* (citations omitted).

structures that create, sustain and degrade sex work also be challenged? Feminists in favor of legalization — this is the postmodern position — argue that, unlike a narrowly defined decriminalization campaign, legalization might significantly improve the lives of sex workers. Legalization, for example, might extend unemployment insurance benefits to sex workers; it might allow sex workers to participate in the social security system; it might prohibit pimping; it might authorize advertising for their business.

Feminists who are against legalization — this is the radical position — envision a decriminalization project that would develop strategies for preventing women from participating in sex work, rather than strategies that would make prostitution a more comfortable line of work. Radical feminists, such as Kathleen Barry, are sympathetic to the plight of sex workers.[20] But their conviction that women are defined as women by their sexual subordination to men leads them to argue that sex workers are particularly victimized by patriarchy and that they should be extricated from their condition rather than supported in their work. These arguments against legalization are in the language of the terrorized female body.

Not all legal feminists believe that prostitutes are terrorized full time. Some feminists — I'll call this group the liberals — believe that at least some sex workers, occasionally, exercise sexual autonomy. But these feminists do not favor assimilating sex work into the wage market. They oppose legalization because they object to the kind of sexual autonomy legalization would support.[21] That is, although they support the right of women to do sex work — even at the cost of reinforcing male dominance — they resist the commodification of women's sexuality.

Sex workers themselves — who inspire the postmodern position as I develop it here — want legal support for sex that is severed from its reproduction function and from romance, affection, and long-term relationships.[22] Because "legal" sexual autonomy is conventionally extended to women only by rules that locate sexuality in marriage or

---

[20] *See* KATHLEEN BARRY, FEMALE SEXUAL SLAVERY 226–37 (1979).

[21] *See* Margaret J. Radin, *Market-Inalienability*, 100 HARV. L. REV. 1849, 1921–25 (1987) (favoring limited decriminalization of prostitution, at least for the short term). *But see* Jody Freeman, *The Feminist Debate Over Prostitution Reform: Prostitutes' Rights Groups, Radical Feminists, and the (Im)possibility of Consent*, 5 BERK. WOMEN'S L.J. 75, 107–08 (1989–1990) (arguing that "the best short-term approach to reform entails removing prostitution from the criminal realm . . . and, at the same time taking affirmative steps to destroy the conditions that create consumption and drive women to the trade").

[22] Not all sex workers seek to legalize as well as decriminalize their work, but many do. *See, e.g.*, GAIL PHETERSON, A VINDICATION OF THE RIGHTS OF WHORES 33–34 (1989); *Draft Statements from the 2nd World Whores' Congress (1986), in* SEX WORK, *supra* note 7, at 307, 307; *International Committee for Prostitutes' Rights World Charter, in* SEX WORK, *supra* note 7, at 305, 305.

by rules that allow women decisional autonomy regarding reproductive issues, arguments in support of law reforms that would legalize sex work conflict with the language of the maternalized female body. The arguments that sex workers are making to assimilate their work into the wage market appeal to a sexualized femininity that is something other than a choice between criminalized and maternalized sex or a choice between terrorized and maternalized sex. This appeal to a fresh image of the female body is based on a reorganization of the three images of femininity I described earlier; it arises within the play of these three images. Its originality suggests, to me, resistance to the dominant images.

It is significant that sex workers have "found" a different voice of feminine sexuality through the process of political organizing, through efforts to speak out against and to change the conditions of their lives. For me, the promise of postmodern legal feminism lies in the juncture of feminist politics and the genealogy of the female body in law. It is in this juncture that we can simultaneously deploy the commonalities among real women, in their historically situated, material circumstances, and at the same time challenge the conventional meanings of "woman" that sustain the subordinating conditions of women's lives.

I do not think that the sex workers' claims for legalization constitute *the* postmodern feminist legal voice. I am also unsure whether I support their position on legalization. But I believe that my analysis of the decriminalization dispute in which they are participating illustrates how postmodern legal feminism can seek and claim different voices, voices which will challenge the power of the congealed meanings of the female body that legal rules and legal discourse permit and sustain.

C. *The Maternalization of the Female Body: Family and Work*

There are a number of legal rules that function to compel or encourage women to bear children and to assume disproportionately larger responsibilities for rearing children than men do. Of these rules, those that regulate biological reproduction or the structure of the family are explicitly engaged in such functions; rules that regulate the wage market or wage market subsidies maternalize the female body more indirectly.

Rules that prohibit, restrict, or hinder access to abortion and rules that prohibit or inhibit the use or distribution of birth control devices prevent women from avoiding unwanted childbirth.[23] These rules have the effect of making some women become mothers against their

[23] Since teenage women are still subject to contraceptive restrictions, despite Eisenstadt v. Baird, 405 U.S. 438 (1972), these rules are not in desuetude.

will. In this way these rules directly conscript the female body in the service of maternity.

Fetal protection rules,[24] decisional law that compels women to undergo unwanted caesareans, and rules that facilitate involuntary sterilization in some circumstances require conduct of pregnant or fertile women that they themselves do not desire or might not otherwise choose. Rules such as these curtail the liberty of some women in order to regulate pregnancy and protect childbirth. In this way, these rules maternalize the female body.

Once women have given birth, legal rules relating to child custody and support disputes compel or encourage women to do more child rearing than men. Sex-specific rules only recently outlawed by the federal and state equality guarantees used to perform these functions quite directly. Pursuant to the maternal preference rule, for example, women were explicitly presumed to be better parents than men; a man could only wrest custody of his children away from their mother if he could prove she was "unfit." This rule not only allocated disproportionately more child rearing responsibilities to women in formal legal disputes; it also signalled to men and women making "private" decisions regarding parenting responsibilities that the legal system expected women to do more parenting and to do it better than men.

Two forms of child support provisions from the not-so-distant past also ensured that women were more likely than men to become primary child caretakers. Under civil and criminal child support rules, states formally imposed support obligations exclusively or primarily on fathers, and, under federal and state welfare benefit rules, widowed or single mothers (but not fathers) were entitled to governmental child support assistance. Both forms of child support provisions "freed" women to abandon or subordinate wage market work in order to care for children.

Although most sex specific provisions have been formally eliminated from custody and child support rules, the neutralized rule system has not significantly reduced the gender lopsidedness of custody and support decisions; judges still impose or approve child custody and support schemes in which women undertake more physical responsibility for child care than men. Thus, the administration of domestic relations law is implicated in helping or making women "mother" their children. The law continues to signal to women and

---

[24] At least 50 cases have been brought against women for "fetal abuse" in giving birth to drug-exposed babies. *See* Dorothy E. Roberts, *The Future of Reproductive Choice for Poor Women and Women of Color*, 12 WOMEN'S RTS. L. REP. 59, 64 n.40 (1990). Some states have expanded the definition of neglected children to include babies who are born addicted to certain classes of drugs. *See* FLA. STAT. ANN. § 415.503(9)(a)(2) (West Supp. 1991); MASS. GEN. L. ch. 119, § 51A (1991). Women have also been charged with vehicular homicide for the death of their fetuses. *See* State v. McCall, 458 So. 2d 875, 877 (Fla. Ct. App. 1984) (count dismissed).

men making "private" decisions about which parent should do more or less child rearing. Mothers receive more legal support for that work than do men.

Moreover, not all sex-specific provisions affecting women's parenting roles have been eliminated from domestic relations law. Procedural and substantive rules relating to the custody and support of children born to unwed parents specifically assume that unwed mothers are (or should be) the primary parents of such children. Similarly, the rules just being developed to resolve disputes over surrogate mother contracts or over the custody of children conceived with technical assistance include a presumption that biological mothers have a more significant claim (or responsibility) for custody than biological fathers.

Historically, then, but also presently, child custody and support rules and enforcement practices assign more women than men the daily responsibilities for child rearing and enforce child support duties in a way that encourages a similar allocation of child care. In this way, family law maternalizes the female body.

Legal rules that regulate the wage market compel or encourage women to bear and to rear children more indirectly than the rules described above. Nevertheless, because wage market rules undervalue the work women do in the wage market, women have much less to lose than men if they abandon, interrupt, or modify their wage market work because of child birth or child rearing. Legal rules that support women's subordinate status in the wage market thus also support (encourage or compel) women to undertake maternal responsibilities.

If employment discrimination rules actually prevented employers from treating women badly in the terms or conditions of their work, the impact of the wage market on the maternalization of the female body would be quite attenuated; it might even be eliminated. To some extent, of course, the advent of employment discrimination rules has improved women's wage work opportunities. However, the gender gap continues to exist in the wage market, partly because of gaps or omissions in the discrimination rules, partly because of the ways in which the rules have been interpreted, and partly because of the limited resources allocated to discrimination law enforcement. Consequently, the legal rules that support the wage market's undervaluation of women and the discrimination rules that don't do enough to curtail that situation support the maternalization of the female body.

Here are several examples of wage market rules that have this effect on women:

1. Although men and women are occupationally segregated into jobs that are disproportionately held by one sex or the other, and although "women's" jobs are less well compensated than "men's," legal rules validate this unequal payment system. It has been widely ar-

gued, for example, that a substantial portion of the wage disparities between sex-segregated job categories could be eliminated by requiring employers to pay wages according to the "comparable worth" of jobs. In most cases, courts have refused to hold that employment discrimination law compels employers to adjust wages in this manner.[25]

2. In most cases hazardous workplace rules that exclude pregnant or fertile women have been upheld,[26] *Johnson Controls*[27] to the contrary notwithstanding.

3. Job allocation schemes that channel disproportionately more men than women into lucrative jobs do not violate employment discrimination rules because of the narrow judicial interpretation of discrimination laws.[28]

4. An unemployment compensation scheme that denies benefits to women who leave work because of childbirth has been upheld under the narrow judicial interpretation of discrimination laws.[29]

[To be worked in, maternalization and paternalization of wage market jobs (pilot/stewardess; doctor/nurse; boss/secretary; principal/teacher)]

D. The Sexualization of the Female Body: Monogamy, Heterosexuality, Passivity

This section describes how legal rules affect the frequency, the character, and the distribution of women's sexual practices. The argument is that by directly or indirectly penalizing conduct that does not conform to a particular set of sexual behaviors, legal rules promote a model of female sexuality; this model is characterized by monogamy, heterosexuality, and passivity. This means that legal rules favor women who marry, who have sex only with their husbands, and who

[25] *See, e.g.*, American Nurses' Ass'n v. Illinois, 783 F.2d 716, 725 (7th Cir. 1986) (holding that a state's refusal to adopt the principle of comparable worth was not actionable); American Fed'n of State, County & Mun. Employees v. Washington, 770 F.2d 1401, 1408 (9th Cir. 1985) (rejecting a union's claim that the state was compelled to restructure its compensation system based on the results of a comparable worth study); Christensen v. Iowa, 563 F.2d 353, 355 (8th Cir. 1977) (finding no prima facie case of sex discrimination under title VII, 42 U.S.C. § 2000e to 2000e-17 (1988), in a state university's practice of paying male physical plant workers more than female clerical workers of equivalent seniority and grade).

[26] *See, e.g.*, Hayes v. Shelby Memorial Hosp., 726 F.2d 1543, 1552 (11th Cir. 1984); Wright v. Olin Corp., 697 F.2d 1172, 1188–91 (4th Cir. 1982).

[27] *See* 111 S. Ct. 1196, 1203 (1991).

[28] *See* EEOC v. Sears, 628 F. Supp. 1264, 1352–53 (N.D. Ill. 1986), *aff'd*, 839 F.2d 302 (7th Cir. 1988); Vicki Schultz, *Telling Stories About Women and Work: Judicial Interpretations of Sex Segregation in the Workplace in Title VII Cases Raising the Lack of Interest Argument*, 103 HARV. L. REV. 1749, 1754–56 (1990).

[29] *See* Wimberly v. Labor & Indus. Relations Comm'n, 479 U.S. 511, 514, 522 (1987).

defer to their husbands in determining when, how often, and in what manner marital sex takes place. In contrast, legal rules discourage women from being celibate or from having sex outside marriage — with one partner, with multiple partners, or with other women; they also deter women from being more assertive than their husbands want them to be about the management of marital sex.

Although law is only one of the cultural factors that influence women's practices, if the legal rules this section describes were different, female sexuality could be different. It is hard to say whether women would have less sex than they do now, or whether they would have more; it is hard to predict how their choice of sex partners would change or how the character of their sexual experiences might be affected. Nevertheless, because the present regime of legal rules induces women to be "good girls" and imposes sanctions on "deviant" sexual conduct, it seems clear that altering the current regime would undermine the current model of female sexual behavior.

Legal rules influence female sexuality by means of three groups of rules or law enforcement practices. One group of legal rules prohibits or promotes certain forms of sex; the two other groups regulate the physical and economic conditions in which sex takes place. The remainder of this section is devoted to explaining how these rules function as a system to encourage women to conform to a monogamous, heterosexual, and passive model of female sexuality.

Legal rules promote sexual monogamy by defining marriage as a union with one other person and by punishing or indirectly penalizing sex outside of marriage. Criminal rules against bigamy prohibit marriage to more than one person at a time, while sex outside of marriage is made a criminal offense, in many states, by rules against fornication and adultery. Legal rules in most states also designate adultery as a marital "offense" that constitutes grounds for divorce. Sex outside of marriage is further discouraged by rules prohibiting prostitution and by contract rules that make agreements between unmarried individuals who live together unenforceable to the extent that they are "based on" sex. These rules encourage women and men to be monogamous by formally restricting sex to the one person to whom they are legally married.

Because the rules against adultery and fornication are only loosely enforced, the legal impact on female sexual monogamy might not amount to much if these rules were the only legal factors affecting women's sexual practices. But this is not the case. The legal rules that regulate the economic consequences of marriage, the legal rules that maintain the inferior status of women in the wage market, and the legal rules that provide women inadequate protection against physical abuse all function to reinforce the impact of the sexual monogamy rules on women. These rules create economic and safety incentives for women to marry and to remain sexually faithful in marriage. Moreover, these rules reduce the power that married and unmarried women have in relationship to men; in this way, these rules make women more susceptible to male demands for sexual fidelity than they might be under conditions of economic equality and physical safety.

Legal rules reduce the economic power of women in relationship to men by maintaining inferior employment opportunities for women in the wage market. At the same time, legal rules make marriage a potential source of income for marital partners, by means of spousal support and property provisions that require economically dominant spouses to share what they have with their partners. In addition, alimony rules sometimes permit economically subordinate spouses to continue to receive support even after their marriages have formally ended. Government benefit rules also structure marriage as an economic enterprise, through rules that provide retirement, death, and disability benefits to the spouses of wage earners.

By structuring marriage as a significant source of financial support, legal rules make marriage a plausible substitute — or supplement — to wage market work for both sexes. However, as a result of their inferior position in the wage market — a position legal rules sustain — women are likely to be more financially dependent on marriage than men. This condition affects the responses they might otherwise have to the lax enforcement of the rules against fornication and adultery. Legal rules induce women to marry, and to stay married, for financial reasons. Even though fornication rules are not stringently enforced, wage market and marital economic benefit rules provide women financial incentives to comply with them. Moreover, married women who are economically dependent on their husbands have economic incentives to have sex only with their husbands. Despite the lax enforcement of anti-adultery rules, the wage market and marital benefit rules function to make divorce financially risky for many women; complying with anti-adultery rules enables them to avoid giving their husbands a legal reason for divorce. By inducing some women to marry and to avoid divorce for financial reasons, wage market and marital economic rules reinforce the impact on women of rules that formally restrict sex to marriage.

The legal rules that regulate social violence reduce women's power in relationship to men because they enhance the significance of the cultural convention that a woman is more likely to be verbally or physically attacked if she is alone or in the company of other women than if she is with an individual man. By ineffectively enforcing legal rules governing rape, sexual assault, and other violent crimes against the person, the social violence rule system places women in physical jeopardy. Women can sometimes mitigate the impact of these circumstances by relying on individual men for protection against violence. To the extent that these rule-enforcement practices provide women with a safety incentive to marry and to stay married, the social violence rule system reinforces anti-fornication and anti-adultery rules that penalize nonmonogamous sexual practices.

By reducing the power of women in relationship to men, the wage market rule system and the social violence rule system provide financial and safety incentives for women to defer to their sexual partners in determining the conditions of intimacy. If their partners value sexual monogamy — an ethic, as we have seen, that legal rules help form — then women are likely to comply with their partners' demands for fidelity. Legal rules make women less inclined to resist such demands than they might be in different circumstances. Legal rules also diminish the ability of women to demand fidelity of intimate partners who are unwilling to give up sexual promiscuity.

I have argued thus far that, by inducing women to marry, by discouraging them from having affairs, and by creating economic and physical conditions that help their sexual partners to impose monogamy on them if they want to, legal rules discourage women from having sex with more than one man. The legal model of female sexual monogamy also gives some women incentives to be more sexually active than they would otherwise be. Sex workers and women who want to be celibate are examples of women whom the sexual monogamy rule system induces into sexual activity.

The legal rules that devalue "women's work" in the wage market make prostitution, like marriage, a significant economic alternative or supplement to wage market labor. Moreover, the rules against prostitution, like the rules against fornication and adultery, are not stringently enforced. Legal rules thus provide de facto protection for prostitution; they enable prostitution to function as a safety valve against the constraints of sexual monogamy. Even though anti-prostitution rules are notoriously enforced more systematically against female sex workers than against male customers, legal rules induce some women to violate the criminal rules against prostitution by making sex work more lucrative than legitimate wage labor.

Legal rules also coerce some sex workers into having more sex than they might otherwise want to by inadequately protecting them from customer abuse, which can include unwanted sex. In addition, legal rules do not protect sex workers against the demands pimps may make of them for sexual activity. Since sex workers are induced to affiliate with pimps in order to defend themselves against customers and in order to broker their way through the criminal justice system when they are caught up in it, legal rules and law enforcement practices are complicit in imposing more sex on these women than they might have if their work were not illegal and if it were physically safe.

The sexuality of women who want to practice celibacy may not be affected by the rules prohibiting bigamy, fornication, adultery, and prostitution. However, by creating economic and safety incentives for women to marry, legal rules encourage some women to abandon celibacy in favor of marriage. Since legal rules in most states provide that refusal to have sex within marriage constitutes grounds for divorce, legal rules inhibit women who marry because of economic or safety incentives from practicing celibacy within marriage.

Legal rules also create economic and safety incentives for women to sacrifice celibacy in order to have sex with men to whom they are not married. In addition to encouraging women to turn to men for physical protection, legal rules reduce women's ability to pay their own way; the wage market treatment of women makes it hard for them to go "dutch treat." These physical and financial pressures encourage unmarried women to yield to the sexual demands of escorts or companions they have turned to — at least in part — for protection against abuse from other men.

Although men and women are both subject to the rules that directly penalize or specifically require sexual monogamy, I have argued that the legal rules establishing the economic and physical circumstances in which women and men have sex encourage women to be more sexually monogamous than men. This sex-based difference in the impact of legal rules on monogamous conduct also has an effect on the character of heterosexual relations. To put this point more bluntly, these rules not only encourage a "double standard" of sexual conduct for women and men; they also enable men to have greater control over the terms of heterosexual intimacy — they give men more power over women in sex. This is one of the ways that legal rules encourage passivity as a model of female sexual conduct.

Women are induced to choose men rather than women as sexual partners — to comply with heterosexuality as the model for female sexual conduct — by legal rules that prohibit sodomy and other sexual acts between individuals of the same sex. Although the criminal rules penalizing homosexual conduct, like the sexual monogamy rules, are not vigorously enforced, decisional law defines marriage as a heterosexual union. Women who might expect that sexual relationships with other women could

[to be completed by:

economic and security incentives that make a male partner more advantageous for non-sexual reasons than a same-sex partner for women.

rules and procedures establishing a passivity norm, which include the marital rape exemption, economic and security incentives for doing what your guy wants, and the lax enforcement of prostitution laws, which induces economically or physically dependent women to let men have their way sexually in order to avoid losing their protectors to illegal sexual competition.]

III. The Politics of Postmodern Feminism: Lessons from the Anti-pornography Campaign

A particular phase of the legal anti-pornography campaign is dead in the water. The ordinance that Catharine MacKinnon and Andrea Dworkin initially authored and then vigorously promoted in Minneapolis, Indianapolis, Cambridge, and other cities would have made pornography a form of discrimination against women. It would have permitted women to bring civil actions against those who produce, make, distribute, or sell pornography, which the ordinance generally defined as "'the graphic sexually explicit subordination of women, whether in pictures or in words.'"[30] It would have provided civil remedies for the harm that pornography causes. But the Supreme Court's summary affirmance of the Seventh Circuit's decision holding the ordinance unconstitutional has rendered continued efforts to enact this particular ordinance very problematic. The campaign to enact the MacKinnon/Dworkin ordinance may, however, offer lessons for other feminist political projects.

The ordinance campaign fascinates me. As a political event involving the community of feminist lawyers, it was a dazzling success and an appalling disaster. It politicized feminist lawyers, by engaging many of us in the practicalities of a grass roots legislative reform effort that was widely publicized and electrifyingly controversial. But it also politicized us by brutally and bitterly fracturing our community. Catharine MacKinnon, in particular, put a high price on feminist opposition to her campaign. In a chapter chillingly entitled "On Collaboration," from her book *Feminism Unmodified*, she charged, with an emotional intensity that also characterized other campaign participants, that "[w]omen who defend the pornographers are defending a source of their relatively high position among women under male supremacy, keeping all women, including them, an inferior class on the basis of sex, enforced by sexual force."[31]

"I really want you to stop your lies and misrepresentations of our position," she continued. "I want you to stop claiming that your liberalism, with its elitism, and your Freudianism, with its sexualized misogyny, has anything in common with feminism."[32]

For reasons I will soon make clear, I don't particularly regret the anti-pornography ordinance defeat. But like the architects of the ordinance, I too believe in using law to oppose the oppression of

---

[30] American Booksellers Ass'n v. Hudnut, 771 F.2d 323, 324 (7th Cir. 1985), *aff'd*, 475 U.S. 1001 (1986) (quoting Indianapolis, Ind. Code § 16–3 (q) (1984)).

[31] MacKinnon, *supra* note 4, at 205.

[32] *Id.*

women. Indeed, the apparent jeopardy of *Roe v. Wade*[33] makes me especially cognizant at this moment that retaining the legalization of abortion may soon become a pressing project requiring astute political skills among feminists forced to seek legislative reform all across the United States. I hope, therefore, that closely examining the ordinance campaign, as a salient incident in the politics of legal feminism, will advance the prospects of an abortion reform effort that the Supreme Court might thrust upon us, as well as the prospects of other future feminist legal projects.

I want to make two points about the campaign. First, I intend to challenge the somewhat familiar criticisms of the campaign by suggesting that some of the campaign's weaknesses can also be understood as political strengths, strengths that might be adapted and deployed in other efforts. That is, my claim will be that the conventional failures of the campaign also constituted the campaign's successes.

Second, I will outline what I think is a new critique of the ordinance campaign. Shamelessly relying on the advantages of hindsight, I will argue that the ordinance proponents were fatally reluctant to apply the theory underlying the campaign to their own efforts. Having brilliantly identified the subordination of women by sex as a linchpin of women's oppression, the ordinance proponents relentlessly perpetuated the dichotomy of gender in the style of their rhetoric, in the content of their arguments, and in the absolutism of the ordinance's structure, which would have rigidly divided pornographic materials into two opposing categories — actionable or unactionable. My claim will be that the greatest strength of the anti-pornography ordinance campaign was also its greatest weakness. Having identified pornography as a cultural practice importantly implicated in the problem of women's condition, the ordinance advocates sought unsuccessfully to use law reform to destroy pornography. I now seek to turn this failure to some profit, by using an analysis of their campaign as an opportunity to deconstruct pornography. The interesting and perhaps troubling question that underlies my own position, however, is what effect this deconstruction would have had on the ordinance campaign.

A word of caution before I proceed. Each of us is likely to have a relatively concrete, relatively firm understanding of what we consider pornography, but we probably disagree about the components of a common conception. When I was twelve, pornography meant a few pages in my parents' copy of *From Here to Eternity*[34] and a few words like "coitus" and "fornicate" thrillingly available in my own dictionary. My personal definition now is more far ranging, but I do not know how widely shared it is.

[33] 410 U.S. 113 (1973).

[34] JAMES JONES, FROM HERE TO ETERNITY (1951).

Two Meese Commission guys recently published a survey in the *Michigan Journal of Law Reform* that comically purports to describe the character of "adults only" pornography currently sold in the United States.[35] The survey classifies the cover photos of books, magazines, and films sold in "adults only" bookstores in four cities. Because the investigation is limited to "adults only" stores, the survey does not include material which I consider part of the pornographic genre. Examples of omitted material I would include are: formula romances; science fiction and comics that feature sexually explicit material; lesbian and gay erotica that is too pretentious for "adults only" bookstores; the dark, serious literature of sex and violence characterized by books like *The Story of O*[36] and Georges Bataille's *Story of the Eye*;[37] and portions of material found in many women's glossy magazines. I am not going to try to solve the problem of confusion that the term pornography generates in listeners by contriving a general, abstract definition that many of you would probably dislike. I simply want to assert that what constitutes pornography is usually a charged and unexplored question in any discussion involving pornography.

A. Conventional Failures Reinterpreted: The Strengths of the Ordinance Campaign

A familiar criticism of the ordinance campaign is the charge that it produced an alliance between ordinance advocates and nonfeminist conservatives. Many feminists during the campaign voiced concern that conservative support for the ordinance indicated their intention to turn the ordinance against material that is offensive only because it describes or depicts "nontraditional" sexuality. Because conservatives have considered the use of birth control devices and sexual activities such as cunnilingus "nontraditional sexual practices," ordinance opponents feared that the ordinance campaign might lead to the repression of sexual freedom rather than to the prevention of sexual oppression.

The conservative alliance might not have occurred had the ordinance advocates been clearer, narrower, and more consistent in their explanation of what constituted pornography. The advocates repeatedly attempted to reassure wary feminists that the ordinance did not need to function to impose an orthodox, traditional form of sexuality on anyone. However, the general definition of pornography as "'the graphic sexually explicit subordination of women, whether in pic-

---

[35] *See* Park E. Dietz & Alan E. Sears, *Pornography and Obscenity Sold in "Adult Bookstores": A Survey of 5132 Books, Magazines, and Films in Four American Cities*, 21 U. MICH. J.L. REF. 7, 10–11 (1987–1988).

[36] PAULINE RÉAGE, THE STORY OF O (Sabine d'Estrée trans., 1965).

[37] GEORGES BATAILLE, HISTOIRE DE L'OEIL (1979).

tures or in words'"[38] was broad enough to encourage the Vanilla-Sex Gestapo that they could get with the ordinance program.

I claim the conservative alliance was a virtue of the ordinance campaign because of its role in extending the ordinance debate beyond predictable feminist constituencies. In contrast to the typically narrow circle, for example, which has exhibited interest in radical legislative reforms related to the anti-family structure of the labor market, the ordinance campaign boldly and successfully engaged nonfeminist political camps. Conservative support for the ordinance undoubtedly posed troublesome management issues for the feminists supporting the ordinance. However, a broad theater of political involvement was obviously vital to the ordinance campaign, and similarly broad coalitions will also be important to the success of other feminist law reform projects.

I acknowledge that extending feminist issues beyond familiar constituencies occurred in the ordinance campaign at the cost of feminist unity. My claim is that breaching this unity is a necessary component of feminist efforts against women's oppressions.

The broad definition of pornography adopted by the ordinance advocates radically challenged a fundamental premise of post-Freudian, Lacanian theories of self, the premise that domination and subordination are an inevitable aspect of interpersonal relations. Ordinance advocates assumed that by eliminating *depictions* of sexual domination, *sexual domination* could be dealt a fatal blow. In contrast, ordinance opponents believed that domination and subordination constitute a psychological structure that does not depend on the pornography industry and that *need not* depend on gender division for its existence.

This dispute involves a profound question about the nature of the self. It is not surprising that people disagree about this issue; it is not surprising that women — indeed, that feminists — disagree about this issue. Although a powerful, broad, and coherent political community is critical to feminist law reform projects, I believe it is a mistake to fear or avoid or condemn differences among feminists as we pursue these projects. Accepting and exploring our differences, in my view, is a critical component of challenging the ideology of gender difference, which includes the assumption that there is a feminine essence that unalterably unites women, binding us together under the generic category "woman."

A second criticism that has been leveled against the ordinance campaign is that it distracted feminists from other work more important to the women's movement. Ordinance advocates argued that

[38] American Booksellers Ass'n v. Hudnut, 771 F.2d 323, 324 (7th Cir. 1985), *aff'd*, 475 U.S. 1001 (1986) (quoting INDIANAPOLIS, IND. CODE § 16-3(q) (1984)).

pornography triggers massive physical violence against women; they claimed that by sexualizing domination and subordination, pornography functions to consign all women to unequal social and economic status on account of their sex; and they asserted that as an eight billion dollar industry, pornography economically exploits the women who participate in its production and drains substantial resources away from other, more significant purposes. In making their criticism that the ordinance campaign was a fruitless diversion, ordinance opponents disputed all these claims.

Opponents claimed that the data causally linking pornography to violence against women was insubstantial, unconvincing, and predicated on a simplistic and unpersuasive theory of causation. They disputed the claim that regulating pornography could have much effect on the subordination of women, arguing, as I have suggested above, that this subordination is not rooted in pornography. Indeed, some feminists claimed that pornography usefully functions in certain cases to channel and subdue troubling fantasies. The opponents were skeptical that bringing down the pornography industry would make eight billion dollars available for women's causes, and they were critical of the costs of pursuing the ordinance campaign.

In contrast to the ordinance opponents, but for different reasons, I believe that concentrating so much effort, energy, expertise, and even money on the anti-pornography issue simplified and thereby facilitated feminist political organizing, much the same way single-issue campaigning often constitutes an organizational advantage in electoral politics. Political success is predictably correlated with coordinating and consolidating efforts.

I also believe the theoretical claim that the subordination of women is rooted in sex is a message that will significantly benefit the feminist movement. This claim radically challenges the traditional focus of feminist concerns. It legitimates pornography as an appropriate field for struggle, analysis, and interpretation. It challenges the traditional feminist agenda of appropriate strategies for contesting the oppression of women. Whatever skirmishes or battles we may have lost because of the anti-pornography diversion will be worth the challenge to conventional attitudes that the theoretical innovations of the movement facilitated. I attribute the exposure and discussion that occurred about this theory to the choice of pornography as the theory's practical target. This suggests to me an important political lesson for feminists. Issue choice affects our political potential, and legislative reform efforts produce political capital beyond the passage or defeat of legislation.

The last criticism of the ordinance campaign I will mention may be less familiar, but I will raise it because of how disappointed I was when the ordinance campaign came to my town in the form of model or boiler plate legislation. By preventing feminists outside the circle of those who originally worked with MacKinnon and Dworkin from having a voice in the structure and scope of their local ordinances, the architects of the ordinance lost the organizing potential and the consciousness-raising benefits that would have inured from wider drafting participation. Moreover, broader drafting consultation or the experimentation in different cities with different ordinances, might have revealed that some of the model legislation provisions were miscalculations, mistakes that could have been corrected as the campaign moved from town to town.

Despite the criticism that using model legislation warrants, I realize that model legislation facilitates publicity and supports scholarship and efficient legal defense work, all of which strengthen local campaigns to enact feminist reform projects. Moreover, the ordinance campaign overall was remarkable for its broadly participatory character. The campaign heavily relied on indigenous, newly formed groups of concerned individuals in each of the targeted towns, and the ordinance utilized the strategy of allowing the victims of pornography to institute claims on their own behalf against pornographers. By eschewing city or state attorneys, the ordinance functioned to empower women. This strategy too could be adaptable and important in other feminist projects.

B. Destroying Pornography or Deconstructing It

I now turn to my claim that the ordinance campaign's greatest strength was also its greatest weakness, my claim that the advocates should have sought to deconstruct pornography rather than single-mindedly seeking to destroy it.

The ordinance campaign's most significant contribution to feminism was its pursuit of Catharine MacKinnon's theoretical insight that the oppression of women occurs through sexual subordination. The anti-pornography campaign allowed MacKinnon and others to dramatize what this theory means in practice, through its focus on a complex cultural phenomenon that is exclusively devoted to sex, a cultural practice consumed with depictions of what "the oppression of women through sexual subordination" means. In pornography, women get fucked.

Now, women get "fucked" in the workplace, too, where we do "women's work" for "women's wages," working for male bosses and working on male schedules. We get assigned to this inferior work track because we are identifiable by our sex. In addition, our past and present economic, social, and physical subordination makes us vulnerable to physical abuse at work, on the way there, and on the way back. We are raped at work or on route to work because of our sex, because we are cunts.

But the moment I say women get "fucked" in the workplace, the clarity of the relationship between women's oppression and sex is jeopardized. "Women's work" is a complicated construction; its origin and perpetuation depends on many factors in addition to misogyny. Pornography is a much cleaner site for demonstrating the practice of the theoretical insight; pornography is about women getting fucked.

I hasten to acknowledge here that pornography is also about violence against women and that ordinance advocates sought to attack pornography in order to prevent women who participate in its production from being harmed and in order to prevent other women from being harmed by the imitative reactions of pornography users. But the ordinance campaign was not restricted to preventing these two forms of harm.

Ordinance advocates also attacked pornography in order to oppose the sexualization of hierarchy and the objectification of women. They understood the ordinance as more than a good example of the truth of feminist theory in practice. They believed that destroying pornography would lead to the end of women's oppression on account of sex. They believed that destroying this particular depiction of women's oppression would change the experience of women's oppression in its many manifestations. I believe this was a fatal miscalculation.

If women's oppression occurs through sex, then in order to end women's oppressions in its many manifestations the way people think and talk and act about sex must be changed. The ordinance campaign was not well organized to change how people think and talk and act about sex. Rather, the ordinance advocates relentlessly utilized and exploited traditional ideas and language regarding sex in all aspects of the campaign.

Let me give just a few examples.

First, the language and rhetorical style of campaign advocacy were characterized by stereotypically masculine attributes. The language and style were militant, authoritative, and riddled with the easy obscenities typical of male talk. (I've done a little male talk myself in this section.) This style was impressively successful — the advocates were powerful campaigners; but the use of additional, less masculine rhetorical styles, which can also be persuasive and moving, would have made the ordinance campaign less gendered.

The campaign also seemed gendered because the arguments of campaign advocates were typically structured by hierarchical dichotomies. Thus, advocates reduced arguments against the ordinance to dismissive epithets: they were "anti-feminist" or "individualistic." Similarly, advocates oversimplified the character of pornography, suggestively referring only to rip and slash material in their discussions rather than acknowledging the complex character of the pornographic genre. Like the style of their rhetoric, the content of their arguments was stirring; it was arousing. But like the ideology of gender, which rigidly divides the world into two sexes, the campaign argument was premised on an assumption that its listeners were divisible into only two camps — those who were pro-woman, and, therefore, pro-ordinance, and those who weren't.

I believe a less dichotomized approach to the problem of the oppression of women by sex would have been more likely to change the way we think and act about sex. By falsely simplifying the content of the pornography genre, the advocates overlooked the way in which some works within the genre already thematically challenge the subordination of women by sex. Not all pornography is simply about women being fucked. There are some pornographic works in which women fuck, for example; some works in which the objectification of the ejaculating penis is not repeatedly depicted and valorized; and many works in which the subjectivity of a female character is a dominant and successful thematic concern. These works do not depict what the ordinance advocates suggested pornography "is."

The ordinance advocates falsely simplified user responses to pornography, assuming in most of their arguments that pornography users mechanistically identify with same-sex characters and mechanistically seek to reproduce pornography scenes in their own lives. This singular reaction does not characterize reader responses to non-pornographic literature or viewer responses to non-pornographic films. Although many individuals may use pornography for sex instruction, it also seems likely that others use pornography as an implement of fantasy, seeking through their reading or viewing to escape lives characterized by chastity, by routinized sex, or by genderized sex. They may also use pornography to transform their lives by a more complicated reaction than simple imitation.

Users would not be interested in or sexually aroused by many forms of pornography if they reacted only by identifying with same-sex characters. Works like sexually explicit formula romances, for example, in which a woman is the principal sexual subject, would most likely be sexually arousing to a male user only if he identified with the female heroine, thereby relinquishing his sex-stereotyped desires to fuck and fantasizing himself instead as fuckee. Similarly, the appeal of lesbian and gay pornography seems to depend on more than mechanistic same-sex identification, in that users must select differences other than biological sex to identify with particular characters.

I hope I am not misunderstood here. I do not want to be understood as a pornography apologist, for I believe that the proliferation and character of the pornography genre is one of the most complicated cultural events of our time, an event whose meanings are still quite indeterminate.

I also do not want to be understood as anti-feminist. The polarization of the feminist legal community during the ordinance campaign was terrifying to me; I understand the instinct to condemn the opposition that caused such division among friends and colleagues. However, I believe the divisions the campaign produced among feminists constituted an important challenge to the polarization of the world by gender. The closing lesson I want to draw from the anti-pornography campaign about feminist organization is the observation that exploring, pursuing, and accepting differences among women and differences among sexual practices is necessary to challenge the oppression of women by sex. Only when sex means more than male or female, only when the word "woman" cannot be coherently understood, will oppression by sex be fatally undermined.

[19]

Post-Colonial Feminism and the Veil: Considering the Differences

Lama Abu-Odeh*

I. Introduction

Since the Iranian Revolution of 1979, the issue of the veil has been the topic of heated debate in Muslim countries; particularly in those countries that witnessed strong fundamentalist movements. Until then, adopting the veil had been the individual choice of Muslim women. The fact that the Islamicists who took power in Iran sanctioned the veil, and penalized those women who chose not to wear it, was a seductive, or alternatively a terrifying, reminder to women in other Muslim countries of what it might be like as a woman under Islamic rule. In countries such as Jordan, Algeria, and Egypt, where fundamentalist movements have mobilized many followers, including large numbers of women who have adopted the veil to signify their initiation into the movement, the question of the legal sanction of the veil has aroused intense reactions from supporters and opponents alike.

In this paper I will try to explore the question of the veil from the complicated perspective of an Arab feminist; one who rejects the veil as a personal choice, but also recognizes its empowering and seductive effect on Arab women. My discussion will be limited to the veil as it plays itself out in an Arab context, since this is what I am most familiar with. The analysis might, or might not, be true in other non-Arab, Muslim countries. Also, my "analysis" will be more of a personal journey of exploration and reflection than a traditional academic or scientific one.

For the purposes of this paper I shall use the term "veil" to mean the current dress adopted by Muslim women in the Arab world, as followers of contemporary fundamentalist movements. In its most common form, the veil entails covering the woman's hair with a scarf that is ordinarily white, leaving the face exposed. All of the body is usually covered with a loose dress of dark colors with buttons from top to bottom. Women typically wear western clothes beneath this dress which they take off, along with the scarf, when they are in the sole company of women. These women do not usually cover their hands with gloves, nor do they wear makeup.

---

* Candidate for S.J.D. at Harvard Law School.

II. From Non-Veil to Veil

In order to make sense of the veil as a social phenomenon, one needs to inspect other types of women's dress that are distinguishable from the veil. This I will do by noting the historical transition that these women have made in their manner of dress, from non-veil to veil.

I would like first, however, to locate the women who adopt the veil in terms of class. This will be rather difficult due to the complexity of class structure in post-colonial societies. In general, these women tend to belong to the urban lower and middle classes. Professionally, they are civil servants, school teachers, secretaries in private enterprise, bank employees, nurses, and university students. They are usually young, in their twenties and early thirties.

In the seventies, these women walked the streets of Arab cities wearing western attire: skirts and dresses below the knee, high heels, and sleeves that covered the upper arm in the summer. Their hair was usually exposed and they wore make-up. These women differed from their mothers, who dressed similarly, in that they were more fashion conscious, more liberal in the coloring of their clothing and more generous in the application of their make-up. Their mothers usually covered their hair with a scarf when they were in public, but in a liberal rather than a rigid way (a good proportion of their hair showed underneath the scarf, in contrast to the scarf of the fundamentalist dress which shows nothing).

If one were to freeze that "moment" in the seventies, in an attempt to understand these women's relationship to their bodies, one would find it multi-layered and highly complex. In a way, their bodies seemed to be a battlefield where the cultural struggles of post-colonial societies were waged. On the one hand, the western attire which covered their bodies carried with it the "capitalist" construction of the female body: one that is sexualized, objectified, thingified, and so on. However, because capitalism never really won the day in post-colonial societies, but managed to cohabit successfully with pre-capitalist social formations (traditionalism), these women's bodies were also simultaneously constructed "traditionally": "chattelized," "propertized," and terrorized as trustees of family (sexual) honor. The cohabitation within the female body of this double construction (the capitalist and the traditional) was experienced by these women as highly conflictual. The former seemed to push them to be seductive, sexy and sexual, the latter to be prudish, conservative and asexual. Whereas the former was supported by the attraction of the market (consumption of western commodities), the latter was supported by the threat of violence (the woman is severely punished, frequently by death, if she risks the family sexual honor).

It is not unusual to find the length of a girl's dress the object of family debate:

Father/Brother: "That dress is too short. No respectable girl would wear it. Ask your daughter (addressing the mother) to take it off."
Mother: "Come on, let her be. Girls these days wear things like that."
Brother: "Let her take it off. My friends follow girls on the streets who wear dresses that short. I won't have my sister going around dressed like that!"
Girl: "But it's so pretty. All my friends wear dresses this short."
Father/Brother: "Maybe they do, but I won't have my daughter/sister walk in the streets with a dress like that. [The girl takes it off.]

Not infrequently, Arabic newspapers carry a story structured along the following lines: *S.M. stabbed his sister K. in a coffee shop across from the university campus. The police are investigating the crime.* A possible scenario for the crime: the woman, a university student belonging to the middle or lower classes, is having coffee with a colleague. Somebody "tips" her brother that she is involved in sexual relations with this man. Provoked by his sister's friendly public behavior with another man, and shamed by other people's thinking that this public behavior has in fact led to illicit sexual contact between them, the brother kills his sister in defense of the family's sexual honor. The time between the "tip" and the actual murder is usually very brief. More concerned with the public perception than with the actual facts, the brother rushes to protect the family honor, promptly and unequivocally. After trial, the brother may be imprisoned for only one year. There is an extenuating circumstance: he has committed a "crime of honor," sanctioned in most Arab penal codes.

The above two stories are points on a continuum. The way the girl dresses and how she behaves have heavy sexual significance. She is continuously subject to the test of "honor" and reputation, which she never really passes. Her sense of disempowerment stems from the terror exercised over her body, death being its infrequent extreme.

The ambivalence that these women felt about their bodies in the seventies was resolved by adopting the Islamic fundamentalist dress in the eighties. The length of a woman's dress was no more the subject of family debate; nor would she be caught having coffee with a colleague in public, thereby risking her own death. Rather than being engaged in keeping the impossible balance of the "attractive prude" or the "seductive asexual," these women chose to "complete" the covering of their bodies, and "consummate" their separation from men. I deliberately use the words "complete" and "consummate" because the veil was only the concealment of an already ambivalently covered body, rather than a radical transition from "revealment" to "concealment." Likewise, segregation by means of the veil was only the completion of an already ambivalent separation between the sexes.

III. The Veil as Empowerment

I earlier identified the women who have adopted the veil as mostly young, working women or students. An important part of their daily life involves walking on the streets and using public transportation to go to work, school, or the university. Public exposure of this kind has never been comfortable for non-veiled women in Arab cities. Unfailingly subject to attention on the streets and on buses by virtue of being women, they are stared at, whistled at, rubbed against, and pinched. Comments by men such as, "What nice breasts you have," or "How beautiful you are," are frequent. Comments may be more subtle in tone, such as, "What a blessed day this is that I have seen you." Ordinarily, women avoid any kind of direct verbal exchange with men when they are so approached. They either give the man a look of disapproval, or simply look ahead, dismayed, and continue on their way. Whatever their reaction, they are always acutely conscious of being looked at.

Exceptionally, a woman might engage in a verbal exchange with the man; where he is insistent in his approaches, continuing to rub his thigh against hers on the bus, despite her attempts at keeping a distance from him. She might retort angrily, "Keep away from me, you pig; don't you have any sisters of your own?" A dramatic public scene usually ensues, whereby the man may jump to his self-defense, denying the allegation. The older men on the bus may condemn such behavior as "unworthy of man who has sisters, and a sign of the corruption of youth these days." The passengers might also chide the woman for failing to dress properly, implying that if she had, such harassment might not have occurred. The bus driver might even gallantly ask the man to leave the bus.

A woman's willingness to raise objections to such male intrusions is notably different when she is veiled. Her sense of the "untouchability" of her body is usually very strong, in contrast to the woman who is not veiled. Whereas the latter would swallow the intrusions as inevitable and part of her daily life, trying to bypass them through any subtle ways she can muster (by looking at the man angrily and moving away from him). The veiled woman, on the other hand, is more likely to confront the man with self-righteousness: "Have you no fear of Allah treating his believers in such shameless fashion?" Public reaction is usually more sympathetic to her as well. The men on the bus may make comments such as, "Muslim women should not be treated like that. Young men should pray more and read the Quran." It is also true that veiled women's exposure to male intrusions in the first place is considerably less than the others.

The importance of these daily experiences and their "existential" effect on women, both veiled and non-veiled, is best understood when put in the context of Arab women's relationship with their bodies. Public sexual harassment seems to reinforce the non-veiled woman's ambivalence about her body, making her powerless in the face of unwelcome intrusions. The problem does not seem to exist for veiled women, since adopting the veil was meant to shield them from such sexual approaches; when such approaches are actually made, they are looked upon as being simply outrageous, both by the veiled women themselves and the public.

IV. The Veil as Disempowerment

As I wrote down the title of this section, I thought that there are, surely, a hundred million ways in which the veil is disempowering to women. But as I searched in my mind for such examples, I discovered that those instances of disempowerment of which I was thinking reflected my own normative assumptions of how the world should be. In other words, they reflected my position as a feminist. Paradoxically enough, and as feminist as I am, instances of the disempowerment of the veil did not present themselves to me as self-evident. While it was obvious to me that the veil remedied the situation of sexual harassment on the street by discouraging men from invading veiled women's space and by empowering the women to raise objections when such invasions took place, it wasn't equally obvious to me that the veil actually weakened women and disabled them from confronting an uncomfortable daily experience.

Even when I activated my own normative assumptions about how the world should be, instances of disempowerment did not become any more self-evident. For instance, my normative assumptions, as an Arab feminist, are based on the premise that Arab women should be able to express themselves sexually, so that they can love, play, tease, flirt and excite. In a social context, such as the one in the Arab world where women can incur violent sanctions for expressing themselves sexually, such acts carry important normative weight to me as a feminist. In them, I see acts of subversion and liberation.

But loving, teasing, flirting, and seducing was not the way these women normatively saw their sexuality. If in all these acts I saw pleasure and joy, they saw only evil. For them, a society in which men and women interact sexually was undoubtedly corrupt. They therefore experience the veil as normatively necessary. Precisely because women should not go around seducing men, they should be veiled. The disempowerment of the veil that I reflected on seemed to express my panicked feminist self, one that sees the veil as threatening to its normative world and sexuality.

In a conversation with a veiled fundamentalist woman in her late twenties, who is single, I ask:

I: "But don't you have sexual needs?"
She: "Sure I do."
I: "What do you do with them?"
She: "Sure I have sexual needs, but nothing that is absolutely over-

whelming and impossible to deal with. I occupy myself all the time. I read books. I love to read books on Islam. To be 'pure' as a single woman is my absolute priority. I do not let these things preoccupy my thinking. It is simply not an issue for me."

In my late twenties and single myself, that was nothing my confused post-colonial feminist self could identify with.

As I wrote the above paragraph about my own normative vision of sexuality, I was fearfully conscious of my father's reaction:

Father: "What is this you're writing? Women going around seducing and teasing??!!"

I: " . . . . "

Father: "Wipe it off. Do you want to shame me?? That's all I need!! My own daughter declaring to the world that she wants women to go around seducing and teasing! How can I show my face to the world??"

I: " . . . . "

Father: "So this is what you want?? This is what your feminism is all about?? Women going around whoring??"

I, desperately searching for words that might fit into his conceptual scheme and finding none, remain silent.

Unless I engaged in intellectual elitism and accused these women of false consciousness and of not knowing their own good, there was no way that I could point to instances of the disempowerment of the veil. What it all sounds like so far is a hopeless clash of normative visions.

V. Preaching to the Unconverted

What about those women who are unconverted, neither feminist nor veiled? Those whose bodies and sexuality have not been constructed by either the veil discourse or the feminist one? What about those whose "moment" in the seventies has lingered, whose ambivalence about their bodies has not been "resolved" by the adoption of the veil? What does a feminist, such as myself, have to offer them and how do I fare in comparison with those who preach the veil? How could what I have to offer them be empowering?

I find that my position, and those of other feminists, is not devoid of ambivalence. We obviously fare worse when it comes to empowering women on the streets. If our remedy for male domination is a long agenda of changing the laws, claiming our right to walk the streets without harassment, and raising consciousness about the "equality" of men and women, then what we have proposed is terribly unattractive. It is long-term (while the veil as a remedy is immediate), sounds hopelessly utopian, and demanding of women to engage in what sounds like a difficult and impossible personal/political struggle. But what is even more serious than all this, in contrast to the image of social respectability that the veil bestows on those who wear it (analogous to the respect afforded a woman dressed like a nun), we seem to offer women a discourse that will make them socially conspicuous, questionable, and suspect. For the ambivalent woman of the seventies, already dogged in her pursuit of a good reputation, what we offer her looks not only unattractive, but almost socially suicidal.

The situation is aggravated further by the fact that most Arab feminists are upper or middle class women, with material resources that enable them to avoid, to a great extent, uncomfortable experiences on the streets (most of them drive their own cars). They also invite instinctive hostility in lower class women by virtue of their class position.

Moreover, feminist discourse sounds quite foreign. It uses concepts such as "equality" and "freedom," which are on the one hand, indeterminate and could easily be appropriated ("equality between men and women means that men should be women's superiors because they are more qualified"), but on the other, they are concepts that need yet to become discourse in the post-colonial context. ("Why should women be free when men are not free either?") Liberalism, which post-colonial feminism seems to be based on, has yet to win the day in these societies.

Regrettably, for the feminist, the import-like quality of her discourse weakens her case even further. Seen as a western product, feminism does not have an obvious list of victories that the post-colonial feminist can lean on. Rape, pornography, and family disintegration in the west are flaunted in the face of such a feminist when she proceeds to preach her politics. Rather than being seen as a political response to these social phenomena, feminism is seen as its cause. It is because western women have become "emancipated" that they are on the streets to be raped, morally corrupt to be playmates, and selfish about their own lives to cause disintegration of the family. In a crude, superficial, partial, empirical way, that might be true. But before the post-colonial feminist steps in to explain the complexity of the situation in the west, she finds herself silenced by the immediate, simple, straightforward, almost magical, rhetoric of the veil. But even if she is allowed to speak, she suddenly finds herself in the uncomfortable position of "defending the west," an anomaly in itself in the post-colonial Muslim societies of the day.

VI. Solidarity with the Veiled

So far I have constructed the positions of the "veiled" and the feminist as being sharply contrasted. I had indicated earlier that they seem to me to represent a hopeless clash of normative visions. But let me step down a little bit and reshuffle the positions I have constructed. Who wants to talk about normative visions anyway? They often seem to lead nowhere. Perhaps the feminist path and the veiled one crisscross. Perhaps they do so to such an extent that they are no longer singularly identifiable as such. To show how they might possibly do that, we need to break them down and attack their coherence.

The coherence of the veiled position breaks down like this: the contemporary veil seeks to address, among other things, sexual harassment on the street. It seeks to protect women on their way to work and to school. Its female subjects are socially conspicuous *a priori*; they are not women who are staying locked indoors. It has come to remedy the uncomfortable daily lives of single, young women, who are leaving the house seeking work and education.

But the veil as rhetoric assumes that women should ideally be inconspicuous. They should be locked indoors, out of men's way so as not to seduce them. They should not go out to work, their rightful place is in the house as wives and mothers, not as wage workers.

The veiled position thus seems to be self-deconstructing. If it seriously pursues its normative vision by inviting women to stay at home, then it loses its attractiveness, and therefore its effectiveness, as a tool; for it was women's conspicuousness that prompted them to adopt the veil in the first place.

Even more paradoxically, fundamentalist idealogy, as the inspiration for the rhetoric of the veil, assumes that women should work only out of necessity, and only in professions that are considered feminine, such as teaching and nursing. Once in the workplace they should minimize their contact with men to the greatest extent possible. Whether during working hours or during break-time, individual women and individual men should not be left alone. Men are presumed to be the leaders in any context, both at work and at home.

Women who adopt the veil for its empowering effect on the street as they go to work, could find themselves seriously disempowered when the veil carries its "logic" to the workplace. Spatial and functional segregation between the sexes, as the fundamentalist ideology of the veil envisages for the workplace, could seriously affect the career prospects of veiled women. Since they live and work in a world where men are the decision makers, and where men are situated higher in the hierarchy of the workplace, minimizing contact between men and women could only result in further isolating women from the positions of power and decision making.

The ambivalence toward their position as veiled women seeking work could be effectively utilized by feminists. Seeing this as a golden opportunity for joining hands with veiled women, feminists can offer their politics as a remedy for the disempowerment veiled women experience at the workplace. Liberal feminist demands, such as equality in the distribution of responsibilities between men and women, equality of promotion opportunities between the sexes, day-care facilities for women, can be offered to these women as empowering political tools for them as wage workers. Such demands will undoubtedly resonate deeply in veiled women's experience at the workplace. Feminism could thus become the empowering politics for the veiled women at work.

The ironic side about all this for feminists, is that all of a sudden, they could find themselves joining hands with veiled women as "comrades" in political action. The coherence of the feminist position could thus become open to question. Post-colonial feminism will have to adjust itself to the fact that its empowered subject are veiled women, not female subjects engaged in a struggle for free and equal interaction with men in a free play of sexuality. In other words, feminist women and veiled women are now sisters.

VII. Veiled and Divided: The Battle Over the Body

I have so far talked about the veiled body as if it were monolithic. Although I believe that the rhetoric of the veil seeks to construct a monolithic female sexuality for its followers, I do not think that upon closer inspection, the community of the veiled reveals any such single construction. Veiled sexuality, it seems to me, reveals a multiplicity that is beyond the feminist's wildest expectations.

True, there are those who can be described as "ideology incarnate." Their relationship with their bodies replicates ideology so well that a shift in this construction looks almost hopeless. They are the leaders, the preachers, the passionate believers, the puritans. They are the ones whose public veiled self takes over, even when they are in the private quarters of women. Their bodies seem to adopt the daily rituals of the veil. They come to look, to the more color-loving, aesthetic eye, rather bland, insipid, and otherworldly. It is the body of the virtuous.

There are, however, those in the community of the veiled who are tentative and wavering. Once secure in the company of women, they reveal bodies that are more colorful, lively, and sexual. One is surprised at the shift their bodies make when they remove the veil. The bland face becomes colorful with creative make-up. The loose dress of the veil, once taken off, reveals fashionable clothing underneath, making more of an individual and personal statement than the collective, public one of the veil. Their sexuality appears to be more forthcoming, assertive, and joyful. Once together, their interaction with each other is not devoid of seductiveness and flirtation. Their private bodies are almost unrelated to their public ones.

There are also those whose private, more colorful bodies shyly, but daringly, push to become more public. They wear make-up with the veil. They are more creative and fashion-conscious in public, so that they constantly attempt to subvert the blandness of the veil. They invent a million ways to tie a colorful scarf on their heads, supplanting the more standard white. The loose dress of the veil suddenly becomes slightly tighter, more colorful, and daring in emulating western fashions, even if it doesn't explicitly reveal more parts of the female body. One also notices them on the streets conversing and strolling with men, subverting the segregation that the veil imposes on the sexes.

There are also those who wear the veil, but retain a fiercely ambivalent relationship with it; wearing it is a decision that is made almost everyday. It is not uncommon to find them wearing it some days and taking it off others. These women might say, "Wearing the veil, I find sometimes encourages me to binge on food since my whole body is covered in public, and I tend to lose touch with it. I feel I need to take it off sometimes. I need the public voyeur's gaze to control myself."

Some women use their bodies and dress as a statement of opposition. They differentiate themselves from others in their environment by wearing the veil, using it as a statement on female subordination in the non-fundamentalist (pseudo-secular, pseudo-religious) Arab households in which they find themselves. Wearing the veil allows them to have a singular and individual voice: "You are all not wearing the veil, but I *am*. I am powerful enough to do it, and this is how I carve myself a space you cannot reach. I disapprove of what you are, who you are, and what you think."

Of course, a veiled woman is not necessarily either "this" or "that." She might shift from one position to another. At times colorful, other times bland, seductive and prudish, publicly and privately. A veiled woman's subjectivity appears to be much more complicated than any meaning the word "veil" could possible convey.

For the feminist, the multiplicity of veiled sexuality could be very exciting, promising rich interaction and dialogue with veiled women. Her position, accordingly, could become more nuanced and multiple. Instead of dismissing them as the enemy, the threat, the falsely conscious, she could see them as the varied, divided, seemingly united, female community trying to survive in an environment that is as hostile to them as it is to her. It is this multiplicity that invites conversation between the "same," rather than the apartness of the "other."

VIII. The Feminist Resituates Herself

In this section, I shall refer to the "rhetoric of the veil"; that is, the fundamentalist construction of the veil as it is circulated ideologically. A woman who decides to wear the veil is usually subjected to a certain ideological indoctrination (by a fundamentalist preacher), in which she is told that every Muslim woman needs to cover her body so as not to seduce men, and that in doing this she obeys the word of Allah. Otherwise, she will face Allah's wrath in the day of judgment. (I have already briefly referred to this in the section entitled "Solidarity with the Veiled.") It is in relation to, and at the same time by means of, this "official" rhetoric that the different women I have just described construct their position of ambivalence or subversion.

In my construction so far, I have largely ignored the question of power. What I mean by power in this context is that which attaches to a particular discourse as the only possible representation of "reality."

This is a particularly important issue for the post-colonial feminist who is interested in understanding, and possibly impacting, the female community of the veiled. The excitement over the multiplicity and richness of such a community for the post-colonial feminist might be immediately dampened by the ideological power of the veil over that community. This will still be the case, despite the variety and richness of veiled women's lives that could be read as subverting the rhetoric of the veil.

It is interesting to note that since the veiled women of the contemporary fundamentalist movements have adopted the veil as a political act (they were not born into it), the rhetoric of the veil has a strong hold over them, because it provides the rationale for their act. In articulating their lives and their relationship with their bodies, they can only engage in such rhetoric. This seems to have the effect, at the end of the day, of reifying the "reality" of their daily lives, by disabling them from seeing the subversions and variations that exist or could exist to disrupt the ideology of the veil.

This seriously complicates the task of the feminist. In order to have a hearing with these women, she needs to "hook up" with their conceptual system (rhetoric). However, she needs to do this in a way that subverts and allows conceptual openings in it through which veiled women can start to see their lives differently. This is a slippery road since she will always risk being overwhelmed by the "logic" of the rhetoric, thereby being rendered ineffective and disabled by it. She will also find herself in the uncomfortable position of having to say things that she "doesn't really mean" in order to have a hearing in the first place. Conscious of having to keep the balance of being both inside and outside the system, the feminist risks being pushed to one side or the other.

> *Feminist*: "I like the way you wear your scarf. It's creative and most unusual."
> *Veiled Woman*: "Thank you. I get bored with the way I look if I wear it the same way everyday."
> *Feminist*: "I thought the whole point was to wear it the same everyday so that you don't attract attention to your body."
> *Veiled Woman*: "It's just that I think people need to look beautiful to others. That doesn't mean they have to seduce them. Allah is beautiful and He likes beauty."
> *Feminist*: "I agree with you. I think women can look beautiful without having to appear as if they are out to seduce men. I believe that women can look both proper and beautiful. In my opinion, you can do that either wearing the veil or even western clothes. I, personally, feel more comfortable wearing the latter. The veil appears to me rather exaggerated."
> *Veiled Woman*: "Except that Allah commanded us to wear the veil. But I've always believed that the important thing is how we feel inside. The important thing is that we feel pure inside, no matter what we wear, whether it is western clothes or the veil."

[20]

ARTICLES

RACISM AND PATRIARCHY IN THE MEANING OF MOTHERHOOD

DOROTHY E. ROBERTS*

I. INTRODUCTION

It is now commonplace for feminist scholars to acknowledge the differences among women.[1] This is a critical observation that is transforming feminist thought. The racial critique of gender essentialism in feminist theory[2] has inspired the ongoing reconstruction of a feminist jurisprudence that includes the historical, economic,

---

* Associate Professor, Rutgers University School of Law-Newark. B.A. 1977, Yale College; J.D. 1980, Harvard Law School. I presented my preliminary thoughts on the subject of this article at Martha Fineman's seminar on Reproductive Issues at Columbia University School of Law. I am grateful to the students for their discussion and Professor Fineman for her generous encouragement. I presented drafts of this article at the Symposium, "Discovering Our Connections: Race and Gender in Theory and Practice of the Law," sponsored by *The American University Journal of Gender & the Law*, and at the Feminism and Legal Theory Project's Workshop on Motherhood at Columbia University School of Law. I benefitted from the comments of participants, particularly Nancy Erickson, Linda McClain, Barbara Omolade, and Ann Shalleck. Kim Taylor provided valuable research assistance.

1. *See, e.g.*, Patricia A. Cain, *Feminist Jurisprudence: Grounding the Theories*, 4 BERKELEY WOMEN'S L.J. 191, 204-05 (1990) (advocating that good feminist thought ought to reflect differences in women's realities).

2. *See, e.g.*, Kimberle Crenshaw, *Demarginalizing the Intersection of Race and Sex: A Black Feminist Critique of Antidiscrimination Doctrine, Feminist Theory and Antiracist Politics*, 1989 U. CHI. LEGAL F. 139, 152-60 (providing examples of how "theory emanating from a white context obscures the multidimensionality of Black women's lives"); Angela P. Harris, *Race and Essentialism in Feminist Legal Theory*, 42 STAN. L. REV. 581, 585 (1990) (demanding that feminist legal theory must account for race differences); Marlee Kline, *Race, Racism, and Feminist Legal Theory*, 12 HARV. WOMEN'S L.J. 115, 124-44 (1989) (examining three critiques, written by women of color, that analyze race essentialism in feminist legal scholarship); *see also* ELIZABETH V. SPELMAN, INESSENTIAL WOMAN: PROBLEMS OF EXCLUSION IN FEMINIST THOUGHT (1988) (arguing that the feminist analysis of gender must include other aspects of identity, such as race and class).

Angela Harris defines gender essentialism as "the notion that a unitary, 'essential' women's experience can be isolated and described independently of race, class, sexual orientation, and other realities of experience." Harris, *supra*, at 585. To claim the existence of a universal "monolithic . . . woman's voice" is in fact to claim that the voice of white, heterosexual, socioeconomically privileged women can speak for all other women. Harris, *supra* at 588.

and social diversity of women's experiences.[3]

This article starts with the presumption that women experience gender in different ways. For example, Black women experience various forms of oppression simultaneously, as a complex interaction of race, gender, and class that is more than the sum of its parts.[4] By focusing on gender as the primary locus of oppression, mainstream feminist legal thought often forces women of color to fragment their experience in a way that does not reflect the reality of their lives.[5] The recognition of women's differences, however, does not negate the fundamental premise of feminism that women are oppressed "as women."[6] It is still, therefore, useful to make patri-

---

3. *See, e.g.*, Cain, *supra* note 1, at 204-05 ("Good feminist thought ought to reflect the real differences in women's realities, in our lived experiences. These include differences of race, class, age, physical ability and sexual preference." (citation omitted)); *see also* AUDRE LORDE, *Age, Race, Class, and Sex: Women Redefining Difference*, in SISTER OUTSIDER 114, 122 (1984) ("Now we must recognize differences among women who are our equals, neither inferior nor superior, and devise ways to use each others' difference to enrich our visions and our joint struggles.").

4. *See* Paulette M. Caldwell, *A Hairpiece: Perspectives on the Intersection of Race and Gender*, 1991 DUKE L.J. 365 (explaining that race and gender interact to form a unique oppression for Black women); BELL HOOKS, AIN'T I A WOMAN: BLACK WOMEN AND FEMINISM 12 (1981) (revealing the failure of the mainstream women's movement to include the Black female experience); Harris, *supra* note 2, at 604 (arguing that Black women, unlike white women, cannot isolate their race from their gender); Judy Scales-Trent, *Black Women and the Constitution: Finding Our Place, Asserting Our Rights*, 24 HARV. C.R.-C.L. L. REV. 9 (1989) (analyzing the unique oppressions experienced by Black women).

5. *See* Harris, *supra* note 2, at 588 ("The result of essentialism is to reduce the lives of people who experience multiple forms of oppression to addition problems: 'racism + sexism = straight black women's experience.' "); *see also* Kline, *supra* note 2, at 135-38 (criticizing Catharine A. MacKinnon's oversimplification of the sites of women's oppression by reducing them to a single, gender-related cause).

"Adding on" race and class to the identities of Black women not only implies that there is a universal, essential gender identity common to all women, but also that white middle-class women have no racial and class identity. SPELMAN, *supra* note 2, at 166-67.

6. *See generally* CATHARINE A. MACKINNON, FEMINISM UNMODIFIED 32-39 (1987) (theorizing that women are oppressed because of their differences as women); Catharine A. MacKinnon, *Feminism, Marxism, Method, and the State: Toward Feminist Jurisprudence*, 8 SIGNS 635 (1983) (analyzing feminism as a theory of power). Professor MacKinnon explains that women's subordination by men forms a system of power relations that is not undercut by women's diversity:

> To speak of being treated "as a woman" is to make an empirical statement about reality, to describe the realities of women's situation. In this country, which parallels other cultures, women's situation combines unequal pay with allocation to disrespected work, sexual targeting for rape, domestic battering, sexual abuse as children, and systemic sexual harassment; depersonalization, demeaned physical characteristics, use in denigrating entertainment, deprivation of reproductive control, and forced prostitution. To see these practices are done by men to women is to see these abuses as forming a system, a hierarchy of inequality.

Catharine A. MacKinnon, *From Practice to Theory, or What is a White Woman Anyway?*, 4 YALE J.L. & FEMINISM 13, 15 (1991). In other words, the practices Professor MacKinnon describes characterize the condition of women as a group, although women experience these practices in diverse ways that depend on their race, class, sexual orientation, and other aspects of their identity and social position.

We must be careful not to confuse this understanding of gender as a political system with the belief that women share a common, essential identity "as women," that can be isolated

archy a focus of feminist inquiry and opposition.[7]

How, then, do we understand our condition as women and work towards our liberation? Recent feminist scholarship has established that racism makes women different, even though women are all subject to patriarchy. What I wish to examine is the relationship between racism and patriarchy.

Racism and patriarchy are not two separate institutions that intersect only in the lives of Black women. They are two interrelated, mutually supporting systems of domination and their relationship is essential to understanding the subordination of all women. Racism makes the experience of sexism different for Black women and white women. But it is not enough to note that Black women suffer from both racism and sexism, although this is true. Racism is patriarchal. Patriarchy is racist. We will not destroy one institution without destroying the other. I believe it is the recognition of that connection — along with the recognition of difference among women — that is truly revolutionary.

This article explores how racism and patriarchy interact in the social construction of motherhood. Motherhood, like sexuality, plays a critical role in women's subordination by men.[8] As Nancy Chodorow notes, "Women's mothering is a central and defining feature of the social organization of gender and is implicated in the

---

from other elements of their identity. *See* SPELMAN, *supra* note 2, at 13 ("[T]he phrase "as a woman "is the Trojan horse of feminist ethnocentrism."). On the other hand, we must avoid "a simplistic anti-essentialism that deconstructs subordinated group identity until subordination no longer seems to exist." Mari J. Matsuda, *Pragmatism Modified and the False Consciousness Problem*, 63 S. CAL. L. REV. 1763, 1774 (1990).

7. Adrienne Rich defines patriarchy as follows:

> Patriarchy is the power of the fathers: a familial-social, ideological, political system in which men — by force, direct pressure, or through ritual, law, and language, customs, etiquette, education, and the division of labor, determine what part women shall or shall not play, and in which the female is everywhere subsumed under the male.

ADRIENNE RICH, OF WOMAN BORN: MOTHERHOOD AS EXPERIENCE AND INSTITUTION 57 (1976). *See* GERDA LERNER, THE CREATION OF PATRIARCHY 239 (1986) (defining patriarchy as "the manifestation and institutionalization of male dominance over women and children in the family and the extension of male dominance over women in society in general."). Both Adrienne Rich and Gerda Lerner note that patriarchy does not imply that women are totally without power.

Patriarchy's ideology, if not its power, is not strictly the domain of white men. As bell hooks explains, "The black male quest for his 'manhood' in American society is rooted in his internalization of the myth that simply having been born male, he has an inherent right to power and privilege." HOOKS, *supra* note 4, at 100. Of course, the Black male's relationship to patriarchy in America is very different from that of white men.

8. *See* CATHARINE A. MACKINNON, *Sex and Violence, in* FEMINISM UNMODIFIED 85, 86 (positing that society's definitions of "normal forms of sexuality" play a role in the subordination of women); *see generally* RICH, *supra* note 7, at 59 (describing how the institution of motherhood oppresses women and suggesting a vision of a liberated motherhood).

construction and reproduction of male dominance itself."[9]

Adrienne Rich distinguishes between the "experience of motherhood" — the relationship between a woman and her children — and "motherhood as enforced identity and as political institution."[10] An unwed Black teenager, for example, may experience motherhood as a rare source of self-affirmation, while society deems her motherhood to be illegitimate and deviant.[11] She may experience caring for her child as a determined struggle against harsh circumstances, while society sees in her mothering the pathological perpetuation of poverty.[12] Some women may experience mothering as debilitating and intrusive, even though patriarchal ideology defines it as woman's instinctive vocation.[13] Some women may experience fulfillment and happiness in mothering, even though feminist theory calls it oppressive.[14]

There are joys and sorrows that most mothers share: the pleasure of nursing her baby; the exhaustion from chasing after her toddler; the gratification of watching her child achieve whatever goal; the terror of unwanted pregnancy; and the despair of surrendering yet another dream in order to care for her child. There are also experiences mothers do not share, in part because of race. Most white mothers do not know the pain of raising Black children in a racist society. It is impossible to explain the depth of sorrow felt at the moment a mother realizes she birthed her precious brown baby into a society that regards her child as just another unwanted Black

---

9. NANCY CHODOROW, THE REPRODUCTION OF MOTHERING 9 (1978). For a critique of Nancy Chodorow's work for failing to account for race and class in the reproduction of mothering, see SPELMAN, *supra* note 2, at 80-113.

10. ADRIENNE RICH, *Motherhood in Bondage*, *in* ON LIES, SECRETS, AND SILENCE 195, 196-97 (1979). *See* Marie Ashe, *Law-Language of Maternity: Discourse Holding Nature in Contempt*, 22 NEW ENG. L. REV. 521, 545-53 (1988) (arguing that individual women experience pregnancy and childbirth very differently within the context of cultural constructs); Iris Marion Young, *Is Male Gender Identity the Cause of Male Domination?*, *in* MOTHERING: ESSAYS IN FEMINIST THEORY 129, 134 (Joyce Trebilcot ed., 1984) [hereinafter MOTHERING] (distinguishing gender differentiation, "a phenomenon of individual psychology and experience," from male domination, a set of "structural relations of genders and institutional forms that determine those structures"); Martha L. Fineman, *Challenging Law, Establishing Differences: The Future of Feminist Legal Scholarship*, 42 FLA. L. REV. 25, 38 (1990) (discussing how society's construction of motherhood influences individual women's experiences of mothering).

11. *See* Regina Austin, *Sapphire Bound!*, 1989 WIS. L. REV. 539, 558-61 (explaining that because of cultural differences Blacks and whites tend to view teenage pregnancy differently).

12. *See* Martha L. Fineman, *Images of Mothers in Poverty Discourses*, 1991 DUKE L.J. 274, 285-89 (discussing how contemporary poverty reform discourse casts single motherhood as pathological and as a primary explanation for poverty).

13. *See* Ashe, *supra* note 10, at 544-45 (indicating that for some women pregnancy is a confining experience); *see also* CHODOROW, *supra* note 9, at 21-22 (presenting the theory believed by some psychoanalysts "and assumed by many people that women have a mothering instinct, or maternal instinct, and that therefore it is 'natural' that they mother.").

14. *See* Ashe, *supra* note 10, at 545 (commenting that pregnancy and childbirth provide some women with strength and insight); *see also* Ashe, *supra* note 10, at 523 (noting that feminists often focus on motherhood as a locus for women's oppression).

charge. Black mothers must bear the incredible task of guarding their children's identity against innumerable messages that brand them as less than human.[15]

There are features of motherhood as a political institution that subordinate women because we are women: our status as childbearer determines our identity, we are assigned the enormous responsibility of childrearing, our work is unpaid and degraded, and to the extent our role as mother is valued, it is only when it "is attached to a legal father."[16] Adrienne Rich argues that motherhood in its present form denies women their potential as full human beings. She writes:

> Institutionalized motherhood demands of women maternal 'instinct' rather than intelligence, selflessness rather than self-realization, relation to others rather than the creation of self. Motherhood is 'sacred' so long as its offspring are 'legitimate' — that is, as long as the child bears the name of a father who legally controls the mother.[17]

Society's construction of mother, its image of what constitutes a good mother and a bad mother,[18] facilitates male control of all women. Women who fail to meet the ideal of motherhood (unwed mothers, unfit mothers, and women who do not become mothers) are stigmatized for violating the dominant norm and considered deviant or criminals.[19] Martha Fineman calls motherhood "[a] colonized [concept] . . . an event physically practiced and experienced by women, but occupied and defined, given content and value, by the

---

15. Patricia Williams mused about a lawsuit brought by a white woman against a clinic that negligently sold her a Black man's sperm.

> I ponder this case about the nightmare of giving birth to a black child who is tormented so that her mother gets to claim damages for emotional distress. I think about whether my mother shouldn't bring such a suit, both of us having endured at least the pain of my maturation in the racism of the Boston public school system. Do black mothers get to sue for such an outcome, or is it just white mothers?

PATRICIA J. WILLIAMS, THE ALCHEMY OF RACE AND RIGHTS 186-87 (1991). *See generally* Dorothy E. Roberts, *Punishing Drug Addicts Who Have Babies: Women of Color, Equity, and the Right of Privacy*, 104 HARV. L. REV. 1419, 1419-46 (pointing out that history's neglect of Black children casts doubt on the state's professed concern for the welfare of the Black fetus).

There are fears peculiar to mothers of other backgrounds, as well. For example, Audre Lorde wrote, "Some problems we share as women, some we do not. You fear your children will grow up to join patriarchy and testify against you, we fear our children will be dragged from a car and shot down in the street, and you will turn your backs upon the reasons they are dying." LORDE, *supra* note 3, at 119; *see also* Harris, *supra* note 2, at 593-94 (commenting on *Santa Clara Pueblo v. Martinez*, 436 U.S. 49 (1978), which involved a Native American mother who is faced with the knowledge that if she, unlike men, marries outside the Pueblo tribe her children will not be full tribal members and will be unable to vote or inherit her rights).

16. RICH, *supra* note 10, at 196-97.

17. RICH, *supra* note 7, at 42.

18. *See, e.g.*, Fineman, *supra* note 12, at 281-82 (stating that a mother's status as good or bad depends on whether or not she is single).

19. *See infra* notes 135-42 and accompanying text.

core concepts of patriarchal ideology."[20]

This is patriarchy's meaning of motherhood, one designed to serve the interests of men. The meaning of motherhood in America, however, is molded, on the basis of race as well as gender.[21] Patriarchy does not treat Black and white motherhood identically. In America, the image of the Black mother has always diverged from, and often contradicted, the image of the white mother.

There are several areas to be examined in the study of racism and patriarchy in the meaning of motherhood. This article is directed to the diverse community of feminist thinkers, as it concerns the construction of motherhood by those in power. The article also raises issues for discussion within the Black community, issues that Black feminist scholars are continuing to address, including: the meaning of motherhood within communities of color;[22] sexism by Black men;[23] and the need for Black women to confront our own differences and to develop solidarity among ourselves.[24] For example, Audre Lorde writes about Black women's need for one another: "There are two very different struggles involved here. One is the war against racism in white people, and the other is the need for Black women to confront and wade through the racist constructs underlying our deprivation of each other. And these battles are not at all the same."[25] My focus here on the dominant meaning of

---

20. Fineman, *supra* note 12, at 289-90.

21. *See* SPELMAN, *supra* note 2, at 80-113 (discussing the importance of race and class in the oppression of mothers).

22. *See, e.g.*, Austin, *supra* note 11, at 553 (arguing that condemnation of unwed mothers is not consistent across "race, sex, and class boundaries"). Professor Austin observes, for example, that "the culture of poor black teens assigns a positive value to being pregnant" and that young Black single mothers receive more tolerance and support from their female relatives and peers than from the rest of society. Austin, *supra* note 11, at 554, 566; *see also* JOYCE A. LADNER, TOMORROW'S TOMORROW: THE BLACK WOMAN 213-14 (1972) (arguing that there are no "illegitimate" children in low-income Black communities). Black mothers' self-definition is a critical aspect of the meaning of motherhood that influences both the dominant society's construction and the feminist reconstruction of mother. On the importance of self-definition for Black women, see PATRICIA HILL COLLINS, BLACK FEMINIST THOUGHT 91-113 (1991). *See also* Harris, *supra* note 2, at 613 (explaining that "society denies [Black] women their full selves" and they must therefore construct their own identity).

23. *See, e.g.*, Crenshaw, *supra* note 2, at 160-66 (addressing the Black community's failure to integrate an analysis of sexism into Black liberation politics); HOOKS, *supra* note 4, at 87-117 (discussing Black male belief in a patriarchal social order); LORDE, *supra* note 3, at 119-20 (discussing "womanhating as a recourse of the powerless" within Black communities).

24. *See, e.g.*, Regina Austin, *Black Women, Sisterhood, and the Difference/Deviance Divide*, 26 N. ENG. L. REV. 877, 879 (1992) ("In the name of 'black sisterhood,' . . . we might respond to female deviance with understanding, support, or praise based on the distinctive social, material, and political interests of black women."); AUDRE LORDE, *Eye to Eye: Black Women, Hatred, and Anger*, *in* SISTER OUTSIDER 145 (1984) (discussing feelings of indignation among Black women).

25. LORDE, *supra* note 24, at 164.

motherhood does not minimize the critical importance of Black and other mothers' self-definition.

This article explores the meaning of motherhood during various periods of American history, from slavery to contemporary poverty discourse. While a complete historical analysis is beyond the scope of this article, my review indicates that the social definition of mother changes along with other social developments. Likewise, the two systems of patriarchy and racism interact in different ways throughout history to produce diverse constructions of motherhood in particular times and places. This dynamic quality of subordination suggests that my inquiry will not produce a grand theory of the relationship between patriarchy and racism.[26] Rather, my inquiry seeks a better understanding of how racism and patriarchy shape the meaning of motherhood in particular contexts, the ways that women resist those meanings, and the implications for future action.

II. SLAVERY: THE FOUNDATION OF RACIST PATRIARCHY IN AMERICA

The intimate intertwining of race and gender in the very structure of slavery makes it practically impossible to speak of one without the other. The social order established by white slaveowners was founded on two inseparable ingredients: the dehumanization of Africans on the basis of race, and the control of women's sexuality and reproduction. The American legal order is rooted in this horrible combination of race and gender. America's first laws concerned the status of children born to slave mothers and fathered by white men: a 1662 Virginia statute made these children slaves.[27]

The experience of Black women during slavery provides the most brutal example of the denial of autonomy over reproduction. Female slaves were commercially valuable to their masters not only for their labor, but also for their ability to produce more slaves.[28] White masters, therefore, could increase their wealth by controlling their slaves' reproductive capacity — by rewarding pregnancy; punishing slavewomen who did not bear children; forcing them to

---

26. *Cf.* Fineman, *supra* note 10, at 25-30 (finding a middle-range feminist legal scholarship "between the extremes of 'grand theory,' which is totalizing in its scope and ambitions, and personal narratives, which begin and end with the presentation of one individual's unique experience").

27. Isabel Marcus, et. al., *Looking Toward the Future: Feminism and Reproductive Technologies*, 37 BUFF. L. REV. 203, 217-18 (1988-89). For a discussion of such laws in Virginia and Georgia, see A. LEON HIGGINBOTHAM JR., IN THE MATTER OF COLOR 42-45, 252 (1978) (reproducing the statutory language of both the Georgia and Virginia statutes which declared that all children born of a slave mother and white father shall be slaves).

28. ANGELA Y. DAVIS, WOMEN, RACE, & CLASS 7-8 (Vintage Books 1983) (1981); JACQUELINE JONES, LABOR OF LOVE, LABOR OF SORROW: BLACK WOMEN, WORK AND THE FAMILY FROM SLAVERY TO THE PRESENT 12 (1985).

breed; and raping them.[29] Racism created for white slaveowners the possibility of unrestrained reproductive control. As Henry Louis Gates, Jr. writes about the autobiography of a slave named Harriet A. Jacobs, it "charts in vivid detail precisely how the shape of her life and the choices she makes are defined by her reduction to a sexual object, an object to be raped, bred or abused."[30] The radical feminist model of motherhood, which is characterized by the patriarchal male's use of a woman's body for reproduction, is epitomized in slavery.[31] Slavery allowed the perfection of patriarchal motherhood. Patriarchy devised the most dehumanizing form of slavery.

Compulsory childbirth was a critical element of the oppression of both Black and white women of the time. A racist patriarchy required that both Black and white women bear children, although these women served different and complementary functions. Black women produced children who were legally Black to replenish the master's supply of slaves.[32] White women produced white children to continue the master's legacy.[33] The racial purity of white women's children was guaranteed by a violently enforced taboo against sexual relations between white women and Black men and by antimiscegenation laws that punished interracial marriages.[34] There was a critical difference in the white patriarch's relationship to these two classes of women. White men accorded some degree of respect

---

29. JONES, *supra* note 28, at 34-35; DOROTHY STERLING, WE ARE YOUR SISTERS: BLACK WOMEN IN THE NINETEENTH CENTURY 24-26 (1984); Catherine Clinton, *Caught in the Web of the Big House: Women and Slavery*, *in* THE WEB OF SOUTHERN SOCIAL RELATIONS 19, 23-28 (Walter J. Raser, Jr. et. al., eds., 1985). The rape of slavewomen by their masters was primarily a weapon of terror that reinforced white domination. DAVIS, *supra* note 28, at 23-24.

On slavewomen's resistance to outsiders' control of their reproductive lives, see DEBORAH WHITE, AR'N'T I A WOMAN? FEMALE SLAVES IN THE PLANTATION SOUTH 76-90 (1985) (analyzing slavewomen's resistance to white control of their activities in general); STERLING, *supra*, at 25-26, 58-61 (providing examples of slavewomen's efforts to keep control of their children).

30. Henry Louis Gates, Jr., *To Be Raped, Bred or Abused*, N.Y. TIMES BOOK REV., Nov. 22, 1987, at 12 (reviewing HARRIET JACOBS, INCIDENTS IN THE LIFE OF A SLAVE GIRL (J. Yellin ed., 1987)).

31. *See* Jeffner Allen, *Motherhood: The Annihilation of Women*, *in* MOTHERING, *supra* note 10, at 315, 317 (confirming that the patriarchy valued Black and white women for little else than their ability to produce children, whether the children were to become slaves or heirs).

32. *See* DAVIS, *supra* note 28, at 7 (stating that Black slavewomen were often viewed as breeders for white slaveholders).

33. *See* EUGENE D. GENOVESE, ROLL JORDAN ROLL: THE WORLD THE SLAVES MADE 414 (1976) (remarking that slaveholders were careful to ensure that wives had children only with their white husbands so the children were "all white" and could inherit the father's name).

34. *See* COLLINS, *supra* note 22, at 50 (providing examples of laws that punished interracial marriage); HIGGINBOTHAM, *supra* note 27, at 45 (describing penalties for white women having children with Black men); RICH, *supra* note 7, at 35 (mentioning some of the penalties for interracial marriages); *cf.* WILLIAMS, *supra* note 15, at 226 ("Is there not something unseemly, in our society, about the spectacle of a white woman mothering a black child?"). These roles for Black and white women are reflected in Black author, James Baldwin's remark to a white Southerner during a television debate: "You're not worried about me marrying *your* daughter. You're worried about me marrying your *wife's* daughter. I've been marrying your daughter ever since the days of slavery." GENOVESE, *supra* note 33, at 414.

and protection to white women, who were their wives, mothers, daughters, and sisters. White patriarchs, however, owed nothing to their female slaves, who were denied even the status of "woman."[35] Black mothers reproduced for white patriarchy, but gained nothing from it.

Paradoxically, the role of Black slavewomen — the quintessential servants of patriarchy — often contradicted the fundamental structure of patriarchy. First, the sexual relationship between female slaves and their white masters impugned the value that white women held under patriarchy as wives and mothers.[36] For example, some Southern white women cited in their divorce actions their husbands' "affection" for slavewomen as the cause for the dissolution of the marriage.[37] Some denounced slavery because of their anger and humiliation at their husbands' sexual exploitation of Black women.[38] Second, giving children born of the union between white masters and Black women the status of slaves violated the central tenet of patriarchy that the status of the child must follow his or her father.[39] Nonetheless, the slave's mother determined her child's

---

35. *See* ELIZABETH FOX-GENOVESE, WITHIN THE PLANTATION HOUSEHOLD 293 (1988) (asserting that only white women were allowed certain privileges which were denied to slavewomen); Barbara Omolade, *The Unbroken Circle: A Historical Study of Black Single Mothers and Their Families*, 3 WIS. WOMEN'S L.J. 239, 242-43 (1987) (illustrating that, because white women were valued as wives and mothers, a Black women's status as wife or mother could not be acknowledged by white society).

36. *See* ADRIENNE RICH, *Disloyal to Civilization: Feminism, Racism, Gynephobia*, *in* ON LIES, SECRETS, AND SILENCE 275, 295 (1979) (noting that, in the times of Southern slavery, many white women had feelings of jealousy towards the Black slavewomen their husbands raped).

37. *See* Clinton, *supra* note 29, at 29-30 (describing a divorce claim in which the wife used the fact that her husband raped a Black slavewoman as grounds for divorce); Martha Minow, *Forming Underneath Everything that Grows: Toward a History of Family Law*, 1985 WIS. L. REV. 819, 862 (establishing that the rape of a Black slavewoman was grounds for divorce).

38. HOOKS, *supra* note 4, at 28. One of the best known examples is Mary Boykin Chestnut, whose diary contains many passages condemning this aspect of slavery, such as the following:

> *[March 14, 1861]* . . . God forgive us, but ours is a monstruous system, a wrong and an iniquity! Like the patriarchs of old, our men live all in one house with their wives and their concubines; and the mulattoes one sees in every family partly resemble the white children.
>
> *[Aug. 22, 1861]* I hate slavery. You say there are no more fallen women on a plantation than in London, in proportion to numbers; but what do you say to this? A magnate who runs a hideous black harem with its consequences under the same roof with his lovely white wife and his beautiful and accomplished daughters?

GENOVESE, *supra* note 33, at 426-27; *see also* FOX-GENOVESE, *supra* note 35, at 339-71 (describing the life and writings of Mary Boykin Chestnut). Elizabeth Fox-Genovese argues that, although Mary Boykin Chestnut complained about certain aspects of slavery, she should not be considered a "feminist-abolitionist." Her diaries also reveal her deep racism, acceptance of slavery as a necessary part of her life, criticism of Harriet Beecher Stowe's abolitionist writings, and resentment that she was childless. FOX-GENOVESE, *supra* note 35, at 339-71.

39. *See* Omolade, *supra* note 35, at 244 (revealing the total hypocrisy of the patriarchy which in all cases, except when the child had a Black mother, dictated that the father determined the race of the child).

identity as slave or free, Black or white.[40] Thus, Frederick Douglass saw no hope for freedom in a biological tie to his master:

> The whisper that my master was my father, may or may not be true; and, true or false, it is of little consequence to my purpose whilst the fact remains in all its glaring odiousness, that slaveholders have ordained, and by law established, that the children of slave women shall in all cases follow the condition of their mothers . . . .[41]

Maintaining racial hierarchy required that the patriarchal blood line be broken, that white men deny their own sons' entitlement to patriarchal power.

III. THE VALUE OF MOTHERHOOD

Motherhood under patriarchy is compulsory.[42] Society exerts structural and ideological pressures upon women to become mothers.[43] Motherhood is women's major social role: all women are socially defined as mothers or potential mothers.[44] No woman achieves her full position in society until she gives birth to a child.[45] Pronatalism is so deeply imbedded in our consciences that even feminist reproductive freedom discourse usually centers on the timing of births and the social arrangements surrounding motherhood; it does not question the assumption that all women will eventually be mothers.[46] Historically, the sanctity of motherhood not only encouraged women to become mothers, but also relieved some of the pain women experienced from their exploitation under patriarchy.[47] Women's labor in the home was compensated by the ideological rewards of motherhood, rather than by economic remuneration or the

---

40. *See* HIGGINBOTHAM, *supra* note 27, at 43 (reprinting a 1662 statute which provided that the mother determined the race of the child).

41. FREDERICK DOUGLASS, NARRATIVE OF THE LIFE OF FREDERICK DOUGLASS: AN AMERICAN SLAVE 49 (Houston A. Baker, Jr. ed., 1982).

42. *See supra* text accompanying notes 9, 13.

43. *See* Fineman, *supra* note 12, at 276 (concluding that there are social and cultural forces that define the 'essential or idealized woman' as a mother). *But see* Fineman, *supra* note 12, at 274 (suggesting that social and cultural forces often discourage poor, unmarried women from motherhood).

44. *See* Martha E. Gimenez, *Feminism, Pronatalism and Motherhood*, *in* MOTHERING, *supra* note 10, at 287 (viewing motherhood as a dimension of a woman's normal adult role that is taken for granted).

45. Martha E. Gimenez, *Feminism, Pronatalism and Motherhood*, *in* MOTHERING, *supra* note 10, at 288.

46. Martha E. Gimenez, *Feminism, Pronatalism and Motherhood*, *in* MOTHERING, *supra* note 10, at 287, 290.

47. Martha E. Gimenez, *Feminism, Pronatalism and Motherhood*, *in* MOTHERING, *supra* note 10, at 304 (commenting on the low paid, undesirable roles for women in the industrialized capitalist system of the early and middle 1900s and arguing that motherhood was seen as preferable to working in a capitalist system that exploited women).

opportunity for self-determination.[48]

Compulsory motherhood under patriarchy is complicated by racism. Our society views childbearing by white women as desirable. For example, Ruth Colker tells the story of her law school classmate who decided to be sterilized.[49] The university physician refused to allow her to undergo the procedure unless she agreed to attend several sessions with a psychiatrist, presumably to dissuade her from her decision.[50] Professor Colker recognizes that the "physician's actions reflect the dominant social message — that a healthy (white) woman should want to bear a child."[51]

Procreation by Black mothers, on the other hand, is devalued and discouraged.[52] The devaluation of Black motherhood is a way of disregarding Black humanity. The value society places on individuals determines whether it sees them as entitled to perpetuate themselves in their children. Denying a woman the right to bear children deprives her of a basic part of her humanity. Patriarchy values women primarily for their procreative capacity: it accords value to white women for nurturing a more valuable fetus, but it denies to Black women even this modicum of value. Black women are deemed not even worthy of the dignity of childbearing. Discouraging Black procreation is also a means of subordinating the entire race; under patriarchy, it is accomplished through the regulation of Black women's fertility.[53]

A popular mythology about Black women, rooted in slavery, portrays them as less deserving of motherhood.[54] One of the most prevalent images of slavewomen was the character of Jezebel, a wo-

---

48. Thus, the voluntary motherhood advocates in the nineteenth century opposed birth control partly because they realized that motherhood was the only source of dignity for women of their time. *See* Linda Gordon, *Why Nineteenth-Century Feminists Did Not Support "Birth Control" and Twentieth-Century Feminists Do: Feminism, Reproduction, and the Family*, *in* RETHINKING THE FAMILY 40 (B. Thorne & M. Yalom eds., 1982) (explaining that the voluntary motherhood movement thought birth control would destroy the sanctity of marriage and harm women socially and economically); *see also* LINDA GORDON, WOMAN'S BODY, WOMAN'S RIGHT: A SOCIAL HISTORY OF BIRTH CONTROL IN AMERICA 111-15 (1976) (describing the voluntary motherhood movement's pro-motherhood ideology that accepted the Victorian mystification of the mother).

49. Ruth Colker, *Feminism, Theology, and Abortion: Toward Love, Compassion, and Wisdom*, 77 CAL. L. REV. 1011, 1067 n.196 (1989).

50. *Id.*

51. *Id.*

52. *See* Austin, *supra* note 11, at 549-58 (discussing negative stereotypes of unwed Black mothers in the media and judicial decisions); Roberts, *supra* note 15, at 1436-50 (describing society's devaluation of Black motherhood).

53. The disproportionate sterilization of Black women, for example, is reversed in the case of men. *See infra* text accompanying notes 70-74. In 1988, only 0.5 percent of Black men were contraceptively sterile, compared with 8.4 percent of white men. Felicia Halpert, *Birth Control for Him*, ESSENCE, Nov. 1990, at 20.

54. I developed parts of this discussion of the devaluation of Black motherhood more fully in Dorothy E. Roberts, *Punishing Drug Addicts Who Have Babies: Women of Color, Equality,*

man governed by her sexual desires.[55] The ideological construct of the licentious Jezebel legitimated white men's sexual abuse of Black women and defined Black women as the opposite of the ideal mother. Jezebel contradicted the prevailing image of the True Woman, who was virtuous, pure, and white. The myth of the sexually loose, impure Black woman was deliberately and systematically perpetuated after slavery ended, and persists in modern American culture.[56]

If the "bad" Black Jezebel represented the opposite of ideal motherhood, the asexual and maternal Black Mammy was the embodiment of the patriarchal ideal.[57] Mammy was both the perfect mother and the perfect slave: whites saw her as a "passive nurturer, a mother figure who gave all without expectation of return, who not only acknowledged her inferiority to whites but who loved them."[58] It is important to recognize, however, that Mammy did not reflect any virtue in Black motherhood. The ideology of Mammy placed no value in Black women as the mothers of their own children. Rather, patriarchy "claimed for the white family the ultimate devotion of black women, who reared the children of others as if they were their own."[59] Because of racism, Black mothers could not be moral authorities, as white mothers were, in relation to their own children.[60] Mammy, while she cared for the master's children, remained under the moral supervision of her white mistress.[61]

---

and the Right of Privacy, 104 HARV. L. REV. 1419, 1436-50 (1990). On Black mothers' tradition of rejecting these images and defining themselves, see COLLINS, *supra* note 22, at 115-137.

55. WHITE, *supra* note 29, at 28-29.

56. *See* HOOKS, *supra* note 4, at 65-67 (recounting examples in major American media which continue to portray negative stereotypes of Black women as bad tempered, mean, and unattractive); Barbara Omolade, *Black Women, Black Men and Tawana Brawley — The Shared Condition*, 12 HARV. WOMEN'S L.J. 12, 16 (1989) (presenting myths in the media about the rape of Black women).

57. For descriptions of the image of the Black Mammy, see Austin, *supra* note 11, at 570; HOOKS, *supra* note 4, at 84-85; GENOVESE, *supra* note 33, at 353-61 (describing the role of Mammies in antebellum plantation homes).

58. HOOKS, *supra* note 4, at 85. *See* GENOVESE, *supra* note 33, at 356 (stating that Mammy "gave the slaves a white-approved standard of black behavior"); WHITE, *supra* note 29, at 58 (describing Mammy as "the personification of the ideal slave, and the ideal woman . . . an ideal symbol of the patriarchal tradition").

59. FOX-GENOVESE, *supra* note 35, at 292; *see also* GENOVESE, *supra* note 33, at 361 (identifying Mammy's "tragedy" as her "inability to offer her individual power and beauty to black people"). Black mothers, in contrast, were pictured as irresponsible and unable to care properly for their own children. *See* Roberts, *supra* note 15, at 1441-42 (discussing the attribution by white census marshals of Black infant deaths to accidental suffocation by their mothers).

60. *See* Ann Ferguson, *On Conceiving Motherhood and Sexuality: A Feminist Materialist Approach*, *in* MOTHERING, *supra* note 10, at 153, 170-71 (arguing that racial stereotyping created a dichotomy where white women were viewed as good, virginal mothers, while Black women were perceived as evil and sexual and thus not as mothers with the authority to care for their own children).

61. Ann Ferguson, *On Conceiving Motherhood and Sexuality: A Feminist Materialist Approach*, *in* MOTHERING, *supra* note 10, at 171.

This ideological devaluation of Black motherhood has been manifested in many ways throughout American history. During slavery, Black women were systematically denied the rights of motherhood, including any legal claim to their children.[62] Slave masters owned both Black women and their children. Slave owners alienated slavewomen from their children through the sale of either mother or child to other slave owners and through the control of childrearing.[63] In *Beloved*, Toni Morrison recounts a slave mother's experience of separation from her loved ones:

> Anybody Baby Suggs knew, let alone loved, who hadn't run off or been hanged, got rented out, loaned out, bought up, brought back, stored up, mortgaged, won, stolen or seized . . . . What she called the nastiness of life was the shock she received upon learning that nobody stopped playing checkers just because the pieces included her children. Halle she was able to keep the longest. Twenty years. A lifetime. Given to her, no doubt, to make up for *hearing* that her two girls, neither of whom had their adult teeth, were sold and gone and she had not been able to wave goodbye.[64]

Patriarchy denied to Black mothers the authority and joy of mothering which it allowed white mothers. Once again, patriarchy was perfected in the treatment of slavewomen.

A contemporary example of the way in which Black motherhood is devalued is the welfare system's disproportionate denial of Black mothers' parental rights.[65] Malcolm X called foster care a system of legalized slavery.[66] He described the state's disruption of his own family in terms that mirrored white slavemasters' control of slave families:

> Soon the state people were making plans to take over all of my mothers' children . . . . A Judge . . . in Lansing had authority over me and all of my brothers and sisters. We were "state children," court wards; he had the full say-so over us. A white man in charge of a black man's children! Nothing but legal, modern slavery — however kindly intentioned . . . . I truly believe that if ever a state social agency destroyed a family, it destroyed ours.[67]

---

62. *See* Anita Allen, *Surrogacy, Slavery, and the Ownership of Life*, 13 HARV. J.L. & PUB. POL'Y 139, 140 n.9 (1990) (suggesting that the institution of slavery made Black mothers de facto surrogates for their masters and mistresses).

63. Id. at 140 n.9; Dorothy Burnham, *Children of the Slave Community in the United States*, 19 FREEDOMWAYS 75, 75-77 (1979). On slave mothers' resistance, see FOX-GENOVESE, *supra* note 35, at 322-24.

64. TONI MORRISON, BELOVED 23 (1987).

65. *See* Sylvia Sims Gray & Lynn M. Nybell, *Issues in African-American Family Preservation*, 69 CHILD WELFARE 513, 513 (1990) (noting that about one-half of the children in foster care are Black).

66. MALCOLM LITTLE, THE AUTOBIOGRAPHY OF MALCOLM X 21-22 (1965).

67. *Id.*

The state intervenes more often in Black homes in part because Black mothers are more likely to be supervised by social workers, because child welfare workers apply culturally-biased standards to Black families, and because the state is more willing to intrude upon the autonomy of Black mothers.[68] Government bureaucrats often mistake Black childrearing patterns as neglect when they diverge from the norm of the white nuclear family.[69]

One of the most extreme forms of devaluation of Black motherhood is the sterilization abuse of Black women.[70] The disproportionate sterilization of Black women enforces society's determination that we do not deserve to be mothers.[71] Black women experience sterilization abuse in the form of blatant coercion, trickery, and subtle influence on their decision to be sterilized.[72] It is performed by individual doctors who encourage Black women to be sterilized because they view Black women's family sizes as excessive and believe we are incapable of using contraceptives.[73] It is also accomplished through government policies that penalize wo-

---

68. *See* Carol B. Stack, *Cultural Perspectives on Child Welfare*, 12 N.Y.U. REV. L. & SOC. CHANGE 539, 541 (1983-84) (arguing that the misunderstanding of cultural family patterns contributes to a disproportionate number of minority children placed in foster homes); Michael S. Wald, *State Intervention on Behalf of "Neglected" Children: Standards for Removal of Children from Their Homes, Monitoring the Status of Children in Foster Care, and Termination of Parental Rights*, 28 STAN. L. REV. 623, 629 nn.21-22 (1976) (arguing that more minority parents are charged with neglect because they are disproportionately on welfare and thus subject to greater social work supervision); *cf.* Martha A. Fineman, *Intimacy Outside of the Natural Family: The Limits of Privacy*, 23 CONN. L. REV. 955, 959 (1991) (distinguishing between "private" families that earn the right to government protection by living up to ideological expectations, and "public" families that are subject to state supervision and control because they deviate from social norms).

69. For descriptions of "deviant" childrearing patterns in the Black community, such as extended kin networks, see ROBERT B. HILL, INFORMAL ADOPTION AMONG BLACK FAMILIES (1977); CAROL B. STACK, ALL OUR KIN: STRATEGIES FOR SURVIVAL IN A BLACK COMMUNITY 62-107 (1974).

70. *See generally* DAVIS, *supra* note 28, at 215-21 (documenting the sterilization abuse of women of color since the 1970s); Laurie Nsiah-Jefferson, *Reproductive Laws, Women of Color and Low-Income Women*, 11 WOMEN'S RTS. L. REP. 15, 30-32 (1989) (setting forth statistics demonstrating the disproportionate sterilization of minority women, particularly Black women, and the factors reflected in the statistics); Charlotte Rutherford, *Reproductive Freedoms and African American Women*, 4 YALE J.L. & FEMINISM 255, 273-75 (1992) (suggesting that historically Black women were more likely to use sterilization as a contraceptive method than were white women because they were subjected to coercion and other abusive tactics). In 1982, 24 percent of Black women were sterilized, compared to 15 percent of white women. *Id.* at 273.

71. Roberts, *supra* note 15, at 1442-43.

72. *See* Nsiah-Jefferson, *supra* note 70, at 30-31 (describing the medical community's targeting of poor Black women to undergo sterilization); Rosalind P. Petchesky, *Reproduction, Ethics, and Public Policy: The Federal Sterilization Regulations*, 9 HASTINGS CENTER REP. 29, 32 (1979) (defining sterilization abuse as the pressuring of an individual into sterilization, which may include: failing to acquire formal or written consent to sterilization, failing to explain the irreversability of the sterilization, failing to address other birth control alternatives to sterilization, threatening the loss of welfare or medical benefits if sterilization is refused, or the making of consent to sterilization necessary in order to receive an abortion).

73. Roberts, *supra* note 15, at 1443.

men on welfare for having babies, but make sterilization the only publicly-funded birth control method readily available to them.[74]

Currently, the image of the undeserving Black mother legitimizes the prosecution of poor Black women who use drugs during pregnancy.[75] Although prenatal substance abuse cuts across racial and socioeconomic lines, the vast majority of women charged with such crimes are poor and Black.[76] These women are more likely to be detected and reported to government agencies, in part because of the racist attitudes of health care professionals.[77] On a deeper level, it is their failure to meet society's image of the ideal mother that makes their prosecution more acceptable. The state does not punish poor crack addicts simply because they may harm their unborn children. Rather, they are punished for having babies because they are deemed unworthy of procreating.[78]

Angela Harris uses the example of beauty to demonstrate the qualitative difference between white and Black women's failure to meet patriarchal standards.[79] She observes that Black women's frustration at being unable to look like the "All-American" woman is not simply a more intense form of white women's frustration. This is because beauty is constructed according to race, as well as gender.[80] Thus, the despair felt by Pecola Breedlove, the character in Toni Morrison's *The Bluest Eye* who spends her childhood praying for blue eyes, is something other than the disappointment felt by a little white girl who despised her features.[81] Pecola Breedlove despairs "not because she's even further away from the ideal of beauty than white women are, but because Beauty [sic] *itself* is white, and she is not and can never be, despite the pair of blue eyes she eventually believes she has."[82]

Similarly, Black women can never attain the ideal image of motherhood, no matter how much we conform to middle-class convention, because ideal motherhood is white. The maternal standards created to confine women are not sex-based norms which Black wo-

---

74. Roberts, *supra* note 15, at 1443-44.
75. Roberts, *supra* note 15, at 1444.
76. Roberts, *supra* note 15, at 1432-36.
77. Roberts, *supra* note 15, at 1432-34.
78. Roberts, *supra* note 15, at 1472.
79. Harris, *supra* note 2, at 596-98.
80. *See* bell hooks, *Theory as Liberatory Practice*, 4 YALE J.L. & FEMINISM 1, 4 (1991) ("[G]ender is not the sole factor determining constructions of femaleness.").
81. TONI MORRISON, THE BLUEST EYE (1970).
82. Harris, *supra* note 2, at 597. *See* SPELMAN, *supra* note 2, at 123 ("An additive analysis treats the oppression of a Black woman in a society that is racist as well as sexist as if it were a further burden when, in fact, it is a different burden.").

men happen to fail. They are created out of raced, as well as gendered, components.

IV. MOTHERHOOD AND DOMESTICITY

During the nineteenth century, the ideology of separate spheres for men and women reinforced women's devotion to motherhood within the orbit of patriarchy. Under this construct, the husband sustained the family economically and represented the family in the public sphere; the wife cared for the private realm of the home.[83] The separate spheres ideology gave women a place, a role, and importance in the home, while preserving male dominance over women.[84] "The cult of domesticity" legitimized the confinement of women to the private sphere by defining women as naturally suited for motherhood and naturally unfit for public life.[85] Justice Bradley expressed this view of women in his notorious concurring opinion in *Bradwell v. Illinois*,[86] which upheld the exclusion of women from legal practice:

> The natural and proper timidity and delicacy which belongs to the female sex evidently unfits it for many of the occupations of civil life. The constitution of the family organization, which is founded in the divine ordinance, as well as in the nature of things, indicates the domestic sphere as that which properly belongs to the domain and functions of womanhood . . . . The paramount destiny and mission of woman [sic] is to fulfil [sic] the noble and benign offices of wife and mother. This is the law of the Creator.[87]

---

83. *See* Frances E. Olsen, *The Family and the Market: A Study of Ideology and Legal Reform*, 96 HARV. L. REV. 1497, 1498-1501 (1983) (suggesting that a dichotomy existed between ideas of market and family in the nineteenth century separate spheres ideology); Wendy W. Williams, *The Equality Crisis: Some Reflections on Culture, Courts, and Feminism*, 7 WOMEN'S RTS. L. REP. 175, 178 (1982) (focusing on the separate spheres ideology as reflected in Supreme Court jurisprudence). For a description of gender conventions in the antebellum South, see FOX-GENOVESE, *supra* note 35, at 192-241.

84. *See generally* Williams, *supra* note 83, at 178 (detailing the Supreme Court's longstanding endorsement of the separate spheres ideology). Martha Fineman contends that nineteenth century feminist domestic ideology had "unrealized radical potential to empower mothers within the family:" it "raised Mother as a powerful symbol;" it was the basis for the movement away from the father's absolute right to custody; and it recognized mothers' socially productive labor. Martha A. Fineman, *The Neutered Mother*, 46 U. MIAMI L. REV. 653, 657-58 (1992). This potential challenge to patriarchy, however, was incorporated into patriarchal ideology and family structure. *Id.* at 657.

85. For a critique of relational feminism as a resurgence of the ideology of domesticity, see Joan C. Williams, *Deconstructing Gender*, 87 MICH L. REV. 797 (1989). Professor Williams argues that relational feminists, such as Carol Gilligan, "reclaim the compliments of Victorian gender ideology while rejecting its insults." *Id.* at 807. She also demonstrates how many of the gender stereotypes derived from domesticity influenced the decision in EEOC v. Sears, Roebuck & Co., 628 F. Supp. 1264 (N.D. Ill. 1968), *aff'd*, 839 F.2d 302 (7th Cir. 1988), which denied women's claims of sex discrimination in commission sales positions. *Id.* at 813-21.

86. 83 U.S. 130 (1872).

87. *Id.* at 141-42 (Bradley, J., concurring). Similarly, Justice Brewer asserted in Muller v. Oregon, which upheld a law limiting the hours women were permitted to work for wages:

The gendered division of labor continues to be an aspect of women's subordination. The American wage labor system is structured as if workers have no child care responsibilities.[88] This assumption systematically disadvantages women since they are assigned the task of childrearing. Men have the privilege of performing as ideal workers (i.e., workers with no child care responsibilities) and consequently earn more money.[89] Although most mothers now engage in wage labor, they must limit their work commitments to accommodate their child-care duties. According to Joan Williams, this gender system leads mothers to marginalize themselves economically by failing to perform as ideal workers, in order to allow their husbands to perform that role and to ensure that their children receive high-quality care.[90]

Black women have historically defied the norm that defines motherhood in opposition to wage labor. The separate spheres ideology dissolved within slavery. While Victorian roles required white women to be nurturing mothers, housekeepers, and companions to their husbands, slavewomen's role required strenuous labor.[91]

Slavewomen's lives of hard physical labor shattered the myth that women were weaker than men and unfit for the public sphere. Thus, in 1851 Sojourner Truth could present to a women's rights convention in Akron, Ohio, a unique denunciation of male justifications for the disenfranchisement of women.[92] Unlike most of the

---

> That woman's physical structure and the performance of maternal functions place her at a disadvantage in the struggle for subsistence is obvious. This is especially true when the burden[s] of motherhood are upon her . . . [A]s healthy mothers are essential to vigorous offspring, the physical well-being of a woman becomes an object of public interest and care in order to preserve the strength and vigor of the race.

208 U.S. 412, 421 (1908).

88. Mary Joe Frug, *Securing Job Equality for Women: Labor Market Hostility to Working Mothers*, 59 B.U. L. REV. 55, 56-61 (1979); Williams, *supra* note 85 at 822; *cf.* Vicki Shultz, *Telling Stories About Women and Work: Judicial Interpretations of Sex Segregation in the Workplace in Title VII Cases Raising the Lack of Interest Argument*, 103 HARV. L. REV. 1750 (1990) (discussing how the structure of workplaces results in sex segregation).

89. Williams, *supra* note 85, at 823 (suggesting an analytical framework for the study of gender in the wage labor structure and how this structure relates to the "systematic impoverishment of women").

90. Williams, *supra* note 85, at 823-24.

91. *See* Roberts, *supra* note 15, at 1438 (quoting Angela Davis' observations about the way Black women were excluded from nineteenth century definitions of femininity).

While Black women performed the male task of working in the field, Black men were not assigned the female task of domestic service. Bell hooks argues that the dynamics of sexist and racist oppression during slavery really centered on the masculinization of the Black female, rather than the more commonly noted de-masculinization of the Black male. HOOKS, *supra* note 4, at 22.

On the sexual division of labor among slaves, see Jacqueline Jones, *"My Mother Was Much of a Woman:" Black Women, Work, and the Family Under Slavery*, 8 FEMINIST STUDIES 235 (1982).

92. DAVIS, *supra* note 28, at 60-61; HOOKS, *supra* note 4, at 159-60.

white women's rights advocates, she could point to her personal experience of field labor as proof that women could perform the same work as men:

> Dat man ober dar say dat women needs to be helped into carriages, and lifted ober ditches, and to have de best place every whar. Nobody eber help me into carriages, or ober mud puddles, or gives me any best place . . . and ar'n't I a woman? Look at me! Look at my arm! . . . . I have plowed, and planted, and gathered into barns, and no man could head me — and ar'n't I a woman? I could work as much and eat as much as a man (when I could get it), and bear de lash as well — and ar'n't I a woman? I have borne thirteen chilern and seen 'em mos' all sold off into slavery, and when I cried out with a mother's grief, none but Jesus heard — and ar'n't I a woman?[93]

Sojourner Truth not only attacked patriarchal images of women, she also challenged white feminists to relinquish their racial privilege.[94] As bell hooks notes, "White women saw black women as a direct threat to their social standing — for how could they be idealized as virtuous, goddess-like creatures if they associated with black women who were seen by the white public as licentious and immoral?"[95] In this way, the construction of an ideal mother that excluded Black women actually ensured white women's allegiance to an oppressive concept of their own womanhood. In order to embrace Ms. Truth's message, the white women present had to reject the racist assumption that because Black women were unworthy of the title "woman" their experiences had no bearing on true womanhood. (At an anti-slavery rally in Indiana, Sojourner Truth bared her breasts to prove that she was indeed a woman.)[96] The women present had to accept Ms. Truth as truly woman and to sacrifice their personal stake in the white ideal of womanhood.

After slavery, Black women continued to work in patterns that diverged drastically from those of white women. Black women joined the wage-earning labor force in proportions three or four times

---

93. OLIVE GILBERT, NARRATIVE OF SOJOURNER TRUTH: A BONDSWOMAN OF OLDEN TIME 134 (1878).

94. *See* Crenshaw, *supra* note 2, at 154 (reflecting on Sojouner Truth's relationship to the tension in feminist theory and politics caused by white feminists' reluctance to sacrifice racial privilege); *see also* DAVIS, *supra* note 28, at 62-64 (describing white women's opposition to allowing Truth to speak at a women's rights convention in Akron); HOOKS, *supra* note 4, at 159-60 (suggesting that the experiences of Black female slaves, as testament to the truth that women "could be the work-equals of men," advanced the white feminist movement's call for the recognition of women's equal rights).

95. HOOKS, *supra* note 4, at 131.

96. HOOKS, *supra* note 4, at 159.

higher than white women.[97] After the Civil War, Black women were encouraged by white politicians and entrepreneurs, as well as by the depressed wages of Black men, to earn a living outside the home.[98] In 1880, fifty percent of Black women were in the labor force, compared to only fifteen percent of white women.[99] The racial disparity among married women was even greater: in 1870 in the rural South, more than four out of ten Black married women had jobs, mostly as field laborers, while 98.4 percent of white wives were housekeepers.[100] In Southern cities, Black married women worked outside the home five times more often than white married women.[101]

The demands of Black women's labor within white homes undermined their own roles as mothers and homemakers.[102] Black domestics, of course, were unable to attend to their children during the day. They returned home late in the evening (if not on weekends) and had to entrust their children to the care of a neighbor, relative or older sibling, or leave them to wander in the neighborhood.[103] The preoccupation with the virtue of white women justi-

---

97. Ferguson, *supra* note 60, at 179 n.12 (setting forth percentages demonstrating that since the Civil War married and unmarried Black women entered the work force in significantly larger numbers than did their white counterparts).

98. Omolade, *supra* note 35, at 252 (stating that because women were a source of cheap labor, young Black girls were socialized to first become workers, then to become mothers and wives).

99. Omolade, *supra* note 35, at 252.

100. *See* JONES, *supra* note 28, at 63 (asserting that the disparity in the number of Black working wives, as opposed to white working wives, stemmed from Black families' heavy dependence on women's field work, which had its roots in the sexual division of labor under slavery).

101. JONES, *supra* note 28, at 113. White women of the nineteenth century, such as the "mill girls" who operated textile mills throughout New England, also confounded the myth of domesticity by working outside the home in significant, though fewer, numbers. *See* DAVIS, *supra* note 28, at 54 (describing the long hours and horrible working conditions endured by mill girls, who were recruited from local farm families under the guise that mill work was an attractive "prelude to married life"); Minow, *supra* note 37, at 869-74 (suggesting that mill girls sought to combine aspirations for economic independence and self-improvement with their inherited roles of daughter, wife, and mother). In addition, white women on Southern tenant farms helped out their male kin as unpaid laborers, often doing a "man's share" of cutting wheat or working tobacco. Dolores Janiewski, *Sisters Under Their Skins: Southern Working Women, 1880-1950*, *in* SEX, RACE, AND THE ROLE OF WOMEN IN THE SOUTH 14-16 (Joanne V. Hawks & Sheila L. Skemp eds., 1983). More affluent women resisted their relegation to the private sphere by engaging in public service activities that they perceived as an extension of their maternal roles. Minow, *supra* note 37, at 877-82; *see also* FOX-GENOVESE, *supra* note 35, at 335 (proposing that nineteenth century women's organizations accepted the separate spheres ideology and "drew upon the idea of women's special mission to justify action outside the home").

102. JONES, *supra* note 28, at 127.

103. *See* JONES, *supra* note 28, at 129 (detailing typical variations of Black domestic servants' daily routines with relation to their employers and their own children); *I Live a Treadmill Life*, *in* BLACK WOMEN IN WHITE AMERICA 227-28 (Gerda Lerner ed., 1973) (relaying an account of a Black woman who rarely sees her own children due to the long hours she spends working for a white family).

fied not only the persecution of Black men, but also the condemnation of "insolent" Black female servants.[104] Black women holding menial jobs were portrayed as unfeminine to justify subjecting them to working conditions that conflicted with the image of delicate womanhood:

> The image of Mammy, "Aunt Jemima," Beulah, and even the emasculating matriarch is that of an overweight, rotund female, devoid of the curves that are indicative of the more seductive examples of her sex. Outfitted in an unflattering dress, apron, and scarf (a "headrag"), she is always ready for work and never ready for bed.[105]

Women of color continue to do most of the domestic service in America, filling jobs such as maids, child care workers, nurse's aides, sewing machine operators, and food preparation workers.[106] In the early twentieth century, nearly two-thirds of all employed Black women in the North were domestic servants or laundresses.[107] It was not until 1970 that Black women were no longer employed primarily as domestic workers or farm laborers.[108] Nevertheless, these jobs remain segregated on the basis of both race and gender, and they pay the lowest wages.[109]

The experience of Black working mothers complicates the feminist response to domesticity in two ways. First, white feminists' view of work, as resistance to motherhood and a liberating force for women, does not account for Black women's experiences. This ideology often focuses on a romanticized middle-class quest for entrance into an elite work force, rather than on the women who have always been exploited as a source of cheap surplus labor.[110] Black women historically experienced work outside the home as an aspect of racial subordination and the family as a site of solace and resistance to

---

104. JONES, *supra* note 28, at 149.

105. Austin, *supra* note 24, at 883. Judith Rollins found in her research that the actual unattractiveness of domestics was due not only to the type of labor they performed but also to their awareness that "the female employer preferred the presence of another woman whose appearance, as well as other attributes, was inferior to her own." JUDITH ROLLINS, BETWEEN WOMEN: DOMESTICS AND THEIR EMPLOYERS 200 (1985).

106. *See* NATIONAL COMMITTEE ON PAY EQUITY: AN ISSUE OF RACE, ETHNICITY AND SEX 20-26 (1987) (setting forth statistical evidence demonstrating that Black women are concentrated in service-oriented occupations).

107. JONES, *supra* note 28, at 164.

108. Omolade, *supra* note 35, at 258-59 (describing the movement of Black women from the ranks of domestics and farm workers into the ranks of white collar, sales, and clerical workers as a manifestation of the changes brought about by the civil rights and women's movements, coupled with the economy's transformation from an industrial to a service employment base).

109. NATIONAL COMMITTEE ON PAY EQUITY, *supra* note 106, at 56-59. On racial segregation within the female labor force, see HOOKS, *supra* note 4, at 132-36; Janiewski, *supra* note 101, at 20-35.

110. HOOKS, *supra* note 4, at 146.

white oppression.[111] Black women's attention to domestic duties within their homes has defied the expectation of total service to whites.[112] Elizabeth Spelman has observed that the oppressive nature of the "housewife" role must be understood in relation to women's other roles, which are raced as well as gendered: "The work of mate/mother/nurturer has a different meaning depending on whether it is contrasted to work that has high social value and ensures economic independence or to labor that is forced, degrading, and unpaid."[113]

Second, Black mothers' work experience raises one way in which racial privilege has helped to maintain the gendered division of domestic work. The employment of Black women as domestic servants in white homes reproduced the mistress-houseslave relationship.[114] White mothers who could afford it reduced the burdens of childrearing by shifting their duties to Black maids.[115] Judith Rollins found in her study of domestics and the women who employ them that the increased participation of middle-class women in the workplace did not change their attitudes towards their role in the home. According to Judith Rollins:

---

111. *See* SPELMAN, *supra* note 2, at 123, 132 (noting that the mother/housewife role does not have the same meaning for Black and white women); Kline, *supra* note 2, at 128-31 (criticizing a feminist analysis of child custody law that neglects the experiences of Black and Native American women); *cf.* Collins, *supra* note 22, at 49 (suggesting that the public/private split for Black women is the line separating the Black community from whites rather than that separating their homes from the community).

112. *See* DAVIS, *supra* note 28, at 16-17 (stating that Black women "were not debased by their domestic functions in the way white women came to be;" rather, domestic life provided slavewomen with the only space where they could truly experience themselves as human beings); Jones, *supra* note 91, at 237 (arguing that for Black women, "full attention to the duties of motherhood deprived whites of their power over these women").

The emphasis in Black feminist scholarship on the benefits of domestic labor, on the other hand, has neglected the exploitative aspects of this work. *See* COLLINS, *supra* note 22, at 44 (suggesting that there is a need for further exploration of "families as contradictory locations that simultaneously confine yet allow Black women to develop cultures of resistance").

113. SPELMAN, *supra* note 2, at 123.

114. *See* DAVIS, *supra* note 28, at 90-91 (describing how Black women in the South worked as cooks, nursemaids, and, chambermaids, while white women rejected this line of work); JONES, *supra* note 28, at 127 (arguing that domestic service restored the mistress-slave relationship); *see generally* ROLLINS, *supra* note 105, at 200-03 (describing the relationship between domestic servants and their female employers as characterized by rituals of deference and maternalism). Moreover, working in white homes subjected many Black women to continued sexual violation by white men. DAVIS, *supra* note 28, at 91-92; Janiewski, *supra* note 101, at 21; JONES, *supra* note 28, at 150.

On Black domestic servants' resistance to oppressive working conditions, see Dorothy Bolden, *Organizing Domestic Workers in Atlanta, Georgia*, *in* BLACK WOMEN IN WHITE AMERICA 234, 236-38 (Gerda Lerner ed., 1973) (describing the organizing efforts of the National Domestic Workers Union of America); Janiewski, *supra* note 101, at 21-22 (discussing ways in which Black domestics won concessions from white employers); ROLLINS, *supra* note 105, at 212-22 (describing how domestics retain a remarkable sense of self-worth despite being treated as "non-persons" by their employers).

115. ROLLINS, *supra* note 105, at 103.

> The middle-class women I interviewed were not demanding that their husbands play a greater role in housekeeping; they accepted the fact that responsibility for domestic maintenance was theirs, and they solved the problem of their dual responsibilities by hiring other women to assist.[116]

Thus, white, middle-class women gained entry to the male public sphere by assigning female domestic tasks to Black women, rather than by demanding a fundamental change in the sexual division of labor.[117]

V. SINGLE MOTHERHOOD AND POVERTY

The sharp increase in the number of single mothers is changing the practice of motherhood in America. As more and more women raise children without husbands,[118] the state responds by increasing its interference in their families and by instituting programs and policies designed to restore the nuclear family by reinstating the missing male.[119]

Contemporary welfare reform measures exemplify this effort. Martha Fineman demonstrates how the new poverty rhetoric blames single mothers for perpetuating poverty and how it proposes as the solution the coupling of poor single mothers with financially secure

---

116. ROLLINS, *supra* note 105, at 104. Rollins noted further that the female employer viewed her maid as an extension of the more menial part of herself rather than as an autonomous employee:

> The female employer, regardless of the degree to which she may have chosen to buy her way out of it, knows that she is seen as responsible for all household maintenance and that this is devalued work. She perceives the person she hires to do such work as doing *her* work in a way the male employer does not. The domestic is something more than an employee: she is an extension of, a surrogate for, the woman of the house. And she operates in what is increasingly the least prestigious realm of women's activities.

ROLLINS, *supra* note 105, at 183.

Rollins found that women also hired domestic servants as a confirmation of social status. ROLLINS, *supra* note 105, at 104-06. Although women performed the day-to-day supervision of domestics' work in the home, their husbands retained ultimate authority over major employment decisions. ROLLINS, *supra* note 105, at 181; *see also* COLLINS, *supra* note 22, at 11-12 (noting that a Black maid's "work of caring for white women allows her an insider's view of some of the contradictions between white women thinking they are running their lives and the actual sources of power and authority in white patriarchal households").

117. Crenshaw, *supra* note 2, at 154 n.35 and accompanying text. *See also* DAVIS, *supra* note 28, at 96-97 (criticizing middle-class feminists for conveniently omitting the exploitation of domestic workers from their agenda).

118. *See* Fineman, *supra* note 12, at 275 n.1 (citing Myron E. Wegman, *Annual Summary of Vital Statistics - 1988*, 84 PEDIATRICS 943, 944-45 (1989) for statistics which demonstrate that during the past decade, an increasing proportion of all births have been to unmarried women).

119. *See* Fineman, *supra* note 12, at 279 (discussing how paternity actions and child support measures authorized by the Family Support Act of 1988 reinforce traditional norms of male-headed households); Fineman, *supra* note 68, at 960 (noting that many reformers urge the state to curb the practice of single motherhood).

males.[120] She links the representation of single motherhood as pathological to patriarchal ideology which defines mother and child by their relationship to fathers.[121] Single mothers are considered deviant because they reject the primacy of sexual affiliation as the basic organizing concept of the family.[122] Professor Fineman concludes that the condemnation of single mothers in current poverty reform discourse is primarily a reflection of patriarchy.[123] Indeed, she declares: "The ideology of patriarchy is the most instrumental force in the creation and acceptance of discourses about Mothers in our society."[124]

Race is very much implicated both in the correlation between poverty and single motherhood and in the discourses that explain it.[125] While the proportion of poor families maintained by women has risen in all racial and ethnic groups, the proportion of poor Black families headed by women is far larger.[126] Single motherhood also

---

120. Fineman, *supra* note 12, at 274-89. Professor Fineman also isolates single motherhood as a social construct that determines society's view of women: "Merely occupying the socially suspect category of single mother makes it more likely that one's actions will come under state supervision." Fineman, *supra* note 68, at 961. Fineman notes that despite differences of race and class, policymakers identify the "missing male" as the core problem facing single mothers. Both divorce reforms, which affect more affluent women, as well as poverty discourse, perceive the need to bring fathers into the family. Fineman, *supra* note 12, at 276. Fineman suggests that at the core of child support legislation is the creation of a legal bond between the mother and father, thereby coupling the "dependent, single mother" with the "economically-viable male." Fineman, *supra* note 12, at 274.

121. Fineman, *supra* note 12, at 289.

122. Fineman, *supra* note 12, at 291. *See* Fineman, *supra* note 68, at 969-71 (explaining how the single mother and her children threaten cultural and social configurations of the family by calling into question the role of men within the family).

123. Fineman, *supra* note 12, at 289.

124. Fineman, *supra* note 12, at 276. I credit this declaration as the inspiration for my article. I was initially taken aback by Professor Fineman's statement attributing the condemnation of single mothers in new poverty discourses primarily to patriarchy. When I read these discourses, I thought, "the ideology of *racism* is the most instrumental force" in their creation and acceptance. In fact, that reaction was the thesis of an article I wrote about the prosecution of women who use drugs during pregnancy. Roberts, *supra* note 15. The strange thing about my response to Professor Fineman's arguments was that I mostly agreed with them. I understood more clearly that both racist and patriarchal ideology work together to construct the meaning of motherhood in our society.

125. *See, e.g.*, WILLIAM JULIUS WILSON, THE TRULY DISADVANTAGED: THE INNER CITY, THE UNDERCLASS, AND PUBLIC POLICY (1987) ("In the early and mid-1960s social scientists such as Kenneth B. Clark, Lee Rainwater, and Daniel Patrick Moynihan discussed in clear and forceful terms the relationship between black poverty and family structure").

126. "The proportion of poor white families maintained by women rose from twenty percent in 1959 to forty-two percent in 1987. During the same period the proportion of poor Black families maintained by women rose from forty-six to seventy-four percent." Audrey Rowe, *The Feminization of Poverty: An Issue for the 90's*, 4 YALE J.L. & FEMINISM 73, 74 (1991) (citing U.S. BUREAU OF THE CENSUS, CURRENT POPULATION REP., SER. P. 60 NO. 163, POVERTY IN THE UNITED STATES: 1987, at 156 (1989)).

The feminist analysis of the "feminization of poverty," which emphasizes the correlation between gender and poverty, obscures the importance of race in analyzing the economic status of female-headed families. *Id.* at 74. *See* Diana M. Pearce, *The Feminization of Poverty: Women, Work, and Welfare*, 11 URB. & SOC. CHANGE REV. 28, 28 (1978) (coining the phrase "feminization of poverty"). The feminization of poverty is attributed largely to the drastic

has deeper roots in the lives of Black women. During slavery, masters forcibly separated many Black mothers from their husbands.[127] Some slave men escaped to freedom or purchased themselves from their masters, leaving their women and children behind.[128] For example, Mississippi marriage registration records from 1864 show that nearly one in five Black women aged thirty and older were separated from their husbands by force.[129] One study of slavewomen in Georgia revealed that over half of the women known to have been mothers appeared to have been living apart from their husbands.[130]

Suzanne Lebsock's research on free Black women in early nineteenth century Petersburg, Virginia, revealed that the most common household structure among free Blacks was the female-headed family containing one woman and her children.[131] Professor Lebsock notes that free Black women had a unique incentive to remain single, arising from their ability to retain legal control over their property.

> For the woman who hoped to buy an enslaved relative, legal wedlock meant that her plan could be sabotaged at any time by her husband or by her husband's impatient creditors. The common-law disabilities of married women added an ironic twist to chattel

---

economic losses white middle-class women and children suffer as a result of divorce. *See, e.g.*, LENORE J. WEITZMAN, THE DIVORCE REVOLUTION: THE UNEXPECTED SOCIAL AND ECONOMIC CONSEQUENCES FOR WOMEN AND CHILDREN IN AMERICA 323 (1985) (finding that divorced women and their minor children experienced a 73 percent decline in their standard of living in the first year after divorce). Research on household composition and poverty suggests that race may produce different paths to poverty: the status of Black single mothers may be "reshuffled poverty," caused when already poor two-parent households dissolve. *See* Maxine Baca Zinn, *Family, Race, and Poverty in the Eighties*, 14 SIGNS 856, 862 (1989) (reporting findings that whites became poorer within the first years after a divorce, while most of the Blacks who were poor after a divorce were poor before the divorce). Moreover, since 1984 over half of all Black families with children have been headed by women who never married. Margaret C. Simms, *Black Women Who Head Families: An Economic Struggle*, *in* SLIPPING THROUGH THE CRACKS: THE STATUS OF BLACK WOMEN 141, 142 (Margaret C. Simms & Julianne M. Malveaux eds., 1986).

127. Omolade, *supra* note 35, at 242.

128. Omolade, *supra* note 35, at 248. After purchasing their freedom, former slaves had to leave their wives and children behind because they could not legally remain in slave-holding areas. Omolade, *supra* note 35, at 248.

129. HERBERT G. GUTMAN, THE BLACK FAMILY IN SLAVERY IN LOW COUNTRY GEORGIA, 1750-1925, at 146 (1976).

130. Betty Wood, *Some Aspects of Female Resistance to Chattel Slavery in Low Country Georgia, 1763-1815*, 30 HIST J. 603, 609 (1987). There was no way of knowing whether the husband was dead, living on a neighboring estate, or had been sold away. *Id.*

131. Suzanne Lebsock, *Free Black Women and the Question of Matriarchy: Petersburg, Virginia, 1784-1820*, 8 FEMINIST STUDIES 271, 273, 285-86 (1982). Professor Lebsock found that over half of the free Black households in Petersburg, Virginia, were headed by women. *Id.* She also gives a fascinating account of how the single, free Black women of Petersburg, Virginia, were able to acquire a significant degree of economic control, in part because of their unmarried status. *Id.* She concludes that "In a slave society of the early nineteenth century, there developed among free blacks a relatively high degree of equality between the sexes." *Id.* at 287.

> slavery's strange fusion of persons and property: [m]atrimony could pose a threat to the integrity of the free black woman's family.[132]

This pattern of Black single-motherhood continued after Emancipation.[133] Between 1880 and 1915, twenty-five to thirty percent of all urban Black families were headed by women.[134]

Ideologically, in America, single motherhood is Black. The current condemnation of unwed mothers is rooted in the myth of the Black matriarch, the domineering female head of the Black family. White sociologists have held Black "matriarchs" responsible for the disintegration of the Black family and the consequent failure of Black people to achieve success in America.[135] Daniel Patrick Moynihan popularized this theory in his 1965 report, *The Negro Family: The Case for National Action*.[136] According to Moynihan:

> At the heart of the deterioration of the fabric of Negro society is the deterioration of the Negro family. It is the fundamental cause of the weakness of the Negro community . . . . In essence, the Negro community has been forced into a matriarchal structure which, because it is too out of line with the rest of the American society, seriously retards the progress of the group as a whole.[137]

Thus, Moynihan attributed the cause of Black people's inability to overcome the effects of racism largely to the independence and dominance of Black mothers.[138]

Underlying the current campaign against poor single mothers is the image of the lazy welfare mother who breeds children at the expense of taxpayers in order to increase the amount of her welfare check.[139] In society's mind, that mother is Black. Writers in the

---

132. *Id.* at 285.

133. JONES, *supra* note 28, at 113.

134. JONES, *supra* note 28, at 113.

135. *See* PAULA GIDDINGS, WHEN AND WHERE I ENTER: THE IMPACT OF BLACK WOMEN ON RACE AND SEX IN AMERICA 325-35 (1984) (discussing how various theorists maintain that by remaining assertive, Black women "were ruining the family and so ruining the race"); HOOKS, *supra* note 4, at 76 (explaining how white male scholars assume that the reason behind the large number of Black female-headed households is the presence of Black "matriarchs"). Hooks explains how white male scholars assume that Black men vacate their parenting roles because of domineering Black women. As hooks points out, the term "matriarch" does not accurately describe the Black woman's role in our society. As the most socially and economically marginalized group in America, Black women do not hold the power the term matriarch implies. HOOKS, *supra* note 4, at 70-83.

136. OFFICE OF PLANNING & POLICY RESEARCH, U.S. DEP'T OF LABOR, THE NEGRO FAMILY: THE CASE FOR NATIONAL ACTION (1965).

137. *Id.* at 5, 29.

138. *Id.* at 29.

139. *See* Fineman, *supra* note 12, at 280-82 (discussing how the image of the "worthy widow" has been supplanted by stereotypical images of welfare mothers who are not interested in marriage, want to avoid work, and are sexually promiscuous); COLLINS, *supra* note 22, at 77 (describing how the welfare mother is typically portrayed as being content to sit around and collect welfare, shunning work and passing on her bad values to her offspring).

1980s, most notably Charles Murray, author of *Losing Ground*, claimed that welfare induces poor Black women to refrain from marriage and to have babies.[140] Society penalizes Black single mothers not only because they depart from the norm of marriage as a prerequisite to pregnancy, but also because they represent rebellious Black culture.[141] To some extent, society punishes white single mothers because they are acting too much like Black women.[142]

The focus entirely on race in analyzing Black single motherhood is also incomplete. The implications of gender also need to be explored. Black feminists have criticized William Julius Wilson's assessment of female-headed households in *The Truly Disadvantaged*,[143] for example, for being essentially an endorsement of patriarchy.[144] While Wilson rejects the theory that poverty is culturally transmitted, he accepts the premise that family structure causes poverty and that rebuilding the traditional family is, therefore, the key to solving Black poverty.[145] It is true that families headed by single Black females are poorer than families with an adult male present.[146] Wilson, however, fails to investigate the economic and social forces that marginalize Black single mothers. He also fails to explore the extent to which Black women have deliberately created single-mother families by dissolving unwanted relationships in response to

---

140. *See* CHARLES MURRAY, LOSING GROUND 154-66 (1984). Other researchers have refuted this claim. *See, e.g.*, William A. Darity & Samuel L. Myers, *Does Welfare Dependency Cause Female Headship? The Case of the Black Family*, 46 J. MARRIAGE & FAM. 765, 773 (1984) (concluding that "[t]he attractiveness of welfare and welfare dependency exhibits no effects on black female family heads"). In fact, Black families headed by women have, on average, about the same number of children as other families (1.89) and less than ten percent of their aggregate income comes from welfare. Margaret C. Simms, *Single-Parent Families Section Introduction*, *in* SLIPPING THROUGH THE CRACKS: THE STATUS OF BLACK WOMEN 139, 139 (Margaret C. Simms & Julianne M. Malveaux eds., 1986).

141. *See* Austin, *supra* note 11, at 557 (discussing how the Girls Club of Omaha fired an unmarried Black teacher because she was pregnant).

142. *See* COLLINS, *supra* note 22, at 74 (explaining how the image of the Black matriarch serves as a symbol for both Black and white women of what can go wrong if they challenge their prescribed roles: they will find themselves abandoned by their men, end up impoverished, and be stigmatized as unfeminine).

143. WILSON, *supra* note 125.

144. *See, e.g.*, Austin, *supra* note 11, at 567-68 (arguing that Wilson's emphasis on the "worsening economic position of Black males as a prime reason for the increase in female-headed families" may be construed as an endorsement of patriarchy as the ideal family structure); Zinn, *supra* note 126, at 870-72 (criticizing Wilson's model because it ignores alternative concepts of family and fails to explore women's opportunities and earning capacities outside of marriage).

145. WILSON, *supra* note 125, at 57-62, 71-92.

146. Simms, *supra* note 126, at 143, 144 table 1; WILSON, *supra* note 125, at 71-72. There is an indisputable correlation between Black single motherhood and family poverty:

> Over one-half of black families headed by women are in poverty and they constitute two-thirds of all black families in poverty. While poverty rates are very high among black families with an adult male present, black families headed by a woman are three times as likely to be poor or near poor.

Simms, *supra* note 126, at 143.

sexism in their homes or other disadvantages of marriage.[147] Wilson's suggestions for reform, aimed at returning Black men to the family, neglect ways to directly empower Black women to improve their economic well-being.[148]

In fact, it is questionable that marriage alone will transform Black women's lives. For pregnant teenagers, marriage is actually correlated with "dropping out of school, having more babies, and ultimately being divorced or separated."[149] Although fundamental social change is required, expanding women's access to day care, low-income housing, nontraditional job markets, and health care are more viable short-term remedies for Black female poverty.[150] Using both race and gender in deconstructing Black single motherhood clarifies that Black women's welfare will not be improved simply by restoring the patriarchal family structure.

In some ways, white mothers' lives are becoming structurally more similar to the lives of Black mothers.[151] Patriarchy in the modern capitalist welfare state is marked by an increased devaluation of motherhood that cuts across racial lines. Indications of this change include: the rise in "illegitimate" single motherhood for both Black and white women; the abandonment of the moral mother ideology and the diminished control of women over childrearing; the replacement of the father by the patriarchal welfare state; the decrease in the amount of mothers' domestic work and increase in the numbers

---

147. *See* Omolade, *supra* note 35, at 273 (stating that even full Black male employment will not solve the problem of Black female poverty and noting that some Black women remain single because of sexism); *cf.* Lebsock, *supra* note 131, at 274, 282, 285 (suggesting that some free Black women in early nineteenth century Petersburg, Virginia may have refrained from legal marriage in order to remain free economic agents and retain legal control over their property). Some of the free Black women of Petersburg who did marry protected their property rights from their husband's grasp:

> Two days before she married Jacob Brander, Nancy Curtis deeded her furniture and livestock to her teenaged children, a clear attempt to protect the rights of her own heirs. Lydia Thomas maintained her property rights in a slave and some furniture, despite her marriage to John Stewart, by entering into a prenuptial contract with him. This gave her a separate estate.

Lebsock, *supra* note 131, at 291 n.47 (*citing* DEEDS IV, 335 (1815); DEEDS V, 288 (1818); MARRIAGES (1814, 1817)).

148. Crenshaw, *supra* note 2, at 165. *See* Austin, *supra* note 11, at 568 (arguing that stressing the need to improve the economic status of Black males perpetuates patriarchy). Austin also points out that Wilson's emphasis on the "marriageability" of Black men exposes Black women to the charge that they are "insufficiently concerned about what racism and economic exploitation do to black men." Austin, *supra* note 11, at 567.

149. Austin, *supra* note 11, at 565-66 (*citing* NATIONAL RESEARCH COUNCIL PANEL ON ADOLESCENT PREGNANCY AND CHILDBEARING, RISKING THE FUTURE 123, 126-29 (1987)). Half of all out-of-wedlock births among Blacks are to teenagers. Simms, *supra* note 126, at 142.

150. Rowe, *supra* note 126, at 77.

151. *See* Fineman, *supra* note 12, at 275 n.1 (citing statistics which demonstrate that since 1980 there has been a 40 percent increase in the number of births to unmarried white women, thereby narrowing the gap between the percentage of Black unmarried mothers compared to white unmarried mothers).

of women in the labor force; and the growing isolation of mothers.[152] In late twentieth century America, more and more white mothers will occupy social positions that were defined for Black mothers.[153] As Black women must see the need to identify and oppose patriarchy in the social control of their families, white women must be wary of the racism in the social control of their families.

It may be in the lives of those most outcast by patriarchy that we will catch a glimpse of a liberated motherhood.[154] Those mothers considered the most deviant may help us to imagine what motherhood might be like in a society where women are "free to develop a sense of self that is our own, and not a mere construct of patriarchy."[155] In other words, we could move from deconstructing soci-

---

152. *See* Ann Ferguson, *On Conceiving Motherhood and Sexuality: A Feminist Materialist Approach*, *in* MOTHERING, *supra* note 10, at 172-75 (arguing that while capitalist patriarchy oppresses women differently depending on their class and race, the conflicts between men and women over parenting, sexuality, and nurturance are becoming structurally similar); Fineman, *supra* note 84, at 658-66 describing how the liberal feminist's goal of a gender-neutral concept of motherhood has contributed to the devaluation of the work mothers perform and actually harms women because it ignores the "very gendered and mothered lives most women live.").

153. This does not mean that white and Black mothers will be treated in the same way. It means that racism helps to determine the social constructs that regulate white as well as Black mothers. *Cf.* DAVIS, *supra* note 28, at 94 ("[T]he wages received by white women domestics have always been fixed by the racist criteria used to calculate the wages of Black women servants"); COLLINS, *supra* note 22, at 75 (observing that the image of the Black matriarch served as a warning to white women who challenged the white patriarch); COLLINS, supra note 22, at 167 (arguing that the historical objectification of Black women's bodies laid the foundation for the portrayal of all women in contemporary pornography); FOX-GENOVESE, *supra* note 35, at 192-241 (describing how slavery as a social system determined Southern gender conventions).

For example, Professor Fineman argues that "[t]he 'public' single mother family is distinguished from her counterpart in the 'private' family" and is subjected to greater state intervention. Fineman, *supra* note 68, at 961. The construction of "public" and "private" families is based on race, as well as patriarchal norms. The state has always considered Black mothers, whether married or single, as needing public supervision and not entitled to privacy. *See supra* Section III. Thus, the "public" single mother has never had a Black counterpart in the "private" family. When white single mothers and their children are considered "public" families, they are placed in a category that has historically been occupied by Black mothers. I suspect that many poor single white mothers will be harmed by welfare reforms really meant for Black women.

154. *See* Robin West, *Jurisprudence and Gender*, 55 U. CHI. L. REV. 1, 47-48 (1988) (discussing Adrienne Rich's feminist vision of a liberated motherhood); ADRIENNE RICH, *Motherhood: The Contemporary Emergency and the Quantum Leap*, *in* ON LIES, SECRETS, AND SILENCE 259, 271-73 (1979) (arguing that destroying the patriarchal institution of motherhood is not the same as destroying motherhood. Rather, by destroying patriarchy, motherhood will be released into "the realm of decision, struggle, surprise, imagination, and conscious intelligence.")

155. Cain, *supra* note 1, at 212. *See* RICH, *supra* note 154, at 270-73 (imagining "a future in which women are powerful, full of our own power not the old patriarchal power-over, but the power to create, power to think, power to articulate and concretize our lives and those of our children"); *cf.* Fineman, *supra* note 84, at 660 (criticizing liberal legal feminists for failing to articulate "an alternative, non-patriarchal legal discourse about Mother"); Fineman, *supra* note 10, at 33 (identifying the presentation of oppositional values as a goal of feminist legal methodology: "In fact, the larger social value of feminist methodology may lie in its ability to make explicit oppositional stances vis-a-vis the existing culture.").

ety's view of these women to actually claiming their oppositional insights as part of our reconstruction of motherhood. Regina Austin challenges us to consider whether Black single motherhood is an example of resistance against patriarchy:

> A black feminist jurisprudential analysis . . . must seriously consider the possibility that young, single, sexually active, fertile, and nurturing black women are being viewed ominously because they have the temerity to attempt to break out of the rigid economic, social, and political categories that a racist, sexist, and class-stratified society would impose upon them.[156]

Of course, this is risky territory. It is difficult to identify the emancipatory moments that spark within the vast realm of subordination. How can we claim what is liberating in the lives of the oppressed without denying all that remains oppressive? How can we discern the transformative potential in what is basically a response to subjugation?[157] We must do the hard work of distinguishing between self-destructive and self-affirming behavior, between resistance and accommodation, between what merely reproduces illegitimate hierarchy and what destroys it.[158]

---

156. Austin, *supra* note 11, at 555. The free Black women of Petersburg, Virginia, who refrained from marriage may also provide such an example. *See* Lebsock, *supra* note 131, at 282-87 (detailing how significant numbers of free Black women shunned lawful matrimony, thus giving them higher economic status than white women of the same community). *But see* FOX-GENOVESE, *supra* note 35, at 52 (arguing that Lebsock's research must be assessed against the evidence that opportunities for marriage during slavery were limited and that Blacks enthusiastically sought legalized marriage after emancipation).

157. For greater insight into reactions to subjugation, see FOX-GENOVESE, *supra* note 35, at 48-49 ("From the perspective of Afro-Americans as a people, should the independence of [slave] women be interpreted as a collective gain, or merely as the confirmation of slave men's weakness relative to white men?"). Suzanne Lebsock, for example, recognizes that the economic gains and unmarried status of free Black women resulted from racial oppression; they were products of a shortage of men and of chronic economic deprivation. Nevertheless she concludes:

> Yet there was autonomy of a kind, and the fact that its origins lay in racial subordination should not detract from its significance . . . . The tragedy for the nineteenth century — or one of many tragedies — was that white people were unable to use the free black example to call their own gender arrangements into question . . ."

Lebsock, *supra* note 131, at 287.

On the dangers of an uncritical celebration of women's "nearly inexhaustible resources for resistance," see Williams, *supra* note 85, at 829, *quoting* T.J. Jackson Lears, *The Concept of Cultural Hegemony: Problems and Possibilities*, 90 AM. HIST. REV. 567, 573 (1985) (finding that social historians are often reluctant to acknowledge the possibility that their subjects may have been assimilated into the dominant culture). While single motherhood defies the dominant norm, many Black teenagers become pregnant for very traditional, rather than subversive, reasons. *See* Austin, *supra* note 11, at 558-60 (observing that some Black teenagers become pregnant in order to secure intimacy, love, attention, and the father's financial assistance). I am indebted to Barbara Omolade for this insight.

158. *See* Austin, *supra* note 11, at 578 (expressing the need to explore whether single Black mothers are symbols of subordination or emancipation).

VI. DISLOYALTY TO FEMINISM

What does this connection between racism and patriarchy mean for the feminist project? How does it test our commitment to a feminist vision of motherhood and of society in general? What does it tell us about the requirements for unity among women who are different? In this section, I will explore the ways in which the interaction between racism and patriarchy tempts both white and Black women to be "disloyal" to feminism.[159]

A. *White Women and White Privilege*

One of the most painful parts of recognizing the relationship between racism and patriarchy is confronting white women's participation in the racial subordination of Black women. During slavery, for example, most white women either silently cooperated with the practice of owning Africans as chattel or actively abused the slaves in their households.[160] Elizabeth Fox-Genovese explains that, although Southern white women grumbled in private about certain aspects of slavery, they failed to attack the entire system that benefitted them in many ways: "Slavery, with all its abuses, constituted the fabric of their beloved country — the warp and woof of their social position, their personal relations, their very identities."[161] Some white women used their power over the slaves owned by their husbands as compensation for their own subjugated position in marriage.[162] Bell hooks suggests that the cruelty white men inflicted on

159. This phrase is a play on the title of Adrienne Rich's essay, *Disloyal to Civilization: Feminism, Racism, Gynephobia*, in which Rich refers to women's disloyalty to patriarchy. RICH, *supra* note 36.

160. Clinton, *supra* note 29, at 28-32. *See* HOOKS, *supra* note 4, at 38-49 (noting that white women "looked-passively" at the torture of Black women and "played as active a role in the physical assaults of Black women as did white men."); BELL HOOKS, FEMINIST THEORY: FROM MARGIN TO CENTER 49 (1984) ("Historically, many black women experienced white women as the white supremacist group who most directly exercised power over them, often in a manner far more brutal and dehumanizing than that of racist white men."); *see generally* FOX-GENOVESE, *supra* note 35 (describing the lives of slavewomen and their mistresses in antebellum plantation households). For an account of women's participation in the abolitionist movement, see DAVIS, *supra* note 28, at 30-45.

161. FOX-GENOVESE, *supra* note 35, at 334.

162. *See* HOOKS, *supra* note 4, at 153 (arguing that the subjugation of Blacks allowed white women to mitigate their subordinate position under patriarchy); RICH, *supra* note 36, at 283 (noting that white women's "only outlet for rage and frustration" was their power over enslaved Blacks). Moreover, slavery was defended as a civilizing institution because it freed white women from degrading labor and afforded them greater equality with men. FOX-GENOVESE, *supra* note 35, at 197-98.

Judith Rollins found a similar relationship among modern Black domestics and their white female employers:

> I submit that this remains one of the functions of the domestic servant — the validation of the employer's class status (and thus the hierarchical class system). And I go further: the presence of the deference-giving inferior enhances the employer's self-

female slaves in the presence of white women served as a warning to their wives, sisters, and daughters to remain obedient.[163]

> Surely, it must have occurred to white women that . . . [if] . . . enslaved black women [were] not available to bear the brunt of such intense anti-woman male aggression, they themselves might have been the victims . . . . Their alliance with white men on the common ground of racism enabled them to ignore the anti-woman impulse that also motivated attacks on black women.[164]

Thus, the subjugation of Black women encouraged white women's allegiance to the patriarchy. This is a critical lesson about the relationship between racism and patriarchy: racism did not perfect patriarchy only by allowing slavemasters the possibility of unrestrained control of Black women. It also secured the compliance of white women by promising them the privileges denied to slaves and threatening them with the punishments meted out to slaves.

Black feminists of the period criticized white women for allowing their affiliation with white men and their interest in the system to limit their opposition to slavery. Ida B. Wells, for example, saw the patriarchal idealization of white womanhood as license for white women's willing or unwilling silence.[165] Anna Julia Cooper charged the contemporary women's movement with opposing only women's domestic confinement rather than the entire system of racial patriarchy.[166] My intention here is not to assess the level of white women's guilt, but to show how white women's stake in patriarchy largely determined their complicity in the institution of slavery. That complicity, in turn, enabled their acquiescence in their own inferior status.

Racism within feminist advocacy concerning motherhood in particular has neglected and even harmed Black women.[167] The feminist birth control movement in the early twentieth century collaborated with the racist eugenics movement of the time.[168] Leading advocates of birth control, such as Margaret Sanger, made accommodations with eugenists and used racist rhetoric urging the

---

> esteem as an individual, neutralizes some of her resentment as a woman, and, where appropriate, strengthens her sense of self as a white person.

ROLLINS, *supra* note 105, at 180.

163. HOOKS, *supra* note 4, at 39-44.

164. HOOKS, *supra* note 4, at 38-39.

165. Harris, *supra* note 2, at 599-600.

166. Harris, *supra* note 2, at 600 n.88.

167. For general accounts of racism in the American women's movements during the nineteenth and twentieth centuries, see DAVIS, *supra* note 28, at 46-86; HOOKS, *supra* note 4, at 119-49.

168. DAVIS, *supra* note 28, at 213-15; GORDON, *supra* note 48, at 274-90. For a general discussion of the collaboration of the birth control and eugenics movements see GORDON, *supra* note 48, at 329-40.

reduction of the birthrates of "undesirables." [169] For example, in "Why Not Birth Control in America?," published in *Birth Control Review* in 1919, Margaret Sanger stated as the feminist movement's objective, "More children from the fit, less from the unfit — that is the chief issue of birth control."[170]

Feminists during this period and into the next century advocated birth control, not as a means of self-determination for all women, but as a tool of social control by the white elite.[171] Their private birth control clinics evaluated clients based on their eugenic worth and advised them on the desirability of their procreative decisions.[172] The first publicly-funded birth control clinics were established in the South in the 1930s as a way of lowering the Black birthrate.[173] During the Depression, birth control was promoted as a means of lowering welfare costs.[174] In 1939, the Birth Control Federation of America proposed a "Negro Project" designed to reduce reproduction by Blacks who "still breed carelessly and disastrously, with the result that the increase among Negroes, even more than among whites, is from that portion of the population least intelligent and fit, and least able to rear children properly."[175]

The focus of contemporary reproductive rights discourse on abortion also neglects the broader range of reproductive health issues that affect Black women.[176] White, middle-class women concern themselves mainly with laws restricting choices otherwise available to them, such as statutes making it more difficult to obtain an abortion.[177] Poor women of color, however, remain primarily concerned with the material conditions of poverty and oppression restricting their choices.[178] For example, the denial of access to safe

169. GORDON, *supra* note 48, at 274-90.

170. GORDON, *supra* note 48, at 281. In *The Pivot of Civilization*, published in 1922, Margaret Sanger advocated society's use of stockbreeding techniques, warning that uncontrolled procreation by the illiterate and "degenerate" might destroy "our way of life." GORDON, *supra* note 48, at 281.

171. GORDON, *supra* note 48, at 276-86.

172. GORDON, *supra* note 48, at 286-87. Birth control clinics also participated in eugenic research. GORDON, *supra* note 48, at 286-87.

173. GORDON, *supra* note 48, at 314-29.

174. GORDON, *supra* note 48, at 329-40.

175. GORDON, *supra* note 48, at 332. For a contemporary version of the "Negro Project" (not connected to feminist reproductive rights advocacy) see *Poverty and Norplant: Can Contraception Reduce the Underclass?*, PHILA. INQUIRER, Dec. 12, 1990, at A18 (suggesting that Black women on welfare be given incentives to use the contraceptive Norplant); Tamar Lewin, *Implanted Birth Control Device Renews Debate Over Forced Contraception*, N.Y. TIMES, Jan. 10, 1991, at A20 (reviewing the debate on the forced use of Norplant).

176. Roberts, *supra* note 15, at 1461.

177. Roberts, *supra* note 15, at 1461.

178. Thus, the pro-choice movement remained relatively complacent about the effective denial of access to abortions for poor women by the Supreme Court's decisions in Maher v. Roe, 432 U.S. 464 (1977), and Harris v. McRae, 448 U.S. 297 (1980), which upheld the denial

abortions, as well as the lack of resources necessary for a healthy pregnancy and parenting relationship, limit the reproductive freedom of poor women of color.[179] Because of racism, it is more likely that the government will interfere with their reproductive decisions; because of their poverty, they are more likely to need the government's assistance to facilitate those decisions.

The mainstream opposition to sterilization reform in the 1970s exemplifies how the focus on "choice" has contradicted the interests of Black women.[180] The Committee to End Sterilization Abuse introduced, in New York City, guidelines designed to prevent sterilization abuse by requiring informed consent and a thirty day waiting period.[181] Planned Parenthood and the National Abortion Rights Action League openly opposed the guidelines on the ground that they restricted women's access to sterilization.[182]

Women's false hope in white privilege continues to thwart any radical assault on gender hierarchy. I discussed earlier how many white women gained entry into the white male working world by shifting female domestic work to Black women, rather than by demanding a fundamental change in the sexual division of labor.[183] Dolores Janiewski describes how racism prevented unity among Southern working women in the 1930s:

> White women prized the tangible benefits of their privileged position as workers and sometimes employers of black women. The intangible benefits of white supremacy's pseudo-homage to white womanhood remained deeply entrenched in these women's notions of self-respect and respectability. Taught to view themselves as "lady-like" when they refrained from heavy labor but to call black women "lazy" when they made the same claims, these women resisted any imputation of "social equality" which would place them on the same level with those they regarded as unclean, immoral, and unlike themselves. Black women's demands for equal treatment threatened white women's deeply held beliefs in a natural, God-given order that established their moral as well as economic superiority over their black co-workers. Organized,

---

of public funding for abortion. Nancy Stearns, *Roe v. Wade: Our Struggle Continues*, 4 BERKELEY WOMEN'S L.J. 1, 7 (1989). The belated mobilization of the pro-choice movement triggered by the Supreme Court's decision in Webster v. Reproductive Health Services, 492 U.S. 490 (1989) (upholding states' ability to restrict access to abortion services), and the resulting spate of state restrictions on abortion seemed motivated by their threat to the reproductive rights of affluent women. *Id.* at 7-9.

179. Roberts, *supra* note 15, at 1461.

180. Roberts, *supra* note 15, at 1461 n.213.

181. Roberts, *supra* note 15, at 1461 n.213. These guidelines were introduced to both the New York City Council and the Department of Health, Education, and Welfare.

182. Roberts, *supra* note 15, at 1461 n.213.

183. *See supra* notes 114-17 and accompanying text.

whenever such organization was successful, by unions that failed to confront white domination, these women never met their black counterparts on equal terms in the workplace, the community, or the union.[184]

Privileged racial identity has always provided whites with a powerful incentive to leave the existing social order intact.[185] W.E.B. DuBois explained white resistance to labor reform during Reconstruction, for example, by the fact that "the white group of laborers, while they received a low wage, were compensated in part by a sort of public and psychological wage."[186] Similarly, the white laboring class never demanded free public education during slavery because they relied on the possibility of becoming slaveholders themselves as their means of social advancement.[187] Freed slaves, not working-class whites, led the first mass movement for publicly-funded education in the South.[188] Women's common oppression has not been any more successful than workers' common oppression at overcoming the stifling effect of racial privilege on movements for radical social change.

Sojourner Truth challenged the women's movement of her time to relinquish any perceived advantage in the cult of white womanhood. Her challenge — the racial challenge to feminism — remains the giant step necessary for radical change. To point out white women's racial privilege is not to deny that white women are oppressed.[189] Indeed, it is to point out a principal means by which white women remain oppressed. Adrienne Rich sees the need to confront racism as a white woman because she understands that only by giving up white privilege will white women be fully capable of dismantling patriarchy.[190] Otherwise, Rich argues, white feminists "might still possess the capacity to delude themselves into some compromise of inclusion into patriarchy, into the white male

---

184. Janiewski, *supra* note 101, at 33-34.

185. *See* Derrick Bell, *After We're Gone: Prudent Speculations on America in a Post-Racial Epoch*, 34 ST. LOUIS U. L.J. 393, 402-03 (1990) (discussing what would happen if all Blacks suddenly left the planet and many whites discovered that they were not as privileged as they had once believed). For the classic statement of whites' "property right" in their superior status, see Plessy v. Ferguson, 163 U.S. 537, 549 (1896) (referring to "the reputation of belonging to the dominant race" as the "property" of the white man).

186. WILLIAM EDWARD BURGHARDT DUBOIS, BLACK RECONSTRUCTION 700-01 (1976).

187. *Id.* at 641.

188. *Id.* at 637-69.

189. *See* Aída Hurtado, *Relating to Privilege: Seduction and Rejection in the Subordination of White Women and Women of Color*, 14 SIGNS 833, 834 (1989) (noting that "white women, as a group, are subordinated through seduction, women of Color, as a group, through rejection"). *But cf.* MacKinnon, *supra* note 6, at 19 (positing the image of white women as " 'women, modified,' this woman discounted by white, meaning she would be oppressed but for her privilege").

190. *See* RICH, *supra* note 36, at 275-310 (discussing the intertwined natures of racism and white privilege).

order."[191]

B. Black Women and Black Nationalism

Catharine MacKinnon recently suggested that some Black women may be disloyal to feminism because of a common struggle with Black men for racial justice:

> I sense here that people feel more dignity in being part of any group that includes men than in being part of a group that includes that ultimate reduction of the notion of oppression, that instigator of lynch mobs, that ludicrous whiner, that equality coat-tails rider, that white woman. It seems that if your oppression is also done to a man, you are more likely to be recognized as oppressed, as opposed to inferior. Once a group is seen as putatively human, a process helped by including men in it, an oppressed man falls from a human standard.[192]

I imagine that most Black women would find it farfetched to seek a greater claim to humanity (in the eyes of the dominant culture) by identifying with Black men, whom society also views as less than human. Our unity with men in the struggle for Black liberation is grounded in the reality that being Black in America is part of *our* identity, critical to what it means for us to be women. We are bound to Black men through the day-to-day struggles of living in a racist society. We know that our liberation as women is linked to the liberation of Black people as a group.

Black women may be guilty of another kind of disloyalty, however. Some of us remain silent about sexism in our own communities, or decline to align with white feminists because of the response of Black men. We fear we will be charged with betraying our common interests as a people. Audre Lorde explained that "the necessity for and history of shared battle have made us, Black women, particularly vulnerable to the false accusation that anti-sexist is anti-Black."[193] The relationship between racism and patriarchy, then, also holds a challenge for Black women. It calls Black feminists to

---

191. RICH, *supra* note 36, at 309. *See* LORDE, *supra* note 3, at 118 ("[W]hite women face the pitfall of being seduced into joining the oppressor under the pretense of sharing power."); *cf.* MacKinnon, *supra* note 6, at 20 (observing that "skin privilege . . . has never insulated white women from the brutality and misogyny of men").

192. MacKinnon, *supra* note 6, at 21-22.

193. LORDE, *supra* note 3, at 120. *See also* Crenshaw, *supra* note 2, at 161 (discussing "the ambivalence among Black women about the degree of political and social capital that ought to be expended toward challenging gender barriers, particularly when the challenges might conflict with the antiracism agenda"). Bell hooks notes, however, that Black women's failure to confront Black sexism results basically from the same forces that cause women of all races to accept sexist-defined roles: "[Black women's] support of patriarchy was not engendered solely by their concern for the black race but by the fact that they live in a culture in which the majority of women support and accept patriarchy." HOOKS, *supra* note 4, at 185. Barbara

inform our communities that patriarchy contributes to Black men's oppression and that feminism is essential to the struggle for the liberation of all Black people.[194]

Perhaps women who occupy different social positions possess differing abilities to identify particular aspects of oppression in each instance of domination. Perhaps some feminists see more clearly the patriarchy in discourses about single mothers, for example, while others see more clearly their racism. We can help each other to understand how the discourses really contain both. We can remind each other that, whatever attraction racist patriarchy holds for us, it is not our order.[195] Comparing oppressions ("I experience sexism the same way you experience racism," or "I experience sexism more painfully than you experience racism," or vice versa) can only be destructive. These comparisons lead us to think, "What you are experiencing is only [or less than] what I have experienced, and therefore I do not need to listen to your story."[196] Recognizing the connection between different forms of subordination leads to a more productive response: "What you are experiencing is linked to what I have experienced, and therefore I need to listen to your story to better understand my own (and our) oppression."

Omolade suggested to me that Black women's reluctance to challenge sexism is manifested more outside the Black community than in our communications with Black men.

194. Audre Lorde wrote of wanting to teach her son this lesson:

> I wish to raise a Black man who will not be destroyed by, nor settle for, those corruptions called *power* by the white fathers who mean his destruction as surely as they mean mine. I wish to raise a Black man who will recognize that the legitimate objects of his hostility are not women, but the particulars of a structure that programs him to fear and despise women as well as his own Black self.

AUDRE LORDE, *Man Child: A Black Lesbian Feminist's Response*, in SISTER OUTSIDER 72, 74 (1984) (emphasis in original). On Black women's involvement with feminism, see HOOKS, *supra* note 4, at 159-96.

195. *Cf.* RICH, *supra* note 7, at 83 (discussing the difficulty men have in giving up patriarchy: "For patriarchy, however much it has failed them, however much it divides them from themselves, is still *their* order, confirming them in privilege.") (emphasis in original).

196. Trina Grillo & Stephanie M. Wildman, *Obscuring the Importance of Race: The Implications of Making Comparisons between Racism and Sexism (or Other -isms)*, 1991 DUKE L.J. 397, 409 n.36.

VII. CONCLUSION: FEMINISM AND ANTI-RACISM

In the past, I don't care how poor this white woman was in the South she felt like she was more than us. In the North, I don't care how poor or how rich this white woman has been, she still felt like she was more than us. But coming to the realization of the thing, her freedom is shackled in chains to mine, and she realizes for the first that she is not free until I am free.

— Fannie Lou Hamer,
"The Special Plight and Role of
Black Women" (1971)[197]

Understanding the connection between racism and patriarchy expands the feminist project. Its goal cannot be to eliminate the subordination of women, divorced from issues of race. Racism subordinates women.[198] "If feminism is to be a genuine struggle to improve the lives of *all* women, then all feminists must assume responsibility for eliminating racism."[199] The struggle against racism is also a necessary part of uniting women in political solidarity. Racism divides women.[200] Some feminists may find their motivation to oppose racism within the dreams of feminism: "It can spring from a heartfelt desire for sisterhood and the personal, intellectual realization that racism among women undermines the potential radicalism of feminism."[201] I do not mean that feminists should see anti-racism as an important extra-curricular project. Because racism is part of the structure of patriarchy in America, anti-racism is critical to dismantling it.[202]

Difference is such a pleasant word. It applies to everyone. It does not call anyone to action. We need only acknowledge that it exists, and then move on with our preconceived plans. *Racism* is quite different. It destroys. It condemns. It speaks of power. It demands a response. Adrienne Rich calls on feminists to use the word, racism:

> If black and white feminists are going to speak of female accountability, I believe the word *racism* must be seized, grasped in our bare hands, ripped up out of the sterile or defensive consciousness in which it so often grows, and transplanted so that it can yield new insights for our lives and our movement . . . . I thought

197. RICH, *supra* note 36, at 278.
198. SPELMAN, *supra* note 2, at 14-15.
199. Kline, *supra* note 2, at 117 (emphasis in original).
200. HOOKS, *supra* note 4, at 156.
201. HOOKS, *supra* note 4, at 157-58.
202. This view of racism and patriarchy rejects the claim that one institution is more fundamental than the other, that one derives from the other, or that it is more critical to destroy one before the other. *See* SPELMAN, *supra* note 2, at 123-24 (criticizing the feminist claim that sexism is more fundamental than racism and that sexism causes racism). I stress the importance of opposing racism here because I am speaking to (mostly white) feminists. Were I speaking to Black liberationists, I would stress the importance of linking the struggle against sexism to the struggle for racial justice.

> of trying to claim other language in which to describe, specifically, the white woman's problem in encountering the black woman; the differences that have divided black and white women; the misnaming or denial of those differences in everyday life. But I am convinced that we must go on using that sharp, sibilant word; not to paralyze ourselves and each other with repetitious, stagnant doses of guilt, but to break it down into its elements, comprehend it as a *female* experience, and also to understand its inextricable connections with gynephobia.[203]

Acknowledging each other's differences is not enough.[204] Relationships of power produce our differences.[205] We must face the awful history and reality of racism that helps create those differences. We do not need to focus less on gender; we need to understand how gender relates to race. If we see feminism as a "liberation project" that seeks the emancipation of all women, then we must address the complexity of forces that bind us.[206] Bell hooks describes the feminist project embracing this holistic understanding of oppression:

> To me feminism is not simply a struggle to end male chauvinism or a movement to ensure that women will have equal rights with men; it is a commitment to eradicating the ideology of domination that permeates Western culture on various levels — sex, race, and class, to name a few — and a commitment to reorganizing U.S. society so that the self-development of people can take precedence over imperialism, economic expansion, and material desires.[207]

When we not only acknowledge our differences, but take up the struggle they demand, we stand a chance of creating that world.

---

203. RICH, *supra* note 36, at 301-04 (emphasis in original).

204. *See* AUDRE LORDE, *The Master's Tools Will Never Dismantle the Master's House*, *in* SISTER OUTSIDER 110, 111 (1984) ("Difference must be not merely tolerated, but seen as a fund of necessary polarities between which our creativity can spark like a dialectic."); SPELMAN, *supra* note 2, at 160-71 (demonstrating how recent concessions in feminist theory to the multiplicity of women nevertheless preserve the privileged focus on white middle-class women).

205. *See* Deborah L. Rhode, *Enough Said*, 4 YALE J.L. & FEMINISM 35, 37-38 (1991) (arguing that discourse on difference must remain sensitive to the power relations that underlie it); Celina Romany, *Ain't I a Feminist?*, 4 YALE J.L. & FEMINISM 23, 29 (1991) (criticizing the postmodern feminist critique of essentialism for failing to "encounter . . . differences at the very concrete level of power differentials and unequal distribution of privileges"). *See generally* MARTHA MINOW, MAKING ALL THE DIFFERENCE: INCLUSION, EXCLUSION, AND AMERICAN LAW (1990) (presenting a relational approach to difference).

206. *See* Romany, *supra* note 205, at 23 (describing the intertwined oppressive natures of racism and sexism).

207. HOOKS, *supra* note 4, at 194-95.

Name Index

www.ingramcontent.com/pod-product-compliance
Ingram Content Group UK Ltd.
Pitfield, Milton Keynes, MK11 3LW, UK
UKHW041846031026
15587UKWH00004B/1038

9 780814 761793